MANAGEMENT PRAGMATICS

Cases and Readings on
Basic Elements of
Managing Organizations

The Irwin Series in Management and The Behavioral Sciences

L. L. Cummings *and* E. Kirby Warren   *Consulting Editors*
John F. Mee, *Advisory Editor*

MANAGEMENT PRAGMATICS

Cases and Readings on
Basic Elements of
Managing Organizations

Edited by
ROSS A. WEBBER
Wharton School
University of Pennsylvania

1979

RICHARD D. IRWIN, INC. Homewood, Illinois 60430
IRWIN-DORSEY LIMITED Georgetown, Ontario L7G 4B3

© RICHARD D. IRWIN, INC., 1979

ISBN 0-256-02232-1
Library of Congress Catalog Card No. 78–70952
Printed in the United States of America

1 2 3 4 5 6 7 8 9 0 K 6 5 4 3 2 1 0 9

To my brothers and sisters . . .

Richard
James Bruce
Robert Alan
Emily Janet
Muriel Lynn

PREFACE

Pragmatic is derived from a Greek word meaning "business," which stems from an even older root meaning "I do." And Pragmatism as a philosophy argues that usefulness of ideas is the best test of their truthfulness. This is the perspective that has shaped the readings selected for inclusion in this volume. In each of the major functional / process areas of management, readings were chosen that appear most helpful to a potential practitioner. Theoretical and experimental reports are minimal.

The first reading in each part is a short poem capturing an artist's perception of the relevant organizational process—for example, William Shakespeare on leadership, Robert Frost on structure, and Ogden Nash on change. The second selection describes a manager who is successfully performing the relevant function—for example, Donald Frey of Bell and Howell, Roy Ash of Addressograph-Multigraph, and Charles Pilliod of Goodyear. The remaining readings in each part offer a variety of conceptual views and applied advice. With the exception of the poems, all of the selections are as recent as possible (all from the 1970s) in order to present material which can be difficult to make available to students. Each part also contains three cases which raise issues especially pertinent to the topics in that part.

The structure of this reader parallels the organization of my text *Management: Basic Elements of Managing Organizations* (rev. ed.; Homewood, Ill.: Richard D. Irwin, 1979) and can be used in conjunction with that book or independently. Additional information and comments on the cases in this volume will be found in the instructor's manual for the text.

The cases and readings have been selected and organized to cover the following topics:

Part One, Individuals and Groups at Work, examines individual needs and motivation along with the meaning of work and money to various people.

Part Two, Managerial Leadership, discusses power / influence and how leadership must fit the task, people, and situation.

Part Three, Planning and Controlling, scrutinizes strategic planning, setting objectives and goals, and control through budgets, policies, and procedures.

Part Four, Structuring Organizational Systems, considers the design of organizations to promote predictable performance.

Part Five, Managing Conflict and Change, investigates various approaches to handling conflict and promoting desired change.

Part Six, Managerial Careers, explores career opportunities and problems common to all young managers, with additional attention to specific problems of females and blacks.

February 1979   **Ross A. Webber**

CONTENTS

INTRODUCTION: THE NECESSITY FOR MANAGEMENT, 3

PART ONE: INDIVIDUALS AND GROUPS AT WORK

READINGS

1–1 The Managers, *W. H. Auden*, 15

1–2 Donald Frey Had a Hunger for the Whole Thing, *Arthur M. Louis*, 16

1–3 What You Really Want from Your Job, *Patricia A. Renwick, Edward E. Lawler, and the* Psychology Today *staff*, 26

1–4 Power Is the Great Motivator, *David C. McClelland and David H. Burnham*, 35

1–5 Femininity and Successful Achievement: A Basic Inconsistency, *Matina S. Horner*, 45

1–6 Entrepreneurship: A New Female Frontier, *Elizabeth Brantley Schwartz*, 52

1–7 Money as a Motivator: Some Research Insights, *David C. McClelland*, 65

1–8 Innovations in Job Design: The Union Perspective, *Bernard J. White*, 74

CASES

1–1 Al Ruskin, 83

1–2 Dixie Hatfield Is Fired, 89

1–3 Metropolis Electric Company Engineering Department, 91

PART TWO: MANAGERIAL LEADERSHIP

READINGS

2–1 Cassius on Caesar, *William Shakespeare*, 99

2–2 Failure Is a Word I Don't Accept: An Interview with John H. Johnson, 101

2–3 What Makes a Manager Good, Bad, or Average? *Jay Hall*, 112

2–4 Why Manage Behavior? A Case for Positive Reinforcement, *Harry Wiard*, 116

2–5 Power, Dependence and Effective Management, *John P. Kotter*, 123

2–6 The Myths of Behavior Mod in Organizations, *Edwin A. Locke*, 133

2–7   The Ambiguity of Leadership, *Jeffrey Pfeffer*, 142

2–8   Leadership and Organizational Excitement, *David E. Berlew*, 152

CASES

2–1   An Attempt to Consolidate Cooperatives in Ecuador, 163

2–2   Open or Closed in the Operating Room? 166

2–3   National Bank of San Francisco, 168

PART THREE: PLANNING AND CONTROLLING

READINGS

3–1   Departmental, *Robert Frost*, 175

3–2   Sterling Swanger—The Man Who Keeps Those Maytag Repairmen
       Lonely, *Edmund Faltermayer*, 176

3–3   Why Corporations Hate the Future, *Arthur R. Roalman*, 182

3–4   How to Design a Strategic Planning System, *Peter Lorange and
       Richard F. Vancil*, 186

3–5   Strategic Goals: Process and Politics, *James Brian Quinn*, 194

3–6   Planning & Control and Accounting: Divide and Conquer,
       Louis N. Redman, 207

3–7   On the Folly of Rewarding A, While Hoping for B, *Steven Kerr*, 211

3–8   Formal Planning in Major U.S. Corporations, *Harold W. Henry*, 221

CASES

3–1   "Unbundling" at World Data Processing, 230

3–2   Henderson Specialties, Incorporated, 232

3–3   Lewis Equipment Company, 247

PART FOUR: STRUCTURING ORGANIZATIONAL SYSTEMS

READINGS

4–1   Winnie the Pooh: In Which a Search Is Organized, *A. A. Milne*, 263

4–2   How General Motors Turned Itself Around, *Charles G. Burck*, 264

4–3   An Introduction to Organizational Design, *Michael B. McCaskey*, 271

4–4   Organization Design: An Information Processing View, *Jay R. Galbraith*, 278

4–5   Two Models of Organization: Unity of Command versus Balance of
       Power, *Stanley M. Davis*, 287

4–6   Diversification Strategies and Organization Policies of Large
       Diversified Firms, *Robert R. Pitts*, 296

4–7   The Third Managerial Revolution, *Lee E. Preston and James E. Post*, 307

4–8   Evolving Organizational Forms, *John Hutchinson*, 316

CASES

4–1   The Hamson Company, 328

4–2   Milano Enterprises, 332

4–3   Grindley School of Business, 339

PART FIVE: MANAGING ORGANIZATIONAL CONFLICT AND CHANGE

READINGS

5–1   Eheu! Fugaces: Or, What a Difference a Lot of Days Make, *Ogden Nash*, 345

5–2   Roy Ash Is Having Fun at Addressogrief-Multigrief, *Louis Kraar*, 346

5–3   An Analysis of Intergroup Conflict and Conflict Management,
      J. David Hunger, 353

5–4   Improving Executive Decisions by Formalizing Dissent: The Corporate
      Devil's Advocate, *Theodore T. Herbert and Ralph W. Estes*, 359

5–5   The Effective Management of Conflict in Project-Oriented Work
      Environments, *Hans J. Thamhain and David L. Wilemon*, 364

5–6   Seducing the Elites: The Politics of Decision Making and Innovation
      in Organizational Networks, *George Kelley*, 376

5–7   Power and Innovation: A Two-Center Theory, *Eberhard Witte*, 384

5–8   Theory of Change and the Effective Use of Management Science,
      Dale E. Zand and Richard E. Sorenson, 394

5–9   Management Development *Is* Organization Development,
      Glenn H. Varney, 401

CASES

5–1   Race Relations in the U.S. Navy, 408

5–2   Saint Martin's Challenge, 410

5–3   Industrial Engineering at Chemtech Corporation, 417

PART SIX: MANAGERIAL CAREERS

READINGS

6–1   Confucius on the Stages of Life, 425

6–2   Charles Pilliod Was the Odd Man In at Goodyear, *Arthur M. Louis*, 426

6–3   Why Bosses Turn Bitchy, *Rosabeth Moss Kanter*, 434

6–4   The Management of Stress, *Karl E. Weick*, 440

6–5   An Assessment of Supervisors' Organizational Loyalty,
      John A. Pearce II, 446

6–6   The Black MBA: The Vanguard Generation Moves Up, 452

6–7   Tokenism: Opportunity or Trap? *Rosabeth Moss Kanter*, 458

6–8   Women in Management: An Endangered Species? *John F. Veiga*, 465

6–9   The Hardest Job of All: Career Planning, *Thomas G. Gutteridge*, 470

CASES

6–1   Young Engineers at Dynamic Tech Corporation, 474

6–2   The Young Supervisor, 476

6–3   Case of the Plateaued Performer, 488

AUTHOR INDEX, 495

INTRODUCTION:
THE NECESSITY
FOR MANAGEMENT

At a number of large universities back in the early 1970s, students organized "free universities" which were open to all comers, with no tuition or academic credentials required. Specialized courses on contemporary and esoteric subjects were offered by volunteer instructors (two examples: Drugs and the Law, Body Awareness). The founders' intentions were to offer a wider choice of courses, more flexibility, and greater individual attention than were available in the regular universities saddled with red tape and bureaucracy. Yet the student founder of the largest of these free universities subsequently resigned with a bitter comment about the growth of stifling bureaucracy and inhibiting rules in the new institution. He was disillusioned about the growth of hierarchy, policies, and rules. Probably they are inevitable. This is not to say that "better" authority systems—more participation, more flexibility, and more humanistic values—are not possible. But any new organizational system will include bureaucracy and rules.

From the dawn of civilization, authority has been manifested in some form of hierarchy. The concept of authority may extend all the way back to our primate forebears who were protected by and paid homage to the tyrant ape dominating the pack. Whether real or imaginary, this authority relationship included only one level, however, whereas a hierarchy includes multiple levels. Cultural historians maintain that the evolution of multiple social levels was relatively slow. Some see the creation of hierarchy and management as virtually synonymous with the beginning of civilization. Differentiated authority marked and facilitated, if it did not cause, the beginnings of history in ancient Sumer and Egypt.

To the laborers on the pyramids of Gîza, the authority hierarchy probably appeared arbitrary and unfair. So it is with hierarchies in politics and education today. In not always polite language, malcontents

The Necessity for Management

stridently question why certain people are where they are and why they make certain decisions—in short, why that nebulous group constituting "the establishment" is at the top of the pyramid, while most of us are on the slopes or near the bottom. Neither such adverse attitudes towards authority nor human struggles to change existing power imbalances are new. In this Introduction, we will use some illustrative anecdotes to introduce central managerial activities, which are discussed in the selected readings.

Managers as Agents of Private Property

Organizational hierarchy traditionally has been explained and justified by ownership. All of the power and authority in a business organization formerly was concentrated in the owner. Since the business was his or her property, and since Judeo-Christian tradition recognizes property as an extension of the owner's person, it was natural that the owner issued orders unilaterally about the use of that property. Adam Smith's *Wealth of Nations* (1776) and the books of the later classical economists recognized that workers' jobs are dictated by technology and the division of labor. But since the manager was still the owner, authority flowed from property.

However valid and valuable may be the institution of private property, it is not a good explanation of the necessity for management—even in business. As corporations grew in America, the ranks of owners swelled, and as ownership became divorced from direct management, hierarchy became even more necessary. In fact, managerial hierarchy is essential even without private property; the critical functions of management would still exist.

Management as a Reflection of Human Differences

Even older than private property as an explanation for hierarchical forms of organization are human differences. Prestige, caste, and class reflect the idea that people are different. Under these concepts, some are born to lead and others to follow, and the prudent people are satisfied with their lot. In the traditional business organization, as well as society, inferiors were expected to obey their betters. The idea of a divinely or naturally ordained social structure, including business, was especially strong in 19th-century Europe. In the early books analyzing the rational aspects of management, the manager's leadership style rested heavily upon class structure and built-in obedience by the working class to their upper-class leaders. In the United States, the more popular explanation of class differences, leadership, and followership was Social Darwinism, which held that some people are born to be more vigorous, competitive, and able. These people supposedly became owners and managers by virtue of their personal characteristics—the winners in life's race.

Psychology has demonstrated that there are indeed differences between people—although they are environmentally caused at least as much as they are determined by genes. For example, greater achievement drives may well explain why some people become managers. Nonetheless, like property, personality is not a sufficient explanation for hierarchy. In a propertyless communist utopia, even if people were all the same in class, ambition, intelligence, and energy, we would still need a management structure. Let us see why.

Formulating Plans and Executing Controls

A century or so ago, anarchists throughout the world instigated a wave of bombings, knifings, and shootings aimed at destroying the established institutions of class and private property. From the aberrant Russian Prince Peter Kropotkin to the 19th-century French beatnik Ravachol, these dedicated anarchists saw themselves as great individualists and libertarians. They hoped to free mankind from oppression by destroying class and property, the twin buttresses for social structure and hierarchy. Princes, presidents, and captains of industry were shot—but the structure did not fall. Instead, anarchism faded away because the movement never consisted of much more than a rabble of dedicated, semicrazed individuals operating independently. Their effectiveness was limited sharply because they never recognized the need for hierarchy and management.

Vladimir Ulyanov saw this need. As Nikolai Lenin, he was the leading power in the development of the Russian Communist Party. His goals were essentially the same as those of the anarchists—the overthrow of property and privilege. He, however, developed the means to achieve them—plans and controls. There was just as much personal commitment among the anarchists as among Lenin's Bolsheviks; many died in the pursuit of their long-range goals. The difference was that Bolshevik leaders developed and imposed operational objectives. Hierarchy and control were vital to their program; "We need iron discipline," stated Lenin.

Strong operational objectives formulated by management created the Communist organization. The Anarchists, in contrast, were never more than isolated activists, because they refused to allow any central direction. They believed that the creation of hierarchy would simply reproduce the autocratic evil they were attempting to overthrow. Operational objectives were left completely to the individual. Without a coordinated plan, the anarchists were annoying—even terrifying —but impotent. With coordinated planning and operational objectives, the Bolsheviks shook the world. The recognition of the essential need for hierarchy and management created an organization that could accomplish far more than the sum of the members working as individuals. In a complex system (a large number of parts that interact in a nonsimple way) the whole is more than the sum of the parts. As Lenin put it in 1913:

The Party is the vanguard of the working class. The force of this vanguard is ten or 100 more times greater than its number. Is that possible? Can a strength of 100 people be greater than that of 1,000 people? It can and is, *when the 100 are organized.* Organization multiplies one's strength tenfold. . . .

So the development and application of operational objectives is an essential reason for hierarchy and management—even without property or individual differences. There are other reasons also.

Structuring Tasks and Making Unpopular Decisions

In addition to the violent anarchists and Bolsheviks, more gentle people dreamed of easing the workers' burden by abolishing private property. The pleas of the Utopian Socialists for business cooperatives predate the call of Karl Marx and Friedrich Engels

for a communist society, but even in such institutions management functions must be performed.

A French cooperative provides an interesting example of the development of management structure in such organization. After the chaos of World War II, some French companies were reconstituted on the basis of cooperative ownership and management. In one of these firms, the workers, as owners, were to receive equal pay and shares of profit. In addition, all would participate in making important decisions, and all were to work at all jobs. In Marx's relatively rare speculation about future communist society, he suggested that eventually all people will be able to decide for themselves what they will work at each day. A broad social commitment should ensure that all necessary duties are performed. This French cooperative attempted to give such a choice—each worker could choose his or her job for each day.

So the free, equal, worker-owners began to labor in their hierarchy-free business. But utopia was not to be. All jobs were not the same; some were dirty or boring or hard, and others were clean or interesting or easy. After a period of voluntary selection of the former, workers began to choose the latter. Free choice did not work; the necessary jobs were not filled. An assignment system was needed to correct the imbalance in job selection. A worker with integrity and popularity was chosen by fellow workers to set up and run a system which would provide a fair method for rotating people equally through all positions. The honored worker was to labor at the regular jobs as well as make the necessary assignments and was to continue to receive the same equal share of profits.

As an example of a worker in such a position, consider Pierre, who was honest and trustworthy but faced several problems. First, what was fair? Should he assign weak, sickly André to arduous duties just

as often as he did strong, healthy Jacques? Should he make this decision himself, or should he raise it with the entire work force? Even more difficult, although Pierre might be scrupulously honest in seeing that everyone worked at desirable and undesirable jobs equally, André and Jacques did not perceive themselves as putting in equal time. Some workers exaggeratedly conceived their assignments to be exceptionally difficult and therefore accused Pierre of bias. He began to feel lonely, alienated from his friends, and distrusted by his associates. In short, his election turned out to be no privilege.

After some time of unhappiness, Pierre went to his fellow workers with an ultimatum: either he got out of his unpleasant duties or he wanted a greater reward. Eventually he received a reduction of duties and an increase in pay. *Voilà!* The result was managerial hierarchy, complete with differentiated power, prestige, and reward.

This evolution of a managerial structure rests on two needs. Allocation of people and positions is the first. Given strong social conscience, freedom **of** choice may work for a while. Buttressed with lengthy consultation, exhortation, and social pressure, it may work for a longer period. Eventually, however, greater direction and central control become necessary. One would be naive to think otherwise. When differentiating between strong Jacques and weak André,

Pierre was making certain allocational and structural decisions. Long ago, management engineers understood that organizational effectiveness is adversely affected when all people perform all tasks. Effectiveness depends upon people doing those jobs for which they are best suited. This requires both assignment of people and structuring of jobs.

More important (and the central moral of this tale of the French cooperative), managers must make unpopular decisions. In all cooperative endeavors, there will be unpleasant duties to be performed and displeasing decisions to be made. Many people, perhaps most, will be upset and will not agree. Some mechanism for reaching these decisions must be provided, and one such mechanism is organizational hierarchy. The Founding Fathers of the United States recognized in the Constitution that the nation's leaders had to be insulated from the people at times in order to allow them to make needed, unpopular decisions. Recall and impeachment were intentionally made difficult so that when not standing for reelection, officials could do what they felt to be correct. In short, no matter how equal or dispersed the ownership of property, no matter how equal and reasonable the people, unpopular decisions must be made. The officials who make these decisions need to be differentiated from the rest of the organization in position and reward. The differential reward may be in power, prestige, or psychic satisfaction rather than money, but it must be there.

Communicating Critical Information

Based upon an analysis of the Socialist Party many years ago, a French scholar described an "Iron Law of Oligarchy." His argument was that hierarchies become strong and organizations become autocratic because it is impossible to keep everyone informed, no matter how much the members may desire democracy. Only a few can monitor the necessary information flows and know enough about what is going on to participate in organizational decisions. These few who occupy critical communication points emerge as leaders who make decisions that affect others.

Human limitations as well as technical problems force us to restrict communications. Human beings have quite limited information-processing capability. We can consider only a relatively few factors at a time; other factors in the system are assumed to be constant. Much perceptual research indicates that we focus our attention because we must. Our communications are thus limited because we are more nearly a serial than a parallel information-processing system. Although some teenagers would seem to be exceptions, we can carry on only one conversation at a time. A one-way announcement or lecture can be addressed to a mass audience, but most other forms of social interactions are sharply limited in this respect. In addition, most

roles impose tasks and responsibilities that are time-consuming. One cannot, for example, behave as a real "friend" with large numbers of people.

New insight into communications is reported by behavorial research on networks. A number of researchers have investigated how the structure of organization affects speed and accuracy in solving problems. The findings suggest an essential aspect of management. In a group structured as a wheel, the person at the hub can communicate with all of the people at the spokes. The latter, however, can communicate only with the hub, not with one another. Regardless of personality, whether a campus politician or bookworm, the person at the hub emerges as the decision maker or leader. An ambitious person at one of the spoke positions may attempt to lead, but among all groups tested, those on the spokes came to recognize that those at the hub must be the decision makers because they can get all the necessary information more easily.

Research has also studied another network in which the participants are arranged in an "all-channel" group in which everyone can communicate with everyone else. In a series of trials, most of the all channel networks found it impractical to operate on this basis, however, and so they transformed themselves into wheel networks. Voluntarily, they restricted their communication links.

In most groups, some individual emerges as the occupant of the critical communica-

Wheel Network   All-Channel Network

tion point at the hub, and the others communicate only with him or her. The process is facilitated if one individual is clearly a leader in terms of personality and presence. Nonetheless, even where the members of the group are balanced as to personality and prestige, the all-channel network tends to convert itself to the wheel structure. Thus management emerges because of the difficulty and inefficiency of transmitting all information to every member of the organization.

Managing Conflict

Ann and Johnny are fighting over who the family's new puppy really "belongs" to—Ann, who asked for it most; Johnny, whom the pup seems to prefer; Daddy, who paid for it; or Mommy, who feeds and cleans up after the darling animal. They run to a parent expecting and hoping that he or she will render a Solomon-like decision that satisfies all parties. Parenthood is filled with such conflict resolution problems. And so is organizational management, because scarce resources and unpopular decisions inevitably involve conflict between people. Increasingly we have come to recognize that conflict does not necessarily indicate managerial failure, but rather is an inevitable and essential part of organizational behavior. Nonetheless, it must be controlled, and managing conflict is one of the manager's most central tasks.

An example is posed by the field engineering group and the electrical engineering department of Metropolitan Electric Company, which must share particularly expensive and sophisticated testing equipment. Neither could utilize it all the time, but conflict occurs when they sometimes want to use it at the same time. Under pressure from the manufacturing division, field engineering wants the equipment *now*. But electrical engineering also wants it now, because they have reached a critical point

in testing the switch gear that failed last week and precipitated an area blackout. Somewhat like Ann and Johnny, they may well run to the vice president for justice.

Perhaps the greatest contribution of hierarchical structure has been in conflict management: the provision of a common superior who can act as judge in the dispute of contending subordinates. The wheellike hierarchy of the past has been a particularly appropriate method of handling conflict over scarce resources and power because it has minimized the number of interconnections between possible rivals and funneled those relations and critical communications through a common superior. In a hierarchy, the manager is at the center in order to reduce the possibility of subordinates' engaging in uncontrolled competition. The manager can act as the allocator of resources by resolving conflicts and balancing the costs and benefits of each post.

Maintaining Stability

Human society embodies a paradox in that we need both stability and change. This tension is especially dramatic in the historical struggle between authority and freedom, control and autonomy. Although stressful and dangerous, we need this struggle. Numerous political observers have suggested that we should maintain balance in the contending forces. Some, like Thomas Hobbes, Jean Bodin, and Nikolai Lenin, were inclined to skew the balance toward authority and control. Others, like John Locke, Thomas Jefferson, and Peter Kropotkin, emphasized freedom and autonomy. Long ago John Stuart Mill indicated the requirement for creative tension when he wrote: "A party of order or stability, and a party of progress or reform are both necessary elements of a healthy state of political life."

So it is with all of society's organizations. Business has emphasized control; management's authority may owe more to Genghis Kahn than to Thomas Jefferson. Given economic realities, the emphasis may not be misplaced. In fact, every organization requires both stability and change. Change is exciting, and much literature is devoted to the manager's responsibility to initiate change. But stability is just as important. Most of the time, administrators are trying to establish and maintain equilibrium in work flow and human relations—not because they fear change, but because individuals and systems can absorb only limited innovation. For effective relations and efficient performance, relative stability is essential. Without such stability, the advantages of division of labor will not be realized, cooperative human relationships will be hindered, and organizational control will be handicapped.

In any organization, jobs are interdependent, and it must be possible to predict the behavior of people in interacting positions. Whether with the engine-block casting operation at Chrysler, the policy underwriting group at Liberty Mutual Insurance, or the students attempting to reform a university, coordinating effort will collapse into confused individual actions unless the behavior of others is predictable.

Stability and predictability are also necessary because of human limitations. We are *ceteris paribus* creatures; we can consider only a relatively few factors at a time, and other factors must be assumed constant. This means that we must focus our attention. Research on the selective nature of perception indicates that we do so by concentrating on matters that are most central to our needs and ignoring those that are peripheral.

Most important, novelty and creativity are unrecognizable unless they emerge from order. In solving problems and adapting to external changes, everyone should not be required to change behavior, only some people. Most effective adaptation seems to occur when some people repeat past practice, while others change behavior completely. Thus a mixture of repetition and change may be the best way to make the transition from past to future. This implies that in order to behave adaptively, management needs stable regulations and procedures that it can employ in carrying out adaptive procedures. That these rules are overdone sometimes is true, but the 300-year-old advice of one church philosopher still has relevance: "When it is not necessary to change, it is necessary not to change."

Managing Change

With his two faces, Janus, the Roman god of beginnings and endings, looked backward and forward. Similarly, because a manager stands at the interface between internal and external worlds, he or she must look inward to the organization and outward to the environment. One of the most difficult responsibilities is to mediate between the demands of organization and environment. This requires internal adaptation in response to changed external conditions.

The military is often cited as an illustration of resistance to change. One of the best (or worst) examples involves a British naval officer in the Far Eastern Fleet, Sir Percy Scott, who in 1897 designed a modification to naval gun mountings that allowed them to be aimed continuously as the ship rolled with the sea. Prior to this, the pointer had to anticipate the roll of the vessel and fire before the sight was on target. Scott's practice firings indicated an improvement in accuracy of some 3,000 percent!

In 1900 Lieutenant William Sims of the U.S. Navy met Scott while on China patrol. Sims was impressed and disturbed that the

United States lagged so far behind the British in this capability. He wrote to the Bureau of Ordnance at the Navy Department, but they ignored his letters. Although he stepped up his campaign, he failed to arouse interest because he was so far away, so low ranked, and so impertinent. Besides, the American navy had just established its power in the Spanish-American War by dealing a crushing defeat to the enemy at Manila Bay, winning the battle under the old system of gunnery. (However, it was later estimated that of some 9,500 shots fired in the engagement, only 121 found their mark!) Success came to the ambitious Sims only when he put his career on the line and went directly to President Theodore Roosevelt. The United States implemented the ordnance modification and Sims ended up an admiral and senior naval officer in World War I.

To the business manager, this story may epitomize the limitations of the military mind. But all minds are quite similar in this regard. We tend to hold on to the past because it usually has worked, and it is comforting. Sometimes we do not want to learn that the world has changed and adaptation is imperative. For these reasons, change agents are essential in organizations. Managers may not always be the initiators, but they must deal with the initiation and facilitate needed innovation.

Tension between Individuals and Organizations

We have presented some practical examples of reasons for hierarchial structure and managerial roles in human organizations. Short-range objectives, unpopular decisions, critical communication links, conflict and change have been described. Underlying these managerial functions are limited resources, which, be they material, financial, temporal, or human, impose restraints

requiring decisions, decision rules, and data communication. If every participant had every resource needed to meet his or her own goals, there would be no need for organizations and no management.

Consider the example of the youthful founder of the free university. This new institution was born as a protest against formal university structure and values. At its high point, several thousand students were attending the open classes of the free university. It was apparently successful, yet the founder resigned. He simply was not aware of the managerial functions necessary in any organization once it grows beyond a very small size.

These functions grew out of scarce resources, from which the initial policies and procedures (the so-called red tape) emerged. Classrooms were limited—and the rooms were not all the same size. Scheduling was necessary: rooms, hours to be used, number of students enrolled for the courses, and so forth. Records were required; comparison, communication, and the exclusion of some students were necessary. This exclusion of students meant making some unpopular decisions. In order to be equitable, admissions criteria were necessary if class size had to be limited. In addition, there was a shortage of professors. Class hours had to be scheduled to fit their availability. Further, professors were to be given complete freedom to teach whatever they wanted, but some effort had to be made to provide courses in a variety of areas, and such efforts required goals and priorities for the free university.

In short, even in such an informal, protest-oriented institution, managerial functions exist. Managers are needed, and policies and procedures are necessary to assist them in administering the organization's activities. It was unfortunate that the founders were ignorant that such policies and procedures would be required. Certainly, rules should be subordinated to desired ends, and flexibility should be maintained so that the red tape does not become an end in itself, but policies and procedures are necessary because they reflect management's basic functions.

For all practical purposes, management and hierarchy may be essential and inevitable. A large proportion of the complex systems in nature exhibit hierarchical structure. Hierarchy is one of the central structural schemes that "the Architect of complexity" uses. The basic form is found in atoms and galaxies, in inanimate computers and living organisms. Complexity and hierarchy are close companions, and this is especially so in human organizations because hierarchy reflects basic aspects of human nature and organizational management. Formulation of operational objectives, structuring duties, assigning people, unpopular decision making, information processing—all of these suggest that some form of organizational structure resembling a hierarchy would be necessary even if people were identical and even if we lived in a utopia without private property or class distinction.

Essential and inevitable as they are, however, hierarchy and organization create problems. People do not behave as they should, not because they are perverse but because life in organizations will always be somewhat aggravating and confining. By definition, organization describes and limits behavior. Few people are so submissive and

authority dependent that they will not feel frustrated from time to time. Most people experience frequent conflict with organizational structure as they attempt to respond to demands, influence behavior, and accomplish objectives. Nonetheless, this inevitable conflict between organization and the individual is not a tragedy, however much some may prefer a simpler existence. A critical factor is how people take it. Do they demonstrate courage and patience, accepting the inevitable restrictions of organization but never easing pressure on those aspects that can be changed? Or do they lose all spontaneity and direction and lapse into a kind of organizational sleepwalking? A paraphrase of the well-known prayer of Alcoholics Anonymous is appropriate: "Give me the patience to accept what cannot be changed in the organization, the courage to change what can be changed, and the wisdom to know the difference."

We do not suggest that present organizational structures or procedures should be unchanged. Reform is desirable. The routes up the hierarchy should be more open to those with ability and promise, rather than just to those with the right sex, skin color, background, or college. Avenues for communication and influence upward should be strengthened. Nonetheless, differentiated positions and managers will still be necessary. The selected cases and readings in the book are organized to illustrate these primary management functions and processes:

Reprinted by permission of the *Chicago Tribune—New York News Syndicate*

Part One: Individuals and Groups at Work. The cases and readings examine individual needs and motivation along with the meaning of work and money to various people.

Part Two: Managerial Leadership. Readings and cases discuss power/influence and how leadership must fit the task, people, and situation.

Part Three: Planning and Controlling. Readings and cases examine strategic planning, setting objectives and goals, and control through budgets, policies, and procedures.

Part Four: Structuring Organizational Systems. Readings and cases consider the design of organizations to promote predictable performance.

Part Five: Managing Conflict and Change. Readings and cases consider various approaches to handling conflict and promoting desired change.

Part Six: Managerial Careers. Readings and cases examine career opportunities and problems common to all young managers with additional attention to specific problems of females and blacks.

PART
ONE

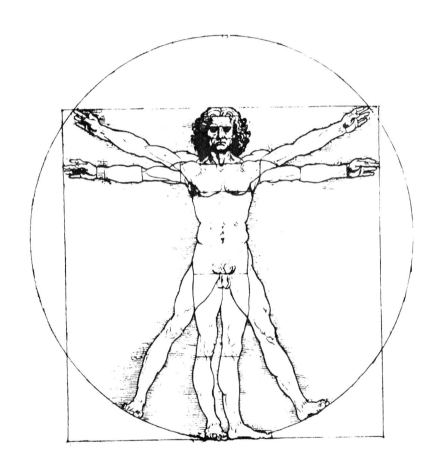

INDIVIDUALS AND
GROUPS AT WORK

READINGS

1–1

"The Managers," W. H. Auden.

1–2

"Donald Frey Had a Hunger for the Whole Thing," Arthur M. Louis.

1–3

"What You Really Want from Your Job," Patricia A. Renwick, Edward E. Lawler, and the *Psychology Today* staff.

1–4

"Power Is the Great Motivator," David C. McClelland and David H. Burnham.

1–5

"Femininity and Successful Achievement: A Basic Inconsistency," Matina S. Horner.

1–6

"Entrepreneurship: A New Female Frontier," Elizabeth Brantley Schwartz.

1–7

"Money as a Motivator: Some Research Insights," David C. McClelland.

1–8

"Innovations in Job Design: The Union Perspective," Bernard J. White.

CASES

1–1   Al Ruskin

1–2   Dixie Hatfield Is Fired

1–3   Metropolis Electric Company Engineering Department

THE MANAGERS*

W. H. AUDEN

In the bad old days it was not so bad:
    The top of the ladder
Was an amusing place to sit; success
    Meant quite a lot—leisure
And huge meals, more palaces filled with more
    Objects, girls and horses
Than one would ever get round to, and to be
    Carried uphill while seeing
Others walk. To rule was a pleasure when
    One wrote a death-sentence
On the back of the Ace of Spades and played on
    With a new deck. Honors
Are not so physical or jolly now,

The last word on how we may live or die
    Rests today with quiet
Men, working too hard in rooms that are too
        big,
    Reducing to figures
What is the matter, what is to be done.
    A neat little luncheon
Of sandwiches is brought to each on a tray,
    Nourishment they are able
To take with one hand without looking up
    From papers; a couple
Of secretaries are needed to file,
    From problems no smiling
Can dismiss; the typewriters never stop
    But whirr like grasshoppers
In the silent siesta heat.

To rule must be a calling,
It seems, like surgery or sculpture, the fun
    Neither love nor money
But taking a necessary risk, the test
    Of one's skill, the question,
If difficult, their own reward.

It's somewhat exceptional for a man to become chief executive of a major company without spending at least a few years working for it. Donald N. Frey, who took over the job at Bell & Howell Co. five years ago, when he was 47, is one of the exceptions. Before his appointment, his only connection with Bell & Howell—the Chicago-based manufacturer of photographic products, business equipment, and educational materials—was as an outside director. He had been on the board nine months.

The appointment as chief executive came suddenly and unexpectedly, and it was indirectly provoked by Richard M. Nixon. Frey's immediate predecessor, Peter G. Peterson, was still in his 40s, and had seemed destined to run the company for many years. But then Nixon urgently demanded that Peterson join his administration as an adviser on foreign economic policy. The Bell & Howell board could detect no suitable replacement for Peterson among the remaining executives, and turned to Frey.

The Boss Wanted to Go Slow

Frey was both delighted and relieved to get the job. For the previous two years, he had been president and chief operating officer of General Cable Corp., a metal fabricator, and he had found it an unsatisfying experience. Although he had helped to stop a steep slide in the company's earnings, he felt restless in his role as second in command. Frey thought General Cable needed a major overhaul, and he was brimming with ideas for reforming it. But his boss had insisted that he proceed slowly.

He had jumped from yet another company at the time he became president of General Cable. The foundation of his business career had been the 17 extraordinary years he spent with Ford Motor Co. Frey piled one outstanding achievement upon another at Ford, and was rewarded with

* Reprinted from the September 1976 issue of *Fortune* Magazine by special permission; © 1976 Time Inc.

Note: Donald Frey is president of Bell & Howell Company.

READING 1–2

Donald Frey Had a Hunger for the Whole Thing*

ARTHUR M. LOUIS

nine promotions, rising all the way from laboratory researcher to group vice president. He even earned a measure of national fame, as one of the principal developers of the spectacularly successful Mustang.

His decision to leave Ford had caused him anguish, but he felt compelled to yield to an inner drive. "I just have to run a *whole* business—it's in here," he explains, clutching his abdomen. "In the crudest sense, you could say it's a need for power. In an esoteric sense, it's a need for completeness. I'm not happy unless I'm dealing with all the pieces. All through the years, regardless of what function I was performing, I had a desire to find out the broader aspects of what I was doing—to see what the next guy was going to do."

Long before he finally left in 1968, it had become clear that he was never going to be the top man at Ford. That position had been preempted, for the foreseeable future, by

Henry Ford II, grandson of the founder. But more to the point, a phenomenal marketer by the name of Lee Iacocca had consistently remained a notch or two above Frey in the Ford hierarchy, and Iacocca was his junior by nearly two years. For a while, Frey had consoled himself with the thought that managing a piece of Ford was like running a "whole business" somewhere else. But eventually, he felt it was time to look elsewhere.

The Brain-Picker

Frey's insatiable curiosity—his drive for "completeness"—had played a large part in propelling him up the corporate ladder at Ford. Originally trained as a metallurgical engineer, he would pry into every corner of the vast Ford empire. While other executives remained immured in their elegant offices, he would stand with the men on the production line and listen to their gripes. He would take finished cars off the line and drive them around the test track, checking for bugs. Notoriously informal, he would appear in the office of a marketing or financial executive, prop his feet up on the desk, and spend hours picking the man's brain. He would barge into the styling studio, brandishing a fat cigar, and bombard the artists with questions and ideas. From these many encounters, he developed a remarkable range of talents.

Just about everyone who has worked with Frey over the years has been struck by the speed with which he grasps and solves problems. "You never have to say something twice to Don," marvels a Bell & Howell vice president. "He understands what you've said before you even finish." But some who have worked with him say that Frey's quickness can lead to impatience with his subordinates—and Frey himself readily agrees. "On occasion, I have to watch myself," he says. "The pressures on a chief executive are all in the direction of hurry-up, but he's also the last person in the

company who should lose his patience, or his temper. I think I'm less impatient now than I used to be."

Frey's intellectual range extends well beyond his own company or industry, and well beyond business in general. He subscribes to 20 different magazines, covering the gamut of developments in business, foreign affairs, science, politics, literature, and the arts, and he reads a book or two a week —usually history or biography.

Where Two Plus Two Equals Four

Frey came from a family with "middle-class values and a strong educational tradition," as he describes it. Both his father, Muir, and his mother had gone to the school of mines and metallurgy at the University of Missouri, and in fact his father was still studying for a master's degree when Donald was born in March 1923.

After getting the degree, Muir Frey worked briefly as an engineer with two companies in Illinois. Then, in 1926, he settled down with John Deere Tractor Co. in Waterloo, Iowa. There the family remained until Donald was 14. "I was born in St. Louis, but I consider myself an Iowan, and I'm proud of it," he says. "Two plus two always equals four in Iowa." In 1937 his father went to work for Republic Steel Corp. in Buffalo, and two years later he was transferred to Detroit, where Donald graduated from high school in 1940.

He earned a scholarship to Michigan State, where he studied engineering, planning to become a metallurgist. He earned straight As in his freshman year, and that summer he worked for Packard Motor Co. It was manufacturing engines for the British Spitfire airplane, and Frey got a dollar an hour for inspecting parts and making sure they conformed to the blueprints.

Back at school, he went into a sophomore slump, and his average plunged to around C, barely high enough to maintain his scholarship. "I discovered that there was a world outside," he explains. "I got interested in parties and girls, and spent very little time in the dormitory studying." The social spree culminated in a sudden marriage—when Frey was only 19—to a coed from East Lansing. The marriage, which produced six children, ended in divorce six years ago. He has since remarried.

Shortly after Pearl Harbor, Frey had gone downtown and volunteered for the Army. But he wasn't taken immediately. He was placed in the Enlisted Reserve Corps, and was sent back to college with the understanding that he could be called at any time. The call hadn't come at the start of his junior year, and he switched to the University of Michigan. His average soared back to the A level. In May 1943, as his junior year was coming to a close, the Army ordered him to report for basic training.

One Way to Make Sergeant

Thanks to one of those delightful snafus for which the wartime Army was so famous, Frey entered basic training as a full-blown sergeant, rather than a buck private. It seems that he had held the rank of sergeant cadet in the Enlisted Reserve Corps, and some bureaucrat had absentmindedly carried the rank over into the army. By the end of 1943, Frey had gone through Officer Candidate School and been commissioned a second lieutenant. He says he would have preferred to be stationed in some major theater of operations—"I wanted to be where the action was"—but he was appointed a gun-control instructor at the Aberdeen Proving Grounds in Maryland. He remained there throughout the war, finally getting discharged from the Army in the summer of 1946.

After earning his bachelor's degree at Michigan in 1947, Frey continued with his studies, intending to make a career as an engineering teacher. Fortunately, he found

a way to supplement his income from the GI bill while doing his doctoral research. He served as an engineer on a project assigned to the University of Michigan by the National Advisory Committee for Aeronautics —the predecessor of NASA. The work involved testing various alloys, to see whether they were strong enough to be used in making jet engines. Frey submitted his findings as a doctoral thesis. "The technical content was okay for its time, but my ability to write English was awful," he recalls. "I have since learned to say what I want to say in a lot fewer words."

He received his Ph.D. in 1950, and the university appointed him an assistant professor of metallurgy for the 1950–51 academic year. But he found himself uncomfortable in that position. "At the age of 28, I was only a few years older than the kids I was teaching, and maybe one chapter ahead in the book. It seemed to me that the ideal engineering professor would be someone who practiced in the real world, then came back to teach how things were done." When a recruiter for Babcock & Wilcox, which includes steel tubing among its many products, visited the university looking for summer help, Frey jumped at the opportunity.

Hot and Smoking in the Real World

The experience couldn't have been more practical. Frey was sent to a plant in Beaver Falls, Pennsylvania, and he spent much of his time at hard labor, as fourth helper on a furnace. "This *was* the real world," he remarks. "It was hot, and dangerous, and smoking. I don't know that my doctor's degree had a hell of a lot of relevance. I would talk to the crew, trying to learn what relevance my studies did have to what was going on there. I guess you could find some if you tried hard enough."

When he wasn't feeding the furnace, he worked as an assistant in the plant laboratory. On one occasion, he and another technician were assigned to deal with a customer who had complained that the company's tubing cracked under normal stress. It was a great thrill for Frey when they came up with a solution to the problem. "In the education of a young man, an experience like that is of enormous importance—to learn how you go about getting things done in the commercial world."

Frey fully intended to return to the university in the fall of 1951, but before the academic year began, he was offered a job at Ford's new scientific-research laboratory. The assistant manager of the lab, Donald McCutcheon, a Michigan graduate, had been combing the faculty for likely prospects. Frey turned him down, but then he was approached again, this time by McCutcheon's boss, Andrew Kutcher. Frey continued to say no, but Kutcher, who was greatly impressed by the young professor, wouldn't give up. "What on earth would it take to get you?" he implored. "How much do you want?" Frey named "the biggest figure I could think of." He had been making $3,600 a year at the university, so he told Kutcher he wanted $10,000. To his amazement, Kutcher agreed.

Frey worked in the laboratory for a little more than six years, moving up to associate director in 1955. Then, in 1957, he became director of Ford's engineering-research office. He got involved in a number of interesting futuristic projects, including one aimed at finding alternatives to the piston engine. He and his colleagues focused their efforts on developing a gas-turbine engine suitable for automobiles, but their research never got anywhere.

In November 1957, Frey was given his first operating job. He was appointed an executive engineer in the car-product engineering office of the company's Ford division. The title may have been a bit muddled, but the duties were clear enough: make sure that the parts fit together, and that the cars

work. Frey was disappointed when he got the job, thinking that it would be less dignified than his work in the lab. "I was still one of those people who felt there was a pecking order, with research ahead of metal bending," he says. But he quickly recovered from his disappointment. "It lasted one hour. I became so busy, and the work was so fascinating—I had a terrific time. Metal bending turned out to be just as challenging."

McNamara's Translator

He proved himself more than equal to the challenge, and the promotions followed in rapid succession. He became assistant chief engineer of the car-product engineering office in 1959, rose to product-planning manager for the entire Ford division in 1961, and then to assistant general manager of the division in 1962. He began to attract favorable attention from executives in the highest echelons of the corporation—including Ernest Breech, Robert McNamara, and Henry Ford himself.

Frey remembers with glee an occasion when he made an indelible impression on McNamara, who served as president of Ford for only a year before becoming Secretary of Defense in 1961. There had been an engineering foul-up somewhere in the Ford division, and McNamara, whose background was financial rather than technical, presided at a meeting where the problem was considered. Frey was sitting in the crowd, while one of his fellow engineers gave a long, dull, complicated explanation.

"I had noticed before this that McNamara, when he got impatient, would pull up his socks," Frey recalls. "As I followed the presentation, I suddenly noticed that he was starting to tug at them. So I decided to break in. I stood up and said, 'What this man is saying, Mr. McNamara, is that the parts broke.' McNamara looked startled, and then he replied, 'Well, why didn't he say so?'

After that, I often served as McNamara's translator. I became known as someone who could go from one camp to another."

"Sir, I'll Fix That"

He also became known as a man who could do a job—any job—quickly and competently. "The guy who gets the job done is the guy who gets promoted," Frey says. "We had a vice president who used to say, 'Every time we give you a job, the son of a bitch works!' He liked that—and so do I, now that I'm running the show. It's good to have someone you can depend on, and you tend to look to him the next time an opening comes. I should add that I wasn't exactly a shrinking violet. If we were at a meeting, discussing some problem, I'd get up and say, 'Sir, I'll fix that.'"

And over the years, there was plenty of fixing to be done. People at Ford still talk about that glorious day in the late 1950s when Frey fixed the window regulators. In its way, this accomplishment was as proud as any of his later, larger successes. "The windows of Ford cars had always been difficult to roll up and down," Frey says. "It took four men, a boy, and a crank to move them. Finally, I went to the general manager of the division and said, 'Look, show me the guy who designs the window regulators.' We finally found him eight levels down.

"I took him to an assembly plant by the scruff of the neck—figuratively speaking, of course—and introduced him to the foreman. The foreman said, 'So you're the son of a bitch!' He just about did take the guy by the scruff of the neck, led him over to where the window regulators were assembled, and said, 'Here, you put 'em together.' And the guy couldn't. He had never been off his drafting board, he had never seen the inside of a plant, and he had no idea what problems he was causing. We got the window regulators redesigned, and we got them fixed."

As he is the first to admit, Frey made a few mistakes himself during his tenure at Ford. To cite the most flagrant example, he was the engineer in charge of the 1961 Thunderbird, one of the great lemons in Ford's history. "It was noisy, it was shaky—it was a dog," says Frey. "It was hard to put together in the assembly plant. The parts didn't fit right. It shook and rattled on rough roads. It was just a poor automobile. We had to shut down the assembly line for two weeks. That's a no-no in the automobile business, shutting down a line in the middle of production. But it just wouldn't go together right, and fixing it on the line was like trying to rebuild a locomotive while going down the track at 60 miles per hour.

"We finally cleaned it up about two-thirds of the way through production, and we made a '62 Thunderbird that was a good automobile. My pride was wounded, of course, and there were a lot of meetings where I had to stand up and take the responsibility. But the important thing in a situation like that is: don't lose heart. It's easy enough to come unglued and throw up your hands. Instead, you should sit down and see what you can do to fix it up."

A Challenge for the Monza

It was during his period of penance that Frey took a step that was to lead to his greatest single triumph at Ford. Early in 1961, after being made product-planning manager, he dropped into the styling studio and said, "I'd like us to have a little sports car. Let's make some models." The Ford division hadn't made a sports car since the mid-50s, when it discontinued the original two-seater Thunderbird, replacing it with the larger, hardtop model. "The two-seater Thunderbird never made any money, but it was an aficionado's car, and people around Detroit were always asking me when we planned to make another." Now he thought the time was ripe. Several months earlier, Chevrolet had come out with a sporty coupe called the Monza—really just the humble Corvair with bucket seats and a floor shift—and it had sold briskly. "You could see that there was some kind of demand out there," Frey says.

At first, the stylists tried to recreate—resurrect, as it were—the two-seater Thunderbird. But Frey quickly realized that something more was required. "The last thing we needed was a warmed-over version of a design that was outmoded," he says. He asked the stylists to come up with some new ideas.

A Few Simple Concepts

After they had produced some fresh designs for two-seaters, Frey invited Lee Iacocca, who then serving as general manager of the Ford division, to take a look. Iacocca spotted a fundamental flaw. "You're making a mistake," he said. "The two-seater Thunderbird didn't sell, and neither will this. You've got to put four seats in. The back seat may be only big enough for small kids or a dog, but it's got to *look* like a family car." Frey says it took him "exactly three seconds" to appreciate the wisdom of Iacocca's comment. The creation of the Mustang became a team effort, with Iacocca as the coach and Frey as the quarterback, to use Frey's own analogy.

"We were looking for what we call 'conquest incremental buying,'" says Frey. "The idea would be to get the long-term General Motors buyer to jump brand loyal ties and buy a Ford product. The key was to get the G.M. buyer—and the Chrysler buyer. This is a tough thing to get done. The whole thing was based upon a few very simple concepts, but simple concepts are of-

ten the hardest to come by. There were really just four basic points in our plan. The car had to be sporty, it had to have four seats, it had to have a low price, and it had to be instantly recognizable—in a pleasant, dramatic, highly acceptable way."

Ironically, Frey stumbled on the design for his new car while thumbing through a picture book of old cars. "I came to a picture of a Fiat, or something like that, from about 1912, with a very long hood and a cute little ass. I said let's try these proportions, the stylists did their creative thing, and there it was." To keep the price down, the engine, transmission, and all the other innards were the same as the Ford Falcon's. Only the body and undercarriage were different. But to the average consumer, that made it a whole new car.

Frey and Iacocca were sure they had come up with a bombshell, but it took many months before they could persuade Henry Ford to go ahead with production. The company was still recovering from its debacle with the Edsel—luckily, neither Frey nor Iacocca had been involved with that project —and the chairman was understandably wary. A debate raged all during 1962, with Frey and Iacocca propagandizing on behalf of the Mustang, and some of Ford's financial executives propagandizing against it.

The financial people pointed to a study by the company's market-research analysts, which indicated that about 86,000 Mustangs would be sold in the first year. At that volume, it would have been only a marginal venture. Frey believed that the company could sell around 200,000 Mustangs the first year. "I just ignored the survey," he says. "How can a consumer make a judgment on something that doesn't exist, that no one ever saw? Sure, you can show scale models to the housewives of Toledo, but that doesn't get at the demand. In a case like this, the judgment has to come from your guts. You say something's right or it's not right. You just know if it's going to work."

An Unwanted Promotion

As things turned out, even Frey's entrails failed to forecast the Mustang's full potential. Henry Ford finally gave his assent, the car went into production, and the first unit went on display at the New York World's Fair in the spring of 1964. Within a year, the company had sold no less than 418,000 Mustangs, and the demand continued to surge, reaching a peak of more than 600,000 in 1966.

As a direct result of the Mustang's success, both Iacocca and Frey received major promotions in 1965. Iacocca was given a newly created position, as vice president of the company's car and truck group, and Frey replaced him as head of the Ford division. The division, with annual sales at the time of $5 billion, was a reasonable facsimile of that "whole business" Frey had always wanted to run. "For the first time," he says, "I had a chance to sell some of the products I had created, to get into the whole marketing and dealer relationship. I was full of my usual self-confidence, and I really enjoyed myself."

His euphoria was shattered just two years later, when he received yet another promotion—one he didn't want. Henry Ford had decided to reorganize the executive hierarchy along functional lines. Frey, who had made his most stunning achievements as a developer of products, was appointed vice president in charge of product development, and soon afterward his title was extended to group vice president. It was a position of tremendous responsibility—to supervise the development of all Ford products—and placed him just under Iacocca, who had been made the executive vice president. But Frey missed the marketing duties that he had come to relish so much. When he protested

the reorganization plan, he was bluntly informed that the decision was final.

He became increasingly restless, but he stayed on in the new structure for more than a year. During that time Semon E. Knudsen, formerly of General Motors, was brought in—ahead of both Iacocca and Frey—to fill the position of president. In July 1968, Frey finally informed his superiors that he planned to leave. "I fussed and I stewed, but then I told myself that the best thing was to face up to the facts. If I was going to run my own company, it wasn't going to be at Ford. I felt I had to go somewhere where my opportunities were not foreclosed by a younger person ahead of me, or by primogeniture."

Comfortable with Wire

He left in September 1968, and remained unemployed for a month while he considered dozens of job offers. Word of his impending departure had been circulating, and he was a prize catch. He didn't have to send out a single copy of his résumé. Frey figured he ought to take a job as a chief operating officer, rather than become a chief executive right away. "At Ford, I had been only a piece of the whole," he explains. "I still had little experience in financial matters. I made up my mind that I would take the second position somewhere, with the understanding that I could someday rise to No. 1."

Frey narrowed the choice to two companies—Varian Associates and General Cable. Varian, based in Palo Alto, California, was an electronics company with revenues of $170 million. General Cable, which was based in New York, was an old company with revenues of $350 million, much of it derived from making wire for independent telephone companies. Frey chose General Cable primarily because of his background in metallurgy. "I felt more comfortable going to a company whose business I could grasp quicker. That would make it easier for me to move on to the problems of marketing and production."

A Good Match—On Paper

The chief executive of General Cable, A. Leon Fergenson, was 11 years older than Frey. A lawyer by training, Fergenson had succeeded James R. MacDonald, a master salesman who had run the company for 11 years. MacDonald had pushed the revenues, earnings, and stock price to record heights before dropping dead of a heart attack in 1966. Unfortunately, he had made no discernible effort to develop management talent in depth, and when Fergenson, who had been vice president and general counsel, took over the company, there was no one who could back him up as chief operating officer. He tried going it alone for a couple of years, but the company began to founder badly, and he started an intensive search for an operating man. He and Frey were brought together by an executive-search specialist who was a friend of Frey.

On paper, it seemed a good match. Fergenson had experience as a financial man and administrator, while Frey could supply the technical and marketing know-how that the chief executive lacked. But when Frey came forward with a number of dramatic proposals for raising profits, it became clear that the two were temperamentally at odds. Fergenson did go along with some of Frey's suggestions—including construction of a scrap-recovery plant in Missouri, and the closing of several marginal plants. But Frey says he greeted others with apathy or opposition. Frey couldn't persuade Fergenson to discontinue two high-overhead, low-margin products—magnet wire and building wire. And Fergenson became perturbed when Frey hired a trader to deal in copper spot and futures markets on General

Cable's behalf. The company had always emphasized direct purchases from producers, and Fergenson insisted on continuing that approach.

In retrospect, Frey feels that he might have made out better at General Cable by discussing his proposals directly with the board of directors—of which he was a member. As an inducement to join the company, Fergenson had actually offered him the right to report formally to the other members of the board. "Through ignorance or naiveté," Frey says, "I never took advantage of my opportunity to keep the board informed and apprised of what I was doing and why." He explains that at Ford he had always dealt with problems "within the context of a strict hierarchical organization." At General Cable he had simply been unable to break the habit.

No "No" for Nixon

Frey had known Peter Peterson since the late 1950s. They had met while Peterson was an executive of a market-research firm, before he joined Bell & Howell, and they had gone on to establish a close relationship. During the 60s they were both among a group brought together by Jerome S. Hardy, who was then publisher of *Life*, for informal discussions of world affairs. Another member of the group was Dr. Jonas Salk, and both Peterson and Frey were tapped to serve as trustees of the Salk Institute. In 1970, when a director of Bell & Howell retired, Chairman Peterson asked his friend Frey to fill the vacancy.

It was in January 1971 that President Nixon summoned Peterson to Washington. Peterson frankly told Nixon that he preferred to remain as chief executive of Bell & Howell. If he left, he stood to lose several $100,000's worth of deferred compensation and stock options. But Nixon refused to take no for an answer, and Peterson soon relented. Nixon was in a hurry, furthermore, and Peterson resigned before a new chief executive was chosen.

Although he had been running Bell & Howell for ten years, Peterson was still only 44, and he had not established a line of succession. His vice chairman, Everett F. Wagner, had a heart condition. His president, Henry E. Bowes, was a competent operating man, but the board did not consider him a contender for the position of chief executive. The board asked Bowes, Wagner, and Lawrence Howe, the senior vice president to run the company while it looked around for a replacement.

Frey objected strenuously to this arrangement. "I told them in an inflamed manner that it wouldn't work—that they had to form a search committee at once and find a chief executive as soon as possible. With a troika, one way or another, it doesn't work out. There's a boss, and there's some subordinates." After the meeting, one of the directors told him, "That was quite a speech. How would *you* like to be considered for the job?" Frey confessed that he would.

By coincidence, one of the other Bell & Howell directors—Austin T. Cushman— was also a director of General Cable. When Frey's name came up, Cushman told him that they both had a duty to let Fergenson know that Frey was being considered for the top job at Bell & Howell. Fergenson accepted the news with equanimity, but other General Cable directors decided that if their own chief operating officer was going to negotiate for another job, it would be appropriate for him to resign from this one. The Bell & Howell appointment came through less than a week later.

A Failure in Home Study

Running Bell & Howell has been no breeze for Frey. The company's revenues and earnings did reach record levels during his first three years as chief executive, but in 1974 the earnings dropped, and last year they collapsed. The company suffered a $5.8 million loss in 1975, on revenues of $398.7 million. Part of the abrupt decline was due to the combination of recession and inflation—but only part. The main problem was the demise of the company's home-study business.

The home-study operation, which offered a variety of technical and accounting courses, had been acquired by Peterson during the 60s, and for a while it had been highly profitable. But in 1973, the Federal Trade Commission, reacting to consumer complaints, imposed some stringent new regulations on the entire correspondence-school industry. Bell & Howell's courses became unprofitable almost overnight.

The most insidious regulation, from the company's point of view, sharply increased the amount of tuition money that had to be refunded to students who dropped out of home-study courses. Since it costs money to recruit students, Bell & Howell began losing on dropouts. The home-study courses went into the red in 1974, and this year Frey shut down the last of them, taking an $18.4-million write-off on the investment.

Dealing with the Pieces

Frey is staking the future of Bell & Howell on his knack for developing successful products. And he is devoting a great deal of his attention to one of Bell & Howell's earliest lines—photography. The photography business became overshadowed during the 50s and 60s, when the company was diversifying into such lines as microfilm equipment, textbooks, and, of course, correspondence courses. Bell & Howell is now developing a sound-movie camera with a self-focusing lens—a combination not yet offered by any competitor. Frey says his guts tell him that it'll be a roaring success.

Having reached the top, Frey is even more compulsively peripatetic than he was as a young executive at Ford. "I like to go out and see what's going on," he says. "I might visit a plant, or I might even visit our distributor in Singapore. To be honest, I'd rather jump out of this building than go to Singapore, but there's a Bell & Howell distributor there, and I'd better see him.

"There are times when I'll make a decision, and then, to see how it works out, I'll go eight links down the chain, to some lowly clerk, and ask him what he's heard about the decision. I may find that he hasn't heard nothin'—to use some bad English. That means I've got to start over, because ultimately he's the one who's got to do what I want done." It's clear that Frey really is dealing with all the pieces—and having the time of his life.

Toward the end of the 19th century, when trade unionism and radical socialism were competing for the soul of the American worker, the country was asking what labor wanted. Samuel Gompers' simple answer was *"more."* The first president of the American Federation of Labor expounded a vision for labor of "more opportunities to cultivate our better natures, to make manhood more noble, womanhood more beautiful, and childhood more happy and bright." The theme became a litany in Gompers' campaigns on behalf of craft unionism. "We want more, we demand more, and when we get that more, we shall insist upon again more and more," Gompers said in a 1902 speech.

Psychology Today's survey of our readers' work satisfaction reveals that you, too, want *more.* But not simply more money and benefits—you were raised in affluence and tend to take these for granted. Instead, you want more psychological satisfactions. More opportunities to learn and grow. More chance to exercise to the fullest your talents and skills. More possibility of accomplishing something worthwhile.

Like your parents, you are willing to work hard and even put in long hours. Although you value your leisure, our survey suggests (in contrast to some other national studies on broader populations) that you still find much of your identity in work. But you want more control over the decisions in the workplace, especially those that affect your own jobs. And you want more freedom to set the pace of your own work, to control your own hours and schedules, to get in an hour of tennis before work or take a long skiing weekend. You have a whole hierarchy of needs, which you see as necessary for what Abraham Maslow called self-actualization.

This emphasis on personal growth has also been noted in previous studies of your generation. What is surprising in our data is that if you do not get what you want, you

What You Really Want from Your Job*

PATRICIA A. RENWICK, EDWARD E. LAWLER, and the *PSYCHOLOGY TODAY STAFF*

may just bug out, take French leave. No less than two-thirds of those who answered the *PT* questionnaire reported there was some likelihood they would change occupations within the next five years (and only a small portion of the sample were young people who are beginning their careers and tend to make more changes).

A total of 23,008 readers returned the 77-item questionnaire in our September issue that asked, "How Do You Like Your Job?" From the survey results and the letters that many of you who wanted to comment in detail sent in, we conclude that most of you are generally satisfied with your jobs for now, but that there is an unmistakable undercurrent of restlessness that may well create problems for your employers as the American economy rambles toward the 1980s. You are potentially quite a mobile generation, with only loose loyalties to a particular corporation or a particular occupation.

* Source: Reprinted from *Psychology Today* Magazine, May 1978. Copyright © 1978 Ziff-Davis Publishing Company.

The questionnaire, developed jointly by the authors and the *PT* staff, also tells us where you stand on a number of social issues related to jobs, ranging from whose career comes first in dual-career families; to who feels discriminated against on the job, and why; to how men and women are dividing the household tasks these days, and how people regard the ethical standards of their companies. Since we drew some questions from items in previous surveys by the Institute for Social Research at the University of Michigan, we can compare what you think with the opinions of other Americans.

Among the more intriguing results of the *PT* survey:

43 percent of *PT* readers felt that they had been victims of job discrimination in the past five years. Yet 82 percent oppose programs of affirmative action to make up for past discrimination against women and members of minorities.

78 percent would like to be able to set the hours that they start and leave work— suggesting strong support for plans such as "flextime."

44 percent feel "locked into," or trapped in, their jobs.

Most people would continue working even if they could live comfortably for the rest of their lives without doing so.

The most popular method of relieving tension from the job was not alcohol or drugs but physical exercise.

Despite the influence of the women's movement, men's careers still come first in two-career families, and women are still stuck with most of the housework.

You Like Your Work—Maybe

Of course, we could not cover everything, and some readers complained, quite rightly, about our omissions. Gays, for example, pointed out we had not included them in an item about job discrimination. Other readers wrote to us about the tensions of having to work at two jobs. A number of people pointed out the special problems and pleasures of work in a small, family-owned business. A few offered some good advice about the importance of having work experience before graduating from school and beginning a career.

As a group, *Psychology Today*'s readers are closer in composition to Daniel Yankelovich's New Breed than to the country as a whole. They tend to be younger, better educated, and higher paid, with a heavy concentration of professionals (43.4 percent vs. a national average of 15.1 percent). In the sampling of questionnaires we analyzed, almost half earned between $10,000 and $20,000 a year. About 44 percent were 25 to 34 years old, which means this group was overrepresented in comparison to the nation.

There were more women than men (52 percent vs. 48 percent), reflecting the population as a whole but not the labor force, which has approximately 12 percent fewer women than the *PT* sample. The racial composition was 92 percent white and 8 percent nonwhite, similar to the ratio in the national labor force.

The majority of our sample had fairly positive attitudes toward their present jobs and were notably free of depression. Their reports on how satisfied they were break

"How likely is it that you will change your occupation in the next five years?"			
Occupation	Likely	Some-what likely	Not at all likely
Semiskilled or unskilled	59 7%	24.8%	15.5%
Clerical workers	59.4	26.5	14.2
Other	52.5	27.7	19.8
Salesman	50.6	21.6	27.8
Foreman or skilled worker	38.7	31.4	30.0
Executive or manager	30.5	28.1	41.4
Professional	25.9	31.4	42.7

down much like the results of the myriad other large-scale national studies of work satisfaction done in recent years: 21 percent said they were *very* satisfied, 20 percent registered some dissatisfaction, and, of these, 6 percent were *very* dissatisfied.

Not surprisingly, managers, executives, and professionals were more satisfied, less often depressed by their work, and less likely to feel trapped in their jobs than semi-skilled, unskilled, and clerical workers. The most dissatisfied workers were the young (under 24), blacks, and those with an annual income between $5,000 and $10,000. These groups also reported the highest levels of depression. (We asked nine questions related to depression, such as, "How often do you feel down-hearted and blue?" and "How often do you feel more irritable than usual?")

Women generally tended to be as satisfied as men, which contradicts some other studies that show them to be more dissatisfied; the evidence from various studies on this point is inconsistent. By the same token, women did not report more depression than the men in our sample.

But men report higher levels of satisfaction than women in five aspects of their work: the opportunities it offers them to learn new things; the freedom they have on the job; the degree of participation in decision making; their chances of promotion; and monetary rewards.

Through a series of questions, we checked to see if there's any truth in the assertion that female bosses have a negative effect on the job satisfaction of their

"All in all, I am satisfied with my job."	
Strongly disagree	7.8%
Disagree	10.6
Slightly disagree	7.5
Neither agree nor disagree	5.7
Slightly agree	15.1
Agree	35.6
Strongly agree	17.6

subordinates. We found no evidence of it. Women with female supervisors, women with male supervisors, men with female supervisors, men with male supervisors—all tended to report roughly the same amount of job dissatisfaction.

Complaints about the Corporation

In general, *PT* readers were dissatisfied with the way rewards are distributed and their performances evaluated in their organizations. As might be expected, they ranked pay and lack of advancement as chief causes of dissatisfaction, but they frequently complained as well about the share of praise they received for doing a good job and the amount of information they are given about their job performance.

Previous studies also suggest that the rewards provided by an organization and the way they are allocated are a major source of worker dissatisfaction. Of course, they probably always will be, so long as budgets are limited and only a few can advance. But there is also evidence that many organizations often aggravate the situation by deciding who gets what in secretive and authoritarian ways—a style hardly calculated to attract the New Breed.

Cynicism about corporate processes was also apparent in the response to a question about how people get promoted. Almost half the people in the survey think that getting ahead in an organization depends more on whom you know than job performance. (Some of this reaction may have been de-

"I often feel trapped in my present job."	
Strongly disagree	16.5%
Disagree	21.9
Slightly disagree	7.6
Neither agree nor disagree	10.1
Slightly agree	18.6
Agree	14.1
Strongly agree	11.3

fensive: people who were dissatisfied with their jobs and less involved in them were more likely to believe that knowing the right people was most important.)

Some writers have argued that most workers have about as much to say in decision making as they really want, and that only social scientists are concerned with giving them more. What did *PT* readers think? Overall, they tended to agree that such influence was desirable and that they wanted more of it. The majority said they had most influence on decisions directly related to their own work—but wanted more. They also said they had relatively little influence on corporate policy in general and on the division of work in their organization. Here, too, they wanted more say. Finally, they reported having the least say in personnel matters, such as firing and promoting others, but they were ambivalent about whether they wanted more influence in those decisions.

Men also reported having more say than women in every area of decision making except in the scheduling of their own work routines. Women seemed less interested in opportunities to make decisions than the men in our sample, for reasons we could not determine.

What's Most Important?

PT readers seem to make a sharp distinction between what they liked about their jobs and what they thought was most important about work in general. When asked how satisfied they were with various aspects of their jobs, the thing that pleased the largest number was the friendliness of their fellow workers.

But when asked to rate the things they felt were most important in work, they told another story. It was the possibilities for self-growth that crowded the head of the list, including opportunities to develop their skills and abilities, to learn new things, and

"How satisfied are you with each of the following aspects of your job? And how important to you is each of them?"

Respondents were asked to choose among different degrees of importance and satisfaction for each job feature. Based on averages of their responses, the numbers below rank each from 1 (most important to the group or most often satisfying) to 18 (least important or least often satisfying).

	Importance	Satisfaction
Chances to do something that makes you feel good about yourself	1	8
Chances to accomplish something worthwhile	2	6
Chances to learn new things	3	10
Opportunity to develop your skills and abilities	4	12
The amount of freedom you have on your job	5	2
Chances you have to do things you do best	6	11
The resources you have to do your job	7	9
The respect you receive from people you work with	8	3
Amount of information you get about your job performance	9	17
Your chances for taking part in making decisions	10	14
The amount of job security you have	11	5
Amount of pay you get	12	16
The way you are treated by the people you work with	13	4
The friendliness of people you work with	14	1
Amount of praise you get for job well done	15	15
The amount of fringe benefits you get	16	7
Chances for getting a promotion	17	18
Physical surroundings of your job	18	13

to accomplish something that would make them feel good about themselves. Among the least important things (though not necessarily unimportant) were fringe benefits, chances for promotion, the physical surroundings at work—and the friendliness of co-workers.

"If you would continue to work, what is the one most important reason?"	Male	Female
I enjoy what I do on my job.	29.0%	28.6%
I derive the major part of my identity.	25.8	27.5
Work keeps me from being bored.	17.4	18.2
My work is important and valuable to others.	13.9	10.8
I enjoy the company of my coworkers.	5.3	8.1
I would feel guilty if I did not contribute to society through gainful employment.	4.4	3.4
I would continue out of habit.	4.2	3.4

Was self-actualization really more important than money? We pressed people on the issue by asking them if they would accept a higher-paying job if it meant less interesting work. Almost two-thirds of the sample were unwilling to do so.

On the other hand, 46 percent said they would not accept a *more* interesting job if it paid less than their present one (41 percent were willing to make such a tradeoff). Those least likely to take a pay cut for more interesting work were divorced women (55 percent), widows (47 percent), women living with someone (47 percent), and married men (49 percent).

The data suggest that people have in mind a level of compensation that they consider adequate for them. If their pay falls below this level, then money becomes more important than interesting work. If wages or salary are above this level, then whether they consider their job interesting assumes more importance.

Who Plans to Change?

The majority of *PT* readers in our sample appear to be having second thoughts about their occupations. Many of those who think

they might make a change in the next five years are, of course, the same people who express overall dissatisfaction with their jobs. Though women seem to be no more dissatisfied than men, they are more inclined to make a change in the next five years.

People are restless for a number of reasons that we can only speculate about. Some go through a mid-career crisis and are forced to reevaluate their previous values and goals. Others discover that because of changes in the economy, their skills are simply no longer in demand and they must learn new ones.

The *PT* survey suggests another reason may be that their choice of career was poorly thought-through in the first place. Almost 40 percent of the reader sample said they had happened into their occupation by chance, without much deliberation. Still another 16 percent reported that they had settled for their present occupation because they couldn't get a job in another one they preferred. Only 23 percent were working in their occupation of choice.

As for the 44 percent who feel "locked in," most of them may think the time isn't right to take a risk or that they have too much at stake in the present job to move. Pay plans, seniority advantages, and fringe benefits are powerful incentives for staying with a company—even if an employee isn't happy there. A tight labor market and high unemployment may contribute to nervousness about a hasty move.

More than half of our sample (54 percent) were optimistic about their ability to find another job at about the same level of pay and benefits as their present one. Managers and executives felt most keenly that they had too much at stake to leave their present positions now. However, it was the semiskilled and unskilled who expressed the strongest feelings about being trapped and thought it would be very difficult to find a job equal to their present one.

How You Cope

The data on job mobility only affirm that work is to this generation of adults more than an economic necessity to be avoided if at all possible. Only 9 percent said they would stop working if they could live as comfortably as they liked for the rest of their lives. Almost 75 percent reported that they would continue to work; and women were as likely as men to want to continue, which suggests, in part, that work now is as important to their identities as it is to men's.

The average *PT* reader spends between nine and 10½ hours a day on work and work-related activities. To be sure, attitudes toward work have changed. For the most part, this generation agrees with Douglas McGregor, author of *The Human Side of Enterprise*, that "work is as natural as play." But work also causes pressures and tensions. How do our readers cope with them?

They appear to make a conscious attempt to separate home and work. Almost 70 percent in our survey said they like to keep the two separate. But the attempt to compartmentalize doesn't always succeed. Three-fourths of those in the sample said they brought their work, troubles, and frustrations home with them.

For our survey members, work was rewarding, but not when it cut into leisure or time with family. About 24 percent of them complained about excessive hours. Another 28 percent felt they had to start work too early or leave too late. Some 20 percent found it difficult to complete assigned work during office hours; 13 percent objected to excessive overtime. And 21 percent reported that their work schedules interfered with their family lives. (Executives and managers complained most about long hours and the impact on their families.)

The data suggest there is considerable potential support for a system such as flex-time, which has been successfully introduced in some government and company offices. Under flextime, an employee must work a set number of hours per week (usually 40), but is given a choice of a few different schedules.

With their long hours and desire for career growth, this generation has its share of tensions and frustrations. They have found their own ways of coping.

In his novel *Something Happened*, Joseph Heller describes salesmen as a "vigorous, fun-loving bunch" who "drink heavily until they get hepatitis or heart attacks or are warned away from drinking for some other reason. . . ." Salesmen are more likely to drink on and off the job than other occupational groups, our survey shows, but they are also more likely to engage in physical exercise. Indeed, physical exercise is the approach to handling job stress cited most frequently by our whole sample.

The next most frequent methods are eating, daydreaming, and buying something for oneself. Women are more likely than men to use all three methods. Along with professionals, they are, as a group, also more likely to seek counseling or therapy to relieve job stress.

Managers and executives are somewhat more inclined than others to drink after work. Foremen and skilled workers are more likely to use drugs on and off the job. In general, clerical workers are more likely to buy something for themselves and, along with professionals, to eat when under stress. Unskilled and semiskilled workers are more likely than others to smoke or daydream. The younger the person, the more likely he or she is to use drugs as a means of coping—including tranquilizers, amphetamines, and marijuana.

The Old Ethic—Not Dead Yet

Although women as well as men seek the psychological satisfactions of work nowadays, this apparently does not spare women from the housekeeping chores. The reports of both men and women on how they divide household tasks indicate that women still do most of the grocery shopping, cleaning, cooking, and clearing away after meals. When there are children, women generally take care of them, including driving them to activities, or they share the responsibilities with their mates. The younger the woman, the more likely she was to report that the household work is shared equally—a sign that changes may be coming, though slowly.

As for household finances, most people reported that they handled the bills themselves or shared the task with their mates. It seems likely that in most cases each partner managed different aspects of the family budget.

The men and women in our sample also displayed traditional attitudes on the issue of whose career comes first when both partners work. Almost all the women in the survey (93 percent) and most of the men (59 percent) were in the dual-career category. About 65 percent of the men said that their careers came first in decisions affecting both parties, while only 9 percent of the women said theirs came first.

Similarly, when we asked men and women whether they would move if their

partner were offered a better job in another city—even if it meant that they might be initially unemployed or underemployed—women were much more likely to pick up stakes and follow their men (64 percent of the women vs. 19 percent of the men would move). The higher a man's income, the more resistant he was to moving under these circumstances. His mate's income had absolutely nothing to do with what he said he would do. It seems that reports of the death of traditional sex roles are greatly exaggerated.

Although a majority of our sample described their politics as liberal (47 percent) or moderate (34 percent), their views seemed conservative on some social issues. For example, 82 percent of the sample opposed a program on affirmative action that would give preference in hiring to women or members of minority groups if their qualifications were not as good as those of other applicants. There was no significant difference in the male/female responses to this question. Our readers took this position even though 43 percent reported that they themselves had been victims of some form of job discrimination within the past five years.

Complaints about discrimination were most numerous among women, blacks, and the young (though people between the ages of 45 and 54 also reported a relatively high incidence of discrimination). Their most frequent complaint was that they had not been able to get a job commensurate with their skills and abilities because of discrimination. Next in frequency, people complained about being denied access to informal communication or other sources of information vital to their jobs. Some people also reported that they had not received equal pay for equal work.

Women were more likely than men to report that they had been expected to do more work or less prestigious work than other workers who had similar jobs. They

"All in all, whose career is given more weight when making decisions that affect both careers?"		
	Male	Female
Mine	65.2%	9.4%
Partner's	1.4	40.7
Equal weight	15.7	32.6
Does not apply	17.6	17.2

"If your partner were offered a better job in another city, how likely is it that you would move even though you might initially be underemployed or unemployed?"		
	Male	Female
Unlikely	69.9%	25.3%
Likely	18.6	63.5
Undecided	11.5	11.1

also said that they were often not invited to take part in informal activities, such as lunch or a drink after work, when they might pick up information useful to their jobs, and were not encouraged, or in some cases even allowed, to join in-house training programs. On the other hand, men were much more likely to complain of "reverse discrimination"—that they had lost out on some opportunities because of preferential treatment of women or members of minorities.

Why do those who themselves have been discriminated against lack sympathy for affirmative action? We suspect this seeming contradiction might reflect older and deeper values, going back to the Protestant ethic. If so, we would expect those in our sample to endorse the values of hard work and individualism. The results support this interpretation. More than 50 percent of the respondents felt that hard work makes you a better person, and more than 75 percent believed that people who were capable of working and chose not to were a drain on society.

Attitudes toward ethics in business were more ambivalent. About 86 percent rejected the suggestion that it was necessary for them to themselves engage in illegal or immoral behavior in their jobs. But when asked if they would report illegal or immoral behavior by their employers, they were generally uncertain. Although 37 percent were quite likely to do it, 26 percent said they were not at all likely to—and the remaining 37 percent were ambivalent. We got similar responses when we asked people if they would confront their employers with such behavior, rather than go to the authorities.

Letters from readers suggest that the main reasons for which they were unwilling to act against their employers were worries about getting another job and supporting their families. One woman wrote that she would be guided by loyalty to her employer in such cases, and would quit her job before turning him in. On the evidence of the *PT* survey, it seems that potential whistle-blowers in the corporation are a minority.

Tomorrow's Turnover

Many of the views of *PT* readers seem to represent a healthy new commitment to the importance of work. But it would be wrong to conclude that their attitudes represent a return to traditional feelings about job values. Healthy, yes; traditional in the spirit of the 40s and 50s, probably not. *PT* readers do not have the strong commitment to working for a particular organization or in a particular occupation that was characteristic of the old days. They appear to be very willing to change jobs if they can better themselves. They also seem very concerned about the decision-making opportunities, interest, and challenge in their jobs. Further, they seem to have little of the social consciousness that was so important to young people in the 60s.

It seems to us that the best term to describe our respondents' approach to work is "self-oriented." The phrase expresses a turning inward that is taking place in the nation as a whole. Americans today seem to have less interest in social reform than they do in securing a satisfying job for themselves.

This high self-orientation should, in some ways, make management of organizations easier than it was in the rebellious 60s and early 70s. People seem to believe again in the value of hard work and in developing themselves at the workplace. On the other hand, they are not likely to be easy to satisfy or retain as employees. They are likely to demand a great deal, and, if they don't receive it, will look elsewhere.

We may be in for a period of increasing instability, because of the turnover of those who can find better jobs and the turnoff of those who can't. Particularly disturbing is the fact that our data come from a sample that contains mostly professional and managerial employees—who are essential to any large organization and who have traditionally had a low rate of turnover. Equally unsettling is the amount of discontent among other critical groups—foremen, clerical personnel, skilled and unskilled workers. They, too, want a satisfying job that offers prospects of personal growth. Instead of seeing opportunities ahead, however, many express feelings of being trapped and show signs of psychological withdrawal.

One thing that organizations can do, in response, is to pay more attention to the needs of their employees. If they want to make the most of their human resources, they had better understand the new job values—and start thinking of ways to improve the quality of work. Even if they do, however, some people will continue to move —and there will be little corporations can do about it. Under the circumstances, the only alternative may be to develop training and recruitment programs that are designed to deal with the turnover from a generation that wants more, more, more, and may worry, above all, about standing still.

What makes or motivates a good manager? The question is so enormous in scope that anyone trying to answer it has difficulty knowing where to begin. Some people might say that a good manager is one who is successful; and by now most business researchers and businessmen themselves know what motivates people who successfully run their own small businesses. The key to their success has turned out to be what psychologists call "the need for achievement," the desire to do something better or more efficiently than it has been done before. Any number of books and articles summarize research studies explaining how the achievement motive is necessary for a person to attain success on his own.[1]

But what has achievement motivation got to do with good management? There is no reason on theoretical grounds why a person who has a strong need to be more efficient should make a good manager. While it sounds as if everyone ought to have the need to achieve, in fact, as psychologists define and measure achievement motivation, it leads people to behave in very special ways that do not necessarily lead to good management.

For one thing, because they focus on personal improvement, on doing things better by themselves, achievement-motivated people want to do things themselves. For another, they want concrete short-term feedback on their performance so that they can tell how well they are doing. Yet a manager, particularly one of or in a large complex organization, cannot perform all the tasks necessary for success by himself or herself. He must manage others so that they will do things for the organization.

[1] For instance, see my books *The Achieving Society* (New York: Van Nostrand, 1961) and (with David Winter) *Motivating Economic Achievement* (New York: Free Press, 1969).

READING 1–4

Power Is the Great Motivator*

DAVID C. McCLELLAND
and DAVID H. BURNHAM

Also, feedback on his subordinate's performance may be a lot vaguer and more delayed than it would be if he were doing everything himself.

The manager's job seems to call more for someone who can influence people than for someone who does things better on his own. In motivational terms, then, we might expect the successful manager to have a greater "need for power" than need to achieve. But there must be other qualities beside the need for power that go into the makeup of a good manager. Just what these qualities are and how they interrelate is the subject of this article.

To measure the motivations of managers, good and bad, we studied a number of individual managers from different large U.S. corporations who were participating in management workshops designed to improve their managerial effectiveness.

The general conclusion of these studies is that the top manager of a company must

* *Harvard Business Review*, March–April 1976, pp. 100–110. Copyright © 1976 by the President and Fellows of Harvard College; all rights reserved.

possess a high need for power, that is, a concern for influencing people. However, this need must be disciplined and controlled so that it is directed toward the benefit of the institution as a whole and not toward the manager's personal aggrandizement. Moreover, the top manager's need for power ought to be greater than his need for being liked by people.

Now let us look at what these ideas mean in the context of real individuals in real situations and see what comprises the profile of the good manager. Finally, we will look at the workshops themselves to determine how they go about changing behavior.

MEASURING MANAGERIAL EFFECTIVENESS

First off, what does it mean when we say that a good manager has a greater need for "power" than for "achievement"? To get a more concrete idea, let us consider the case of Ken Briggs, a sales manager in a large U.S. corporation who joined one of our managerial workshops. Some six or seven years ago, Ken Briggs was promoted to a managerial position at corporate headquarters, where he had responsibility for salesmen who service his company's largest accounts.

In filling out his questionnaire at the workshop, Ken showed that he correctly perceived what his job required of him, namely, that he should influence others' success more than achieve new goals himself or socialize with his subordinates. However, when asked with other members of the workshop to write a story depicting a managerial situation, Ken unwittingly revealed through his fiction that he did not share those concerns. Indeed, he discovered that his need for achievement was very high—in fact over the 90th percentile—and his need for power was very low, in about the 15th percentile. Ken's high need to

achieve was no surprise—after all, he had been a very successful salesman—but obviously his motivation to influence others was much less than his job required. Ken was a little disturbed but thought that perhaps the measuring instruments were not too accurate and that the gap between the ideal and his score was not as great as it seemed.

Then came the real shocker. Ken's subordinates confirmed what his stories revealed: he was a poor manager, having little positive impact on those who worked for him. Ken's subordinates felt that they had little responsibility delegated to them, that he never rewarded but only criticized them, and that the office was not well organized, but confused and chaotic. On all three of these scales, his office rated in the 10th to 15th percentile relative to national norms.

As Ken talked the results over privately with a workshop leader, he became more and more upset. He finally agreed, however, that the results of the survey confirmed feelings he had been afraid to admit to himself or others. For years, he had been miserable in his managerial role. He now knew the reason: he simply did not want to nor had be been able to influence or manage others. As he thought back, he realized that he had failed every time he had tried to influence his staff, and he felt worse than ever.

Ken had responded to failure by setting very high standards—his office scored in the 98th percentile on this scale—and by trying to do most things himself, which was close to impossible; his own activity and lack of delegation consequently left his staff demoralized. Ken's experience is typical of those who have a strong need to achieve but low power motivation. They may become very successful salesmen and, as a consequence, may be promoted into managerial jobs for which they, ironically, are unsuited.

If achievement motivation does not make a good manager, what motive does? It is not enough to suspect that power motivation may be important; one needs hard evidence that people who are better managers than Ken Briggs do in fact possess stronger power motivation and perhaps score higher in other characteristics as well. But how does one decide who is the better manager?

Real-world performance measures are hard to come by if one is trying to rate managerial effectiveness in production, marketing, finance, or research and development. In trying to determine who the better managers were in Ken Brigg's company, we did not want to rely only on the opinions of their superiors. For a variety of reasons, superiors' judgment of their subordinates' real-world performance may be inaccurate. In the absence of some standard measure of performance, we decided that the next best index of a manager's effectiveness would be the climate he or she creates in the office, reflected in the morale of subordinates.

Almost by definition, a good manager is one who, among other things, helps subordinates feel strong and responsible, who rewards them properly for good performance, and who sees that things are organized in such a way that subordinates feel they know what they should be doing. Above all, managers should foster among subordinates a strong sense of team spirit, of pride in working as part of a particular team. If a manager creates and encourages this spirit, his subordinates certainly should perform better.

A Need for Power

In examining the motive scores of over 50 managers of both high and low morale units in all sections of the same large company, we found that most of the managers —over 70 percent—were high in power motivation compared with men in general. This finding confirms the fact that power motivation is important for management. (Remember that as we use the term *power*

motivation, it refers not to dictatorial behavior, but to a desire to have impact, to be strong and influential.) The better managers, as judged by the morale of those working for them, tended to score even higher in power motivation. But the most important determining factor of high morale turned out not to be how their power motivation compared to their need to achieve but whether it was higher than their need to be liked. This relationship existed for 80 percent of the better sales managers as compared with only 10 percent of the poorer managers. And the same held true for other managers in nearly all parts of the company.

In the research, product development, and operations divisions, 73 percent of the better managers had a stronger need for power than a need to be liked (or what we term *affiliation motive*) as compared with only 22 percent of the poorer managers. Why should this be so? Sociologists have long argued that, for a bureaucracy to function effectively, those who manage it must be universalistic in applying rules. That is, if they make exceptions for the particular needs of individuals, the whole system will break down.

The manager with a high need for being liked is precisely the one who wants to stay on good terms with everybody, and, therefore, is the one most likely to make exceptions in terms of particular needs. If a male employee asks for time off to stay home with his sick wife to help look after her and the kids, the affiliative manager agrees almost without thinking, because he feels sorry for the man and agrees that his family needs him.

When President Ford remarked in pardoning ex-President Nixon that he had "suffered enough," he was responding as an affiliative manager would, because he was empathizing primarily with Nixon's needs and feelings. Sociological theory and our data both argue, however, that the person whose need for affiliation is high does not make a good manager. This kind of person creates poor morale because he or she does not understand that other people in the office will tend to regard exceptions to the rules as unfair to themselves, just as many U.S. citizens felt it was unfair to let Richard Nixon off and punish others less involved than he was in the Watergate scandal.

Socialized Power

But so far our findings are a little alarming. Do they suggest that the good manager is one who cares for power and is not at all concerned about the needs of other people? Not quite, for the good manager has other characteristics which must still be taken into account.

Above all, the good manager's power motivation is not oriented toward personal aggrandizement but toward the institution which he or she serves. In another major research study, we found that the signs of controlled action or inhibition that appear when a person exercises his or her imagination in writing stories tell a great deal about the kind of power that person needs.[2] We discovered that, if a high power motive score is balanced by high inhibition, stories about power tend to be altruistic. That is, the heroes in the story exercise power on behalf of someone else. This is the "socialized" face of power as distinguished from the concern for personal power, which is characteristic of individuals whose stories are loaded with power imagery but which show no sign of inhibition or self-control. In our earlier study, we found ample evidence that these latter individuals exercise their power impulsively. They are more rude to other people, they drink too much, they try to exploit others sexually, and they collect symbols of personal prestige such as fancy cars or big offices.

---

[2] David C. McClelland, William N. Davis, Rudolf Kalin, and Erie Warner, *The Drinking Man* (New York: The Free Press, 1972).

Individuals high in power and in control, on the other hand, are more institution minded; they tend to get elected to more offices, to control their drinking, and to want to serve others. Not surprisingly, we found in the workshops that the better managers in the corporation also tend to score high on both power and inhibition.

PROFILE OF A GOOD MANAGER

Let us recapitulate what we have discussed so far and have illustrated with data from one company. The better managers we studied are high in power motivation, low in affiliation motivation, and high in inhibition. They care about institutional power and use it to stimulate their employees to be more productive. Now let us compare them with affiliative managers—those in whom the need for affiliation is higher than the need for power—and with the personal power manager—those in whom the need for power is higher than for affiliation but whose inhibition score is low.

In the sales division of our illustrative company, there were managers who matched the three types fairly closely. *Exhibit 1* shows how their subordinates rated the offices they worked in on responsibility, organizational clarity, and team spirit. There are scores from at least three subordinates for each manager, and several managers are represented for each type, so that the averages shown in the exhibit are quite stable. Note that the manager who is concerned about being liked by people tends to have subordinates who feel that they have very little personal responsibility, that organizational procedures are not clear, and that they have little pride in their work group.

In short, as we expected, affiliative managers make so many ad hominem and ad hoc decisions that they almost totally abandon orderly procedures. Their disregard for pro-

EXHIBIT I

Average Scores on Selected Climate Dimensions by Subordinates of Managers with Different Motive Profiles*

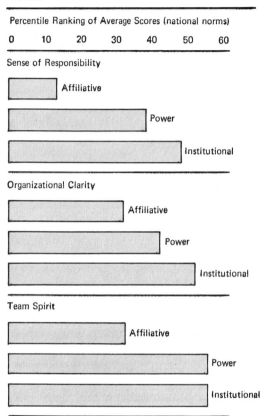

Percentile Ranking of Average Scores (national norms)

0   10   20   30   40   50   60

Sense of Responsibility

Affiliative

Power

Institutional

Organizational Clarity

Affiliative

Power

Institutional

Team Spirit

Affiliative

Power

Institutional

* Scores for at least three subordinates of·

Affiliative managers (affiliation greater than power, high inhibition)

Personal power managers (power greater than affiliation, low inhibition)

Institutional managers (power greater than affiliation, high inhibition)

effective. They are able to create a greater sense of responsibility in their divisions and, above all, a greater team spirit. They can be thought of as managerial equivalents of successful tank commanders such as General Patton, whose own daring inspired admiration in his troops. But notice how in *Exhibit 1* these men are still only in the 40th percentile in the amount of organizational clarity they create, as compared to the high power, low affiliation, high inhibition managers, whom we shall term *institutional*.

Managers motivated by personal power are not disciplined enough to be good institution builders, and often their subordinates are loyal to them as individuals rather than to the institution they both serve. When a personal power manager leaves, disorganizational often follows. His subordinates' strong group spirit, which the manager has personally inspired, deflates. The subordinates do not know what to do for themselves.

Of the managerial types, the institutional manager is the most successful in creating an effective work·climate. *Exhibit 1* shows that his subordinates feel that they have more responsibility. Also, this kind of manager creates high morale because he produces the greatest sense of organizational clarity and team spirit. If such a manager leaves, he or she can be more readily replaced by another manager, because the employees have been encouraged to be loyal to the institution rather than to a particular person.

cedure leaves employees feeling weak, irresponsible, and without a sense of what might happen next, of where they stand in relation to their manager, or even of what they ought to be doing. In this company, the group of affiliative managers portrayed in *Exhibit 1* were below the 30th percentile in morale scores.

The managers who are motivated by a need for personal power are somewhat more

Managerial Styles

Since it seems undeniable from *Exhibit 1* that either kind of power orientation creates better morale in subordinates than a "people" orientation, we must consider that a concern for power is essential to good management. Our findings seem to fly in the face of a long and influential tradition of organizational psychology, which insists that authoritarian management is what is wrong with most businesses in this country. Let us say frankly that we think the bogeyman of authoritarianism has in fact been wrongly used to downplay the importance of power in management. After all, management is an influence game. Some proponents of democratic management seem to have forgotten this fact, urging managers to be primarily concerned with people's human needs rather than with helping them to get things done.

But a good deal of the apparent conflict between our findings and those of other behavioral scientists in this area arises from the fact that we are talking about *motives*, and behaviorists are often talking about *actions*. What we are saying is that managers must be interested in playing the influence game in a controlled way. That does not necessarily mean that they are or should be authoritarian in action. On the contrary, it appears that power-motivated managers make their subordinates feel strong rather than weak. The true authoritarian in action would have the reverse effect, making people feel weak and powerless.

Thus another important ingredient in the profile of a manager is his or her managerial style. In the illustrative company, 63 percent of the better managers (those whose subordinates had higher morale) scored higher on the democratic or coaching styles of management as compared with only 22 percent of the poorer managers, a statistically significant difference. By contrast, the latter scored higher on authoritarian or coercive management styles. Since the better managers were also higher in power motivation, it seems that, in action, they express their power motivation in a democratic way, which is more likely to be effective.

To see how motivation and style interact, let us consider the case of George Prentice, a manager in the sales division of another company. George had exactly the right motive combination to be an institutional manager. He was high in the need for power,

low in the need for affiliation, and high in inhibition. He exercised his power in a controlled, organized way. His stories reflected this fact. In one, for instance, he wrote, "The men sitting around the table were feeling pretty good; they had just finished plans for reorganizing the company; the company has been beset with a number of organizational problems. This group, headed by a hard-driving, brilliant young executive, has completely reorganized the company structurally with new jobs and responsibilities. . . ."

This described how George himself was perceived by the company, and shortly after the workshop he was promoted to vice president in charge of all sales. But George was also known to his colleagues as a monster, a tough guy who would "walk over his grandmother" if she stood in the way of his advancement. He had the right motive combination and, in fact, was more interested in institutional growth than in personal power, but his managerial style was all wrong. Taking his cue from some of the top executives in the corporation, he told people what they had to do and threatened them with dire consequences if they didn't do it.

When George was confronted with his authoritarianism in a workshop, he recognized that this style was counterproductive —in fact, in another part of the study we found that it was associated with low morale —and he subsequently changed to acting more like a coach, which was the scale on which he scored the lowest initially. George saw more clearly that his job was not to force other people to do things but to help them to figure out ways of getting their job done better for the company.

The Institutional Manager

One reason it was easy for George Prentice to change his managerial style was that in his imaginative stories he was already having thoughts about helping others, characteristic of men with the institution-building motivational pattern. In further examining institution builders' thoughts and actions, we found they have four major characteristics:

1. They are more organization-minded; that is, they tend to join more organizations and to feel responsible for building up these organizations. Furthermore, they believe strongly in the importance of centralized authority.

2. They report that they like to work. This finding is particularly interesting, because our research on achievement motivation has led many commentators to argue that achievement motivation promotes the Protestant work ethic. Almost the precise opposite is true. People who have a high need to achieve like to get out of work by becoming more efficient. They would like to see the same result obtained in less time or with less effort. But managers who have a need for institutional power actually seem to like the discipline of work. It satisfies their need for getting things done in an orderly way.

3. They seem quite willing to sacrifice some of their own self-interest for the welfare of the organization they serve. For example, they are more willing to make contributions to charities.

4. They have a keen sense of justice. It is almost as if they feel that if a person works hard and sacrifices for the good of the organization, he should and will get a just reward for his effort.

It is easy to see how each of these four concerns helps a person become a good manager, concerned about what the institution can achieve.

Maturity

Let us consider one more fact we discovered in studying the better managers at George Prentice's company. They were more mature. Mature people can be most simply described as less egotistic. Somehow their positive self-image is not at stake in what they are doing. They are less defensive, more willing to seek advice from experts, and have a longer range view. They accumulate fewer personal possessions and seem older and wiser. It is as if they have awakened to the fact that they are not going to live forever and have lost some of the feeling that their own personal future is all that important.

Many U.S. businessmen fear this kind of maturity. They suspect that it will make them less hard driving, less expansion-minded, and less committed to organizational effectiveness. Our data do not support their fears. These fears are exactly the ones George Prentice had before he went to the workshop. Afterward he was a more effective manager, not despite his loss of some of the sense of his own importance, but because of it. The reason is simple: his subordinates believed afterward that he genuinely was more concerned about the company than about himself. Where once they respected his confidence but feared him, they now trusted him. Once he supported their image of him as a "big man" by talking about the new Porsche and the new Honda he had bought; when we saw him recently he said, almost as an aside, "I don't buy things anymore."

CHANGING MANAGERIAL STYLE

George Prentice was able to change his managerial style after learning more about himself in a workshop. But does self-knowledge generally improve managerial behavior?

How did the managers change? Sometimes they decided they should get into another line of work. This happened to Ken Briggs, for example, who found that the reason he was doing so poorly as a manager was because he had almost no interest in influencing others. He understood how he would have to change if he were to do well in his present job, but in the end decided, with the help of management, that he would prefer to work back into his first love, sales.

Ken Briggs moved into "remaindering," to help retail outlets for his company's products get rid of last year's stock so that they could take on each year's new styles. He is very successful in this new role; he has cut costs, increased dollar volume, and in time has worked himself into an independent role selling some of the old stock on his own in a way that is quite satisfactory to the business. And he does not have to manage anybody anymore.

In George Prentice's case, less change was needed. He was obviously a very competent person with the right motive profile for a top managerial position. When he was promoted, he performed even more successfully than before because he realized the need to become more positive in his approach and less coercive in his managerial style.

But what about a person who does not want to change his job and discovers that he does not have the right motive profile to be a manager?

The case of Charlie Blake is instructive. Charlie was as low in power motivation as Ken Briggs, his need to achieve was about average, and his affiliation motivation was above average. Thus he had the affiliative manager profile, and, as expected, the morale among his subordinates was very low. When Charlie learned that his subordinates' sense of responsibility and perception of a reward system were in the 10th percentile and that team spirit was in the 30th, he was shocked. When shown a film depicting three managerial climates, Charlie said he preferred what turned out to be the authoritarian climate. He became angry when the workshop trainer and other members in the group pointed out the limitations of this

managerial style. He became obstructive in the group process and objected strenuously to what was being taught.

In an interview conducted much later, Charlie said, "I blew my cool. When I started yelling at you for being all wrong, I got even madder when you pointed out that, according to my style questionnaire, you bet that that was just what I did to my salesmen. Down underneath I knew something must be wrong. The sales performance for my division wasn't so good. Most of it was due to me anyway and not to my salesmen. Obviously their reports that they felt very little responsibility was delegated to them and that I didn't reward them at all had to mean something. So I finally decided to sit down and try to figure what I could do about it. I knew I had to start being a manager instead of trying to do everything myself and blowing my cool at others because they didn't do what I thought they should. In the end, after I calmed down on the way back from the workshop, I realized that it is not so bad to make a mistake; it's bad not to learn from it."

After the course, Charlie put his plans into effect. Six months later, his subordinates were asked to rate him again. He attended a second workshop to study these results and reported, "On the way home I was very nervous. I knew I had been working with those guys and not selling so much myself, but I was very much afraid of what they were going to say about how things were going in the office. When I found out that the team spirit and some of those other low scores had jumped from around 30th to the 55th percentile, I was so delighted and relieved that I couldn't say anything all day long."

When he was asked how he acted differently from before, he said, "In previous years when the corporate headquarters said we had to make 110 percent of our original goal, I had called the salesmen in and said, in effect, 'This is ridiculous; we are not going to make it, but you know perfectly well what will happen if we don't. So get out there and work your tail off.' The result was that I worked 20 hours a day and they did nothing.

"This time I approached it differently. I told them three things. First, they were going to have to do some sacrificing for the company. Second, working harder is not going to do much good because we are already working about as hard as we can. What will be required are special deals and promotions. You are going to have to figure out some new angles if we are to make it. Third, I'm going to back you up. I'm going to set a realistic goal with each of you. If you make that goal but don't make the company goal, I'll see to it that you are not punished. But if you do make the company goal, I'll see to it that you will get some kind of special rewards."

When the salesmen challenged Charlie saying he did not have enough influence to give them rewards, rather than becoming angry Charlie promised rewards that were in his power to give—such as longer vacations.

Note that Charlie has now begun to behave in a number of ways that we found to be characteristic of the good institutional manager. He is, above all, higher in power motivation, the desire to influence his salesmen, and lower in his tendency to try to do everything himself. He asks the men to sacrifice for the company. He does not defensively chew them out when they challenge him but tries to figure out what their needs are so that he can influence them. He realizes that his job is more one of strengthening and supporting his subordinates than of criticizing them. And he is keenly interested in giving them just rewards for their efforts.

The changes in his approach to his job have certainly paid off. The sales figures for his office in 1973 were up more than 16 percent over 1972 and up still further in 1974

over 1973. In 1973 his gain over the previous year ranked seventh in the nation; in 1974 it ranked third. And he wasn't the only one in his company to change managerial styles. Overall sales at his company were up substantially in 1973 as compared with 1972, an increase which played a large part in turning the overall company performance around from a $15 million loss in 1972 to a $3 million profit in 1973. The company continued to improve its performance in 1974 with an 11 percent further gain in sales and 38 percent increase in profits.

Of course not everyone can be reached by a workshop. Henry Carter managed a sales office for a company which had very low morale (around the 20th percentile) before he went for training. When morale was checked some six months later, it had not improved. Overall sales gain subsequently reflected this fact since it was only 2 percent above the previous year's figures.

Oddly enough, Henry's problem was that he was so well liked by everybody that he felt little pressure to change. Always the life of the party, he is particularly popular because he supplies other managers with special hard-to-get brands of cigars and wines at a discount. He uses his close ties with everyone to bolster his position in the company, even though it is known that his office does not perform well compared with others.

His great interpersonal skills became evident at the workshop when he did very poorly at one of the business games. When the discussion turned to why he had done so badly and whether he acted that way on the job, two prestigious participants immediately sprang to his defense, explaining away Henry's failure by arguing that the way he did things was often a real help to others and the company. As a result, Henry did not have to cope with such questions at all. He had so successfully developed his role as a likeable, helpful friend to everyone

in management that, even though his salesmen performed badly, he did not feel under
any pressure to change.

CHECKS AND BALANCES

What have we learned from Ken Briggs,
George Prentice, Charlie Blake, and Henry
Carter? Principally, we have discovered
what motive combination makes an effective manager. We have also seen that
change is possible if a person has the right
combination of qualities.

Oddly enough, the good manager in a
large company does not have a high need
for achievement, as we define and measure
that motive, although there must be plenty
of that motive somewhere in his organization. The top managers shown here have a
high need for power and an interest in
influencing others, both greater than their
interest in being liked by people. The manager's concern for power should be socialized—controlled so that the institution as a
whole, not only the individual, benefits.
Men and nations with this motive profile
are empire builders; they tend to create high
morale and to expand the organizations
they head.

But there is also danger in this motive
profile; empire building can lead to im-
perialism and authoritarianism in companies
and in countries.

The same motive pattern which produces
good power management can also lead a
company or a country to try to dominate
others, ostensibly in the interests of organizational expansion. Thus it is not surprising
that big business has had to be regulated
from time to time by federal agencies. And
it is most likely that international agencies
will perform the same regulative function
for empire-building countries.

For an individual, the regulative function
is performed by two characteristics that are
part of the profile of the very best managers
—a greater emotional maturity, where there
is little egotism, and a democratic, coaching
managerial style. If an institutional power
motivation is checked by maturity, it does
not lead to an aggressive, egotistic expan-
siveness.

For countries, this checking means that
they can control their destinies beyond their
borders without being aggressive and hostile. For individuals, it means they can control their subordinates and influence others
around them without resorting to coercion
or to an authoritarian management style.
Real disinterested statesmanship has a vital
role to play at the top of both countries and
companies.

Summarized in this way, what we have
found out through empirical and statistical
investigations may just sound like good
common sense. But the improvement over
common sense is that now the characteristics of the good manager are objectively
known. Managers of corporations can select
those who are likely to be good managers
and train those already in managerial positions to be more effective with more
confidence.

Although Mead first made this observation in 1949, it continues to be significant in today's society. Both in theory and in practice, the role of women in American society (which is primarily an achievement-oriented system) has over the years been little understood and much ignored by psychologists. A peculiar paradox arises in the society because we have an educational system that ostensibly encourages and prepares men and women identically for careers that social and, even more importantly, internal psychological pressures really limit to men. This paradox is reflected by the feelings of the women who somehow overcome these pressures and pursue a particular career: they feel anxious, guilty, unfeminine, and selfish.

Women as well as men in this society are immersed in a culture that rewards and values achievement and that stresses self-reliance, individual freedom, self-realization, and the full development of individual resources, including one's intellectual potential. In *The Achieving Society* (1961), McClelland has carefully elaborated how these values and attitudes (which are rooted in Max Weber's "Protestant Ethic") effect child-rearing practices that foster the development of achievement motivation. Winterbottom's (1958) work has shown that, when early self-reliance and mastery are expected and rewarded by the parents, the child internalizes these values and is prone to develop a high achievement motive (*n* Achievement). (This behavior will not occur, however, if the parents' high standards of excellence and independence reflect authoritarianism or rejection or simply the desire to make their own burdens less.)

Despite the prevalence of these values in most middle-class American homes, femininity and individual achievement continue to be viewed as two desirable but mutually exclusive ends. The cultural attitudes toward sex roles have truly limited the horizons of women. As a result, there is a sig-

Femininity and Successful Achievement: A Basic Inconsistency[*]

MATINA S. HORNER

Each step forward in work as a successful American regardless of sex means a step back as a woman. . . . (Margaret Mead, *Male and Female*)

nificant and increasing absence of American women in the mainstream of thought and achievement in the society. For instance, the *proportion of* women college *graduates* is smaller today than it was 30 years ago, even though in absolute numbers more women are being educated. Furthermore, although the *number* of working women is increasing, the vast majority are found in low-skilled jobs and a very small proportion are working at a level close to that reflecting their education or professional training. Whereas the number of professional women in Europe has doubled in the past 30

* Extensively abridged from "Femininity and Successful Achievement: A Basic Inconsistency" by Matina S. Horner, in *Feminine Personality and Conflict* by J. M. Bardwick, E. Douvan, M. S. Horner, and D. Gutmann. Copyright © 1970 by Wadsworth Publishing Company, Inc. Reprinted by permission of the publisher, Brooks/Cole Publishing Company, Monterey, California, and the author.

years, the number in America has actually declined. There are fewer women in upper-echelon positions now than there were before World War II. Thus a great number of women have been highly educated and trained for various professions or positions of leadership but are not using their skills, even though they may be part of the labor force at some lower level. This situation reflects the greatest loss of potential.

Although the social structure decries the terrible loss of female potential in both economic and personal terms, it provides few, if any, positive incentives or sanctions for career-oriented women. This situation is particularly noticeable for women of middle- or upper-class status who want to work for reasons other than economic necessity or survival. For women the distinction between a "job" and a "career" is very important.

Recently the "intellectual community" has been exerting effort to come to some understanding of the loss of human potential and resources that is reflected in this pattern of behavior. The experimental data to be presented later . . . show that, despite the removal for women of many legal and educational barriers to achievement, which existed until the 20th century, there remains a *psychological barrier* that is considerably more subtle, stubborn, and difficult to overcome. I refer to this barrier as the *motive to avoid success* (M_{-s}). This "fear of success" receives its impetus from the expectancy held by women that success in achievement situations will be followed by negative consequences, including social rejection and the sense of losing one's femininity. . . .

NEGATIVE CONSEQUENCES OF SUCCESS

What exactly are the negative consequences of success in competitive achievement activity for women, and why has it taken us so long to recognize them? Perhaps part of our inability to recognize the problems results from a general lack of awareness of the extent to which we have been influenced by the image of woman and her sex role that has evolved over the centuries. Aristotle claimed that women never suffered from baldness because they never used the contents of their heads. That image of woman appears to have persisted over the centuries. . . . Let us consider what happens when women stray from the image and do use their heads.

If not rejected, they are praised (or castigated) for having Masculine Minds. Clare Booth Luce rejected that kind of praise from a colleague by saying: "I must refuse the compliment that I think like a man. Thought has no sex. One either thinks or one does not." Other women who are actively engaged in professional pursuits find themselves constantly trying to establish or prove their femininity, often going to great efforts and sometimes to extremes to display in dress and speech the obvious popular standards of femininity. Conrad suggested that "A woman with a masculine mind is not a being of superior efficiency; she is simply a phenomenon of imperfect differentiation—interestingly barren and without importance."

Unfortunately, many people unconsciously connect sex with certain characteristics and occupations. Although there is nothing intrinsically feminine about typing or teaching, or intrinsically masculine about medicine, physics, investment counseling, preaching, or just plain "thinking," for that matter, we have had difficulty adjusting to this idea psychologically. As a whole, society has been unable to reconcile personal ambition, accomplishment, and success with femininity. The more successful or independent a woman becomes, the more afraid society is that she has lost her femininity and therefore must be a failure as a wife and mother. She is viewed as a hostile and destructive force within the society. On the other hand, the more successful a man is in his work (as reflected in his high status, salary, and administrative powers—all of which are in keeping with his masculinity), the more attractive he becomes as a spouse and father. Whereas men are unsexed by failure (Mead, 1949), women seem to be unsexed by success.

Maccoby (1963) has pointed out that "the girl who maintains qualities of independence and active striving (achievement-orientation) necessary for intellectual mastery defies the conventions of sex appropriate behavior and must pay a price, *a price in anxiety*." This observation may help explain why, after four years at a very high-ranking women's college (during which time they became "more liberal and independent"—that is, more masculine—in their values and attitudes), girls show a higher incidence of anxiety and psychological disturbance than they did when they were freshman (Sanford, 1961, chap. 24).

At a symposium on the potential of women in which Mannes (1963) discussed the problems of the creative woman and described the "entrance charges" she must pay for the approval of men and other women, the point was made that "nobody objects to a woman's being a good writer or sculptor or geneticist *if*, at the same time, she manages to be a good wife, a good mother, good-looking, good-tempered, well-dressed, well-groomed, and *unaggressive*."

Most American women faced with the conflict between maintaining their feminine image and developing their ability compromise by disguising that ability and abdicating from competition in the outside world. Consider little Sally (from the *Peanuts* comic strip), who remarked, "I never said I wanted to be someone. All I want to do when I grow up is be a good wife and mother. So—why should I have to go to kindergarten?" We are all familiar with the American coed who is intelligent enough

to do well but also too intelligent to get all *As* and thereby lose her man. She knows she will be more "desirable" if she needs the assistance of a male Galahad to help her understand her work. Women have been choosing—perhaps unconsciously—not to develop either their potential or their individuality but rather to live through and for others. This behavior is consistent with Rousseau's idea that a woman's "dignity consists in being unknown to the world; her glory is in the esteem of her husband; her pleasures in the happiness of her family."

Thus, while society has been legally opening its doors to women and decrying the loss of female potential, it has been teaching them to fail outside the home. No one ever seriously objects to a woman's education or intellectual development, provided its objective is to make her a more entertaining companion and a more enlightened, and thus better, wife and mother. Only when her objective is an independent personal career does a problem arise. Mead suggested that intense intellectual striving (of the kind necessary for the serious pursuit of a career) is viewed as "competitively aggressive behavior." The aggressive overtones of competition and success are evident in the fact that each time one person succeeds, someone else fails or is beaten. This situation may well be the basis of fear of success. It seems there is nothing more distasteful than an "uppity" woman who opts to beat a man, especially at "his own game"—be it law, medicine, physics, or rational thought. She will evoke the wrath not only of men but also of other women. Riesman (1964) points out that "women, as with many minority groups, bitterly resent and envy those among them who break out of confinement" and are frequently "shrewish and vindictive toward them."

Freud (1965) pointed out that the whole essence of femininity lies in repressing aggressiveness. A woman is threatened by success because unusual excellence in academic and intellectual areas is unconsciously equated with loss of femininity; as a result, the possibility of social rejection becomes very real. A woman who achieves success may lose her self-esteem and her sense of femininity, which is an internalized standard acquired early in the socialization process. Thus, regardless of whether anyone else finds out about her success, the inconsistency between femininity and successful achievement is so deeply embedded that most women, as Rossi (1965) has indicated, believe that even wanting something more than motherhood is unnatural and reflects emotional disturbance within them. Social rejection following success can also prevent a woman from fulfilling her other needs for affection, love, marriage, and children. Kagan and Moss (1962) summarize the problem and its consequences as follows:

The typical female has greater anxiety over aggressiveness and competitive behavior than the male. She therefore experiences greater conflict over intellectual competition which in turn leads to inhibition of intense strivings for academic excellence.

Assuming that, for most men, active striving for success in competitive achievement activity is consistent with masculinity and self-esteem and does not give rise to the expectancy of negative consequences, it may be that the motive to avoid success is one of the major factors underlying sex differences detected in research on achievement-related motivation and performance. . . .

EMPIRICAL EVIDENCE

I will now present some of the empirical evidence in support of the ideas that have thus far been proposed and discussed.

Sex Differences in the Motive to Avoid Success

The first goal was to determine the extent of any sex differences in the motive to avoid success, and a measure to assess individual differences in this motive was developed (Horner, 1968). It involved a standard TAT (Thematic Apperception Test) for the achievement motive, except that four verbal, rather than pictorial, cues were used. An additional verbal lead was included that could be scored for motive to avoid success. For the 90 women in the study, the cue used was "After first-term finals, Anne finds herself at the top of her medical-school class." The cue for the 88 men in the sample was "After first-term finals, John finds himself at the top of his medical-school class." The subjects in this study were predominantly freshmen and sophomores at a large Midwestern coeducational university. . . .

The subjects' responses can be readily classified into three main groups.

1. Fear of Social Rejection This reaction appeared most frequently. The negative affect and consequences described were rooted mainly in affiliative concerns, including fear of being socially rejected and fear of losing one's friends or one's datability or marriageability. Fear of isolation or loneliness as a result of the success, as well as the desire to keep the success a secret and pretend that intelligence is not there, were also included. The following are examples of stories in this category.

Anne has a boyfriend, Carl, in the same class, and they are quite serious. Anne met Carl at college, and they started dating about their sophomore year in undergraduate school. Anne is rather upset and so is Carl. She wants him to be higher scholastically than she is. Anne will deliberately lower her academic standing the next term, while she does all she subtly can to help Carl. His grades come up and Anne soon drops out of med school. They marry and he goes on in school while she raises their family.

Anne doesn't want to be number one in her class. She feels she shouldn't rank so high because of social reasons. She drops down to ninth in the class and then marries the boy who graduates number one.

2. Concern about One's Normality or Femininity

This group comprises stories in which negative affect and consequences are free of any affiliative concern and independent of whether anyone finds out about the success. Typical reactions in this category include doubting one's femininity, feeling guilt or despair about the success, and wondering about one's normality.

Anne is completely ecstatic but at the same time feels guilty. She wishes that she could stop studying so hard, but parental and personal pressures drive her. She will finally have a nervous breakdown and quit med school and marry a successful young doctor.

Anne cannot help but be pleased; yet she is unhappy. She had not wanted to be a doctor . . . she had half hoped her grades would be too poor to continue, but she had been too proud to allow that to happen. She had worked extraordinarily hard and her grades showed it. "It is not enough," Anne thinks. "I am not happy." She is not sure what she wants—only feels the pressure to achieve something, even if it's something she doesn't want. Anne says "To hell with the whole business" and goes into social work—not hardly as glamorous, prestigious, or lucrative; but she is happy.

The great amount of confusion manifested in this last story was not uncommon.

3. Denial

The stories in this third group were remarkable for their psychological ingenuity. Some of the girls denied the reality or possibility of the cue by actually changing its contents, distorting it, or simply refusing to believe it. Others tried to absolve Anne of responsibility for her success—as if it were some antisocial act. Also included in this group are the stories in which the success was attributed to cheating rather than to the girl's ability. Stories involving denial of various types made up the second largest category and were particularly interesting.

Anne is a *code* name for a nonexistent person created by a group of med students. They take turns taking exams and writing papers for Anne. . . .

Anne is really happy she's on top, though Tom is higher than she—though that's as it should be. . . . Anne doesn't mind Tom winning.

Anne is talking to her counselor. The counselor says she will make a fine nurse. She will continue her med-school courses. She will study very hard and find she can and will become a good nurse.

It was luck that Anne came out on top of her med class because she didn't want to go to med school anyway.

This last comment is an interesting reversal of the sour-grapes theme.

Several of the girls became very personally involved with Anne's dilemma: "I don't know. Her problem is apparently insoluble, because she is really a good student. Will she humble herself? Wait and see" or "I wonder if she will ever marry" or "The last I heard, she was still in school but had broken off her engagement." Others assumed the role of society and punished her for her accomplishment. The intensity, hostility, and symbolic quality of the language used by some of the girls was somewhat startling. They accused Anne of being a "social pariah"—someone who must "justify her existence." They attacked her physical attractiveness, her virtue, her sexuality, and sometimes even her person. For instance, in one story her classmates, "disgusted with her behavior . . . jump on her in a body and beat her. She is maimed for life." These stories in general tend to support Honoré de Balzac's contention that "A woman who is guided by the head and not the heart is a social pestilence: she has all the defects of a passionate and affectionate woman, with none of her compensations: she is without pity, without love, without virtue, without sex."

Overall, the two most common themes in the stories dealt with Anne's physical unattractiveness and with her "lonely Friday and Saturday nights." This result receives further support from some recent data gathered at an outstanding Eastern women's college. In an interview, the girls were told: "Anne is at the top of her med-school class. Describe her." More than 70 percent of them described Anne as having an unattractive face, figure, or manners. Interestingly enough, more than 50 percent described her as "tall" (perhaps reducing the number of men who would find her attractive). . . .

The sheer magnitude of the differences in the kind of responses made to the TAT cues by men and women in the first study was very striking. As had been hypothesized, the women did in fact show significantly more evidence of motive to avoid success than did the men. Only 8 out of 88, or less than 10 percent, of the men, compared with 59 out of 90, or more than 65 percent, of the women, wrote stories high in fear-of-success imagery. The percentage of white women showing fear-of-success imagery in response to this cue has been consistently between 62 percent and 75 percent in all the subsequent studies.

Perhaps the best way to understand the sex differences found is to consider a few of the typical stories written by men.

John is a conscientious young man who worked hard. He is pleased with himself. John has always wanted to go into medicine and is very dedicated. His hard work has paid off. He is thinking that he must not let up now, but must work even harder than he did before. His good marks have encouraged him (he may even consider going into research now). While others with good first-term marks sluff off, John continues working hard and eventually graduates at the top of his class.

The positive affect, increased striving, and heightened level of aspiration following success that are found in this and many of the other male stories are strikingly different from the typical female responses. The fol-

lowing story clarifies the positive impact that successful achievement has on the social relationships of men.

John is very pleased with himself, and he realizes that all his efforts have been rewarded: He has finally made the top of his class. John has worked hard, and his long hours of study have paid off. He spent hour after hour in preparation for finals. He is thinking of his girl, Cheri, whom he will marry at the end of med school. He realizes he can give her all the things she desires after he becomes established. He will go on in med school making good grades and be successful in the long run.

Relating Motive to Performance

We have observed great differences in the presence of fear-of-success imagery in men and women based on differences in the expected consequences of successful achievement. It is reasonable therefore to speculate that the motive to avoid success is in fact a major variable underlying previously unresolved sex differences in studies of achievement motivation.

The next issue to consider is how—if at all—individual differences in the motive to avoid success affect behavior in achievement-oriented situations. Inasmuch as motives affect performance only when they are aroused, we should expect to see the behavioral manifestations of motivation to avoid success only in competitive achievement conditions in which success implies aggressiveness and behavior unbecoming to a "lady." Anxiety aroused by the expectancy of negative consequences of successful competition and by its aggressive overtones is assumed to be most prevalent in the most able or highly motivated women who are competing against men, particularly if they are doing so in male-dominated fields.

In the study designed to explore some of these hypothesis (Horner, 1968), each girl was administered a number of tasks in a large mixed-sex competitive condition (not

TABLE 1
The Motive to Avoid Success and Performance in Competitive and
Noncompetitive Achievement Situations

Motive to Avoid Success	Performed Better in Noncompetitive Situation	Performed Better in Competitive Situation
High	13	4
Low	1	12

unlike a large classroom or lecture situation). The girls were then randomly assigned to three other experimental conditions. Some were placed in a strictly noncompetitive (NC) situation in which they worked on a number of tasks guided only by tape-recorded instructions. The rest of the girls were divided at random between two competitive situations in which they worked on the same tasks and followed the same instructions as did those girls in the NC situation. In one of these two groups each girl competed against one male and in the other group against one female. None of the girls knew or had previous contact with the competitors. Performance in the initial large group condition was most highly related to that in the two-person, opposite-sex competitive condition. This result is reasonable, since the large group also involved members of both sexes. Only the 30 subjects in the NC condition worked in both a competitive and a noncompetitive situation.

It was important to exert some control over initial ability differences between the subjects; otherwise, I could not have determined how much of the difference in performance stemmed from motivation and how much from initial ability differences. In this study the best control possible was letting each subject act as her own control —that is, perform in both the competitive and noncompetitive setting. Thus the performance of the 30 women in the NC situation was compared with their own previous performance in the large mixed-sex situation. The tasks involved were two standard, similar, and highly correlated verbal tasks.

The results from this part of the study are shown in Table 1. Clearly, the women who score high in fear-of-success imagery do better working alone than they do in the competitive condition, whereas those who score low in fear-of-success imagery do better in the competitive condition. The performance of this latter group of women resembles that of the men, who are generally low in fear-of-success imagery and two-thirds of whom do better in the competitive than in the noncompetitive situation.

What man has not yearned to create a profitable venture as his own boss? Most of our major corporations are such dreams made reality. Today, something new is on the "profitable venture horizon"—i.e., women, in increasing numbers, also want to start their own companies.

Why should women risk entrepreneurship when statistics show that about 72 percent of all new ventures fail within the first two years? A Dun and Bradstreet survey revealed a 6 percent rise in small business failures for 1974; dollar losses surpassed $3 billion.[1] New, inexperienced firms accounted for most of the losses; specifically, companies five years old or less were responsible for 60 percent of the total failures.

Sufficient capital, sound ideas, and hard work are not always enough to make a profitable new venture. However, the simple fact that thriving self-employed people are still around is testimony enough that the odds are surmountable; and, increasingly, women want to take their chances.

ENTREPRENEUR DEFINED

Basically, the entrepreneur is an innovative individual who creates and builds a business from nonexistence. The entrepreneur assumes responsibility for not only the development and management of the enterprise but also for the risk of gain or loss from the venture. Classical economists viewed entrepreneurs as capitalists who financed and directed factors of production into marketable products. Now it is believed that entrepreneurs should have certain personal characteristics in addition to being risk-takers and manager/owners.[2] For instance, a corporate manager who supervises

---

[1] *Dun and Bradstreet Small Business Survey* (1975).

[2] Michael Palmer, "The Application of Psychological Testing to Entrepreneurial Potential," *California Management Review*, vol. 13, no. 3, pp. 32–38.

Entrepreneurship: A New Female Frontier*

ELEANOR BRANTLEY SCHWARTZ

and performs delegated tasks is not an entrepreneur, although he or she may perform entrepreneurial tasks.[3] Often, the entrepreneur is not the best manager for a company as it matures since he or she generally may be "unable to allocate administrative responsibility and to set up procedures and controls." Problems typically arise "after a new company reaches sales of $6 million."[4]

THE STUDY

While female corporate executives/managers have been the subject of recent research, little attention has been given to female entreprepreneurs.[5] In contrast, the

---

* *Journal of Contemporary Business*, Winter 1976, pp. 47–76.

[3] Herbert E. Kierulff, "Can Entrepreneurs Be Developed?" *MSU Business Topics* (Winter 1975), p. 40.

[4] "Venture Capital and Management," *Proceedings, Second Annual Boston College Management Seminar* (May 1970), p. 83.

[5] A recent pilot study, *The Female Entrepreneur* (1975), was conducted by James W. Schreier at the Wisconsin Center for Venture Management. His study included an examination of entrepreneurial activity among Milwaukee, Wisconsin, women who started their own businesses.

entrepreneurial behavior of males has been researched extensively with conclusions rendered regarding the characteristics, psychology, and management styles of these male entrepreneurs. The purpose of this study is to discern the set of characteristics, motivation, and attitudes of female entrepreneurs; e.g.,

Who is the female entrepreneur? Do women who start their own business possess characteristics similar to those of men who start their own business?

Why do some women shun the security of more traditional paths to strike out on their own?

How do women view themselves in their entrepreneurship role? How do their attitudes toward their entrepreneurial roles compare to the general essentials of entrepreneurship concluded from research on male entrepreneurs?

How do women perceive the attitudes of males and females (e.g., lenders, investors, suppliers, customers, employees) who do business with or work for them?

What deterrents to success can women identify as unique to them as females (in contrast to their male counterparts)?

Can women develop the qualities considered essential to entrepreneurship?

To determine answers to these questions, we reviewed literature from 1958 to 1975 on male entrepreneurs, and 25 female entrepreneurs were interviewed, either in person, by telephone, or by mail. Twenty female entrepreneurs participated in the survey; this represented an 80 percent response. The female entrepreneurs were not characterized by geographic location, and they represented a variety of businesses, although most of them fell within the "services" category.

The goal of the study was to develop a better understanding of female entrepreneurs—the kind of women, as compared to

the kind of men, who become entrepreneurs—and what they go through to build and maintain a new business. This understanding can help determine the special education and training needs of self-employed women and of those who want to become self-employed. As a result, educational programs to provide needed skills to existing and potential female entrepreneurs can be planned better. And, importantly, many of the 7.2 million women who head families may see broader directions for career opportunities.[6]

THE FINDINGS

The study focused on perspectives from the female entrepreneurs as they correlated to or contrasted with the findings of research literature on male entrepreneurs. Perceptions of the surveyed female entrepreneurs are presented as major findings and then related to research on male entrepreneurs in the discussion that follows.

Finding 1 Major motivators for becoming entrepreneurs were perceived to be the need to achieve, the desire to be independent, the need for job satisfaction, and the necessity—economically

Discussion Some researchers have concluded that most entrepreneurs have a long, lonely, and difficult road; those who follow it must be a special breed. Numerous studies offer insight into the psychology and characteristics of male entrepreneurs. They generally conclude that individuals with entrepreneurial drive are not drawn randomly from the population. On the contrary, they are likely to be found in certain social structures, to possess common behavioral traits and to emerge especially when the economy displays certain characteristics.[7]

---

[6] As of March 1975.

[7] In addition to personal motivations and characteristics, individuals tend to become entrepreneurs in proportion to entrepreneurial opportunity;

For instance, "social marginality"[8] appears to be one of the most likely forces motivating a man to set up his own business.[9] The owner/manager role is chosen to develop an acceptable self-identity. Discrepancy between perceived ability in one's self and work roles available creates an inconsistency resolved only in being one's own boss.[10] For example, an "educationally unsuccessful" person from a modestly well-off family needs "paper qualifications" for corporate management mobility. Rather than accepting a corporate situation with less status, he develops his own business.[11]

Some research presents evidence that entrepreneurs are motivated strongly by an almost overwhelming ego (desire to succeed, self-esteem)[12] and perhaps, ultimately, self-fulfillment needs. Safety and physiological needs of entrepreneurs tend to be low, but need for self-esteem is great.

Self-esteem needs must be satisfied almost entirely before self-actualization factors motivate. Once met, the entrepreneur may seek to self-actualize through other new ventures to build from scratch. The entrepreneur may talk about retiring, but seldom does. If the business is sold, usually another is started eventually.[13]

Almost all studies on entrepreneurs show the desire for independence as a motivation to become one's own boss. Entrepreneurs tend to strongly dislike authority, especially when they feel they can do a better job than their superiors.

However, perhaps, the strongest research-supported motivator is the need for achievement—the desire to do well—not for social prestige, but for a feeling of accomplishment.[14] A high need for achievement leads people to:

behave in most of the ways they should behave if they are to fulfill the entrepreneurial role successfully. . . . The achievement motive should lead individuals to seek out situations which provide moderate challenge to their skills, to perform better in such situations, and to have greater confidence in the likelihood of their success. It should make them conservative where things are completely beyond their control, as in games of chance, and happier where they have some opportunity of influencing the outcome of a series of events by their own actions and of knowing concretely what those actions have accomplished. . . . Finally, it should encourage them to value money not for itself but as a measure of success.[15]

Although the entrepreneurs often think they are motivated by money, in reality, it is "the achievement of creating an organi-

---

i.e., rising income per capita in an expanding economy leads to investment opportunity. In turn, increased investment promotes entrepreneurial growth. Also, high levels of change combined with economic expansion (as, for example, the 10- to 15-year period after World War II) provides entrepreneurial opportunities.

[8] Discontinuity between how one perceives oneself and roles available to him in society. For a review of the "social marginality" concept, see H. P. Dickie-Clark, *The Marginal Situation* (Routledge & Kegan Paul, 1966).

[9] O. F. Collins, D. G. Moore, and D. B. Unwalla, "The Enterprising Man," *MSU Business Topics* (1964).

[10] Second-generation entrepreneurs appear to have a much lower level of social marginality than their parents. Frequently they admit that if they had not inherited it, they would not have created the business. See Charles B. Swayne and William R. Tucker, *The Effective Entrepreneur* (New Jersey: General Learning Press, 1973), p. 14.

[11] A socially marginal person with a blue-collar background is believed to be more likely to choose an extreme political ideology or trade union role than to become an owner/manager.

[12] According to A. H. Maslow, *Motivation and Personality* (Harper & Row, 1954), ego needs involve self-esteem (self-respect, self-confidence, autonomy) and reputation (status, recognition, appreciation, and respect of others).

[13] Swayne and Tucker, *Effective Entrepreneur*, chap. 3.

[14] David C. McClelland, J. W. Atkinson, R. A. Clark, and E. L. Lowell, *The Achievement Motive* (New York: Appleton-Century-Crofts, Inc., 1953).

[15] David C. McClelland, *The Achieving Society* (Princeton, N.J.: Van Nostrand, 1961), p. 238.

zation" that motivates them. Money is but a criterion of the degree of success.[16]

To determine if females are motivated differently than male entrepreneurs, the entrepreneurs surveyed were asked to rank from "insignificant" to "considerably strong" the role of the following motivators in their decision to start their own business: achievement, independence, status, money, power, competition, affiliation,[17] security, and job satisfaction. Many of the respondents included the rationale for their rankings, and the responses showed that women who decided to start their own business are motivated the same as men who do. Just as in Schreier's study,[18] a significant number of women indicated that economic necessity was a basic reason. (None of the respondents started their business as a hobby.) Some female entrepreneurs were heads of household and felt they went into business out of economic necessity (they felt they could make more money on their own than in working for someone else). However, most of the respondents, just as the male entrepreneurs, seemed to be motivated primarily by achievement and self-actualizing needs. "Ability versus opportunity" reasons given for leaving a corporate position could lead to the conclusion that "social marginality" was also a major motivator.

Interestingly, significantly more than half of the respondents had a management, or semiadministrative, position for two or more years before going into business for

themselves. They left for achievement, independence, or job satisfaction needs; e.g., one entrepreneur commented, "I started my own business mainly because I couldn't get the kind of job I felt my background warranted." Another entrepreneur got only so far; management was unwilling to give her more challenge. "I could not achieve my personal career goals. I got frustrated, definitely bored, and left to be my own boss." Another relatively new entrepreneur left her management position after four years because:

Much of the work I could not justify as meaningful. I found myself on a treadmill, my creativity and initiative suppressed; everything had to be done the "organization's way." I was miserable. Rather than thwart my goals to succeed, I set up my own company.

Another entrepreneur left a well-paying corporate position to set up her own company because:

I got tired of being promoted again and again only to find the job had been narrowed or that I reported to someone on the "totem hierarchy" lower than my male predecessor did.

Other comments, such as the following, further supported female entrepreneurs' needs for achievement, independence and job satisfaction:

I wanted to be master of my own fate. I deliberately went after the education, technical and business; and, more important, gained experience in other people's companies to ready myself for the big step.

I feel like I've earned something by the sweat of my brow.

Being my own boss is a continual learning experience. It's forced me to be creative when I thought I couldn't be. I've had to shift gears when things went wrong. I must depend on my own sense of self-confidence and courage. Besides, it's a great feeling to break new ground.

I wasn't getting anywhere. I was frustrated and depressed, though I told myself to "keep smiling." I didn't want to lose sight of my goal,

---

[16] Ralph M. Hogdill, *Individual Behavior and Group Achievement* (Oxford University Press, 1969), chap. 5.

[17] Affiliation was included because traditionally women have been labeled as having high affiliation needs in contrast to high achievement needs. See Finding 6.

[18] The women surveyed in Schreier's study, *The Female Entrepreneur*, started their businesses (1) out of economic necessity (whether prompted by a specific financial crisis or a family crisis—e.g., a divorce), (2) as a hobby, or (3) because they saw a marketing opportunity and seized it.

but after so long I couldn't persevere any longer. I left and set up my own business. I no longer have "just a job." And I've proved to myself that a woman can do almost anything if she wants to badly enough. Women's place, no matter what anyone says, is where she *wants* to be.

I figured I'd never make it to the top of a corporation, so I just decided to create my own.

Research by Professor Eugene Jennings[19] highlighted a tendency for women high-achievers to become disenchanted in a mature organizational environment. While some high achievers (male and female) can compromise with corporate requirements, one type of person cannot. Jennings found that after ten years, and often less in management, female high-achievers had learned how to carry authority and to manage profit objectives. Many of them made $20,000 to $40,000 and were managers of a branch office, department, or zone but, at this point, left the company. Three alternatives, according to Jennings, were likely to attract high female achievers:

- One's own business.
- Small, service-oriented corporations that require initiative and creativity.
- Staff position (perhaps in the same corporation) in, for example, planning, advertising, personnel, or some aspect of finance.

Finding 2 The most important personality traits for success as an entrepreneur were thought probably to be strong ego and achievement drives.

Discussion An almost "consuming desire to succeed," "capacity to work hard for long hours," and "willingness to forego immediate satisfactions for future gain" were considered to be absolutely necessary to "make it" as an entrepreneur. Not only were

these items self-requirements, but also entrepreneurs want to hire (in the words of one of them) "only energetic achievers who are unafraid to work 18-hour days and really want to get ahead." As many as half of the respondents believed an entrepreneur could overcome most "reasonable" economic barriers if the personality makeup combined a strong desire to succeed with willingness to work hard (see Finding 6).

The majority of respondents felt that not only must entrepreneurs want to succeed but also that they must be confident they have what it takes to achieve the results they want. In a *New York Times* study, a female entrepreneur expressed this self-confidence as well as an intuitive ability to read the market: " . . . . My guts just told me this was the right thing to do. I can't say why. And I always find a way to come out on my feet. There's something in my nature that just doesn't allow me to fail."[20]

Almost all of the female entrepreneur respondents felt they and other entrepreneurs are nonconformers. Evaluations, decisions, and actions are made in terms of what the entrepreneur wants or thinks must be done.[21] They believe their success requires aggressive determination to "make things happen." "Being an entrepreneur just simply requires a certain amount of toughness," said one entrepreneur. Interestingly, one researcher emphasized a necessity for strong empathy to balance ego toughness. A weak ego and strong empathy combination was found to result in a "nice guy" who is inadequately assertive to fight the new firm's survival battle. A strong ego with weak empathy is sufficiently assertive, but insensitivity to needs and feelings of others

---

[19] As reported by John Cunniff, "Obstacles for Female Managers" (by Professor Eugene Jennings, Michigan State University), *Atlanta Journal* (11 July 1975).

[20] Jean Lipman, "Female Entrepreneurs Like Del Goetz Make 'Man's Work' Pay Off," *New York Times*, vol. 219, pp. 1, 19.

[21] Scheier's study, *The Female Entrepreneur*, showed a tendency for entrepreneurs not to communicate what is on their mind—not that they do not mean to, but because they just do not think to do it.

causes resistance to seemingly "bulldozer" tactics. An individual with both weak ego and weak empathy is a follower-type.[22] These female entrepreneurs indicated comfortableness with their highly developed aggressiveness and leadership behavior, although they also indicated awareness that many traditionally oriented people often are not comfortable with this determination and assertiveness. A substantial majority acknowledged that an entrepreneur must be able to endure high levels of stress. Said one respondent, "The entrepreneur must be able to maintain control in unusual situations and still be innovative after intensive demands."

Finding 3   Most of the women entrepreneurs tend to closely watch and control their business operations, thus leaning toward an autocratic management style.

Discussion   "Maximizing sales and controlling costs is a major concern," said one of the women entrepreneurs reflecting the view of all the entrepreneurs surveyed. "I must maintain an adequate cash position." Research shows that the leadership style most characteristic of male entrepreneurs in the first stages of their company's growth also tends to be autocratic. Although male entrepreneurs tend to have a "Theory Y" style, neither Theory X nor Y appears to be a better entrepreneurial style.[23] Fighting survival in an uncertain environment, however, most entrepreneurs tend to make decisions in favor of sales, production, or costs over "people" considerations. A business name must be established, consumer acceptance gained, competitors combatted; the major goal is to create a profitable base and, therefore, survival. The company depends on the drive and resources of the entrepreneur, so authority revolves around the entrepreneur, who, incidentally, rarely delegates well anyway.[24] As the organization matures, a more balanced approach appears to emerge among the male entrepreneurs. People increasingly are recognized as essential to the company, though many of them may not commit the same energy to their jobs as the entrepreneur. On the other hand, entrepreneurs are eternally aware that not even one unproductive employee can be afforded. The "basic design of a small business is its lean and thin structure."[25]

In general, research shows male entrepreneurs to be fair-to-good planners and intuitive, keen market analysts. Short-term plans are stressed with concentration on tactical plans to achieve them. Less time may be devoted to organizing and staffing, except in selecting good personnel. The entrepreneurs in this study recognized the importance of all the management functions, especially planning and staffing (see Finding 5). Generally, persuasive leaders tend to motivate and control their support people effectively.

As a company matures, a leadership crisis may occur.[26] Emphasis must move from an entrepreneurial to a managerial orientation.[27] Research indicates that most entrepreneurs are unsuited temperamentally to manage as the firm moves into a stage[28] that needs professional management. For the organization to remain effective, the entrepreneur must delegate—decentralize control—and adapt to sophisticated man-

[22] Swayne and Tucker, *Effective Entrepreneur,* p. 25.

[23] Douglas McGregor, *The Human Side of Enterprise* (New York: McGraw-Hill, 1960).

[24] Robert Blake and Jane Mouton, *The Managerial Grid* (Houston, Tex.: Gulf Publishing Company, 1964).

[25] Swayne and Tucker, *Effective Entrepreneur,* p. 14.

[26] Rohrer, Hibler, and Replogh, *Managers for Tomorrow* (New American Library, 1969), p. 258.

[27] Richard Ivan Henderson, "The Best of Two Worlds: The Entrepreneurial Manager," *Journal of Small Business Management,* p. 5.

[28] According to economic life-cycle models, a business develops through four stages: (1) birth and struggle for survival, (2) adolescence and rapid growth, (3) maturity, and (4) senescence and death.

agement. Few entrepreneurs can so drastically change their management style.[29] In cases in which the entrepreneur is concerned "with specifics and views the business as an extension of himself," the company as it matures needs a professional manager concerned with "integration of systems and the long-range planning necessary for long-term growth."[30] The female entrepreneurs surveyed in this study had not been in business long enough to draw any conclusions about how their management style might evolve as their businesses mature. Only one comment was made which may be a clue, "I'm a builder, not a manager."

Finding 4   The initial and major barrier experienced was felt to be credit discrimination during the capital formation stage. Many of the responding female entrepreneurs said credit was denied just because they were women. In general, however, they found that once established both women and men would do business with them.

Discussion   In an open-end question,[31] the respondents were asked to give the biggest obstacles(s) they had encountered, which was unique to them as females, in getting their business off the ground. See Table 1 for the barriers indicated most often.

Putting together the necessary capital was felt to be the greatest challenge. Though they recognized that this also was possibly true for males, women felt that it was more of a barrier for them. The major

TABLE 1
Major Barriers Experienced Most Frequently by New Female Entrepreneurs

Barriers	Times Mentioned
Obtaining lines of credit	17
Weak collateral position	11
Lack of business training and knowledge	13
Lack of management experience (staffing, supervising, directing)	12
Lack of respect for women	3
Demands of the company affecting stability of marriage	9
Overcoming some of society's belief that women are not as serious as men about business matters	4

sources of initial capital reported included their own savings; loans (or gifts) from husband, father or relative; and bank loans. Many of them felt that, generally, of commercial loan sources, clearing banks had the lowest interest rates and simplest procedures for getting a loan. Said one female entrepreneur, "Banks determine the entrepreneurs of tomorrow." She stresses that banks, in general, need to be more lenient toward small business. She found the small entrepreneur stands a better chance with a smaller bank: "In the process of growing itself, the bank is more willing to take a chance." The general consensus of those who had experienced difficulty obtaining credit was that, because of the Equal Credit Opportunity Act,[32] future female entrepreneurs would not be as likely to have this problem "just because they are women." All of the respondents felt it absolutely essential to establish and maintain a good credit rating.

Research shows that the odds against any new entrepreneur obtaining venture capital are high—perhaps as high as 50 to 1. Lack

[29] Larry E. Greiner, "Evolution and Revolution as Organizations Grow," *Harvard Business Review* (July–August 1972), p. 39.

[30] Swayne and Tucker, *Effective Entrepreneur*, p. 16.

[31] The question asked the respondents was: "Aside from general obstacles to entrepreneurial success for anyone (e.g., unfavorable economic climate, governmental restrictions, and so on), what particular barriers have you experienced which you feel were unique to you as a female entrepreneur?"

[32] The Equal Credit Opportunity Act (effective 28 October 1975) prohibits discrimination against credit applicants on the basis of sex or marital status. It covers all those who regularly extend credit to individuals, including banks, finance companies, department stores, credit card issuers, and government agencies, such as the Small Business Administration.

of knowledge and communication of information on the venture capital process among entrepreneurs, capital sources, and intermediaries were often major impediments. Not only do new entrepreneurs not have access to all venture capital sources, but also government tax and regulatory policies can impede the flow of venture capital.[33] Importantly, most venture capital financiers weigh the entrepreneur's management capabilities as much as the merit of the venture idea. Consequently, entrepreneurs should have business plans, financial requirements, and repayment proposals well thought out, with a professional appearance (typed, etc.). Useful persons to consult in the mechanics of starting a business include an accountant and lawyer. A company's profitability depends, to a large extent, on strategic accounting, taxation and legal arrangements.[34]

Those respondents who saw their biggest obstacle as overcoming their lack of training and business knowledge indicated they had to learn basic things such as how to:

. . . tackle business problems as a leader.
. . . wade through confusing and often hazy details to get at the crux of the business problem.
. . . compensate for lack of experience (a) from no formal education in schools of business and finance, and (b) at management levels in the business world itself.
. . . deal with available sources of credit and financing.
. . . negotiate contracts and, in some cases, deal with unions.
. . . wade through the myriad laws and regulations on how business must report its activities.[35]

[33] "Venture Capital and Management," p. 52.

[34] Ibid.

[35] New female entrepreneurs expressed amazement at learning the seeming endlessness of regulations that affected them at city (e.g., business license, zoning restrictions), state (e.g., sales and income taxes, workers' compensation), and federal (e.g., payroll tax, social security, income tax, unemployment tax) levels, for example.

Lack of management experience (staffing, supervising, directing) did not concern the respondents as much as lack of access to credit and need for more business knowledge. A number of respondents had learned that "acquiring an efficient working team is a trial and error process." They pinpointed three critical principles important to building an effective workforce: (1) good selection procedures, (2) incentives to motivate good performers to stay with the firm, and (3) prompt dismissal of inefficient people.

Almost all the respondents would not marry unless the "partner could understand and fit into the female entrepreneur's business owner role." Combining the demands of marriage, and especially a family, with the demands of a business seemed hazardous to both the marriage and the business unless the partner was understanding and cooperative when the business had to take a dominant role. However, the entrepreneurs married to such a partner felt that their husband's understanding and support was a decided asset. A small percentage of the respondents said their business caused their divorce. Many unmarried women said they had little time for frivolous dating or a social life, but expressed no regret for the business's erosion into their personal lives.

Finding 5 The greatest common mistake the majority of the female entrepreneurs felt they had made was underestimating the cost of operating their business and marketing their product or service.

Discussion The respondent's biggest fiasco was "running out of money," which was felt to result largely from a lack of experience in handling money. Almost equally blamed was that they "did not plan well enough." The general consensus was that everything had to be soundly planned for—from the cost of marketing to the building up of the marketing organization. As expressed by one respondent. "You have to have an idea, but you also have to have the capital and management if you are to succeed with the idea. The idea must be marketed, and this costs money. The capital goes fast, at first, with no income. But regardless of how good the product or service is, you have to have customers. You can't cut marketing costs easily, or taper them down quickly, if you want to get where you want to go. Instead, you must plan carefully and then through good management handle your financial affairs prudently."

The importance of managing money is supported further by a recent quote of a female entrepreneur in the moving and storage business, "Building equity is top priority now. We got through a very rough winter because I know how to handle cash."[36] Lack of experience and success in handling money is a major problem for male entrepreneurs also.[37] Inept management has been shown to be the major cause for business failure; the Dun and Bradstreet 1974 survey showed it to be the contributing factor in nine out of every ten failures. Modern operations, and particularly today's uncertain economic conditions, demand management expertise. Inexperienced entrepreneurs are apt to go under quickly. The Dun and Bradstreet survey showed key management problems responsible for the percents shown in Table 2 of this total failure rate:

Companies with small financial reserves were involved in approximately 68 percent of the total failures. The difficulties of striking out on one's own have increased because of rising costs, expensive credit, and an uncertain business climate.

Finding 6 The female entrepreneurs strongly felt that women, just as men, have entrepreneurial qualities to some extent and in some combination. They believe that

---

36 Lipman, "Female Entrepreneurs," pp. 1, 19.
37 "Venture Capital and Management."

TABLE 2
Key Management Problems

Key Problem	Percent of Total Failure Rate
Lack of experience in the line	15%
Lack of managerial experience	14
Unbalanced experience	22
Incompetence	40

these abilities can be developed with an understanding of the qualities important to entrepreneurship.

Discussion The respondents felt, almost unanimously, that women who demonstrate entrepreneurial characteristics and inclinations have as good a chance to become successful entrepreneurs as men who have these traits and desires. They have to learn, just as do men, how to create and take advantage of business opportunities and solve business problems. As one of the female entrepreneurs pointed out, "The rules of the game must be known before either a man or a woman can play the game." Ambition, high self-esteem, energy, competitiveness, achievement motivation, willingness to assume risk, and a high need for independence were considered necessary qualities for entrepreneurial success. Women have these potentials, which, under the proper conditions, can be developed. Generally all the respondents felt about themselves as this female entrepreneur, "I have never for a minute thought I couldn't do something just because I'm a woman. Or that I should be a certain way just because I'm a woman. I'm a person first. I always intended to be in a business of my own in some form at some time. I don't think it was a new or urgent drive that impelled me into business—just a simple ambition that had been with me as long as I can remember." Increasingly, research shows that neither sex exclusively possesses a certain aptitude or ability. Where women generally excel, there are men who also excel and vice versa.[38]

Research supports the notion that entrepreneurial abilities can be developed in male adults (based on researcher/psychologist David McClelland's work in India).[39] McClelland found the "need for achievement" to be the major force motivating entrepreneurship among males. Three factors were found to be important in the development of achievement motivation in males: (1) the parents' high achievement standards; (2) encouragement and warmth in the home; and (3) a nondominating, nonauthoritarian father. Females traditionally have been thought to be motivated by a "need for affiliation or external social approval" rather than by an "internalized desire to excel."[40] Little research has been done specifically on the development of achievement needs and entrepreneurial behavior in females. However, a few studies have been conducted on development of achievement needs in career-oriented women in a corporate environment. For example, sociologist Jean Lipman-Blumen showed that career women tend to have a dominant or dissatisfied mother (or equal dominance between the parents). The female tends to pursue a domestic life style if the father is dominant. A dissatisfied mother's influence is stronger than a dominant father, however. Neither the parents' income, occupation, or education, nor number of siblings or

mother's career was found to have any relationship in shaping career versus domestic goals.[41]

Margaret Henning studied 125 U.S.-Canadian female corporate presidents and vice presidents and found that these achieving women tended to be either only children or the oldest in an all-girl family; had strong self-esteem; and were close to their fathers. Because their parents had the same ambitions for them as for a son, they grew up with the same choices boys have. They were not a "girl's girl"; rather, they liked intellectually serious girls. They dated males who respected a woman's intellect. Once in the business world, they became a protege of a male executive several levels higher in the company and related to him as they once had to their father (e.g., role model and security base).[42] Another study indicated that only moderate levels of warmth and permissiveness, coupled with high achievement expectations by parents, facilitated female achievement behavior. It was postulated that if females are oversocialized with too much warmth or too much restrictiveness, they tend to develop conforming, dependent (traditionally feminine) behavioral patterns. Further, fathers may be particularly important in encouraging independence and achieving behavior in females, especially if the mothers are traditional women. Achievement behavior can be reinforced or negated by other adults, e.g., as in the case of teachers who react negatively to task-oriented behavior in bright girls but positively to socially oriented behavior.[43]

---

[38] A nonprofit, New York-based firm with 12 testing facilities across the country that has tested for differences in male and female aptitudes since 1922. Thousands of men and women of all ages have been tested; however, the largest sample has been young high school graduates.

[39] David C. McClelland, "Achievement Motivation Can be Developed," *Harvard Business Review*, vol. 43, no. 6 (November–December 1965).

[40] Aletha Huston Stein and Margaret M. Bailey, "The Socialization of Achievement Orientation in Females," *The Psychological Bulletin 80* (November 1973), pp. 345–66.

---

[41] Jean Lipman-Blumen, "What Shapes a Woman's Wish for a Career or To Be A Full-time Housewife?" *Scientific American* (May 1973).

[42] Margaret Henning (Ph.D. dissertation Simmons College).

[43] See U. Bronfenbrenner, "Some Familial Antecedents of Responsibility and Leadership in Adolescents," in L. Petrullo and B. M. Bass, eds., *Lead-*

Interestingly, research also shows that females achieve well during early school years, but their achievement efforts tend to diminish as they reach adolescence and adulthood.[44] Doing well in school does not appear to make a female more intellectual or interested in intellectual pursuits. On the other hand, school as a contributing factor to later work achievement does not promote better school performance among males.[45] Perhaps this is because society has not expected women to "succeed" or wield power in the business world, but to be "feminine" —i.e., submissive, unassertive, emotional, and sociable. These expectations can become self-fulfilling prophecies. To succeed in the business world, qualities such as determination, assertiveness, and objective and analytical thinking are needed, whether male or female. The problem has been that a man with these traits is a "great guy" while a woman traditionally has been "unfeminine." This has put many nontraditionally achieving women into a doublebind. A frustration expressed by one respondent who was a corporate manager before setting up her own company was having to tread a thin line between "too little assertion" to get results and too much assertion "for a woman." Another respondent, also a corporate manager before becoming an entrepreneur, said,

Soon after I married I knew the little bride's role was not for me. I committed myself to a career. I soon ran straight into conflict with my desire to succeed and other expectations of what I should and should not be like. While

trying to resolve my achievement-femininity conflict, I recalled my efforts to avoid successful competition with my male peers. For a while, it was easier to internalize their low expectations of me than to swim upstream. Fortunately, I decided this was dishonest to myself and what I wanted. When I kept running into people—men and women—who saw my achieving behavior as offensively overaggressive (and with the encouragement of my husband), I left the company to go into business for myself.

Willingness to risk generally is conditioned by how a person sees the costs versus the benefits of a particular action. Until the last five to ten years, most women have perceived the risks as being unworthy of the costs of surmounting the significant barriers to success. A female entrepreneur said,

Women are still a minority in the business world because their expectations haven't been there for as long as men's have. As attitudes continue to change—women will become inspired as they watch other women succeed and as they themselves get more technical training and experience as well as get used to thinking and doing for themselves. They'll not be so afraid to take on responsibility or of making mistakes. They'll no longer be caught between "fear of failure" and "fear of success."[46]

Just as more women now are moving into the management mainstream, more women are likely to assume the risks of entrepreneurship. Most people—men or women— are more self-confident and willing to risk when they understand a situation, their role in it, and have a reasonable chance to succeed.

IN PERSPECTIVE

The entrepreneur must be able to spot opportunistic changes in the market and economy, risk the capital needed to imple-

---

ership and Interpersonal Behavior (New York: Holt, 1961), pp. 239–71; and W. C. Becker, "Consequences of Different Kinds of Parental Discipline," in M. L. Hoffman and L. W. Hoffman, eds., Review of Child Development Research, vol. 7 (New York: Russell Sage, 1964), pp. 169–208.

[44] Jean D. Grambs and Walter B. Waetjen, "Being Equally Different: A New Right for Boys and Girls," The National Elementary Principal, vol. XLVI, no. 2 (November 1966), p. 63.

[45] Ibid., p. 62.

[46] See Matina S. Horner, "Toward an Understanding of Achievement—Related Conflicts in Women," Journal of Social Issues 28 (1972), pp. 157–76.

ment them, and develop and manage a growing small business. This demands certain abilities whether the entrepreneur is male or female. Interviews with female entrepreneurs indicate little difference in the basic makeup of female and male entrepreneurs. Female entrepreneurs are special people—just as their male counterparts—who work, achieve, fight for their judgments, and sacrifice private time and emotional energy. Once proven knowledgeable and professional, women entrepreneurs felt they received the same respect and admiration, for the most part, as a man. The women interviewed communicated extreme confidence in their abilities and comfortableness with their aggressive drive to compete successfully—an attitude that probably helps create their good business relationships and overall high productivity.

Some evidence exists that entrepreneurial characteristics can be developed. Perhaps what is first required is an understanding of the qualities that are essential to entrepreneurship, the social and psychological factors that encourage or inhibit entrepreneurial drive, and the business tools and concepts the entrepreneur must learn in order to succeed. David McClelland has postulated the need for achievement as the entrepreneur's primary motivator. The needs of high-achievement motivation have been traced back to early childhood. Interestingly, most researchers hypothesized a greater female need for affiliation than achievement. Traditionally, women have been socialized to "achieve" in directions other than owning and managing their own business (e.g., wife, mother, or supportive —affiliation—role in an "acceptable"—culturally approved—occupation for women). Thus, for entrepreneurship to attract many women, and for them to be successful entrepreneurs, these women will have to be resocialized first. An appraisal of currently changing female attitudes reflects more independent thinking about what they can

and cannot do and should or should not be, and a strong indication of more of an achievement orientation outside the traditionally "feminine" areas. Certainly, the old myths no longer hold true. On the other hand, many women will not ever want to live around the clock with their work to the extent they would if they owned their own business and had to live with make-or-break decisions. But, then, neither do many men.

Moreover, while achievement motivation is essential, it alone is not enough. Skills are needed to transform desires and hopes into overt actions. Similarly, skills without motivation are unlikely to gain success. Those interested in developing entrepreneurial ability need to focus on both the appropriate psychological makeup and functional skills (ability to handle money, find risk capital, market, manage, etc.).[47]

More research needs to be done to help women assess their entrepreneurial potential and education needs. It also could assist the entrepreneur in general by refocusing upon the special training needs of the small business owner and manager. For instance, most business schools train people to fit into a corporate environment. This is of little help to the entrepreneur; administration of a small company is largely different. Just to mention only ways: short-term planning is emphasized over long-term planning, and the entrepreneur needs to be more of a generalist (know a little about everything) than the corporate executive.

Advice from these experienced entrepreneurs to other women who want to start their own business emphasized the all-consuming need for money (and energy), especially during the start-up period; a real interest in the business; the ability to risk

[47] Douglas E. Durand, "Training and Development of Entrepreneurs: A Comparison of Motivation and Skills Approaches," *Journal of Small Business Management*, vol. 12, no. 4 (12 October 1971), p. 26.

and sacrifice friends, sports, or hobbies; the need for those who live with them to understand them; and a continuing willingness to modify the product or service to what the customer wants.

Many of the entrepreneurs previously employed confided an "identity crisis" during the first year on their own. Suddenly they were no longer defined by salary, title, or tasks assigned by others. "Employee benefits" were nonexistent—i.e., paid vacations, sick leave, medical care or pension plans. No one said, "You're getting in over your head," or "You're not doing the job right," or whatever. If the work situation is not exactly right, it is the responsibility of the owner/boss to change it. Most of the problems are directly traceable to the owner, anyway. In the words of one of the interviewees, "Some aspects of owning your own business are good, some bad; but almost all are of your own doing." The entrepreneur is free from "being bossed," meetings, office politics, and any other activities which may have been done in a corporate setting. On the other hand, the entrepreneur has to become a good "self-manager." Unproductive days are no longer paid for by someone else.

In final perspective, the mood of the mature 1970s supports the increased involvement of women in all facets of our society, and especially in business. A redefinition of sex roles in America has been taking place. Men and women have begun to share the pressures and excitement of the working world. Increasingly, more options are opening up for both sexes. Entrepreneurship is a new frontier for women, offering unlimited opportunities. The extent to which women have, in the past, assumed an entrepreneurial role is statistically difficult to determine. However, the Census Bureau is conducting the first nationwide headcount of women in business for the U.S. Department of Commerce's Office of Minority Business Enterprise. Information is being gathered on partnerships, sole proprietorships, and corporations. The report will break down various categories of geograhic areas, industry, and employment. While the 1970 Census reported 1,060,000 self-employed women, the new survey (base year 1972) will show for the first time how many women actually own businesses. And it is highly probable that in the next decade we will see the emergence of many more female owners/managers of small businesses. Successful women entrepreneurs will attract other women to the entrepreneurial role.

For nearly half a century, industrial psychologists have been demonstrating that money isn't nearly so potent a motivating force as theory and common sense suggest it ought to be. Elton Mayo's 1922 study of work output in a Philadelphia textile mill set the tone of what was to follow. Management had found that incentive payment schemes had not succeeded in increasing work or decreasing turnover in a department where the jobs were particularly monotonous and fatiguing. Mayo found, on the other hand, that allowing the men to schedule the work for themselves brought dramatic increases in productivity. Where money incentives hadn't proven effective, psychic rewards worked.[1]

Over and over again, later students[2] of industrial psychology emphasized the same point: Money isn't everything. Its meaning is in the eye of the beholder. It functions only as a symbol representing more important psychological factors in the work situation.

Why, then, in spite of all the evidence, do people still take money so seriously as a motivator? In the first place, money obviously is very important. Work, unless it is volunteer or "play," involves a contract between two parties "guaranteed" by the payment of money. The pay may symbolize the psychological realities of the contract imperfectly—which may be all the psychologists are saying. The employee may think he is working for it, and the manager

Money as a Motivator: Some Research Insights*

DAVID C. McCLELLAND

may think he is using it to get the employee to work, but both are only partly right. To understand the situation better, particularly if we wish to manage motivation or behavior, we must penetrate beyond the money itself and consider what it really represents to employer and employee.

MONEY MISCONCEPTIONS

But it is not just man's tendency to confuse symbols with realities that leads him to talk as if money were an end in itself. There are at least three other reasons why he does so. In the first place, no idea is more deeply entrenched in contemporary American psychology than the notion that in the end all learning is based on a few simple material rewards. I suspect practically all top managers today learned in Psychology I that there are so-called primary material rewards, such as food and water, and that all other rewards are "secondary," getting their "motivating value" from learned associations with the primaries. Money obviously falls into the secondary category.

---

[1] Cf. S. W. Gellerman, *Motivation and Productivity*, New York: American Management Association, 1963.

[2] Cf. R. Likert, "A Motivational Approach to a Modified Theory of Organization and Management" in *Modern Organization Theory*, M. Haire, ed., New York: Wiley, 1959; F. Herzberg, B. Mausner, and B. Snyderman, *The Motivation to Work*, 2d ed., New York: Wiley, 1959; W. F. Whyte, *Money and Motivation*, New York: Harper, 1955; D. McGregor, *The Human Side of Enterprise*, New York: McGraw-Hill, 1960. For review of these studies see *Motivation and Productivity, op. cit.*

---

* Reprinted by special permission from the Fall 1967 issue of *The McKinsey Quarterly*.

This notion involves some major misconceptions, and there is no good reason why it should continue to shape the thinking of men who are interested in managing motivation. But it has persisted because of its appealing simplicity, and because the alternatives to it are hard to formulate so neatly.

Let me, however, illustrate one of these alternative approaches by a quick analogy. Think of what goes on in a man's mind as if it were a computer printout of a lot of miscellaneous material. In commonsense terms, a lot of thoughts buzz through a man's head during any given time. As anyone who has tried to do content analysis of computer printouts knows, the periods or other punctuation marks are of key importance. That is, if you are to search and simplify what is otherwise a bewildering mass of material, it is first necessary to break it up into units within which co-occurrences can be noted.

In real life, rewards or incentives are like punctuation marks. They break up sequences or call attention to them. In psychological terms, they are attention-getting, affect-producing mechanisms, rather than substitutes for something else. As such they are of tremendous importance in producing organization or order in thought and action. Note, however, that they are only one possible type of attention-getting mechanism. Bright lights and colors, changes in rest periods, reorganizations of work flow—all sorts of things—can also get attention.

In short, rather than being some kind of a substitute for simpler material rewards, money is more sensibly regarded as *one of a class* of attention-getters. And, like other members of its class, it can lose its attention-getting power with repetition.[3]

A second reason why managers go on thinking that money is a prime motivator

is that most of them are highly achievement-oriented; in the psychologist's terms, they are "high in *n* Ach." We know that such men attach special significance to money rewards. They are strong believers in steeply increasing financial rewards for greater accomplishment. Because they themselves are particularly interested in some concrete measure that will sensitively reflect how well they have done, it is easy and natural for them to mistake this idea for a related one—namely, that the more money you offer someone the harder he will work.

Obviously, believing in more pay for more work is simply not the same as saying that more pay will lead *to* more work. But the fallacy in this reasoning is not only logical but psychological, for other experimental evidence shows that even men who score high in *n* Ach are not themselves spurred to greater efforts by money incentives. While they attribute greater importance to money as a motivator, it doesn't motivate *them* to work harder.

The apparent explanation: They seek financial reward, not for its own sake, but because it tells them how well they are doing. As Saul Gellerman has pointed out, the incentive value of top executive salaries must lie primarily in their "merit badge" quality, since high taxes result in rather minor differences in take-home pay at this level of compensation. So managers believe money is important in motivating others because they mistakenly think it motivates themselves. Actually, while it *is* more important to them as a measure of accomplishment, it doesn't really motivate them. And it doesn't motivate others either, except indirectly—as workers and others are ready to point out whenever they are asked.

Finally, the third reason why managers keep coming back to money as a way of motivating people is because at the practical level it is the one thing they can manipulate rather easily. After all, it is part of their

[3] See J. Kagan, "On the Need for Relativism," *American Psychologist*, 1967, pp. 22, 131–42.

job to motivate the people working for them, to get more work out of people, or at the very least to make sure that people aren't loafing. The higher their achievement motivation, the more they will want to show an improvement in the quality or quantity of the work done by their people. They may listen patiently to the psychologists and sociologists who seek to convince them that money isn't important for its own sake, but then what can they do to change those other psychological factors which are supposedly more important? Payment plans are real and manipulable. Plans for dealing with psychological factors often seem nebulous.

What, then, does all this add up to? Are we left with the conclusion that the nature of incentive plans makes no difference at all? Hardly. It is one thing to say that psychological factors will modify how incentive plans work; it is quite another to conclude that variations in incentive plans do not make any difference.

What we need is a change in orientation. The problem is managing motivation—not managing work, but managing the *desire* of men to work. This means seeing incentive plans as a particular means of achieving specific objectives within the larger framework of the work situation.

THE WORK VARIABLES

It has recently been shown[4] that a work situation involves four sets of variables which must be accurately diagnosed before a "prescription" can be written for improvement:

1. The motives and needs of the persons working at the task.
2. The motivational requirements of the task they have to perform.

3. The motives (or strengths and limitations) of the manager.
4. The organizational climate.

Once a manager knows where he stands on these variables in a particular work situation, he is in a position to do various things. For example, if he finds that most of his workers are strongly achievement-oriented, while the tasks to be performed are assembly-line work that doesn't satisfy this motivation, he has an obvious mismatch. To bring the interests of the people into line with the motivational requirements of the job, he can get a different type of worker or change the nature of the task.

Our focus, here, however, is narrower: Given different settings on these four types of variables, how can management use payment plans to help motivate men? Obviously, there can be no simple sovereign payment system that will work best for all people under all conditions. But we can give illustrations.

Variations in the Motives of Workers

Whether workers or managers are high or low in achievement motivation makes a real difference in the effectiveness of financial incentives. Several studies have shown that offering additional financial rewards for doing a task does not make strongly achievement-oriented people work harder or better.[5] A group of aggressive, achievement-minded salesmen would certainly be angry if their extra efforts were not recognized with a much greater financial reward;

[4] G. H. Litwin and R. A. Stringer, *Motivation and Organization Climate*, Cambridge: Harvard, 1967.

[5] J. W. Atkinson and W. R. Reitman, "Performance as a Function of Motive Strength," *Journal of Abnormal and Social Psychology*, 1956, pp. 53, 361–66; J. W. Atkinson, ed., *Motives in Fantasy, Action and Society*, Princeton, N.J.: D. Van Nostrand, 1958; C. P. Smith, "The Influence of Testing Conditions on Need for Achievement Scores and Their Relationship to Performance Scores," in *A Theory of Achievement Motivation*, J. W. Atkinson and N. T. Feather, eds., New York: Wiley, 1966, pp. 277–97.

yet offering them bonuses is not what produces the extra effort. This may seem like a psychological distinction without a difference, but the interpretation of the meaning of the bonus plan genuinely affects performance, as a later example will show.

People with relatively low achievement motivation, on the other hand, *will* work harder for increased financial rewards. It is not the task itself that interests them, however, nor does the money they get by doing it interest them primarily as a measure of accomplishment. Rather, it has other values for them.

Two consequences flow from this simple fact. First, if there is any way to get the reward without doing the work, they will naturally tend to look for it. This means that managers who rely primarily on money to activate people who are low in achievement motivation will have a much harder job of policing the work situation than they would if the work satisfied certain other motivational needs. This conclusion will hardly come as news to managers who have been struggling with employee incentive plans over the past generation.

The second implication is that such employees will have to want something that the money can buy. Obviously, there are lots of important things that money *can't* buy: tolerable working conditions, friendship, and job security, to name a few. As a number of studies have shown, even the material possessions that most middle-class managers assume everyone wants, such as a home of one's own, are in fact not wanted by many of the people he is trying to motivate. It follows that if a manager must deal largely in financial incentives for these people, he will have to give some thought to creating psychological wants that money will satisfy—such as more education for children, a happier retirement, a more exciting (and expensive) vacation, etc.

But money can also have other values for

people who are most strongly motivated by needs for social approval and solidarity with others in the work group. One study found, somewhat to the experimenters' surprise, that girls who scored high in *n* Affiliation actually worked harder for money prizes than girls who scored low on this factor, whereas there had been no difference between the two types of girls when the extra incentives were not offered.[6] Evidently the money helped to create a general expectancy on the girls' part that they should work hard to please the experimenters. The moral again is simple: For a working force that scores high on this factor, incentive plans and payments should be framed in terms of working together for the common good, not—as achievement-oriented managers nearly always assume—of working for one's own gain.

Finally, another study showed that college students who scored high in *n* Power spend more money on prestige supplies— expensive liquor, college insignia, powerful motorcycles or cars, etc.—in other words, on things which will make them feel or seem big, strong, powerful and respected.[7] If a manager finds his staff scores high in *n* Power, then he ought to administer his financial incentives in different ways, perhaps even presenting some of them in the form of prestige supplies—such as a trip to Europe or a new Cadillac—for especially outstanding performance.

One simple lesson to be learned from all these studies is that the motivational characteristics of the staff make a lot of difference. Even with the cost of incentives held constant, their form and meaning have to be shaped to fit the needs of the people they are designed to influence.

---

[6] *Journal of Abnormal and Social Psychology,* op. cit.

[7] D. G. Winter, "Power Motivation in Thought and Action," unpublished Ph.D. thesis, Harvard University, 1967.

Variations in the Motivational Requirements of Tasks

Researchers have suggested some simple measuring devices for the motivational requirements of different tasks.[8] For instance, the job of an assembly-line worker has more "affiliation" than "achievement" elements, because workers must interact with each other. Successful task accomplishment depends on the cooperation of co-workers, stable working relationships over time, etc. If this is so, how can incentive plans help? Actually they are more likely to hinder, because most incentive plans are based on the assumption that all tasks primarily involve achievement. And in fact such plans usually make less than 10 percent of the people into "ratebusters," while they make the rest of the work force angry because the extra incentives reinforce behavior which is in direct opposition to the affiliation requirements of the task.[9] Such "gung-ho" achievers often disrupt normal working patterns and lower average productivity over the long run.

Even at the sales level this can be true. While, generally speaking, successful salesman are strongly achievement- and power-oriented and low in affiliation needs, at least one sales situation has been identified in which the very best salesmen scored only moderately high in achievement orientation, quite a bit higher in affiliation orientation than most salesmen, and lower in power orientation.[10] These particular salesmen were involved in a task which, in the researchers' words, required "a much greater emphasis on coordinating the efforts of the sales and service function, and on building long-term close customer relationships in-

volving at high degree of trust, than on entrepreneurial selling." Here an incentive plan based on sales volume alone could easily attract the wrong men (those too high in *n* Ach) into sales, or influence existing salesmen to neglect the long-term consumer relationships that experience shows to be necessary for success in this job. Money payments have to fit not only the characteristics of the people in a work force, but also the nature of the jobs they have to perform.

Variations in the Motives of Managers

As we have seen, unless the manager understands his own motives, he may project them onto others. It is all too easy for a manager, in making plans for other people, to assume that they are like himself. But if he knows what *he* wants, he may be able to avoid falling into the trap. He may, for example, even be able to see when his own motivations are leading him to propose new ideas that have little chance of success. I have sometimes wondered how many personnel managers think up new incentive plans in order to convince *their* superiors that they are high achievers, deserving of a special bonus. Actually, a personnel man ought to be specially rewarded for picking and keeping outstanding men, but such day-to-day performance may be less promptly noticeable and rewardable than the installation of a brand new incentive plan. Here again, the pay system may tend to distort the personnel job by treating and rewarding it as a straightforward achievement proposition.

Beyond such considerations, a manager must understand himself well enough to know what he can or should do in a given organizational situation. Thus he may discover that, while his staff is heavily affiliation-oriented and therefore wants and needs many signs of approval and friendship, he himself is rather aloof, priding himself that

---

[8] *Motivation and Organization Climate*, op. cit.

[9] *Money and Motivation*, op. cit.

[10] G. H. Litwin and J. A. Timmons, *Motivation and Organization Climate: A Study of Outstanding and Average Sales Offices*, Boston: Behavioral Sciences Center, 1966.

he got where he is today by not wasting time with "the boys." This kind of self-understanding should help him create the kind of climate that will make the incentive system work under a given set of conditions.

Variations in Climate

Two researchers, G. H. Litwin and R. A. Stringer, have identified some nine different dimensions on which organizational climates can vary.[11] They hypothesize that each of these variables has different effects on the motivations of people working in the organization. For example, a high degree of *structure* (rules, regulations, going through channels), reflecting an emphasis on power and control, should reduce affiliation and achievement needs among its employees, but at the same time make them more power-oriented. Similarly, a high degree of risk or challenge in the tasks to be performed should arouse achievement motivation but have little or no effect on worker's affiliation or power needs.

Consider how these climatic factors may operate when the incentive system is held constant. In one study[12] four outstanding sales offices were contrasted with four average sales offices, not only in terms of climate differences as perceived by the salesmen, but also in terms of actual observations of how managers interacted with their men during the day.

The incentive system in all offices was the same and men in the outstanding and the average offices were equally satisfied with it. Yet other climate variables apparently made for very different performance averages. The outstanding offices, as perceived by their salesmen, had more structure, evoked more identity and loyalty, and were warmer and friendlier. The salesmen from these outstanding offices also felt that

higher standards were being set and that they were more often rewarded by the manager for their efforts than criticized for nonperformance. Their views were substantiated by observation of managers in the two types of offices. Those in the outstanding offices gave almost twice as much praise and encouragement as the managers from the average offices. To quote from the study,

. . . the outstanding manager makes it a habit to compliment a man sincerely on a job well done; a personal thank-you is always given over the phone and in person. He might also drop the man a note of congratulation and thanks for a successful sale. He also typically thanks the customer in the same manner and makes a real effort to visit the new installation with the salesman and compliment the salesman's efforts before the customer. In contrast, the average manager's attitude is that "these men are on very large commissions and that's what makes them hustle. They know they can got out on any day of the week and get a raise just by selling another piece of equipment. Oh, I *might* buy them a drink, but it's money that motivates these guys."[13]

Once again we see that nonfinancial, situational factors are important, but with a difference. Furthermore, we have a nice illustration of how too exclusive a concern for money can distract a manager's attention from other psychological variables that he ought to be taking into account.

INCENTIVE PLAN VARIABLES

But it is no use repeating that everything depends on the way financial plans are perceived. If variations in the incentive plan really matter, we should be able to discover just what difference they make by investigating them while holding situational variables constant. Until such specific studies have been made, we cannot generalize very confidently about the important varia-

---

[11] *Motivation and Organization Climate*, op. cit.
[12] Ibid.

[13] Ibid, p. 13.

bles in the incentive plan itself. But on the basis of some theory and laboratory research it may be permissible to speculate about three of these variables: the probability of success (winning the incentive award), as perceived by participants in the plan; the size of the incentive offered; and the nature of the response-reward relationship.

Probability of Success

Experimental evidence indicates that moderate probabilities of winning an incentive reward produce better performance than either very low or very high probabilities.[14] In general, one researcher has shown, a person who has one chance in two of getting a reward will work harder than if he has a lower or higher probability of getting it, regardless of the strength of his achievement motivation or the size of the money incentive.[15] A study of my own confirmed the fact that students will work harder when the odds are lower than three chances out of four.[16] The generalization seems likely to hold for financial incentive plans, though the optimum probability for winning a special reward obviously would need to be worked out for each particular situation. John W. Atkinson's estimate that it is somewhere around the one-chance-in-two level is not a bad place to start.[17]

We know two further facts about this phenomenon. First, strongly achievement-oriented individuals work best under odds as slim as one in three, or even longer.[18] Thus, an incentive plan for a strongly achievement-oriented sales force should obviously offer a different set of odds from a plan designed for a group of clerical workers who score low in n Ach.

Second, we know that the perceived probability of success changes with experience. This is probably why achievement-oriented people work better under somewhat longer odds than the average person. They know from past experience that they tend to be more successful than the average person in tasks they undertake. Therefore, what to the outsider observer is a one-in-three chance of winning for an average worker is correctly perceived by the high achiever as a one-in-two chance for him.

Many of the difficulties that incentive plans get into flow from the fact that experience changes the perceived probability of success. Suppose a salesman or a worker exposed to a new incentive plan works extra hard and gets a special bonus. Then what does he do in the next time period? If he notices that a lot of other people have made it, and if he makes it again, he may fear that management will raise the normal standard. Management, on its side, may wonder how it can keep the perceived probability of success at the optimal level without raising standards as individuals get better at their jobs. Most managers are unhappy if incentive plans stop working after a while. Yet, theory suggests that, because experience changes perceived probability of success, plans would have to be changed regularly in order to keep expectancies of winning at an optimal level for producing performance.

Size of Incentive

Offered $2.50 for the best performance, a group of college students solved more arithmetic problems than when they were offered only $1.25—regardless, again, of their level of achievement, motivation, or the odds under which they were attempting

---

[14] *Motives in Fantasy, Action and Society,* op. cit.; *A Theory of Achievement Motivation,* op. cit.

[15] *Motives in Fantasy, Action and Society,* p. 296.

[16] D. C. McClelland, *The Achieving Society,* Princeton, N.J.: Van Nostrand, 1961.

[17] *Motives in Fantasy, Action and Society,* op. cit.

[18] Ibid.; see also *The Achieving Society,* op. cit.

to win the prize.[19] Obviously, then, size of reward makes a difference.

Just as obviously, "size" is a relative matter—relative, that is, to one's own starting point and to what other people are getting. Five hundred dollars is much more of an incentive to a $5,000 wage earner than to a $50,000 executive. Almost certainly, the increment in money necessary to create a "just noticeable incentive" is some kind of constant fraction of the base. But, again, this function has yet to be determined for real-life situations. It would probably be easier to work out in a personnel recruiting context, where the incentive effect of additional pay is more obvious than that of incentives offered for increased output in a given work setting.

Many authors have recently turned their attention to how large a man perceives an incentive to be, in comparison not with his own starting level but rather with what others like him are getting.[20] Here, oddly enough, the yardstick seems to be more absolute than relative. That is, for a man earning $50,000, $500 may not seem like much of an incentive relative to his own past earnings, but it could become an important incentive if it puts him clearly ahead of another man whom he sees as a competitor.

The Response-Reward Relationship

Even in seniority systems where a man gets more pay as he grows older, the tacit assumption is that, with greater experience on the job, he is presumably doing the job better, even though it would be impractical to try to measure exactly how. This suggests the first variable in the incentive situation: how specifically the desired response is de-

fined. If a person doesn't know what he is supposed to do to earn the reward, he will obviously be less able to do it. So, in general, the supposition is that the more clearly specified the behavior, the greater the incentive value of the reward.

In some jobs—selling, for example—desired performance is relatively easy to define, while in others, such as the job of a personnel manager, it is quite difficult. In any case, it seems probable that successful incentive plans involve goals worked out as specifically as possible in advance, between superior and subordinate, so that the subordinate will know whether he is achieving his goals.

Two types of errors are commonly made in specifying the response for which the reward is offered. First, the manager may assume that the task primarily involves work output and may specify the expected responses in those terms, whereas a careful job analysis would show that other factors are important to success. A case in point is the sales offices mentioned previously, where too much emphasis on selling interfered with service functions and actually lowered performance.

Second, the manager may believe he is rewarding better performance from his staff, when in fact he is primarily rewarding other kinds of behavior, such as being loyal to him or "not rocking the boat." A comparative study of two large business organizations in Mexico provides an interesting illustration.[21] In Company A, where rewards were clearly given for better performance, men with high achievement motivation got significantly more raises over a three-year period. However, in Company P, where men were highly regarded if they were loyal to the boss and stayed in line, men who scored high in n Power were more

[19] *Motives in Fantasy, Action and Society*, p. 293.

[20] See R. L. Opsahl and M. D. Dunnette, "The Role of Financial Compensation in Industrial Motivation," *Psychological Bulletin*, 1966, pp. 66, 94–118.

[21] J. D. W. Andrews, "The Achievement Motive in Two Types of Organizations," *Journal of Personality and Social Psychology*, June 1967.

often promoted. Company A was growing much more rapidly than Company P. Yet the president of Company P declared that he was interested in better performance for his top executives and couldn't understand why his company was not growing faster. He did not realize, though his subordinates did, that he was actually dispensing financial rewards primarily for loyalty to himself.

Another important characteristic of the response is whether it is expected from a group or from individuals. Should incentives be prorated on the basis of group performance, as in profit-sharing plans, or given for individual performance alone? No easy generalization is yet possible, though everyone agrees that each work situation should be carefully analyzed to see which type of performance it is most appropriate to reward in a given case. For example, where the staff is strongly affiliation-oriented and the job requires lots of interpersonal cooperation, some kind of group incentive plan would obviously be more effective than one rewarding individual excellence.

Still another important variable is the delay between the response and the reward. How often should bonus reviews be held monthly, semiannually, or annually? Most studies with lower animals in simple learning situations suggest that the shorter the delay, the greater the incentive value of the reward. Applying this principle to the design of an individual incentive plan could lead to "atomizing" expected improved responses so that a person could accumulate "points" every time he showed a better response, the points to be totaled and cashed in for money at regular intervals. The difficulty of measuring performance in a given work situation will almost certainly decide how often and how immediately rewards can be given. Generally speaking, such variations in timing are probably less important than the other variables mentioned, since most adults, and certainly most managers, are able to work for rewards deferred at least a month, and often a year or even longer.

In summary, then, money is one tool among many for managing motivation. It is a treacherous tool because it is deceptively concrete, tempting many managers to neglect variables in the work situation and climate that really affect productivity. In the near future, there will be less and less excuse for neglecting these variables, as the behavioral sciences begin to define them and explain to management how they can be manipulated just as one might change a financial compensation plan.

Incentive plans will continue to play an important role in the overall management framework. But the effective manager will also need to diagnose the needs of his staff, the motivational requirements of their jobs, his own motives, and the climate of the present organizational setup. Then he can rationally plan how to improve productivity by improving the climate; by developing certain motives in key people; by making a better match between the needs of the people and the needs of the job; or, finally, by specifically gearing incentive plans to the organizational situation.

Several years ago at a conference dealing with a then-novel topic, "Job Design and the Quality of Work," John Dunlop (who at the time was U.S. Secretary of Labor) delivered the keynote address on the presumably problematic state of job design and work organization in the United States. In his remarks he demonstrated an unwillingness to subscribe to a thesis of widespread worker alienation or to endorse a massive program of radically innovative job design and work structuring. Rather, he urged the conferees to be careful and objective in assessing evidence, to be aware of and sympathetic to institutional and economic realities, and, most important, to recognize the enormous *diversity* which characterizes the real world of work.

Dunlop's advice is cited here for two reasons. First, as we examine the response of the labor movement and individual unions to the issue of innovative job design, many of us, especially the true believers, are likely to be frustrated by organized labor's caution and skepticism. A union leader's interpretation of evidence on job design experimentation is bound to be different, and in some ways perhaps more objective, than an advocate. Also, the union leader is responsible for the viability and well-being of an organization whose institutional role is, in a hundred subtle ways, questioned, threatened, and criticized by many forms of innovative job design and work structuring.

The great diversity of the American workplace, as pointed out by John Dunlop, is important in the context of the present paper. If we focus only on the question, "What has been the response of U.S. labor unions to the issue of innovative job design?" we are likely to find diversity in

1. The forms of the work innovations themselves, job enrichment, semiautonomous work groups, flextime, and new compensation arrangements.

Innovations in Job Design: The Union Perspective[*]

BERNARD J. WHITE

2. The responses of various unions.
3. The official (stated) response versus the actual (behavioral) response within any one union.
4. The official and actual responses at different organizational levels within the same union.

It is evident that the first element of diversity cited above is real. The third and fourth elements of diversity (between official and actual policy and across hierarchical levels) are, of course, found in any organization of any significant policy-related issue.

Evidence of diversity in the responses of various unions (the second element) is readily available. For an example, one need look no further than the contrasting statements of two union leaders on a key element in job design decisions, namely, assumptions about the motives which individuals bring to the workplace. In an often-quoted passage from a 1973 *American Federationist* article, William Winpisinger of the Inter-

---

[*] *Journal of Contemporary Business*, vol. 6, no. 2 (Spring 1977), pp. 23–35.

national Association of Machinists suggested that:

If you want to enrich the job,
   enrich the paycheck.
The better the wage,
   the greater the job satisfaction.
If you want to enrich the job,
   begin to decrease the number of
   hours a worker has to labor.
If you want to enrich the job
   do something about the nerve-
   shattering noise, the heat, and
   the fumes that are deafening,
   poisoning, and destroying the
   health of American workers."[1]

Winpisinger presented these comments as part of a spirited attack on the premises of the job enrichment movement and in defense of traditional union demands on behalf of their members.

On the other hand, George Nestler, a representative of the Amalgamated Meatcutters' International in Pittsburgh, responded to the question of individual motives in the following way:

What do workers want? They want to identify with the company, the union, the product, and the group they work with. They want responsibility, they want communication, and they want to contribute. They want to participate in their jobs, to have input. These things are meaningful to workers. They want to care about people. They want a sharing of the aims and goals, and of the financial rewards. Initially, financial rewards are what everyone looks at. This diminishes after a period of time. They are looking for new skills in their work, and for training. They want job security. And they want the right to question what's going on in their environment, in their workplace.[2]

Clearly, the contrast between Nestler's views and Winpisinger's suggests the in-

herent dangers in generalizing about "*the union response.*"

Indeed, the theme of diversity—in individual motives, in the nature of the workplace, in the forms of job design innovations, in the stances of various unions and union leaders, in official versus actual union policy, and in the postures of various levels of union hierarchy—is an important issue on which this paper will focus. Drawing valid generalizations about "the union response" or "the union role" is risky in the face of such diversity. Yet there are some generalizations to be drawn, there are predictions to be made and there is experience from which to learn. The objective of this paper is to accomplish these tasks without doing violence to the real world's rich diversity about which Mr. Dunlop wisely reminded us.

LABOR UNIONS AND JOB DESIGN

Recently, the author completed a major study[3] of the response of labor unions to the related issues of job dissatisfaction and innovative job design.[4] It contained a content analysis of union policy statements and addresses by union leaders, along with a review of published information about job design experimentation involving unionized employees. In addition, the author con-

---

[1] William Winpisinger, "Job Satisfaction: A Union Response," *AFL-CIO American Federationist* (February 1973), pp. 8–10.

[2] *World of Work Report*, vol. 1, no. 4 (June 1976), p. 10.

---

[3] Bernard J. White, "*Union Response to Job Dissatisfaction and Work Innovations*" (Ph.D. diss., The University of Michigan, 1975).

[4] Innovative job designs can be classified as (a) *changes in the work content*, for example, increasing the variety of tasks performed by each worker; (b) *changes in the work environment*, for example, changes in technology, in the physical location of the job, or in methods of pay; and/or (c) *changes in decision-making authority*, for example, control by work groups over the distribution and timing of tasks. This classification scheme is adapted from J. Erfurt and A. Foote, *Overcoming Barriers to Technological Innovations in Industrial Settings* (The University of Michigan, Institute of Labor and Industrial Relations, and Wayne State University, July 1973).

ducted interviews with a number of consultants, managers and union leaders who have been involved directly in such experimentation. Some key findings of that study are presented in this article in the following form:

1. A summary and evaluation of the *criticisms* directed at unions by certain advocates of the job dissatisfaction thesis and proponents of innovative job design.

2. Some lessons from cooperative ventures and union response to management-initiated innovations.

3. A number of predictions concerning likely future directions of union response to these issues.

The Critic's View: Lack of Union Initiative

Critics contend that increased satisfaction from the work itself is an emerging need among union members whose more basic physiological, security, and social needs are, for the most part, satisfied. Similarly, they claim that job dissatisfaction is a growing problem among some union members. Therefore, they suggest that union leaders should incorporate "increasing members' job satisfaction" or "resolving the problem of job dissatisfaction" into the set of union objectives which traditionally has consisted of (1) increasing pay, (2) increasing job and economic security, (3) increasing time off and away from the job, and, to a lesser extent, (4) improving the physical work environment. Unions, they claim, should in particular initiate collective bargaining demands in pursuit of greater job satisfaction and, in general, serve as a positive force to focus attention on the problem of job dissatisfaction.[5]

Critics also have labeled unions an "organizational obstacle" to the implementation of work innovations by management.[6] They claim that this is ironic since, in their opinion, union demands for innovations in their members' job design represent: (1) an ideal policy by which to pursue and achieve the objective of reducing job dissatisfaction and (2) a logical means of enhancing the power and control of workers in the workplace, which is presumably another objective of unions. In this sense, work innovations are viewed as a significant *opportunity* which unions possess the distinctive competency to exploit on behalf of their members.

The evidence from the author's study confirms, with only minor modifications, the charge made by critics that unions have not expanded their objectives to include increased satisfaction with the work itself. A study by Blum, Moore, and Fairey[7] reveals that only an infinitesimal percentage of contract clauses negotiated by unions relate, even under the broadest criteria, to making the work itself more satisfying. Articles in union journals and most public statements by individual union spokesmen, other than representatives of the United Automobile Workers and a few others, constitute nearly unanimous agreement that dissatisfaction with the job is not as severe or as widespread as critics suggest and that further advances in traditional union objectives should continue to take precedence over the objective of increasing job satisfaction.[8] Of course, one

---

[5] See, for example, Albert Blum, "Union Prospects and Programs for the 1970's," *Proceedings of the Twenty-second Annual Winter Meeting* (Madison, Wis.: Industrial Relations Research As-

sociation, 1969), pp. 136–43; ———, Michael Moore, and B. Parker Fairey, "The Effect of Motivational Programs on Collective Bargaining," *Personnel Journal* (July 1973), pp. 633–41.

[6] See *Work in America* (Cambridge, Mass.: The M.I.T. Press, 1972); and David Jenkins, *Job Power* (New York: Doubleday and Co., 1973).

[7] Blum, Moore, and Fairey, "The Effects of Motivational Programs on Collective Bargaining."

[8] See, for example, a series of articles in the *American Federationist*, 1972–74, including

must conclude that the same logic is implied in the case of the many unions which have made no public statement on the job dissatisfaction issue—those unions which similarly have made no move to incorporate reduction of job dissatisfaction into their set of objectives. Notable as exceptions are the positions represented in the statements of several officers of the U.A.W. and in the bargaining behavior of the union with respect to job dissatisfaction. The dominant spokesmen for the U.A.W. on this issue[9] have stated that while workers themselves are not explicitly demanding more satisfying work, the role of the worker should be expanded and his or her influence increased at the workplace. They suggest, at least as a minimum, that this possibility should be explored, in part to render work a more satisfying, meaningful, and "humanized" experience.[10] In addition, the U.A.W., in its 1973 contract talks with General Motors, Chrysler, and Ford, initiated a demand for cooperation with the companies in efforts to "improve the work environment as a means of making work a more satisfying and stimulating experience." This demand resulted in letters of intent between the companies, and the union appended the 1973 contract to establish a formal role for the

union in innovative job design efforts.

In general, why have unions not expanded their objectives to include initiating demands for increased satisfaction with the job itself, an objective which innovative job design might be instrumental in achieving? There are three major reasons: one is related to *members' needs* in this area; another lies in the *attitudes* of union leaders and the influence of *precedents and structures;* and a third is the *source* of demands that unions be more proactive.

The probability that some issue will become a union (bargaining) objective is, to a large extent, a function of an interplay between the *degree of commonality* of the members' needs in that area and the *relative saliency* of those needs. That is, a narrowly held but very salient need may be about as likely to become a union objective as a widely held but relatively less salient need. What are the implications of this theory for the job dissatisfaction/innovative job design issue?

Recent reviews of survey evidence on job satisfaction cast serious doubt on three hypotheses:

1. That many or most people are dissatisfied with their jobs.

2. That dissatisfaction is on the increase.

3. That "interesting work" is the factor of greatest concern to most people with respect to their attitude toward their job.

Kahn noted that the modal response (to the question "How satisfied are you with your job?") is on the side of neutrality— "pretty satisfied."[11] Over the years, a consistently small percentage of working people (10–20 percent) report job dissatisfaction. Quinn et al. demonstrated that there

---

Thomas R. Brooks, "Job Dissatisfaction: An Elusive Goal" (October 1972), pp. 1–7; William Winpisinger, "Job Satisfaction: A Union Response" (February 1973), pp. 8–10; and William Gomberg, "Job Satisfaction: Sorting Out the Nonsense" (June 1973), pp. 14–19.

[9] Irving Bluestone, Douglas Fraser, and Donald Elphin.

[10] See Douglas Fraser, "The Importance of the U.A.W./Chrysler Agreement; Organized Labor and the Future of the Quality of Work" (Speech before the National Conference on the Quality of Work Controversy, Chicago, 10 December 1973); the comments of Irving Bluestone in "Worker Involvement in 'Managing the Job,'" *World of Work Report,* vol. 1 no. 8 (October 1976), pp. 1,8–9; and Donald Ephlin, "The Union's Role in Job Enrichment Programs," *Proceedings of the Twenty-sixth Annual Meeting* (Madison, Wis.: Industrial Relations Research Association, 1973), pp. 219–23.

[11] Robert L. Kahn, "The Meaning of Work," in A. Campbell and P. Converse, eds., *The Human Meaning of Social Change* (New York: The Russell Sage Foundation, 1972).

is no significant trend, upward or downward, in this percentage,[12] and White suggested that a careful disaggregation and analysis of key national survey data reveals "interesting work" to be only one of many factors affecting job satisfaction, with more traditional considerations (pay, job security, etc.) being more salient for many workers.[13]

The point of these findings is simply that from the vantage point of most union leaders, there has been, and continues to be, little impetus to modify existing and gradually evolving union objectives in favor of increased satisfaction with the job itself through innovative job design. The need, in most cases, is neither widespread nor highly salient.

Interestingly, one union representing members in workplaces where alleviation, boredom, and dissatisfaction *do* seem to be genuine issues (namely, on auto assembly line work) has been exceptionally active in both initiating and cooperating in job design experimentation. The difference in the U.A.W. position on job dissatisfaction may be explained in part by a difference in the needs of its members. Survey evidence suggests that unskilled workers, in general, and unskilled auto workers, in particular, constitute one of the identifiable groups in the work force most dissatisfied with the nature of their jobs. Of course, work on the assembly line is the stereotypical example of a fractionated, repetitive, monotonous, and, therefore, dissatisfying job. Thus, even though fewer than one third of the U.A.W. membership hold assembly line jobs, and

even though a high degree of job dissatisfaction among that one third may not be universal, it is likely that alleviating job dissatisfaction is a more widespread and more salient need of U.A.W. members than of members of most other unions.

There are other reasons for organized labor's general caution and skepticism. One is appropriately labeled inertia. In the policy formulation/objective-setting process in any organization, there is, other things being equal, a natural preference for existing objectives over new and unfamiliar ones. In part, this preference is rooted in the cognitive processes of leaders and, in part, it is a fraction of the existing organization structure which limits and biases strategy formulation and the choice of objectives. Commitment to more traditional objectives is institutionalized in the form of union staff departments and individuals charged with developing proposals and analyzing alternatives in *existing* areas. An additional reason for union caution and skepticism is the nature of the *source* of external demands for a more positive union response. A traditional and partially justified mistrust of behavioral scientists, who represent a large proportion of those people advocating the job dissatisfaction/innovative job design issue, exists among many union leaders.[14] This mistrust has been exacerbated by the more recent general estrangement of academics and liberals from union leaders. Organized labor has learned to do without the full support of these parties in recent years. Thus, one could predict accurately that their influence efforts would be unlikely to have much effect.

In summary, with the notable exception of the U.A.W., union caution and skepticism on the job dissatisfaction/innovative job design issue can be attributed to:

---

[12] R. Quinn, T. Mangoine, and M. S. Baldi de Mandilovitch, "Evaluating Working Conditions in America," *Monthly Labor Review* (November 1973), pp. 32–41.

[13] Bernard J. White, "Organization Policies and Members' Needs: A Critical Analysis," *Proceedings of the 19th Annual Conference of the Midwest Academy of Management* (St. Louis, Mo.: Midwest Academy of Management, 1976), pp. 65–77.

---

[14] Loren Baritz, *The Servants of Power* (Middleton, Conn.: Wesleyan University Press, 1960).

1. The nature of their members' needs in this area.
2. Structural realities in the union organization which are not conducive to developing initiatives in the area.
3. The attitude of union leaders toward the issue and its proponents.

Cooperative Ventures and Union Response to Management-Initiated Innovations

A discrepancy between the articulated and actual response of labor unions to innovative job design seems to be a continuing reality since 1970. Interviews with managers and consultants associated with innovative efforts suggest strongly that actual union response has been consistently more "neutral to positive" than policy statements and remarks by union leaders would suggest. In addition, it appears that there has been a gradual shift over the last several years in both articulated and actual union response to the innovative job design issue, toward a more "neutral/positive" stance and away from a predominantly negative one.

There are several possible explanations for the perceived discrepancy in the articulated/actual union position, as well as for the trend toward a more positive stance.

First, the more vocal union spokesmen have held relatively extreme, and typically negative, views on the innovative job design issue. The considerably more neutral majority has been underrepresented in public statements, and thus in perceptions of "the union response." Actual response, because it is inevitably evoked by management-initiated innovations from a broader and more representative sample of union leaders, has been considerably closer to neutral.

Second, a cautious, critical and even hostile union stance on an issue makes a great deal of sense as an *initial bargaining position*. From the union perspective, taking a tough and protective stance with respect to any innovation which threatens previously won rights and prerogatives, particularly those which insure job control, is good strategy. As the author has pointed out previously:

Because of the increased economic benefits, job security, and employment opportunities which breaking out and demarcating jobs has meant to unions and their members, unions have traditionally been more-than-willing partners with management in dividing operations into ever-smaller jobs. Thus even the most common type of work innovation, one which simply "puts back together" a function which had been fractionated into several repetitive and monotonous jobs, can be a complex and debatable proposition for a union, in that it may imply real costs not just to the union as an organization, but also to some individual (inevitably senior) members in the form of loss of certain prerogatives and advantages earned during years of working into their present jobs under the existing system of job design and work organization. Therefore, even under the assumption that workers have a high priority need for greater job satisfaction through more "humanized" work, union leaders in determining their policy on work innovations must weigh the value of potential gains in job control, or at least against the cost of bargaining new provisions to reestablish the degree of job control held prior to the innovations.[15]

It is easy enough for the union to grant waivers of specific rights and provisions in order to facilitate an innovation on an *ad hoc* basis as a function of the perceived value of the tradeoff. The author's field research, as well as published reports of job design innovations involving unionized employees, suggests that this process has been

---

[15] Bernard J. White, "Union Response to the Humanization of Work: An Explanatory Proposition," *Human Resource Management* (Fall 1975), pp. 2–9.

part of the mechanism which has permitted successful introduction of job design innovations in the face of highly restrictive contractual provisions.

Finally, the discrepancy between more positive actual versus more negative articulated union responses to innovative job design appears to be a function of the rapidly increasing use of *joint labor-management committees* as a structural mechanism to facilitate the implementation of innovations. Such committees at the local level have been a key element of several demonstration projects being managed by the National Quality of Work Center and evaluated by the Institute for Social Research of the University of Michigan. These include (1) the Rushton Mining Company/United Mineworkers of America; (2) Harman International (Bolivar)/United Automobile Workers; (3) Tennessee Valley Authority/Tennessee Valley Engineers Association and Office Professional Employees Union; and (4) Mount Sinai Hospital/National Union of Hospital and Health Care Employees, New York State Nurses Association, and Committee of Interns and Residents of the City of New York.[16]

Consultants in the Quality of Work Program report that the joint labor-management committee typically has been a product of several agreements between local union leaders and management. These include: (1) equal representation; (2) areas delineated in which the committee can institute changes in the workplace; (3) the ability to suspend certain prescribed areas of the contract in creating new experiments in job design; (4) no rights to institute any changes that "harm" anyone in the plant, for example, no reductions in force; and (5) a provision for dissolution of the Com-

mittee by either party on 24-hours' notice. Such committees have proven to be a highly effective alternative to the problem of, on the one hand, either avoiding *any* potential contract violations (which severely limits the range of possible job design innovations) or accepting the cost in labor unrest of violating many contractual provisions or, on the other hand, renegotiating each restrictive clause (a long, arduous and costly process).

What does seem clear from experience in introducing job design innovations to organized employees is that the concerns of local union leaders are *not* philosophical and ideological. Rather, they are *practical*. As one report put it, "The union's biggest concern at first was that the contract would be circumvented, and that the project was just another trick of the 'bad guys.' "[17] Will job security be protected? What about transfers and downgrading? Will seniority rules hold? Will pay rates and job classifications be affected? If management is responsive to these concerns, ideally through involvement (*genuine* participation) of local union leaders in a joint committee with representatives of management, they need not be an overwhelming obstacle to the effective implementation of significant innovations in job design. That both the articulated and actual responses of many unions to the issue of innovative job design seem to be growing more positive may be evidence that enlightened management strategies are, in fact, being pursued.

Innovative Job Design and the Role of Labor Unions: Some Predictions

What are some of the likely future developments in organized labor's response to the issue of innovative job design? Extrapo-

---

[16] *The Quality of Work Program: The First Eighteen Months* (Ann Arbor: The University of Michigan National Quality of Work Center and the Institute for Social Research, 1975).

[17] *Recent Initiatives in Labor-Management Cooperation* (Washington, D.C.: National Center for Productivity and Quality of Working Life, 1976).

lations from the past weighted in favor of recent developments suggest the following trends:

1. Most unions in the United States will not adopt the very active role demanded by their critics (and which some European unions have played) in advocating and working toward more satisfying work, and specifically toward more *direct* worker control of the job and the enterprise. To the extent that they do so, it will be largely as a response to external criticism (which appears to be waning) and unfavorable comparisons with the "broader goals" of European unions.[18]

2. In collective bargaining demands, union objectives in general will continue to focus on traditional members' needs, particularly those relating to wages and benefits, job security and working conditions. These needs are likely to become *more* salient relative to needs for greater intrinsic job satisfaction as a function of problematic economic and employment conditions forecast for the short- and mid-term future. Relief from dissatisfaction with the job itself will continue to be sought through improved compensation, more time off and away from the job, and earlier retirement. These "solutions" are more quantifiable, more familiar, and less risky to the union as an organization than are innovations in job design.

3. Clashes between unions and management are inevitable in cases in which management unilaterally initiates major and extensive work innovations involving violations of or changes in contract provisions covering the jobs of organized employees. Conflicts will arise specifically over violations of contractual provisions assuring job control to union members; for example, seniority rights, transfer rules, job classifications, and pay schemes.

4. Managements are more likely than unions to raise the issue of work innovations through collective bargaining in an effort to obtain waivers or to ease contract provisions which restrict management's ability to implement significant and extensive work innovations. Unions will seek, and management will be obliged to give, assurances such as job security for a specified period in exchange for waivers easing such restrictions.

5. The primary vehicle for facilitating innovative job design will continue to be some form of joint labor-management committee. Such committees are essential to: (1) give the local union a necessary voice and means of influence over job-related factors affecting their members; (2) combat the traditional adversary model of union-management relations which generates an atmosphere that is not conducive to job design innovation; and (3) deal on an expedited, *ad hoc* fashion with contractual provisions which would restrict the range of alternative innovations severely. While the popularity of joint committees seems to be increasing, questions of their "cooptive effect" have been raised by some observers. Such concerns, if they are articulated and widely shared, make the committees politically unattractive to union leaders and thus limit their use. Whether this will occur remains an open question.

6. In the absence of effectively functioning joint committees, management may be forced to choose between dealing with a storm of union protests over contract violations or bargaining to gain flexibility in contract provisions necessary to implement innovative job designs. Faced with such a choice, some managements may well decide

---

[18] For discussions of the role of European unions in "work innovations," see Y. Delamotte and K. Walker, "Humanization of Work and the Quality of Working Life—Trends and Issues," *International Institute for Labor Studies Journal*, no. 11 (1974), pp. 3–14; J. Clerc, "Experiments in Humanizing the Organization of Industrial Work: Some Points from a Symposium," *International Institute for Labor Studies Journal*, no. 11 (1974), pp. 21–24.

that the potential benefits of such innovations simply do not outweigh these costs; thus, they will abandon their innovation efforts with organized employees.

7. Management will continue to concentrate innovative efforts in new plants and on the jobs of unorganized employees in order to avoid the necessity of dealing with "the union variable."

8. The United Automobile Workers union may be expected to continue pursuing its unique objectives and policy with respect to job dissatisfaction and work innovations for the reasons mentioned previously: the special needs of its members; the union's susceptibility and sensitivity to external criticism; and the philosophical and ideological orientations of its leaders. However the specific direction of its future response inevitably will be affected by the union's experience in innovative efforts it cosponsors or in which it participates, such as the U.A.W.-Harman International Industries program and the Swedish auto plant visit by six U.A.W. members. What the U.A.W. (and a few other unions) has shown is a willingness to experiment on a relatively small scale. Through experimentation the union generates better information on which to base policy decisions on innovative job design, which will have a larger impact on longer-time implications.

In short, it is clear that for management and unions, the 1970s are years of job design experimentation. Whether actual union response in the years ahead will grow more positive, accepting, and flexible or more negative, resistant, and inflexible certainly will be a function of the individual and shared experiences of the "advanced guard" of unions participating in such experimentation. While diversity of response is likely to remain a reality for years to come, certain very significant trends already have begun to emerge.

CASES FOR PART ONE

Case 1–1
AL RUSKIN*

Al Ruskin dropped in to see one of his professors at the Harvard Business School. Al Ruskin had graduated from the school three years earlier. The following conversation took place.

After a few pleasantries about families and friends, Al began to talk about his current job situation. With the professor interjecting an occasional question and expression of interest, Al proceeded to tell the following story.

Al: I guess you know I'm still working for Amalgamated Industries.

Professor: Well, I wasn't sure.

Al: I've been in their sales department ever since I left the School. As you know, we have a huge sales organization. I've had two or three different jobs, but right now I'm working in the market research division, and there are about 30 of us in that outfit. The work of the division is broken down into four different sections, and then there is another group of clerical people who do the actual figure calculations and help get out the analytical reports of the division. I'm working in one of these four sections as an analyst. There are about six of us doing that kind of work in the section I'm in. We report to our section chief, and then the division has a couple of assistant managers and then a manager of the division who reports to a vice president.

Professor: What kind of work do you do?

Al: Well, I'm an analyst, and we work on different management problems that are sent down to us. There's always more than enough work to do. Right now I'm pretty discouraged about the setup around there. The trouble is with the supervision up the line. Some of them up there either don't know about some of the problems or just don't face up to what's going on. As far as I can see, all of them are trying to act like super-analysts instead of like supervisors. For a while on this job I was able to look at what was going on in a detached way, and it didn't bother me very much. Sometimes another fellow who graduated from HBS and myself get together and discuss these problems and enjoy talking about them. But lately it's been getting under my skin.

Let me give you an instance of what is bothering me. Let me tell you about the first big report I worked on. I got really excited about that job. It involved an issue as to whether or not the company should continue with a certain product line. They had about decided to discontinue it when I started digging into some of the figures, and it seemed to me that the figures indicated they might come out with a different answer. I worked on it very hard. I spent a number of nights working on it and got quite excited about the project. When I had finished my report I let my section chief know about it, and he came right over to my desk. He held out his hand for the report and I gave it to him and he turned around and walked out of the office and went up to see the vice president. The other two analysts who were in the office with me had been watching this. As soon as the door was closed they looked over at me and one of them said, "Well, how does it feel, Al? Do you like the way it feels?" Then they laughed and said, "Don't worry, Al, after that's happened to you about half a dozen times you'll get sort of used to the way it feels, and it won't be quite so tough."

Professor: Did you ever hear anything more about the report?

Al: Well, a couple days later the chief mentioned to me that he had taken it upstairs and the people there weren't too impressed with the potential profits that could be realized with my proposal. Of course, I don't think my chief or the people he was talking with really understood what I was proposing. But that was the end of it. I think he was a little let down that they didn't get more excited about it. I know I certainly was. You see part of the problem is that our supervisors have the notion that they have to do their own analysis job on all the reports that we turn in to them. They sort of think that they have to have all the answers at their fingertips when they go to talk to the people up the line that the reports are being prepared for.

Professor: Do most of your reports get prepared for the top management group?

Al: Yeh, that's who they're for. We work them up for them. For instance, some fellow at the top of the organization will think of a question that he would like to get an answer on. For instance, he will wonder what the profit picture is or is going to be on some particular product. He will ask the question, and then it filters down to our group, and we have to go out and dig up or develop all the data and prepare the report for him. I don't think the people at the top often realize how much work is going into those reports, and I don't think we analysts always realize just what problem the executive is really concerned with.

These requests affect our district offices, too. You see, for six months before I got into this headquarters group, I was working as a field analyst in one of our district offices. The three analysts there spent their time running around getting data that were requested by headquarters. None of them had time to be of help to the local sales force. I was sent out on temporary duty so I did have time to help the local people on a couple of the studies they were interested in. They really appreciated the help. Those field men impressed me as being "on the ball" and very desirous of having the help of good analytical stuff. They knew what they wanted and used the figures in directing their sales efforts when they got them; but they couldn't get much help from their own analysts because they were so busy doing work for headquarters. The fellow I was working for out there asked me if I would like to go to work for them on a permanent basis and painted a good picture of the job. I told them I would be interested if it could be arranged. I really enjoyed that kind of work. You felt that you had some notion of what you were accomplishing by your efforts. But there's quite a story on why I didn't get that job.

Professor: I'd be interested to hear something about it.

Al: Well, apparently that fellow at the district office really went to bat to try to get my services. What it involved was getting a transfer for me. He came in here to headquarters with this request and got the approval of the fellow that's head of market research. I didn't learn all this until after the request had finally been turned down. The trouble came up when the division head checked with one of the assistant managers who had known me and my work. Apparently the assistant manager told the manager that he knew me and liked my work and would like to keep me in this organization. That stopped the transfer. No one asked me about it. I don't doubt the assistant manager who did it thought he was doing it not only for the good of our local section but probably also for my good. But it isn't exactly the way I'd go about doing that kind of thing. I don't think it even occurred to him to check with me on it.

Professor: How do you account for that?

Al: Well, I'm not sure just how to account for it. The problem seems to go quite a way up. They tell me that even the vice president that we report to sits down and adds up the figures again on any report or study that is brought to him. I guess when the rest of the supervisors see him doing that they figure they've got to sit down and recheck everything and add up all the figures before they pass it on. They've got a lot of people working for them, but they never think of themselves as doing a supervising job.

Every job that comes along in this division is handled as a crisis. I thought when I first arrived here that the job that was hot when I arrived was an unusual thing—that this was a rush job, and that things would quiet down shortly. They never have quieted down. Every job is a crisis. You are always working against extremely tight deadlines, and you always have to do a sort of halfway job. You never know exactly what it is you're supposed to be doing, so you just grind it out as best you can. It seems as if you always make a few mistakes when you're doing it that way.

People in this organization seem to delight in finding the mistakes of others. For instance, our group turns out a periodic letter on commercial operations, and apparently almost everybody else in the department immediately reads this letter to see if they can find any mistakes in it. Within a matter of a few minutes after the letter is released, we start getting phone calls from people who have spotted things that are wrong. I don't mean by this that they find matters of real significance that are wrong but rather such things as a misspelling or a figure that is slightly in error.

It seems as if all the supervisors up the line feel that they are in direct competition with one another. They are all concentrating on trying to impress their immediate boss as being a particularly keen analyst. They never seem to have time to look at what is going on in their own group. You can imagine what that does to the state of mind of the fellows who are at the bottom of the organization. It isn't so bad on me and the other fellow down here from HBS because we have the feeling, rightly or wrongly, that we can leave this company and go get good jobs in other organizations. We don't feel tied to this organization for our career. But that isn't true of most of the fellows in this department. Most of them do not know of any other place that they can work. They feel that they have to make the best of this situation for their career. After they have worked around here for a while, most of them seem to get pretty bitter.

I know the senior analyst that I work with is still a pretty young man, but he's amazingly cynical and bitter about this organization. I try to be careful not to be too influenced by his views of the thing because pretty clearly he is seeing the worst side of things. But that's apt to happen to people after they've been around for a while. However, I think most of the people, that have no choice but to stay, don't really dare to take a close look at what is going on in the organization and face up to whether or not it is worthwhile. They do seem to get used to the constant state of tension and crisis around the place and sort of resign themselves to it.

Let me see if I can give you some examples of the kind of problems that keep coming up. Just a few weeks ago I got caught in the bind on a situation that is typical of the sort of thing that is apt to happen. In order to get a report of mine out in time to meet a deadline, I needed the help and cooperation of a group of the clerical people who were handling the figures. There were several people in that group who were involved in doing this for me. I had the feeling that there was some confusion about what was needed and when it was needed. On several occasions I went to my boss and asked him if he would call a meeting for me with the supervisors who were concerned with helping me on the job. I told him I thought we needed it in order to get a clear understanding of who was to do what, and when. Each time he told me I was making too much of a fuss about it and that he didn't see any reason why we needed to get together to get the job done. He said it was perfectly evident that the other people had the responsibility for doing their part of it, and it was up to them to do it. You see I didn't think it was a matter of their being willing to do it; I think it was a matter of some confusion about just what was needed. But as I feared, the jobs that I needed them to do for me did not get done as they should have been done and at the right time. I talked to them about it over there personally, but they still were not getting done on time. So at the last minute I felt I had to go to my boss and tell him that the work of the other group was not being done properly and on time. He then went over to the boss of these people and told the story and then they got called on the carpet by their boss for not keeping up with our schedule. Of course, they think now that I'm a real s.o.b. for having done this to them. I guess it's not quite that bad. I think we understand each other pretty well, but it was a messy situation, and I could see it coming and could see no way of avoiding it. I couldn't seem to get the point across to my boss that we needed to get together to make sure that everybody knew what was being done.

I could give you a couple of other instances of the way my particular boss works with me. Just for example a while back he passed me in the hall and, just as a passing remark, said that I'd be getting a raise in my next check. Nothing more was said. I suppose that's the way a lot of people handle an announcement of that kind, but it's not my idea of how to let a fellow know that he's got a raise. I muttered something about "Thank you," and that was the extent of the conversation. I think if I was giving a person a raise I'd use that as an occasion to sit down and tell him about the things he's been doing well and maybe point out some things he's not doing too well.

On another occasion my boss asked me to get out a fairly simple little statement about some distribution figures. He and the senior analyst and myself were sitting around the desk with these reports in front of us, and he asked me to simply draw out and restate in summary form certain figures that were on a piece of paper there. He took his pencil and pointed to the items on the list that he wanted me to make a summary of. I didn't know anything about what the job was for and simply did as he told me. I took out the particular items and sent in the report. Well it turned out to be wrong. We forgot to include some item that should have been included, and, because the mistake wasn't caught until some time later, a good deal of work had to be redone in another part of the office. When the mistake was found, my boss called me in and said he was taking the responsibility for the error. Then he proceeded for the next 15 minutes to tell me, in effect, that I'd better be careful not to make mistakes of that kind again. Well, what you can do when something like that happens to you? I guess I don't blame him too much. It's just that he and a bunch of other fellows are caught in this system of trying to be perfect and not admit any mistakes. It's funny, too, but in that kind of an organization I think all of us make more mistakes than we normally would. Everything is done at such a hectic pace, and there's so many changes being made at the last minute when you're trying to get out a report. You always seem to be making very simple little mistakes. These turn up later on to everybody's embarrassment. As I said before, they say that the vice president still gets out his pencil and checks questionable figures, and the awful part of it is he still finds mistakes that weren't caught coming all the way up the line.

You know I really like this analytical work that I'm doing, but I'm getting terribly discouraged with this job. I guess part of the trouble is that you never know just what's being done with the reports and studies that you do turn out. Sometimes I wonder if I have a tendency to exaggerate these problems, but then some new incident comes along and convinces me that this is the way things are, the way they're probably going to stay. Lately I've been doing a little outside job for a small company on some of my weekend time. I'm helping the owner to use available market information in planning his operations and distribution setup. It's a funny thing, but I've been getting more fun out of doing that on my own spare time than I ever get out of my regular job. You really get a feeling you're accomplishing something when you do a job for an outfit like that.

I just don't know whether it's worthwhile to stay with this organization or not. I really believe that I have a fairly decent chance to move on up the line in this organization. I think if I stuck around another five or ten years I would be getting up the line. Maybe I'm kidding myself, but I think, without any false modesty, my prospects are pretty good. But I'm not at all sure it's worth the effort. I'm not at all sure I'd be able to do anything that would really help the situation very much.

Professor: You don't see any way you can contribute and change this pattern you see?

Al: Well, I really don't from my level of the organization. I think you could if you were higher up the line. I don't know if it would be too easy even then. You see, it takes a lot of courage to say what needs to be said in order to get these things straightened out. I guess by the time you get up that way most of the fellows are so worried about their jobs that they don't dare say some of the things that they think ought to be said even if they know what needs to be done. At my level right now I don't know just what you could do. I try to talk to my boss about some of these things, but it doesn't seem to make much difference. I know my senior analyst tells me he's written a number of reports and recommendations suggesting some changes that he thinks would begin to get at some of these problems. He has always submitted them to his boss, and nothing more has ever happened to them. At least as far as he knows nothing has happened at all, and his boss hasn't really explained to him why he hasn't done anything with them. I I suppose over a lifetime in this organization you could really make a little headway, but I don't know. I'm beginning to think life's too short to spend all your time bucking that kind of a situation.

Questions

1. What kind of a person does Al appear to be? What is he seeking from work?
2. Why is he frustrated with his main job? How does he contribute to this?
3. Why does Al derive more satisfaction from his field and part-time work?
4. What does Al seem to fear? Why is he apparently considering staying?
5. How has Al contributed to his situation?
6. What would you recommend to Al?

Case 1–2
DIXIE HATFIELD IS FIRED

When Dixie Hatfield became manager of the Metropolis Rockets baseball team, it was the fulfillment of a life's dream. He had made the trip from the minor to major leagues twice: once as a player and once as a manager. Born 49 years earlier on a farm in Alabama, Dixie had toiled for seven years in the bush leagues, riding dusty buses, sleeping in flea-bag hotels, and receiving only $300 per month. He was never a natural talent, but he worked hard, scrambling for walks or singles and being hit by pitches. Leo Durocher was his hero, and his play reflected Leo's philosophy. The Texas League double was the extent of his power. When he made it to the big leagues, he never let up, hustling everywhere and all the time. During 11 years in the majors, he won the batting title twice, averaged exactly .300, and developed a reputation for ferocious competitiveness. His top salary before his retirement in 1960 was $40,000, reached the year after his second batting title. He took maximum pay cuts in each of his last two years as his speed and legs gave out.

After that, it was back to the minors as a coach and manager—at less than half his playing salary. The buses and hotels were newer, but not much improved over 20 years before. Dixie was an effective if not lovable manager. Threatening, policing, fining, and publicly berating his combination of young boys and old men who either dreamed of a major league future or feared the end of a career, he rewarded good plays and hits with $20 bills and won pennants in the minors.

When the parent club called him up to the big time again, Dixie was happy and optimistic. True, the Rockets had never won even a division title, but they had almost reached .500 the preceding season. More important, they had at least three real stars, fellows with the natural talent never possessed by Dixie. With hard work, sacrifice, and courage, Dixie thought the team could be a winner.

It never was; Dixie failed to achieve the hoped-for results. The players did not seem to try as hard as he thought was necessary. They would sneak out of the tough spring conditioning drills. Two of his stars even missed all of spring training because of deadlocked salary negotiations. During the year, the $50 fines imposed for not running out grounders and for committing mental errors had no impact. Once Dixie instituted a bonus incentive system under which a player would receive $500 cash for a homer, $300 for a triple, and so on, but the Commissioner of Baseball vetoed the plan because performance-based bonuses were against new baseball regulations. Things seemed to go from bad to worse when Dixie ordered his players to shave their mustaches and trim their hair. Communications with his black athletes especially collapsed. Not long afterward, Dixie was unemployed.

The following article appeared a few days later in the national press:

> Dixie Hatfield, recently fired manager of the Metropolis Rockets, says that the salary situation in baseball has stripped managers of their chief motivational weapon and could lead to a dangerous situation provoking some cases of "unintentional complacency."
>
> "I don't want anyone to think I'm saying a player shouldn't get all he's worth, but how're you going to make any player do something when he gets a raise whether his production warrants it or not?
>
> "Where's the incentive?" Disappearing, according to Hatfield, in a baseball economy that "has really exploded in the last six to seven years with television coming into the picture and more money in the pot to give out and being given out."
>
> But it's not the $500,000 salaries for the game's superstars that disturbs the Rockets' ex-manager as much as raises handed out indiscriminately. "The owners and general managers aren't as tough as they used to be because they want to make the players happy," Hatfield explained. "There are guys in the $100,000 class who hit .300 one year, .260 the next, and wind up with raises. With that kind of situation there's no way to make a player do extra work or drive himself if he doesn't want to. Whether we like it or not, fear is the thing that still governs all of us, and the fear of getting a pay cut is disappearing.
>
> "That leads to a situation in which the player doesn't intend to lose his drive, his incentive, but he does anyway. It's not intentional, it's unconscious. But it begins to happen because some of the incentive's gone."
>
> Hatfield underscored the fact that this situation could lead to some abuses the manager can no longer control by raising the spectre of salary decreases. Hatfield then explained that there were three differences between the incentive for a ball player in his day and one today. "First, when I played, money was quite an incentive and you didn't get a raise unless you have a heckuva year. Second, the World Series money meant an awful lot to you if you were only making $10,000. And third, a player who didn't produce found himself out of the majors a lot quicker than with today's expanded leagues."

Questions

1. What leadership style did Hatfield demonstrate? What assumptions did he make?
2. Analyze the possible reasons for the failure of Hatfield's leadership.
3. Using the probabilistic influence model, analyze the apparent changes in money as a motivator.
4. Given the realities of his situation, how might Hatfield have managed differently? Why might this have been more effective?
5. If you were the owner of the team, what kind of a person would you select as the new manager?
6. What recommendations would you make to the new manager for motivating and leading his team?

Case 1–3
METROPOLIS ELECTRIC COMPANY
ENGINEERING DEPARTMENT

The Metropolis Electric Company is an operating utility providing electric and gas service to the Metropolis metropolitan area. The total area served covers 2,400 square miles, with a population of 2 million. The company carries on a continuous expansion and construction program. During a recent five-year period, gross property additions and retirements amounted to $972 million and $98 million, respectively, resulting in an increase of more than 60 percent in utility plant. Capital expenditures for plant additions and improvements to meet the continuing growth in customer needs are expected to approximate $1.6 billion for the next five years. All of this expansion and construction is under the direction of the Engineering Department, which employs approximately 350 graduate engineers and 200 technical personnel. Exhibit 1 is the organization chart for the department, and Exhibit 2 lists the position levels.

Most engineers have graduated from local colleges and universities. Many grew up perceiving the electric company as a most desirable place to work. Turnover has been very low, with many men remaining for their entire careers. In short, company management is pleased with the personnel situation in the Engineering Department.

A questionnaire was recently administered to all managerial and professional personnel in the department by a newly appointed department manager (who had just come from another department in the company). The results indicated a relationship between attitudes and age or seniority. Answers to a number of questions are summarized in Exhibit 3.

EXHIBIT 1
Metropolis Electric Company: Engineering Department

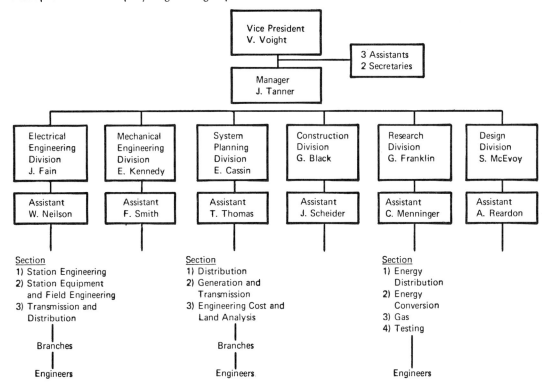

Section
1) Station Engineering
2) Station Equipment
   and Field Engineering
3) Transmission and
   Distribution

Branches

Engineers

Section
1) Distribution
2) Generation and
   Transmission
3) Engineering Cost and
   Land Analysis

Branches

Engineers

Section
1) Energy
   Distribution
2) Energy
   Conversion
3) Gas
4) Testing

Engineers

EXHIBIT 2
Metropolis Electric Company: List of Position Levels in Engineering Department

1. Vice president
2. Department manager
3. Division manager
4. Assistant division manager
5. Section engineer in charge
6. Assistant engineer in charge
7. Branch supervising engineer
8. Senior engineer
9. Engineer
10. Assistant engineer
11. Technicians, draftsmen, clerks, and other nonprofessional personnel

EXHIBIT 3
Metropolis Electric Company: Questionnaire Results (age and years with company, distribution of professionals in engineering department)

Age		Years with Company	
20–29	21% (46 returns)	0–4	20% (43 returns)
30–39	17 (37)	5–9	7 (16)
40–49	32 (71)	10–19	22 (48)
50–59	23 (50)	20–29	36 (86)
60–69	6 (12)	30–39	10 (21)
		40–49	4 (8)

The marks on the following questions indicate the average responses to each question by people in each of the indicated position and age categories

1. In general, how satisfied are you with your job? (percentage distribution)

	Very unhappy 1	2	3	4	5	6	7 Very satisfied
Division Manager							▨
Section Head						■	
Branch Supervisor						▨	
Senior Engineer					■		
Engineer						▨	
Assistant Engineer					■		

2. How challenging do you find your job?

	Not challenging at all 1	Seldom challenging 2	Sometimes challenging 3	4	Often challenging 5	Usually challenging 6	Always challenging 7
Division Manager						▨	
Section Head						■	
Branch Supervisor						▨	
Senior Engineer					■		
Engineer					▨		
Assistant Engineer				■			

3. Is there considerable misutilization of people in your organization, that is, too many professional people working on details that others could handle?

	Strongly agree (yes) 1	2	3	4	5	6	7 Strongly disagree (no)
Division Manager					■		
Section Head			▨				
Branch Supervisor			■				
Senior Engineer			▨				
Engineer			■				
Assistant Engineer			▨				

4. How would you rate the time demands of your present job? E.g., the number of hours you must work are:

	Unreasonable (too great) 1	2	3	Reasonable 4	5	6	7 Too little
Division Manager		▨					
Section Head		■					
Branch Supervisor			▨				
Senior Engineer				■			
Engineer						▨	
Assistant Engineer						■	

EXHIBIT 3 (continued)

5. Company assistance to personal professional development is:

	Inadequate						Excellent
	1	2	3	4	5	6	7
Age (20-29)			▨				
(30-39)				■			
(40-49)					■		
(50-59)					▨		
(over 60)					■		

6. How frequently are you delayed in your work because your superior is not available?

	Never						Always
	1	2	3	4	5	6	7
Age (20-29)					▨		
(30-39)				■			
(40-49)				▨			
(50-59)			■				
(over 60)			▨				

7. Organizational environment:

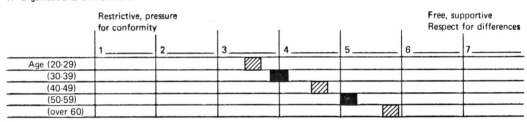

	Restrictive, pressure for conformity					Free, supportive Respect for differences	
	1	2	3	4	5	6	7
Age (20-29)			▨				
(30-39)				■			
(40-49)					▨		
(50-59)					■		
(over 60)						▨	

8. Degree of mutual support:

	Every one for themselves					Genuine concern for each other	
	1	2	3	4	5	6	7
Age (20-29)			▨				
(30-39)				■			
(40-49)					▨		
(50-59)						■	
(over 60)						▨	

Of the Following, Which Three Would You Consider the Most Important Reasons for Working at Metropolis Electric? Relative to Other Organizations, M.E. Offers (mark three):

Frequency Distribution of All Answers

31	High pay
154	High security
93	Nice people to work with
7	Low pressures to perform
10	Habit, just never looked elsewhere
0	Rapid promotion
2	Don't think I could find another job
1	High status in community
134	Interesting work
35	Autonomy and freedom on the job; people leave you alone.
86	Opportunity to solve interesting problems.

Frequency Distribution
of All Answers (cont.)

33 . . . . Opportunity to help people and contribute to society
30 . . . . High fringe benefits
 5 . . . . Opportunity to have substantial control over money and people
17 . . . . Other

Sample of Responses to Question: "What Is the Most Frustrating and Dissatisfying Aspect of Your Job?"

1. Due to heavy work load, one never is able to do a *really good* job on any of his numerous assignments. This is frustrating if you take pride in doing good work.
2. Not having time to finish a project to my satisfaction before something more urgent supersedes it.
3. Not enough time; having to abandon one job because another has higher precedence.
4. Lack of time to properly institute new procedures for new equipment.
5. Not being able to follow projects to completion. Receiving inaccurate information from other divisions. Having to pay IEEE dues. No personal benefit is received from being a member. I feel the company should pay this fee and also the PSPE dues. If an individual is willing to be a working member and spend several evenings a year of his own time attending meetings, the fees should be paid.
6. Waiting for action and/or results on my recommendations (not from my direct supervisor but from those above him).
7. The seemingly dead hand of bureaucracy and clerk-mindedness of the system.
8. The small amount of authority given to me. Almost every decision, no matter how small, must be approved at a higher level before it can be acted on.
9. My objection focuses on the mechanism which permits each level of management to modify or compromise my solutions according to their views of the problem. A nontechnical problem has as many solutions as persons attempting to interpret the problem. To get an authorization is unlikely from a probabilistic point of view. Each level reviewing a request has a probability of rejecting it. To get all persons at each level to agree is difficult.
10. Working for a supervisor whom I consider a very poor handler of personnel. He is, however, probably one of the most technically competent men under whom I have served.
11. Having to deal with a supervisor who, in my opinion, is a pathological faultfinder. The long-run net result is a slow destruction of one's confidence and self-esteem. The man is very technically competent but should not be supervising people since he refuses to apply even the most basic principles of human relations. He would make an excellent staff or research engineer but should not be entrusted with the well-being of any subordinates.
12. Taking over work which has been started by others and finding there is no way to tell how the job was being done or how information was obtained.
13. Lack of adequate record keeping by my peers, so that when they are unavailable, one can determine job status or history. Reasons why certain decisions are made are all too often kept only in the minds of those making them. The successes or mistakes of the past (which I feel are essential to know in the present) are too often forgotten.
14. Poor and inadequate filing systems—spend too much time locating information.
15. Atrocious stenographic service. Not the fault of my present secretary—a very diligent individual. She has too many men to serve and too many extra duties.
16. The total lack of clerical and technician-grade help. Programmers, junior engineers, and keypunching are nonexistent in my area. Projects must stop in order that I take care of work which could be done by someone with much less training. Due to lack of support, projects must be constantly stopped and started so that all get attention.
17. Lack of clerical assistance to retrieve files, Xerox papers, obtain copies of drawings, etc. Limitation of job assignments to those which fit into the scope of my present branch. Inability of construction forces to complete field work because of lack of manpower.

Sample of Responses to Question: "What Company Policies or Conditions Interfere with the Performance of Your Job?"

1. Upper management becomes too involved with decisions that should be made at the engineering level and approved at the branch head level. Management at the division level and above gets too involved in the details of a project. This increases the time pressure on us and restricts our efforts in carrying out the project.
2. All decisions up the line are based on outguessing of top-level opinion. It seems there is too much effort to look good rather than tell it like it is.
3. Paternalism of M.E.: "The Company is too tolerant of poor performers." "Too much coddling of inept, inefficient employees."
4. Clerical support: totally inadequate. "Also, a poor filing system currently exists—not enough room for personal files."
5. Data processing facilities: Keypunch facilities inadequate. Also, resentment exists over control of the data processing facilities by the financial department.
6. "En masse" promotions: "Nothing I do will help me get promoted."
7. Telephone arrangements are insufficient—not enough telephones per office; annoyance over the use of a single extension number for multistaffed office; M.E. directory needs to be updated.
8. Noise level in the office is annoying. "I need a place where I can go when I concentrate on a difficult problem."
9. Often I feel like I'm not treated like a professional.
10. There's a factory atmosphere here. I feel like I'm constantly being watched (e.g., strict adherence to 8:15–5:00 work hours).

Questions

1. Do you think the department has any problems with job attitudes?
2. In what ways do attitudes vary with age, seniority, and level?
3. What aspects of the work and organization are considered satisfying? What aspects are considered dissatisfying?
4. Why do you think the younger engineers are less satisfied than the older ones?
5. Should management do anything? What recommendations would you make?

PART TWO

MANAGERIAL

LEADERSHIP

READINGS

2-1

"Cassius on Caesar," William Shakespeare.

2-2

"Failure Is a Word I Don't Accept: An Interview with John H. Johnson."

2-3

"What Makes a Manager Good, Bad, or Average?" Jay Hall.

2-4

"Why Manage Behavior? A Case for Positive Reinforcement," Harry Wiard.

2-5

"Power, Dependence, and Effective Management," John P. Kotter.

2-6

"The Myths of Behavioral Mod in Organizations," Edwin A. Locke.

2-7

"The Ambiguity of Leadership," Jeffrey Pfeffer.

2-8

"Leadership and Organizational Excitement," David E. Berlew.

CASES

2-1   An Attempt to Consolidate Cooperatives in Ecuador

2-2   Open or Closed in the Operating Room?

2-3   National Bank of San Francisco

Cassius on Caesar*

WILLIAM SHAKESPEARE

BRUTUS
What means this shouting? I do fear, the people
Choose Cæsar for their king.

CASSIUS
                    Ay, do you fear it?
Then must I think you would not have it so.

BRUTUS
I would not, Cassius, yet I love him well.
But wherefore do you hold me here so long?
What is it that you would impart to me?
If it be aught toward the general good,
Set honour in one eye and death i' the other,
And I will look on both indifferently:
For let the gods so speed me as I love
The name of honour more than I fear death.

CASSIUS
I know that virtue to be in you, Brutus,
As well as I do know your outward favour.
Well, honour is the subject of my story.
I cannot tell what you and other men
Think of this life, but, for my single self,
I had as lief not be as live to be
In awe of such a thing as I myself.
I was born free as Cæsar; so were you:
We both have fed as well, and we can both
Endure the winter's cold as well as he:
For once, upon a raw and gusty day,
The troubled Tiber chafing with her shores,
Cæsar said to me 'Darest thou, Cassius, now
Leap in with me into this angry flood,
And swim to yonder point?' Upon the word,
Accoutred as I was, I plunged in
And bade him follow: so indeed he did.
The torrent roar'd, and we did buffet it
With lusty sinews, throwing it aside
And stemming it with hearts of controversy;
But ere we could arrive the point proposed,
Cæsar cried 'Help me, Cassius, or I sink!'
I, as Æneas our great ancestor
Did from the flames of Troy upon his shoulder

The old Anchises bear, so from the waves
    of Tiber
Did I the tired Cæsar: and this man
Is now become a god, and Cassius is
A wretched creature, and must bend his body
If Cæsar carelessly but nod on him.
He had a fever when he was in Spain,
And when the fit was on him, I did mark
How he did shake: 'tis true, this god did shake;
His coward lips did from their colour fly,
And that same eye whose bend doth awe the
    world
Did lose his lustre: I did hear him groan:
Ay, and that tongue of his that bade the
    Romans
Mark him and write his speeches in their books,
Alas, it cried, 'Give me some drink, Titinius,'
As a sick girl. Ye gods! it doth amaze me
A man of such a feeble temper should
So get the start of the majestic world
And bear the palm alone.   [*Shout. Flourish*

BRUTUS
Another general shout!
I do believe that these applauses are
For some new honours that are heap'd on
    Cæsar.

_____
* *Julius Cæsar*, act I, ii.

99

CASSIUS

Why, man, he doth bestride the narrow world
Like a Colossus, and we petty men
Walk under his huge legs and peep about
To find ourselves dishonourable graves.
Men at some time are masters of their fates:
The fault, dear Brutus, is not in our stars,
But in ourselves, that we are underlings.
Brutus, and Cæsar: what should be in that
    Cæsar?

Why should that name be sounded more than
    yours?
Write them together, yours is as fair a name;
Sound them, it doth become the mouth as well;
Weigh them, it is as heavy; conjure with 'em.
Brutus will start a spirit as soon as Cæsar.
Now, in the names of all the gods at once,
Upon what meat doth this our Cæsar feed,
That he is grown so great?

HBR: Mr. Johnson, an admirer of yours quotes you as saying, "Success in business is a time-honored process involving hard work, risk-taking, money, a good product, maybe a little bit of luck, and most of all a burning commitment to succeed." We'd like to talk about most of these, but we'd like to start with the last one. What do you mean by a burning commitment to succeed?

Johnson: I don't see, never did see, failure as an option. When *Life* went out of business, the guys who made the decision to discontinue it knew that it was not going to disturb their lives. As a matter of fact, Time, Inc's stock went up that day. But if *Ebony* didn't succeed, it was going to destroy my life. So I had total commitment; my whole life depended on *Ebony*. I had no options. So I had to learn the rules of the game to win.

HBR: What kind of rules do you mean?

Johnson: If you're drowning, and two guys are standing above you, one with a long stick and one with a short stick, and the one with the short stick tosses it to you, you can say, "Oh, no, I want the longer stick." But if there's only one stick there, you're going to take it, whatever it is.

For instance, once I was trying to get a second-class permit for *Tan*, which had some suggestive stories in it. When I went to the post office, the man said he didn't like *Tan*, he couldn't approve it. I tried all kinds of ways to get him to approve it, including saying, "Well, gee, you must be prejudiced because I'm black, and you've okayed similar magazines, like *True Story*, *True Confessions*, and so on. Why do you want to do this to me?" But the man just kept rejecting my application. So finally I went down to see him again, and I said, "Mr. So-

READING 2–2

Failure Is a Word I Don't Accept: An Interview with John H. Johnson*

and-So, I've got to have this second-class permit. I can't survive without it. You're in charge, and I've concluded that the only thing I can do is to do what you want. Will you please tell me what you want me to do?" He said, "Now you're talking, Johnson." And then, really, he told me to do what I was doing right then, namely, being persistent but not hostile. I learned the rules of the game. It wasn't always easy, but I learned them.

HBR: Are you aware of any sacrifices or personal compromises you've had to make?

Johnson: I don't think I've had to compromise any integrity along the way. I can't recall any instance when I knowingly did it. I think I have stooped to conquer. I saw I wasn't go-

* *Harvard Business Review*, March–April 1976, pp. 79–88. Copyright © 1976 by the President and Fellows of Harvard College; all rights reserved.

Note: John Johnson is editor and publisher of Johnson Publishing Company which issues *Ebony*, *Jet*, *Ebony, Jr.*, *Black Stars*, and *Black World*.

ing to get anywhere by burning things down. So I tried not to let anger and emotions interfere with logical decisions.

HBR: How do you deal with the anger?

Johnson: If I'm mad at somebody, I just go in a room, close the door, and cuss him or her out where nobody can hear me. Sometimes I write a letter that I don't mail. I've done a lot of that. I think we have to let the steam off, but I can't recall when I've openly expressed anger in front of anyone or to anyone for a very long time. You just lose. You really do. Fussing and arguing just don't work, so I try to avoid them.

HBR: Have you ever wanted to lash out rather than figure a way around a problem?

Johnson: Yes, all the time. All of us would like to lash out sometimes. I think you always have to keep in mind what your goal is, though; and lashing out will not achieve it. You see, one disadvantage blacks have with anger and dealing with it is not knowing how to behave in a business situation. Most don't know, so they may respond inappropriately and get very frustrated. I was lucky; at a very early age—18 —when I graduated from high school and went to work at Supreme Life Insurance Company as an office boy, I was a kind of flunky to Harry H. Pace, who was the president of the company. He took great pride in developing young people, and he regarded me as one of his discoveries. So he spent a lot of time with me, telling me about business, and why certain decisions had been made. I learned a lot by just being with him and listening to him.

One valuable lesson I learned was that you have to work with people you don't like, and you have to be willing to forgive and forget if what you've objected to has been corrected.

HBR: Do you apply that lesson to the way you manage?

Johnson: I sure do. Just yesterday I was talking to one of our vice presidents. He had fired a certain guy in anger, and this person was the best we had for the particular job he was in. So I said to the vice president, "Now, let's bring the guy to Chicago. Let's sit down and talk to him together. Let's give him another chance, and if he apologizes, and if he has learned his lesson, let's go with him again." I think many people would be inclined to say, "Well, that guy's no good; he insulted me, and I'm never going to deal with him again." I think we have to be prepared to deal with anybody and anything if the circumstances change. And we have to be prepared to go with what we've got. I always remind myself that my employees are the best people I have, and they're the only people I have. So I have to work with them.

HBR: It sounds as if you're translating your own success or philosophy of success into a management style. Would that be a fair statement?

Johnson: Yes, it would. Back in 1954, I made up a list of 25 or 30 people that I thought I needed to run the magazines. I have a secret office in the heart of my company in which I keep those names before me at all times. I try to think of all the things that I can do to make those people happy and well-satisfied with their work here. This often involves more than salary. It involves an upgrading in title, maybe occasional trips, recognition of something well-done, like a little note thanking them for it, calling attention to an outstanding job. It may involve my asking some private club to invite them to be a member, if that's what they want. I think you have to understand the people that work for you, find out what they want, and try to respond to it, because these are the people you need to succeed.

HBR: Traditionally, the entrepreneur is the person who wants to do it all on his own. It seems you recognized early on that you couldn't do it all yourself.

Johnson: I want to be big and I want to be bigger, and I can't do it all by myself. So I try to do only those things that I can't get anybody else to do. In other words, I don't really have a job at Johnson Publishing Company. Everything here is supposed to be done by somebody else. My job is to see that they do it, or to show them how.

HBR: So you see part of your function as teaching people?

Johnson: Teaching, training, leading, and demonstrating. I try hard to save people now, much harder than I did in my younger years. Most of the people we employ, less now than before, are people who were previously in something else. We have had to convert them. For example, most of our ad salesmen had never sold ads for anybody else. They were Urban League secretaries, school teachers, and post office workers. We had to mold these people, and train and direct them into becoming marketing experts and advertising salespeople.

HBR: Is training one of the responsibilities of all your managers?

Johnson: A key responsibility; the best manager is a good teacher. To give you an example, three years ago we started a cosmetic company called Fashion Fair, which is now very successful.

Now, there were no black people trained in that area. Before then, black people had not worked at high levels in the cosmetic industry. We looked around, and there were no black salesmen working for Revlon or Estée Lauder. They were not going to send black people in to sell Marshall Field and Bonwit Teller, so there was no company we could really raid.

HBR: What did you do?

Johnson: We made our own experts. For instance, Mr. J. Lance Clarke, who is our vice president of sales of cosmetics, had never worked in this field before. He didn't know how to go into a store like Marshall Field or Bonwit Teller. So I took him with me, and he and I together opened accounts in about 20 stores. He listened to what I said, he watched when I backed off, he watched when I went forward. And he learned. It isn't really that I'm a better salesman than he is; it's that there was and still is more mystique connected with me. I'm the head of the business. So I can sometimes get more done simply because of who I am. For this reason, there are still certain store accounts I have to open myself, but by and large, Mr. Clarke's doing it himself. And he's doing it because he watched me, and he learned.

HBR: Do you get personally involved in the selection of employees?

Johnson: Yes, yes. If I told you, you wouldn't believe it. Along with the personnel manager, I interview every person that we employ for our Chicago building. I don't do it for the New York office or for other offices, but for this building, yes. I don't say that it guarantees you'll like everybody. There're still a lot of people I don't particularly like for one reason or another. But because I'm interested, I think my interviewing guarantees that I'm getting the best people I can get. It also lets me learn enough about them so that I can get as much out of them as I know how.

HBR: Do you think it difficult to manage when you know everybody personally?

Johnson: Yes. But it has its advantages and disadvantages. The advantage is that we don't have a union. The disadvantages are that you genuinely have to work and help people. You just can't say you're going to do it. You've got to do it. Their concerns have to be your concerns. For example, if I know someone has died in an employee's family, and he's got to travel some distance and might be short of cash, I've got to offer to help.

HBR: How do you deal with the people who can't make it?

Johnson: As a matter of fact, I only fuss with the people I love. Of course, some people say I shouldn't love them so much. I try to push and fuss and cajole and do whatever I can to get the most out of them. But after we fuss and fight and argue, if nothing changes, we fire them. There's nothing else to do. If you do all that you can do—you warn people, you set goals, you tell them what the issues are, you tell them what's expected— and if they fail over and over again, then you have to get rid of them. We have no other choice. We reward success, and we punish failure. It's a known policy; it's not a secret. If people do well, we're going to find some way to reward them. If they do badly consistently, then we have to dismiss them. And it works.

HBR: How do you recognize a good man or woman?

Johnson: By observing. I look for dedication and commitment, and willingness to learn. I think it's more the last than it is anything else, because an intelligent person can be taught almost anything that's not purely technical. So we look primarily for a desire to learn and a dedication to the job. If they have these, we can teach them the rest.

HBR: How do you teach judgment, which takes time to acquire?

Johnson: I work with my people day in and day out. When I was young, I would see an employee doing something wrong and I'd let it go by instead of stopping it. Eventually, the employee would get to the point where I would have to dismiss him. Now that's a waste. I learned early in the game that if you dismiss the people you have, then the new people you hire are sometimes worse than the ones you dismissed. Very often, just the shock of having the kind of conversation we had with the guy we brought to Chicago to talk to will turn a man around. Another way to have turned him around, of course, would have been to challenge him on every little defection. We try to teach the regular corrective process to our managers so that they don't rush out and do something that we'll be sorry for.

HBR: Doesn't your persistence sometimes frighten people?

Johnson: If I've been really, really hard on a person, then I'll back off and let a few things go by. Very often, the people will correct themselves. If you've really been riding somebody, say, about coming to work on time, sometimes when they try real hard, they'll be late just from trying so hard. Then it's better to step back and let things ride for a few days rather than to sit in the lobby every day to see whether or not they come on time. Not long ago I wrote a memo giving everybody hell for coming to work late. I haven't even been in the lobby since I did that. But next week I'm going to be there.

HBR: Being visible is important, then?

Johnson: Well, as a matter of fact, when people visit the building, they're shocked to see me walking around the floors or riding on the elevator. If I want to see someone, I don't order him up to my office. I go down and see him. I'm all over the building all the time. It's not a thing I plan; it's just a thing I do. I know my people, I socialize with them, and we're friends.

HBR: There isn't any tension between your roles as friend and as employer?

Johnson: I don't think I've lost anything by being friendly with the people on the staff. If they get out of line, I challenge them. I say, we're friends, but this is the way it has to be. I don't find it to be a problem, but I guess there's always some tension. We don't have Christmas parties anymore because people would very often have too much to drink and say things either to me or to some manager that they shouldn't have said. We've lost several people through Christmas parties.

HBR: In effect, you're making it difficult for people to get out on a limb?

Johnson: That's right. If somebody challenges you out in the open, you've got to do something about it. You can be visible and available and friendly, but not too social with most of the people. You're never quite sure that your position will be respected. I don't want to be exposed to something that I'll have to take recognition of, and yet I think it's a risk I have to run.

HBR: How do you handle that tension in making business decisions?

Johnson: When we have staff meetings, I will listen very patiently to everyone's opinions. If I feel really strongly about something, the chances are I will try to put my own ideas over. But I cannot ever recall doing anything that everybody was against. If all of the people in whom I have confidence were against something, I would not go forward with it no matter how much I wanted to do it. I'd think that if all these people were against it, there must be something wrong with it.

HBR: Do you ever simply lay down the law?

Johnson: Not really, but if there's a tie, or a division of opinion, then I'll do as I feel. Or if I feel so strongly about something that I know that it's absolutely the right thing to do, then I don't call a meeting at all. I just say we're going to do it. I used to call employees together if there was a big dispute to see if I could mediate it. I didn't want one to think that I said anything that the others didn't know about. But that's a mistake, because all they did was scream and holler at each other. You're much better off to meet with each employee privately, and try to get each one to commit himself to a change of attitude without bringing them together for a confrontation.

HBR: From sitting on the boards of companies and universities, do you have a sense of how other people manage their businesses in ways distinct from the ways you do?

Johnson: I think our management is more personal and more direct. In most large corporations, the board and the management are so far removed that they'll have maybe only three people reporting to them. That's all the chief executive officer's exposed to. In my case, I have the heads of every department reporting directly to me. Not only that, but I talk directly to people, if I want to. As a matter of fact, if something is really wrong, anybody can petition to see me, if he or she really feels he or she has been mistreated. In any event, my theory is that even though you have a lot of people who could see you, you really have to deal only with those who have a problem.

HBR: You are chief executive officer at Supreme Life Insurance Company. Are things the same there? In one article about you, your business methods at Supreme were described as "arrogant and ruthless."

Johnson: Before I became CEO at Supreme, no matter what you did there, you couldn't get fired. Management just kept transferring people from one job to another. (I understand that they did that at the *Saturday Evening Post* too, which is probably why they folded.) When I went to Supreme, I made one statement: no one could be transferred. You had to succeed in your job; you were going to be given an adequate opportunity, but if you didn't succeed in that job, you were going to be dismissed, no matter how many years you had been there. Now, that was called arrogant. Maybe it was, but it turned the company around.

HBR: You didn't bring in your own management staff?

Johnson: No, we didn't change the people; we changed the method of operation. For instance, Supreme's executives and supervisors were supposed to go to work at 9:00, and the lowly employees were supposed to go to work at 8:30.

Well, the executives really came in around 10:00. So we changed that; everybody had to come to work at 9:00. The guy who said I was arrogant was probably one of the people who had to start coming to work at the same time all the other employees did.

HBR: Do you find that you now can manage both companies the same way?

Johnson: Yes, because we have a very good president at Supreme now. I think the two companies' problems are basically the same. You've got to look after the interest of the employee and then insist that the employee look after the interest of the company. In other words, in both organizations we paid the employees more money, we gave them more liberal benefits, and then we insisted that they do their work. I used to tell a joke about my New York manager. We gave him a big office. We paid him a big salary. We gave him a beautiful secretary. And then we threatened to take it all away from him. You'd be surprised how much we got out of him.

HBR: Do you think, using your own or other black companies as examples, that black organizations operate differently from white organizations?

Johnson: Generally, black organizations are more sentimental, more emotional, and less businesslike than white organizations, I think. We work with people we like a little bit more than we should.

HBR: Why is it more than you should?

Johnson: Well, when you dismiss people, it gives you a bad reputation in the black community, which is small. For example, in the early days I was known as someone who was ruthless in terms of dismissing people. That's partly why I got the reputation, which I often said was well-earned. If people didn't do their work, they were dismissed, period.

HBR: Do you think that black companies ought to try to stay separate from large white organizations?

Johnson: Well, you have to understand that I don't believe in black capitalism. Black people ought to have the right to become capitalists, but black capitalism presupposes that you're only going to sell to black people. If I sold only to black people, I wouldn't have a very successful company. Most of my subscriptions and newsstand sales are made to blacks, but 90 percent of my advertising is made to whites. So I don't believe that we ought to limit our sales to the black community. I think a black businessman ought to strive to be a businessman and to sell to any customers who will buy from him. If Kentucky Fried Chicken can sell chicken to blacks, we ought to be able to sell something to whites.

HBR: You have been quoted as saying, "I do not believe that the overriding desire to succeed has reached the desired intensity in minority business." Why do you think that's so?

Johnson: I said that because I meet so many men who want to go into business, and they can't because the SBA won't give them a loan. Now, if you truly want to go into business and you try all the banks and they say no, and you try all the SBAs and governmental agencies and they say no, then you have to talk individual people into buying stock and making investments.

HBR: It sounds as if what's missing is the motivation to go out there and succeed.

Johnson: That's the whole point. If blacks had the motivation, we would do some of these things. We would not give up our dream of going into business simply because a particular agency would not let us have the money to do it. I think the culture is such that we are taught to believe that everything good has happened, that all the new businesses have been started, that this is the age of big business, and that without friends and influence one cannot succeed.

HBR: Do you think that's the system's message?

Johnson: Yes, and I think that's bad. Most people don't believe success is possible. So they get discouraged before they start. They think that all the cards are stacked against them; and many blacks think the white man's not going to let him succeed. I was interviewed on television not long ago, and the interviewer was telling me that Chicago's a terrible town, that Mayor Daley's doing this and Mayor Daley's doing that. I said, Mayor Daley's not keeping anybody from succeeding. Mayor Daley's not keeping anyone from going to school, he's not keeping anybody from getting a job. Many of these things are within our own power to do, and so we can't blame the system for everything. Anger and fear of failure get in the way.

HBR: And the lack of successful models?

Johnson: Yes, you do need visible successful models. I think it's very important for a black person to see another black person, someone like himself, who is doing the thing that he wants to do. It lets him know, particularly in a country like ours, where you read so much about racial barriers and difficulties, that in spite of all those difficulties, it is still possible to make it.

That's very important for black people to know.

HBR: And this is what *Ebony* is all about.

Johnson: Absolutely. That's why we always play a positive role. It is why we are telling people what they can do rather than what they cannot do. Enough people are out there giving examples of what you can't do. Whenever there is a black person doing a successful job in a unique situation, there is an *Ebony* story. We want to show our readers, "Look, he's doing it in transportation, he's doing it in this, he's doing it in that. And if he can do it, you can do it."

HBR: There is a nice dualism in the role that *Ebony* plays in the black world. It is a symbol of black success, it is a success, and it has success as its main product. One could look at you in the same way. Do you see yourself as in a sense your own best product?

Johnson: Well, I think that might be overly immodest. But I would say that I see myself as representing what I'm trying to sell in *Ebony*, yes. Yes, I do. I'm one of the models. There are a lot of them now, but I'm one of them. I'm one of the people who says you can succeed against the odds. I'm not saying the odds aren't there. Many people assume that *Ebony* is saying everything is just great. But we're not saying that. We're saying we have to deal with the world as we find it. And within the context of what we find, these are the ways we think you can succeed within the system.

HBR: So in a sense you're creating a whole new cultural ideal or concept?

Johnson: Well, we're trying to apply the American culture to the black experience, to bring them together. If we learned anything during the 1960s, it was that perhaps we can make the system a little more responsive. We really can't change it, even if we wanted to. And the only way to succeed in the system is to learn the rules, and to try as nearly as possible to play by those rules.

HBR: What about the young blacks who are in large corporations? How would you advise them to stay with the system, to be active rather than angry?

Johnson: I think they have to find ways to get their bosses to help them without admitting guilt, without feeling uncomfortable. The boss is not going to promote you if in the process he has to admit that he was wrong all the years that he didn't move you up. He's got to somehow feel that you did something that came to his attention and that justifies the promotion in the present.

HBR: You've got to let everybody save face.

Johnson: Yes, that's right. Face-saving is important. But also, I think young people can be uniquely qualified. The important thing for all of us to have, particularly blacks, is some kind of power. And power comes in many forms. It comes in knowledge, it comes in experience, it comes in being beautiful. Some women have power by being beautiful; they can use their beauty, and that's power. It comes with sex. They can use sex, and that's power. It comes from being better at your job than anybody else, and that's power. For example, somebody here who can do a better job than anybody else has got a whole lot of power with me. They have what it takes to command a lot from me.

HBR: What if the corporation or system doesn't recognize power, or allow it. What can young blacks do then?

Johnson: I think they are obligated to try to make each system work, and to try to persuade the people who could make the system more responsive. Failing that, if they still want to work for a large company, then I think they need to try another one. I don't think we ought to say that all big business is bad simply because a particular company has not treated somebody fairly.

HBR: What can large white corporations do to keep young blacks motivated to stay?

Johnson: Well, I think they can do this by trying to promote them according to their abilities. I'm not sure that some of the large corporations are yet ready to do that for blacks. In many instances, the policy is straight at the top; management enunciates an equal opportunity policy, and I believe that many of the people on the board and in top management believe in it. But the policy is interpreted and operated on at a lower level, and here the prejudices of local supervisors can completely negate what top management would genuinely like to do.

HBR: Do you think then that white managers should deal with black subordinates differently from the way they do whites?

Johnson: No, I just think they should deal with them equally.

HBR: How can top management be sure this happens?

Johnson: Well, let me put it this way. I think that large white corporations ought to have an equal opportunity auditing committee. I never really thought about that before, but since you've asked me, I'll expand. Just as we have Arthur Andersen and Peat, Marwick come in and look over our business records to determine if the people lower down are doing what in fact they tell us they are doing, an equal opportunity auditing committee ought to examine the qualifications of the various people in the company and determine whether the blacks, based on their experience and qualifications, are in fact being given equal opportunity according to the policies announced. An audit would make the guys who are making the promotions and who are looking into the situation think more seriously about it.

HBR: Do you finance black enterprises on your own?

Johnson: No, no. I never invest in any business that I don't control. And I just don't believe that it's my obligation to finance every guy who wants to go into business. I believe it's my obligation to try to be a successful model, to build businesses, to contribute to the community in other ways, but I don't believe it's my obligation to invest every time some guy believes he's got a good idea.

HBR: When you encourage young blacks to start their own businesses, what new markets do you see? These are tight times!

Johnson: They are. To tell you the truth, if I were starting out, I would go into some phase of the franchise food business. Fortunes are being made every day because people have to eat. Look at MacDonald's and Kentucky Fried Chicken. Some blacks should move in quickly. Not only have whites taken over fried chicken, which black people cook better, but they've also now taken over ribs, which we cook better, too. I say, when they take ribs, they're going too far! So if I didn't have any other business, I'd start a chain of chicken shacks. Or I'd start an insurance agency, selling insurance on a brokerage basis. These are things that you wouldn't need capital for.

HBR: How would you feel about someone taking over the lead in your field?

Johnson: I would consider it a personal failure if someone took over. I wouldn't feel bad if someone started a new, good magazine, but if someone could move past me in circulation and in advertising, I would consider that a personal failure. And failure is a word I don't accept. I don't really think anybody could do it, though. I have a circulation of 103 million . . . what would I be doing while somebody else was getting 103 million?

I have a little niece who's always saying, "There's a big bully in our school." She says, "When I grow up, I'm going to punch him in the nose, and hit him in the mouth." I always say to her, "When you grow up, he's going to be bigger." You know, she keeps thinking that she's going to grow up, and he's going to stay where he is. If somebody came in the field, while he was getting successful, what would I be doing? I'd be working like hell to maintain my lead. As a matter of fact, I'm not too sure some good competition wouldn't be a good thing.

HBR: From what you say, your position seems secure. Do you have specific anxieties or fears connected with the future?

Johnson: I'm afraid I cannot maintain my position. Life is very like a merry-go-round—you can't slow it down, and you don't want to get off. There are times when I feel that I would rather not be working as hard as I am. I'm actually working harder now than I did when I started, and that's because I want to maintain my leadership position. The responsibility of trying to be

a leader and of trying to maintain that leadership is heavy. But I see my success here as something that I can't walk away from. And I can't slow it down.

HBR: Do you ever experience doubts?

Johnson: Yes, there are doubts and fears. Each time I started a new magazine, I had a certain amount of fear about it. I wondered, Well, will it succeed? Is this the right time? Am I making a mistake? I think all of us have fears. But in the end, it's what you come out with that makes the difference; it's what finally emerges as your decision. And my decision has always been to go forward.

HBR: Risk-taking is part of your formula for success.

Johnson: It's true. You have to dare to do things that you're afraid of. As a matter of fact, my editors often identify a hot story, one that will sell in *Ebony*, as one that I'm afraid to publish. Some of our best articles have been ones that I had a certain amount of fear about publishing. For example, I was fearful of the one called "Was Abraham Lincoln a Segregationist?" But it succeeded. Then we devoted a whole issue to the "white problem" in America; I was afraid of that. But in each case, after thinking about it and weighing all the circumstances, I'd say, "I've got to go forward with this."

HBR: Were the fears in those instances that you'd lose some of your advertisers?

Johnson: Right. I thought it was going too far and that advertisers would reject it. And *Ebony* has to have advertising. Yes, I was fearful of that. As a matter of fact, I remember the night before we went to press, one of the editors, it was a woman, said, "Boss, do you know what you're doing?" And I said, "No, I really don't, but I'm going to do it anyway."

HBR: So there is a fear that the system could suddenly turn on you?

Johnson: Oh yes, I always have that fear now. Don't get me wrong. I'm not saying that I'm going around strongly confident. I live in fear all the time. I run scared all the time. I think you have to in order to make it in business. I really don't think you can ever get the knots out of your stomach. It's never going to get better than it is now. You've just got to keep trying; when it's easy, you're dead.

HBR: Does this fear get in your way?

Johnson: I don't tell others what I'm telling you. I walk around here with great confidence. I issue edicts and statements and policy as though it were the final word, and I'd gotten it from on high. But I'm trembling in my boots. I think that's what a good manager has to do. Once I decide I'm really going to do something, I psych myself up and convince myself that I'm going to do it. And in effect I gain confidence from expressing confidence.

HBR: So living with fear can be an asset?

Johnson: I think it's very important to live with fear. One of the things that fear tells you is that you care about what you are doing.

When they start their careers, most managers expect to succeed. They have their dreams, for themselves and their families. But achieving these dreams takes more than desire. It takes knowledge, knowledge of what a person must do to be an effective manager.

An entire industry has been created to capitalize on this need. If all the books, articles, and tapes telling us how to be better than we are were thrown into a single bonfire, they would make a lovely flame. Not much light, probably, but a lot of heat.

Nowhere is the plague of miracle cures more prevalent than in management. Today's business literature is a smorgasbord from which each aspiring manager may choose according to his appetite—winning through intimidation, being an OK boss, avoiding group think, or even learning how to say "no" convincingly.

Unfortunately, much of the advice is long on inspiration but stingy on fact. It slides down easily, but an hour later your brain rumbles for more solid fare. We recently completed a five-year research project at Teleometrics that fills the need for evidence of what makes for executive success—what it takes to climb the ladder fast. By studying 16,000 male bosses, we discovered several specific ways in which managers who do well act differently from those who are average or worse.

Up the Ladder

Since our business is to apply behavioral science to business organizations, we routinely collect data on the values and day-to-day actions of individuals who make their organizations function as they do. To get more data, we gave additional tests to managers and their subordinates at more than 50 businesses of all sizes.

Knowing how managers acted wasn't much use without a reliable way of distinguishing between those who were suc-

READING 2–3

What Makes a Manager Good, Bad, or Average?*

JAY HALL

cessful and those who weren't. We had to know what good managers did, or didn't do, that their less-successful peers didn't do, or did. We felt that learning what didn't work would be just as useful as learning what actions pay off in job and salary.

We developed a variation on the Managerial Achievement Quotient (MAQ) developed by industrial engineer Benjamin Rhodes. It takes into account how far an individual has climbed on the organizational ladder in relation to his age and the number of career moves necessary to reach the top of his organization.

To test how accurately the MAQ reflected success in real life, we collected biographical data on more than 5,000 managers, aged 19 to 64, in 26 different types of companies. When we worked up MAQ scores for each, and analyzed the results, we found that the MAQ was a reliable indicator of success. For the rest of our study, we categorized managers with MAQ scores of 60 or above as high achievers, those with 41 to 59 as average achievers, and those with 40 or below as low achievers.

Now that we had an objective, reliable way of telling good managers from bad, we were ready to see what they did that made the difference. We knew from earlier studies that managerial effectiveness could be measured in terms of three factors— motivation, the participative ethic, and interpersonal competence—and in terms of managerial style, a synthesis of the first three factors.

Motivation has sometimes been overlooked in understanding managers because analysts have assumed that managers are just naturally motivated by strong drives for power, success, achievement, etc. If they weren't, they wouldn't be managers. The fact is, managers have different motivations, differences which influence how well they do their jobs and permit subordinates to do theirs.

To test this idea, we gave groups of managers and their employees two tests. We had 1,265 managers and 3,500 subordinates take the Hall and Williams Work Motivation Inventory, a test which measures the needs most important to individuals in their jobs. We gave another 664 managers a companion test, the Management of Motives Index, which shows how much a manager stresses a particular need in his handling of others.

The tests measure two kinds of needs. One consists of creature comforts and safety—needs that psychologist Frederick Herzberg calls *hygiene* and *maintenance* factors. Managers who feel these are important are usually negative people, interested mainly in keeping things smooth and avoiding trouble. Managers who are concerned mainly with *motivator needs* (ego status and self-actualization) are positive fellows, out to get things done without worrying much about security and comfort.

Back and Forth

When we compared our good, bad, and indifferent managers on this basis, we found that motives were a good predictor of effectiveness. Good managers were driven mainly by the need for *self-actualization*. Average managers were concerned with *ego status*. And poor managers were caught in a double bind, equally preoccupied by safety and ego-status needs. They wavered back and forth trying to satisfy both needs, and failed to accomplish either very well.

When we looked at how their subordinates answered these same questions, we found they read their boss's message loud and clear. Good managers seem to create, or find, subordinates who get the job done. Play-it-safe bosses also shape employees in their own image—timid souls who worry mainly about job security, put their time in, and get their kicks elsewhere. Good managers challenge their people; poor ones comfort them.

So now we knew what made good managers tick: the drive to succeed, to satisfy themselves, and to accomplish as much as they could. But how did this translate into action? What did good managers do that others didn't?

Much of the difference lies in a boss's willingness to let his people participate in the decisions that affect them. We confirmed this by giving the Personal Reaction Index to more than 2,000 individuals who worked for 731 good, bad, and indifferent managers. The PRI, in addition to assessing how much a manager allows subordinates to influence decisions, also gauges the subordinates' job satisfaction, sense of responsibility, pride in work, and so on— the factors that reflect a good or bad work climate.

A good manager believes five heads are better than one in solving a problem. And this turns out to be good for his career, because as head head he gets most of the credit when the right decisions are made.

Encouraging people to share in decisions which affect them is an important part of being a good boss. But the stage must be set. A good manager needs interpersonal competence, the ability to create an open work climate in which his subordinates feel free to suggest and act. We administered a Personnel Relationship Survey to 1,691 managers to see how they dealt with subordinates, colleagues, and superiors, and gave a companion test—the Management Relations Survey—to 1,884 of their subordinates as a check to see how they rate their bosses' way of handling people.

We found two things:

1. Good, bad, and average managers dealt with people in substantially different ways.
2. The subordinates' ratings of their managers' interpersonal competence matched how the managers described themselves.

So what *is* interpersonal competence? According to what good managers said— and, more important, what their subordinates said about them—it means accepting responsibility for your own ideas and feelings, being open to your own and others' sentiments, experimenting with new ideas and feelings, and helping others accept, be open to, and experiment with their own ideas and attitudes.

Cluster of Actions

Some of these attributes are particularly important. Accepting responsibility for ideas is so common among managers that it doesn't mean much in terms of interpersonal competence; in fact, excessive preoccupation with his own ideas and feelings can make a manager authoritarian rather than sharing. That description fits many average managers. Being open with others,

willing to experiment and help subordinates do the same is much rarer, and is a potent predictor of high interpersonal competence and high achievement.

These three factors—motivation, participatory management, and interpersonal competence—combine to create managerial style: a cluster of actions and values that interact to form a new element that is hard to define but easy to recognize. To assess it objectively, we examined the interplay between a manager's two most important considerations, production and people.

We gave the Styles of Management Inventory to 1,878 managers and the Management Appraisal Survey to their subordinates to see how good, bad, and indifferent bosses scored in these two areas. Again the managers and subordinates agreed. Good managers are deeply interested in both people and production (high task/high relationship oriented, to use the pertinent psychological jargon). They use an integrative style of management in which production goals and people's needs are equally important.

Average managers were pegged by their subordinates as high task/low relationship people, so preoccupied with getting the job done that they often forget about the people who have to do it. Poor bosses employ a low task/low relationship style. The personnel manual and standard operating procedures are their guides and self-preservation their goal.

The good manager, it seems, needs to find meaning in his work and strives to give the same meaning to others. What he does flows from his view that work is both a challenge and an opportunity for self-expansion. He looks upon innovation as an opportunity rather than a threat and is therefore willing to take risks. He believes that to be successful he must work with people under him and create opportunities for them to succeed. He is, in a phrase, an apostle of enlightened self-interest.

As a behaviorist, I believe strongly that we are what we do. This is fortunate for most of us because it means that success as an executive doesn't depend on personal traits or extraordinary skills unique to a few outstanding individuals. It depends, rather, on how we *behave* in our work, on the values we hold about personal and interpersonal potentials. All of these can be learned. The key to becoming a good manager—a success, if you will—is to learn to behave like one.

In the past 20 years, our basic management philosophies have become increasingly results-oriented. In spite of this orientation, the hoped-for results have become more and more elusive. Managers now find themselves needing to acquire new skills which can enable them to improve performance. The most sought-after new skills have been based on traditional motivation theories; and while they have been exciting to work with, there is little evidence that they represent the optimal strategy of helping people perform better. Operating on the far end of the continuum from traditional theorists, behavioral psychologists have accumulated data which leads to two primary suggestions:

1. Traditional approaches to improved performance have been ineffective because they focus on presumed deficiencies in people, rather than on performance itself—on getting the job done.
2. Behavior technology can be effective in improving performance because it is very heavily performance oriented.

While these may be only suggestions, they are based on a **great** deal of clinical and real-world research.

They are also the source of a great deal of controversy. Since controversy is usually the child of confusion, I would like to devote this article to those areas of confusion most commonly encountered when dealing with behavior technology in the management environment, particularly with positive reinforcement.

How Behavior Technology Differs from Motivation Theory

Motivation theory is the product of traditional psychology—which has always considered itself to be the science of the mind. If we were able to peel back the top of the human skull, all we would see would be viscous gray matter. Our most acute phys-

READING 2-4

Why Manage Behavior? A Case for Positive Reinforcement*

HARRY WIARD

ical examination could not begin to reveal the workings of the human mind. The psychologist who deals with the mind on a very intimate basis is unable to tell us much more than we might observe ourselves through the magic skull flap. The result of this lack of information has been a very loosely-formed system of deductive logic that we refer to as "analysis."

The basic premise of the analytic school seems to be that any form of undesired or strange behavior can be traced back to some underlying mental disorder which can then be cured, thereby eliminating undesired behavior. While this may sound reasonable, it's really not. If we take a good hard look at the situation, we see that people don't get locked up for thinking crazy, people get locked up for acting crazy. You might think that they would be *unlocked* when they stopped acting crazy, but this generally isn't

* Reprinted from *Human Resource Management*, Summer 1972, pp. 15–20, Graduate School of Business Administration, University of Michigan, Ann Arbor, Michigan.

so because the analyst has yet to find and root out the "actual" disorder. While this desire to cure the *actual disorder* is enviable, there is little evidence to indicate that the cure ever happens; what does take place is an exercise of the loosest form of conjecture. One of the highlights of my undergraduate career was a psychology professor who delighted in telling his classes bizarre stories of a "textbook paranoiac" whom he was currently treating. It seemed that the only patients he paid any attention to were those who demonstrated that they were messed up (to him, that demonstration was progress). Unfortunately, as long as they continued demonstrating that they were *not functioning,* there was little hope that they would ever get out of therapy.

We see this same phenomenon in management. There are many managers who feel that they should counsel their employees and try to motivate them. While there are a lot of managers who want to motivate their employees, there are maybe ten times as many employees who don't want to be motivated. We all know who these employees are—they are our unmotivated employees. The motivational manager—just like the analytical therapist—seems willing to sacrifice performance for the sake of motivation itself. This seems somewhat a waste, especially when there is little chance that he can tell what it *is* that motivates a single worker (much less his entire workforce). Louis Armstrong, when he was listening to a jazz drummer at the Newport Festival some years ago, said something that succinctly expresses the plight of the analytical therapist and the motivating manager; he said, "He's trying to find where it's at, and he don't even know what it is."

The principles of positive reinforcement are premised on two very basic principles: (1) people perform in the ways that they find most rewarding to them; (2) by providing the proper rewards, it's possible to improve people's performance. If these statements seem abrupt, B. F. Skinner is more succinct yet when he states, "Behavior is determined by its consequences."

The consequences of our day-to-day relationships with other people are *reward* and *punishment.* Unfortunately, punishment is used to change performance more frequently than reward is. Its basic value is derived more from its threat than its administration, as long as the threat value is not diminished by long periods of time or overadministration of the actual punishment.

The overall punishment strategy is really very illogical. When we consistently use punishment to improve performance, it often becomes a reward. The reward comes when we don't punish for not performing in a specified manner. We then assume that if people do *not* perform in the ways that we *don't* want them to, that they *will* perform in the ways that we *do* want them to.

If overall punishment strategies are not too logical, our choice of punishments is sometimes absurd; for example, consider these illustrations:

One frustrated mother (all mothers are frustrated) laid down the law to her children that every piece of their clothing that she had to pick up was going to cost them a penny. At the end of a week she presented them with a bill for 27 cents. Her children promptly paid the bill, added a 10-cent tip, and a note thanking her for the terrific job that she had done.

In one southern prison, the recidivism or return rate for solitary confinement was abnormally high. Some simple research revealed that ten days in solitary, on bread and water, represented a substantial status symbol to the prison population. The diet was changed to baby food, and the recidivism rate dropped substantially. Apparently ten days on baby food wasn't much of a status symbol.

There may be cases where the use of punishment has resulted in improved performance, but they are few and far between.

The pitfalls of punishment can be encountered with any indirect approach. The specified goals are often *negative goals* such as the elimination of poor performance, with little consideration as to what it is that constitutes good performance.

What Is Positive Reinforcement?

Positive reinforcement is directly oriented to desired results, so it provides a more direct approach to the solution of performance problems. The theories of positive reinforcement are premised on the fact that people perform for one of two reasons (or, you might say, for one of two kinds of rewards): first, because a specific type or level of performance is consistently rewarding, or, second, because a specific pattern of performance has at one time been rewarded so handsomely, that it will be repeated in hope that the reward will be repeated. Let's take a closer look at each type.

The first type is fairly straight-forward; it merely implies that people perform in manners that they find rewarding. Apply this to one of your subordinates. His salary pays him for a level of performance determined by and/or equal to his peers; if you want him to perform better than his peers, you reward him. In most cases the reward need not be monetary; when he does a better job and you recognize it as such by telling him that he has done a better job, the chances are very high that if you consistently tell him when he does better, that he will consistently do better. If you expect him to be "good for nothing," he will probably fulfill your expectation of him.

The second type of reward is not as straight-forward. While there are probably situations in business that exemplify it, a more understandable example can be observed in the casinos in the Bahamas or Nevada. Those of you who have spent any time in Reno or Las Vegas have probably been amazed that people will stand and play the same slot machine for eight hours, have the machine locked to protect their investment, go to dinner, and come right back to play the same machine for another eight hours. The next time you go out there, look a little closer; invariably you will find that the machines pay jackpots only and those people stand there for hours on end working for the big pay-off. Since really big pay-offs are fairly difficult to build into manager-subordinate relationships, we'll concentrate, for the sake of space and practicality, on consistent performance through consistent reward.

There is no reason why you can't use positive reinforcement to gain desired performance through built-in rewards. There are three considerations in the successful implementation of any positive reinforcement program.

One *Desired levels of performance should be very specifically determined, and once determined, they should be clearly stated.* The determination of standard levels of performance is a most important step in the management process and in the process of using positive reinforcement. More often than not, performance standards are determined only on the basis of what we feel should be, or could be, or needs be; there is very little attention paid to what *is*. A reality-based determination of present performance is achieved through the use of accurate measurement. It achieves two ends: you know exactly where you are in relation to where you would like to be, and you have arrived at a base line from which you can begin the process of improving performance through the use of positive reinforcement. Once you have determined what your performance standards are going to be, inform people who are going to have to maintain those standards; in many cases, a standard, once determined, often gets buried in some procedures manual, and your people are the last ones to know. Performance standards really become effective when there is constant measurement and feedback and they become an integral factor in the communication link between manager and subordinate.

Two *Rewards for desired performance should be appropriate to the performance, but above all they should be rewarding.* Reward selction can be a subtle task, but it's not really difficult. Gilbert and Sullivan maintained that the punishment should fit the crime; the guideline for positive reinforcement might well be *let the reward fit the performance.* The appropriateness of rewards can be measured by the extent to which they change performance. When one of your people improves his performance, you should be as specific as possible as to why it is that you are rewarding him. Let's assume that George has exceeded his current level of production, and you reward him with "Good job, George." While that's a reward, it won't have the impact on his performance that this will: "George, you did well yesterday; your production was up 10 percent." Well, admittedly, the idea of complimenting subordinates on their work is obvious; but on the other hand, how many people do you know who *dislike* hearing good things about themselves?

The most commonly-thought-of reward is money. Money has a great deal of impact, but for many there are more effective rewards. The real advantage of the nonmonetary reward is visibility. A visible reward is more accessible, and subsequently, more effective in improving performance. The most striking example of an effective nonmonetary reward is the trading stamp. Trading stamps have created droves of fanatically loyal shoppers. In industry, the trading stamps have been effective in two performance-oriented organizations. One steel plant in the midwest rewarded the families of employees with trading stamps for uninterrupted periods of attendance. As a consequence, the absentee rate has been reduced considerably. In the second case, a company in Massachusetts has a practice of calling the families of their employees and asking them for the current safety message. If they answer correctly, they are rewarded with trading stamps. Both of these programs were well-thought-out; by making the stamps available to the families they ensured visibility, and the effectiveness of the program could be easily measured by the number of winners.

If there is ever any question as to what it is that might be rewarding, you might follow the example of a young manager at one of the major automobile manufacturers. After having been put in charge of a line that assembled rear-end units for trucks and buses, he discovered that while the standard was 72 units an hour, the men were lucky if they completed 45. Being fairly new with the company, the young manager went to the people working that particular line and asked them what it would take for them to bring their output up to standard. After talking it over, they decided that if they were able to get in an extra smoke break once in a while, it would justify an increased effort on their part. The final deal was that once they had completed 72 units in a given hour, the rest of that hour was theirs for a smoke break. It was only about a week before the men took 35 minutes to produce standard—and they were taking the other 25 minutes for their smoke break.

Both the manager and the men were aware that the situation could not go on, so they proceeded to renegotiate and this time the standard was raised to 92 units per hour, which they were able to produce and still get a ten-minute smoke break. Everything was fine until one of the divisional vice presidents, hearing of the improved production, came down to see what was going on. As luck would have it, he showed up in the middle of a break and raised the roof; increased production not withstanding, those men were being paid to *work* eight hours a day, and that was exactly what they were going to do.

Needless to say, the men went back to "working" eight hours a day, and the production went back to below the original standard. The new supervisor's unorthodox reward was visible and accessible, and there was no doubt that it was effective. The real question evolved around the choice of having a labor force which produces, or a labor force which puts in its time.

Three *Rewards should follow desired performance as closely as possible.* When the specific purpose of a reward is to improve performance, that reward will be much more significant if it follows closely the incidence of performance. Again, if we look at the trading stamp program, we see that it was effective because it followed very closely the desired performance. The ability to reward promptly assumes the existence of a fast and accurate feedback system. Since all effective management systems are dependent on feedback systems, the use of positive reinforcement pays off not only in improved performance but with more effective feedback systems.

Does Positive Reinforcement Really Work?

The answer is an unqualified yes. Positive reinforcement can be an invaluable management skill. Two case studies demonstrate some of its potential (the first discusses its potential in a nonmanagement area, but is amusing enough to "reward" you for reading this far).

In the early part of World War II, the vastness of the Pacific Theater made apparent the need for a more far-reaching weapon than the airplane—which was then considered to be the ultimate weapon. It was at this point that serious development of the guided missile began. One of the first missiles was the Pelican. Its development presented many unique problems, but one was outstanding: the missile was capable of carrying only such a limited weight that if it carried a payload, there was no way that it could carry a guidance system; or if it carried a guidance system, there was no way that it could carry a payload.

Dr. B. F. Skinner suggested that a lightened guidance system could be developed through the use of a lower order animal which was conditioned through positive reinforcement to fly the missile. The animal Skinner selected was the pigeon. Pigeons are small, readily available, and, most important, possess excellent eyesight. In testing out his notion in a very primitive simulator, Skinner proved that it was not only possible to train pigeons to guide missiles, it was possible to train them perfectly. His research was ignored until the summer of 1942, when the vice president of research at General Mills suggested that the company might, as a patriotic service, develop the pigeon guidance system for the government. By the summer of 1943, General Mills was awarded a modest grant by the Office of Scientific Development to develop a homing device. Using a pigeon-sized link-type trainer, Skinner was able to condition the pigeons to guide the missiles with appalling accuracy. When they were confronted with the pigeons' competence, the government people expressed a great concern over the fact that *one* little pigeon was to have total control over a highly explosive missile.

To assure the government people, Skinner trained the pigeons to work in teams. This placed the burden of target selection on two out of a team of three pigeons. Again, the pigeons were able to track and select targets accurately. The government was still not satisfied, and after the pigeons were trained to function in teams of five, just as effectively, the entire proposal was quietly dismissed by the government.

The relevance of Skinner's accomplishment can be measured by the way that the enemy solved their guidance system problem. Their "solution" was just a little heavier—it was a kamikazi pilot. If we were to consider training pigeons to fly missiles in today's times, the whole idea would be at best ludicrous. But if we pause to consider Skinner's success, three implications might follow for managers who want to develop their ability to improve performance.

1. If Skinner was able to use behavior technology to train pigeons to fly planes in about half the time that it takes to train a man to do the same job, then the use of the same techniques should substantially reduce the time that it takes to train people to perform a wide variety of skills.
2. Skinner's techniques are so effective in training that we might question the efficiency of "traditional approaches" toward the same end—bringing the worker to perform at set levels of performance.
3. The pigeons we have been feeding in the park for so many years are much smarter than we anticipated; a similar conclusion might be drawn about the people who work for us.

The second case study comes from Emery Air Freight. While it is not as spectacular as pigeons flying missiles, there are significant implications as to the use of behavioral techniques within the business community. Emery survives and grows on its ability to provide shipping that is faster and more dependable than a land-carrier. Prerequisite to its providing this service is its ability to provide customer information which is just as fast and dependable as the shipping. The first step in the customer information service is handled at a large table where telephones and a computer terminal are manned by the requisite number of peo-

ple. Since supplying information is often contingent upon the information's availability, and delays are often inevitable, the management considered it essential to set certain objectives for the information teams. These objectives are:

1. When a phone rings, it should be answered within the first three rings.
2. If the desired information is not immediately available, and the customer is put on hold, he must be gotten back to within a specified period of time and assured that the information is still being searched for.
3. In the event that information is not available, the customer should be called back within specified periods of time and given progress reports until that time when the information is available.

When Emery set the objectives, they measured the teams to see if they were already meeting the objectives. It was determined that the teams were not even close to meeting the specified objectives. Using the original measurement as a baseline for comparison, Emery continued measuring the teams on an hourly basis, and made it a point to inform the members of the team of their results. By keeping track of the results, and keeping the team members informed of those results, management provided them with feedback which functioned as positive reinforcement. The team improved their percentage of accomplished objective by 60 percent in the first day.

When the team was deprived of the feedback, its percentage of objectives dropped back to the point of the original baseline measurement. When Emery decided that continuous feedback was a positive factor in the accomplishment of objectives, they assigned one member of the team—on a rotational basis—to do nothing but measure the other members of the team. The end result was a greatly improved customer service in spite of the fact that one of the team members was occupied with measurement and feedback.

The work with their telephone team has been a small part of the behavioral program which has been installed at Emery. The results of the above study indicate that the management of performance is not expensive, and that the potential payoffs for management indicate that the extra effort was, and is, well worth it.

Let's say a word about the arguments which adamantly oppose the idea of behavior technology. Those who are aware of the work of Skinner pay him a very high compliment by inferring that his techniques, applied to people, constitute a threat to our classical concept of personal autonomy. Dr. Skinner's work in conditioning animals proved that his applied theories are most effective; but the assumption that Skinner wants to condition society in the same manner as he has conditioned his pigeons is not only false, it's malicious.

Behavior technology is a science concerned with the changing of environments, not people; actions, not feelings; and, in general, man's external condition rather than his outlook or philosophy. In a society where we are dithered by computers, traffic jams, pollution, fast food, aerosol cans, etc., an environment which *responds positively* to human results will contribute to the reinforcement—rather than the destruction—of human autonomy. Any "threat" involved in behavior technology is directed towards the maintenance of a substantial amount of ritualized, nonproductive, and, more often than not, frustrating behavior which at this point has become an integral element of our day-to-day lives.

A second but more specific objection to the behavioral approach is the concept that rewarding or reinforcing performance is tantamount to bribery. In many working environments, the assumption prevails that working people have an instinctive desire to "succeed" regardless of reward. To assume that people will maintain the desire to succeed without tangible reward is not only unreal, it's absurd. If we want more-than-acceptable performance, we must make the performance worthwhile to the performer, and the process of making that performance worthwhile to the performer can hardly be termed bribery.

The last argument against behavior management implies that it is difficult to use with large groups of people, and that it is expensive. For the most part, the use of behavioral techniques requires that performance be very closely monitored, and when it is warranted, that it be reinforced as quickly as possible. Keeping track of performance is a manager's job; and improving performance implies that he will also be rewarded. Taking the trouble to reinforce people for doing a good job is not that difficult, or that expensive. The ultimate payoff could be a lot more people doing many more good things, and that can only lead to a better world.

Americans, as a rule, are not very comfortable with power or with its dynamics. We often distrust and question the motives of people who we think actively seek power. We have a certain fear of being manipulated. Even those people who think the dynamics of power are inevitable and needed often feel somewhat guilty when they themselves mobilize and use power. Simply put, the overall attitude and feeling toward power, which can easily be traced to the nation's very birth, is negative. In his enormously popular *Greening of America*, Charles Reich reflects the views of many when he writes, "It is not the misuse of power that is evil; the very existence of power is evil."[1]

One of the many consequences of this attitude is that power as a topic for rational study and dialogue has not received much attention, even in managerial circles. If the reader doubts this, all he or she need do is flip through some textbooks, journals, or advanced management course descriptions. The word *power* rarely appears.

This lack of attention to the subject of power merely adds to the already enormous confusion and misunderstanding surrounding the topic of power and management. And this misunderstanding is becoming increasingly burdensome because in today's large and complex organizations the effective performance of most managerial jobs requires one to be skilled at the acquisition and use of power.

From my own observations, I suspect that a large number of managers—especially the young, well-educated ones—perform significantly below their potential because they do not understand the dynamics of power and because they have not nurtured and developed the instincts needed to effectively acquire and use power.

[1] Charles A. Reich, *The Greening of America: How the Youth Revolution Is Trying to Make America Liveable* (New York: Random House, 1970).

READING 2–5

Power, Dependence, and Effective Management*

JOHN P. KOTTER

In this article I hope to clear up some of the confusion regarding power and managerial work by providing tentative answers to three questions:

1. Why are the dynamics of power necessarily an important part of managerial processes?
2. How do effective managers acquire power?
3. How and for what purposes do effective managers use power?

I will not address questions related to the misuse of power, but not because I think they are unimportant. The fact that some

* *Harvard Business Review*, July–August 1977, pp. 125–36. Copyright © 1977 by the President and Fellows of Harvard College; all rights reserved.

Author's note: This article is based on data from a clinical study of a highly diverse group of 26 organizations including large and small, public and private, manufacturing and service organizations. The study was funded by the Division of Research at the Harvard Business School. As part of the study process, the author interviewed about 250 managers.

managers, some of the time, acquire and use power mostly for their own aggrandizement is obviously a very important issue that deserves attention and careful study. But that is a complex topic unto itself and one that has already received more attention than the subject of this article.

RECOGNIZING DEPENDENCE IN THE MANAGER'S JOB

One of the distinguishing characteristics of a typical manager is how dependent he is on the activities of a variety of other people to perform his job effectively.[2] Unlike doctors and mathematicians, whose performance is more directly dependent on their own talents and efforts, a manager can be dependent in varying degrees on superiors, subordinates, peers in other parts of the organization, the subordinates of peers, outside suppliers, customers, competitors, unions, regulating agencies, and many others.

These dependency relationships are an inherent part of managerial jobs because of two organizational facts of life: division of labor and limited resources. Because the work in organizations is divided into specialized divisions, departments, and jobs, managers are made directly or indirectly dependent on many others for information, staff services, and cooperation in general. Because of their organization's limited resources, managers are also dependent on their external environments for support. Without some minimal cooperation from suppliers, competitors, unions, regulatory agencies, and customers, managers cannot

help their organizations survive and achieve their objectives.

Dealing with these dependencies and the manager's subsequent vulnerability is an important and difficult part of a manager's job because, while it is theoretically possible that all of these people and organizations would automatically act in just the manner that a manager wants and needs, such is almost never the case in reality. All the people on whom a manager is dependent have limited time, energy, and talent, for which there are competing demands.

Some people may be uncooperative because they are too busy elsewhere, and some because they are not really capable of helping. Others may well have goals, values, and beliefs that are quite different and in conflict with the manager's and may therefore have no desire whatsoever to help or cooperate. This is obviously true of a competing company and sometimes of a union, but it can also apply to a boss who is feeling threatened by a manager's career progress or to a peer whose objectives clash with the manager's.

Indeed, managers often find themselves dependent on many people (and things) whom they do not directly control and who are not "cooperating." This is the key to one of the biggest frustrations managers feel in their jobs, even in the top ones.

As a person gains more formal authority in an organization, the areas in which he or she is vulnerable increase and become more complex rather than the reverse. It is not at all unusual for the president of an organization to be in a highly dependent position, a fact often not apparent to either the outsider or to the lower level manager who covets the president's job.

A considerable amount of the behavior of highly successful managers that seems inexplicable in light of what management texts usually tell us managers do becomes understandable when one considers a man-

---

[2] See Leonard R. Sayles, *Managerial Behavior: Administration in Complex Organization* (New York: McGraw-Hill, 1964) as well as Rosemary Stewart, *Managers and Their Jobs* (London: Macmillan, 1967) and *Contrasts in Management* (London: McGraw-Hill, 1976).

ager's need for, and efforts at, managing his or her relationships with others.[3] To be able to plan, organize, budget, staff, control, and evaluate, managers need some control over the many people on whom they are dependent. Trying to control others solely by directing them and on the basis of the power associated with one's position simply will not work—first, because managers are always dependent on some people over whom they have no formal authority and, second, because virtually no one in modern organizations will passively accept and completely obey a constant stream of orders from someone just because he or she is the "boss."

Trying to influence others by means of persuasion alone will not work either. Although it is very powerful and possibly the single most important method of influence, persuasion has some serious drawbacks too. To make it work requires time (often lots of it), skill, and information on the part of the persuader. And persuasion can fail simply because the other person chooses not to listen or does not listen carefully.

This is not to say that directing people on the basis of the formal power of one's position and persuasion are not important means by which successful managers cope. They obviously are. But, even taken together, they are not usually enough.

Successful managers cope with their dependence on others by being sensitive to it, by eliminating or avoiding unnecessary dependence, and by establishing power over those others. Good managers then use that power to help them plan, organize, staff, budget, evaluate, and so on. *In other words, it is primarily because of the dependence inherent in managerial jobs that the dy-*namics of power necessarily form an important part of a manager's processes.

ESTABLISHING POWER IN RELATIONSHIPS

To help cope with the dependency relationships inherent in their jobs, effective managers create, increase, or maintain four different types of power over others.[4] Having power based in these areas puts the manager in a position both to influence those people on whom he or she is dependent when necessary and to avoid being hurt by any of them.

Sense of Obligation

One of the ways that successful managers generate power in their relationships with others is to create a sense of obligation in those others. When the manager is successful, the others feel that they should —rightly—allow the manager to influence them within certain limits.

Successful managers often go out of their way to do favors for people whom they expect will feel an obligation to return those favors. As can be seen in the following description of a manager by one of his subordinates, some people are very skilled at identifying opportunities for doing favors that cost them very little but that others appreciate very much:

Most of the people here would walk over hot coals in their bare feet if my boss asked them to. He has an incredible capacity to do little

---

[3] I am talking about the type of inexplicable differences that Henry Mintzberg has found; see his article "The Manager's Job: Folklore and Fact," *HBR*, July–August 1975, p. 49.

[4] These categories closely resemble the five developed by John R. P. French and Bertram Raven; see "The Bases of Social Power" in *Group Dynamics: Research and Theory*, Dorwin Cartwright and Alvin Zandler, eds. (New York: Harper & Row, 1968), chap. 20. Three of the categories are similar to the types of "authority"-based power described by Max Weber in *The Theory of Social and Economic Organization* (New York: Free Press, 1947).

things that mean a lot to people. Today, for example, in his junk mail he came across an advertisement for something that one of my subordinates had in passing once mentioned that he was shopping for. So my boss routed it to him. That probably took 15 seconds of his time, and yet my subordinate really appreciated it. To give you another example, two weeks ago he somehow learned that the purchasing manager's mother had died. On his way home that night, he stopped off at the funeral parlor. Our purchasing manager was, of course, there at the time. I bet he'll remember that brief visit for quite a while.

Recognizing that most people believe that friendship carries with it certain obligations ("A friend in need. . . ."), successful managers often try to develop true friendships with those on whom they are dependent. They will also make formal and informal deals in which they give something up in exchange for certain future obligations.

Belief in a Manager's Expertise

A second way successful managers gain power is by building reputations as "experts" in certain matters. Believing in the manager's expertise, others will often defer to the manager on those matters. Managers usually establish this type of power through visible achievement. The larger the achievement and the more visible it is, the more power the manager tends to develop.

One of the reasons that managers display concern about their "professional reputations" and their "track records" is that they have an impact on others' beliefs about their expertise. These factors become particularly important in large settings, where most people have only secondhand information about most other people's professional competence, as the following shows:

Herb Randley and Bert Kline were both 35-year-old vice presidents in a large research and development organization. According to their closest associates, they were equally bright and competent in their technical fields and as managers. Yet Randley had a much stronger professional reputation in most parts of the company, and his ideas generally carried much more weight. Close friends and associates claim the reason that Randley is so much more powerful is related to a number of tactics that he has used more than Kline has.

Randley has published more scientific papers and managerial articles than Kline. Randley has been more selective in the assignments he has worked on, choosing those that are visible and that require his strong suits. He has given more speeches and presentations on projects that are his own achievements. And in meetings in general, he is allegedly forceful in areas where he has expertise and silent in those where he does not.

Identification with a Manager

A third method by which managers gain power is by fostering others' unconscious identification with them or with ideas they "stand for." Sigmund Freud was the first to describe this phenomenon, which is most clearly seen in the way people look up to "charismatic" leaders. Generally, the more a person finds a manager both consciously and (more important) unconsciously an ideal person, the more he or she will defer to that manager.

Managers develop power based on others' idealized views of them in a number of ways. They try to look and behave in ways that others respect. They go out of their way to be visible to their employees and to give speeches about their organizational goals, values, and ideals. They even consider, while making hiring and promotion decisions, whether they will be able to develop this type of power over the candidates:

One vice president of sales in a moderate-size manufacturing company was reputed to be so much in control of his sales force that he could get them to respond to new and different marketing programs in a third of the time taken by the company's best competitors. His power over his employees was based primarily on their strong identification with him and what he stood for. Emigrating to the United States at age 17, this person worked his way up "from nothing." When made a sales manager in 1965, he began recruiting other young immigrants and sons of immigrants from his former country. When made vice president of sales in 1970, he continued to do so. In 1975, 85 percent of his sales force was made up of people whom he hired directly or who were hired by others he brought in.

Perceived Dependence on a Manager

The final way that an effective manager often gains power is by feeding others' beliefs that they are dependent on the manager either for help or for not being hurt. The more they perceive they are dependent, the more most people will be inclined to cooperate with such a manager.

There are two methods that successful managers often use to create perceived dependence.

Finding and Acquiring Resources   In the first, the manager identifies and secures (if necessary) resources that another person requires to perform his job, that he does not possess, and that are not readily available elsewhere. These resources include such things as authority to make certain decisions; control of money, equipment, and office space; access to important people; information and control of information channels; and subordinates. Then the manager takes action so that the other person correctly perceives that the manager has such resources and is willing and ready to use them to help (or hinder) the other person. Consider the following extreme—but true —example.

When young Tim Babcock was put in charge of a division of a large manufacturing company and told to "turn it around," he spent the first few weeks studying it from afar. He de-

cided that the division was in disastrous shape and that he would need to take many large steps quickly to save it. To be able to do that, he realized he needed to develop considerable power fast over most of the division's management and staff. He did the following:

1. He gave the division's management two hours' notice of his arrival.
2. He arrived in a limousine with six assistants.
3. He immediately called a meeting of the 40 top managers.

Face-to-Face Influence

The chief advantage of influencing others directly by exercising any of the types of power is speed. If the power exists and the manager correctly understands the nature and strength of it, he can influence the other person with nothing more than a brief request or command:

Jones thinks Smith feels obliged to him for past favors. Furthermore, Jones thinks that his request to speed up a project by two days probably falls within a zone that Smith would consider legitimate in light of his own definition of his obligation to Jones. So Jones simply calls Smith and makes his request. Smith pauses for only a second and says yes, he'll do it.

Manager Johnson has some power based on perceived dependence over manager Baker. When Johnson tells Baker that he wants a report done in 24 hours, Baker grudgingly considers the costs of compliance, of noncompliance, and of complaining to higher authorities. He decides that doing the report is the least costly action and tells Johnson he will do it.

Young Porter identifies strongly with Marquette, an older manager who is not his boss. Porter thinks Marquette is the epitome of a great manager and tries to model himself after him. When Marquette asks Porter to work on a special project "that could be very valuable in improving the company's ability to meet new competitive products," Porter agrees without hesitation and works 15 hours per week above

EXHIBIT 1
Methods of Influence

Face-to-face Methods	What They Can Influence	Advantages	Drawbacks
Exercise obligation-based power.	Behavior within zone that the other perceives as legitimate in light of the obligation.	Quick. Requires no outlay of tangible resources.	If the request is outside the acceptable zone, it will fail; if it is too far outside, others might see it as illegitimate.
Exercise power based on perceived expertise.	Attitudes and behavior within the zone of perceived expertise.	Quick. Requires no outlay of tangible resources.	If the request is outside the acceptable zone, it will fail; if it is too far outside, others might see it as illegitimate.
Exercise power based on identification with a manager.	Attitudes and behavior that are not in conflict with the ideals that underlie the identification.	Quick. Requires no expenditure of limited resources.	Restricted to influence attempts that are not in conflict with the ideals that underlie the identification.
Exercise power based on perceived dependence.	Wide range of behavior that can be monitored.	Quick. Can often succeed when other methods fail.	Repeated influence attempts encourage the other to gain power over the influencer.
Coercively exercise power based on perceived dependence.	Wide range of behavior that can be easily monitored.	Quick. Can often succeed when other methods fail.	Invites retaliation. Very risky.
Use persuasion.	Very wide range of attitudes and behavior.	Can produce internalized motivation that does not require monitoring. Requires no power or outlay of scarce material resources.	Can be very time-consuming. Requires other person to listen.
Combine these methods.	Depends on the exact combination.	Can be more potent and less risky than using a single method.	More costly than using a single method.
Indirect methods			
Manipulate the other's environment by using any or all of the face-to-face methods.	Wide range of behavior and attitudes.	Can succeed when face-to-face methods fail.	Can be time-consuming. Is complex to implement. Is very risky, especially if used frequently.
Change the forces that continuously act on the individual: Formal organizational arrangements. Informal social arrangements. Technology. Resources available. Statement of organizational goals.	Wide range of behavior and attitudes on a continuous basis.	Has continuous influence, not just a one-shot effect. Can have a very powerful impact.	Often requires a considerable power outlay to achieve.

and beyond his normal hours to get the project done and done well.

When used to influence others, each of the four types of power has different advantages and drawbacks. For example, power based on perceived expertise or on identification with a manager can often be used to influence attitudes as well as someone's immediate behavior and thus can have a lasting impact. It is very difficult to influence attitudes by using power based on perceived dependence, but if it can be done, it usually has the advantage of being able to influence a much broader range of behavior than the other methods do. When exercising power based on perceived expertise, for example, one can only influence attitudes and behavior within that narrow zone defined by the "expertise."

The drawbacks associated with the use of power based on perceived dependence are particularly important to recognize. A person who feels dependent on a manager for rewards (or lack of punishments) might quickly agree to a request from the manager but then not follow through—especially if the manager cannot easily find out if the person has obeyed or not. Repeated influence attempts based on perceived dependence also seem to encourage the other person to try to gain some power to balance the manager's. And perhaps most important, using power based on perceived dependence in a coercive way is very risky. Coercion invites retaliation.

For instance, in the example in which Tim Babcock took such extreme steps to save the division he was assigned to "turn around," his development and use of power based on perceived dependence could have led to mass resignation and the collapse of the division. Babcock fully recognized this risk, however, and behaved as he did because he felt there was simply *no other way* that he could gain the very large amount of quick cooperation needed to save the division.

Effective managers will often draw on more than one form of power to influence someone, or they will combine power with persuasion. In general, they do so because a combination can be more potent and less risky than any single method, as the following description shows:

One of the best managers we have in the company has lots of power based on one thing or another over most people. But he seldom if ever just tells or asks someone to do something. He almost always takes a few minutes to try to persuade them. The power he has over people generally induces them to listen carefully and certainly disposes them to be influenced. That, of course, makes the persuasion process go quickly and easily. And he never risks getting the other person mad or upset by making what that person thinks is an unfair request or command.

It is also common for managers not to coercively exercise power based on perceived dependence by itself, but to combine it with other methods to reduce the risk of retaliation. In this way, managers are able to have a large impact without leaving the bitter aftertaste of punishment alone.

Indirect Influence Methods

Effective managers also rely on two types of less direct methods to influence those on whom they are dependent. In the first way, they use any or all of the face-to-face methods to influence other people, who in turn have some specific impact on a desired person.

Product manager Stein needed plant manager Billings to "sign off" on a new product idea (Product X) which Billings thought was terrible. Stein decided that there was no way he could logically persuade Billings because Billings just would not listen to him. With time, Stein felt, he could have broken through that barrier. But he did not have that time. Stein also realized that Billings would never, just because of some deal or favor, sign off on a product he did not believe in. Stein also felt it not worth the risk of trying to force Billings to sign off, so here is what he did:

On Monday, Stein got Reynolds, a person Billings respected, to send Billings two market research studies that were very favorable to Product X, with a note attached saying, "Have you seen this? I found them rather surprising. I am not sure if I entirely believe them, but still. . . ."

On Tuesday, Stein got a representative of one of the company's biggest customers to mention casually to Billings on the phone that he had heard a rumor about Product X being introduced soon and was "glad to see you guys are on your toes as usual."

On Wednesday, Stein had two industrial engineers stand about three feet away from Billings as they were waiting for a meeting to begin and talk about the favorable test results on Product X.

On Thursday, Stein set up a meeting to talk about Product X with Billings and invited only people whom Billings liked or respected and who also felt favorably about Product X.

On Friday, Stein went to see Billings and asked him if he was willing to sign off on Product X. He was.

This type of manipulation of the environments of others can influence both behavior and attitudes and can often succeed when other influence methods fail. But it has a number of serious drawbacks. It takes considerable time and energy, and it is quite risky. Many people think it is wrong to try to influence others in this way, even people who, without consciously recognizing it, use this technique themselves. If they think someone is trying, or has tried, to manipulate them, they may retaliate. Furthermore, people who gain the reputation of being manipulators seriously undermine their own capacities for developing power and for influencing others. Almost no one, for example, will want to identify with a manipulator. And virtually no one accepts, at face value,

a manipulator's sincere attempts at persuasion. In extreme cases, a reputation as a manipulator can completely ruin a manager's career.

A second way in which managers indirectly influence others is by making permanent changes in an individual's or a group's environment. They change job descriptions, the formal systems that measure performance, the extrinsic incentives available, the tools, people, and other resources that the people or groups work with, the architecture, the norms or values of work groups, and so on. If the manager is successful in making the changes, and the changes have the desired effect on the individual or group, that effect will be sustained over time.

Effective managers recognize that changes in the forces that surround a person can have great impact on that person's behavior. Unlike many of the other influence methods, this one doesn't require a large expenditure of limited resources or effort on the part of the manager on an ongoing basis. Once such a change has been successfully made, it works independently of the manager.

This method of influence is used by all managers to some degree. Many, however, use it sparingly simply because they do not have the power to change the forces acting on the person they wish to influence. In many organizations, only the top managers have the power to change the formal measurement systems, the extrinsic incentives available, the architecture, and so on.

GENERATING AND USING POWER SUCCESSFULLY

Managers who are successful at acquiring considerable power and using it to manage their dependence on others tend to share a number of common characteristics:

1. They are sensitive to what others consider to be legitimate behavior in acquiring and using power. They recognize that the

four types of power carry with them certain "obligations" regarding their acquisition and use. A person who gains a considerable amount of power based on his perceived expertise is generally expected to be an expert in certain areas. If it ever becomes publicly known that the person is clearly not an expert in those areas, such a person will probably be labeled a "fraud" and will not only lose his power but will suffer other reprimands too.

A person with whom a number of people identify is expected to act like an ideal leader. If he clearly lets people down, he will not only lose that power, he will also suffer the righteous anger of his ex-followers. Many managers who have created or used power based on perceived dependence in ways that their employees have felt unfair, such as in requesting overtime work, have ended up with unions.

2. They have good intuitive understanding of the various types of power and methods of influence. They are sensitive to what types of power are easiest to develop with different types of people. They recognize, for example, that professionals tend to be more influenced by perceived expertise than by other forms of power. They also have a grasp of all the various methods of influence and what each can accomplish, at what costs, and with what risks. (See *Exhibit 1*.) They are good at recognizing the specific conditions in any situation and then at selecting an influence method that is compatible with those conditions.

3. They tend to develop all the types of power, to some degree, and they use all the influence methods mentioned in the exhibit. Unlike managers who are not very good at influencing people, effective managers usually do not think that only some of the methods are useful or that only some of the methods are moral. They recognize that any of the methods, used under the right circumstances, can help contribute to organiza-

tional effectiveness with few dysfunctional consequences. At the same time, they generally try to avoid those methods that are more risky than others and those that may have dysfunctional consequences. For example, they manipulate the environment of others only when absolutely necessary.

4. They establish career goals and seek out managerial positions that allow them to successfully develop and use power. They look for jobs, for example, that use their backgrounds and skills to control or manage some critically important problem or environmental contingency that an organization faces. They recognize that success in that type of job makes others dependent on them and increases their own perceived expertise. They also seek jobs that do not demand a type or a volume of power that is inconsistent with their own skills.

5. They use all of their resources, formal authority, and power to develop still more power. To borrow Edward Banfield's metaphor, they actually look for ways to "invest" their power where they might secure a high positive return.[5] For example, by asking a person to do him two important favors, a manager might be able to finish his construction program one day ahead of schedule. That request may cost him most of the obligation-based power he has over that person, but in return he may significantly increase his perceived expertise as a manager of construction projects in the eyes of everyone in his organization.

Just as in investing money, there is always some risk involved in using power this way; it is possible to get a zero return for a sizable investment, even for the most powerful manager. Effective managers do not try to avoid risks. Instead, they look for prudent risks, just as they do when investing capital.

---

[5] See Edward C. Banfield, *Political Influence* (New York: Free Press, 1965), chap. 11.

6. Effective managers engage in power-oriented behavior in ways that are tempered by maturity and self-control.[6] They seldom, if ever, develop and use power in impulsive ways or for their own aggrandizement.

7. Finally, they also recognize and accept as legitimate that, in using these methods, they clearly influence other people's behavior and lives. Unlike many less effective managers, they are reasonably comfortable in using power to influence people. They recognize, often only intuitively, what this article is all about—that their attempts to establish power and use it are an absolutely necessary part of the successful fulfillment of their difficult managerial role.

---

[6] See David C. McClelland and David H. Burnham, "Power Is the Great Motivator," *HBR*, March–April 1976, p. 100.

Behavior modification, the application of behavioristic conditioning principles to practical problems, has proliferated in the last decade. While the earliest applications were to such fields as education, clinical psychology (psychotherapy), and behavior management in institutions (e.g., mental hospitals, homes for delinquents), recent attempts have been made to apply these ideas to management of employees in work organizations (13, 16, 28, 29, 30, 43, 52). One article claims: "The long range potential for behavior modification seems limitless" (31, p. 46).

Behaviorism asserts that human behavior can be understood without reference to states or actions of consciousness (54, 55). Its basic premises are:

1. Determinism: With respect to their choices, beliefs, and actions, individuals are ruled by forces beyond their control (according to behaviorism, these forces are environmental). Individuals are totally devoid of volition.
2. Epiphenomenalism: People's minds have no causal efficacy; their thoughts are mere by-products of environmental conditioning and affect neither their other thoughts nor their observable actions.
3. Rejection of introspection as a scientific method. It is unscientific, and its results (the identification of people's mental contents and processes) are irrelevant to understanding their actions (23).

The major theoretical concept in Skinner's (54) version of behaviorism, the one most often applied to industry, is that of reinforcement. Behavior, Skinner argues, is controlled by its consequences. A reinforcer is some consequence which follows a response and makes similar responses more likely in the future. To change the probability of a given response, one merely modifies either the contingency between the response and the reinforcer or the reinforcer itself. The concept of reinforcement is, by design, de-

The Myths of Behavior Mod in Organizations*

EDWIN A. LOCKE

void of any theoretical base, e.g., the experiences of pleasure and pain. The term is defined by its effects on behavior and only by these effects. Reinforcements modify responses automatically, independent of the organism's values, beliefs or mental processes, i.e., independent of consciousness.

While this theory of behavior may be appealing in its simplicity, the facts of human behavior do not correspond to it. All behavior is not controlled by reinforcements given to an acting organism. People can learn a new response by seeing other people get reinforced for that response; this is called "vicarious reinforcement" (17). People sometimes learn by imitating others who are not reinforced for their actions; this is called "vicarious learning" (33). Some behaviorists now acknowledge that people can control their own thoughts and actions by "talking to themselves," i.e., thinking. This is called "self-reinforcement" (18) or "self-instruction." These last two concepts flatly contradict the assumption of determinism.

* *Academy of Management Review*, October 1977, pp. 543–53.

Recent experiments and reviews of the learning literature have further undermined the behaviorist position. Not only do an individual's values, knowledge, and intentions have a profound effect on behavior (9, 22), but even the simplest forms of learning may not occur in the absence of conscious awareness on the part of the learner (8).

Studies of actual practices of behavior modifiers show that their techniques implicitly contradict all the main premises of behaviorism. For example, the procedures employed by behavioral psychotherapists assume that: (a) patients are conscious; (b) they can understand the meaning of words and can think; (c) they can introspect; and (d) they can control the actions of their own minds and bodies (6, 23, 32).

In view of conclusions drawn about behavior modification in other areas, will the same hold true when behavior modification principles are applied to industrial-organizational settings? One thesis to be explored here is that "behavior mod" applications to industry do not actually rest on behaviorist premises—they do not ignore the employee's consciousness and/or assume it to be irrelevant to the employee's behavior.

If true, this thesis would mean that, since organizational changes do not automatically condition the employee's response, attention must be paid to what the employee *thinks* about such changes. Are they wanted? Are they understood? What are they expected to lead to, etc?

A second issue concerns the originality of the techniques used by behavior mod practitioners in industry. Because the concept of reinforcement is defined solely by its consequences, if an alleged reinforcer does not reinforce, it is not a reinforcer. If it does, it is. Since the concept of reinforcement itself has no content (no defining characteristics independent of its effects on behavior), how are behavior modifiers to know what to use as reinforcers? In practice, behaviorists must use rewards and incentives which they observe people already acting to gain and/or keep; they must cash in on what they already know or believe people value or need. Thus when it comes to the choice of reinforcers, behavior mod can offer nothing new (4). A second thesis is that the actual techniques used by behavior modifiers in industry to "reinforce" behavior are no different from the rewards and incentives already used by nonbehaviorist practitioners in this field or related fields.

If this thesis is true, then the claims of originality by behavior mod practitioners are spurious and the attention of researchers would be focused best on further development of existing approaches to motivating employees (e.g., human relations, job enrichment, incentives).

Behavior mod advocates might reply that even if the particular reinforcers they use are not new, they do have something original to offer the practicing manager, namely, the idea of contingency. While the contingency idea is emphasized strongly in behaviorism, it is certainly not new. It has been used, if inconsistently, for centuries by animal trainers, parents, diplomats, and employers. Furthermore the principle does not work unless the individual is aware of the contingency (8). Finally, the principle is of limited usefulness in real life work situations where the manager cannot control everything that happens to subordinates (4).

Supporters of behavior mod might also argue that an original aspect of the behavior mod approach to management is its exclusive emphasis on the use of positive rewards and the avoidance of punishment. Such an argument would be misleading, since behaviorists are by no means averse to the use of punishment. Electric shock is often used to change the habits of unruly, disturbed children and to "cure" homosexuals. Furthermore, there is an element of arbitrariness in the behaviorist definition of this and related terms. Punishment is defined as an aversive stimulus which decreases the frequency of a response when it follows the response. Withholding a positive reinforcer, such as food, is not called punishment but extinction. A starving schizophrenic who is told, "No work, no food" might see the withholding of food as very punishing, despite the benign label "extinction" which the behaviorists attach to the process. Similarly, "negative reinforcement," the removal of an aversive stimulus when the organism does what you want, may be viewed justifiably as very punishing and coercive.

Performance Standards with Feedback

Perhaps the most well known applications of behavior mod to industry are Feeney's quasi-experiments at Emery Air Freight (5, 42, 48, 60, 61). Related ideas are presented by Hersey and Blanchard (14) and Morasky (38). Feeney's basic procedure is to:

1. Specify the desired level or standard of performance, preferably in quantitative terms. The concept of "performance standard" in this context is clearly a behavioristic euphemism for "goal."
2. Provide immediate, quantitative feedback informing employees of their level of performance in relation to the standard (preferably this feedback will come directly to the employees such as through performance records which they keep themselves).
3. Provide positive reinforcement in cases where the feedback indicates that performance meets the standard, and encouragement in cases where it does not meet the standard. Praise is recommended as the most practical positive reinforcer.

The evidence indicates that praise is not essential to achieve output gains. When the frequency of praise is decreased, no performance decrement results; but when feedback is eliminated, performance immediately drops to its previous level. According to Feeney, "feedback is the critical variable in explaining the success of the program" (5, p. 45). Another writer offers a feedback explanation to explain the productivity increases observed in the Hawthorne studies (46).

Both writers favor a behavioristic interpretation of the effects of feedback. They argue that feedback automatically reinforces the behavior which precedes it, and that the existence of the feedback explains the results of the foregoing studies.

Taken literally, this claim is absurd. If feedback *as such* automatically reinforced previous behavior, people should never change since the feedback would reinforce whatever they did previously. (Feeney's methods actually violate good behaviorist technique since the feedback is not contingent on high performance.)

Parsons' (46) hypothesis about the Hawthorne studies is refuted by findings obtained in one of those very studies. In the Bank-Wiring Observation Room individual output was recorded daily; "each man seemed to know just where he stood at any time [during the day]" (51, p. 428). In spite of this, output among these workers did not go up; it remained at a fairly constant level because the employees were deliberately restricting their output.

There are additional facts that do not coincide with the behavioristic interpretation of the effects of feedback. In Feeney's studies (5), performance in the customer service offices improved "rapidly"—in one case from 30 percent to 95 percent of standard in a single day! In the container departments, container use jumped from 45 percent to 95 percent, and in 70 percent of the cases this improvement also occurred within a day (42). Since genuine conditioning is asserted to be a gradual process, the very speed of these improvements militates against a conditioning explanation of the results. More likely what occurred was a conscious *redefinition of the job* resulting from the new standards and the more accurate feedback regarding performance in relation to those standards.

Further support for this interpretation comes from the extensive research on feedback and knowledge of results which do *not* automatically lead to performance improvement (3, 26, 27). The effects of feedback on subsequent performance depend upon such factors as: (*a*) amount and usefulness of information (knowledge) provided by the feedback; (*b*) degree to which the information source is trusted; and (*c*) utilization of the feedback to set goals and/or to regulate one's performance in relation to these goals.

The results obtained by Feeney are more logically explained by the joint operation of explicit goal-setting and feedback regarding performance in relation to the goals, i.e., by the employee's conscious self-regulation of action, than by the concept of automatic conditioning through reinforcement.

Another study claiming to illustrate the positive effects of behavior mod in improving employee performance can be interpreted similarly. Adam (1) instructed the line supervisors of a die-casting department to meet with each operator weekly and to provide him or her with feedback concerning performance quantity and quality, either on an absolute basis or in relation to set standards, as well as in relation to the shift and department averages. Operators with average or below average quality scores were asked explicitly to improve, although the supervisors evidently stressed quantity more than quality during their daily interactions with the operators. The use of goal-setting led to a significant increase in work quantity but no change in quality.

The concepts of goal and feedback or knowledge of results are in no sense be-havioristic concepts. The term *goal*, as used in industrial contexts, refers to the *consciously* held aim of an action, e.g., a work norm or an output standard. The concept of knowledge refers to the *awareness* of some fact of reality. Both concepts refer to states or actions of consciousness.

Furthermore, the concepts of goal and feedback are not new, not even as applied to industry. There is little difference between Feeney's ideas and some key elements of Scientific Management presented more than 60 years ago by Taylor (57). Taylor's central concept, the task, which consisted of an assigned work goal (with the work methods also specified), is virtually identical in meaning to Feeney's concept of a *performance standard*, a term which also was used by advocates of Scientific Management. Similarly, Taylor argued that work should be measured continually and the results fed back to employees so that they could correct errors and improve or maintain their quantity of output. Taylor favored a monetary bonus as a reward for increased productivity while Feeney's results indicate that this may not be necessary.

Latham and his colleagues also obtained dramatic results in industry by the use of goals and feedback without monetary incentives (19, 20, 21). Their work was based on the results of laboratory studies of goal setting which had an explicit nonbehavioristic base (22).

Monetary Incentives

The effectiveness of monetary incentives in improving work performance has long been recognized in industry. The use of large bonus payments for reaching assigned tasks or work goals was a cornerstone of Scientific Management (57), although the use of piece-rate payment systems was common even before the turn of the century.

Payment programs designed explicitly around behavior mod principles and employing behavior mod terminology have been rare in industrial settings. Yukl and Latham (62) compared the effect of continuous and variable ratio piece-rate bonuses among tree planters. Contrary to predictions, the continuous schedule yielded the highest level of performance. One reason for less effectiveness of the variable ratio schedules was that some members of work groups receiving those schedules were consciously opposed to the program, some on the grounds that "gambling" was immoral, and some due to general distrust. Clearly the effect of the so-called reinforcers was far from automatic.

Other studies have used monetary reinforcers or their equivalent (e.g., valued prizes such as appliances) to reduce absenteeism (44, 47). Either payments were made to all individuals showing perfect attendance for a given time period, or rewards were based on lottery drawing with only those with perfect attendance being eligible.

Nord (44) observed that such systems may become progressively less effective with time, although no explanation was offered for this finding. Presumably the reinforcers are no longer as reinforcing, but this does not explain anything (24).

A striking finding of the Pedalino and Gamboa (47) study was that employees in the experimental lottery group showed a significant reduction in absenteeism during the very first week of the program, *before anyone in the group had been, or could have been, reinforced* (34).

The concept of conditioning through reinforcement cannot account for these results since the behavior change *preceded* the reinforcement. Obviously the employees' expectations of and desire for the reward caused their change in behavior. Expectation and desire are not behavioristic concepts since they refer to states and ac-

tions of consciousness. Furthermore, these expectations were not, according to any evidence presented, generated by past reinforcements (lottery experiences) but by the explanation of the proposed incentive system to the employees.

Conclusion

The conclusion is inescapable that behavior mod in industry is neither new nor behavioristic. The specific techniques employed by behavior mod advocates have long been used in industry and other fields. What the behaviorists call reinforcers do not condition behavior automatically, but affect action through and in conjunction with the individual's mental contents and processes (integrations, goals, expectancies, etc.). While operant conditioning principles avoid the necessity of dealing with phenomena which are not directly observable, such as the minds of others, for this very reason they lack the capacity to explain human action (24).

The typical behaviorist response to arguments like the foregoing is, in effect, "Who cares why the procedures work, so long as they work?" (60). This is the kind of pragmatic answer one might expect from primitive witch doctors who are challenged to explain their "cures." One has the right to expect more from a modern-day scientist.

Unless one knows why and how something "works," one does not know *when* it will work or even *that* it will work in a given circumstance. Many things which behaviorists do to change behavior, do, in fact, change it. But many of them do not, and most behaviorists do not have the slightest idea what accounts for these inconsistencies. Post-hoc speculations about past conditioning or improper scheduling of the reinforcements do not solve this problem.

Skinner has long argued that resorting to mentalistic concepts tends to prematurely cut off the search for the real causes of behavior (55). While this may be true if the mentalistic concepts involved are pseudo-scientific, semimystical constructs like Freud's "id," the opposite is the case if the mentalistic concepts are clearly definable and verifiable through introspection. It is empty behavioristic concepts like "reinforcement" which delude investigators into thinking they understand the organism's behavior, and thus cut off the search for the real causes, i.e., those characteristics of the organism, including its mental contents and processes, which explain why it reacted as it did in response to, or in the absence of, the so-called reinforcements (24).

As Argyris (4) and Mitchell (37) have pointed out, there are numerous contextual assumptions which are untrue, nonuniversal or inappropriate in most applied settings, which behaviorists make when applying their techniques. Examples are the assumptions that individuals are basically passive responders to external stimulation; and that when subjects are being exposed to reinforcers, they will not think about what is happening, talk to anyone else about it, focus on the long-term implications or consider their own goals.

There is a common element in the above assumptions, a premise which underlies and unites all of the behaviorist theories of human behavior and of management. It is the premise that *humans do not possess a conceptual faculty*. The frequently made distinction between metaphysical and methodological behaviorism does not contradict this characterization of behaviorism since, in practice, both versions amount to the same thing. While Skinner does not openly deny that people have minds, he does assert that the environment is the ultimate cause of all thinking and action (54, 55). *But if mind is an epiphenomenon, then, for all practical purposes, it does not exist.*

Only if humans were by nature limited to the perceptual level of functioning, like dogs or cats, could one reasonably argue that they were passive responders to outside influences and that they would do nothing that they were not conditioned to do.[1] To quote Ayn Rand, a critic of behaviorism, on the issue of human nature:

Man's sense organs function automatically; man's brain integrates his sense data into percepts automatically; but the process of integrating percepts into concepts—the process of abstraction and of concept-formation—is *not* automatic.

The process of concept-formation does not consist merely of grasping a few simple abstractions, such as "chair," "table," "hot," "cold," and of learning to speak. It consists of a method of using one's consciousness, best designated by the term *conceptualizing*. It is not a passive state of registering random impressions. It is an actively sustained process of identifying one's impressions in conceptual terms, of integrating every event and every observation into a conceptual context, of grasping relationships, differences, similarities in one's perceptual material and of abstracting them into new concepts, of drawing inferences, of making deductions, of reaching conclusions, of asking new questions and discovering new answers and expanding one's knowledge into an ever-growing sum. The faculty that directs this process, the faculty that works by means of concepts, is: *reason*. The process is *thinking*.

Reason is the faculty that perceives, identifies, and integrates the material provided by man's senses. It is a faculty that man has to exercise *by choice*. Thinking is not an automatic function. In any hour and issue of his life, man is free to think or to evade that effort. Thinking requires a state of full, focused

---

[1] Even the assertion that animals are passive organisms is misleading. While animals lack free will (i.e., they cannot choose to think), they are still motivated by internal states (e.g., needs, wants, experiences of pleasure and pain). They are only passive by comparison to humans in that they cannot (through thinking) choose their wants nor means of achieving them. Nor can they reflect on the significance of what they are doing. Thus through arranging suitable external conditions, much of their behavior can be controlled.

awareness. The act of focusing one's consciousness is volitional. Man can focus his mind to a full, active, purposefully directed awareness of reality—or he can unfocus it and let himself drift in a semiconscious daze, merely reacting to any chance stimulus of the immediate moment, at the mercy of his undirected sensory-perceptual mechanism and of any random, associational connections it might happen to make (50, pp. 20–21).

Since people can choose to think (a fact which can be validated by introspection), the behaviorist view of human nature is false. Thus the claim that behaviorism, taken literally, can serve as a valid guide to understanding and modifying human behavior in organizations is a myth.

REFERENCES

1. Adam, E. E. "Behavior Modification in Quality Control," *Academy of Management Journal*, vol. 18 (1975), 662–79.

2. Ammons, R. B. "Effects of Knowledge of Performance: A Survey and Tentative Theoretical Formulation," *Journal of General Psychology*, vol. 54 (1956), 279–99.

3. Annett, J. *Feedback and Human Behaviour* (Baltimore: Penguin, 1969).

4. Argyris, C. "Beyond Freedom and Dignity by B. F. Skinner (An Essay Review)," *Harvard Educational Review*, vol. 41, no. 4 (1971), 550–67.

5. "At Emery Air Freight: Positive Reinforcement Boosts Performance," *Organizational Dynamics*, vol. 1, no. 3 (1973), 41–50.

6. Bergin, A. E., and R. M. Suinn, "Individual Psychotherapy and Behavior Therapy," *Annual Review of Psychology*, vol. 26 (1975), 509–56.

7. Bolles, R. C. "Reinforcement, Expectancy, and Learning," *Psychological Review*, vol. 79 (1972), 394–409.

8. Brewer, W. F. "There is No Convincing Evidence for Operant or Classical Conditioning in Adult Humans," in W. B. Weimer and D. S. Palermo (eds.), *Cognition and the Symbolic Processes* (Hillsdale, N.J.: Erlbaum, 1974), pp. 1–42.

9. Dulany, D. E. "Awareness, Rules and Propositional Control: A Confrontation with S-R Behavior Theory," in T. R. Dixon and D. L. Horton (eds.), *Verbal Behavior and General Behavior Theory* (Englewood Cliffs, N.J.: Prentice-Hall, 1968), pp. 340–87.

10. Fry, F. L. "Operant Conditioning in Organizational Settings: Of Mice or Men?" *Personnel* (July–August 1974), 17–24.

11. Gagné, R. M. "Military Training and Principles of Learning," *American Psychologist*, vol. 17 (1962), 83–91.

12. Goldstein, A. P., and M. Sorcher. *Changing Supervisory Behavior* (Elmsford, N.Y.: Pergamon Press, 1974).

13. Hamner, W. C. "Reinforcement Theory and Contingency Management in Organizational Settings," in R. M. Steers and L. W. Porter (eds), *Motivation and Work Behavior* (New York: McGraw-Hill, 1975), pp. 477–504.

14. Hersey, P., and K. H. Blanchard. "The Management of Change," *Training and Development Journal*, vol. 29, no. 2 (1972), 20–24.

15. Jabara, R. F. *A Comparison of Programmed Instruction and Text Methods of Presentation, With Time Controlled* (Master's Thesis, University of Maryland, College Park, 1970).

16. Jablonsky, S. F., and D. L. DeVries. "Operant Conditioning Principles Extrapolated to the Theory of Management," *Organizational Behavior and Human Performance*, vol. 7 (1972), 340–58.

17. Kanfer, F. H. "Vicarious Human Reinforcement: A Glimpse into the Black Box," in L. Krasner and L. P. Ullman (eds.), *Research in Behavior Modification* (New York: Holt, Rinehart and Winston, 1965), pp. 244–67.

18. Kanfer, F. H., and P. Karoly. "Self-Control: A Behavioristic Excursion into the Lion's Den," *Behavior Therapy*, vol. 3 (1972), 398–416.

19. Latham, G. P., and J. J. Baldes. "The 'Practical Significance' of Locke's Theory of Goal-Setting," *Journal of Applied Psychology*, vol. 60 (1975), 122–24.

20. Latham, G. P., and S. B. Kinne. "Improving Job Performance Through Training in Goal-Setting," *Journal of Applied Psychology*, vol. 59 (1974), 187–91.

21. Latham, G. P., and G. A. Yukl. "Assigned Versus Participative Goal Setting with Educated and Uneducated Woods Workers," *Journal of Applied Psychology*, vol. 60 (1975), 299–302.

22. Locke, E. A. "Toward a Theory of Task Motivation and Incentives," *Organizational Behavior and Human Performance*, vol. 3 (1968), 157–89.

23. Locke, E. A. "Is 'Behavior Therapy' Behavioristic? (An Analysis of Wople's Psychotherapeutic Methods)," *Psychological Bulletin*, vol. 76 (1971), 318–27.

24. Locke, E. A. "Critical Analysis of the Concept of Causality in Behavioristic Psychology," *Psychological Reports*, vol. 31 (1972), 175–97.

25. Locke, E. A. *A Guide to Effective Study* (New York: Springer, 1975).

26. Locke, E. A., and J. F. Bryan. "The Directing Function of Goals in Task Performance," *Organizational Behavior and Human Performance*, vol. 4 (1969), 35–42.

27. Locke, E. A., N. Cartledge, and J. Koeppel. "Motivational Effects of Knowledge of Results: A Goal-Setting Phenomenon?" *Psychological Bulletin*, vol. 70 (1968), 474–85.

28. Luthans, F. "An Organizational Behavior Modification (O. B. Mod) Approach to O. D." Paper presented at the National Academy of Management, Seattle, 1974.

29. Luthans, F., and R. Kreitner. "The Management of Behavioral Contingencies," *Personnel* (July–August 1974), 7–16.

30. Luthans, F., and R. Kreitner. *Organizational Behavior Modification* (Glenview, Ill.: Scott Foresman, 1975).

31. Luthans, F., and D. D. White. "Behavior Modification: Application to Manpower Management," *Personnel Administration*, vol. 34, no. 4 (1971), 41–47.

32. Mahoney, M. J. *Cognition and Behavior Modification* (Cambridge, Mass.: Ballinger, 1974).

33. Marlatt, G. A. "A Comparison of Vicarious and Direct Reinforcement Control of Verbal Behavior in an Interview Setting," *Journal of Personality and Social Psychology*, vol. 16 (1970), 695–703.

34. Mawhinney, T. C. "Operant Terms and Concepts in the Description of Individual Work Behavior: Some Problems of Interpretation, Application, and Evaluation," *Journal of Applied Psychology*, vol. 60 (1975), 704–12.

35. McKeachie, W. J. "Instructional Psychology," *Annual Review of Psychology*, vol. 25 (1974), 161–93.

36. Meichenbaum, D. "Self-Instructional Methods," in F. H. Kanfer and A. P. Goldstein (eds.), *Helping People Change* (Elmsford, N.Y.: Pergamon, 1974).

37. Mitchell, T. R. "Cognitions and Skinner: Some Questions about Behavioral Determinism." Paper presented at the National Academy of Management, Seattle, 1974.

38. Morasky, R. L. "Self-Shaping Training Systems and Flexible-Model Behavior, i.e., Sales Interviewing," *Educational Technology*, vol. 11, no. 5 (1971), 57–59.

39. Moses, J. E. "A Behavioral Method of Evaluating Training or: A Light at the End of the Tunnel." Paper presented at National Society for Performance and Instruction, New York, 1974.

40. Moses, J., and D. Ritchie, "Assessment Center Used to Evaluate an Interaction Modeling Program," *Assessment and Development*, vol. 2, no. 2 (1975), 1–2.

41. Nash, A. N., J. P. Muczyk, and F. L. Vettori. "The Relative Practical Effectiveness of Programmed Instruction," *Personnel Psychology*, vol. 24 (1971), 397–418.

42. "New Tool: 'Reinforcement' for Good Work," *Business Week*, December 18, 1971, 76–77.

43. Nord, W. R. "Beyond the Teaching Machine: The Neglected Area of Operant Conditioning in the Theory and Practice of Management," *Organizational Behavior and Human Performance*, vol. 4 (1969), 375–401.

44. Nord, W. R. "Improving Attendance Through Rewards," *Personnel Administration*, vol. 33, no. 6 (1970), 37–41.

45. O'Day, E. F., R. W. Kulhavy, W. Anderson, and R. J. Malczynski. *Programmed Instruction, Techniques and Trends* (New York: Appleton-Century-Crofts, 1971).

46. Parsons, H. M. "What Happened at Hawthorne?" *Science*, vol. 183 (1974), 922–32.

47. Pedalino, E., and V. U. Gamboa. "Behavior Modification and Absenteeism: Intervention in One Industrial Setting," *Journal of Applied Psychology*, vol. 59 (1974), 694–98.

48. "Performance Audit Feedback, and Positive Reinforcement," *Training and Development Journal*, vol. 29, no. 11 (1972), 8–13.

49. Pressey, S. L. "Teaching Machine (and Learning Theory) Crisis," *Journal of Applied Psychology*, vol. 47 (1963), 1–6.

50. Rand, A. "The Objectivist Ethics," in A. Rand, *The Virtue of Selfishness* (New York: New American Library, 1964), pp. 13–35.

51. Roethlisberger, F. J., and W. J. Dickson. *Management and the Worker* (Cambridge, Mass.: Harvard, 1956).

52. Schneier, C. E. "Behavior Modification in Management: A Review and Critique," *Academy of Management Journal*, vol. 17 (1974), 528–48.

53. Skinner, B. F. "Teaching Machines," *Science*, vol. 128 (1958), 969–77.

54. Skinner, B. F. *Beyond Freedom and Dignity* (New York: Alfred A. Knopf, 1971).

55. Skinner, B. F. "The Steep and Thorny Way to a Science of Behavior," *American Psychologist*, vol. 30 (1975), 42–49.

56. Sorcher, M., and A. P. Goldstein. "A Behavior Modeling Approach to Training," *Per-*

sonnel Administration, vol. 35, no. 2 (1972), 35–41.

57. Taylor, F. W. *The Principles of Scientific Management*, 1911 (New York: Norton, 1967).

58. Thorndike, E. H. *Human Learning*, 1931 (Cambridge, Mass.: M.I.T. Press, 1966).

59. Welsh, P., J. A. Antoinetti, and P. W. Thayer, "An Industrywide Study of Programmed Instruction," *Journal of Applied Psychology*, vol. 49 (1965), 61–73.

60. "Where Skinner's Theories Work," *Business Week*, December 2, 1972, 64–65.

61. Wiard, H. "Why Manage Behavior? A Case for Positive Reinforcement," *Human Resource Management*, vol. 11, no. 2 (1972), 15–20.

62. Yukl, G. A., and G. P. Latham. "Consequences of Reinforcement Schedules and Incentive Magnitudes for Employee Performance: Problems Encountered in an Industrial Setting," *Journal of Applied Psychology*, vol. 60 (1975), 294–98.

Leadership has for some time been a major topic in social and organizational psychology. Underlying much of this research has been the assumption that leadership is causally related to organizational performance. Through an analysis of leadership styles, behaviors, or characteristics (depending on the theoretical perspective chosen), the argument has been made that more effective leaders can be selected or trained or, alternatively, the situation can be configured to provide for enhanced leader and organizational effectiveness.

Three problems with emphasis on leadership as a concept can be posted: (a) ambiguity in definition and measurement of the concept itself; (b) the question of whether leadership has discernible effects on organizational outcomes; and (c) the selection process in succession to leadership positions, which frequently uses organizationally irrelevant criteria and which has implications for normative theories of leadership. The argument here is that leadership is of interest primarily as a phenomenological construct. Leaders serve as symbols for representing personal causation of social events. How and why are such attributions of personal effects made? Instead of focusing on leadership and its effects, how do people make inferences about and react to phenomena labelled as leadership (5)?

THE AMBIGUITY OF THE CONCEPT

While there have been many studies of leadership, the dimensions and definition of the concept remain unclear. To treat leadership as a separate concept, it must be distinguished from other social influence phenomena. Hollander and Julian (24) and Bavelas (2) did not draw distinctions between leadership and other processes of social influence. A major point of the Hollander and Julian review was that leadership research might develop more rapidly if more general theories of social influence

The Ambiguity of Leadership*

JEFFREY PFEFFER

were incorporated. Calder (5) also argued that there is no unique content to the construct of leadership that is not subsumed under other, more general models of behavior.

Kochan, Schmidt, and DeCotiis (33) attempted to distinguish leadership from related concepts of authority and social power. In leadership, influence rights are voluntarily conferred. Power does not require goal compatibility—merely dependence—but leadership implies some congruence between the objectives of the leader and the led. These distinctions depend on the ability to distinguish voluntary from involuntary compliance and to assess goal compatibility. Goal statements may be retrospective inferences from action (46, 53), and problems of distinguishing voluntary from involuntary compliance also exist (32). Apparently there are few meaningful distinctions between leadership and other concepts of social influence. Thus, an understanding of the phenomena subsumed under the

---

* *Academy of Management Review*, January 1977, pp. 104–12.

rubric of leadership may not require the construct of leadership (5).

While there is some agreement that leadership is related to social influence, more disagreement concerns the basic dimensions of leader behavior. Some have argued that there are two tasks to be accomplished in groups—maintenance of the group and performance of some task or activity—and thus leader behavior might be described along these two dimensions (1, 6, 8, 25). The dimensions emerging from the Ohio State leadership studies—consideration and initiating structure—may be seen as similar to the two components of group maintenance and task accomplishment (18).

Other dimensions of leadership behavior have also been proposed (4). Day and Hamblin (10) analyzed leadership in terms of the closeness and punitiveness of the supervision. Several authors have conceptualized leadership behavior in terms of the authority and discretion subordinates are permitted (23, 36, 51). Fiedler (14) analyzed leadership in terms of the least-preferred co-worker scale (LPC), but the meaning and behavioral attributes of this dimension of leadership behavior remain controversial.

The proliferation of dimensions is partly a function of research strategies frequently employed. Factor analysis on a large number of items describing behavior has frequently been used. This procedure tends to produce as many factors as the analyst decides to find, and permits the development of a large number of possible factor structures. The resultant factors must be named and further imprecision is introduced. Deciding on a summative concept to represent a factor is inevitably a partly subjective process.

Literature assessing the effects of leadership tends to be equivocal. Sales (45) summarized leadership literature employing the authoritarian-democratic typology and concluded that effects on performance were small and inconsistent. Reviewing the literature on consideration and initiating structure dimensions, Korman (34) reported relatively small and inconsistent results, and Kerr and Schriesheim (30) reported more consistent effects of the two dimensions. Better results apparently emerge when moderating factors are taken into account, including subordinate personalities (50), and situational characteristics (23, 51). Kerr, et al. (31) list many moderating effects grouped under the headings of subordinate considerations, supervisor considerations, and task considerations. Even if each set of considerations consisted of only one factor (which it does not), an attempt to account for the effects of leader behavior would necessitate considering four-way interactions. While social reality is complex and contingent, it seems desirable to attempt to find more parsimonious explanations for the phenomena under study.

THE EFFECTS OF LEADERS

Hall asked a basic question about leadership: is there any evidence on the magnitude of the effects of leadership (17, p. 248)? Surprisingly, he could find little evidence. Given the resources that have been spent studying, selecting, and training leaders, one might expect that the question of whether or not leaders matter would have been addressed earlier (12).

There are at least three reasons why it might be argued that the observed effects of leaders on organizational outcomes would be small. First, those obtaining leadership positions are selected, and perhaps only certain, limited styles of behavior may be chosen. Second, once in the leadership position, the discretion and behavior of the leader are constrained. And third, leaders can typically affect only a few of the variables that may impact organizational performance.

Homogeneity of Leaders

Persons are selected to leadership positions. As a consequence of this selection process, the range of behaviors or characteristics exhibited by leaders is reduced, making it more problematic to empirically discover an effect of leadership. There are many types of constraints on the selection process. The attraction literature suggests that there is a tendency for persons to like those they perceive as similar (3). In critical decisions such as the selections of persons for leadership positions, compatible styles of behavior probably will be chosen.

Selection of persons is also constrained by the internal system of influence in the organization. As Zald (56) noted, succession is a critical decision, affected by political influence and by environmental contingencies faced by the organization. As Thompson (49) noted, leaders may be selected for their capacity to deal with various organizational contingencies. In a study of characteristics of hospital administrators, Pfeffer and Salancik (42) found a relationship between the hospital's context and the characteristics and tenure of the administrators. To the extent that the contingencies and power distribution within the organization remain stable, the abilities and behaviors of those selected into leadership positions will also remain stable.

Finally, the selection of persons to leadership positions is affected by a self-selection process. Organizations and roles have images, providing information about their character. Persons are likely to select themselves into organizations and roles based upon their preferences for the dimensions of the organizational and role characteristics as perceived through these images. The self-selection of persons would tend to work along with organizational selection to limit the range of abilities and behaviors in a given organizational role.

Such selection processes would tend to increase homogeneity more within a single organization than across organizations. Yet many studies of leadership effect at the work-group level have compared groups within a single organization. If there comes to be a widely shared, socially constructed definition of leadership behaviors or characteristics which guides the selection process, then leadership activity may come to be defined similarly in various organizations, leading to the selection of only those who match the constructed image of a leader.

Constraints on Leader Behavior

Analyses of leadership have frequently presumed that leadership style or leader behavior was an independent variable that could be selected or trained at will to conform to what research would find to be optimal. Even theorists who took a more contingent view of appropriate leadership behavior generally assumed that with proper training, appropriate behavior could be produced (51). Fiedler (13), noting how hard it was to change behavior, suggested changing the situational characteristics rather than the person, but this was an unusual suggestion in the context of prevailing literature which suggested that leadership style was something to be strategically selected according to the variables of the particular leadership theory.

But the leader is embedded in a social system, which constrains behavior. The leader has a role set (27), in which members have expectations for appropriate behavior and persons make efforts to modify the leader's behavior. Pressures to conform to the expectations of peers, subordinates, and superiors are all relevant in determining actual behavior.

Leaders, even in high-level positions, have unilateral control over fewer resources and fewer policies than might be expected.

Investment decisions may require approval of others, while hiring and promotion decisions may be accomplished by committees. Leader behavior is constrained by both the demands of others in the role set and by organizationally prescribed limitations on the sphere of activity and influence.

External Factors

Many factors that may affect organizational performance are outside a leader's control, even if he or she were to have complete discretion over major areas of organizational decisions. For example, consider the executive in a construction firm. Costs are largely determined by operation of commodities and labor markets; and demand is largely affected by interest rates, availability of mortgage money, and economic conditions which are affected by governmental policies over which the executive has little control. School superintendents have little control over birth rates and community economic development, both of which profoundly affect school system budgets. While the leader may react to contingencies as they arise, or may be a better or worse forecaster, in accounting for variation in organizational outcomes, he or she may account for relatively little compared to external factors.

Second, the leader's success or failure may be partly due to circumstances unique to the organization but still outside his or her control. Leader positions in organizations vary in terms of the strength and position of the organization. The choice of a new executive does not fundamentally alter a market and financial position that has developed over years and affects the leader's ability to make strategic changes and the likelihood that the organization will do well or poorly. Organizations have relatively enduring strengths and weaknesses. The choice of a particular leader for a particu-

lar position has limited impact on these capabilities.

Empirical Evidence

Two studies have assessed the effects of leadership changes in major positions in organizations. Lieberson and O'Connor (35) examined 167 business firms in 13 industries over a 20-year period, allocating variance in sales, profits, and profit margins to one of four sources: year (general economic conditions), industry, company effects, and effects of changes in the top executive position. They concluded that compared to other factors, administration had a limited effect on organizational outcomes.

Using a similar analytical procedure, Salancik and Pfeffer (44) examined the effects of mayors on city budgets for 30 U.S. cities. Data on expenditures by budget category were collected for 1951–68. Variance in amount and proportion of expenditures was apportioned to the year, the city, or the mayor. The mayoral effect was relatively small, with the city accounting for most of the variance, although the mayor effect was larger for expenditure categories that were not as directly connected to important interest groups. Salancik and Pfeffer argued that the effects of the mayor were limited both by absence of power to control many of the expenditures and tax sources and by construction of policies in response to demands from interests in the environment.

If leadership is defined as a strictly interpersonal phenomenon, the relevance of these two studies for the issue of leadership effects becomes problematic. But such a conceptualization seems unduly restrictive, and is certainly inconsistent with Selznick's (47) conceptualization of leadership as strategic management and decision making. If one cannot observe differences when leaders change, then what does it matter who occupies the positions or how they behave?

Pfeffer and Salancik (41) investigated the extent to which behaviors selected by first-line supervisors were constrained by expectations of others in their role set. Variance in task and social behaviors could be accounted for by role-set expectations, with adherence to various demands made by role-set participants a function of similarity and relative power. Lowin and Craig (37) experimentally demonstrated that leader behavior was determined by the subordinate's own behavior. Both studies illustrate that leader behaviors are responses to the demands of the social context.

The effect of leadership may vary depending upon level in the organizational hierarchy, while the appropriate activities and behaviors may also vary with organizational level (26, 40). For the most part, empirical studies of leadership have dealt with first line supervisors or leaders with relatively low organizational status (17). If leadership has any impact, it should be more evident at higher organizational levels or where there is more discretion in decisions and activities.

THE PROCESS OF SELECTING LEADERS

Along with the suggestion that leadership may not account for much variance in organizational outcomes, it can be argued that merit or ability may not account for much variation in hiring and advancement of organizational personnel. These two ideas are related. If competence is hard to judge, or if leadership competence does not greatly affect organizational outcomes, then other, person-dependent criteria may be sufficient. Effective leadership styles may not predict career success when other variables such as social background are controlled.

Belief in the importance of leadership is frequently accompanied by belief that persons occupying leadership positions are selected and trained according to how well they can enhance the organization's performance. Belief in a leadership effect leads to development of a set of activities oriented toward enhancing leadership effectiveness. Simultaneously, persons managing their own careers are likely to place emphasis on activities and developing behaviors that will enhance their own leadership skills, assuming that such a strategy will facilitate advancement.

Research on the basis for hiring and promotion has been concentrated in examination of academic positions (e.g., 7, 19, 20). This is possibly the result of availability of relatively precise and unambiguous measures of performance, such as number of publications or citations. Evidence on criteria used in selecting and advancing personnel in industry is more indirect.

Studies have attempted to predict either the compensation or the attainment of general management positions of MBA students, using personality and other background information (21, 22, 54). There is some evidence that managerial success can be predicted by indicators of ability and motivation such as test scores and grades, but the amount of variance explained is typically quite small.

A second line of research has investigated characteristics and background of persons attaining leadership positions in major organizations in society. Domhoff (11), Mills (38), and Warner and Abbeglin (52) found a strong preponderance of persons with upper-class backgrounds occupying leadership positions. The implication of these findings is that studies of graduate success, including the success of MBAs, would explain more variance if the family background of the person were included.

A third line of inquiry uses a tracking model. The dynamic model developed is one in which access to elite universities is affected by social status (28) and, in turn, social status and attendance at elite universities affect later career outcomes (9, 43, 48, 55).

Unless one is willing to make the argument that attendance at elite universities or coming from an upper-class background is perfectly correlated with merit, the evidence suggests that succession to leadership positions is not strictly based on meritocratic criteria. Such a conclusion is consistent with the inability of studies attempting to predict the success of MBA graduates to account for much variance, even when a variety of personality and ability factors are used.

Beliefs about the bases for social mobility are important for social stability. As long as persons believe that positions are allocated on meritocratic grounds, they are more likely to be satisfied with the social order and with their position in it. This satisfaction derives from the belief that occupational position results from application of fair and reasonable criteria, and that the opportunity exists for mobility if the person improves skills and performance.

If succession to leadership positions is determined by person-based criteria such as social origins or social connections (16), then efforts to enhance managerial effectiveness with the expectation that this will lead to career success divert attention from the processes of stratification actually operating within organizations. Leadership literature has been implicitly aimed at two audiences. Organizations were told how to become more effective, and persons were told what behaviors to acquire in order to become effective, and hence, advance in their careers. The possibility that neither organizational outcomes nor career success are related to leadership behaviors leaves leadership research facing issues of relevance and importance.

THE ATTRIBUTION OF LEADERSHIP

Kelley conceptualized the layman as:

an applied scientist, that is, as a person concerned about applying his knowledge of causal relationships in order to *exercise control* of his world (29, p. 2).

Reviewing a series of studies dealing with the attributional process, he concluded that persons were not only interested in understanding their world correctly, but also in controlling it.

The view here proposed is that attribution processes are to be understood not only as a means of providing the individual with a veridical view of his world, but as a means of encouraging and maintaining his effective exercise of control in that world (29, p. 22).

Controllable factors will have high salience as candidates for causal explanation; while a bias toward the more important causes may shift the attributional emphasis toward causes that are not controllable (29, p. 23). The study of attribution is a study of naive psychology—an examination of how persons make sense out of the events taking place around them.

If Kelley is correct that individuals will tend to develop attributions that give them a feeling of control, then emphasis on leadership may derive partially from a desire to believe in the effectiveness and importance of individual action, since individual action is more controllable than contextual variables. Lieberson and O'Connor (35) made essentially the same point in introducing their paper on the effects of top management changes on organizational performance. Given the desire for control and a feeling of personal effectiveness, organizational outcomes are more likely to be attributed to individual actions, regardless of their actual causes.

Leadership is attributed by observers. Social action has meaning only through a phenomenological process (46). The identification of certain organizational roles as leadership positions guides the construction cf meaning in the direction of attributing effects to the actions of those positions. While Bavelas (2) argued that the functions of leadership, such as task accomplishment and group maintenance, are shared throughout the group, this fact provides no simple and potentially controllable focus for attributing causality. Rather, the identification of leadership positions provides a simpler and more readily changeable model of reality. When causality is lodged in one or a few persons rather than being a function of a complex set of interactions among all group members, changes can be made by replacing or influencing the occupant of the leadership position. Causes of organizational actions are readily identified in this simple causal structure.

Even if, empirically, leadership has little effect, and even if succession to leadership positions is not predicated on ability or performance, the belief in leadership effects and meritocratic succession provides a simple causal framework and a justification for the structure of the social collectivity. More importantly, the beliefs interpret social actions in terms that indicate potential for effective individual intervention or control. The personification of social causality serves too many uses to be easily overcome. Whether or not leader behavior actually influences performance or effectiveness, it is important because people believe it does.

One consequence of the attribution of causality to leaders and leadership is that leaders come to be symbols. Mintzberg (39), in his discussion of the roles of managers, wrote of the symbolic role, but more in terms of attendance at formal events and formally representing the organization. The symbolic role of leadership is more important than implied in such a description. The leader as a symbol provides a target for action when difficulties occur, serving as a

scapegoat when things go wrong. Gamson and Scotch (15) noted that in baseball, the firing of the manager served a scapegoating purpose. One cannot fire the whole team, yet when performance is poor, something must be done. The firing of the manager conveys to the world and to the actors involved that success is the result of personal actions, and that steps can and will be taken to enhance organizational performance.

The attribution of causality to leadership may be reinforced by organizational actions, such as the inauguration process, the choice process, and providing the leader with symbols and ceremony. If leaders are chosen by using a random number table, persons are less likely to believe in their effects than if there is an elaborate search or selection process followed by an elaborate ceremony signifying the changing of control, and if the leader then has a variety of perquisites and symbols that distinguish him or her from the rest of the organization. Construction of the importance of leadership in a given social context is the outcome of various social processes, which can be empirically examined.

Since belief in the leadership effect provides a feeling of personal control, one might argue that efforts to increase the attribution of causality to leaders would occur more when it is more necessary and more problematic to attribute causality to controllable factors. Such an argument would lead to the hypothesis that the more the *context* actually affects organizational outcomes, the more efforts will be made to ensure attribution to *leadership*. When leaders really do have effects, it is less necessary to engage in rituals indicating their effects. Such rituals are more likely when there is uncertainty and unpredictability associated with the organization's operations. This results both from the desire to feel control in uncertain situations and from the fact that in ambiguous contexts, it is easier to attribute consequences to leadership without facing possible disconfirmation.

The leader is, in part, an actor. Through statements and actions, the leader attempts to reinforce the operation of an attribution process which tends to vest causality in that position in the social structure. Successful leaders, as perceived by members of the social system, are those who can separate themselves from organizational failures and associate themselves with organizational successes. Since the meaning of action is socially constructed, this involves manipulation of symbols to reinforce the desired process of attribution. For instance, if a manager knows that business in his or her division is about to improve because of the economic cycle, the leader may, nevertheless, write recommendations and undertake actions and changes that are highly visible and that will tend to identify his or her behavior closely with the division. A manager who perceives impending failure will attempt to associate the division and its policies and decisions with others, particularly persons in higher organizational positions, and to disassociate himself or herself from the division's performance, occasionally even transferring or moving to another organization.

REFERENCES

1. Bales, R. F. *Interaction Process Analysis: A Method for the Study of Small Groups* (Reading, Mass.: Addison-Wesley, 1950).

2. Bavelas, Alex. "Leadership: Man and Function," *Administrative Science Quarterly*, vol. 4 (1960), 491–98.

3. Berscheid, Ellen, and Elaine Walster. *Interpersonal Attraction* (Reading, Mass.: Addison-Wesley, 1969).

4. Bowers, David G., and Stanley E. Seashore. "Predicting Organizational Effectiveness with a Four-Factor Theory of Leadership," *Administrative Science Quarterly*, vol. 11 (1966), 238–63.

5. Calder, Bobby J. "An Attribution Theory of Leadership," in B. Staw and G. Salancik (eds.), *New Directions in Organizational Behavior* (Chicago: St. Clair Press, 1976), in press.

6. Cartwright, Dorwin C., and Alvin Zander. *Group Dynamics: Research and Theory*, 3d ed. (Evanston, Ill.: Row, Peterson, 1960).

7. Cole, Jonathan R., and Stephen Cole. *Social Statification in Science* (Chicago: University of Chicago Press, 1973).

8. Collins, Barry E., and Harold Guetzkow. *A Social Psychology of Group Processes for Decision-Making* (New York: Wiley, 1964).

9. Collins, Randall. "Functional and Conflict Theories of Stratification," *American Sociological Review*, vol. 36 (1971), 1002–19.

10. Day, R. C., and R. L. Hamblin. "Some Effects of Close and Punitive Styles of Supervision," *American Journal of Sociology*, vol. 69 (1964), 499–510.

11. Domhoff, G. William. *Who Rules America?* (Englewood Cliffs, N.J.: Prentice-Hall, 1967).

12. Dubin, Robert. "Supervision and Productivity: Empirical Findings and Theoretical Considerations," in R. Dubin, G. C. Homans, F. C. Mann, and D. C. Miller (eds.), *Leadership and Productivity* (San Francisco: Chandler Publishing Co., 1965), pp. 1–50.

13. Fiedler, Fred E. "Engineering the Job to Fit the Manager," *Harvard Business Review*, vol. 43 (1965), 115–22.

14. Fiedler, Fred E. *A Theory of Leadership Effectiveness* (New York: McGraw-Hill, 1967).

15. Gamson, William A., and Norman A. Scotch. "Scapegoating in Baseball," *American Journal of Sociology*, vol. 70 (1964), 69–72.

16. Granovetter, Mark. *Getting a Job* (Cambridge, Mass.: Harvard University Press, 1974).

17. Hall, Richard H. *Organizations: Structure and Process* (Englewood Cliffs, N.J.: Prentice-Hall, 1972).

18. Halpin, A. W., and J. Winer. "A Factorial Study of the Leader Behavior Description Questionnaire," in R. M. Stogdill and A. E. Coons (eds.), *Leader Behavior: Its Description and Measurement* (Columbus, Ohio, Bureau of Business Research, Ohio State University, 1957), pp. 39–59.

19. Hargens, L. L. "Patterns of Mobility of New Ph.D.s Among American Academic Institutions," *Sociology of Education*, vol. 42 (1969), 18–37.

20. Hargens, L. L., and W. O. Hagstrom. "Sponsored and Contest Mobility of American Academic Scientists," *Sociology of Education*, vol. 40 (1967), 24–38.

21. Harrell, Thomas W. "High Earning MBAs," *Personnel Psychology*, vol. 25 (1972), 523–30.

22. Harrell, Thomas W., and Margaret S. Harrell. "Predictors of Management Success." *Stanford University Graduate School of Business, Technical Report No. 3 to the Office of Naval Research.*

23. Heller, Frank, and Gary Yukl. "Participation, Managerial Decision-Making, and Situational Variables," *Organizational Behavior and Human Performance*, vol. 4 (1969), 227–41.

24. Hollander, Edwin P., and James W. Julian. "Contemporary Trends in the Analysis of Leadership Processes," *Psychological Bulletin*, vol. 71 (1969), 387–97.

25. House, Robert J. "A Path Goal Theory of Leader Effectiveness," *Administrative Science Quarterly*, vol. 16 (1971), 321–38.

26. Hunt, J. G. "Leadership-Style Effects at Two Managerial Levels in a Simulated Organization," *Administrative Science Quarterly*, vol. 16 (1971), 476–85.

27. Kahn, R. L., D. M. Wolfe, R. P. Quinn, and J. D. Snoek. *Organizational Stress: Studies in Role Conflict and Ambiguity* (New York: Wiley, 1964).

28. Karabel, J., and A. W. Astin. "Social Class, Academic Ability, and College 'Quality'," *Social Forces*, vol. 53 (1975), 381–98.

29. Kelley, Harold H. *Attribution in Social Interaction* (Morristown, N.J.: General Learning Press, 1971).

30. Kerr, Steven, and Chester Schriesheim. "Consideration, Initiating Structure and Organizational Criteria—An Update of Korman's 1966 Review," *Personnel Psychology*, vol. 27 (1974), 555–68.

31. Kerr, S., C. Schriesheim, C. J. Murphy, and R. M. Stogdill. "Toward A Contingency Theory of Leadership Based Upon the Consideration and Initiating Structure Literature," *Organizational Behavior and Human Performance*, vol. 12 (1974), 62–82.

32. Kiesler, C., and S. Kiesler. *Conformity* (Reading, Mass.: Addison-Wesley, 1969).

33. Kochan, T. A., S. M. Schmidt, and T. A. DeCotiis. "Superior-Subordinate Relations: Leadership and Headship," *Human Relations*, vol. 28 (1975), 279–94.

34. Korman, A. K. "Consideration, Initiating Structure, and Organizational Criteria—A Review," *Personnel Psychology*, vol. 19 (1966), 349–62.

35. Lieberson, Stanley, and James F. O'Connor. "Leadership and Organizational Performance: A Study of Large Corporations," *American Sociological Review*, vol. 37 (1972), 117–30.

36. Lippitt, Ronald. "An Experimental Study of the Effect of Democratic and Authoritarian Group Atmospheres," *University of Iowa Studies in Child Welfare*, vol. 16 (1940), 43–195.

37. Lowin, A., and J. R. Craig. "The Influence of Level of Performance on Managerial Style: An Experimental Object-Lesson in the Ambiguity of Correlational Data," *Organizational Behavior and Human Performance*, vol. 3 (1968), 440–58.

38. Mills, C. Wright. "The American Business Elite: A Collective Portrait," in C. W. Mills, *Power, Politics, and People* (New York: Oxford University Press, 1963), pp. 110–39.

39. Mintzberg, Henry. *The Nature of Managerial Work* (New York: Harper and Row, 1973).

40. Nealey, Stanley M., and Milton R. Blood. "Leadership Performance of Nursing Supervisors at Two Organizational Levels," *Journal of Applied Psychology*, vol. 52 (1968), 414–42.

41. Pfeffer, Jeffrey, and Gerald R. Salancik. "Determinants of Supervisory Behavior: A Role Set Analysis," *Human Relations*, vol. 28 (1975), 139–54.

42. Pfeffer, Jeffrey, and Gerald R. Salancik. "Organizational Context and the Characteristics and Tenure of Hospital Administrators," *Academy of Management Journal*, vol. 20 (1977), in press.

43. Reed, R. H., and H. P. Miller. "Some Determinants of the Variation in Earnings for College Men," *Journal of Human Resources*, vol. 5 (1970), 117–90.

44. Salancik, Gerald R., and Jeffrey Pfeffer. "Constraints on Administrator Discretion: The Limited Influence of Mayors on City Budgets," *Urban Affairs Quarterly*, in press.

45. Sales, Stephen M. "Supervisory Style and Productivity: Review and Theory," *Personnel Psychology*, vol. 19 (1966), 275–86.

46. Schutz, Alfred. *The Phenomenology of the Social World* (Evanston, Ill.: Northwestern University Press, 1967).

47. Selznick, P. *Leadership in Administration* (Evanston, Ill.: Row, Peterson, 1957).

48. Spaeth, J. L., and A. M. Greeley. *Recent Alumni and Higher Education* (New York: McGraw-Hill, 1970).

49. Thompson, James D. *Organizations in Action* (New York: McGraw-Hill, 1967).

50. Vroom, Victor H. "Some Personality Determinants of the Effects of Participation," *Journal of Abnormal and Social Psychology*, vol. 59 (1959), 322–27.

51. Vroom, Victor H., and Phillip W. Yetton. *Leadership and Decision-Making* (Pittsburgh: University of Pittsburgh Press, 1973).

52. Warner, W. L., and J. C. Abbeglin. *Big Business Leaders in America* (New York: Harper and Brothers, 1955).

53. Weick, Karl E. *The Social Psychology of Organizing* (Reading, Mass.: Addison-Wesley, 1969).

54. Weinstein, Alan G., and V. Srinivasan. "Predicting Managerial Success of Master of Business Administration (MBA) Graduates," *Journal of Applied Psychology,* vol. 59 (1974), 207–12.

55. Wolfle, Dael. *The Uses of Talent* (Princeton, N.J.: Princeton University Press, 1971).

56. Zald, Mayer N. "Who Shall Rule? A Political Analysis of Succession in a Large Welfare Organization," *Pacific Sociological Review,* vol. 8 (1965), 52–60.

In the past several years, an increasing number of individuals—often new graduates and professionals—have rejected secure positions in apparently well-managed organizations in favor of working alone or joining up with a few friends in a new organization. Usually they are not protesting, but searching for "something more." The nature of this "something more" is the subject of this article.

Current Leadership Models

Almost without exception, theories of managerial leadership currently in vogue postulate two major dimensions of leadership behavior.[1] One dimension concerns the manager's or leader's efforts to accomplish organizational tasks. Various writers have given this dimension different names, including task or instrumental leadership behavior, job-centered leadership, initiating structure, and concern for production. The second dimension is concerned with the leader's relations with his subordinates; it has been labelled social-emotional leadership behavior, consideration, concern for people, and employee-centered leadership. Measures of the effects of leadership also usually fall into two categories: indices of productivity and of worker satisfaction. A leader or manager who is good at organizing to get work done and who relates well to his subordinates should have a highly productive group and satisfied workers.

There is nothing wrong with two-factor models of managerial leadership as far as they go, but they are incomplete. They grew out of a period in history when the goal was to combine the task efficiency associated with scientific management with

READING 2–8

Leadership and Organizational Excitement*

DAVID E. BERLEW

the respect for human dignity emphasized by the human relations movement. They did not anticipate a time when people would not be fulfilled even when they were treated with respect, were productive, and derived achievement satisfaction from their jobs. As a result, two-factor theories of managerial leadership tell us more about management than about leadership. They deal with relationships between man and his work, and between men and other men, but they do not tell us why some organizations are excited or "turned-on" and others are not. They do not help us understand that quality of leadership which can ". . . lift people out of their petty pre-occupations . . . and unify them in pursuit of objectives worthy of their best efforts."[2]

* © 1974 by the Regents of the University of California. Reprinted from *California Management Review*, vol. 17, no. 2 (Winter 1974), pp. 21–30, by permission of the Regents.

Note: Published originally in David A. Kolb, Irwin M. Rubin, and James M. McIntyre, *Readings in Organizational Psychology*, 2d ed. (Prentice-Hall, 1974).

[1] Robert J. House, "A Path Goal Theory of Leader Effectiveness," *Administrative Science Quarterly*, 16, no. 3 (1971), pp. 321–38; and Abraham K. Korman, "Consideration, Initiating Structure, and Organizational Criteria—A Review," *Personnel Psychology*, vol. 19 (1966), pp. 349–61.

[2] John W. Gardner, "The Antileadership Vaccine," *Annual Report of the Carnegie Corporation of New York*, 1965.

FIGURE 1
Organizational Emotions and Modes of Leadership

	Stage 1	Stage 2	Stage 3
Emotional tone:	Anger or Resentment	Neutrality	Satisfaction Excitement
Leadership mode:	CUSTODIAL	MANAGERIAL	CHARISMATIC
Focal needs or values:	Food Shelter Security Fair treatment Human dignity	Membership Achievement Recognition	Meaningful work Self-reliance Community Excellence Service Social responsibility
Focal changes or improvements:	Working conditions Compensation Fringe benefits Equal opportunity Decent supervision Grievance procedures	Job enrichment Job enlargement Job rotation Participative management Management by objectives Effective supervision	Common vision Value-related opportunities and activities Supervision which strengthens subordinates

Leadership and Emotion in Organizations

In an effort to help fill that void, the outline of a model relating types of leadership to the emotional tone in organizations is presented in Figure 1. Stages 1 and 2 of the model are derived from familiar theories of work motivation and the two-factor models of leadership discussed earlier. Angry or resentful workers (Stage 1) are primarily concerned with satisfying basic needs for food, shelter, security, safety, and respect. Organizations in Stage 1 try to improve their situations by eliminating "dissatisfiers" through improved working conditions, compensation, and fringe benefits, and by providing fair or "decent" supervision. The type of leadership associated with a change from an angry or resentful emotional tone to one of neutrality, or from Stage 1 to Stage 2, has been labelled *custodial*. The workers are neutral, lacking either strong positive or negative feelings about their work or the organization. In the absence of "dissatisfiers," they tend to become increasingly concerned with group membership or "belonging" and opportunities to do inherently satisfying work and to receive recognition. In order to increase employee satisfaction, organizations at Stage 2 introduce improvements such as job enrichment, job enlargement, job rotation, participative management, and effective (as opposed to decent) supervision. Changes are oriented toward providing work that is less routine and more interesting or challenging, building cohesive work teams, and giving employees more say in decisions that directly affect them. The type of leadership associated with this movement from neutral to satisfied workers, or from Stage 2 to Stage 3, has been labelled *managerial*.

Most of the advances in organization theory and management practice in the past few decades have related to Stage 2: defining and controlling the elements of supervision and the organizational environment that result in high productivity with high satisfaction. While these advances have been substantial and have led, in most cases, to healthier, more effective organizations, they have not prevented the increasing alienation of professional employees.

The addition of Stage 3 to the model to extend the emotional tone continuum to include *organizational excitement* is an attempt to deal with a phenomenon of the 70s—the increasing number of professionals and new graduates who are rejecting secure positions in established organizations. The model suggests that for this small but growing element of the population, the satisfaction of needs for membership, achievement, and recognition is no longer enough. The meaning they seek has less to do with the specific tasks they perform as individuals than the impact of their individual and collective efforts—channeled through the organization—on their environment. The feelings of potency which accompany "shaping" rather than being shaped or giving up (and dropping out) are a source of excitement. So, too, are the feelings that stem from commitment to an organization that has a value-related mission and thus takes on some of the characteristics of a cause or a movement. At the extreme, this can lead to total involvement or total *identification*—the breaking down of boundaries between the self and the organization so that the "individual becomes the organization" and the "organization becomes the individual."

Stage 3 Leadership

Although Stage 3 leadership must involve elements of both custodial and managerial leadership, the dominant mode is charismatic leadership. The word *charisma* has been used in many ways with many meanings. Here we will define it in terms of three different types or classes of leadership behavior which provide meaning to work and generate organizational excitement. These are:

1. The development of a "common vision" for the organization related to values shared by the organization's members.
2. The discovery or creation of value-related opportunities and activities within the framework of the mission and goals of the organization.
3. Making organization members feel stronger and more in control of their own destinies, both individually and collectively.

The first requirement for Stage 3 or charismatic leadership is a common or shared vision of what the future *could* be. To provide meaning and generate excitement, such a common vision must reflect goals or a future state of affairs that is valued by the organization's members and is thus important to them to bring about.

That men do not live by bread alone has been recognized for centuries by religious and political leaders. All inspirational speeches or writings have the common element of some vision or dream of a better existence which will inspire or excite those who share the author's values. This basic wisdom too often has been ignored by managers.

A vision, no matter how well articulated, will not excite or provide meaning for individuals whose values are different from those implied by the vision. Thus, the corporate executive who dreams only of higher return on investment and earnings per share may find his vision of the future rejected and even resented by members of his organization. Indeed, he may even find his vision of a profitable corporate future questioned by stockholders concerned with the social responsibility of corporations. Progressive military leaders may articulate a vision or mission congruent with the needs and values of the young people they are trying to attract to an all-volunteer service, only to discover that the same vision conflicts with the values of their senior officers.

An important lesson from group theory and research is that informal groups tend to select as leader the individual who is most representative of the group's needs and values. Thus his hopes and aspirations, and the goals toward which he will lead the group, are automatically shared by the group's members.

One problem for heads of complex organizations is that if they are to function as leaders (as opposed to custodians or managers) they must represent and articulate the hopes and goals of many different groups—the young and the old, the unskilled and the professional, the employee and the stockholder, the minority and the majority, union, and management. Only the exceptional leader can instinctively identify and articulate the common vision relevant to such diverse groups. But to fail to provide some kind of vision of the future, particularly for employees who demand meaning and excitement in their work, is to make the fatal assumption that man *can* live by bread alone.

There are dangers as well as advantages to a common vision. If top management does not sincerely believe in the desirability of the vision they articulate, they are involved in an attempt to manipulate which will probably backfire. Another danger might be called the *Camelot phenomenon:* the articulation of a shared vision that is both meaningful and exciting, but so unrealistic that people must inevitably be disillusioned. Whether the responsibility in such cases lies with the seducer or the seduced is difficult to say, but the end result is a step backward into cynicism.

Finally, the effectiveness of the common vision depends upon the leader's ability to "walk the talk": to behave in ways both small and large that are consistent with the values and goals he is articulating. In this regard, my experience in the Peace Corps taught me that the quickest way to destroy or erode the power of a common vision is for the leader to allow himself to be sidetracked into bargaining over details instead of concentrating all of his attention

on identifying, tracking, and talking to the value issue involved. For example, at a meeting where volunteers are reacting negatively to a proposed reduction in their living allowance, the Peace Corps director or leader cannot afford to get involved in a discussion of whether or not female volunteers will be able to afford pantyhose with their reduced allowance. The role of the leader is to keep alive the common vision which attracted volunteers to the Peace Corps in the first place: in this case, the idea of a group of Americans whose help will be more readily accepted if they live at about the same standard as their local co-workers.

Value-Rated Opportunities and Activities

It is a mistake to assume that individuals who desert or reject established organizations are basically loners. In fact, many start or join new organizations, often at considerable personal sacrifice in terms of income, security, and working conditions. It is revealing to analyze these "new" organizations for sources of meaning or excitement which may be lacking in more mature organizations. A list of opportunities present in many of the younger organizations in our society is presented in Figure 2, along with values related to those opportunities.

A Chance To Be Tested Many of us go through life wondering what we could accomplish if given the opportunity. Our Walter Mitty fantasies place us in situations of extreme challenge, and we come through gloriously. Few of us, however, have an opportunity to test the reality of our fantasies, as society increasingly protects us from getting in over our heads where we might fail and thus hurt the organization or ourselves. This is especially true of corporations where managers are moved along slowly, and only after they have had sufficient training and experience to practically insure that they will not have too much difficulty with their next assignment.

As a Peace Corps country director in the mid-60s, I was struck by the necessity of having to place many volunteers without adequate training or experience in extremely difficult situations, and the readiness—even eagerness—of most volunteers to be tested in this way. Some volunteers rose to the challenge in remarkable ways, others held their own, and some could not handle the stress. Volunteers who were severely tested and succeeded were spoiled for the lockstep progression from challenge to slightly more difficult challenge which most established organizations favor to protect both themselves and the individual from failure. The same thing happens in wars and other emergency situations where planned development and promotion systems break down.

The point is that many people want an opportunity to be tested by an extraordinary challenge, and such opportunities rarely exist in established organizations. As a result, some who are most able and most confident leave the shelter of the established organization to measure themselves against a value of independence and self-reliance.

Social Experimentation   A great deal has been written about the increasing superficiality of personal relationships in our society and the resulting loneliness and alienation. Organizations have responded with efforts to build cohesive work teams and to provide individuals doing routine, independent work with opportunities to talk with co-workers on the job. These gestures have not begun to meet the needs of persons who have been influenced by the counter-culture's emphasis on authentic relationships as opposed to role-regulated relationships and the need to reduce social fragmentation by carrying out more of life's functions—working, child rearing, playing, loving—with the same group of people.

Established organizations do not provide these kinds of opportunities. Many prohibit husbands and wives from working together. Child-care centers, if they exist, are separate from the parents' workplace, and the workplace is geographically and psychologically separated from the home. As a result, individuals who desire more integrated lives often leave established organizations and form new organizations, such as businesses in which wives and children

FIGURE 2
Sources of Meaning in Organizations: Opportunities and Related Values

Type of Opportunity	Related Need or Value
A chance to be tested; to make it on one's own.	Self-reliance Self-actualization
A social experiment, to combine work, family, and play in some new way.	Community Integration of life
A chance to do something *well*—for instance, return to real craftsmanship; to be really creative.	Excellence Unique accomplishment
A chance to do something *good*—for instance, run an honest, no "rip-off" business, or a youth-counselling center.	Consideration Service
A chance to change the way things are—for instance, from Republican to Democrat or Socialist, from war to peace, from unjust to just.	Activism Social responsibility Citizenship

can play a role and professional firms whose members live as well as work together.

A Chance To Do Something Well   Established organizations fight a continual battle between controlling costs and maintaining standards of excellence; and standards are usually compromised. This is not cynicism: a group of skilled metal workers, machinists, and mechanics can nearly always produce a better automobile than General Motors if cost is no object. The opportunity to seek true excellence, to produce the very best of something, is a strong attraction, even though the market may be extremely limited and the economic viability of the venture questionable. Individuals frustrated by the need to cut corners in established organizations find the alternative of a new organization committed to excellence an attractive one, and they will work long hours at low pay to make it financially viable.

A Chance To Do Good   Still others desert established organizations in the belief that they are compromising standards of honesty and consideration in their struggle to survive in "the capitalistic jungle." They form organizations to do *good*: to provide honest, no "rip-off" services or products, or services which they believe a "good" community should have, such as free schools, legal, medical, and counselling services for the deprived, or low-income housing.

A Chance To Change Things   Finally, many thoughtful individuals leave established organizations because they view them as too interwoven with or dependent upon the system to be an effective force for change. So they form new organizations as vehicles for bringing about change, whether it is to increase our appreciation of art, eliminate discrimination, or protect the environment.

The critical difference between these new organizations and established organizations is that the newer ones provide opportunities

and activities closely related to the values of their members within the framework of the mission and goals of the organization. This is true even when the organization is as intent on making money as any established corporation (as they often are), and when they resemble a modern version of a 19th-century sweatshop (as they often do). Members of these organizations are not against profit-making *per se* or hard work or putting the organization before the individual. But there must be a reason for doing these things: they are not ends in themselves. The reason comes from a common vision of what they are trying to create together, as well as opportunities to behave in a value-congruent manner. These factors justify and even make desirable those characteristics of organizations which otherwise would be rejected as unnecessary or exploitative.

Few, if any, progressive executives will find the types of opportunities and values noted above distasteful or undesirable. Many, however, will conclude that it is simply unrealistic to expect to find such opportunities in a large corporation or government agency under pressure from stockholders or the voting public to maximize profits or minimize expenditures.

However, such opportunities *do* exist in large, established organizations, and where they do not, they can often be created. For example, established organizations do not have to be tied to a step-by-careful-step advancement ladder. AT&T, for example, has experimented with a system whereby potential new hires for management positions are offered exceptionally challenging year-long assignments and are told that depending on their performance, they will either leapfrog ahead or be asked to leave the company. It provides confident individuals with a series of opportunities to test themselves. If implemented successfully, it benefits the organization by attracting and developing self-reliant managers while quickly weeding out security seekers and poor performers.

While it takes managerial leadership to introduce such changes, it takes charismatic leadership to recognize the value relevance of such a program and to integrate it with the organization's mission in such a way that it creates and sustains excitement. Too often such programs go unrecognized or un-exploited as sources of increased organizational excitement simply because of a limited conception of leadership.

Our organizations and institutions have, for the most part, been quite uncreative about countering or controlling the increasing fragmentation of work and family life and the many problems that result. I know from my relationships with my wife and children now that I work at home a few days a week compared to when I spent 50 to 80 hours at the office or out of town and came home tired and irritable, often with homework. I doubt if I am much different from most other professionals in this regard. Why not actively recruit husbands and wives as work teams when possible, with child-care facilities nearby? Or, where possible, encourage employees to work at home on individual projects when they may have fewer interruptions than at the office?

Many organizations have a manifest commitment to excellence in their products and services and to carrying out their corporate responsibilities toward the community. Occasionally they are in a position to spearhead social change. Too frequently, however, the value-relevent message seems directed toward customers or stockholders and only secondarily toward organization members. When it is directed toward members, it usually comes from a staff department such as corporate relations or the house organ rather than directly from the senior-line officers. This is public relations, not leadership, and whereas charisma might substitute for public relations, public rela-tions, no matter how good, cannot substitute for charisma.

Making Others Feel Stronger

The effective Stage 3 leader must lead in such a way as to make members of his or-ganization feel stronger. To achieve the or-ganization's goals as well as to meet the needs of his more confident and able em-ployees, his leadership must encourage or enable employees to be Origins rather than Pawns.

Richard deCharms has described Origins and Pawns in the following terms:

An Origin is a person who feels that he is director of his life. He feels that what he is doing is the result of his own free choice; he is doing it because he wants to do it, and the consequences of his activity will be valuable to him. He thinks carefully about what he wants in this world, now and in the future, and chooses the most important goals ruling out those that are for him too easy or too risky . . . he is genuinely self-confident because he has determined how to reach his goals through his own efforts . . . he is aware of his abilities and limitations. In short, an Origin is master of his own fate.

A Pawn is a person who feels that someone, or something else, is in control of his fate. He feels that what he is doing has been imposed on him by others. He is doing it because he is forced to, and the consequences of his activity will not be a source of pride to him. Since he feels that external factors determine his fate, the Pawn does not consider carefully his goals in life, nor does he concern himself about what he himself can do to further his cause. Rather he hopes for Lady Luck to smile on him.[3]

Clearly, there may only be a few people in the real world of human beings who are

[3] Richard deCharms, *Personal Causation* (New York: Academic Press, 1968); and Richard deCharms, "Origins, Pawns, and Educational Prac-tice," in G. S. Lessor, ed., *Psychology and the Edu-cational Process* (Glenview Ill.: Scott, Foresman and Co., 1969).

always guiding their own fate, checking their own skill, and choosing their own goals, but some people act and feel like Origins more of the time than do other people. Similarly, there are only a few people who *always* feel pushed around like Pawns. Some individuals—parents, teachers, managers—have the ability to relate on a one-on-one basis in ways that make another person feel and behave more like an Origin and less like a Pawn. Certain types of leaders can apparently affect entire groups of people the same way.

In an experiment conducted at Harvard University, a group of business school students were shown a film of John F. Kennedy delivering his inaugural address. After viewing the film, samples of the students' thoughts or fantasies were collected by asking them to write short imaginative stories to a series of somewhat ambiguous pictures. The thoughts of students exposed to the Kennedy film reflected more concern with having an impact on others and being able to influence their future and their environment than the thought samples of students exposed to a neutral control film. J.F.K. made them feel like Origins.[4]

Replicating this experiment in a number of leadership training sessions, I have found the same thing: exposure to a certain type of leader—such as John F. Kennedy—leaves people feeling stronger, more confident of being able to determine their own destinies and have an impact on the world. It was this type of reaction to J.F.K. that attracted many young people to the Peace Corps to "change the world" during the early and mid-60s.

It is difficult to assess precisely what it was about Kennedy's leadership that had this strengthening effect. We do know that he articulated a vision of what could be which struck a resonant chord, particularly in young people and citizens of developing nations. He also projected extremely high expectations of what young people could do to remake their country, if not the world.

Although most organization leaders cannot count on such dramatic moments as a presidential inauguration, or perhaps on their oratorical powers, they nevertheless do have a powerful effect on whether those around them feel and behave like Origins or Pawns. A number of factors determine the effect they have on others in this critical area.

Beliefs about Human Nature One important factor is the manager's beliefs or assumptions about human nature. If he believes that the average human being has an inherent dislike of work and will avoid it if he can, that most people must be coerced or controlled to get them to put forth effort toward the achievement of organizational objectives and that they wish to avoid responsibility, have relatively little ambition, and want security above all, then the manager will organize and manage people as if they were Pawns, and they will tend to behave as Pawns. If, on the other hand, the manager believes that the expenditure of physical and mental effort in work is as natural as play or rest, that individuals will exercise self-direction and self-control in the service of objectives to which they are committed, and that commitment to objectives is a function of the rewards associated with their achievement, including psychological rewards, then he will organize and manage people in quite a different way, with the result that they will tend to behave more like Origins than like Pawns.[5]

[4] David G. Winter, *Power Motivation in Thought and Action* (Ph.D. dissertation, Harvard University, Department of Social Relations, January 1967).

[5] Douglas McGregor, *The Human Side of Enterprise* (New York: McGraw-Hill Book Company, 1960).

High Expectations Another important factor is the expectations a manager has about the performance of his subordinates. To some extent, all of us are what others expect us to be, particularly if the others in question are people we respect or love. A dramatic demonstration of this phenomenon is the strong positive relationship between a teacher's expectations of how well a student will do and the student's actual performance, a relationship which persists even when the teacher's positive expectations are based on invalid information.[6] A second study, done in a corporate setting, demonstrated that new managers who were challenged by their initial assignments were better performers after five years than new managers who were initially assigned to relatively unchallenging tasks, despite the fact that the potential of the two groups was about the same.[7]

Reward Versus Punishment Some managers tend to focus their attention on mistakes—to intervene when there are problems, and to remain uninvolved when things are going well. Other managers look for opportunities to reward good performance. An overbalance in the direction of punishing mistakes as opposed to rewarding excellence lowers self-confidence and is relatively ineffective in improving performance. Rewarding examples of effective action, however, both increases self-confidence and improves performance.

Encouraging Collaboration Americans have a tendency to compete when the situation does not demand it and even sometimes when competition is self-defeating (as when individuals or units within the same organization compete). Diagnosing a situa-

tion as win-lose, and competing, insures that there are losers; and losing is a weakening process. If a situation is *in fact* win-lose in the sense that the more reward one party gets the less the other gets, competition and the use of competitive strategies is appropriate. This is usually the situation that exists between athletic teams or different companies operating in the same market. Diagnosing a situation as win-win and collaborating is a strengthening process because it allows both parties to win. A situation is *in fact* win-win when both parties may win or one can win only if the other succeeds, as is usually the case *within* a company or a team.

The leader who is effective in making people feel stronger recognizes collaborative opportunities where they exist and does not allow them to be misdiagnosed as competitive. When he identifies instances of unnecessary competition within his organization, he uses his influence to change the reward system to induce collaborative rather than competitive behavior. If confronted with a competitive situation which he cannot or does not want to alter, however, he does not hesitate to use competitive strategies.

Helping Only When Asked It is extremely difficult to help someone without making them feel weaker, since the act of helping makes evident the fact that you are more knowledgeable, powerful, wise, or rich than the person you are trying to help. Those familiar with this dynamic are not surprised that some of the nations that the United States has most "helped" through our foreign aid resent us the greatest, particularly if we have rubbed their noses in their dependence by placing plaques on all the buildings we have helped them build, the vehicles we have provided, and the public works projects we have sponsored.

Yet the fact remains that there are real differences between individuals and groups in an organization, and help-giving is a real

6 Robert Rosenthal and Lenore Jacobson, *Pygmalion in the Classroom* (New York: Holt, Rinehart and Winston, Inc., 1968).

7 David E. Berlew and Douglas T. Hall, "The Socialization of Managers: Effects of Expectations on Performances," *Administrative Science Quarterly*, 11, no. 2 (1966), pp. 207–23.

requirement. The effective Stage 3 leader gives his subordinates as much control over the type and amount of help they want as he can without taking untenable risks. He makes his help readily available to those who might come looking for it, and he gives it in such a way as to minimize their dependence upon him. Perhaps most important, he is sensitive to situations where he himself can use help and he asks for it, knowing that giving help will strengthen the other person and make him better able to receive help.

Creating Success Experiences   A leader can make others feel stronger, more like Origins, by attempting to design situations where people can succeed and where they can feel responsible and receive full credit for their success. People, whether as individuals or organizations, come to believe in their ability to control their destiny only as they accumulate successful experiences in making future events occur—in setting and reaching goals. The leader's role is to help individuals and units within his organization accumulate such experiences.

When an organization, through its leadership, can create an environment which has a strengthening effect on its members, it leads to the belief that, collectively, through the organization, they can determine or change the course of events. This, in turn, generates organizational excitement. It also becomes an *organization* which has all the characteristics of an Origin.

Some Unanswered Questions

In this article, I have tried to analyze one aspect of the problem of alienation in the workplace: the increasing attrition of professionals and new graduates from established organizations. I have tried to suggest the nature and source of the meaning and excitement they are seeking in their work and the type of organizational leadership required to meet their needs. However, a number of questions have been left unasked which must be explored before any conclusions can be drawn.

One question concerns the relationship between organizational excitement and productivity. We know there are many productive organizations—some of our major corporations, for example—which cannot be called excited or "turned-on." We have also seen excited organizations expending tremendous amounts of energy accomplishing very little. In the case of excited but unproductive organizations, it is clear that they are overbalanced in the direction of Stage 3 leadership and need effective *custodial* and *managerial leadership* to get organized and production-oriented rather than solely impact-oriented. The case of efficient and productive organizations that are not excited is more complex. Would General Motors or ITT be better off if they could create a higher level of organizational excitement? Would they attract or hold better people, or are they better off without those who would be attracted by the change? Are such corporations headed for problems which can only be dealt with by an emphasis on Stage 3 leadership, or have we overstated the magnitude of the social change that is taking place?

A second question concerns the relevance of the model to different types of organizations. There is little question of the relevance of charismatic leadership and organizational excitement to such as the Peace Corps, the United Nations, religious organizations, political groups, community action organizations, unions, and the military. The same is true of start ups where new industrial or business organizations are competing against heavy odds to carve out a piece of the market. What is not so clear is whether it is any less relevant to large, established corporations and government bureaucracies. Quite possibly, it is precisely the element that is missing from some government agencies and is one of the key elements that gives one great corporation the edge over another.

While more questions have been raised than answered, there should be no confusion about one point: just as man cannot live by bread alone, neither can he live by spirit alone. Organizations must have elements of custodial and managerial leadership to achieve the necessary level of efficiency to survive. It is not proposed that Stage 3 or charismatic leadership increases efficiency; indeed, it may reduce the orderly, professional, totally rational approach to work which managerial leadership tries to foster. However, it does affect motivation and commitment, and organizations will face heavy challenges in these areas in the coming decade.

* * * *

CASES FOR PART TWO

Case 2–1

AN ATTEMPT TO CONSOLIDATE
COOPERATIVES IN ECUADOR

A credit cooperative is known to most persons in the United States as a credit union or a savings and loan cooperative. Members place their savings in the cooperative, as they would in a bank, but loans are available only to members, hopefully at a lower rate of interest. Yearly, all profits are returned to the members based on the amount of savings they have in the cooperative.

A cooperative is normally governed by a five-member board elected from the membership. These members include a president, a vice president, treasurer, and the heads of the credit and supervisory committees. The credit committee approves all loans, and the supervisory committee insures that the cooperative is being operated according to its by-laws. Professional managers can be hired by the cooperative, but this is only feasible when the cooperative is of a large size.

Credit cooperatives have been formed in many underdeveloped areas because of the lack of credit facilities at reasonable interest rates for the small merchant and farmer. Credit cooperatives provide this source. At the same time, they mobilize capital in the community by teaching the members the importance of regular savings.

Credit cooperatives were started in Ecuador for these purposes. Ecuador is a small country, larger only than Uruguay in South America, with a population of about 5 million. It is an extremely poor country relying on the export of bananas for most of its income. It has a geographic handicap for future economic development because the Andes Mountains run completely through the center of the country. The ruggedness of these mountains makes trade and communication between areas very difficult, and may partially explain why the coastal region of Ecuador has had a better record of cooperative development than has had the mountain region.

As a young American member of the Peace Corps, I was assigned to work with the credit cooperatives in Cuenca, the third largest city in Ecuador with a population of about 80,000 persons. Cuenca is situated in the mountain region, eight hours from the coast and 15 hours from the capital city, Quito. Thus, it is not surprising that the cooperatives in Cuenca have been doing so poorly that most people in the city had never even heard of credit cooperatives.

There were three formally organized cooperatives in Cuenca. After an initial period of growth, two of them were stagnating. The third cooperative simply had failed completely.

The best of the three cooperatives was called "La Merced," after the patron saint of the neighborhood in which the cooperative was formed. The president, Sr. Caldera, and the treasurer, Sr. Marchan, were knowledgeable in the mechanics of operating a cooperative but were not aggressive in promoting the concept. As a result, the cooperative had only 100 members and $100 in capital. Most of its members were women, small businessmen, and merchants, which hampered the economic growth of the cooperative. If the cooperative was to give its intended service, the membership had to be expanded. Unfortunately, the cooperative had not attracted many new members in the last six months.

The other functioning cooperative in Cuenca was headed by Sr. Mendosa. Sr. Mendosa exhibited tremendous pride in being the founder and president of an organization of this kind. He ran the entire show, and he took great pride in doing so. He was not only the president, but the treasurer; he approved all the loans (which, by the way, is illegal). He just did not delegate any authority, and he resented criticism of his operation by anyone. He restricted membership to only his friends and spoke of his role as one of looking out for their welfare, but of course their voice in the cooperative was insignificant.

The third cooperative was made up of local carpenters. It failed because the membership did not seem to understand what a credit cooperative was or how it was to operate. The cooperative was never officially disbanded, and only a complete transfusion could save it. But even this was doubtful, since it had a reputation of failure.

After having worked with these cooperatives for a few months, I felt that Cuenca should have more people involved in credit unions than just the 200 now participating. I thought the idea of a single large cooperative for the entire city was desirable and feasible. Instead of independently improving the three existing cooperatives, I thought it would be more sensible to merge them into one. This would result in a nucleus of trained personnel to manage the cooperative and a base of 200 members from which to convince others that the cooperative was a success.

Because I thought I could make a substantial contribution to the economic life of the city, with great excitement I set up appointments with the presidents of the three cooperatives.

I approached each of the cooperatives with my idea. Sr. Mendosa strongly rejected the plan and dismissed me, saying that the other cooperatives should be dissolved, with their members joining his organization. The other two cooperatives, in turn, rejected Mendosa's position, but they did agree to discuss consolidation of their two groups.

When the meeting was held, the purpose of the merger was explained, and how it was to be accomplished was carefully detailed. Each cooperative would officially withdraw from the National Federation and a new one would immediately be established so that there would be no loss in services for the present members. With the larger amount of members and capital, the new cooperative would be able to make larger loans to its members with greater regularity. All old officers of the two cooperatives would resign and a new directorship would be elected by the new, combined membership.

At this point the idea began to run into difficulties. The president of "La Merced," Sr. Caldera, did not like the idea of disbanding his cooperative, because the name would be changed. He felt that the name had religious significance and should be retained. The president of the carpenters, Sr. Maldonado, on the other hand, did not want to retain the name of "La Merced" because it would seem as if they were being forced to capitulate to the other cooperative—and besides he didn't like the religious association. The subsequent argument forced a polarization of those present, each backing the position of their own cooperative; each side became more adamant in their position as time went by.

When the discussion turned to the election of officials, fear was expressed that if one cooperative outnumbered the other, their directors might be completely reelected, leaving the other cooperative without representation. This problem was partially bypassed when it was suggested that the president should be elected from one cooperative, a vice president from the other, etc. This, however, met with resistance on the point of which cooperative was to elect the president. Each cooperative wanted to retain their own president, and neither president wanted to accept the second position in favor of the other. The mistrust by members of one cooperative toward the members of the other gradually became obvious.

The meeting was finally adjourned with no progress toward consolidation and with heightened suspicion and animosity between the two cooperatives. Later, when I met with individuals in each cooperative, I could see that they did not want to discuss the matter further. Future plans were dropped and the idea died.

Questions

1. Analyze why the United States Peace Corps member failed to influence the Latin Americans.
2. What personal objectives was the North American striving to achieve? How did they relate to the others' objectives?
3. What motivational assumptions did the North American make? What was wrong with them?
4. What leadership style did the North American demonstrate? Why was it ineffective?
5. How do you think he should have proceeded?

Case 2–2

OPEN OR CLOSED IN THE OPERATING ROOM?

Operating room nurses work together more frequently and intensely than nurses do in any other hospital activity. Precise and consistent procedures are essential to meet the surgeon's demands and the patient's needs. In addition, safety is paramount because sedated patients, sharp instruments, flammable anesthetics, electrical equipment, and the need for speed all present constant danger. To handle this complexity, surgical teams work out very detailed rules on how instruments are to be cleaned, stored, sterilized, and handled from aid to nurse to surgeon. Everyone is very conscious of time and motion economy.

A proposed change in sterilization technique presented a problem for the operating room of Mercy Care Hospital, a medium-sized institution in a semirural, small-city area.

Three years ago, Beatrice Hunt, the registered nurse who was the operating room supervisor, attended a three-day workshop for operating room nurses given by a university medical center in Chicago. Her subordinate nurses resented her going on the coveted trip because they had heard that she was leaving the hospital in a few months. Upon her return, she announced that it was no longer considered adequate to sterilize instruments with their locks closed. She directed that the procedures be changed so that the hemostats would be sterilized and handled in an open position.

The hemostat, the most commonly used surgical instrument, consists of two serrated jaws to occlude (close) a blood vessel, two rings (like the handle of a pair of scissors) for the thumb and third or fourth finger, and the working joint between the handle and the jaws (see Exhibit 1). In most cases there is a ratchet on the handle by which the jaws can be locked shut until the blood vessel is ligated (sewed closed), when the ratchet is released by the operator. While there are hundreds of sizes, shapes, and names for hemostatic forceps, the basic design is the same: jaws, handles, joint, and ratchet. It had been recognized for some time that the serrated jaws and the "screw lock" or "box lock" joints were the most difficult part to sterilize, even with steam under pressure, the most satisfactory method in use at the time. Traditionally, however, except when actually using or cleaning them, the instruments were handled in a closed position.

Some reasons for keeping the instruments closed were:

1. The jaws are less likely to be knocked out of line if kept closed.
2. The instrument is less likely to catch on sterile gloves, drapes, or other instruments when kept closed.
3. The instrument is less awkward to pass to the surgeon in the closed position.
4. The trays and shelves are neater.

Hunt's directive aroused much complaining and minimal compliance unless she was present and insistent, in which case torn gloves, dropped in-

EXHIBIT 1
Basic Design of Hemostat

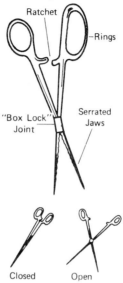

Ratchet

Rings

"Box Lock" Joint

Serrated Jaws

Closed   Open

struments, and swearing doctors were all too common. The hemostats were still generally stored, sterilized, and handled in the closed position. When she left the hospital a few months later, the directive simply was forgotten.

Helen Petrosky is now operating room supervisor, having moved up from head nurse to replace Hunt when she left two and a half years ago. Petrosky has been reconsidering the hemostat sterilization issue because several articles have recently appeared in professional journals recommending open sterilization and handling. Spot checks taken by culturing swabs from instruments sterilized by aids at Mercy Care rarely indicate contamination. Even when they do, there are several possible explanations: the elderly sterilizers, faulty operation or timing, improper cleaning before sterilization, overloading the sterilizer, or not allowing air to clear from the chamber. Nonetheless, Petrosky feels that the present procedure should be changed.

Questions

1. Describe and analyze Hunt's change style. What were her assumptions?
2. Analyze why Hunt's directive did not change behavior as she desired.
3. How is Petrosky's situation different from Hunt's?
4. What are Petrosky's alternatives?
5. Recommend a detailed change plan for Petrosky.

Case 2–3

NATIONAL BANK OF SAN FRANCISCO*

The National Bank of San Francisco operates 13 branches that receive deposits and make loans to both businesses and individual depositors. Deposits have grown from $14 million to $423 million within the past 20 years, and the directors have opened more branches as population and business activity in the Bay area have increased.

The Bank has generally been characterized by aggressive marketing including give-away promotions for new deposits and extremely competitive interest rates on loans. President E. F. Wellington has prided himself on his ability to appoint entrepreneurial branch managers and loan officers who have pushed new business development.

In response to a question at a board meeting two years ago concerning a noticeable rate of increase in operating and overhead expenses, Wellington announced that he would undertake a study of ways the bank might lower, or at least hold the line on, these costs.

Shortly thereafter, he called in James Nicholson, one of his two assistants, described the general problem of reducing costs, and told him that the bank had reached the size where it needed a man to devote his full time to operating methods and facilities. He said that he had talked this matter over with Mr. Simmons, manager of personnel, and that both of them had agreed "that you would be a fine man for this position." He also explained that Mr. Simmons would be simultaneously promoted to vice president and put in charge of all equipment purchases, the maintenance of all bank buildings, and personnel relations. "Simmons and I feel that you might have a permanent advisory committee made up of one man from each branch, and that such a group can be really effective in deciding on ways to utilize our banking buildings and equipment, and our people, more effectively. Unless you have some objection, each of the branch managers will appoint a man to meet with you regularly."

Within three months of the original reference to the subject at the directors' meeting, Simmons had been promoted to vice president, Nicholson received the title of manager of personnel and equipment planning, and all branch managers had appointed, at Wellington's request, a man to what became known as the "systems committee." At the present time, two years later, the committee appears to have taken its work seriously, as evidenced by (1) a record of regular meetings held over a period of 18 months; (2) the transcripts of those meetings and exhibits, which show that all seven men entered the discussions; (3) 17 recommendations in writing, supported by a total of 1,800 pages of research data and reasoning; (4) the fact that meetings often lasted four to five hours, extending after working hours; and (5) the statements of all seven members of the committee to the effect that they enjoyed the work, felt that they were accomplishing something for

---

* Copyright 1978, Charles E. Summer, University of Washington.

the bank, and had personally enjoyed being on the committee with the other members. All men have also expressed their high regard for Jim Nicholson and feel that he has done a good job.

The 17 recommendations cover such matters as salary scales, a policy on days off for personal business, a policy on central purchasing of janitorial supplies, and a recommendation that certain models of typewriter and dictating machine be adopted uniformly in all branches.

Office Space and Furnishings

About a year ago, both Simmons and Nicholson had made inspection trips to the branches and had come to the conclusion that there was much wasted space in branch offices and that this situation had been brought about principally because officer personnel and clerical personnel had been, over a period of years, buying equipment—such as desks, telephone stands, and extra tables—that pleased them personally but that, in many instances, was also "too large and expensive" for what the bank needed to keep up its public appearance. In addition, loan officers in some branches had succeeded in having the managers construct walls for unnecessary private offices. Nicholson had obtained the services of the bank's architect and also of systems engineers from two large equipment manufacturers; together they made a "general estimate, to be confirmed by further fact-finding" that the bank could save $80,000 a year over a 30-year period if (1) furniture were to be standardized with functional equipment that was modest in design but met the essential requirements of dignity for the branches and if (2) henceforth, only branch managers could have private offices.

Before the meeting of the systems committee last week, Simmons expressed concern to Nicholson that his committee had not taken up these two problems.

> Your committee could have done some real research on these questions. I hope that you will put them on the agenda right away and agree, let's say in six months, on standard layouts and equipment. You and I both know, for instance, that the loan officers at San Mateo and Menlo Park have entirely too much space, should not be in those large offices, and perhaps should have three standard pieces of equipment—a desk, chair, and small bookcase. There should be no telephone stands like those that were purchased there last year for $90 each.

Relations with Branch Managers

Branch managers have been kept informed of the committee's general work over the 18-month period. Most managers selected a loan officer (assistant manager) to represent them, and these officers made a real effort to let their managers know what was going on. Dick May, representative of the Burlingame branch, reports that he has been spending at least an hour a week with his boss telling him what the committee is doing and asking for his ideas. James Strickland of the Market Street branch says that he has been able to confer briefly with his boss about once a week on the subjects the committee is working on. Other members report that they, too, have been able to keep their managers informed and that the latter exhibit a good deal of interest in the committee's work. In all cases except Burlingame, however, men say that their managers quite naturally do not have the time to go into the details of committee recommendations and that they, the managers, have not been particularly aggressive or enthusiastic about putting any of those recommendations into effect.

The committee has talked about the best way to get its recommendations adopted. Dick May claims that his manager is ready to put many of them into effect immediately and that it is up to each man to convince his own manager. All others say they believe that the president should issue the recommendations as instructions over his signature. The reason given by Strickland is typical:

> We're convinced that the recommendations are best for the bank, but the managers just won't buy them. The only way to get the managers to carry them out is to have Mr. Wellington lay them out as official and let it be known that they are going to be put into effect. Of course, they would have to be acknowledged as being drawn up by the Department of Personnel and Equipment, with some advice from our committee.

James Nicholson reported in his own weekly meeting with the president that it looked as if it is going to be "rather touchy" to get managers to accept the recommendations. Mr. Wellington thereupon stated that his own knowledge of the committee recommendations was rather sketchy, even though he had discussed them in part with Nicholson each week for a year. He therefore decided to call a meeting of all branch managers and committee members at the same time so that he and everyone concerned could be acquainted in detail with them. This meeting took place one week ago.

Informal Comments of Branch Managers

Most of the branch managers dropped in to the officers' dining room for lunch before the meeting. After the usual banter, the conversation naturally drifted onto the proposals of the systems committee.

> Sure hope my secretary likes those new typewriters. I can't spell, and if Sally left I'd be sunk.
>
> So what, Joe, you always talk better than you write.
>
> Say, I sure hated to come in here this afternoon. Ever since Smedley Scott became president of Menlo Laboratories I've been trying to convince him to do all his banking with us. Had to break a date with him, and in my office, too. If we start spending all our time buying mops, our development program goes out the window.
>
> How are you making out with your two (officer) trainees, Carl? I have one smart boy coming right along, but he won't be happy under the proposed salary schedule.

The best young man we have came from the credit department a year ago. He sure gets around. Tennis matches, hospital drives, U.N. meetings; always on the go. I thought of him when I read that proposal for days off. How do you decide when a guy like that is working? Granted his work gets behind sometimes. That's better than drawing pay for just sitting at his desk. I get a kick out of bringing a man like that along. And he is building a lot of good will for the bank in my area.

Well, I kind of like that days-off rule. It would save a lot of complaints and conversation about grandfather's weak heart.

It might be just fine for you, Tyson, but not so good for Pete. Why not let each manager decide for himself? After all, each of us is paid to run his branch in the best interests of the bank, and we wouldn't be in our present positions if we weren't doing it. What do you think, Oscar?

Guess I have longer service than any of the rest of you. It will be 39 years in September. But I'd say there isn't a manager who doesn't run his branch just as though it was his own business.

And the record is not bad either. Deposits are going up and the bank is making money.

It's making money that counts. (This from a manager of one of the slower-growing branches.)

I heard from somebody about a year ago that the committee was going to study office space and equipment and that someone figured they could save $1 million over a period of years. But apparently they didn't get around to that.

Don't worry. We're building a real base for the future. By the way, did you see the latest report on Zenith Radio?

Just before the meeting with the systems committee, Simmons called Jim Nicholson into his office to have a brief discussion of the recommendations. The two men read over the list of 17 final recommendations; then Nicholson explained briefly the reasons why each recommendation was made and how it would help the bank to reduce costs.

The Meeting of the Committee and Branch Managers

The meeting started at 2:00 P.M. and was scheduled to last until 5:00 P.M., but actually ran over until six o'clock. The committee, branch managers, Wellington, and Simmons were present. Wellington opened the meeting by stating that its purpose was to study the committee recommendations and, it was hoped, to arrive at a decision on whether they should be accepted and put into effect.

In fact, however, after a reading of the 17 recommendations, the entire meeting was taken up by a discussion of the first two recommendations.

1. It is recommended that the following pay scales be adopted for clerical and nonofficer personnel in all branches. (This was followed by a list of positions and grades—the bank had had some uniformity before, but the recommendation specified absolute uniformity and also changed

some of the classifications, thus meaning, for instance, that head tellers would in the future receive more than head bookkeepers, whereas both had received the same in the past.)

2. Employees should be allowed two days per year off with pay for miscellaneous personal business, such days to be granted at the discretion of managers. Because of the possibility of abuse of this privilege, days in excess of two must be taken without pay. This limitation does not apply to sickness or death in the immediate family.

In the discussion, the branch managers found a great many points on which (a) they disagreed among themselves, and (b) they agreed among themselves but disagreed with the committee. For instance, they all agreed that uniformity was in the interest of the bank but disagreed on many of the salary scales and classifications. On this point, they cited many instances in which one competent employee would feel hurt if the scales were arranged in the way the committee recommended.

The committee members had talked confidentially among themselves before the meeting and agreed that Jim Nicholson must be the one to present the findings and, by and large, the one to defend them. This plan was carried out, and after the meeting, the president remarked to Jim that

> the combined thinking of the managers, with all of their experience, made quite an impression on Simmons and me. We have confidence in you, and you know that, but I can't help but wonder if your committee really worked out the "best" recommendation for all on this salary matter. If you had, why couldn't you convince the managers instead of raising all of the criticism?

Yesterday, Wellington and Simmons met to consider the recommendations privately. Simmons again expressed the same idea that Wellington passed on to Nicholson, wondered out loud whether the committee should be sent back to do more research on the recommendation. Both men expressed concern that two years had elapsed since the committee was established without any recommendations having been accepted and put into effect.

Questions

1. How would you characterize Wellington's leadership? How did he apparently hope that his system would work? Why didn't it?
2. How would you characterize Nicholson's leadership? What is his problem now? How did he contribute to his situation?
3. What was the problem confronted by the committee members?
4. How should Wellington and Nicholson have proceeded (if they could go back in time and begin again)?
5. What do you recommend now?

PART THREE

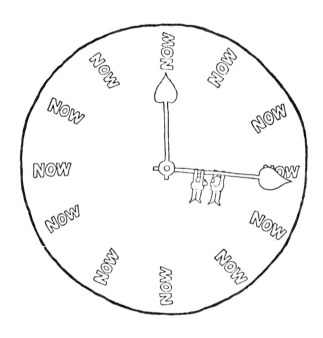

Courtesy Sperry Univac Division of the Sperry Rand Corporation

PLANNING AND
CONTROLLING

READINGS

3–1

"Departmental," Robert Frost.

3–2

"Sterling Swanger—The Man Who Keeps Those Maytag Repairmen Lonely," Edmund Faltermayer.

3–3

"Why Corporations Hate the Future," Arthur R. Roalman.

3–4

"How to Design a Strategic Planning System," Peter Lorange and Richard F. Vancil.

3–5

"Strategic Goals: Process and Politics," James Brian Quinn.

3–6

"Planning & Control and Accounting: Divide and Conquer," Louis N. Redman.

3–7

"On the Folly of Rewarding A, While Hoping for B," Steven Kerr.

3–8

"Formal Planning in Major U.S. Corporations," Harold W. Henry.

CASES

3–1   Unbundling at World Data Processing

3–2   Henderson Specialties, Incorporated

3–3   Lewis Equipment Company

An ant on the table cloth
Ran into a dormant moth
Of many times his size.
He showed not the least surprise.
His business wasn't with such.
He gave it scarcely a touch,
And was off on his duty run.
Yet if he encountered one
Of the hive's enquiry squad
Whose work is to find out God
And the nature of time and space,
He would put him onto the case.
Ants are a curious race;
One crossing with hurried tread
The body of one of their dead
Isn't given a moment's arrest—
Seems not even impressed.
But he no doubt reports to any
With whom he crosses antennae,
And they no doubt report
To the higher up at court.
Then word goes forth in Formic:
'Death's come to Jerry McCormic,
Our selfless forager Jerry.
Will the special Janizary
Whose office it is to bury
The dead of the commissary
Go bring him home to his people.
Lay him in state on a sepal.
Wrap him for shroud in a petal.
Embalm him with ichor of nettle.
This is the word of your Queen.'
And presently on the scene
Appears a solemn mortician;
And taking formal position
With feelers calmly atwiddle,
Seizes the dead by the middle,
And heaving him high in air,
Carries him out of there.
No one stands round to stare.
It is nobody else's affair.

It couldn't be called ungentle.
But how thoroughly departmental.

Departmental*

ROBERT FROST

  * From *Complete Poems of Robert Frost*, Holt,
Rinehart & Winston, 1936.

If cartographers made maps of the American appliance industry like the elegant wine maps of France, they would surely reserve a special one—like the dab of purple that designates, say, a fabled district in the Côte d'Or—for Newton, Iowa. There, in a town of 16,000 set in rolling cornfields, the Maytag Co. turns out clothes washers of legendary reliability, as well as sturdy dryers, top-rated dishwashers, and garbage disposers that can chew up 16-penny nails.

A growing number of consumers clearly believe in the superiority of Maytag appliances, which have won wider market shares in recent years. The most complicated product, the automatic clothes washer, commands a premium of roughly $70 at retail. Last month Consumers Union once again picked it over all other makes, as it has four of the last five times, citing among other things its "much better than average" repair record. Maytag's sales climbed to a record $275 million in 1976. Its profits are perennially fat; it earned 26.4 percent on shareholders' equity last year, compared with 15.9 percent at rival Whirlpool, the leading maker of home laundry equipment.

Many people deserve laurels for Maytag's performance, not least a board of directors that exalts quality and abhors wasteful model changes, and a research department that quietly goes on modifying product designs "under the hood" to lessen vibration, wear, and breakdown. The chief defender of Maytag's reputation, however, is the man in charge of turning laboratory prototypes and books of specifications into gleaming appliances mass-produced at a rate of hundreds per hour—appliances that will perform so well in millions of homes that at least some Maytag repairmen will really lead the lonely lives celebrated in television commercials. That crucial person is Maytag's vice president for manufacturing.

Sterling Swanger—The Man Who Keeps Those Maytag Repairmen Lonely*

EDMUND FALTERMAYER

Gears in the Desk Drawers

As you approach Maytag headquarters to meet him, stereotypes crowd the mind. Is he a Rickover of the Corn Belt, similar to the dictatorial types who really did rule Maytag's production lines from time to time in the past? Or a charismatic Knute Rockne who cheers on his subordinates to feat after feat? Sterling O. Swanger, who has held the top manufacturing job for the past two years, is in fact a study in understatement, all amiability and soft-sell.

"I'm not the bull-of-the-woods type of manager," Swanger confesses in a flat Iowa drawl. Indeed, your first impression on meeting this trim man of 55, who puts on no airs, and who sits in a windowless office with desk drawers full of gears and other appliance innards, is that of someone two

---

* Reprinted from the November 1977 issue of *Fortune* Magazine by special permission; © 1977 Time Inc.

Note: Sterling Swanger is vice president of manufacturing for the Magtag Co.

levels further down in the organization. That impression lasts about three minutes.

As Swanger begins to talk with authority about the "Maytag philosophy" of doing things right, you begin to feel the quiet, sustained energy he emits, the way one starts to feel the sun on a beach. You notice that the benign, Nordic-blue eyes behind his steel-rimmed glasses are probing and insistent. And his firm mouth, set in a smile, conveys an expectation of performance.

Swanger is an executive of great staying power, who can gently monitor, decide, and goad. "I'm not hesitant about putting the pressure on," he says. Swanger has a higher position in his company's hierarchy than is usually accorded to manufacturing bosses these days. His salary and bonus, the third highest at Maytag, totaled $74,823 last year. Swanger is given a very free hand with production, normally meeting with Daniel J. Krumm, Maytag's president and c.e.o., only once a week or so.

Like Horatius at the bridge, Swanger has held the line on quality in an era of widespread temptation to do otherwise. Like many appliance makers, in fact, Maytag is producing a more reliable machine than ever. In the mid-1950s, when the company's late president, Fred Maytag II, laid down a standard of ten years' trouble-free operation, the company's average automatic clothes washer was three years short of the target. Today, grueling "lifetime" tests show, a typical machine leaving the loading platform should run 14 years without serious trouble.

At the same time, the manufacturing division has chipped away at production costs. The plastic top of the water pump in a clothes washer, for example, was formerly put in place with 13 screws; now it is quickly sealed on with the application of heat. This year, the division expects to beat its goal of $4.3 million worth of money-saving changes in methods and materials, up

from a smaller goal that was also exceeded in 1976. Such savings, of course, cannot make up for the ever-rising prices of purchased materials or for increases in wages. Along with the Frigidaire division of G.M., Maytag has the highest wages in the industry. Under an escalator provision in its contract with the United Auto Workers, it recently raised the average worker's hourly compensation to $6.86 plus fringes. But economizing has enabled Maytag to hold its price increases to about 40 percent over the past five years, less than the 46 percent rise in the general cost of living.

Maytag's production lines, with extensive automation and 25 miles of overhead conveyors, are awesomely intricate and vulnerable to stoppage at dozens of points. But Swanger has the plants running with the dependability of—well, a Maytag washer. The worst production loss in the past 12 months occurred when a freak accident in a big press forced a brief four-hour shutdown of the clothes-washer line.

The manufacturing division is also three-quarters of the way through an expansion program to raise Maytag's overall capacity by 75 percent, and is right on schedule. "My claim to fame," Swanger says serenely and with no tone of boastfulness, "is the implementation of our expansion program on time and under the estimated cost." In this era of overruns, that is no mean trick.

Cynics Need Not Apply

It helps, of course, that the place is Iowa and the company is Maytag. The work ethic is strong in those parts—sufficiently strong so that Maytag has twice considered, then dropped, the idea of expanding elsewhere. Not that the company's 2,100 production workers, many of them men and women in their 20s, are exactly docile. Maytag had to take a five-month strike in 1971 when the U.A.W. unsuccessfully challenged its incentive-pay system. But the work force consists largely of people off the farm who, in the words of Dan Krumm, Maytag's president, "expect to work eight hours for eight hours' pay."

Maytag's corporate way of life, too, is fertile soil in which someone like Swanger can thrive. The whole organization, most of it right in Newton, has the sort of uncynical air that the founders of work communes dream about. The top people are obsessed with the patient, painstaking pursuit of better products and production methods.

The new products come forth only when Maytag is good and ready. The company's first automatic clothes washer did not appear until 1949, a decade behind the nation's first "home laundry." Since then Maytag washers have gone on to outsell every competing make except Whirlpool (whose sales include the Kenmore line produced for Sears) and General Electric. Maytag has slowly brought out other appliances, but only when it was sure that they could win a place at the top of the market.

Since the product mix is limited and model changes are rare, the manufacturing people can concentrate on honing the production process. They can do so, moreover, without fear of being suddenly dispatched to a different task in a faraway location, as Maytag—whose stock sells at a premium—is in no immediate danger of being taken over by a larger company.

Like so many executives in the manufacturing division, Swanger comes from a rural Iowa background and holds an engineering degree from the state university at Ames. He arrived at Maytag in 1947, when the company still produced nothing but wringer washers. In those days the manufacturing vice-president was J. A. Rose, an abrasive but benevolent tyrant formally addressed by all subordinates as "Mr. Rose," who brought in many manufacturing innovations. Within a year and a half, Swanger was one of two employees dispatched to a

six-week course at Lake Placid, New York, run by Allan Mogensen, the apostle of so-called "work simplification." Upon their return, Swanger and his colleague set up an Employees' Idea Plan at Maytag.

The plan turned into a real winner. Work simplification is a systematic way of boosting productivity through suggestions provided by both rank-and-file workers and management. Thanks to a ten-hour training program that all employees are offered and prizes of up to $4,000 for hourly workers' ideas that actually save money, an astounding 90 percent of those workers turn in suggestions. Recently the top award went to Irvin J. McCombs of the sheet-metal department, who suggested that a smaller blank be used in stamping out base frames for washers; this reduced the amount of steel needed, as well as trim scrap.

In five of the last six years, Maytag has been cited by the National Association of Suggestion Systems for the highest participation rate of any company with fewer than 6,000 employees. Workers' ideas account for only 14 percent of the money saved through productivity gains, most of which are initiated by management. But their enthusiastic participation, Swanger and others say, makes them more receptive to management's cost cutting.

In 1952, Swanger was moved out of "industrial engineering," which at Maytag focuses on the worker and his motivation, and into "methods engineering," which involves such things as plant layout, work flow, and cost analysis. This is the field in which he really got noticed over the next 16 years. Almost immediately, he was put in charge of the team that designed Maytag's first assembly line to make clothes dryers. A few years later, he was given the task of revamping the trouble-prone area where big presses bend and stamp sheet metal to make cabinets and other parts. "We relocated every major press," he recalls proudly, "without shutting any production lines."

The Last Word in Porcelain

Throughout this period, Swanger was also involved in keeping the company abreast of the latest advances in production technology. In the late 1960s the company installed a new type of porcelain furnace for fusing a protective layer of powdered glass to washer tubs and other wear-prone parts. It still represents the last word in the field, Swanger says.

As Swanger moved higher with successive promotions, his time-consuming involvement in projects like these came to an end. Today he functions mainly as a maestro, coaxing the best possible performance out of seven department heads who report to him. One of them, Gene Nicol, runs the actual assembly lines and operates largely on his own; on a typical day he spends only a half hour with Swanger, going over production reports. Swanger spends far more time on the other aspects of manufacturing, each of which has some special Maytag touches.

Quality control, for example, is strongly based on the premise that reliability cannot be "inspected" into a product. There's inspection aplenty, of course. Every Maytag appliance is operated just before it is packed for shipment. Clothes washers are hooked up on a slowly revolving "merry-go-round" and run through every function in a 15-minute test. Machines that don't work perfectly go to the "boneyard" for repair or dismantlement. (Whirlpool and G.E. also make a final test of every function on each machine and say that their tests, while shorter, are just as good as Maytag's.)

Educating the Timer People

Long before the machines reach the final testing stage, inspectors from the 177-person quality-control department have watched them take shape at critical points on the assembly lines, and before that have sampled and tested the purchased materials and parts that went into them. Maytag is very fussy with suppliers, and in recent years has been working with them to improve the quality of such potentially troublesome components as motors and timers. Thanks to this effort, Swanger says, Maytag repairmen are sending back fewer defective motors and timers than ever. The timer has been the biggest headache. In the language of a diplomat, Swanger discloses that "we've had trouble convincing the timer people of our quality level."

The real key to quality control, however, is the attitude of the individual Maytag worker. The main role of inspectors, Swanger says, is to "audit" a quality-control job that must be done by everybody. Pride helps. Every few weeks, Swanger hears of a worker who has scornfully commented that "this is not a Maytag-quality part," and has put it aside even when it was from a shipment passed by inspectors.

The snug wire connections in Maytag appliances, Swanger says, provide incontrovertible proof that the workers give a damn. The connections are mostly of the push-on type, and to all intents and purposes there is no way to prevent a slovenly worker from failing to push them home, nor can inspectors begin to catch all the loose connections. The appliance world, Swanger says, is full of products whose circuitry holds up during final tests in the plant—but shakes loose during shipment or in the home. Relatively few of them are Maytags, he asserts. Swanger recalls visiting the General Motors Vega plant at Lordstown during its highly publicized start-up troubles several years ago. "They were automated to the teeth," he says, "but they didn't reckon on the workers' attitude. There's no way they could have produced a quality product."

Enlarging the Worker's Job

Even as he watches over quality control, Swanger also nudges along the industrial-engineering department's search for new ways to get the maximum output from those highly paid workers. Incentive pay already keeps them moving fast, and the union has not made a big issue of it in the last two contract negotiations. Maytag has also raised productivity, here and there, through so-called "job enlargement."

Company officials scoff at the idea that most assembly-line workers are bored and frustrated. Nevertheless, Swanger says, "we've been aware of the Iron Monster of the assembly line for a long time." In the late 1950s, before the quality of work became a fashionable topic, Maytag found that some workers really do prefer to work at their own speed and to get recognition for their contribution to quality. One of Swanger's predecessors ordered that the assembly of control panels and transmissions be converted to bench-style operations.

Formerly, a half dozen people had put together these subassemblies as they moved down a production line. With *job enlargement*—a term Maytag prefers to the newer term *job enrichment*—each worker puts the whole unit together and stamps his own number on it. The worker can set his own pace, and he also tends to make fewer mistakes on parts of this type. Bench assembly, Maytag officials say, has cut defects on clothes-washer transmissions by 62 percent, and in 1977 alone will save the company $43,000 compared to the old method. The transmissions control the rotation of agitator and tub at varying speeds, and can cause all kinds of trouble if put together wrong.

Though less than 100 workers are involved in all, job enlargement is still being expanded at Maytag. Two years ago, when planning got under way for the company's new dishwasher assembly line, Swanger told his engineers to see if any operations could be converted to the bench method. Since last summer, when the new line started up, individual workers have been putting together entire dishwasher doors.

For a Tardy Supplier, the Guillotine

Swanger also steps in whenever the purchasing department encounters tough problems with suppliers. His most anguished experience of the past 12 months occurred last summer, when production of the company's new commercial clothes washers and dryers was held down for want of enough of the chromium-plated parts that make up the coin slot. The parts were arriving late and, Swanger declares with narrowed eyes, "you can't run a mass-production facility on that basis." Maytag had "some very frank discussions" with the tardy supplier, he says, and for three months' running he spent from 15 minutes to two hours on the problem every day or so, including some evenings and weekends. "We finally decided they just weren't going to make the grade for us," Swanger says. He ordered a switch to a more dependable source.

The final decision on whether to go on buying a part at all, or to make it under Maytag's own roof, is Swanger's. The company, he says, is more self-sufficient than most competitors. Maytag has long made the water seals and most of the rubber hoses for its clothes washers, molded many of its plastic parts, and formed many of its gears from powdered metal. It even makes a lot of its screws and, starting three years ago, began to put the plastic covering on all of its copper wire. Generally, the company switches to making its own parts for cost reasons, Swanger says, but later finds that it can improve quality, too. Swanger expects the trend to self-sufficiency to go right on.

One of Swanger's most important jobs these days is to make sure the company's expansion program stays on schedule. The final phase includes an enlargement of zinc-plating capacity. Fanatically dedicated to rustproofing, Maytag uses zinc the way a pizza parlor uses cheese. The plating on vulnerable parts is up to three times as thick as on some competing makes, company officials claim. The detailed engineering work on the plating project is handled by a task force headed by Jerry Jones, Swanger's manager of production engineering. Jones has plenty of opportunity to observe his boss's operating style.

"He believes in an intense follow-up," Jones says. "I've learned to do my own follow-up with people under me, because I know Sterling will be asking." In meetings, Jones adds, Swanger almost never settles disagreements among subordinates with edicts, preferring to move the discussion toward a consensus with carefully directed questions. Keith Nielsen, who runs quality control, marvels at Swanger's ability to stay cool. "I've never been in a situation where he raised his voice," he says. "I've seen him stay calm when a guy was blowing his top. I would have gone sky high."

Spurning the Headhunters

"My mission," Swanger observes over lunch at the Newton Country Club, "is to get people enthusiastic about keeping our costs down and quality up, right down to the assembly line." Like any top executive, Swanger must also spend a good deal of his time preparing for Maytag's future. Promising young executives must be groomed for higher posts, and Maytag must be kept informed of new manufacturing technology.

Swinger reads a half dozen trade journals and does most of the reading at home outside his regular 50-hour workweek. He also finds time for racquet ball, which he plays one or two evenings a week during the winter, and golf. Vacation trips take him far from Newton and its assembly lines— last year to Spain, this year to Ireland.

If there is an essential ingredient in Maytag's success, it is the methodical perseverance that Swanger himself epitomizes. "The Maytag people are not manufacturing geniuses, they're just diligent," says James I. Magid, a security analyst at General American Investors Co. who has long followed the appliance industry. Even the machinery in Maytag's plants, Swanger admits, is "fairly standard" throughout the industry —though he quickly adds that Maytag people have shown "creativeness" in modifying it. From time to time, Swanger gets feelers from headhunters on whether he might wish to take his diligence elsewhere. But he plans to stay put, he says. "I like working for a quality outfit."

There's an absorbing motion picture, distributed by Pyramid Films of Santa Monica, California, called *An American Time Capsule*. The film, which first achieved fame on television, attempts to show the entire history of the United States in three minutes. "It's one of the most popular shorts we've ever had," says Robert Gilhooley, Pyramid's director of marketing.

The film is an illustration, in exaggerated form, of a well-known fact: change is occurring at phenomenal rates. All managed entities must recognize that fact and attempt to cope with it in some way. Most of them do so by setting up various planning operations and procedures. But establishing a planning operation doesn't automatically solve the problem of coping with change.

"Strategic planning? We have it, but that's a point above and a step beyond," says the vice president of a large (assets of about $400 million) company that currently is in deep trouble, mainly because it didn't keep abreast of recent changes in money markets and take decisive action to respond to those changes as they emerged. "Plan for tomorrow?" says a senior vice president with one of the country's largest service companies. "Hell, we haven't caught up with today!"

"Maybe 95 percent of all companies really don't pay much attention to the future," says Dale H. Marco, who heads the industrial management group at Peat, Marwick, Mitchell and Co. one of the big eight auditing firms that makes available management consulting services as well as accounting. "They react to history—history that is anywhere from one day to a few centuries old.

"About 4.5 percent of companies *try* to guess what's ahead. But they do it in such a haphazard fashion that they guess wrong as often as they guess right. It can be profitable to work for these companies during a right-guessing cycle. It can be costly to work

READING 3–3

Why Corporations Hate the Future*

ARTHUR R. ROALMAN

for them during a wrong-guessing period. This is the crap-shooter's paradise.

"That leaves about 0.5 percent of the nation's companies that work hard and well at projecting the future. They know that today you can see the long-range impact of emerging technologies. These companies are right much more often than they are wrong. They are highly profitable, have relatively few inefficiences, are fun and exciting places to work, and are great places to enjoy a long, rich career."

Marco claims that he is probably too optimistic in his percentages. However, the situation may be changing. There are a number of indications that long-range planning may be gaining more widespread acceptance. For example:

The World Future Society—a group of corporate and government planners and academicians who joined together to study what they call "alternative futures"—has grown in ten years of existence to more than

---

* Reprinted with permission from the November 1975 *MBA*. Copyright © 1975 by MBA Communications, Inc.

16,000 members. The society's second world conference was held this summer and attracted more than 2,500 people. WFS also publishes a sound and improving monthly magazine that often provides valuable insight into current developments that are likely to have an impact on our future.

Mitchell Energy & Development, a Houston-based company, is working with the University of Houston to conduct, every other year for the next ten years, programs that will bring together top-level "futures" thinkers and speakers. The first of the programs, called "Limits to Growth '75," was held in October. The programs hope to get top executives and other national leaders thinking about emerging national problems before they explode over us as knee-buckling catastrophes.

In a recent study conducted by publishers of *The Gallagher Presidents' Report*, 46 percent of the 154 presidents responding reported that they had "early warning" systems to monitor changes in social attitudes and opinions. Slightly more than half of these had initiated their early-warning mechanisms since 1970.

There's a proliferation of planning—or, at least, efforts to cope with change in some levels of the educational structure. Some 400 high schools, according to the National Educational Association, now conduct "futures" weeks, consisting of five days of futures orientation, in an attempt to discover what's ahead in such fields as mathematics, biology, English, and so on. "We need such weeks," says Robert Mercier, head of the mathematics department at Willowbrook High School in Villa Park, Illinois, and organizer of one of these programs. "Students have been growing apathetic in the face of the awesome changes all of us have seen in recent years. Their attitude, increasingly, is one of resignation, of inability to cope. Futures weeks are one way of showing them that change is inherent to society, how to recognize change, and how

to cope with it." (Colleges and universities, by and large, are lagging far behind high schools in the teaching of futurism. The reason is that universities are tied to established departmental structures. Nobody has a doctorate in futurism, so it will probably be some years before college students are taught applied futurism.)

There is also a boom in books dealing with the future. Nobody knows how big the boom is, but Julia Larson, librarian for the World Future Society Book Service, estimates that she has 140 books on the subject, compared with only two in 1966.

Still, we have a way to go before futures studies can be regarded as a mature and sophisticated field of endeavor. Much current planning is little more than projecting into the future what has happened in the past.

"The future is simply a niggle in the mind of most businesses," says Professor Lawrence Lavengood of Northwestern's graduate school of management. "Businesses have come across so many unexpected developments in the past ten years that they know they ought to develop some more revealing approach to the future. But many business executives tend to think in rather parochial terms."

Lavengood, who has developed a course in environmental forecasting at Northwestern, claims that most currently used planning techniques badly approximate the face of the future. "We need something other than quantitative measures in assessing probability," Lavengood says. "I don't want to underevaluate extrapolation, but technical forecasters have come to realize that social and political components are as important as economic ones in considering the future. For example, much of the effort in technical development is sponsored by the government, which means that politics is involved. I think it was really along this ledge of technical forecasting that minds began to crawl out to examine systemic relationships."

To make long-range planning pay, it takes, first of all, a real commitment to planning on the part of management. Most good managers will go *this* far, although many of them go, to put it mildly, reluctantly. The next step is to find able people to staff the planning function. This is not as easy as it sounds. The field has its legion of charlatans, as well as scientists who may be enormously able in their areas of expertise but are unable to synthesize and conjecture for effective decision-making purposes.

Finally, top-level operations people have to accept the planning concept and the planning programs. This can be the toughest problem of all.

"They don't understand what we're doing," moans the head of the long-range planning group working for one of the nation's largest corporations. A scientist with more than one doctorate, he finds it almost impossible to penetrate the operating people's mentalities and to get them to work with him in the planning process or with the results of planning efforts. The problem—common to many planning functions—is that he is too far ahead of the operating people, who generally are used to measuring their worth by quarterly profit statements, not by what is likely to happen in 1982. This man's planning operation is a classic case of underutilization—in both the planning and operating groups—of high-priced people, frustration all around, and missed opportunities.

The problem of acceptance of the planning process can take many forms. "The roughest thing to get rid of is the Persian messenger syndrome, where the bearer of bad tidings is beheaded by the king," says William S. Woodside, recently named president of American Can Company. "You should lean over backwards to reward the guy who is first with the bad news. Most companies have all kinds of abilities to handle problems, if they only learn about them soon enough."

Or take the case of a giant, Washington-based association whose directors instructed its planning group to construct a computerized model that would allow association members to plug in and get a better handle on such things as future capital-formation needs, plant locations, personnel needs, and so on. Early in the process, the association planners made a decision to build the best model possible, the most sophisticated device for giving insights into what was likely to happen in future years. They opted for this sort of model instead of one that would be less refined but easier to use and understand.

The result? Eighteen months after the model was made available, only five of the association's 167 members have used it. In effect, it is a very expensive white elephant.

Why are so many planning efforts floundering? There is no single reason, but the paramount one is that the planners don't know how to market their wares. In fact, it seems that there is a growing need for a new corporate specialty—marketing planning concepts and results to operating people. Increasingly, CEOs point out that this is one of their most difficult jobs.

"Top managements are responsible when the planning function flounders," says Dr. John G. Keane, president of Managing Change Inc., a Barrington, Illinois, firm that specializes in helping corporations spot emerging trends. "Either they don't know what good planning is or they allow themselves to be overpowered by short-term concerns. This is especially true in the present economic atmosphere.

"Of course," he adds, "going more deeply into the subject, you have to look at the corporate rewards system. And it is geared to the short term."

In addition, many companies are afflicted with the Jeanne Dixon syndrome; that is, they see planning as an effort to predict the future. They don't realize that, in reality, planning is a complex, sophisticated process of isolating developments that may have an impact on the future; monitoring the growth —or death—of these developments; and making adjustments as new facts are made available and placed alongside assumptions.

Other companies are afflicted with the solution-to-everything syndrome. Their managers may start off with an antiplanning posture. Then they get religion and see planning as a surefire solution to everyday problems. Finally, when they discover that it is not—as, inevitably, they must—they go full circle and abandon planning altogether.

Many planning efforts fail because companies don't realize that it is a specialized function that requires people of special skills. An organization might be suddenly told by top executives that they *will* plan. But that is like asking a track mile runner to become the driver of a high-powered race car. Superior operating people don't quickly make superior planners. At the same time, planners often don't appreciate what it takes for operating people to be successful in a highly competitive, real-world marketplace.

The gap between these two groups of people is like the chasm between tomorrow and today. To work, planning must involve healthy interchanges and understanding between operating people and planners. Planning cannot be imposed on a large group, like fog, but must grow and become whole through understanding, challenges to proposals, adaptation, and renovation.

Every business carries on strategic planning, although the formality of that process varies greatly from one company to the next. Conceptually, the process is simple: managers at every level of a hierarchy must ultimately agree on a detailed, integrated plan of action for the coming year; they arrive at agreement through a series of steps starting with the delineation of corporate objectives and concluding with the preparation of a one- or two-year profit plan. However, the *design* of that process—deciding who does what, when—can be complex, and it is vital to the success of the planning effort.

A strategic planning system is nothing more than a structured (that is, designed) process that organizes and coordinates the activities of the managers who do the planning. No universal, off-the-shelf planning system exists for the simple and obvious reason that companies differ in size, diversity of operations, the way they are organized, and managers' style and philosophy. An effective planning system requires "situational design"; it must take into account the particular company's situation, especially along the dimensions of size and diversity.

While providing in this article some guidelines for designing strategic planning systems, we caution the reader to recognize that, for the reasons just stated, such generalizations can be treacherous. We do not aspire to prescribe a planning system for your organization; you must do the tailoring.

But some useful generalizations are possible, particularly in distinguishing between large companies and small ones and between highly diversified companies and less diversified ones. Size and diversity of operations generally go hand-in-hand, although exceptions to that rule are common. Several of the large airlines, for example, are in one business, and a number of miniconglomerates with sales of less than $100 million have divisions in disparate industries. For

How to Design a Strategic Planning System[*]

PETER LORANGE and
RICHARD F. VANCIL

convenience here, we shall talk about companies as "small" or "large," defining those labels in terms of the typical characteristics shown in *Exhibit 1*.

While your company may not neatly match either set of characteristics, an understanding of why an effective strategic planning system is different in these two types of companies may enable you to design a system that fits your situation. We should note that the characteristics of small companies also describe a "typical" division in a large, diversified business. Therefore, division managers in such companies can follow our discussion at two levels simultaneously: (1) In their role as a part of the corporate planning process, and (2) in their strategic planning role for their own "small" businesses.

There are six issues on which a choice must be made while designing a strategic

---

[*] *Harvard Business Review*, September–October 1976, pp. 75–81. Copyright © 1976 by the President and Fellows of Harvard College; all rights reserved.

EXHIBIT 1
Characteristics of "Small" and "Large" Companies

	"Small" Companies	"Large" Companies
Annual sales	Less than $100 million	More than $100 million
Diversity of operations	In a single industry	In two or more different industries
Organization structure	Functional departments	Product divisions
Top executives' .... expertise in industries in which company operates	Greater than that of functional subordinates	Less than that of divisional subordinates

planning system. With each issue the proper choice for large companies will be different in most cases from the one for small companies. The issues are: communication of corporate performance goals, the goal-setting process, environmental scanning, subordinate managers' focus, the corporate planner's role, and the linkage of planning and budgeting. We shall describe each of these issues in turn and briefly discuss why the design choice differs in the two corporate settings.

COMMUNICATION OF CORPORATE GOALS

A common roadblock in designing a formal planning system occurs when second-level managers ask headquarters for guidelines to focus the preparation of their strategic plans. These managers, uncertain how to tackle the assignment, may ask, implicitly or explicitly, "Tell us where you want us to go and the performance you expect from us, and we'll give you a plan of how to achieve it." These questions are not unreasonable, but acceding to them may violate the very purpose for undertaking strategic planning. To determine how goals should be communicated and how specific they should be is an important matter in planning system design.

When the president of *a small company* (or the general manager of a division of a diversified company) initiates the strategic planning process, he shares with his functional subordinates his thoughts about the objectives and strategy of the business. In most situations, however, he does not make explicit his performance goals. Instead, he asks his functional managers to devise a set of action programs that will implement the strategy of the business in a manner consistent with its objectives. In a pharmaceutical company that we observed, the R&D, manufacturing, and marketing functions jointly proposed a series of possible programs for developing various new drugs and modifying existing ones. But often, of course, this "programming" process involves only a single department.

Usually, the managers concerned realize that there is no need to anticipate the results of their planning efforts by trying to establish goals before establishment and evaluation of the programs. This would be time-consuming and burdensome and might also create false expectations among the functional managers.

The programming process is oriented much more toward analysis of alternative actions than toward establishment of corporate goals, primarily because the functional managers involved in programming tend (properly) to have a parochial point of view. They have a somewhat shorter time horizon than the president and focus their attention on their own areas of the business. The president is the one who selects the action programs for achieving the goals he has set for the business. Functional managers do not need to know the president's performance goals, only that he wants the managers to recommend the best set of programs.

Because of its action orientation, the programming process usually lacks continuity from one year to the next. The objectives and strategy of the business may remain the same, but each year it is necessary to re-examine all existing programs and try to devise new ones. As a consequence, even though the programming activity commonly uses a three- to five-year time horizon, management pays little attention to the tentative goals established in the preceding year. Instead, the focus is on the current situation, the best set of action programs now, and the development of an achievable goal for the forthcoming year.

The diversity of the portfolio of businesses in *large companies* is often so great that it limits top management's capacity for in-depth perception and familiarity with each business. Consequently, management has to rely on the relatively unconstrained inputs from the divisions.

Division managers do heed corporate guidance in the form of broad objectives, but, as a rule, top management should delay development of a statement of performance goals for the corporation. Usually, a division manager is in a better position to assess the potential of his own business if he is unbiased by corporate expectations. Delay also permits the top executives to change their approach to the task. In the absence of a formal strategic planning process, top management may have developed explicit goals for itself; but it cannot be sure of the appropriateness of the goals when viewed in the context of a set of independently arrived-at divisional goals. Divisional recommendations stimulate a better job of corporate goal setting.

GOAL-SETTING PROCESS

From the division manager's viewpoint, should he or corporate management set the division's goals? This issue is sometimes cast as a choice between "top-down" and "bottom-up" goal setting. Actually, of course, management at both levels must agree on divisional goals. An important issue, however, remains: Which level in the hierarchy should initiate the process? In a homogeneous company, the same issue arises concerning the general manager and functional managers. The design of the planning system can strongly influence how this issue is resolved.

The goals that emerge from the programming process in *a small company* are tied to an approved set of action programs. Until the president has decided on the programs, no functional manager can set goals for his sphere of activity. Selection of a set of action programs, therefore, more or less automatically determines the performance goals for each functional unit. In many small companies—such as the pharmaceutical concern we spoke of—a "package" of action programs spells out the functional goals for every department, because of the interdependence of all the departments.

In a sense then, functional goal setting is a top-down process. The functional managers propose action programs, but the president with his business-wide perspective determines the programs and goals for his functional subordinates.

In *a large company* with a relatively diversified group of businesses, "capacity limitations" at the corporate level dictate a more or less bottom-up approach. The divisions initiate much of the goal setting, since it requires intimate knowledge of the industry-specific set of business conditions.

Establishing an effective corporate-divisional goal-setting climate in a large company is not easy. For the first year or two of a formal planning effort, the best approach in most situations is to allow the initiative for recommending divisional goals to rest with the division manager. This approach gives him support in running his business and encourages strategic thinking at the divisional level.

Later, after the corporate and divisional managers have gained experience in hammering out a mutually agreeable set of divisional goals, the division manager's annual proposal for divisional goals will become more constrained than in the early years. In a divisionalized, consumer goods manufacturer we know of, the first years of carrying on the planning process were viewed frankly as a learning experience for division managers in making plans operational as well as for top management in learning to appreciate the strategic problems of each business of the company.

The cumulative experience of negotiating the goal setting over the years improves the effectiveness of the process. Corporate management can help nurture this development by creating a system that maintains a proper top-down/bottom-up balance. One way to achieve this balance is by withholding an explicit statement of corporate goals for the first year or two, while requiring the division manager to recommend goals for his division.

ENVIRONMENTAL SCANNING

A strategic planning system has two major functions: to develop an integrated, coordinated, and consistent long-term plan of action, and to facilitate adaptation of the corporation to environmental change. When introducing and developing such a system, companies commonly concentrate on its integrative aspects. The design of the system, however, must also include the function of environmental scanning to make sure that the planning effort also fulfills its adaptive mission.

Corporate management, of course, provides subordinates with a set of forecasts and assumptions about the future business environmnet. Since each manager, initially at least, draws the strategic plans for his sphere of responsibility more or less independently of his counterparts, all managers must have access to the same set of economic and other environmental forecasts.

Environmental scanning in *small companies* is a strategically oriented task that can go far beyond the mere collection of data about markets, competitors, and technological changes. A company that, for example, enjoys a large share of the market for a product used by middle- and upper-income teenagers and young adults may devote considerable effort in analyzing demographic trends and changes in per capita income. A fairly accurate forecast of market size five years hence is possible to make and would be useful in appraising the potential for the company's growth.

The task of monitoring detailed environmental changes in *large companies* is too difficult to be performed by top management alone. Division management, therefore, is expected to study the external environment that may be relevant to their particular businesses. In these circumstances, headquarters typically provides only a few environmental assumptions—mainly economic forecasts.

Environmental scanning may play another important role in large companies that are interested in diversification through acquisitions. In one diversified electronics and high-technology company that set out to decrease its dependence on defense contracts, the vice-president in charge of planning spent most of his time searching for acquisition opportunities. After establishing close ties with the investment community and certain consultants, he spread word of his company's intentions.

SUBORDINATE MANAGERS' FOCUS

In a strategic planning effort, where should the second-level managers direct their attention? What roles do the division manager, functional manager, and top management play? We shall consider these questions in terms of whether plans should be more quantitative or more qualitative, more concerned with financial detail or with strategic analysis.

Preparation of a functionally coordinated set of action programs for *a small company* may require a great deal of cross-functional communication. Much of this interchange is most efficiently expressed in dollar or other quantitative terms, such as numbers of employees, units of product, and square feet of plant space. Use of financial or quantitative data is appropriate for two reasons: (1) it helps each functional manager understand the dimensions of a proposed program and forces him to think through the implications of executing it; (2) it permits the president to select more confidently the set of programs to be implemented. The pharmaceutical company previously referred to, for instance, focuses on the funds flows that might be expected from the various strategic programs suggested by the functional departments.

In practice, the financial and quantitative aspects of functional planning become progressively detailed as the programming process continues, culminating in very specific plans that constitute the operating budget.

In a diversified *larger company,* top management wants each division to adopt a timely strategic outlook and division management to focus primarily on achieving that outlook. Particularly during the early years of the planning program, division managers should be permitted to develop as much financial detail in support of their proposals as they think desirable. As a result,

they may generate more financial detail than necessary for strategic business planning. After a year or two, therefore, the corporate requirements for financial detail to support division proposals should be made explicit —and should be explicitly minimal.

Division managers should be asked to shift the focus of their efforts to identification and analysis of strategic alternatives, using their expertise to estimate quickly the financial implications. This focus has been a goal from the beginning, of course, but it is difficult to achieve at the outset. Failing to shift the focus is an even greater danger; the planning activity becomes a "numbers game" and never achieves its purpose.

Considering that the division manager may never have seen, much less prepared, long-range financial projections for his business, drawing them up should be a useful activity. Such projections help him lengthen the time horizon of his thinking; they oblige him to make his intuitive economic model of the business more explicit, which in turn enables him to forecast changes in financial performance. As a result, a division manager's initial planning efforts tend to be financially oriented and, in many respects, analogous to long-range budgeting. Corporate management should design the requirements of the system to mitigate the pressures that initiation of formal planning poses for a division manager.

One important caveat for the chief executive of a large company: he should never allow himself to get so involved in the development of business plans that he assumes the division managers' planning job. A situation that we investigated concerned the newly appointed president of a multinational company in the consumer products business, whose experience was mainly in marketing. He could not resist "helping" one of his divisions develop a detailed, more aggressive marketing plan. Such interference often inhibits the division from coming up with a realistic plan to which it can commit itself. In this case, quiet resistance effectively shelved the president's ideas.

CORPORATE PLANNER'S ROLE

A major issue in the design of the planning system is where the corporate planner fits. Strategic planning is a line management function; a sure route to disaster is to have plans produced by staff planners and then issued to line managers. Strategic planning is essentially a people-interactive process, and the planner is only one in the cast of characters involved. If the process is to function effectively, he must clearly understand his proper role. The corporate planner's function in small and large companies is quite different.

In *a small company* (or a product division of a large company), the planner performs the function of staff planning assistant to the president (or the general manager). While coordinating the planning activities of the functional managers, he concerns himself with the president's problem of selecting the best set of action programs. Only the president—and his planning assistant—has a business-wide perspective of the choices, and the assistant must do the bulk of the analysis.

Cast in this role, the planner may become a very influential member of the president's (or the general manager's) executive team. If he uses his power sensitively, he need not lose effectiveness with his peers running the functional departments. They can appreciate the necessity for cross-functional analysis of program alternatives. Managing the planning process is an almost incidental role for the assistant, since he merely formalizes the analysis that leads to a coordinated set of action programs.

In *a large company*, the corporate planner's organizational status can have significant symbolic value in conveying to division managers the importance of formal strategic planning and the difference between

it and conventional budgeting. The planner's role initially is that of a catalyst, encouraging line managers to adopt a strategic orientation. He helps corporate management do a better job of resource allocation among the divisions, partly by assisting the division managers in strategic planning for their businesses. But he must not succumb to the temptation to become more involved in formulating the plans, or he may lose his effectiveness.

System maintenance and coordination is the planner's primary function as the planning effort matures; he monitors its evolution and maintains consistency. His tasks differ greatly from the mainly analytical role of the planner in the small company.

LINKAGE OF PLANNING AND BUDGETING

The steps in a typical planning system represent an orderly, gradual process of commitment to certain strategic alternatives. Each step is, theoretically at least, linked to those preceding. In financial terms this linkage may be quite explicit; for instance, a division's profit forecast prepared in the first planning cycle may become the profit commitment for next year's operating budget. Although few companies expect to achieve this financial linkage in narrowing the choices, all the parties involved in the process should understand the intended relationship between the cycles.

How fast this narrowing should be is a situational design question that depends on the particular corporate setting. A tight linkage between planning and budgeting indicates that more strategic commitments have been made at an earlier stage. A loose linkage, on the other hand, implies that the narrowing process is slower and will occur mainly late, in the budgeting stage of the process.

Exhibit 2 shows examples of slow versus rapid narrowing profiles. Notice that a com-

EXHIBIT 2
Slow versus Rapid Narrowing Profiles in the Planning Process

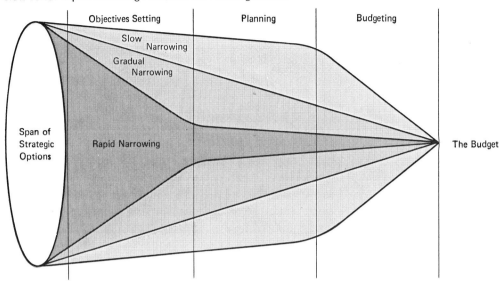

pany that does little narrowing in the early stages faces the task of considering a large number of strategic issues in the budgeting stage. This implies that either the company is equipped with an adequate organization to process an immense and "peaky" budgeting workload, or it will neglect some choices altogether, with the likely result that the quality of its allocation decisions suffers.

A small company with little diversity in its operations may wish to adopt an early or rapid narrowing process, since the functional and corporate executives involved are thoroughly familiar with the strategy of the few businesses in question. Then functional managers can proceed directly to the development of action programs to continue implementation of that strategy. Quantitative financial linkage between the selected programs and the resulting budgets is feasible, and "tight" linkage of this type is common practice.

In *a large company,* linkage is usually looser and the narrowing process more gradual. During the start-up phase top management should give division managers plenty

of time to devote to strategic thinking about their businesses—but the lower-level executives must remember to differentiate that activity from long-range budgeting, with its related requirement of divisional performance fulfillment.

As the system matures, however, management can gradually accelerate the narrowing process without jeopardizing the creative aspect of planning. A natural result of this progress is a more precise definition of the linkage between the planning cycle and the budgeting cycle. A large producer of heavy equipment we know of, for instance, has "tightened up" the linkage between planning and budgeting. The top executives believe that this development is a natural consequence of their increasingly cohesive strategic points of view.

EVOLVING SYSTEMS

In sum, significant differences exist between the planning procedures used in the two types of companies we have examined. The issues that management must address,

EXHIBIT 3
Approaches to Planning System Design issues

		Situational Settings	
		"Large" Companies	
Issues	*"Small" Companies*	*New Planning System*	*Mature Planning System*
Communication of corporate goals	Not explicit	Not explicit	Explicit
Goal-setting process	Top-down	Bottom-up	"Negotiated"
Corporate-level environmental scanning	Strategic	Statistical	Statistical
Subordinate managers' focus	Financial	Financial	Strategic
Corporate planner's role	Analyst	Catalyst	Coordinator
Linkage of planning and budgeting	Tight	Loose	Tight

and our attempt to delineate what is good practice in small and large companies, are summarized in *Exhibit 3*.

In companies that are not very diversified and are functionally organized—as well as product units of diversified corporations—top management carries on the strategic thinking about the future of the business. In such companies, a formal process to help organize that reflective activity is frequently unnecessary, in view of the few managers involved. Instead, formal strategic planning focuses on the development and review of innovative action programs to implement the strategy. The planning system reflects that focus: goal setting is top-down, linkage to the budget is tight, and the staff planning officer plays a major role as cross-functional program analyst and environmental scanner.

In companies that operate in several industrial sectors and are organized into product divisions, initiating a formal strategic planning process is a major task. The first year or two of such an effort must be viewed as an investment in fostering a planning competence among division managers; the payoff in better decisions at the corporate level must wait until the system matures.

If the planning system is to survive as more than an exercise in pushing numbers into the blank space on neatly designed forms, it must evolve rapidly along several dimensions. A mature system, however, can be invaluable, helping both corporate and divisional executives make better and better-coordinated strategic decisions.

Any company—indeed, any organization—is a dynamically evolving entity whose situational setting is subject to change Accordingly, to remain effective, the design of the planning process is a continuous task requiring vigilance and insight on the part of management.

Executives are constantly under pressure to:

Define specific goals and objectives for their organizations.

State these goals clearly, explicitly, and preferably quantitatively.

Assign the goals to individuals or organizational units.

Control the organization toward established measurable goals.

These have become almost biblical mandates for most managers. Yet at the strategic level in large companies one often finds that successful executives announce only a few goals. These are frequently broad and general. Only rarely are they quantitative or measurably precise. Further, managements tend to arrive at their strategic goals through highly incremental "muddling" processes rather than through the kinds of structured analytical processes so often prescribed in the literature and "required" according to management dogma.

This article documents why top managers act as they do. It also asserts that their practices are purposeful, politically astute, and effective. They do not represent breakdowns in management technique, sloppiness, or lack of top management sophistication—as critics of these practices so often suggest. Managers at all levels can be more effective if they understand the logic and process considerations behind such "broad goal setting" and "incremental" techniques.

The conclusions in this article come from systematic observation of some ten organizations over a period of several years. Examples are selected from these observations, from secondary sources, and from a current project on "Strategy Formulation in Major Organizations," in which the author has interviewed some 100 top managers in large U.S. and European companies.

194

READING 3-5

Strategic Goals: Process and Politics[*]

JAMES BRIAN QUINN

WHY NOT ANNOUNCE GOALS?

Why don't top executives simply arrive at goals and announce them in the precise, integrated packages advocated by theoretical strategists and expected by their organizational constituents? In fact, they may establish a few broad goals by decree. But more often—and for good reason—they avoid such pronouncements. Why?

Undesired Centralization

Effective top managers understand that goal "announcements" centralize the organization. Such statements tell subordinates that certain issues are closed and that their thoughts about alternatives are irrelevant. Successful top executives know they cannot have as much detailed information about products, technologies, and customers needs as their line compatriots do. In formulating goals, they want both to benefit from this knowledge and to obtain the genuine

* *Sloan Management Review*, Fall 1977, pp. 21–37. Reprinted by permission.

participation and commitment of those who have it. For example:

Mr. James McFarland said that shortly after he became Chief Executive Officer, "I asked myself what was expected of me as CEO. I decided that my role was really to build General Mills from a good into a great company. But I realized this was not just up to me. I wanted a collective viewpoint as to what makes a company great. Consequently, we took some 35 top people away for three days to decide what it took to move the company from 'goodness' to 'greatness.' Working in groups of six to eight, we defined the characteristics of a great company from various points of view, what our shortcomings were, and how we might overcome these." Over time these broad goals were translated into charters for specific divisions or groups. They became the initial guidelines that stimulated the company's very successful development over the next decade.

The president of another large consumer products company was trying to develop a posture to deal with ever-increasing government regulation in his field. He said, "I have started conversations with anyone inside or outside the company who can help me. I don't know yet what we should do. And I don't want to take a stand we can't all live with. Before we make any irrevocable decisions, I'll want a lot of advice from those people in the company who understand the specific problems better than I do. And I'll want everyone pulling together when we do set our course."

Far from stimulating desired participation, goal announcements can centralize the organization, rigidify positions too soon, eliminate creative options, and even cause active resistance to the goals themselves.

Focus for Opposition

Further, explicitly stated goals—especially on complex issues—can provide focal points against which an otherwise fragmented opposition will organize. Anyone with political sensibilities will understand this phenomenon. For example, President Carter's stated energy plan immediately drew the adverse comments of many parochial interests who only opposed a specific part of the plan. But soon these highly fragmented forces appeared unified in their opposition to the total plan, and each fragment gained added credibility from this apparent unity. In a like manner, a "land use plan" or a "zoning ordinance" quickly becomes a coalescing element for many disparate interests in a town. In industry, department or division heads, who compete fiercely on most issues, can become a formidable power bloc against some announced thrust which affects each only marginally. For example:

In a textile fibers company strong marketing, production, and R&D managers—who fought each other constantly—formed a potent coalition to resist a "product management" scheme to coordinate the very things that caused their friction. And in decentralized companies powerful product division heads have forced new CEOs to give up, get out, or revert to acquisitions—rather than accept new interdivisional goals pushed from the top.

Because of such potential opposition, experienced executives are reluctant to put forward complete "goal packages" which could contain significant points of controversy. Instead they progress by building consensus around one—or a few—important new goal(s) at a time. This in part explains the "incrementalism" so often observed in organizations.

Rigidity

Once a top executive publicly announces a goal, it can become very difficult to change. Both the executive's ego and those of people in supporting programs become identified with the goal. Changing the goal broadcasts that the executive was in error and that all those pursuing the goal were on the wrong track. As a consequence, people doggedly prolong outmoded—but publicly committed—goals, rather than swallow losses and move on.

The government constantly continues obsolete military, energy, and social programs for just such reasons. Corporate bankruptcy lists are rampant with conglomerates, banks, transportation companies, and real estate ventures under duress because their officers tried frantically to fulfill announced—but unrealistic—growth goals.

By contrast, the vice chairman of a multibillion dollar consumer products company said, "We don't announce growth goals in new areas precisely because we don't want to be trapped into doing something stupid. We might be tempted to acquire a company when we shouldn't. Or we might hang on to an operation we really should sell off. Public statements can sometimes generate powerful expectations—internally and externally—that can pressure you to do the wrong thing."

Top managers generally like to keep their options open as long as possible, consistent with the information they have. One way to accomplish this is to define only broad directions, then respond to specific, well-documented proposals. There is an additional advantage to this approach. The proposers are more likely to identify with their proposition and see it through. Again, this is part of the logic behind incrementalism.

As one vice president in charge of diversification said, "Our management doesn't state a specific diversification goal requiring so many millions in profits and sales within five years. Instead we say 'we want to be a competitive factor in [a designated] industry in five years.' This keeps us free to approach each field flexibly as opportunities develop. And we don't get committed until we have concrete numbers and proposals to look at."

Security

There are still other good reasons why effective top managers do not announce

goals explicitly or widely. In any healthy organization good people constantly bubble out to head other enterprises. Thus top executives are justifiably reluctant to provide potential competitors with specific information about their future moves.

When talking to the investment community or his vice presidents, Tex Thornton was never very specific about the sequence and timing of "his plan" during Litton's rapid growth phase. Advance knowledge of Litton's interest could have inflated an acquisition's stock price, activated other potential acquirers, or caused third parties to intervene. With large numbers of Litton executives being sought by other companies, it would have been folly to disclose acquisition goals in detail. In addition, more general goals allowed Litton needed flexibilities to consider new opportunities as they became available.

Further, as one chief executive said, "the future can make fools of us all." There are many examples of former high executives ousted because unforeseen events made it impossible to fulfill ambitious announced goals.

In the late 1960s the president of a large consumer products company announced to all his goal of 10 percent profit growth per year. But many in the company regarded this as "his goal"—not theirs. Despite some impressive successes the president was hung for a failure to meet this goal in two successive years while he was trying to develop some entirely new ventures within the company. When these were slow in materializing, his vice presidents gleefully saw that the original goal was well remembered at the board level. The embarrassed board, which had earlier approved the goal, terminated the president's career.

There are many other situations—like divestitures, consolidations, or plant closures—where managers may not announce goals at all until after they are accomplished facts. These are just some of the reasons why top managers do not follow the conventional wisdom about announcing goals.

The few goals top managers do announce tend: (1) to reflect or help build a developing consensus, (2) to be broad enough in concept to allow opportunism, and (3) to be sufficiently distant in time that a number of possible options could ensure their achievement.

WHEN SHOULD GOALS BE GENERAL?

Conventional wisdom also requires that effective goals be specific, measurable, and preferably quantitative. Many managers actually express embarrassment or frustration when they cannot reach this "ideal." But more sophisticated executives find such highly precise goals useful only in selected circumstances. As an executive vice president of a major automobile company said:

The decisions where we can set specific numerical goals are the easy ones. Establishing the image of your car line, deciding what posture to take vis-à-vis developing legislation, determining what features the public will want in a car three years from now, setting goals for dealing with worker representation or host country demands abroad . . . those are the tough questions. And they don't have numerical answers.

One can attempt to be verbally precise in such areas. Yet very often a broad goal statement is more effective than its narrower, more measurable counterpart might be. Why?

Cohesion

A certain generality in goals actually promotes cohesion. Many can support "continued growth," "greater freedom," "equal opportunity," "full disclosure," or "quality products" as organizational goals. But oddly enough, adding more specific dimensions to these broad concepts may quickly complicate communications, lose some individuals' support, and even create contention.

If a community tries to agree on its precise goals in building a new school, it may never reach a sufficient consensus for action. People can differ irreconcilably on whether a traditional, experimental, precollege, classical, or vocational approach should predominate. Yet they might easily agree on a goal "to build a new school." Once the broad program is approved, they can resolve some very fundamental value differences by compromising on the much less emotionally charged architectural details.

Similarly, top managers can often avoid serious rifts by focusing agreement on very broad objectives where substantial agreement exists, then treating more specific goal issues as decisions about concrete proposals or program details. Again, incrementalism is logical. For example:

The new principal stockholder in a mechanical equipment company wanted the company to grow relatively rapidly by selective acquisitions. One of the stockholder's board representatives prepared a detailed outline containing proposed areas for growth and diversification. Some other board members—based on limited experience—immediately took a rigid stance against one specific proposal, i.e. acquisitions in "service areas" supporting the company's line. Little progress could be made until the principal stockholder's representatives went back and sold the board on an idea they could all agree to, i.e. growth through acquisition. As the board becomes more comfortable with this broad concept, the principal stockholder's representatives still hope to bring in some "service company" candidates and allay their fellow directors' fears in terms of a specific example.

Identity and Élan

Broad goals can create identity and élan. Effective organizational goals satisfy a basic human need. They enable people to develop an identity larger than themselves, to participate in greater challenges, to have influence or seek rewards they could not achieve alone. Interestingly enough, many employees can better identify with broad goals like being "the best" or "the first" in an area than they can with more specific numerical goals. As the chief executive of a major consumer products company said:

We have slowly discovered that our most effective goal is *to be best* at certain things. We now try to get our people to help us work out what these should be, how to define *best* objectively, and how to *become best* in our selected spheres. You would be surprised how motivating that can be.

Most companies devote great attention to measurable output goals—like size, productivity, profits, costs, or returns—that lack charisma and provide no special identity for their people. Yet they often fail to achieve these goals precisely because their people do not identify sufficiently with the company. To forge a common bond among individuals with widely diverse personal values, expectations, and capacities, such numerical goals must be teamed with goals that satisfy people's more basic psychological needs: to produce something worthwhile, to help others, to obtain recognition, to be free or innovative, to achieve security, to beat an opponent, or to earn community respect. While such organizational goals must be general enough to achieve widespread support, they must also clearly delineate what distinguishes "us" (the identity group) from "them" (all others).

To improve their competitive postures, executives often consciously define the "uniqueness" or "niche" of their company's products, processes, technologies, services, or markets. More thoughtful top managers also carefully analyze whether one strategic goal or another will better at-

tract the skilled people and personal commitments they want. These people's talent and dedication then become the central strengths upon which the organization's success is built. An IBM salesman, a Bell Labs researcher, a *New York Times* stringer, or a Steuben glassblower all enjoy a special élan—as do millions of others whose organizations achieve a unique identity. This élan provides a special psychic compensation for the people involved, and symbiotically it becomes their organization's most priceless asset. More often than not such élan develops around broad conceptual goals, rather than precise mathematical targets.

WHEN SHOULD GOALS BE SPECIFIC?

Contrary to conventional wisdom, relatively few strategic goals need to be mathematically precise. Properly derived, those few can provide essential focal points and stimuli for an organization. However, they should be generated with care and used with balance.

Precipitating Action

By making selected goals explicit at the proper moment, managers can create a challenge, precipitate desired discussions or analyses, or crystallize defined thrusts. For example:

The president of a major packaging company wanted to move his organization in new directions. He first unleased a series of management, staff, and consulting studies to help define the company's weaknesses and major opportunities for improvement. These were circulated as "white papers" for discussion by his top management team. After a while consensus began to emerge on critical issues and options. The president began to reinforce one: "the need to work existing assets much harder." In further discussions his organization crystallized this concept into a specific target return on net assets—vastly higher than the current return—as a principal goal for 1981. This goal triggered the shutdown of excess facilities, a new focus on profitability rather than volume, and a profit-centered decentralization of the whole organization.

Under these circumstances, after building consensus around a broad goal, the top executive may merely approve its specific manifestation. Although the goal is a challenge, his own organization has recommended it. The executive knows that it is feasible, and key people understand and support the goal. The time horizon is sufficiently distant to allow for alternative approaches which will insure its achievement.

Major Transitions

Specific new goals can also help signal a major change from the past. Properly developed, they can challenge lower levels to propose specific solutions, yet not unduly constrain their approaches. To be effective they must build on some accepted values in the organization and leave time enough for proposed new programs to reach fruition. For example:

After much discussion, an aerospace company's top management established the goal of moving 50 percent into nongovernment business within a decade. This started a furor of creative proposals. Research put forward new technical concepts. Each division proposed how it could best realign its own business. Corporate staff units investigated industries and specific companies for acquisitions. The administrative vice president recommended a new control system to handle diversification. Revised banking relations were proposed. And so on. From all these thrusts top management slowly chose its desired pattern of internal vs. external growth, market sectors, organizational form, and financial structure. Throughout, lower levels felt their ideas were appreciated, and they identified with changes made.

After a prolonged disaster or a major trauma, an organization often needs distinct and clear new goals. Typically, these must combine a broad definition of longer-term success and some specific, achievable, short-term goals to build confidence. Without visible intermediate goals, people can become frustrated and give up on the ultimate challenge.

Only a Few

At any given moment, an executive can push only a few specific new goals, giving them the attention and force they need to take hold. Fortunately, a top executive rarely needs to press more than a few significant changes simultaneously. In fact, the essence of strategy is to identify this small number of truly essential thrusts or concepts and to consciously marshal the organization's resources and capabilities toward them. Then—to capture the organization's attention—the executive must consistently reinforce these strategic goals through his statements, his decision patterns, and his personnel assignments. He must be willing to put his credibility on the line and use the power and sanctions of his office to achieve them. Still, the typical organization's ongoing momentum and resource commitments will allow it to absorb only a few major changes at once.

Two examples illustrate the complex interactions that lead to success or failure when setting specific goals at the top level:

In 1969, RCA's chairman, Robert Sarnoff, initiated several major new thrusts simultaneously. While repositioning RCA in its traditional electronics-communications markets, he actively diversified the company through acquisitions. At the same time he also strove: (1) to build RCA's computer activities into an effective direct competitor of IBM, (2) to move the company's technological efforts from research toward applications, and (3) to strengthen the company's lagging marketing capabilities. He implemented much of this through an enlarged central corporate staff. It was difficult for the organization to absorb so much top-level-initiated change at once. Various aspects of the program met intense resistance from existing divisions. The computer venture failed, and Mr. Sarnoff's credibility with the organization became strained to the breaking point.

By contrast, shortly after Philip Hofmann became chairman of Johnson and Johnson, he announced a specific new goal of $1 billion in sales (with a 15 percent after tax return on investment) before his retirement some seven years later. Annual sales were then approximately $350 million. Though the challenge was startling in scale, it built upon an established growth ethnic in the company, and it did not constrain potential solutions. Instead it simulated each division to define how it could best respond, thus maintaining the company's intended decentralization. It also allowed sufficient time for managers to propose, initiate, and carry out their new programs. Performance ultimately surpassed the goal by a comfortable margin.

At some point, of course, planning processes must refine goals into specific operational targets. As the examples of successful goal setting illustrate, this is best achieved through incremental, iterative processes which intimately involve those who have to implement the proposed strategic thrusts.

ARE EFFECTIVE GOALS SO IMPORTANT?

All of the concepts above help insure that strategic goals are set: (1) at the right time, (2) with maximum input from those who have the most specific knowledge, and (3) with the genuine commitment of those who must achieve results. Why should managers take such care in developing and expressing organizational goals? Effective strategic goals do more than provide a basis for direction setting and per-

formance measurement. They are essential to establishing and maintaining freedom, morale, and timely problem sensing in an enterprise. The benefits of effective goal setting are greatest when people throughout the organization genuinely internalize the goals and "make them their own."

Freedom with Control

If people share common purposes, they can self-direct their actions with minimum coordination from executive or staff groups. This is especially critical for creative groups like research, advertising, or strategic planning. Without such goal congruence, control of these activities is impossible. No amount of ex post facto performance measurement can insure that creative people imaginatively identify proper problems, generate imaginative alternatives, or invent new or responsive solutions. Such actions must be stimulated before the fact by ensuring that well-selected people understand and internalize goals.

Morale

Morale is a goal-oriented phenomenon. In a "high morale" organization people intensely share common performance goals. They ignore internal irritations and adapt rapidly to external stimuli which help or hinder goal accomplishment. Entrepreneurial organizations, project teams on urgent tasks, dedicated medical groups, or even whole societies (like Israel or Japan) exhibit these characteristics. A specific industrial example suggests how powerful the symbiotic effect of a stimulating goal and talented people can be:

From 1970–76 tiny KMS Industries supported the world's most advanced laser fusion program for commercial energy production. As one executive said, "I don't know any of us who didn't agree that this was the most important task in the world. We thought we could lick the fight. If successful, we would have a new basis for creating energy, hydrogen, and hydrocarbons. It would make the United States and other nations independent of world energy markets. People on the fusion program had extremely high morale. They would work all night. They were thoroughly committed." On May 1, 1974—despite much larger AEC and Russian expenditures in the field—a KMS team achieved the world's first "unambiguous" release of neutrons from laser fusion.

A contrasting example makes the opposite point:

The dominantly shared goal of many a government (or staff) department is the preservation of its members' positions and budgets. Lacking shared—or often even understood—performance goals, such organizations become "hotbeds of inertia." They focus extraordinary energies on minor internal irritants. When disturbed by external stimuli they operate with awesome tenacity to reestablish accepted interpersonal and political equilibria—even to the point of negating their own output and jeopardizing their continuation.

Often managers spend enormous time trying to ease or resolve the interpersonal tensions in such organizations, but they accomplish little until they can get people to accept a new sense of common purpose.

Problem Sensing

Finally, goals help define problems. Organizations without a strong sense of broad purposes can precipitate their own demise by ignoring major problems or overlooking alternatives. Some companies define their services, concepts, and goals with such limited vision that they screen out major opportunities. Others have elaborately worked out goal statements covering broad issues, but their control and reward systems reinforce—and cause people to internalize—only a few. When people do not internalize an adequate range of goals, the consequences can be extremely costly.

In the late 1960s many conglomerates proudly concentrated on "managing business as a financial enterprise." Their control and reward systems focused so much attention on continuously improving short-term financial performance that their managers often screened out other important issues as "nonproblems." This led them to undercut research and technology, product and personnel development, plant investments, international relations, and perhaps even ethics to an extent that sometimes jeopardized their companies' very viability.

Recently, the chairman of a multibillion dollar diversified company publicly decried the $35 million his divisions would expend on depollution measures. It was clear that he perceived "environmentalism" only as a threat. Yet one division of his company (auto exhaust systems) was likely to sell an additional $600+ million of its product annually—with corresponding profits—because of the same environmental standards he resisted as "a total loss to the company."

WILL CONVENTIONAL PROCESSES WORK?

If goals are to stimulate freedom with control, high morale, and creative problem solving, people throughout the organization must understand and actively identify with them. Usually this requires the genuine participation of many individuals in setting and modifying the goals. Yet the manager must not lose control over this vital process. He must carefully blend consultation, participation, delegation, and guidance to achieve his purposes. How can he manage this complex art?

Bottom Up

The philosophers' ideal is to arrive at goal consensus through democratic discussion or through "bottom up" proposals. These views often prevail within small-company, Japanese, or "Theory Y" managements, and they clearly have merit for some organizations.

However, such approaches are very time consuming and can prove to be frustrating, wasteful, or even divisive. Opaque committee discussions can go on endlessly and still leave individuals with different views of what goals were agreed on. People may expend extraordinary time and energy on proposals that management later rejects as "irrelevant." They feel angry or manipulated when "their" carefully prepared proposals or goals are overruled for other organizational purposes only fully appreciated from on high.

Unwitting Bureaucracy

Managers of larger enterprises rarely feel they can afford a purist approach to democratic goal setting. At the same time, they sense the shortcomings of goals announced from above. Consequently, a pragmatic compromise emerges. Top managers often provide a framework of broad goals for their subordinate units. They then encourage lower-level managers to make proposals which respond to these goals through planning, budgetary, and ad hoc processes. Before the proposals reach final approval stages, a series of staff interventions, personal discussions, and intermediate reviews tune them toward what various people think top management wants and will accept.

This process brings a kind of "collective wisdom" to bear. There is some personal involvement at all levels. But often a bland, committee-like consensus emerges. This process works moderately well for routine modifications of existing thrusts, but it discourages significant changes in organizational goals. Thus, unwittingly, most large enterprises become conservatively bureaucratized. They continue existing momenta

and overlook major external changes or new opportunities.

HOW DO MANAGEMENTS EVOLVE EFFECTIVE STRATEGIC GOALS?

Dramatic new strategic goal-sets rarely emerge full blown from individual "bottom up proposals" or from comprehensive "corporate strategic planning." Instead a series of individual, logical, perhaps somewhat disruptive decisions interact to create a new structure and cohesion for the company. Top managers create a new consensus through a continuous, evolving, incremental, and often highly political process that has no precise beginning or end. A well-documented example—one with which many readers will be familiar—illustrates important dimensions of this "logical incremental" approach to strategic goal setting.

IBM's strategic goal of "Introducing its 360 computers simultaneously as a single line with compatibility, standard interface, business and scientific capability, hybrid circuitry, and the capacity to open new markets" probably started in 1959 when T. Vincent Learson became head of the Data Systems and General Products divisions. The divisions' product lines had begun to overlap and proliferate, causing software, cost, and organizational problems. Top managers sensed this, but no clear solutions were at hand.

In 1960–61 various specific decisions began to eliminate alternatives and define key elements of the new goal. Proposals for two new computers. "Scamp" and the 8000 series, were killed to avoid further proliferation. In mid-1961 Learson and a subordinate. Bob O. Evans, arrived at a broad concept "to blanket the market with a single product line," and they initiated exploratory studies on a new product line called simply "NPL." During 1961 a special Logic Committee recommended that IBM use "hybrid circuitry"—rather than integrated circuits—in any major new line. In late 1961 NPL was foundering. Learson and chairman Watson started a "series of dialogues on strategy" with division heads, but no clear concept emerged. Consequently, they formed the SPREAD committee of key executives to hammer out basic concepts for a new line. In January 1962, the committee reported and top management approved its recommended concepts for a new integrative product line, now worked out in some detail. Broad top management support and a genuine organization momentum were building behind the new concept.

In 1962 development began in earnest, and IBM's board approved a $100-million manufacturing facility for hybrid circuits. Still, technical difficulties and differences in viewpoint persisted. In late 1962 a special programming meeting was held at Stowe to discuss software development, but major programming problems remained unresolved. In 1963 various groups openly resisted the new line. The opposition was broken up or removed. In December 1963, **Honeywell** precipitated action by announcing a **strong** competitor for IBM's successful 1401 **computer.** Shortly thereafter, in January 1964, **Learson** conducted a performance "shoot out" **between** the 360/30 and the 1401. The 360/30 **was judge**d good enough to go ahead. Final **pricing,** marketing, and production studies were now made. In March 1964, top management approved the line in a "final risk assessment session" at Yorktown. And on April 7, 1964, Watson announced the 360 line. The decision now appeared irrevocable.

But in 1965 and later, new time-sharing features, smaller and larger computers, and peripheral equipment units were announced or "decommitted." IBM raised $361 million of new equity in 1965 to support the line—ultimately investing some $4.5 billion in the 360. Further changes occurred in the line and its supporting hardware and software. Finally, well into the 1970s, the 360 series provided IBM's essential strategic strength, its massive installed computer base. The decision and its impact extended over some 15 years.

The pattern is common. At first there are simply too many unknowns to specify a cohesive set of new directions for the enterprise. More information is needed. Technical problems must be solved to determine feasibilities. Investments must be made in programs with long lead times. Trends in the market place must crystallize into sufficiently concrete demands or competitive responses to justify risk taking. Various resource bases must be acquired or developed. Different groups' psychological commitments must be diverted from ongoing thrusts toward a new consensus. Lead times for all these events are different. Yet logic dictates that final resource commitments be made as late as possible consistent with the information available—hence incrementalism.

To reshape an organization's accepted culture significantly, an executive must often overcome some potent psychological/political forces. His success will depend on the very group whose perceptions he may want to change. If he moves too precipitously, he can undermine essential strengths of his organization. All too easily he can alienate his people, lose personal credibility, and destroy the power base his future depends on. Unless a crisis intervenes, he cannot change the organization's ethos abruptly. Instead he usually must build commitment—and his own political support—incrementally around specific issues or proposals. The real art is to thoughtfully blend these thrusts together, as opportunities permit, into patterns which slowly create a new logical cohesion.

Changing strategic goals typically involves managing a complex chain of interacting events and forces over a period of years. How do successful managers approach this challenge?

Managing the Incremental Process

For the reasons cited above, a kind of "logical incrementalism" usually dominates strategic goal setting. This process is purposeful, politically astute, and effective. It starts with needs that may only be vaguely sensed at first and incrementally builds the organization's awareness, support, and eventual commitment around new goals. The stages in this process—though not always the same—commonly recur. These are set forth below. The management techniques used at each stage—also outlined below—are not quite the textbook variety. But seeing these in the context of the total process helps explain their wide use and notable effectiveness. It also explains some of the seeming anomalies and real frustrations of management in large organizations. Managers at all levels should understand how this process operates and how they can best fit into and manage their roles in it.

Sensing Needs Top executives very often sense needs for strategic change in quite vague or undefined terms, like IBM's "organizational overlap" or "too much proliferation." Early signals may come from almost anywhere, and they may initially be quite indistinct. Long lead times are often needed to make significant changes. Consequently, effective executives —like Mr. Learson—consciously seek multiple contact points with managers, workers, customers, suppliers, technologists, outside professional and government groups, and so on. They purposely short-circuit all the careful screens an organization builds to "tell the top only what it wants to hear" and thus delay important strategic signals. They constantly move around, show up at unexpected spots, probe, and listen.

Building Awareness The next step is very often to commission study groups, staff, or consultants to illuminate problems, options, contingencies, or opportunities posed by a sensed need. These studies sometimes lead to specific incremental decisions. More often they merely generate broadened or intensified perceptions of fu-

ture potentials. At this stage managers may need to offset the frustration of study groups, who frequently feel they have "failed" because their studies do not precipitate direct action. But the organization is not yet ready for a decision. Key players are not yet comfortable enough with issues, variables, and options to take a risk. Building awareness, concern, and a "comfort factor" of knowledge about a situation is a vital early link in the practical politics of change.

Broadening Support This stage usually involves much unstructured discussion and probing of positions. Earlier studies may provide data or the excuse for these discussions—as in the case of the "strategic dialogues" at IBM. At this stage top executives may actively avoid decisions, other than agreeing to explore options. Instead, they may encourage other key players to see opportunities in a new light, define areas of indifference or concern, and identify potential opponents and points of contention. Whenever possible, the guiding executive lets others suggest new thrusts and maintains the originator's identity with the idea. He encourages concepts he favors, lets undesired or weakly supported options die, and establishes hurdles or tests for strongly supported ideas he may not agree with, but does not want to oppose openly. His main purpose is to begin constructive movement without threatening major power centers. Typically, goals remain broad and unrefined.

Creating Pockets of Commitment Exploratory projects—like NPL—may be needed to create necessary skills or technologies, test options, or build commitment deep within the organization. Initially, projects may be small and ad hoc, rarely forming a comprehensive program. The guiding executive may shun identity with specific projects to avoid escalating attention to one too quickly or losing credibility if it fails. To keep a low profile he may encourage, discourage, or kill thrusts through subordinates, rather than directly. He must now keep his options open, control premature momentum, and select the right moment to meld several successful thrusts into a broader program or concept. His timing is often highly opportunistic. A crisis, a rash of reassignments, a reorganization, or a key appointment may allow him to focus attention on particular goals, add momentum to some, or perhaps quietly phase out others.

Crystallizing a Developing Focus This is another step. Ad hoc committees—like the SPREAD committee—are a favorite tool for this. By selecting the committee's membership, charter, and timing, the guiding executive can influence its direction. A committee can be balanced to educate, evaluate, or neutralize opponents. It can genuinely develop new options, or it can be focused narrowly to build momentum. Attention to the committee's dynamics is essential. It can broaden support and increase commitment significantly for new goals. Or it can generate organized opposition—and a real trauma—should top management later overrule its strong recommendations.

At crucial junctures the guiding executive may crystallize an emerging consensus by hammering out a few broad goals with his immediate colleagues and stating some as trial concepts for a wider group to discuss. He may even negotiate specific aspects with individual executives. Finally, when sufficient congruence exists or the timing is right, the goal begins to appear in his public statements, guidelines for divisions, and other appropriate places.

Obtaining Real Commitment If possible, the executive tries to make some individual(s) explicitly accountable for the goal. But he often wants more than mere accountability—he wants real commitment. A major thrust, concept, product, or problem solution frequently needs the nurtur-

ing hand of someone who genuinely identifies with it and whose future depends on its success. In such cases, the executive may wait for a "champion" to appear before he commits resources, but he may assign less dramatic goals as specific missions for ongoing groups. Budgets, programs, proposals, controls, and reward systems must now reflect the new goal, whether or not it is quantitatively measurable. The guiding executive sees to it that recruiting and staffing plans align with the new goal and, when the situation permits, reassigns its supporters and persistent opponents into appropriate spots.

Continuing Dynamics All of the above may take years to effect—as it did in IBM's case. Over this time horizon, the process is rarely completely orderly, rational, or consistent. Instead the executive responds opportunistically to new threats, crises, and proposals. The decision process constantly molds and modifies his own concerns and concepts. Old crusades become the new conventional wisdom; and over time, totally new issues emerge.

Once the organization arrives at its new consensus, the executive must move to ensure that this does not become inflexible. In trying to build commitment to a new concept, one often surrounds himself with people who see the world the same way. Such people can rapidly become systematic screens against other views. Hence, the effective executive now purposely continues the change process with new faces and stimuli at the top. He consciously begins to erode the very strategic goals he has just created—a very difficult psychological task.

CONCLUSION

Establishing strategic goals for complex organizations is a delicate art, requiring a subtle balance of vision, entrepreneurship, and politics. At the center of the art one finds consciously managed processes of "broad goal setting" and "logical incrementalism." Management styles vary, but effective top executives in larger enterprises typically state a few broad goals themselves, encourage their organizations to propose others, and allow still others to emerge from informal processes. They eschew the gimmickry of simplistic "formal planning" or "MBO" approaches for setting their major goals. Instead they tend to develop such goals through very complicated, largely political, consensus-building processes that are outside the structure of most formal management systems and frequently have no precise beginning or end.

Those who understand these processes can contribute more effectively, whatever their position in the organization. Those who wish to make major changes in organizations should certainly comprehend these processes, their rationale, and their implications. Those who ignore them may find the costs very high.

REFERENCES

Bower, J. L. "Planning within the Firm." *American Economic Review,* May 1970.

Bowman, E. H. "Epistemology, Corporate Strategy, and Academe." *Sloan Management Review,* Winter 1974, pp. 35–50.

Cohen, K. J., and Cyert, R. M. "Strategy, Formulation, Implementation, and Monitoring." *Journal of Business,* July 1973.

Frank, A. G. "Goal Ambiguity and Conflicting Standards." *Human Organization,* Winter 1958.

Guth, W. D. "Formulating Organizational Objectives and Strategy: A Systematic Approach." *Journal of Business Policy,* Autumn 1971.

Hall, W. K. "Strategic Planning Models: Are Top Managers Really Finding Them Useful?" *Journal of Business Policy,* Winter 1972/1973, pp. 33–42.

Hunger, J., and Stern, C. "An Assessment of the Functionality of the Superordinate Goal in Reducing Conflict." *Academy of Management Journal,* December 1976.

Latham, G. P., and Yukl, G. A. "Review of Research on the Application of Goal Setting in Organizations." *Academy of Management Journal,* December 1975.

Lindblom, C. E. "The Science of 'Muddling Through.'" *Public Administration Review,* Spring 1959.

Mintzberg, H. "Strategy-Making in Three Modes." *California Management Review,* Winter 1973.

Pfiffner, J. M. "Administrative Rationality." *Public Administration Review,* 1960, pp. 125–32.

Simon, H. A. "On the Concept of Organization Goal." *Administrative Science Quarterly,* June 1964.

Soelberg, P. O. "Unprogrammed Decision Making." *Industrial Management Review,* Spring 1967, pp. 19–29.

Tosi, H. L.; Rizzo, J. R.; and Carroll, S. J. "Setting Goals in Management by Objectives." *California Management Review,* Summer 1970, pp. 70–78.

Vancil, R. F. "Strategy Formulation in Complex Organizations." *Sloan Management Review,* Winter 1976, pp. 1–18.

Traditionally, historical accounting data has served as source information for the decision making process in business. More recently, the need to provide information in a timely manner and structured to facilitate day-to-day operational decision making has been of increasing concern. Much criticism has been directed toward accountants for their inability to provide relevant and timely data, presented in a manner which (1) supports the operational decision-making process and (2) is a useful tool for measurement and control of the business.

The purpose of this article is not to defend the capability of the accountant, but to identify problem areas related to data preparation, data gathering, and data reporting for all levels of management and to recommend a solution.

The conclusions reached result from the writer's experience as an accountant who strongly felt an obligation to serve the informational needs of all levels of management.

As controller, it was my responsibility to direct accounting, planning, and budgeting activities of the company, to analyze operating results as compared to plan and budget, and to cause to have prepared the related comments and reports. Nothing unusual in any of this—in fact, it is a classic description in broad terms of what is expected of the controller and his staff in many companies.

In evaluating our staff, we felt that we had an excellent group of management accountants who were extremely knowledgeable, hard working, loyal, and willing to serve management.

Why, then, were we failing to meet the requirements of operating management for information so vital for the day-to-day decision making and control of the business?

We were aware that we were not performing satisfactorily in this area by sev-

READING 3–6

Planning & Control and Accounting: Divide and Conquer*

LOUIS N. REDMAN

eral indicators: (1) we were not invited into operating management meetings—an indication that our input was not felt necessary; (2) we were called "string savers" and "pencil pushers" and similar "endearing" terms; (3) we could see others hired to do analytical work within the operations, such as industrial engineers or methods engineers, which could have been performed better by the management accountant with his complete knowledge of the business; and (4) at times, we were told so by the president and the managers themselves.

How was it, then, that a staff as capable as ours was failing in one of its major areas of responsibility—that of providing management information which served as the basis for day-to-day decision making and control in our operations?

Of greater concern was the question that if we recognized that we were not

---

* *Managerial Planning*, vol. 25, no. 1 (July–August 1976), pp. 15–17.

meeting the challenge, why didn't we take the necessary steps to correct the situation?

Any good planner and analyst knows that before a situation can be resolved, and corrective action taken, the causes must be clearly defined. It was in identifying the causes as we saw them behind our inability to perform our assigned task that we recognized how difficult the corrective steps were and, therefore, why corrective action had not been taken.

To begin with, we concluded that the work load placed on our staff had increased in volume and content, as demand for more diversified and timely information came from all levels of management. The advent of the computer provided a high powered tool capable of producing a great wealth of management information which, if it was to be useful, had to be structured and managed. This represented an additional burden to the staff. In addition, the pressure of competition and the increase in managerial skill accompanying technological advances in our business added further to the demand for a more sophisticated information system.

No longer could financial data such as operating statements, balance sheets, and related statistics and ratios provide the source for decision making at all management levels. This historical information provides a record of how effective the management process has been as related to expectations and, for the most part, is timely enough for decisions to be made at the policy-making level of the company. In addition, a reporting system is required which is expressed in terms understood by operating management, measures the effects of the decision-making process on a day-to-day basis, and which is used to project operating results from a given set of operating conditions.

The first of these data systems relates to the accounting activity and the latter to planning and control.

The responsibility for data development, recording, reporting, and analyzing has traditionally been assigned to the finance or accounting group in most companies. As demand for management information increased, so did the work load for the accountant. The question wasn't asked as to logic of this group providing the required data. There was little or no attempt to identify skills required in the planning and control function as related to the traditional accountant's role. Some schools of thought concluded that a new designation for the accountant to indicate a higher degree of involvement in the development and use of operating data would somehow provide a solution—so, we now have management accountants.

Our experience indicated, in spite of the dedicated staff of management accountants we had, that we failed to respond to information requests from operating management in a satisfactory manner.

The analysis of our problem revealed that the inability of our staff to meet requirements of management was far more complex than one of background, education, or capability. Determined to do something about it, we examined, in addition to skills and capabilities, our organizational structure and reached the following conclusions:

The result is that operating management is often faced with a delay in response to its request for information. It should be of no surprise that, irrespective of staff skills or capabilities, operating management is often critical of the accounting department. From the standpoint of service and of providing information as needed when needed, the priorities were arranged in reverse order. It is of extreme importance that information be made available to operating management that is timely and relevant to facilitate day-to-day decision making and to identify profit and performance improvement opportunities as they occur.

In recognition of the difference in skill requirements and the functional differ-ence between accounting and planning and control, the problem is identified. It is logical to conclude that the accounting function should be divided into two func-tions: (1) accounting and financial control and (2) planning and operational control.

EXHIBIT 1

1. The accounting responsibility in the company, simply stated, was to:
   (a) Process, accumulate, summarize, record, report, analyze, and interpret data.
   (b) Monitor operations for compliance with company policies, pro-cedures, and programs.

2. That this responsibility logically could break down into two separate and distinct skill categories in respect to 1 (9).

A. *Process, Accumulate, Summarize, Record, and Report*	B. *Analyze, Interpret, Record, and Report*
Technical capabilities and training in a specific area	General competence in all facets of the business
Statistically oriented	Statistically and operations oriented
Ability to communicate within this area of com-petence in terms related to specific requirements	Ability to communicate with all management levels in terms understood by each
Relates well personally to those who have sim-ilar background, train-ing, and interest	Must relate well personally with those who have varying backgrounds, training, and work interests
Performs work on a sched-uled basis as defined in es-tablished procedures	A self-starter who indentifies problems and is capable of working in an unstructured environment

3. That if we would hang the tag of accounting on "Process, Accumu-late, Summarize, Record, and Report" and planning and control on "Analyze, Interpret, Record, and Report," we could identify a functional incompatibility.

Accounting and Financial Control	*Planning and Operational Control*
Highly structured in all areas	Conceptual in nature but structural to meet financial requirements
Time-oriented	Project-oriented
Required	Management option
Oriented toward executive management requirements and policy decision making	Oriented toward operational management requirements and operating decisions making

4. That when the assignment for providing all management information rests with one group, priority would be given to required informa-tion which is subject to time constraints and fulfills executive man-agement requirements.

Accounting and financial control is to be a management function, self-contained, which reports to the chief financial officer on a line basis. *Planning and operational control* is to be a function of management, this function to report directly to the management it serves with guidance provided on a functional basis from the chief planning officer of the company to assure uniformity in data preparation, recording, and reporting.

The benefits to be gained by this separation of responsibility are expected to be:

1. The staff will be more responsive to the requirements of the management effort it serves.
2. Management capabilities will be strengthened in a historically weak area.
3. Quality and timing in providing required information will be improved.
4. Individual skills can be utilized more fully.
5. A continuous and coordinated planning effort will be possible.
6. Development of the Management Information System will be expedited.

The extent to which costs are increased due to this organization realignment depends upon the degree to which the staff has been utilized, staff size, and the sophistication of the information system. In any event, the economics should be favorable in light of the benefits which can be achieved.

The physical division of the work load into two areas of responsibility will be difficult to accomplish and the details will vary from company to company. It is well to remember that people keep unto themselves that which they like to do. Care must be taken to insure a continuity in working relationships during the transition period. In order to ascertain that data developed within each function is available to and used by the other, procedures must be carefully documented. Source data, whether financial or statistical, must be consistent at all management levels. The reports and analyses of the planning and control function must complement and be compatible with the financial reporting system. A development program must be organized and implemented which involves not only the functions concerned but the management they serve.

Without this change in organization, operational planning, analysis, and data development will either be relegated to a position of secondary importance due to the nature of the accounting function, or will become an unstructured, informal reporting system within each operation.

The information from this source is far too important as a communication tool to permit these things to happen. It is time to up-grade our data reporting systems to provide equal status to operational planning and control. Organize to provide the right climate.

Whether dealing with monkeys, rats, or human beings, it is hardly controversial to state that most organisms seek information concerning what activities are rewarded, and then seek to do (or at least pretend to do) those things, often to the virtual exclusion of activities not rewarded. The extent to which this occurs of course will depend on the perceived attractiveness of the rewards offered, but neither operant nor expectancy theorists would quarrel with the essence of this notion.

Nevertheless, numerous examples exist of reward systems that are fouled up in that behaviors which are rewarded are those which the rewarder is trying to *discourage*, while the behavior he desires is not being rewarded at all.

In an effort to understand and explain this phenomenon, this paper presents examples from society, from organizations in general, and from profit-making firms in particular. Data from a manufacturing company and information from an insurance firm are examined to demonstrate the consequences of such reward systems for the organizations involved, and possible reasons why such reward systems continue to exist are considered.

SOCIETAL EXAMPLES

Politics

Official goals are "purposely vague and general and do not indicate . . . the host of decisions that must be made among alternative ways of achieving official goals and the priority of multiple goals . . ." (8, p. 66). They usually may be relied on to offend absolutely no one, and in this sense can be considered high acceptance, low quality goals. An example might be "build better schools." Operative goals are higher in quality but lower in acceptance, since they specify where the money will come

READING 3–7

On the Folly of Rewarding A, While Hoping for B*

STEVEN KERR

from, what alternative goals will be ignored, etc.

The American citizenry supposedly wants its candidates for public office to set forth operative goals, making their proposed programs "perfectly clear," specifying sources and uses of funds, etc. However, since operative goals are lower in acceptance, and since aspirants to public office need acceptance (from at least 50.1 percent of the people), most politicians prefer to speak only of official goals, at least until after the election. They of course would agree to speak at the operative level if "punished" for not doing so. The electorate could do this by refusing to support candidates who do not speak at the operative level.

Instead, however, the American voter typically punishes (withholds support from) candidates who frankly discuss where the money will come from, rewards politicians who speak only of official goals, but hopes that candidates (despite the reward system) will discuss

* *Academy of Management Journal*, December 1975, pp. 769–83.

the issues operatively. It is academic whether it was moral for Nixon, for example, to refuse to discuss his 1968 "secret plan" to end the Vietnam war, his 1972 operative goals concerning the lifting of price controls, the reshuffling of his cabinet, etc. The point is that the reward system made such refusal rational.

It seems worth mentioning that no manuscript can adequately define what is "moral" and what is not. However, examination of costs and benefits, combined with knowledge of what motivates a particular individual, often will suffice to determine what for him is "rational."[1] If the reward system is so designed that it is irrational to be moral, this does not necessarily mean that immortality will result. But is this not asking for trouble?

War

If some oversimplification may be permitted, let it be assumed that the primary goal of the organization (Pentagon, Luftwaffe, or whatever) is to win. Let it be assumed further that the primary goal of most individuals on the front lines is to get home alive. Then there appears to be an important conflict in goals—personally rational behavior by those at the bottom will endanger goal attainment by those at the top.

But not necessarily! It depends on how the reward system is set up. The Vietnam war was indeed a study of disobedience and rebellion, with terms such as *fragging* (killing one's own commanding officer) and *search and evade* becoming part of the military vocabulary. The difference in subordinates' acceptance of authority between

World War II and Vietnam is reported to be considerable, and veterans of the Second World War often have been quoted as being outraged at the mutinous actions of many American soldiers in Vietnam.

Consider, however, some critical differences in the reward system in use during the two conflicts. What did the GI in World War II want? To go home. And when did he get to go home? When the war was won! If he disobeyed the orders to clean out the trenches and take the hills, the war would not be won and he would not go home. Furthermore, what were his chances of attaining his goal (getting home alive) if he obeyed the orders compared to his chances if he did not? What is being suggested is that the rational soldier in World War II, *whether patriotic or not*, probably found it expedient to obey.

Consider the reward system in use in Vietnam. What did the man at the bottom want? To go home. And when did he get to go home? When his tour of duty was over! This was the case *whether or not* the war was won. Furthermore, concerning the relative chance of getting home alive by obeying orders compared to the chance if they were disobeyed, it is worth noting that a mutineer in Vietnam was far more likely to be assigned rest and rehabilitation (on the assumption that fatigue was the cause) than he was to suffer any negative consequence.

In his description of the "zone of indifference," Barnard stated that "a person can and will accept a communication as authoritative only when . . . at the time of his decision, he believes it to be compatible with his personal interests as a whole" (1, p. 165). In light of the reward system used in Vietnam, would it not have been personally irrational for some orders to have been obeyed? Was not the military implementing a system which *rewarded* disobedience, while *hoping* that soldiers (despite the reward system) would obey orders?

[1] In Simon's (10, pp. 76–77) terms, a decision is "subjectively rational" if it maximizes an individual's valued outcomes so far as his knowledge permits. A decision is "personally rational" if it is oriented toward the individual's goals.

Medicine

Theoretically, a physican can make either of two types of error, and intuitively one seems as bad as the other. A doctor can pronounce a patient sick when he is actually well, thus causing him needless anxiety and expense, curtailment of enjoyable foods and activities, and even physical danger by subjecting him to needless medication and surgery. Alternately, a doctor can label a sick person well, and thus avoid treating what may be a serious, even fatal ailment. It might be natural to conclude that physicians seek to minimize both types of error.

Such a conclusion would be wrong.[2] It is estimated that numerous Americans are presently afflicted with iatrogenic (physician *caused*) illnesses (9). This occurs when the doctor is approached by someone complaining of a few stray symptoms. The doctor classifies and organizes these symptoms, gives them a name, and obligingly tells the patient what further symptoms may be expected. This information often acts as a self-fulfilling prophecy, with the result that from that day on the patient for all practical purposes is sick.

Why does this happen? Why are physicians so reluctant to sustain a type 2 error (pronouncing a sick person well) that they will tolerate many type 1 errors? Again, a look at the reward system is needed. The punishments for a type 2 error are real: guilt, embarrassment, and the threat of lawsuit and scandal. On the other hand, a type 1 error (labeling a well person sick) "is sometimes seen as sound clinical practice, indicating a healthy conservative approach to medicine" (9, p. 69). Type 1 errors also are likely to generate increased income and a stream of steady customers

who, being well in a limited physiological sense, will not embarrass the doctor by dying abruptly.

Fellow physicians and the general public therefore are really *rewarding* type 1 errors and at the same time *hoping* fervently that doctors will try not to make them.

GENERAL ORGANIZATIONAL EXAMPLES

Rehabilitation Centers and Orphanages

In terms of the prime beneficiary classification (2, p. 42), organizations such as these are supposed to exist for the "public-in-contact," that is, clients. The orphanage therefore theoretically is interested in placing as many children as possible in good homes. However, often orphanages surround themselves with so many rules concerning adoption that it is nearly impossible to pry a child out of the place. Orphanages may deny adoption unless the applicants are a married couple, both of the same religion as the child, without history of emotional or vocational instability, with a specified minimum income and a private room for the child, etc.

If the primary goal is to place children in good homes, then the rules ought to constitute means toward that goal. Goal displacement results when these "means become ends-in-themselves that displace the original goals" (2, p. 229).

To some extent these rules are required by law. But the influence of the reward system on the orphanage's management should not be ignored. Consider, for example, that the:

1. Number of children enrolled often is the most important determinant of the size of the allocated budget.

---

[2] In one study (4) of 14,867 films for signs of tuberculosis, 1,216 positive readings turned out to be clinically negative only 24 negative readings proved clinically active, a ratio of 50 to 1.

2. Number of children under the director's care also will affect the size of his staff.
3. Total organizational size will determine largely the director's prestige at the annual conventions, in the community, etc.

Therefore, to the extent that staff size, total budget, and personal prestige are valued by the orphanage's executive personnel, it becomes rational for them to make it difficult for children to be adopted. After all, who wants to be the director of the smallest orphanage in the state?

If the reward system errs in the opposite direction, paying off only for placements, extensive goal displacement again is likely to result. A common example of vocational rehabilitation in many states, for example, consists of placing someone in a job for which he has little interest and few qualifications, for two months or so, and then "rehabilitating" him again in another position. Such behavior is quite consistent with the prevailing reward system, which pays off for the number of individuals placed in any position for 60 days or more. Rehabilitation counselors also confess to competing with one another to place relatively skilled clients, sometimes ignoring persons with few skills who would be harder to place. Extensively disabled clients find that counselors often prefer to work with those whose disabilities are less severe.[3]

Universities

Society *hopes* that teachers will not neglect their teaching responsibilities but *rewards* them almost entirely for research and publications. This is most true at the large and prestigious universities. Cliches such as "good research and good teaching

go together" notwithstanding, professors often find that they must choose between teaching and research-oriented activities when allocating their time. Rewards for good teaching usually are limited to outstanding teacher awards, which are given to only a small percentage of good teachers and which usually bestow little money and fleeting prestige. Punishments for poor teaching also are rare.

Rewards for research and publications, on the other hand, and punishments for failure to accomplish these, are commonly administered by universities at which teachers are employed. Furthermore, publication-oriented resumés usually will be well received at other universities, whereas teaching credentials, harder to document and quantify, are much less transferable. Consequently it is rational for university teachers to concentrate on research, even if to the detriment of teaching and at the expense of their students.

By the same token, it is rational for students to act based upon the goal displacement which has occurred within universities concerning what they are rewarded for. If it is assumed that a primary goal of a university is to transfer knowledge from teacher to student, then grades become identifiable as a means toward that goal, serving as motivational, control, and feedback devices to expedite the knowledge transfer. Instead, however, the grades themselves have become much more important for entrance to graduate school, successful employment, tuition refunds, parental respect, etc., than the knowledge or lack of knowledge they are supposed to signify.

It therefore should come as no surprise that information has surfaced in recent years concerning fraternity files for examinations, term paper writing services, organized cheating at the service academies, and the like. Such activities constitute a personally rational response to a reward sys-

---

[3] Personal interviews conducted during 1972–73.

tem which pays off for grades rather than knowledge.

BUSINESS RELATED EXAMPLES

Ecology

Assume that the president of XYZ Corporation is confronted with the following alternatives:

1. Spend $11 million for antipollution equipment to keep from poisoning fish in the river adjacent to the plant.
2. Do nothing, in violation of the law, and assume a one in ten chance of being caught, with a resultant $1 million fine plus the necessity of buying the equipment.

Under this not unrealistic set of choices it requires no linear program to determine that XYZ Corporation can maximize its probabilities by flouting the law. Add the fact that XYZ's president is probably being rewarded (by creditors, stockholders, and other salient parts of his task environment) according to criteria totally unrelated to the number of fish poisoned, and his probable course of action becomes clear.

Evolution of Training

It is axiomatic that those who care about a firm's well-being should insist that the organization get fair value for its expenditures. Yet it is commonly known that firms seldom bother to evaluate a new GRID, MBO, job enrichment program, or whatever, to see if the company is getting its money's worth. Why? Certainly it is not because people have not pointed out that this situation exists; numerous practitioner-oriented articles are written each year to just this point.

The individuals (whether in personnel, manpower planning, or wherever) who normally would be responsible for conduct-

ing such evaluations are the same ones often charged with introducing the change effort in the first place. Having convinced top management to spend the money, they usually are quite animated afterwards in collecting arigorous vignettes and anecdotes about how successful the program was. The last thing many desire is a formal, systematic, and revealing evaluation. Although members of top management may actually hope for such systematic evaluation, their reward systems continue to *reward* ignorance in this area. And if the personnel department abdicates its responsibility, who is to step into the breach? The change agent himself? Hardly! He is likely to be too busy collecting anecdotal "evidence" of his own, for use with his next client.

Miscellaneous

Many additional examples could be cited of systems which in fact are rewarding behaviors other than those supposedly desired by the rewarder. A few of these are described briefly below.

Most coaches disdain to discuss individual accomplishments, preferring to speak of teamwork, proper attitude, and a one-for-all spirit. Usually, however, rewards are distributed according to individual performance. The college basketball player who feeds his teammates instead of shooting will not compile impressive scoring statistics and is less likely to be drafted by the pros. The ballplayer who hits to right field to advance the runners will win neither the batting nor home run titles and will be offered smaller raises. It therefore is rational for players to think of themselves first and the team second.

In business organizations where rewards are dispensed for unit performance or for individual goals achieved, without regard for overall effectiveness, similar attitudes often are observed. Under most Management by Objectives (MBO) systems, goals in areas where quantification is difficult often go un-specified. The organization, therefore, often is in a position where it *hopes* for employee effort in the areas of team building, inter-personal relations, creativity, etc., but it for-mally *rewards* none of these. In cases where promotions and raises are formally tied to MBO, the system itself contains a paradox in that it "asks employees to set challenging, risky goals, only to face smaller paychecks and possibly damaged careers if these goals are not accomplished" (5, p. 40).

It is *hoped* that administrators will pay attention to long-run costs and opportu-nities and will institute programs which will bear fruit later on. However, many organi-zational reward systems pay off for short-run sales and earnings only. Under such circumstances it is personally rational for officials to sacrifice long-term growth and profit (by selling off equipment and prop-erty, or by stifling research and develop-ment) for short-term advantages. This prob-ably is most pertinent in the public sector, with the result that many public officials are unwilling to implement programs which will not show benefits by election time.

As a final, clear-cut example of a fouled-up reward system, consider the cost-plus contract or its next kin, the allocation of next year's budget as a direct function of this year's expenditures. It probably is con-ceivable that those who award such budgets and contracts really hope for economy and prudence in spending. It is obvious, how-ever, that adopting the proverb "to him who spends shall more be given," rewards not economy, but spending itself.

An Insurance Firm

The Group Health Claims Division of a large eastern insurance company provides a rich illustration of a reward system which reinforces behaviors not desired by top management.

Attempting to measure and reward accu-racy in paying surgical claims, the firm sys-tematically keeps track of the number of returned checks and letters of complaint received from policyholders. However, un-derpayments are likely to provoke cries of outrage from the insured, while overpay-ments often are accepted in courteous si-lence. Since it often is impossible to tell from the physician's statement which of two surgical procedures, with different allowable benefits, was performed, and since writing for clarifications will interfere with other standards used by the firm concerning "per-centage of claims paid within two days of receipt," the new hire in more than one claims section is soon acquainted with the informal norm: "When in doubt, pay it out!"

The situation would be even worse were it not for the fact that other features of the firm's reward system tend to neutralize those described. For example, annual "merit" in-creases are given to all employees, in one of the following three amounts:

1. If the worker is "outstanding" (a select category, into which no more than two employees per section may be placed): 5 percent.
2. If the worker is "above average" (nor-mally all workers not "outstanding" are so rated): 4 percent.
3. If the worker commits gross acts of neg-ligence and irresponsibility for which he might be discharged in many other companies: 3 percent.

Now, since (a) the difference between the 5 percent theoretically attainable through hard work and the 4 percent attainable merely by living until the review date is small and (b) since insurance firms seldom dispense much of a salary increase in cash (rather, the work-er's insurance benefits increase, causing him to be further overinsured), many employees are rather indifferent to the possibility of obtaining the extra 1 percent reward and therefore tend to ignore the norm concerning indiscriminant payments.

However, most employees are not indifferent to the rule which states that, should absences or latenesses total three or more in any six-month period, the entire 4 or 5 percent due at the next "merit" review must be forfeited. In this sense the firm may be described as *hoping* for performance, while *rewarding* attendance. What it gets, of course, is attendance. (If the absence-lateness rule appears to the reader to be stringent, it really is not. The company counts "times" rather than "days" absent, and a ten-day absence therefore counts the same as one lasting two days. A worker in danger of accumulating a third absence within six months merely has to remain ill (away from work) during his second absence until his first absence is more than six months old. The limiting factor is that at some point his salary ceases, and his sickness benefits take over. This usually is sufficient to get the younger workers to return, but for those with 20 or more years' service, the company provides sickness benefits of 90 percent of normal salary, tax-free! Therefore . . .)

CAUSES

Extremely diverse instances of systems which reward behavior A although the rewarder apparently hopes for behavior B have been given. These are useful to illustrate the breadth and magnitude of the phenomenon, but the diversity increases the difficulty of determining commonalities and establishing causes. However, four general factors may be pertinent to an explanation of why fouled up reward systems seem to be so prevalent.

Fascination with an "Objective" Criterion

It has been mentioned elsewhere that:

Most "objective" measures of productivity are objective only in that their subjective elements are (a) determined in advance, rather than coming into play at the time of the formal evaluation, and (b) well concealed on the rating instrument itself. Thus industrial firms seeking to devise objective rating systems first decide, in an arbitrary manner, what dimensions are to be rated, . . . usually including some items having little to do with organizational effectiveness while excluding others that do. Only then does Personnel Division churn out official-looking documents on which all dimensions chosen to be rated are assigned point values, categories, or whatever (6, p. 92).

Nonetheless, many individuals seek to establish simple, quantifiable standards against which to measure and reward performance. Such efforts may be successful in highly predictable areas within an organization, but are likely to cause goal displacement when applied anywhere else. Overconcern with attendance and lateness in the insurance firm and with number of people placed in the vocational rehabilitation division may have been largely responsible for the problems described in those organizations.

Overemphasis on Highly Visible Behaviors

Difficulties often stem from the fact that parts of the task are highly visible while other parts are not. For example, publications are easier to demonstrate than teaching, and scoring baskets and hitting home runs are more readily observable than feeding teammates and advancing base runners. Similarly, the adverse consequences of pronouncing a sick person well are more visible than those sustained by labeling a well person sick. Team building and creativity are other examples of behaviors which may not be rewarded simply because they are hard to observe.

Hypocrisy

In some of the instances described the rewarder may have been getting the desired behavior, notwithstanding claims that the behavior was not desired. This may be true, for example, of management's attitude toward apple-polishing in the manufacturing firm (a behavior which subordinates felt was rewarded, despite management's avowed dislike of the practice). This also may explain politicians' unwillingness to revise the penalties for disobedience of ecology laws and the failure of top management to devise reward systems which would cause systematic evaluation of training and development programs.

Emphasis on Morality or Equity Rather than Efficiency

Sometimes consideration of other factors prevents the establishment of a system which rewards behaviors desired by the rewarder. The felt obligation of many Americans to vote for one candidate or another, for example, may impair their ability to withhold support from politicians who refuse to discuss the issues. Similarly, the concern for spreading the risks and costs of wartime military service may outweigh the advantage to be obtained by commiting personnel to combat until the war is over.

It should be noted that only with respect to the first two causes are reward systems really paying off for other than desired behaviors. In the case of the third and fourth causes the system *is* rewarding behaviors desired by the rewarder, and the systems are fouled up only from the standpoints of those who believe the rewarder's public statements (cause 3), or those who seek to maximize efficiency rather than other outcomes (cause 4).

CONCLUSIONS

Modern organization theory requires a recognition that the members of organizations and society possess divergent goals and motives. It therefore is unlikely that managers and their subordinates will seek the same outcomes. Three possible remedies for this potential problem are suggested.

Selection

It is theoretically possible for organizations to employ only those individuals whose goals and motives are wholly consonant with those of management. In such cases the same behaviors judged by subordinates to be rational would be perceived by management as desirable. State-of-the-art reviews of selection techniques, however, provide scant grounds for hope that such an approach would be successful (for example, see 12).

Training

Another theoretical alternative is for the organization to admit those employees whose goals are not consonant with those of management and then, through training, socialization, or whatever, alter employee goals to make them consonant. However, research on the effectiveness of such training programs, though limited, provides further grounds for pessimism (for example, see 3).

Altering the Reward System

What would have been the result if:

1. Nixon had been assured by his advisors that he could not win reelection except by discussing the issues in detail?
2. Physicians' conduct was subjected to regular examination by review boards for type 1 errors (calling healthy people ill) and to penalties (fines, censure, etc.) for errors of either type?
3. The President of XYZ Corporation had to choose between (a) spending $11 million dollars for antipollution equip-

ment, and (b) incurring a 50–50 chance of going to jail for five years?

Managers who complain that their workers are not motivated might do well to consider the possibility that they have installed reward systems which are paying off for behaviors other than those they are seeking. This, in part, is what happened in Vietnam, and this is what regularly frustrates societal efforts to bring about honest politicians, civic-minded managers, etc. This certainly is what happened in the insurance company.

A first step for such managers might be to find out what behaviors currently are being rewarded. Perhaps an instrument similar to that used in the manufacturing firm could be useful for this purpose. Chances are excellent that these managers will be surprised by what they find—that their firms are not rewarding what they assume they are. In fact, such undesirable behavior by organizational members as they have observed may be explained largely by the reward systems in use.

This is not to say that all organizational behavior is determined by formal rewards and punishments. Certainly it is true that in the absence of formal reinforcement some soldiers will be patriotic, some presidents will be ecology minded, and some orphanage directors will care about children. The point, however, is that in such cases the rewarder is not *causing* the behaviors desired but is only a fortunate bystander. For an organization to *act* upon its members, the formal reward system should positively reinforce desired behaviors, not constitute an obstacle to be overcome.

It might be wise to underscore the obvious fact that there is nothing really new in what has been said. In both theory and practice these matters have been mentioned before. Thus in many states Good Samaritan laws have been installed to protect doctors who stop to assist a stricken motorist. In states without such laws it is commonplace for doctors to refuse to stop, for fear of involvement in a subsequent lawsuit. In college basketball additional penalties have been instituted against players who foul their opponents deliberately. It has long been argued by Milton Friedman and others that penalties should be altered so as to make it irrational to disobey the ecology laws, and so on.

By altering the reward system the organization escapes the necessity of selecting only desirable people or of trying to alter undesirable ones. In Skinnerian terms (as described in 11, p. 704), "As for responsibility and goodness—as commonly defined —no one . . . would want or need them. They refer to a man's behaving well despite the absence of positive reinforcement that is obviously sufficient to explain it. Where such reinforcement exists, 'no one needs goodness.' "

REFERENCES

1. Barnard, Chester I. *The Functions of the Executive* (Cambridge, Mass.: Harvard University Press, 1964).
2. Blau, Peter M., and W. Richard Scott. *Formal Organizations* (San Francisco: Chandler, 1962).
3. Fiedler, Fred E. "Predicting the Effects of Leadership Training and Experience from the Contingency Model," *Journal of Applied Psychology*, vol. 56 (1972), 114–19.
4. Garland, L. H. "Studies of the Accuracy of Diagnostic Procedures," *American Journal of Roentgenological, Radium Therapy, Nuclear Medicine*, vol. 82 (1959), 25–38.
5. Kerr, Steven. "Some Modifications in MBO as an OD Strategy," *Academy of Management Proceedings*, 1973, pp. 39–42.
6. Kerr, Steven. "What Price Objectivity?" *American Sociologist*, vol. 8 (1973), 92–93.
7. Litwin, G. H., and R. A. Stringer, Jr. *Motivation and Organizational Climate* (Boston: Harvard University Press, 1968).
8. Perrow, Charles. "The Analysis of Goals in Complex Organizations," in A. Etzioni (ed.), *Readings on Modern Organizations* (Englewood Cliffs, N. J.: Prentice-Hall, 1969).
9. Scheff, Thomas J. "Decision Rules, Types of Error, and Their Consequences in Medical

Diagnosis," in F. Massarik and P. Ratoosh (eds.), *Mathematical Explorations in Behavioral Science* (Homewood, Ill.: Irwin, 1965).

10. Simon, Herbert A. *Administrative Behavior* (New York: Free Press, 1957).

11. Swanson, G. E. "Review Symposium: Beyond Freedom and Dignity," *American Journal of Sociology*, vol. 78 (1972), 702–5.

12. Webster, E. *Decision Making in the Employment Interview* (Montreal: Industrial Relations Center, McGill University, 1964).

As the world about us changes, managers in all types of institutions try to cope in a variety of ways. In the early 1960s, many corporate managers realized they could not make sound decisions about future business activities in an expedient, reactive manner because their firms were growing very large and complex with new technologies, products, markets and competition to deal with. As a result, formal planning techniques which had been used in narrow functional applications were introduced on a much broader scale and formal long-range planning became popular. New corporate planning functions appeared in many companies, as well as new staff planning specialists and planning executives. I conducted a field study on the design of these systems in the mid-1960s and that showed great promise for improved management.[1]

With this history in mind, we might ask why such subjects as "planning techniques" and "problems of implementation" are still topics of concern. It would seem that such techniques would be well known and established in most firms after 10–15 years. However, this is not the case, for during a second field study of corporate planning systems which was completed in 1976 I found that many corporations, including some of the largest ones, had redesigned their planning systems in the early 1970s, essentially making a fresh start at formal long-range planning.

This finding was quite surprising and might be explained in various ways:

1. Perhaps the original planning systems were not properly designed or implemented.
2. Perhaps stable conditions and satisfactory performance in the 1960s caused managers to become complacent and let the planning systems stagnate.

[1] Harold W. Henry, *Long-Range Planning Practices In 45 Industrial Companies* (Englewood Cliffs, N.J.: Prentice-Hall, Inc., 1967).

READING 3–8

Formal Planning in Major U.S. Corporations*

HAROLD W. HENRY

3. Perhaps changes occurred in the external environment of firms which were so complex or unusual that the existing planning systems could not deal with them effectively.

Each of these general explanations has some validity, based on the specific factors cited by planners and executives in these companies.

However, the most obvious conclusion from my recent field study was that all corporations experience problems in implementing and using a formal planning system. The nature of these *problems* and some possible *remedies* are the subjects I will focus on in this article.

After identifying and listing several problems which were reported, I examined them for similarities and found they could be grouped into three broad categories:

1. Problems related to *management attitudes and values* (philosophy of management).

* *Long Range Planning*, vol. 10, no. 5 (October 1977), pp. 40–45.

2. Problems related to the *design* of the formal planning system.
3. Problems related to the *method of introducing and administering* the system.

I will discuss the problems in each area in the order listed.

Management Attitudes and Values

Since formal planning systems were first introduced in business corporations, the attitude of top managers has been the most critical factor in attaining effective planning and improved performance. This finding was very evident in the study of several early planning systems I completed in the mid-1960s. At that time, I concluded that "the success of long-range planning efforts in each business corporation seemed to be directly related to the extent of active interest and leadership of the president and other top executives."[2] Many other studies of planning systems have reached the same conclusion.

In my most recent study, the vital role of the top executive was again evident. For example, two contrasting executive views were reflected in these comments I received:

Company A: The president does not want much formality.

Company B: The president sends each division head a letter stating acceptance (of the division's plan) and giving guides on how to correct deficiencies and a pep talk on what he thinks should be emphasized.

You can imagine that these two presidents get different results from their division heads. The problem illustrated may be stated as follows: *When top management views systematic, future-oriented planning as unimportant, the thought and effort exerted by lower-level managers will be minimal.*

---

2 Ibid., p. 28.

Another evidence of the way top management views formal planning is the weight assigned to this activity in performance evaluations and reward systems. If compensation and promotions are based strictly on short-term profit performance, that area will receive the most attention. This is an age-old problem and may be stated as follows: *If top management does not reward systematic planning efforts and results, this activity will not receive adequate attention.*

Another problem reported which reflected the philosophy of management of top executives was *lack of direction from top management in the form of corporation goals, statements of mission, or corporation strategies.* Perhaps some managers believed in decentralization so strongly that they did not want to channel or restrict division managers. Perhaps it was the easiest thing to do and was really an abdication of responsibility. In any case, division managers in several companies felt the need for more guidance to avoid random, wasteful searches for new business activities and the effort to develop plans which had to be redrawn or discarded due to unknown constraints.

In some companies, even when goals were formulated and stated, one problem was the *lack of commitment to the objectives by key executives, operating managers, and staff specialists.* If goals were stated merely because they were required, without a firm belief that they were desirable and attainable, they did not serve as effective focal points for creating and implementing action plans. One vice president summed it up when he said, "Planning without commitment to objectives doesn't accomplish much."

Finally, *if top management views the planning process as more important than the thinking and action it is supposed to stimulate, results are often disappointing.* For example, a new planning director was hired in one corporation and he, along with the president, prepared a planning manual and insisted that everybody follow it precisely. Thus, the planning effort was more form than substance. Division heads could get by if they followed the procedures and the value to them for improving the way they managed was missed. Again, the attitude of top management toward formal planning and its role was the root of the problem.

System Design

The largest group of problems found seemed to fall in the category of improper system design. Of course, the design often reflected top management philosophy, and the way a system was implemented could reflect on the design, so it is impossible to clearly separate the three classes of problems I have identified.

A basic problem of many companies is that *the planning system is too informal.* Without clearcut responsibility assignments for who does what in planning for the future, effective planning is left to chance, and the most likely results are many gaps in performing vital planning activities and some duplication of effort. In the broadest sense, the problem is the lack of organization. Also, if some guidelines, premises, and schedules are not established, the results are likely to be incompatible, and the efforts will be very inefficient.

On the other hand, some *planning systems are too formal,* with thick planning manuals, excessive required documentation, and extensive number exercises. In such systems, rigid compliance to the formal procedures is usually required. Such a design may not lead to better management, as stated above under the problem of "process orientation" of top management. This problem seems to be one of the primary reasons why many planning systems became ineffective and gradually disinte-

grated in the 1960s. For example, one executive reported that "a comprehensive planning system was developed in 1967 or 1968 for the operating units, but much documentation was required and it got burdensome." This result, coupled with the autonomy of division managers in this company and the indifference of the top manager toward formal planning, caused the formal planning system to "fizzle out." A similar pattern was cited in other companies which had renewed their planning efforts in the 1970s.

Another design problem is that the *planning staff can be too large and dominant.* For example, one company had nearly 80 persons assigned to a planning unit at one time. The fact that this system is now defunct may tell us something (of value). Such a system often places much reliance on staff efforts, so operating managers who have important experience and technical knowledge to contribute to the planning process may become indifferent or resentful. In either case, their essential inputs are lost.

A structural flaw which affects planning systems as well as other functions in business corporations is that of *excessive centralization.* This usually reflects the philosophy of top management and may be related to the scope of the product lines or required activities in the company. In addition to the dominant role assigned to planning staffs, top executives may feel compelled to make all major decisions, with very little delegation of authority. If this situation exists, the experience, ideas, and values of other managers are not utilized fully and the stimulus to thinking which results from interactions between managers is never realized.

However, the pendulum may swing too far in the opposite direction, so that the problem becomes *excessive decentralization.* If division heads or local managers have too much authority, their actions may not be in the best interest of the corporation, and their plans may reflect narrow interests or self-serving ventures. Even divisional planners may become very independent and resent any guidance or intrusion by corporate planning specialists or executives. In such a situation, resources may be wasted due to investments which are inconsistent with a corporation strategy and inefficiencies will result from the lack of cooperative effort.

A problem which is believed to be widespread and very serious is the *failure to forge a link between strategic planning and operational planning*. Again, the system design is critical, but top management attitudes and implementation methods also inflence the way managers perceive the relation between strategic and operational planning. There are sound reasons for separating the process of preparing each of these plans, and some companies made a deliberate effort to do so. First, it is only logical to determine major objectives and strategies before operational plans can be developed, for the strategic plan "drives" or determines the type of operations to be performed. Therefore, a strategic planning cycle precedes an operational planning cycle in many firms. Other firms believe it is essential to separate these two types of planning in order to get any strategic planning done at all. Thus, they designate their long-range planning effort as strategic planning in order to get managers to view the business in a broader manner and to avoid any number exercises (to project sales and budgets) which are part of operational planning. Thus, these reasons for separation may be summarized as (1) to concentrate on strategy formulation and (2) to avoid budget projections (which are usually based on the current strategy and prevent any consideration of alternatives).

The problem arises when the results of the strategic planning process are ignored when operational plans are developed. In some cases, different people may be involved in the two processes. Also, the strategies developed may be stated in very broad, general terms which are not understandable or very difficult to translate into operational plans. Finally, inertia tends to keep managers following familiar paths, so they may incorporate too much of current activities and policies in their plans for the future.

In companies which include strategic and operational plans in one set of plans, this last reason for ineffective integration of new strategies into operational plans may cause strategy formulation efforts to be very weak and perfunctory. In other firms, strategic planning may be given very little emphasis in the planning process. Thus, the overall problem which exists in many different types of planning systems is the failure to formulate sound strategies and to reflect them in operational plans. System design can have an important impact both in causing and overcoming this problem.

The final design problem I will discuss is the *imbalance in planning activities* which sometimes exists. For example, a great amount of time and effort may be spent in developing forecasting models, while social, political and technological changes in the external environment are not monitored or evaluated. In other companies, long-range planning efforts may be dominated by financial analysis or by product planning or by marketing considerations. In fact, formal planning systems have evolved in many companies from one specialized function such as long-range financial or product planning or economic analysis. Ideally, a comprehensive planning system should involve every major functional, product, and territorial area within a corporation as well as the major segments of the external environment—social, political, economic, physical, and technological.

Planning System Implementation

When a decision is made to *introduce a formal planning system* in a corporation, it is sometimes made *without consulting or involving many other executives or lower level managers.* Formal planning may be recommended by a consulting firm or a major competitor may start or revive formal planning, so the decision to do it seems logical and everyone is expected to agree. However, it is one thing to get reluctant acquiescence and another to get eager involvement. One vice president said, "If you have to give a directive, it usually not too successful," and thus implied that imposed systems don't work. If managers do not understand the reasons for formal planning and are not involved in discussions or exercises or conferences where the need is recognized, they may be unwilling or indifferent planners and may actively resist and hinder planning efforts. At best, their motivation will be weaker than if they are involved in the initial decision to plan formally.

Another very serious problem in implementing formal planning systems is the *lack of training of managers* to use such a system. Most managers are strongly oriented toward day-to-day operational problems and achieving short-term results they are responsible for. When they are suddenly asked to become future oriented and think about what the world might be like in the distant future, they face a difficult transition. Also, when they are asked to formulate strategies which will lead to the achievement of important and hard-to-reach goals, they wonder where the bolt of lightning came from. To illustrate this problem—the corporate planner in one large firm would talk to operating managers to learn their broad plan of attack for achieving major goals. Then he would write out the strategy he perceived and send it to them to see if he stated their strategy correctly. This little

game was triggered by the inability of the operating managers to write sensible strategy statements in their formal plans.

Also, when managers are asked to look for various types of external changes and trends which may become threats or opportunities, they wonder where to start. In addition, their entire process of thinking must shift from tangibles to intangibles, from actuals to possibilities, from the present to the future, to scenarios, probabilities, priorities, and desirable future goals for the corporation instead of how to get results tomorrow. I think it is too much to expect the average operating manager and many experienced executives to become instant long-range strategic planners. I have heard different planners and executives say that a few years are required to develop an effective planning system in which managers become thinkers and not merely extrapolators. For example, a recent *Business Week* article (Nov. 10, 1975) about Potlatch Corporation stated that a new president set out to reeducate managers to become strategic planners and within about four years, performance was vastly improved.

When formal planning is introduced, the *additional work load on managers* is a significant implementation problem. The number of forms to fill out, the options to evaluate, and the calculations to make require much time and effort and the initial shock may be great. Some managers learn to cope with the increasing paperwork burden (from corporation staffs, governmental units, and universities) by filling out forms faster and faster and providing less and less meaningful data. In other cases, the work is delegated to a subordinate who does not have the knowledge or experience to provide the best inputs. In either situation, the quality of the plans developed and the future performance of the corporation are the things which suffer.

One of the most critical parts of formal planning and one of the most difficult ones to implement is that of capital allocation. Funds are limited in the biggest and best corporations (and even in the U.S. Government) and many managers in each firm are competing to get part of the limited resources. If the *planning process does not include an understandable, logical, consistent, and fair way of allocating capital funds,* managers will lose confidence in it and their planning efforts will decline rapidly. If the allocation system is slow, arbitrary, and unpredictable, managers will engage in "gamesmanship" to get their part. In addition to seriously undermining the planning system, desirable ventures may be delayed, cancelled, or restructured, and corporation performance may decline. In one large chemical corporation, a new formal planning system is struggling to "wean" key managers from making "emergency" capital requests at any time for any purpose.

Remedies for Planning System Problems

In this section, I will outline some possible actions to overcome the problems discussed thus far. At least some of these and perhaps all have been tried in various corporations.

1. Encourage top executives who practice informal planning to attend conferences on planning, to read articles and books on formal planning, and to discuss with executives in other companies various management techniques and results. I know of no other way to get executives enthused about formal planning except through awareness of what others are doing, and a personal evaluation and decision to try new ways of management.

2. To motivate managers to plan beyond the current accounting year, it seems that a specific incentive must be provided in the evaluation and reward system. A factor such as "effectiveness in strategic planning" should be specified as one performance evaluation factor and a definite, significant weight should be assigned to it. To measure performance, "effort" may have to be measured at first by determination of time spent in planning alone, time spent in training sessions, or time spent in actual planning activities with other persons. The "quality" of strategies and plans submitted can also be evaluated by line and staff teams. Finally, actual "results" which may be attributed to each manager's planning efforts can be measured as time goes on. Plans submitted each year should be filed and reviewed in later years to find relationships between plans and subsequent results. Also, each manager can be asked to identify such links.

3. To get more guidance from top executives in the form of corporation goals and strategies, division heads can exert pressure on them to say what is expected. This has happened in some companies, for the division heads have said in effect—we have the resources and capabilities to do many different things; what do you want us to do? Another development which has caused top executives in other companies to give more attention to corporation goals and strategies has been the realization that fragmented, overlapping, or incompatible divisional activities resulted from the lack of corporation direction.

4. Special programs on "commitment" for managers or for all employees can be conducted in a company in an effort to motivate people to commit themselves to goal fulfillment. A "Management by Objectives" program may also be effective for this purpose. In any case, the emphasis on commitment must come through the authority hierarchy from top to bottom, perhaps starting with the board of directors. At the same time it should be stressed that goals must be desirable or worthwhile, realis-

tic or attainable, and also challenging.

5. To shift the thinking of top management and lower level managers away from the planning process and the completion of forms, a review session in which each key manager has to give an oral summary of his goals, premises, strategies, and action plans before a group of fellow managers should be beneficial. Of course, open discussion should follow each presentation and staff assistance and "crutch" charts should be minimized. This requirement to tell others should stimulate the thinking of managers, just as required presentations in the classroom or in graduate-faculty seminars motivate the speaker to prepare more thoroughly.

6. To attain the optimal level of formality in a planning system, especially in regard to the plan required from key managers, it seems better to start in a simple way and increase the complexity rather than starting with a voluminous set of instructions and forms. In the simple approach, managers are not "shellshocked" by the size of the undertaking, they do not have a large increase in work load, and they can understand the reasons for their efforts if the requirements are smaller in scope. As a result, acceptance should be better and efforts should be more conscientious. Also, the learning process and attitudinal changes will advance with increasing planning system sophistication. As managers understand and become more proficient in planning, they will see the need for additional types of analysis. In fact, I think a great deal of flexibility should be permitted in plans so that managers can add parts they consider important. Many companies permit such flexibility.

7. Planning staffs should be kept small at both the corporate and divisional levels. In some companies, a person with only a part-time assignment to coordinate the planning process is very effective in getting line managers and functional staff specialists to develop strategic long-range plans. Sometimes, functional staffs are located in close proximity and one or more persons from each staff has a key role in reviewing plans or in making inputs to the planning process. In other cases, various types of staff specialists are pulled together in one unit under a director of planning or vice president-planning.

In contrast to these arrangements where staff personnel have some operational assignments and some strategic planning assignments, some companies designate a planning staff or executive staff to be strictly a strategic planning unit whose job is to identify and evaluate alternative corporate strategies. In this situation, the staff could play a dominant role unless corporate executives were effective in challenging, evaluating, and modifying strategies proposed by the staff unit. Thus, various staff arrangements can be effective as long as both line managers and staff specialists recognize their respective roles and contribute fully to the planning process.

8. The degree of decentralization of authority which exists in a company is usually a direct reflection of the management philosophy of the chief executive officer and the basic type of organization structure employed. For example, subsidiaries, product divisions, and geographical divisions will be more independent than functional operating units in a corporation. Some managers want to make all major decisions while others believe that much autonomy should be granted to division managers. As a general guideline, divisions should not get so independent in planning and action that they fail to act in the best interest of the corporation. On the other hand, decisions should not be so centralized that division managers are prevented from using their knowledge and experience fully, for they will lose the incentive to be innovative, and the company

will not develop promotable managers very fast.

If an existing organization structure is not suitable for strategic planning by groups, divisions, or departments because one unit does not contain all critical activities related to one business or because it contains two or more businesses, a structure for planning purposes can be superimposed on the existing structure. This has been done successfully in some corporations and such units are called Strategic Business Units.

9. To ensure that strategic planning receives adequate attention, I think it is best to design a formal planning procedure with a two-stage cycle, the first one for strategic planning and the subsequent one for operational planning. To link the two stages, the approved strategic plan should be summarized at the beginning of operational plans and specific proposed programs or activities should be related directly to the strategies indicated.

Independent reviews of submitted plans by line managers and staff groups or by specially-designated evaluation committees should look for direct linkages between operational and strategic plans. If inconsistencies are found, plans should be returned for revision.

10. Planning activities can be balanced by first involving every line and staff unit in the planning process. Then to prevent imbalance between functional plans or other elements of a plan, independent reviews by internal managers and/or external consultants could be made periodically.

11. When introducing a formal planning system, several different approaches may be used. I will review briefly two of these. In the first one, the top manager meets with the vice presidents to discuss problems, needs, goals, and issues in the company. Ideas from all should be sought and then a list of major needs and ways to attain them can be compiled. This process is continued by each vice president with his own subordinates (division heads) and by each division head with his respective subordinates. Then the ideas flow upward and are discussed and integrated at each level. When the top executive level is reached, some concrete ideas on desirable goals and ways to achieve them should emerge. This is the beginning of formal planning, and all key managers have been involved in the process.

A second method is to schedule a management conference at a remote location for 100 or more key managers, with a schedule of activities to include outside speakers from other companies or universities or consulting firms who discuss the changing world and how corporations can cope with changes in the future. Informal buzz group sessions to get ideas from all participants should be included with reports from each group and a master compilation of needs, goals, proposed strategies and action plans. This also provides a foundation for formal planning which includes much involvement by many managers.

12. To provide training for managers on how to plan, some companies have extensive in-house programs, often at remote training centers, and involve corporate executives as well as outsiders in leading the training programs. In some companies, participants in such programs return to their units and train their own subordinates, using visual aids, reading materials, sample plans, and guidebooks provided by the planning staff.

Additional training opportunities exist at strategic planning conferences in other institutions.

13. Managers can avoid excessive work loads and still do effective planning by using the conventional remedies of hiring more support personnel and by delegating more duties and authority to line and staff subordinates.

14. To allocate capital in a consistent, fair manner, proposed capital spending plans should be classified in various ways so that priorities can be determined in relation to the major goals to be sought and the strategies to be employed. For example, some spending plans may be for new ventures, others to expand and improve existing facilities, and others to develop new products. The degree of importance can be indicated, as well as the time period when funds will be needed and the likely impacts if implementation is delayed.

In conclusion, if formal planning systems are to be effective, problems should be identified as soon as possible in each corporation and remedies used by other firms or new ones designed internally should be employed to solve each problem. If one solution doesn't work, others should be tried. There is no cook-book formula which can be applied in every firm, but the most important ingredient is to find or develop managers who want to do a better job of managing.

CASES FOR PART THREE

Case 3-1
"UNBUNDLING" AT WORLD DATA PROCESSING

World Data Processing Company is a giant of the computer field. One of the first to become involved with electronic digital computers, its sales are now in the billions per year. Although its products are not technically superior to its competitors, the company has bettered the others by virtue of its aggressive marketing and servicing. Whereas its largest competitor hired engineers and trained them as salesmen, WDP looked for sales types regardless of education and gave them strong technical support. Until four years ago, WDP marketed through salespeople and systems engineers located all over the country. A salesperson and a systems engineer worked together as a team with the salesperson assigned total customer responsibility while the systems engineer provided technical expertise. The entire marketing program of preproposal studies, proposals, sales, installation, and service was conducted as a sales and systems team effort. In many cases the team worked so closely that roles overlapped.

The systems engineer, therefore, played a key role in WDP's marketing strategy. Continued technical support after sale was a central selling feature because computers require substantial debugging and training of user personnel after delivery. The owner just can't plug it in and expect it to work on Monday morning (although many of them thought so when they first signed the sales contract). In many large accounts, this support required permanent assignment of WDP systems engineers to a customer computer center. All of this service was provided free. When WDP sold or rented a computer, a person went along with it at no extra charge.

In January four years ago, the attorney general of the United States filed an antitrust suit against WDP designed to reduce its primacy in the computer field. The company immediately announced the formation of a special study committee composed of top executives "to investigate the changing data processing market." Data processing had expanded in size and complexity over the years. In addition to equipment manufacturers, the industry now included leasing companies, software houses selling programs, service bureaus, consulting firms, and data processing schools. The results of the study were to be published in six months.

Nothing more was heard about the government suit, the company's response, or the committee's deliberations until June when an announcement summoned all field personnel to their regional offices around the country for a mandatory two-day meeting. It was announced by an executive from the headquarters that marketing and service would be separated or "unbundled." The salesperson would handle all sales but was now to sell equipment and services separately. The systems engineer would report to a different superior and would charge for services at a rate that combined time and task complexity. All other services would also have a price tag including education, manuals, books, and programs.

The new policy would be in full effect immediately along with a 3 percent across-the-board reduction in rental prices. This reduction was described as being the cost of services formerly provided free. Prices to purchase equipment were unchanged. Finally at the end of the meeting, the executive stated that failure to strictly adhere to the policy would be grounds for dismissal.

The company's voluntary policy change was reputedly to appease the federal government and discourage further intervention and prosecution. Whatever it was, the announcement was a complete shock to employees, customers, and competitors. Anger and confusion were rampant for a long time. The systems engineers felt that their status was undetermined because they were no longer part of a professional sales team in this marketing-oriented organization. Indeed, they became a little uneasy because their activity was entirely dependent on the sales of a salesperson who might be more interested in selling hardware than services. Whereas sitting in the office rapping with fellow engineers might have been fun sometimes in the past, after the policy change it engendered fear that they had nothing to do and were expendable. In general, salespeople found it difficult to sell something that they formerly had given away free. The close relations between salespeople and engineers were severed. And field management was often confused about what specifically was included under the new sales and rental contracts.

The difficulties in the policy change were reflected in a series of modifications in the compensation plan for salespeople and systems engineers. In the first year after the announcement, salespeople were paid 50 percent salary and 50 percent commission based on sales of both equipment and services. The systems engineers were paid 80 percent salary and 20 percent commission based on exceeding an office services quota. Few salespeople made their goals that year, and fewer engineers received any bonus. Complaints among both groups increased.

The next year, WDP put systems engineers on straight salary. The salespeople's salary percentage was raised to 60 percent and commissions were based only on selling equipment. An extra bonus could still be made for selling services however.

In the third year after the change, salespeoples' salary percentage was further increased to 90 percent with 10 percent commission based solely on equipment sales. There was no bonus for service sales. As the years have passed, however, local management has become more and more lenient in its interpretation of company policy regarding free technical service to customers.

Since WDP was the dominant computer company, management assumed that their competitors would also separate sales and services. Some did so, but others did not. Management also assumed that customers would spend on services approximately the amount by which rental charges were reduced. This prediction was in error. Small companies spent much more because they were so dependent on WDP, but the larger customers decided to develop their own service capability by hiring their own engineers and computer specialists. Their use of WDP systems engineers dropped greatly and total sales were less than predicted.

Questions

1. What was the WDP Company's strategic response to the government antitrust action? What was the objective in this response? Was it achieved?
2. Why was the company's former marketing strategy superior to the separated sales of equipment and services?
3. Why did the company fail to achieve its sales goals in the two years after the change?
4. Should the field managers, salespeople, and engineers have been consulted by corporation executives in formulating the new policy? What might they have told the executives? How should the company have developed and announced the policy change?
5. Why do you think the company changed the compensation plans for salespeople and engineers? What plan do you recommend?

Case 3–2

HENDERSON SPECIALTIES, INCORPORATED*

Rossall J. Johnson

Henderson Specialties was a manufacturer and distributor of food products. The company's main products included food colors, artificial flavors, cake icings, baking chocolate, ice cream, spices, and pudding powders. In 1967 the company bought approximately 40 percent of its products in a finished or semifinished state from other manufacturers in order to carry a full line.

The company was located in a metropolitan area of approximately 300,000 and limited its sales to bakeries, restaurants, and hotels in the local area. All products were sold under the Henderson Specialties label.

Although the Henderson Specialties line had a good reputation, the company encountered strong competition from two other manufacturers of similar products located in the same city. In recent years these competitors had succeeded in increasing their market share. This was attributed to more

* *Executive Decisions*, South-Western Publishing Co., Cincinnati, Ohio, 1970, p. 208.

aggressive marketing methods and faster delivery service. The latter was particularly important because the majority of bakeries, restaurants, and hotels were relatively small, and customarily bought small quantities on a hand-to-mouth basis.

The customer seemed to be mainly interested in price and service. Thus the quality and price of the various products were about the same among the competitors. Even ice cream was of almost uniform quality from one company to another. The salespeople felt that the customers were a fickle group in that the first salesperson to walk in the doors was likely to get the order. There was little evidence of loyalty to a company or a brand.

Henderson Specialties, Incorporated, was formerly owned and operated by two partners, William Henderson and his brother, Alvin Henderson. The two brothers founded the company in the 1940s and had succeeded in selling their products nationally in the 50s. In 1958 William Henderson left the company after he had suffered a substantial gambling debt that seriously impaired the company's financial condition. In 1963, Alvin Henderson, then 54, became seriously ill and was no longer able to participate actively in management. Sales declined from $2 million in 1960 to $300,000 in 1967 (see Exhibit 1).

On January 1, 1968, Jack Shanks, 28 years of age, bought the company and incorporated. Mr. Shanks held approximately 80 percent of the company's stock, and a few relatives held the remainder. Mr. Shanks, who had recently received a Ph.D. in economics, had approximately two years of practical business experience. He was elected the president after the incorporation. When asked by a friend, Bob Rogers, why he had invested money in the company, the following conversation took place:

Shanks: I think the company is almost on the rocks. But it has great potential. After all, a few years ago it was the leading company in the field. I think I can shape it up and make it profitable again. If not, I can sell it in a few years. It certainly is worth the risk. I like this chal-

EXHIBIT 1

HENDERSON SPECIALTIES, INCORPORATED
Income Statement
For Year Ended December 31, 1967

Net sales		$303,000
Cost of goods sold:		
Inventory, January 1	$ 39,000	
Purchases	192,000	
Cost of merchandise available	$231,000	
Less inventory, December 31	51,000	
Cost of goods sold		180,000
Gross profit on sales		$123,000
Selling expenses	$ 78,000	
General and administrative expenses	39,000	117,000
Net profit before taxes		$ 6,000

lenge, Bob. I believe I can build this company into the largest of its kind in the area.

Rogers: But you have very little business experience and practically none in the food line, Jack.

Shanks: That's true. But I think I'm not exactly stupid. Besides, there are a few good people in the company. Take Mr. Green, the production manager, for example. He has served an apprenticeship as a baker and has been with the company for over ten years. I think he is a very competent man and a nice guy besides (see Exhibit 2).

Rogers: How about the other people?

Shanks: There is Mr. Dillen, the controller and office manager. He has been with the company for almost 20 years. Although he seems to know his business, I think he is a little narrow minded. I bet he watches every penny in the company. Well, I suppose he has to. The financial position of the company is not exactly rosy. Mr. Dillen is about 50 and pretty well set in his ways. I hope I can get along with him. You know, Bob, it is not exactly easy for him to take his orders from a man so much younger than himself.

Rogers: And how about the sales manager, Jack?

Shanks: To tell you the truth, there is none. Old Mr. Henderson used to handle that, and I think I'm going to shape up the sales force myself. You know, I have always been interested in the marketing end of business. I will be plenty busy in this respect: The company's sales force is too small. Packaging is old-fashioned. And as far as merchandising and advertising are concerned, I think these people have never even heard the words!

EXHIBIT 2
Organization Chart

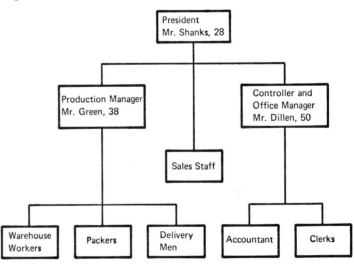

During the first week of January, 1968, Mr. Shanks had a conference with Mr. Green and Mr. Dillen.

Shanks: Mr. Dillen, can you give me your candid thoughts on our financial position?

Dillen: Rather strained. For one thing, we are very short on cash. All our money is tied up in receivables and inventory (see Exhibit 3). We almost never take advantage of cash discounts because we have trouble meeting our obligations on time. For another thing, I think we should concentrate more on the profitable items in our line.

Shanks: If I understand you correctly, we have to reduce the amount of money tied up in inventory and push some profitable items that we can produce ourselves. I don't think we can do too much about our money tied up in receivables because of the terms of the industry.

Dillen: That is correct.

Shanks: Mr. Green, which items in our line are relatively cheap to produce and permit a good markup?

Green: I would say ice cream and cake icing. I have also been thinking that, with our equipment, we could manufacture artificial honey which would be ideally suited for baking.

Shanks: An excellent idea, Mr. Green. We will look into that more thoroughly after I've talked with our salespeople. In conclusion, I would like to say that I am convinced that we can compete successfully and regain a large part of the market share which the company has lost under the previous management. It will take a lot of hard work on the part of all of us. But as we grow, you'll grow with the company. I will appreciate your help and cooperation. Thank you, gentlemen.

EXHIBIT 3

HENDERSON SPECIALTIES, INCORPORATED
Balance Sheet
December 31, 1967

Assets			Liabilities and Capital		
Current assets:			Current Liabilities:		
Cash		$ 5,000	Accounts payable		$ 57,000
Accounts receivable ..		39,000	Notes payable		21,000
Inventory		51,000	Total current liabilities		$ 78,000
Total current assets		$ 95,000			
Fixed assets:			Net worth:		
Delivery equipment ..	$ 9,000		Henderson, capital		$120,000
Furniture and fixtures	5,000				
Machinery	89,000				
Total fixed assets		103,000	Total liabilities and		
Total assets		$198,000	net worth		$198,000

In the spring of 1968, Henderson Specialties introduced its honey which, after initial sales resistance, became a full success. Mr. Green, the production manager, also experimented with new ice-cream flavors, and in the summer of 1968, the company entered the market with a complete line of ice cream. Mr. Shanks spent much of his time in the field working with the sales force. He hired several new salespeople and developed new accounts. Together with the office manager, Mr. Dillen, the president designed new packages and containers in order to give the products a modern, high-quality image. Mr. Shanks and Mr. Dillen spent many evenings together in order to determine how the company's cash position could be improved. On several occasions Mr. Shanks visited the office after hours to find the production manager, Mr. Green, working on new recipes, whistling while he was experimenting.

The income statement as of December 31, 1968, indicated that the company had increased sales substantially and had increased its profits (see Exhibits 4 and 5).

Shanks sought additional capital for expansion purposes but found that the banks had little interest in negotiating a loan. Loans based on the highly perishable food inventory were difficult to obtain. Even when successful, a loan of only about one-tenth of the value of the inventory was possible.

In the fall of 1968 Shanks investigated the possibility of expanding by merging with the Sidney Food Flavoring Company. Before making overtures to the Sidney Company, Shanks sounded out Dillen and Green. Dillen was apprehensive and cautious about the financial position of the Sidney Company. He felt a merger "at this time" should be given a great deal of thought. He stated that Henderson Specialties was still in shaky financial condition.

Green was more concerned about Mr. Sidney, the owner. Henderson Specialties purchased large amounts from Sidney Food Flavoring, and through this contact Green had become acquainted with Sidney. Green felt that Sidney was hardheaded and gave the following as an example: "I have occasionally asked him to modify this or that product for us, but, although

EXHIBIT 4

HENDERSON SPECIALTIES INCORPORATED
Income Statement
For Year Ended December 31, 1968

Net sales		$541,000
Cost of goods sold:		
Inventory, January 1	$ 51,000	
Purchases	258,000	
Cost of merchandise available	309,000	
Less inventory, December 31	38,000	
Cost of goods sold		271,000
Gross profit on sales		$270,000
Selling expenses	$162,000	
General and administrative expenses ..	56,000	218,000
Net profit before taxes		$ 52,000

EXHIBIT 5

HENDERSON SPECIALTIES, INCORPORATED
Balance Sheet
December 31, 1968

Assets			*Liabilities and Net Worth*	
Current assets:			Current liabilities:	
Cash	$ 11,000		Accounts payable	$103,000
Accounts receivable ..	152,000		Notes payable	29,000
Inventory	38,000		Total current liabilities ..	$132,000
Total current assets	$201,000			
Fixed assets:			Net worth:	
Delivery equipment .. $9 ,000			Capital stock	$170,000
Furniture and fixtures 5,000				
Machinery 87,000				
Total fixed assets	101,000		Total liabilities and net worth	$302,000
Total assets	$302,000			

I'm sure that it would have increased his sales to other customers as well, he never did." Green did go on to say that he felt that Sidney knew his food chemistry and that the Sidney Food Flavoring products were of good quality.

Both Dillen and Green queried Shanks as to the advantages of such a merger. Shanks stated his reasons:

Shanks: We need additional production facilities, additional management "know-how," and an expanded sales force. To build these characteristics into our business will take time and more capital than we now have or can get. But we can obtain all of these things if we merge. There are several other advantages to this merger. We can reduce our production and administrative costs, broaden our product line, and increase sales. In addition, we can be sure of our source of supply. You must remember that a company which stands still is a dying company. We have to grow if we expect to survive.

The Sidney Food Flavoring Company

The Sidney Company was a manufacturer of a few specialty items in the food industry. Food flavors and colors accounted for the majority of the company's sales, which amounted to approximately $112,000 in 1967 (see Exhibits 6 and 7). The Sidney Company sold direct to bakeries, restaurants, and hotels and also to several manufacturers of food products, including Henderson Specialties, Incorporated.

Customer contacts were made either by the one salesman, John Reiner, or by Mr. Sidney personally. Mr. Sidney was also in charge of the company's production, employing one or several employees on a part-time basis when business conditions required it. Mr. Sidney delivered most orders

EXHIBIT 6

SIDNEY FOOD FLAVORING COMPANY
Income Statement
For Year Ended December 31, 1967

Net sales		$112,000
Cost of goods sold:		
Inventory, January 1	$ 11,000	
Purchases	78,000	
Cost of merchandise available	$ 89,000	
Less inventory, December 31	10,000	
Cost of goods sold		$ 79,000
Gross profit on sales		$ 33,000
Selling expenses	$ 21,000	
General and administrative expenses ..	8,000	29,000
Net profit before taxes		$ 4,000

EXHIBIT 7

SIDNEY FOOD FLAVORING COMPANY
Balance Sheet
December 31, 1967

Assets			*Liabilities and Capital*		
Current assets:			Current liabilities:		
Cash		$ 3,000	Accounts payable		$25,000
Accounts receivable ...		31,000	Notes payable		6,000
Inventory		10,000	Total current liabilities ...		$31,000
Total current assets		$44,000			
Fixed assets:			Net worth:		
Delivery equipment ...	$ 6,000		Sidney, capital		40,000
Furniture and fixtures	2,000				
Machinery	19,000				
Total fixed assets		27,000	Total liabilities and net worth		$71,000
Total assets		$71,000			

personally in his station wagon. In the evenings Sidney did some paper work, although he employed a full-time bookkeeper-secretary, Miss Miller. The company was located in an old, ill-laid-out building, and storage was often a problem. But the main problem seemed to center around the machinery, which either needed to be replaced or to be completely overhauled.

In October 1968, Mr. Sidney discussed the possibility of a merger with his salesman, John Reiner.

Sidney: You know, John, Shanks of Henderson Specialties was over the other day sounding me out about merging with them. I think a merger at this time would not be a bad idea.

Reiner: They have a pretty good name, but haven't they been going down hill?

Sidney: Not since Shanks took over as president. He is a young and relatively inexperienced man, but he has a lot of drive and initiative. I think they did pretty well this year, especially as far as their ice-cream sales are concerned.

Reiner: I guess you're right at that. They did sell quite a bit of that stuff. But where do we fit in?

Sidney: Well, our products are definitely related, John. We may do quite well together. Besides, this place is too small for us, and our machinery is old. I hate to admit it, but their production facilities are better than ours.

Reiner: If you say so, boss. But we have been doing all right so far.

Sidney: Sure. But I'm too old to handle everything alone. I would like to concentrate on production and let other people do the paper work and the selling.

Reiner: So you want to make an ice-cream salesman out of me. I thought I would never see the day when I would be peddling that stuff. It's like putting a new ball-point pen on the market!

Sidney: Come on now, John. We have been together for a long time. I'm going to see that you handle most of our old customers.

Reiner: Well, if you put it this way, boss, I think it's all right.

The Merger

On January 1, 1969, the two companies merged, retaining the name Henderson Specialties, Incorporated. Mr. Shanks, the major stockholder, remained president, and Mr. Sidney, now a stockholder in the merger, became production manager. Mr. Green remained in charge of production of some of the company's products.

In March 1969, the following exchange took place between Sidney and Green:

Sidney: Mr. Green, would you give me a hand mixing these dyes?

Green: Sorry, Mr. Sidney, but I'm pretty busy getting the ice-cream production on the way. Easter is just around the corner and the orders will be pouring in within the next few days.

Sidney: If we don't get these dyes mixed, you won't have any coloring for your ice cream.

Green: I have enough in stock to carry us through Easter.

Sidney: You must think the whole company centers around your ice cream, don't you?

Green: It did last year. This is our profit-making product. If we don't sell this, we're out of business.

In the spring of 1969, after the Easter rush, Mr. Shanks called a sales meeting to discuss "common problems."

Shanks: Gentlemen, I have asked you to come here today in order to discuss our plans for the months ahead. As you know, we're going all-out this year to promote our ice cream and our cake icings. These two items are of excellent quality and are very profitable. This does not mean, of course, that you should neglect our other products. But before I go on, I would like to hear your opinions. You are, of course, best qualified to tell just what our customers think of us and our products. Please feel free to speak your mind.

Salesperson: Some of my customers complain about our long delivery periods. Our competitors are willing and able to deliver their orders within 24 hours.

Shanks: Yes, I know. I am planning to purchase two additional delivery trucks in the very near future in order to make us more competitive in this respect.

Salesperson: Mr. Shanks, I don't think that we get enough sales promotion support. I find it difficult to introduce some of our newer items.

Shanks: I certainly appreciate this handicap. As you know, our funds are rather limited at this time. However, I'll see if we cannot start a mail advertising campaign in order to entrench our product image more thoroughly and to make selling easier for you.

Salesperson: I think that our take-home pay should be increased. Although I consider myself a pretty good salesman, I find it difficult to support a family on a straight commission basis alone. Competition is tough enough, and we have to do a lot of missionary work before we can sell some of the newer items.

Shanks: I'll take this matter up with the controller and see what we can do. As I said before, we're more or less starting from scratch and our funds are rather limited at this time. But I'll do what I can. Are there any other comments? Well, then, let us discuss our plans for this summer. . .

Several weeks after this meeting, the company purchased the two delivery trucks and also started a mail advertising campaign. On June 30, 1969, the president went over the interim financial statements submitted to him by the controller. Mr. Shanks noticed that sales were behind forecasts and that production costs were out of line and called Mr. Sidney in his office.

Shanks: Mr. Sidney, our production costs seem to be way out of line. What, in your opinion, is the reason for it?

Sidney: I don't think that our production costs are too high at all. But we could possibly lower them if I could get a little more cooperation from Mr. Green.

Shanks: I don't quite understand. I have always thought that Mr. Green was a very competent man. What is the trouble?

Sidney: Well, for one thing, I don't think that Green cares very much how we are doing. He puts in his eight hours a day all right, but that's about all. When I ask him to give me a hand on a job, he usually replies that he is busy with other production work. All he cares about is his ice cream and his recipes. For another thing, he never consults me when he orders any supplies. He goes directly to the controller. How can I exercise cost control if I don't know what's going on in the department?

Shanks: I'll talk to Mr. Green about it. Thanks for coming in.

On the same day Shanks talked to Green:

Shanks: Mr. Green, I just talked to Mr. Sidney about our production costs and, frankly, I just think they are too high. Do you know what's wrong?

Green: I'm not sure, sir, that I know any more what's going on.

Shanks: Come on now, Mr. Green, there is something on your mind. We have always trusted each other, haven't we?

Green: There are several things on my mind, but I was not so sure that anybody was interested in my opinion.

Shanks: I have always valued your opinion, Mr. Green.

Green: Well, first of all, I don't quite like the way in which Sidney runs things. If I give an instruction to one of the packers or boys in the warehouse, I often find that Mr. Sidney changes my instructions. I don't know any more whether or not I'm boss in my own house.

Shanks: I see. Go on, Mr. Green.

Green: For another thing, Sidney often changes the instructions I give to our delivery people. Yesterday, for example, Sidney told one of our drivers to deliver an order immediately to one of his old customers. The driver had to drop everything and run off just with this one order. No wonder our costs are going up!

Shanks: I'll take up the matter with Mr. Sidney. Thank you for your frankness, Mr. Green.

In January Mr. Dillen presented the company's 1969 financial statements to the president (see Exhibits 8 and 9). After studying the statements, Mr. Shanks called a conference with Mr. Sidney and Mr. Dillen.

EXHIBIT 8

HENDERSON SPECIALTIES, INCORPORATED
Income Statement
For Year Ended December 31, 1969

Net sales		$752,000
Cost of goods sold:		
Inventory, January 1	$ 48,000	
Purchases	442,000	
Cost of merchandise available	$490,000	
Less inventory, December 31	41,000	
Cost of goods sold		449,000
Gross profit on sales		$303,000
Selling expenses	226,000	
General and administrative expenses	70,000	296,000
Net profit before taxes		$ 7,000

EXHIBIT 9

HENDERSON SPECIALTIES, INCORPORATED
Balance Sheet
December 31, 1969

Assets			*Liabilities and Net Worth*	
Current assets:			Current liabilities:	
Cash		$ 8,000	Accounts payable	$145,000
Accounts receivable		198,000	Notes payable	37,000
Inventory		41,000	Total current liabilities ..	$182,000
Total current assets		$247,000		
Fixed assets:			Net worth:	
Delivery equip.	$ 24,000		Capital stock	$210,000
Furniture and				
fixtures	7,000			
Machinery	114,000			
Total fixed assets		145,000	Total liabilities and	
Total assets		$392,000	net worth	$392,000

Shanks: Mr. Dillen, would you be kind enough to interpret these statements for us?

Dillen: Well, our financial position is not very good. Our cash position is very strained, despite the fact that we managed to turn over our inventory ten times this year. Sales are below budget. Selling expenses have increased several percent during the last six months, and production costs are far too high.

Sidney: Maybe we are spending too much money on all that fancy stuff: containers, packages, advertising, etc. I suspect that some of these containers cost almost as much as the products we put into them. And I can't see any sense in advertising. I bet our customers don't even read the literature we send them.

Shanks: These promotional expenditures are necessary, Mr. Sidney. We are facing a highly competitive market, and many items in our line just aren't competitively priced because of their high production cost.

Sidney: In other words, it's my fault that sales are below budget.

Shanks: I did not say that, Mr. Sidney. All I said is that many items in our line cost too much to produce when compared with the production costs of previous years. Can you explain that, Mr. Sidney?

Sidney: As I've told you before, I don't get the cooperation I need in the production department, neither from Mr. Green nor from some of the other men. And I'm just about sick and tired of it. For another thing, our machinery is old and inefficient.

Shanks: But we used the same machinery last year. And this year we added a brand new, automatic mixing unit for $6,000.

Dillen: Plus a heating unit for $4,000.

Shanks: What heating unit?

Sidney: I ordered it. It was absolutely necessary.

Shanks: But you should have cleared this purchase with me first. You know that . . .

Sidney: Just a minute, Shanks. I'm a major stockholder in this company and just as interested in profitable operations as you are. Don't forget that. The machine was necessary, as I explained to Mr. Dillen at the time of its purchase. You were in the field when I ordered the unit, so I could not check with you. Besides, you did not consult me either when you purchased your delivery trucks.

Shanks: In the future, I must insist that you clear matters of this importance with me first, Mr. Sidney.

Sidney: Let me ask you something, Shanks: John Reiner told me that he lost most of his old customers because of a reshuffling of sales territories. What's going on in the field? You know, I wouldn't mind being told about these things occasionally?

Shanks: Well, it was necessary to change the boundaries of some sales territories and to reallocate some of the accounts. Before the merger, Reiner sold only your products. Now he is selling our entire line and, his territory is, necessarily, somewhat smaller.

Sidney: Well, Reiner doesn't like it. And I cannot blame him. After all, he lost some of his best accounts.

Shanks: The very same thing happened to a lot of our old salespeople. They don't particularly like it either, I'm sure, but I hope they understand why it was necessary and that they will be better off in the future: broader line, less traveling, more selling time, and most important—more frequent calls. As you all know, most of our customers are small and are buying on a hand-to-mouth basis from any salesperson that just happens to be calling on them. In other words, we have to call on all small bakeries, restaurants, and hotels at least every 14 days. In a sense our salespeople are merely order-takers for the standard products (food colors, artificial flavors, cake icings, baking chocolate, pudding powders, etc.). But, at the same time, they can be missionaries for our newer products (new ice-cream flavors, baking honey, etc.). Our marketing strategy, then, should be somewhat as follows: First, frequent personal calls to pick up all the orders for our standard products we can possibly get. It is, in my opinion, better to take several small orders that the average customers can pay for within 30 days or so, rather than to load them up with a lot of stuff which might spoil if they do not need it right away and for which they cannot pay within a reasonable period of time. Second, because our clients have usually very little time to listen to long sales presentations, and because of the greater impact on the client, our salespeople should present only one new product at each call, thus functioning as missionary salespeople. This technique, together with reenforcing mail advertising, smart packaging, fast delivery, and reasonable prices should, in my opinion, manifest itself in success.

In February 1970, Shanks hired Mr. Young, 48, for the position of assistant to the president (see Exhibit 10). Young was a college graduate and had over 20 years of experience in the marketing of food products. His job assignment was to coordinate the production, financial, and marketing activities of the company and to report directly to the president.

Shortly after he had joined the company, Young talked to Sidney.

Young: Hello, Mr. Sidney. How are things in production these days?

Sidney: Not so good. I just can't get any cooperation from Green. We are doing a lot of unnecessary work. The best thing would be to get rid of him. Then I could get things done around here.

Young: Well, Mr. Green has been with the company for a long time. Mr. Shanks thinks highly of him. I'll talk to Green and see what I can do.

Sidney: You do that, but don't forget that I'm part owner of this company.

Young talked to both Green and Dillen. Green admitted to having differences with Sidney but didn't know what could be done. Young pointed out that the whole team had to "pull together" and suggested that Green attempt to work with Sidney.

EXHIBIT 10
Organization Chart

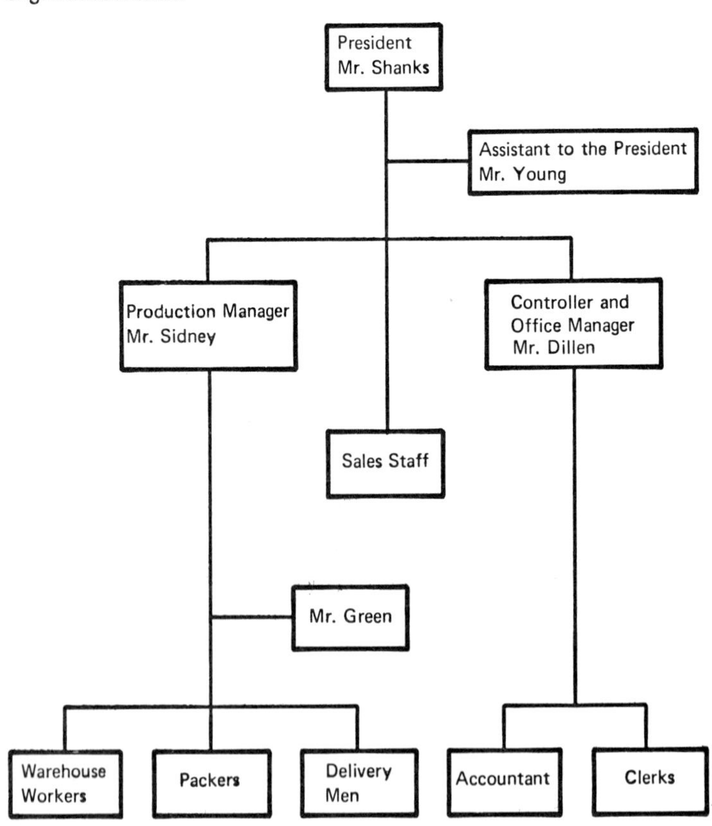

Young asked Dillen about obtaining purchase approvals. Dillen replied that his job was to pay the bills that were approved by any responsible person such as Green, Sidney, or Shanks. Dillen pointed out that he was not in a position to question the decisions of these people.

Young later requested Dillen to submit semimonthly statements and budget reports. Dillen questioned the necessity of these, but Young insisted that these statements and reports were necessary.

In April 1970, Jim Miller, a Henderson salesman, and Paul Olson met by chance on the street. Olson had recently resigned from the sales staff of Henderson.

Miller: Hi, Paul! It's good to see you. I heard you quit?

Olson: That's right, Jim. I quit last week. I was pretty fed up with the money I was making during the last few months.

Miller: I don't blame you, Paul. Our products are overpriced and competition is tough. It's almost impossible to make a living on a straight commission basis.

Olson: That wasn't the only reason I quit, Jim. I didn't like the reallocation of sales territories. Here I was, trying to build up a good bunch of customers and before you know it, they change the territories around. You know what I mean.

Miller: I sure do. One never knows what's going on. I wish Shanks would tell us occasionally about their plans, *before* they make all these changes, I mean.

Olson: I bet Young has a lot to do with all this reshuffling of territories. Shanks is a nice guy, but I don't think he really knows too much about selling.

Miller: May be. You can't learn that in college. Where are you working now, Paul?

Olson: I got a pretty good job lined up with the Top Brand Company: guaranteed minimum salary plus 0.5 percent commission on sales.

Miller: Sounds good. Maybe I should start looking around for another job myself.

In September 1970, Mr. Dillen met Mr. Green on his way home.

Dillen: How about a cup of coffee, Joe?

Green: I could stand one after *this* day, Bill!

Dillen: What's the matter? Young getting you down?

Green: He's all right, although I can't quite figure him out. In my opinion he is a "middle-of-the-roader." He came down to see me a few times trying to iron things out between Sidney and myself. But, as you know, Bill, it's almost impossible to get along with Sidney.

Dillen: I guess you're right. I think that's one reason why the boss hired Young. This way Shanks doesn't have to talk to Sidney too often. I know one thing, though: Young is sure causing me a lot of extra work with all the reports he wants.

Green: Are they really worth all the trouble?

Dillen: I'm not so sure. Analyzing reports is one thing, making the appropriate decision is another.

Green: How are things, financially?

Dillen: Not very good, Joe. Not very good at all. I think we are heading for serious trouble in the very near future (see Exhibits 11 and 12).

Green: I didn't know that things were that bad. What does the boss say?

Dillen: Not very much. He's out in the field most of the time and lets Young pretty well run the house. Things sure have changed.

Green: You can say that again, Bill! It isn't as it was a couple of years ago. Sure we had to work like mad, but it was fun then.

Dillen: I feel the same way, Joe.

EXHIBIT 11

HENDERSON SPECIALTIES, INCORPORATED
Income Statement
For Year Ended December 31, 1970

Net sales		$729,000
Cost of goods sold:		
Inventory, January 1	$ 41,000	
Purchases	473,000	
Cost of merchandise available	$514,000	
Less inventory, December 31	39,000	
Cost of goods sold		475,000
Gross profit on sales		$254,000
Selling expenses	$234,000	
General and administrative expenses	77,000	311,000
Net loss		($ 57,000)

EXHIBIT 12

HENDERSON SPECIALTIES, INCORPORATED
Balance Sheet
December 31, 1970

Assets			*Liabilities and Net Worth*		
Current assets:			Current liabilities:		
Cash	$ 4,000		Accounts payable ...	$203,000	
Accounts receivable	213,000		Notes payable	55,000	
Inventory	39,000		Total current liabilities		$258,000
Total current assets		$256,000			
Fixed assets:			Net worth:		
Delivery equipment .	$ 24,000		Capital stock	$210,000	
Furniture and fixtures	7,000		Earned surplus (deficit)	57,000	
Machinery	124,000		Total net worth		$153,000
Total fixed assets		$155,000	Total liabilities and net worth		
Total assets		$411,000			$411,000

Green: Keep me posted, Bill, will you?
Dillen: You bet.

Questions

1. What problems confront Henderson Specialties? What are the causes?
2. What was Shanks's product and marketing strategy for the firm? What were its strengths and weaknesses?
3. What were Shanks's personal objectives? How did the firm's strategy fit with his personal objectives?
4. What is the control system in the organization? What are its strengths and weaknesses?
5. What recommendations would you offer Shanks?

Case 3–3
LEWIS EQUIPMENT COMPANY*

When William Conrad, a case writer, approached Samuel Coates, the plant manager at Lewis Equipment, about case possibilities, he found that Coates did have a number of concerns that sounded like good case leads. Coates explained that, even though he had been promoted to his present assignment several months earlier, he did not feel that he had as yet made nearly as many improvements in the plant's operations as he believed were possible. In particular, Coates expressed concern about his general foremen (see Exhibit 1 for a partial organization chart of the company).

Sam went on to explain that he personally was under considerable pressure from his superiors to improve factory performance. He did not believe these demands were entirely reasonable, but he believed he could make progress in meeting these demands if only he could find a way to get better coordination between his foremen. Sam also wanted his foremen to spend more of their time and interest on helping their own people overcome the daily problems on the factory floor. He believed his foremen were often too distracted to attend to the practical issues of training and encouraging their employees in getting their work done properly and on time. He wanted his foremen to feel responsible for all aspects of their unit and to fight for the things they felt were necessary to make their unit effective. Sam reported that he was having difficulty in getting his foremen thinking and working along these lines. Starting with this lead, William Conrad decided

---

* This case was prepared by Gerald C. Leader under the supervision of Prof. P. R. Lawrence. All names have been disguised. Copyright © 1963 by the President and Fellows of Harvard College. Reproduced by permission.

EXHIBIT 1
Partial Organization Chart

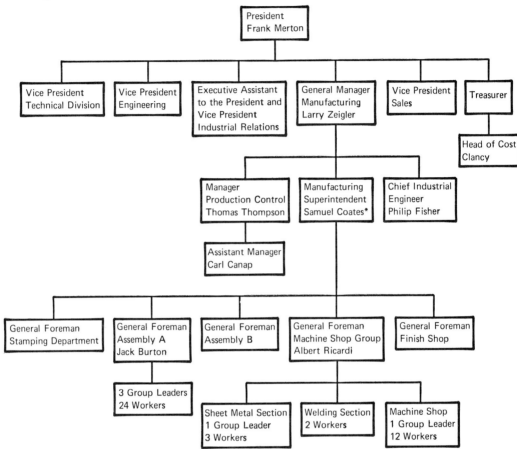

* Mr. Coates had left his former position as general foreman of the stamping department about a year earlier.

to spend some time with two of the foremen involved to learn more about the situation.

Company Background

The Lewis Equipment Company had been started some 15 years earlier as a science-based company producing an increasing line of equipment and instruments that were used primarily in the oil industry. After a period of early financial success and rapid growth, the company had, in recent years, experienced severe competition and had been operating at a loss for about two years. At this time the company employed approximately 900 people, of which a considerable number were engineers and scientists. The factory operated on a job-order basis, and most of the products were produced to customer specifications.

Assembly Department A

The first department that Conrad chose to study was assembly department A under the general foremanship of Jack Burton. During their first conversation Jack explained about the nature of his work and his problems.

Burton: I have one main final assembly line that makes up 12 different types of equipment that are each produced two to six times a year. There are ten people in this production line along with a group leader. I also have a subassembly line that makes small quantities of a variety of components and also finishes some assemblies that are produced only once or twice a year. Then I have the wire and harness line—these are the harnesses and cables used in the finished assemblies.

We're having a lot of trouble with the specifications. The trouble is that we are not given enough time to work out the problems in specifications when they come to us. I have to accept what the engineers give me as the bible, even though there are plenty of errors from the engineers. All the control around here is really in the engineering department. The final test is also done by the engineers, but there is a logic in this because we could develop our own slipshod technique if we did not have the engineers for final tests.

I get a monthly schedule in rough-draft form from production control that tells me what to do and when to do it. It keeps the material flowing. I usually get the report on the first of each month which I don't like, because if I knew in advance what the work would be like for the ensuing months I could go around to the paint foreman, etc., and put pressure on him to get the specific materials that I need for a crash program, so I would be better off.

I get a weekly direct labor utilization report made out by accounting. The accounting department makes this report up from the time cards and tells me what percentage of productivity resulted from our past weekly efforts. My yearly percentage of productivity to date is 62 percent, officially, but this note on the side of the sheet shows that actually I should be at 64 percent productivity. Only a small amount of the jobs are actually timed. The standards on about 90 percent of the jobs are estimated. Management is interested in improving the percentage of productivity over last year's productivity. For instance we are now at 62 percent while last year this department was at a 45 percent productivity. But that improvement isn't much help, because the selling price and the budget are based on the standard times so that no matter how high the productivity is, if it is anything lower than 100 percent, they always complain.

We would show an even better percentage productivity figure if the rework hours were counted in the proper place. For example, last January we had 21 percent rework. On rework we have to eat it. If a late engineering spec change causes rework, we have to eat it, as far as the productivity figures go.

I think they are hiding their heads in the sand. They don't want to know the true cost picture. If they cross-charged rework costs to the department that caused the trouble it would be waving a red flag in their faces and showing where the real problem lies.

The Direct Labor Utilization Report

Burton's frequent reference to the direct labor utilization report prompted Conrad to look into this subject. He learned that this particular control system had been initiated by Mr. Merton, the company president, shortly after he had arrived at the company some three years previously. This system, designed to alert management of possible problem areas and to assist in product and inventory control, encompassed all of the company's manufacturing and assembly activities and a somewhat smaller proportion of the remaining hourly paid labor force. Mr. Merton had made every attempt to have all of the manufacturing jobs and assembly operations rated, but with frequent design modifications requested by customers and the frequent introduction of new products, this goal had never quite been achieved. Currently, some 70 percent of the direct labor force in the manufacturing division were working on rated jobs.

Generally the control system was not unlike progressive cost accounting procedures found in other medium-sized firms working on a job order basis. It was primarily aimed at controlling manufacturing labor costs by comparing the total actual time expended in manufacturing work to the accumulated standard times for each part or assembly produced. These standard times for manufacturing the necessary individual parts and for their assembly were determined by industrial engineering.

The cost accounting department distributed weekly, on Friday afternoon, a direct labor utilization report for each department covered by the system along with a summary for the total factory organization and the total company (see Exhibit 2 for a guide to the method of calculation of the various items). The two most significant measures upon which subordinate organizations were evaluated were known as the productivity and efficiency ratings. Of these two ratings, the productivity figure was the more frequently quoted and discussed rating. Conrad asked James Clancy, the head of cost accounting, what the significance was of these weekly reports. The latter commented as follows:

Clancy: The reports are of some significance since the president looks at the figures every week. He usually gets the productivity and efficiency for total company and total manufacturing and plots them on a big chart in his office, which goes back several years. Sometimes he asks for reports on individual departments, but he never looks at them for more than ten minutes. I would say Mr. Zeigler[1] better be interested in them,

---

[1] Mr. Zeigler was the general manager of manufacturing.

EXHIBIT 2
Sample Direct Labor Utilization Report With Guide to Method of Calculation

1.	Total hrs. available	= The total hours recorded on the time cards of the employees in the department concerned during the reporting period
2.	Hrs. used on indirect labor	= % of group leader's time spent on supr. plus inspector's and clerical help's time $\times$ $\dfrac{8\,\text{Hrs.}}{\text{day}}$ $\times$ Number of working days in reporting period
3.	Hrs. available for direct labor	= #1 minus #2
4.	Hrs. direct labor on nonrated jobs	= Total hours expended on jobs that industrial engineering hasn't rated and/or on special jobs requested by other departments
5.	Hours variance	= Hours expended due to "acts of God" (e.g., machine breakdowns, power failures, snow storms) plus total rework hours*
6.	Hours direct labor on rated jobs	= #3 minus (#4 plus #5)
7.	Std. hrs. produced	= Standard hours allowed for each job $\times$ Jobs completed in reporting period
8.	% Efficiency on rated jobs	= #7 divided by #6
9.	% Total Productivity	= #7 plus #4 divided by #1
10.	Rework* a. Responsible b. Not responsible	

* Work hours expended on rework were broken down into two classifications:
  a. The unacceptable workmanship of the particular organization being measured.
  b. The rework occasioned by subsequent faulty work in other departments or by revisions in product design made by engineering, necessitating a rework of the job.

(Mention was usually made at the bottom of the Utilization Report of the absolute amounts of rework completed during the reporting period.)

since he knows Merton is going to talk to him every week manufacturing's performance doesn't look good. . . . A lot of the managers say that the system is a bunch of rubbish—Mr. Zeigler always says that he doesn't believe in the system. But I know they're concerned because Merton believes in it. You watch them on Friday pacing up and down, waiting to see what the results are. Their actions show that they are interested in it.

The total factory productivity and efficiency percentages were currently averaging approximately 69 percent and 79 percent respectively which were slight increases over the previous two years. Exhibit 3 charts the productivity and efficiency percentages for the factory by months for the two preceding years. The company percentages followed closely the total factory figures, owing to the fact that of the total company hours available, 75 percent were made up of hours contributed by the factory. Exhibit 4 is a sample of the actual reports that were distributed on a weekly basis to the managers and foremen concerned.

EXHIBIT 3
Total Factory Labor "Efficiency" and "Productivity"

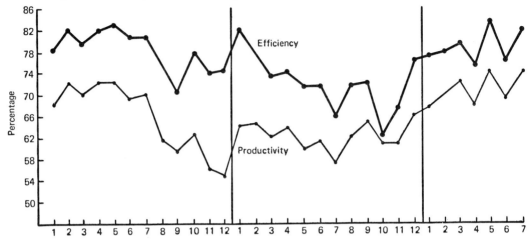

EXHIBIT 4
Direct Labor Utilization Report, Total Machine Shop Group (including the sheet metal and welding shops)

	Week Ending 6/4	Week Ending 6/11	Week Ending 6/18	Week Ending 6/25	Week Ending 7/2	Total Month Ending 7/2
1. Total hours available	565	892	946	800	812	4015
2. Hours used on indirect labor	59	86	85	90	89	409
3. Hours available for direct labor	506	806	861	710	723	3606
4. Hours direct labor on nonrated jobs	8	26	37	44	17	132
5. Hours variance	18	19	13	16	5	71
6. Hours direct labor on rated jobs	480	761	811	650	701	3403
7. Standard hours produced	303	388	508	484	266	1949
8. Percent efficiency on rated jobs (standard hours produced/hours on rated jobs 7/6)	58	51	63	74	38	57
9. Percent total productivity (standard hours + nonstandard hours/ hours available 7 + 4/1)	55	46	58	66	35	52
Rework						
a. Responsible	0	0	0	0	0	0
b. Not responsible ...	18	19	13	16	5	71

Conrad also secured direct evidence of Mr. Zeigler's concern with the productivity records. At the end of the first quarter of the current year when labor utilization percentages were dropping in successive weeks, Mr. Zeigler sent the following note to his subordinates:

> Please write up your suggestions on how we are to salvage this situation. Remember, last month's productivity was only 69 percent. By Tuesday I will expect concrete courses of action from each of you, if you are to meet or beat budget.

Conrad learned that Mr. Zeigler had sent similar notes on other occasions. Fortified with this information, Conrad went back to observing activities in assembly department A.

The Pump Episode

On one of his early trips to the assembly department Jack Burton started telling Conrad of a problem he was having:

Burton: A little while ago my group leader of the subassembly group brought to my attention a problem concerning this pump unit. He was asking me how we could put them together and be sure they would pass final test. I noticed that there might be a chance of having some brass filings get in the critical parts if we were not careful. My group leader dug up the assembly specs which the engineers had drawn up in order to put this critical subassembly together. It called for cleaning the parts twice so that there would be positive assurance of a positive test. Then the group leader saw that the industrial engineers had not allowed enough time for the double cleaning. My group leader actually timed how long it took him to make the double cleaning, and it was considerably over the allotted time. I had the group leader figure the correct amount it would take so that we could resubmit it and get the actual time put down that we were spending on this cleaning operation.

Later in the afternoon when the case writer was talking to Burton, Phil Fisher the head of the industrial engineering department, came up and raised the topic of the standard allowed time on the cleaning operation.

Fisher: What's wrong on this pump assembly operation?

Burton: Come over and look at this. Our cleaning operation on the pump assembly is taking more time than you people have allowed.
[*Hands him the engineering assembly sheet which describes the dual cleaning operation*]

Fisher: [*After reading the sheet*] I can't understand why they have duplicate cleaning operations on this. I don't think it's needed. Look, they've got 16 operations for this part. Look, the three sections to this assembly procedure shows that parts A and C are almost the same thing. They're exactly alike.

Burton: I've got to have those chips out of there to get these pumps past final assembly test. We go by the engineering specifications. Look, this is the engineering assembly S.O.P.[2] It says that we should have two cleaning operations.

Fisher: There's not such a thing as an engineering S.O.P. concerning assembly. I'm going up and see about this. I'm going to see if we can't get one of the duplicate operations for cleaning taken out of the specifications. We've got an ultrasonic cleaner that will do this job perfectly and eliminate one of these operations. That's what we've got the cleaner for anyway, to do jobs like this. This is ridiculous having so many operations. We'll be spending more time cleaning it than it takes to make it. How are we going to make any money doing this?

[Fisher leaves the room]

Burton: *[To case writer]* He's worried about the cost of this—claiming that we will never be able to make a profit on the product if we have to have so many operations. Look at him worried about something like this. That's the chief engineer's job. The chief engineer is the one to worry about whether or not we can make a profit using so many operations with such designs. It's up to the chief engineer to determine whether we can sell a product and make a profit. It's not up to Phil Fisher.

[Jack Burton leaves the room and the case writer talks to Phil Fisher who is coming into Burton's office as the latter leaves]

Fisher: *[To case writer]* Boy, I just can't understand it. If I were to have seen that specification sheet with that many operations on it, I would have blown my top. Some engineer started on this and because he didn't know what he was doing, he just kept applying more operations on operations. I know that if I was a foreman, I wouldn't allow that specification to come into my department without saying anything about it. How is the company going to make any money anyway?

[Jack Burton comes back into his office]

Fisher: I want to try and clean a couple of pumps, using just one operation. I've got an idea how we can cut this down.

Burton: Oh no you're not. I want to first check and see what final test has to say about the ones we've already done using two cleaning operations. I'm not going to have you trying to clean them with only one operation when maybe they aren't getting a positive test with two.

[Burton goes out and talks to the final test engineer and returns]

Burton: *[To Fisher]* The test engineer said that the one we cleaned using the double operation didn't test positively. I'm not going to have you try to make a single operation out of it when we can't even get it with a double. I'm way behind on rework anyway and I can't afford the time messing around with it.

---

[2] Standard Operating Procedure.

A little later on in the afternoon the case writer had a chance to talk to Jack Burton further about the pump-cleaning incident.

Burton: [*To case writer*] You know what Phil Fisher tried to do? He got my group leader behind my back and asked him to make up two complete units so he could test them, using only one cleaning operation. My group leader said, "Definitely no." I'd already warned the group leader of what Phil might do, and I told him not to play his game. It's this kind of thing that he does behind my back that really makes me mad. This is no isolated incident. This happens every day around here with him. He's always going off on a different set of directions. He tells me every once in a while that I'm not cooperating with him. I don't know why I have to keep shuffling my people around to try out his ideas when I am so far behind on my work. If they want to test some parts and make a better operation, they can do it themselves. They can set it up. I'm not going to have them disrupting my operation.

A little while later Fisher approached Burton.

Fisher: Hey, Jack. Come on in the test room. I want to show you what we're doing.

[*The group moves to the test room*]

Look, we have a valve on the pump in the ultrasonic cleaner. Using this device, we could eliminate the operation "C" [*pointing to the engineering specifications*]

Burton: I don't care what you do. I just want a final result!

Fisher: I just wanted to show you what we were doing to keep you up to date. This way we can be sure that the top isn't scarred when we put it in the tester.

Burton: [*Caustically*] I don't care if there's any scars on the top!

Fisher: I thought you said it had to pass final test with a good visual inspection?

Burton: It's the fingerprints and the filings inside the pump that cause the trouble. I'm not interested in the outward appearance. It goes in a shield anyway.

Fisher: Oh. It goes in a shield? I didn't know that.

In a later interview with the case writer, Fisher had a chance to explain some of his motives and methods in running the industrial engineering department.

Fisher: This pump-cleaning operation is the type of thing that Jack Burton should be doing and working on. That's the foreman's job. Jack's a good man, but he doesn't have enough work to do. When Burton and I get together, it's rather rough between us. He's firm in his opinion, and I'm firm in mine.

I guess some people consider me the most hated man in the firm, but I'm rather proud of that position if we can get out of our present rut. I just don't have enough men in the industrial engineering department to do any real big work so I have to rely on the foremen doing the job. What I have to do is to create a big stink or something so that we get some reaction from these people. We raise the commotion in the department and let the foremen take over and do the improvements from there. I think we're on the verge of a breakthrough here if we can get these foremen up using a stop watch and watching these people and seeing if they're using the correct procedures. Why, on this pump-cleaning operation—sure we're spending. We've got two of our men spending two hours of their time this afternoon in order that we can save a half-hour when we finally go to assembly. But if this works out, we'll save the company a lot of money. You've got to spend a dollar in order to make $3.

Later, Jack Burton told the case writer some of his views on Philip Fisher.

Burton: Phil Fisher isn't held in very high esteem because when he came in to the company a little less than a year ago he had too much initiative and tried to do too many things. He got so many projects going that he hasn't had time to finish them up.

I really don't know what the industrial engineers do. It's all I can do to compose myself when I have to talk about them. I get so mad when I think about all their activities. Fisher has them doing so many projects that they don't have time to do the things that they're really supposed to be doing. Take, for instance, the harness board that I showed you earlier this morning. They're supposed to be making those up for us. The boards take about four hours to make up so that we can begin assembly. We're having to make up our own boards, eight hours of nonproductive time that we get charged with. The last run-through, we had to clear the boards that we already made several weeks before. It took one hour to clear them and then four hours of nonproductive time to build new ones. This is the type of job that they should be doing. They should be working on giving us better standards too. The standards are way off because they are based on methods that haven't been worked out yet. That makes the productivity report an unfair basis for measuring our work. That's my big gripe with industrial engineering.

Final Assembly Shutdown

When William Conrad arrived at the plant on the following day, he found that the main final assembly line had been temporarily shut down. This was necessary because production scheduling was unable to supply some front plates that were essential. The required plates had just been started into the paint shop that morning.

Burton: This shutdown is not unusual because we always have this. It's typical. Tom Thompson[3] works his production schedule from a pre-

---

[3] Production control manager.

dicted percentage of productivity figure that Zeigler gives him. I don't know where they get the figure. I know that recently they were talking about an 85 percent productivity. I don't know where they got that. I think it was something about fixing up the line so it would be more efficient, but it certainly has never reached that level of productivity. That 85 percent figure means Purchasing has to hurry up and buy some more parts and materials. Then someone gets blamed for high inventories and it swings way over the other way.

The Machine Shop

Knowing that Sam Coates was also particularly concerned about the machine shop, Conrad decided to spend a few days observing this department and its foreman, Albert Ricardi.

In one of their early conversations Ricardi explained.

Ricardi: When I took over this shop last year it was rapidly moving backwards. I took over and started instituting some changes. We've made some real progress, but it doesn't show in the figures. Accounting has been cutting us into bits. The standards being used are not real standards. They're guesses—pulled out of the air. Then we get hit with the productivity report and we're bums. All they're interested in is making us look bad. I have to spend about 97 percent of my time just coddling all the people who come down here from other departments.

The case writer came in early the following Monday morning and was present when Tom Thompson, the production control supervisor for the manufacturing division, came into Ricardi's office.

Thompson: Al, we really need this job. There's only one operation left on it and it has to be done. Al, I know you're in a bind, but we need this by today. Is there anything you can do?

Ricardi: We're really shorthanded today. Well, I could see what we could do about putting it in the process.

Thompson: I've talked to Brown over in the model shop and he said he could do it for me, that is, if it's all right with you.

Ricardi: No. We don't get any credit on it that way. We've started the job and I want to finish it.

Thompson: Well, Al, I understand how you feel about it, and I know it will disrupt your operation.

Ricardi: Well, we'll see what we can do about it, but I'm not guaranteeing anything. Maybe we can get it out this afternoon.

[*Thompson leaves*]

Conrad: Well, Al, how do you feel on this blue Monday?

Ricardi: Not so good. All my good workers and good machinists are out and I don't know what I'm going to do. My inspector is out, and I'm really going to be running around like a chicken with his head cut off. I guess when your luck runs out, it really goes all at once. Saturday we were running around and found that the drill press operator had drilled the counterbore shallow on those plates we were doing. We had to run 84 of those pieces over again. You don't have to be a machinist to see that the men around here leave a lot to be desired. And then there's Tom Thompson coming down here. If they would leave us alone we would get ahead and get something running and we wouldn't have all these rush jobs. Every time they send in and ask us to do something of a rush nature, that cuts out our general efficiency and we just can't get ahead. That's why I ignored Thompson. When the men quit a job in the middle of it, they get confused or forget and make mistakes. It takes them time to get started again. Here's Thompson asking me to do a rush job. I just can't afford to do it.

Scheduling Problems

Several days later Conrad was walking through the shop with Ricardi when he commented on a pile of finished parts.

Conrad: These castings really look nice, Al. I think Archie did a pretty good job on them.

Ricardi: Yes, they look nice all right, there is no doubt about that. But we have another lot of 50 more coming along right now. I just got the order in today.

Conrad: What? I thought Archie just finished up this lot.

Ricardi: Yes, I know. They should all have been done at the same time. If we had had the order of 50 that we got today, it would have been a complete gift. As it is now we will have to set up the machines again and run the whole batch through. They really don't know how much it is costing them. That is what is wrong with this company. They are afraid to ask how much something costs. When someone asks them or they try to price a product they use the standard hours but the standard hours aren't near what we actually spend on making the product. They don't allow us any time for setups or making fixtures or for any unforeseen events. Those are the main times that are involved. I asked the accounting department one day how much it really cost to make a product and they gave me the computations from the standard hours. I told them that they were no good. They were left without any answer.

Machine Shop and Production Control

In the course of a number of conversations with Sam Coates, Conrad learned that Coates was well aware of the same signs of trouble in the assembly department and the machine shop that Conrad had seen. For instance, Coates told Conrad of a recent talk he had had with Ricardi.

Coates: Just today I happened to mention the production control group to Ricardi, and he about exploded. He started pacing up and down. He said that Carl Canap, the assistant production control manager, was personally out for him. I was shocked by the vehemence. When he calmed down I asked him, "Al, what have I been saying to you!" He stopped. "You are running the shop, not Sam Coates or Larry Zeigler or Production Control. Now why do you feel threatened? Don't you realize that you have forgotten more machine shop operations and the scheduling of machine shop work than Carl Canap will ever learn." I told him that he had to assert himself in a positive way. I told him that he was running the shop and no one else.

Mr. Coates told the case writer that since this conversation he was attempting to remedy the conflict between Ricardi and Carl Canap by having the latter's boss, Tom Thompson, temporarily work with Ricardi instead of Mr. Canap. Sam continued, "If Tom can charm Al so that they work well together, then, later, when Al deals with Canap, he'll let all the little things that have been bothering him go by. Just for Al to be with Thompson will help out a lot in smoothing over the relationship between Al and Carl."

In the morning of the day following the Ricardi-Coates conversation, Conrad observed Tom Thompson talking to Ricardi about scheduling problems and procedures. Carl Canap had not made an appearance. Later in the day Coates and Ricardi were sitting in the former's office, when Ricardi's assistant came in and stated that Carl Canap had just requested that the machine shop stop production of an item that was only partially completed and substitute a "rush job" which used the same machine. Ricardi immediately commented to Coates.

Ricardi: See, Sam, this is the type of thing that I have been talking about. We lose all our efficiency by breaking down in the middle of an operation.

Coates: Al, what have I been telling you for the last week and a half? You don't stop an order in the middle of production. You clear out the job before you start another.

Ricardi: [*After a long pause*] What do I do?

Coates: Al, you're the foreman, not Carl Canap. You're the foreman of this shop, not anyone else.

Ricardi: [*Turning to face the assistant*] Don't do anything.

Approximately 15 minutes later Coates and Ricardi were interrupted in their conversation by Carl Canap, who burst through the doorway and with an angered tone of voice questioned Mr. Coates.

Canap: Sam, I understand you and Al won't allow that rush job to be substituted. Is that true?

Coates: Don't look at me, Carl. Al is the foreman of this outfit, you talk to him.

Canap: What about that, Al?

Ricardi: [*Pause*] That's right.

Canap: Do you realize you are hurting the company, losing sales, losing money? What is this company coming to if we can't rearrange the schedule a little just because somebody wants to get a little extra credit on the weekly report. Do you realize what this means?

Coates: [*Angrily*] Listen here, Carl, Al is right. We're not going to switch and henceforth you'll not be stopping production in the middle of any operation. This is my decision and I want you to stick by it.

Canap: [*Walking out of the office*] If that's the way you want it, that's the way it will be.

Sam Coates' Views

Some few days later Sam Coates was talking to the case writer about the general situation:

Coates: Higher management has become so concerned with the figures that they forget about what we're actually producing, what's finished, and what's good quality. The figures get divorced from what they stand for. But if you're going to have the system, you have to play along with it. I'm sure there are a lot of details about the figures that my foreman and particularly Al are overlooking. In fact, I think he's making himself look poor. His desk is in such a disarray and things come so fast that he just gives up and says, "Oh, to hell with it!" Al has got to learn that he can't work on a bunch of long and hard jobs at the same time and expect to get a good productivity rating. He's got to get his work finished up by Saturday so he can get credit for it. He's not making the most of what he's got down there.

Questions
1. What are the firm's problems? What are the causes?
2. How do the objectives of manufacturing, production control, and industrial engineering appear to conflict?
3. What is industrial engineering trying to get manufacturing to do?
4. How does the control system (the direct labor utilization report) contribute to the firm's problems?
5. What would you recommend to the president? Why?

PART FOUR

STRUCTURING
ORGANIZATIONAL
SYSTEMS

READINGS

4–1

"Winnie the Pooh: In Which a Search Is Organized," A. A. Milne.

4–2

"How General Motors Turned Itself Around," Charles G. Burck.

4–3

"An Introduction to Organizational Design," Michael B. McCaskey.

4–4

"Organization Design: An Information Processing View," Jay R. Galbraith.

4–5

"Two Models of Organization: Unity of Command versus Balance of Power," Stanley M. Davis.

4–6

"Diversification Strategies and Organization Policies of Large Diversified Firms," Robert R. Pitts.

4–7

"The Third Managerial Revolution," Lee E. Preston and James E. Post.

4–8

"Evolving Organizational Forms," John Hutchinson.

CASES

4–1   The Hamsun Company

4–2   Milano Enterprises

4–3   Grindley School of Business

Pooh was sitting in his house one day, counting his pots of honey, when there came a knock on the door.

"Fourteen," said Pooh. "Come in. Fourteen. Or was it fifteen? Bother. That's muddled me."

"Hallo, Pooh," said Rabbit.

"Hallo, Rabbit. Fourteen, wasn't it?"

"What was?"

"My pots of honey what I was counting."

"Fourteen, that's right."

"Are you sure?"

"No," said Rabbit. "Does it matter?"

"I just like to know," said Pooh humbly. "So as I can say to myself: 'I've got fourteen pots of honey left.' Or fifteen, as the case may be. It's sort of comforting."

"Well, let's call it sixteen," said Rabbit. "What I came to say was: Have you seen Small anywhere about?"

"I don't think so," said Pooh. And then, after thinking a little more, he said: "Who is Small?"

"One of my friends-and-relations," said Rabbit carelessly.

This didn't help Pooh much, because Rabbit had so many friends-and-relations, and of such different sorts and sizes, that he didn't know whether he ought to be looking for Small at the top of an oak-tree or in the petal of a buttercup.

"I haven't seen anybody today," said Pooh, "not so as to say 'Hallo, Small,' to. Did you want him for anything?"

"I don't *want* him," said Rabbit. "But it's always useful to know where a friend-and-relation *is*, whether you want him or whether you don't."

"Oh, I see," said Pooh. "Is he lost?"

"Well," said Rabbit, "nobody has seen him for a long time, so I suppose he is. Anyhow," he went on importantly, "I promised Christopher Robin I'd Organize a Search for him, so come on."

Pooh said good-bye affectionately to his fourteen pots of honey, and hoped they were fifteen; and he and Rabbit went out into the Forest.

"Now," said Rabbit, "this is a Search, and I've Organized it——"

"Done what to it?" said Pooh.

"Organized it. Which means—well, it's what you do to a Search, when you don't all

READING 4–1

Winnie the Pooh: In Which a Search Is Organized*

A. A. MILNE

look in the same place at once. So I want *you*, Pooh, to search by the Six Pine Trees first, and then work your way towards Owl's House, and look out for me there. Do you see?"

"No," said Pooh. "What——"

"Then I'll see you at Owl's House in about an hour's time."

"Is Piglet organdized too?"

"We all are," said Rabbit, and off he went.

With giant corporations as with giant oil tankers, bigness confers advantages, but the ability to turn around easily is not one of them. Though General Motors does some things very well, one just doesn't expect it to be nimble. In so huge an organization, decision-making processes are inherently complex, and sheer mass generates a great deal of inertia. Four years ago, however, G.M. came up against the sort of challenge foreseen by Alfred Sloan. Though the company seemed ill prepared for change, it not only met the challenge but did so with a resounding success that surprised many observers of the U.S. auto industry.

The clearest evidence of G.M.'s effective response to that challenge is the transformation of its product line to meet the demands of the marketplace—and the federal government—for better gas mileage. When the Arab oil embargo hit at the end of 1973, G.M. had the worst average gas mileage among U.S. automakers—a dismal 12 miles per gallon. As buyers turned away from gas-guzzlers in panic during the following year, G.M.'s share of the U.S. new-car market slid to 42 percent, the lowest point since 1952 (not counting the strike year of 1970). Just three years later, in the 1977-model year, the average mileage of G.M. cars, 17.8 mpg, was the *best* among the Big Three automakers. G.M.'s big cars alone averaged 15 mpg, or 3 mpg better than the entire 1974 fleet. Largely as a result, the company's market share has rebounded to about 46 percent.

At the center of this product revolution was G.M.'s downsizing strategy, which began last year with the big cars. G.M. gambled that it could redefine the meaning of "big" in the American marketplace, from its traditional connotation of exterior bulk to a more functional, European-style definition based on interior space and driving quality. The gamble succeeded. In what proved to be a good year for big cars in general, G.M.'s more than held their own

READING 4–2

How General Motors Turned Itself Around*

CHARLES G. BURCK

against the conventional offerings of Ford and Chrysler.

The downsizing strategy is also the key to G.M.'s hopes for the future. Despite the many difficulties and uncertainties of the auto market, General Motors is notably more confident than the other U.S. automakers of its ability to meet the government's tightening schedule of mileage laws for the years to come with cars that will still satisfy the American consumer. Says President Elliott M. Estes: "We're working on three or four scenarios for getting to 27.5 miles per gallon by 1985. It's a problem now of economics—how can we do it for the least cost?"

G.M.'s headquarters are awash in self-assurance these days. There is more than a hint of that spirit in Chairman Thomas Aquinas Murphy's outspoken optimism about the economy, the automobile industry, and General Motors itself. Most remarkable is Murphy's unabashed deter-

---

mination to increase market share as much as possible—indeed, he has said on more than one occasion that he will not be satisfied "until we sell every car that's sold." That's an astonishing departure from the posture of earlier G.M. chief executives, who avoided *any* talk about expanding market share for fear of unleashing the hounds of antitrust.

Murphy explains his outspokenness by asking and then answering a rhetorical question. "Should there be a limit to our return or our market penetration? I say no. The risks of the business today are as high as or higher than they've ever been, and the returns ought to be high. And if we're obeying the law, doing the best job of serving the customer, and discharging all the other responsibilities we have as a good employer and responsible citizen, then we've earned whatever we get."

Such spirit was nowhere to be found at G.M. four years ago. Nineteen seventy-four, in fact, seemed to confirm what many observers had been suspecting for some time—that G.M. was losing its capacity to lead the industry. Sloan, the man who established that leadership in the first place during the 1920s, had observed that "success may bring self-satisfaction . . . the spirit of venture is lost in the inertia of the mind against change," and it appeared in the early 1970s that his own company was fulfilling the prophecy.

Between 1962 and 1972, G.M.'s market share drifted down from its all-time high of 51.9 percent to 44.2 percent. Most of the lost sales went to imports and did not greatly trouble G.M. Following a strictly financial logic, the company concluded that it was sensible to stick with its traditional policies, which had earned it dominance of the highly profitable big-car market, rather than compete head-on in the less profitable small-car field.

For a while, events seemed to justify this reasoning. Measured in dollars, sales continued to rise. G.M. indisputably knew who the prime automobile customers were and how to make what they wanted.

But G.M. was slow to realize what besides efficiency made the imports so attractive: agility and a certain sporty functionalism were increasingly appealing to a broader public than what G.M. understood as the economy market. There were executives at G.M. in 1970 who actually thought that—as one explained to a reporter—"there's something wrong with people who like small cars." G.M.'s domestic and foreign competitors, knowing better, captured a lot of the growth while G.M.'s chosen territory was contracting. Ford's market share during those years slipped only two percentage points, to 24.3, while Chrysler's actually rose.

G.M. also seemed fundamentally out of touch with the outside world. Its size made it a natural target for antibusiness critics—especially the militant autophobes who held the auto industry responsible for everything from urban pollution to suburban sprawl. The company's reaction to its critics, as well as to the pollution and safety legislation pushed forth by the government, was defensive and even uncomprehending. Its labor relations presented a similarly sorry sight. The problems of the highly automated plant at Lordstown, Ohio, for example, which began building Vegas in 1971, became celebrated as a classic management failure to understand or communicate with employees.

Yet despite G.M.'s insularity and self-preoccupation, managerial machinery was grinding along, resolutely if ponderously, in search of new directions. Sloan had, after all, set up a management system predicated upon change. But even important management decisions rarely show up visibly or dramatically on the outside. As Thomas Murphy says, "Drama in business lies mostly in doing well the job right before you."

New policies, moreover, like new cars, require lead times. Indeed, G.M.'s top officers are not inclined to react with high emotion to the events of any given year, for the practical reason that in so massive an institution there is little they can do to affect the short run in any case. Experience has taught patience. They know, for example, that even a new division head cannot do much that will influence his division's results for a good 20 to 30 months. Asked about the process of change at G.M., they invariably reply that it is "evolutionary, not revolutionary."

It is a characteristic of evolutionary processes, of course, that they are hard to perceive until after they have been going on for a while. G.M.'s first response to those social-minded critics was aloof and almost brusque. But after handily turning aside their most flamboyant challenge—"Campaign G.M.," at the 1970 annual meeting—the company set up extensive machinery to bring new and critical thinking into its corporate planning process. It created a new public-policy committee, staffed entirely with outsiders, and the fresh viewpoints the committee brought to G.M. were listened to. The company also hired a number of important managers from outside—a radical departure from the tradition of near-exclusive reliance on internal management development. These people were assigned to key posts. For example, Stephen H. Fuller, who had been professor of business administration at Harvard Business School, was put in charge of the personnel administration and development staff. Ernest S. Starkman, from the school of engineering at the University of California, Berkeley, was made head of environmental activities.

The rapid turnaround of G.M.'s product line over the past three years could not have been accomplished without a good deal of earlier thinking and planning. As far back as 1972, the board of directors created an ad hoc group called the energy task force, headed by David C. Collier, then G.M.'s treasurer and now head of the Buick division. Collier's group included people from manufacturing, research, design, finance, and the economics staff, and it spent half a year on its research. "We came to three conclusions," said Collier. "First, that there was an energy problem. Second, the government had no particular plan to deal with it. Third, the energy problem would have a profound effect upon our business. We went to the board with those conclusions in March of 1973."

Collier's report made for a good deal of discussion throughout the company in the months following. "We were trying to get other people to think about it," says Richard C. Gerstenberg, who was then chairman of G.M. Meantime, Collier's group was assigned to examine G.M.'s product program, and when Collier reported back to the board again in October, the talk turned to what Gerstenberg refers to as "getting some downsizing in our cars."

The embargo, of course, intruded dramatically upon this rather studied planning process. But while no specific decisions had yet been made on the basis of Collier's report, the work of the task force had done much to create the right frame of mind at all levels of management. G.M.'s board was able within two months to approve several specific proposals. Two were "crash" decisions for the 1976-model year. The Chevette would be built, using component designs from Opel and other overseas divisions, mainly Brazil; and so would the car that would become the Seville, under consideration for more than a year. And then, as Gerstenberg says, "the possible long-term program was to find a way to redesign all of our regular lines so we could get them all in a much more fuel-efficient area."

G.M.'s product-policy committee had already decided, in April, to scale down the 1977 standard cars, but the reductions were to be modest, totaling about 400 pounds, and they were calculated to improve economy by only about one mile per gallon. By the end of 1973, however, mileage had suddenly become the overriding concern, and it was clear that practically the entire product line would eventually have to be redesigned. The biggest question, recalls Pete Estes, then executive vice president in charge of operations staffs, was where to begin. The committee's deliberations were intense, but not lengthy. The consensus that emerged, says Estes, was that "our business was family cars, so we had to start there. If we had started at the bottom, there would have been a gap for a year or so where the competition could have moved in."

The policy committee's new proposals went to the executive committee, which makes all of G.M.'s major operational decisions (its members include the seven top officers). In December the executive committee instructed the company's engineers to come up with a plan for substantial reductions in the 1977 big cars, and to start on the reductions for other body sizes in the years after.

Even as the product plans were being redrawn, G.M. was taking a broader look at itself—investigating how it had failed to deal with its problems, and working up recommendations for change. Every summer, the executive committee undertakes what Gerstenberg calls "an inventory of people"—a review of the company's 6,000 or so top managers for possible promotion and replacement. In 1974, moreover, it was charged with picking successors to Gerstenberg and President Edward N. Cole, both of whom were retiring. In addition, the board asked the committee to take an inventory of G.M.'s problems. Both inventories, in turn, were presented to the newly created organization review committee, consisting mainly of the outside directors who serve on G.M.'s bonus and salary committee. The

job of this review committee was to analyze the problems and propose organizational solutions.

Many of those problems were in the process of being dealt with, of course— particularly in the transformation of the product line. But some of the most important were not so easily defined or specifically addressed. The process of running G.M. had grown considerably more complex since the 1950s. The business environment was still uncertain, and outside constraints had to be taken increasingly into account. The review committee wrestled with the implications of such matters during that summer; toward the end of its assignment, it was augmented by Murphy, who had been nominated to replace Gerstenberg as chairman.

What the committee recommended, in September 1974, was a major reorganization at the top. That reorganization, says Murphy, "expanded importantly the top management group. Looking beyond where we were at the time, we designed it to bring new executives into a higher echelon." Complicated in its details, the reorganization upgraded the responsibilities of the executive vice presidents, and added a fourth to the three already existing. The upgrading brought forward four relatively young men, all future prospects for the top, to serve on the board and the executive committee. Since the divisions now answer to top management through those executive vice presidents, the reorganization strengthened lines of authority and communication.

The reorganization also redefined and strengthened the jobs of the president and of the new vice chairman, Richard L. Terrell. Supervision of G.M.'s eight operating staffs had previously been split between the president and the vice chairman; all were brought together under Terrell. That move freed the new president, Estes, to concentrate more fully on operations—and especially upon overseas operations, which were transferred to him from the vice chairman. Along with Ford and Chrysler, G.M. is planning a growing number of "world cars"—essentially similar models that can be built in the United States, Europe, or anywhere else. Though the first of those, the Chevette, was barely on the drawing boards for the United States that year, G.M. reasoned that overseas and domestic work could be more directly and effectively integrated if both divisions reported to Estes.

If the reorganization was a landmark event, it was in some ways less important than another change wrought in 1974—the adoption of the project center, a new concept in engineering management, devised to coordinate the efforts of the five automobile divisions. A G.M. project center, made up of engineers lent by the divisions, has no exact counterpart elsewhere in the auto industry—and perhaps in all of U.S. industry. NASA used the concept for the space program, and Terrell spotted it there when he was head of the nonautomotive divisions, one of which—Delco Electronics —was a NASA contractor. Sloan himself would have appreciated the concept, for it is right in line with the coordinated-decentralization approach to management.

G.M. adopted the project-center idea in order to meet the special demands created by the downsizing decision. Coordinating the development of a new body line among the various divisions is a complex undertaking even in normal times. To do what it wanted, the company would have to engineer its cars in a new way, using new design techniques and technologies, during a time when the margins for error and correction would be tighter than usual. Particularly under these circumstances, G.M. could no longer afford the old problem (by no means unique to G.M.) of what Estes calls "N-I-H, not invented here, a kind of disease engineers have." An engineer suffering from N-I-H resists new ideas that originate outside his bailiwick.

The project center is not a permanent group. Every time a major new effort is planned—a body changeover, say—a project center is formed, and it operates for the duration of the undertaking. Thus the A-body center, which shepherded this year's intermediates through development, ran from late 1975 until this past fall. The X-body center is now at work on next year's front-wheel-drive compacts. All project centers report to a board composed of the chief engineers of the automotive divisions.

Project centers work on parts and engineering problems common to all divisions, such as frames, electrical systems, steering gear, and brakes. Many of these are identical in every division; many others are what G.M. calls "common family parts"— e.g., shock absorbers—that are basically the same but are calibrated or adjusted to divisional specifications. The project augments, but does not replace, G.M.'s traditional "lead division" concept, in which one division is assigned primary responsibility for bringing some technical innovation into production.

The project center was probably G.M.'s single most important managerial tool in carrying out that bold decision to downsize. It has eliminated a great deal of redundant effort, and has speeded numerous new technologies into production. Its success, however, rests on the same delicate balance between the powers of persuasion and coercion that underlies G.M.'s basic system of coordinated decentralization. "We become masters of diplomacy," says Edward Mertz, assistant chief engineer at Pontiac, who was manager of the now-disbanded A-body project center. "It's impossible to work closely on a design without influencing it somewhat. But the center can't force a common part on a division." Indeed, many of G.M.'s engineers feel the project-center innovation has actually helped enhance the divisions' individuality, by freeing some of them to work on divisional projects.

The turnaround of the past few years has worked powerfully to lift G.M.'s self-esteem and spirit. Spirit, of course, is a nebulous part of management, difficult to quantify. G.M.'s state of mind has always been particularly hard to assess. Its elaborate management systems seem designed to function almost regardless of the people who work in them, and G.M. officers rarely waste much time telling outsiders how they feel about themselves or their company. They are practical men who choose to be judged by results.

Nevertheless, there is an inescapable difference between the spirit at G.M. headquarters these days and what was observable a few years back. John DeLorean, who was one of G.M.'s rising management stars, quit the company in 1973 complaining that it had "gotten to be totally insulated from the world." And Edward N. Cole retired from the presidency in 1974 with the gloomy remark that "the fun is gone . . . I wouldn't go into the automobile business again."

Today it is hard to find a top executive at G.M. who does not evidence enthusiasm for what he or the company is doing.

Indeed, the bottom line of change at G.M. is the company's state of mind—which today reflects a revivified sense of purpose and a much sharper understanding of the external world.

More fundamentally, G.M.'s entire approach to its business has changed. The company's downsizing plan was its first comprehensive new strategic attack upon the marketplace in many years. And it was shaped by a far better understanding of the market's changing nature than the strategies of the immediate past. The new top-management team that took over in 1974, moreover, was especially capable of making the new strategies work. To a degree rare among G.M. top managers over the years, Murphy, Estes, and Terrell are all confident, relaxed, and straightforward men, good at

speaking and at listening, and broad in their vision and experience.

Indeed, a case can be made that G.M. has passed through one of the major turning points of its history. One authority who holds this view is Eugene E. Jennings, professor of management at Michigan State University, a consultant to top executives of numerous American corporations and a close observer of G.M. for more than 20 years. "In the late 1960s and early 1970s, G.M. was one of the most insular and inner-directed companies around," he says. "Now, more than any other company in the auto business, and more than most companies anywhere, it has moved up to a higher level of organizational effectiveness. It has learned how to be outer-directed and strategic—to use its head, rather than trying to use it clout." Jennings thinks those practical managers at G.M. don't fully realize as yet what they have accomplished —but he predicts that they will within a few years as they see the results accumulate.

There are tough years ahead for General Motors, unquestionably, as well as for the rest of the industry. The tug-of-war between emissions controls and fuel economy, for example, will intensify sharply under the proposed emissions standards for 1981. Publicly, G.M. is committed to good citizenship on the subject—the company has learned to its sorrow that credibility suffers badly when it complains about unreachable standards and then subsequently manages to meet them. But by any realistic measure, the 1981 standards are irrationally severe, and, in terms of their costs, will levy enormous social disbenefits. People at G.M. do not talk much about the problem at present, but they may have to make the issue public at some point in the future.

The coming year, moreover, may challenge G.M.'s downsizing strategy. The new G.M. intermediates are not the spectacular improvements over their predecessors that the standard cars were, and they face much stiffer competition. Ford's compact Fairmont and Zephyr, for example, are elegant designs, cleverly engineered, and are functionally comparable to the G.M. intermediates.

The costs of redoing the entire product line are enormous, of course. G.M.'s R. and D. expenditures are running at an annual rate of well over $1 billion, which is equivalent to more than a third of 1976 net income ($2.9 billion, on revenues of $47 billion). By 1980, G.M. estimates, capital expenditures for the decade will have amounted to more than $25 billion, most of which will go to meet the demands of emissions, safety, and downsizing. And some tactical requirements are costly too. The company is selling Chevettes at a loss right now, for example—G.M. feels it must pay that price to establish itself more securely in the small end of the market.

Along with the problems, however, come opportunities. By downsizing the top of its line first, while competitors started from the bottom, G.M. has ended up with the standard-car market almost to itself for the next year or so. And that market is hardly the dinosaur preserve it may seem to be. Although all American cars are growing smaller, some will always be bigger than others. G.M. estimates that around 25 per-

cent of the public will continue to want six-passenger cars into the foreseeable future.

Small cars, moreover, are turning out to be a great deal more profitable than the industry once believed them to be. Consumers at all but the rock-bottom level are evidently opting for as much automotive luxury as they can afford. As domestic automakers emerge from the struggle of meeting a concentration of expensive government demands, they can almost surely look to climbing rates of return. Those enormous capital outlays will be making a positive contribution too—they are hastening plant overhaul, providing opportunities for productivity gains and new operating efficiencies. Murphy sees no reason why G.M.'s return on shareholders' equity should not climb back to the level of the mid-1960s—consistently above 20 percent.

Indeed, to G.M.'s officers these days, the problems of the future look pretty pallid in comparison with those of the past few years. The system that Sloan built, with its capacity for change and evolution, has weathered a major crisis of adaptation and emerged stronger than ever. It is hard to imagine what might come along in the foreseeable future that could test General Motors more severely.

How does a manager choose among organizational design alternatives? How does he, for example, decide how precisely to define duties and roles? Should decision making be centralized or decentralized? What type of people should he recruit to work on a particular task force? Organization design tries to identify the organizational structures and processes that appropriately "fit" the type of people in the organization and the type of task the organization faces.

Organizational design determines what the structures and processes of an organization will be. The features of an organization that can be designed include: division into sections and units, number of levels, location of decision-making authority, distribution of and access to information, physical layout of buildings, types of people recruited, what behaviors are rewarded, and so on. In the process of designing an organization, managers invent, develop, and analyze alternative forms for combining these elements. And the form must reflect the limits and capabilities of humans and the characteristics and nature of the task environment.[1]

Designing a human social organization is extremely complicated. An organization is a system of interrelated parts so that the design of one subsystem or of one procedure has ramifications for other parts of the system. Furthermore, the criteria by which a system design is to be evaluated (economic performance, survival capability, social responsibility, and the personal growth of organizational members) cannot be maximized simultaneously: the design of a human social organization can never be perfect or final. In short, the design of organizational arrangements is intended to devise a complex set of trade-offs in a field of changing people, environment, and values.

READING 4-3

An Introduction to Organizational Design*

MICHAEL B. McCASKEY

Minor adjustments in organizational design are always being made during the life of an organization, but the times for major concentration on organizational design are:

- Early in the life of an organization, most likely after the basic identity and strategy have been largely worked out.
- When significantly expanding or changing the organization's mission.
- When reorganizing.

Who designs the organization, organizational units, and task forces? Since organizational design concerns the arrangement of people and the division of tasks, a designer or planner has to have some influence or control over these variables. This task is most often handled by middle-level managers and up. However, the charter to design could be broadened to give organizational members at all levels more of a say in organizational design matters.

[1] Herbert A. Simon, *The New Science of Management Decision* (New York: Harper and Brothers, 1960), pp. 2, 43.

* © 1974 by the Regents of the University of California. Reprinted from *California Management Review*, vol. 17, no. 2 (Winter 1974), pp. 13–20, by permission of the Regents.

Key Concepts and Questions

In approaching an organization design problem, some of the important questions to be answered are:

1. How uncertain is the task environment in which the organization operates?
2. In what ways should the organization be mechanistic and in what ways organic?
3. How should the subtasks be divided and how should the organization be differentiated? Should subsystems be organized by the *functions* people perform, by the *products* or services the company provides, or should some other form such as a matrix organization be used?
4. What kind of people are (or can be recruited to become) members of the organization? Under what conditions do they work and learn best?
5. How are activities to be coordinated and integrated? What mechanisms will be used, involving what costs?

Research and theory provide some findings that can be used as design guidelines, and we turn to consider them now.

Mechanistic Patterns of Organizing Tom Burns' and G. M. Stalker's 1961 study[2] of electronics firms and firms contemplating entering the electronics industry in Scotland and England contributed the important design principle of distinguishing between mechanistic and organic patterns of organizing.

Mechanistic organizational units are the traditional pyramidal pattern of organizing. In a mechanistic organizational unit, roles and procedures are precisely defined. Communication is channelized, and time spans and goal orientations are similar within the unit. The objective is to work toward machine-like efficiency. To that end the task is broken into parts that are joined together at the end of the work process. Authority, influence, and information are arranged by levels, each higher level having successively more authority, more influence, and more information. Decision making is centralized at the top, and it is the top levels that make appreciative judgments[3] to determine what is important in the environment. Top levels also determine the channels whereby the lower echelons will gather and process information.

Thus the social organization is designed as a likeness of a machine. People are conceived of as parts performing specific tasks. As employees leave, other parts can be slipped into their places. Someone at the top is the designer, defining what the parts will be and how they will all fit together.

Under what conditions is this pattern of organization appropriate? When the organizational unit is performing a task that is stable, well-defined, and likely to be programmable, or when members of the organization prefer well-defined situations, feel more secure when the day has a routine to it, and tend to want others to supply direction, the mechanistic pattern is applicable. Organization design findings show that, to the extent these conditions hold, a mechanistic form of organizing is more likely to result in high performance.

The mechanistic form is efficient and predictable. For people with a low tolerance for ambiguity it provides a stable and secure work setting. However, the mechanistic form is less flexible: once a direction and procedures have been set, it is hard to change them. Furthermore, mechanistic forms also entail the danger of stultifying their members with jobs that are too simple, with little responsibility, and no sense of worthwhile accomplishment.

---

[2] Tom Burns and G. M. Stalker, *The Management of Innovation* (London: Tavistock, 1961).

[3] Geoffrey Vickers, *The Art of Judgment* (New York: Basic Books, 1965).

Organic Patterns of Organizing   In contrast to mechanistic units, organic organizational units are based on a more biological metaphor for constructing social organizations. The objective in designing an organic unit is to leave the system maximally open to the environment in order to make the most of new opportunities. The demands of the task environment are ambiguously defined and changing, so people have multiple roles which are continually redefined in interaction with others. All levels make appreciations and there are few predetermined information channels. Decision making is more decentralized, with authority and influence flowing to the person who has the greatest expertise to deal with the problem at hand. An organic organizational unit is relatively heterogeneous, containing a wider variety of time spans, goal orientations, and ways of thinking. The boundaries between the system and the environment are deliberately permeable, and the environment exerts more influence over the activities of the system than is true for the mechanistic unit.

An organic form is useful in the face of an uncertain task or one that is not well enough understood to be programmed. The organic form is also appropriate for people who like the disorder of an ambiguous setting, for people who prefer variety, change, and adventure and who grow restless when they fall into the same routine day after day. The organic form is flexible and responds quickly to unexpected opportunities. However, the organic form is often wasteful of resources. Not having precisely defined authority, control, and information hierarchies, time can be wasted in search activities that duplicate the efforts of other members. Furthermore, the stress of uncertainty and the continual threat of power struggles can be exhausting.

Making the Choice   The choice of the most suitable form of organization is *contingent* upon the task and the people involved. There is no one form of organization that will work best in all situations, in all

cultures, with every type of person. Organization design scholars using a contingency theory approach emphasize the need to specify the particular conditions under which a given form is most appropriate.

Note, too, that the same organizational unit can change its position on the organic/mechanistic continuum over time. The unit might start out being very mechanistically organized. But as the environment or staff change, the unit might move toward the organic end of the continuum. In fact, if the unit does not change its structures and processes to meet changed conditions, it is likely to suffer lower performance.

Even more important, one organization is likely to contain both organic units and mechanistic units at the same time. Burns and Stalker[4] characterized whole organizations as mechanistic or organic; but Paul Lawrence and Jay Lorsch[5] found that these descriptions more accurately described units of an organization. They researched and elaborated on a major contribution to organization design in the concepts of differentiation and integration (D&I).

Differentiation

Differentiation, the creation or emergence of differences in the organization, can take place in several ways:

- Vertically—into levels.
- Horizontally—into sections, departments, divisions, and so on.
- Division of labor—into occupational roles.
- Patterns of thinking—differences between units in members' goals, time, and interpersonal orientations.

---

[4] Burns and Stalker, *loc. cit.*

[5] Paul R. Lawrence and Jay W. Lorsch, *Organization and Environment* (Boston: Graduate School of Business Administration, Harvard University, 1967).

By differentiating, the organization gains the advantages of both economies of scale and people becoming experts in particular areas like production, accounting, contracting, and so on.

Lawrence and Lorsch found horizontal differentiation and the differentiation of patterns of thinking to be the most important types of differentiation for organizational design. The organization segments the environment into parts so that organizational units interact with different subenvironments. While marketing interacts with the media, ad agencies, legal departments, competitors' advertising, and the other elements that make up the marketing subenvironment, production is dealing with the machines, labor market, scheduling, cost consciousness, and safety regulations that pertain to their subenvironment. Furthermore, the structure and setting for each unit must supply the appropriate training and support for different job demands. Scientists, for example, need a milieu that will supply specialized information as well as support in projects that may take years to complete.

An important question in organization design, therefore, is how differentiated should the organization be? How should the environment be segmented and what activities should be grouped together? To what extent should the units differ in structures and procedures, types of people, and patterns of thinking?

Research indicates that business organizations in newer and more uncertain industries, like aerospace and electronics, need to be more highly differentiated because they face a greater range of subenvironments. As James Thompson[6] argues, organizations try to shield their technical core from the uncertainties of the environment. The subenvironment of the core technology unit, then,

will be relatively stable and call for more mechanistic patterns of organizing. The units having uncertain subenvironments (often the R&D subenvironment) will need to be more organically organized. Looking at the organization as a whole, the differences between the units will be significant because the range of unit organizational patterns extends from the mechanistic end to the organic end of the continuum.

Conversely, research indicates that organizations in older, more established, and more certain industries need to be less differentiated. They face a narrow range of subenvironments near the certainty end of the spectrum, and will probably pursue the efficiency given by more mechanistic patterns of organizing. An organization in a relatively stable and certain environment benefits from having uniform rules and procedures, vocabulary, and patterns of thinking throughout the organization. The problem of integration for these organizations, therefore, is less demanding.

Integration

At the same time the organization is differentiated to work more effectively on tasks, some activities of organizational units must be coordinated and brought together, or integrated. The manager/designer must resist differentiating the organization too radically—the greater the differences between the units, the harder it is for them to coordinate activities with each other. If all the units have similar goals, values, and time horizons, messages and meanings are more likely to be clear. But when an organization is highly differentiated, people have to spend more effort translating and appreciating the frameworks of people in different units. Most people habitually think in their own terms, and it takes increased effort to move into another's frame of reference. The chances for misunderstandings increase in a highly differentiated organization.

---

[6] James D. Thompson, *Organizations in Action* (New York: McGraw-Hill, 1967).

The greater the differentiation, the heavier the burden on information processing and upon decision making in the organization. This shows up in the array of techniques for coordinating the activities of a firm:

1. The use of rules and procedures along with the hierarchy of authority.
2. If two units are crucial and have trouble integrating, the appointment of a liaison.[7]
3. The building of a new unit into the work flow to serve as an integrating department.

This list of coordinating mechanisms shows progressively more elaborate ways to achieve integration. With greater differentiation, an organization has to spend more effort integrating and use the more expensive devices.

So in addition to asking how much the organization should differentiate to meet environment and people requirements, another question must simultaneously be raised. How much differentiation, at that cost, can the organization successfully integrate? How should people be grouped to provide the best working conditions for individuals *and* to secure the most advantageous work flow for the whole organization? A manager/designer works for the best practical answer to these questions. Many times he may decide to stop short of differentiating to perfectly meet task environment demands because his staff would find it too great a strain or because it would be too costly. Research findings show that in uncertain environments, the most successful organizations are the most highly differentiated *and* the most integrated. The difficult design decision of how to differentiate and how to integrate is often framed as the choice between product or functional organization,[8] or some newer form like a matrix organization.[9]

Work Yet to Be Done

Our knowledge of organizational design is still growing. Some of the important subjects which need further research are:

1. We need a better understanding of the *dynamics* of an organization developing a good fit to its environment and its members. The processes that span organization and environment, such as planning and selecting, recruiting and socializing new members, need to be researched. In addition to learning more about the enduring structural patterns, we also need to learn about the ways in which organization and environment adjust to one another.

2. We must consider the assertion of power in the interaction of organizations and their environments. How do organizations seek to make the environment more favorable to their operations? How does the environment coerce or influence the organization to meet its demands? What are the consequences of one element gaining sizeable amounts of control over the other? We need to learn about the processes which mediate this contest for control and influence.

3. Up until now researchers have mainly relied upon the criterion of economic performance to assess good fit. Clearly, using economic criteria alone is too limited. How can we judge goodness of fit in terms of

---

[7] Paul R. Lawrence and Jay W. Lorsch, "New Management Job: The Integrator," *Harvard Business Review* (November–December 1967), pp. 142–51.

[8] Arthur H. Walker and Jay W. Lorsch, "Organizational Choice: Product Versus Function," *Harvard Business Review* (November–December 1968), pp. 129–38; and Jay R. Galbraith, *Designing Complex Organizations* (Reading, Mass.: Addison Wesley, 1973).

[9] Donald Ralph Kingdon, *Matrix Organization: Managing Information Technologies* (London: Tavistock, 1973).

people outcomes? Moreover, what about the people who are content to follow orders from the organization? Some argue that we cannot be normative on this value question. If a person is satisfied to be passive and dependent on the job, who can insist that he take more control over his own work life? My view is that a democracy can hardly afford a work system which mainly trains people to be docile, to follow orders, and above all to be loyal to the organization. But others emphasize that many prefer following orders, and this is where the issue is joined.

4. A related issue is the possible conflict between efficiency and human needs. Some elements of organization design concern social engineering to devise the most efficient organization to accomplish a task. Other elements of organization design are concerned with the full growth and development of individuals. It is too optimistic to assume that efficiently designed organizations will always or even usually be conducive to human intercourse. Mammoth operations built to meet economies of scale considerations teach us that efficiently engineered operations can be inhumane. If we had better noneconomic measures of outcomes, maybe we could more accurately assess the design tradeoffs. As it stands now, much of organization design emphasizes an engineering approach, neglecting human growth aspects. Another challenge: How can we design organizations to meet both people and engineering concerns?

5. We also need to learn more about how facilities design supports or detracts from the intent of an organization design. How does the physical layout influence the pattern of social interaction? How does the visual display of information affect decision making? At what distance for what types of activities does physical separation of people or units greatly strain the organization's ability to integrate? How can facilities be designed so that physical spaces can be re-

arranged to fit changes in organizing patterns? Robert Propst,[10] Fritz Steele,[11] and Thomas Allen[12] have begun work on some of these questions.

Summary

A convenient guideline for reviewing what we know about designing organizations is the continuum from mechanistic to organic patterns of organizing. Most suited to stable, certain environments and a staff that prefers stability, the mechanistic form is the traditional hierarchical pyramid that is controlled from the top and programs activities tightly. Most suited to an unstable, uncertain environment and people tolerant of ambiguity, the organic pattern of organizing is more collegial and stresses flexibility in rules, decision-making authority, procedures, and so on. Of course, there are more than these two types of organizing patterns. They should be considered the ends of a continuum of types of organizing patterns.

An organization is likely to contain both organically and mechanistically organized units. How widely the units should range on the mechanistic/organic continuum is part of the question of differentiation. How great should the differences be between units in terms of structures, types of people, and patterns of thinking? Overall, organizations in mature and stable industries contain units that face more or less well-defined and certain subenvironments. Therefore, to meet environmental demands,

---

[10] Robert Propst, *The Office: A Facility Based on Change* (New York: Taplinger Publishing Co., 1968).

[11] Fred I. Steele, "Physical Settings and Organizational Development," in H. Hornstein, *et al.* (eds.), *Social Intervention: A Behavioral Science Approach* (New York: The Free Press, 1971).

[12] Thomas J. Allen, "Communication Networks in R&D Laboratories," *R&D Management, 1*, 1 (1970) Oxford, England, pp. 14–21.

the units should generally be more mechanistically organized, and the organization as a whole will be less differentiated.

On the other hand, organizations in dynamic new industries must have some units organically organized to deal with an uncertain subenvironment. At the same time it should devise more mechanistic units (for example, production and accounting) to face more stable subenvironments. To cover that range of subenvironments, the manager/organization designer creates or allows to develop greater differences between the units. In addition, the organization tends to create more job roles (occupational differentiation) and more levels (vertical differentiation) in response to environmental diversity. The organization, therefore, becomes more highly differentiated.

The opposite tendency from differentiation is the need to integrate, to coordinate the activities of different parts of the organization. The greater the differentiation, the harder it is to integrate. The choice of a particular integrating mechanism, such as a liaison in addition to rules, signals the manager/designer's decision to expend a certain amount of effort to coordinate activities. Concurrent with designing the extent of differentiation in an organization, a manager must consider what effort at what cost will be needed to integrate those differences. The greater the differentiation, the more elaborate and costly are the mechanisms needed for integration.

Organizational design choices are trade-offs between good fit to the task environment and people characteristics, to monetary and human costs, and to short-term and long-term consequences. Such a design is never perfect or complete. Organizational design seeks to build knowledge about and provide guidelines for designing more efficient and more human organizations.

THE INFORMATION PROCESSING MODEL

A basic proposition is that the greater the uncertainty of the task, the greater the amount of information that has to be processed between decision makers during the execution of the task. If the task is well understood prior to performing it, much of the activity can be preplanned. If it is not understood, then during the actual task execution more knowledge is acquired which leads to changes in resource allocations, schedules, and priorities. All these changes require information processing *during* task performance. Therefore *the greater the task uncertainty, the greater the amount of information that must be processed among decision makers during task execution in order to achieve a given level of performance.* The basic effect of uncertainty is to limit the ability of the organization to preplan or to make decisions about activities in advance of their execution. Therefore it is hypothesized that the observed variations in organizational forms are variations in the strategies of organizations to (1) increase their ability to preplan, (2) increase their flexibility to adapt to their inability to preplan, or (3) to decrease the level of performance required for continued viability. Which strategy is chosen depends on the relative costs of the strategies. The function of the framework is to identify these strategies and their costs.

THE MECHANISTIC MODEL

This framework is best developed by keeping in mind a hypothetical organization. Assume it is large and employs a number of specialist groups and resources in providing the output. After the task has been divided into specialist subtasks, the problem is to integrate the subtasks around the completion of the global task. This is the prob-

READING 4-4

Organization Design: An Information Processing View[*]

JAY R. GALBRAITH

lem of organization design. The behaviors that occur in one subtask cannot be judged as good or bad *per se*. The behaviors are more effective or ineffective depending upon the behaviors of the other subtask performers. There is a design problem because the executors of the behaviors cannot communicate with all the roles with whom they are interdependent. Therefore the design problem is to create mechanisms that permit coordinated action across large numbers of interdependent roles. Each of these mechanisms, however, has a limited range over which it is effective at handling the information requirements necessary to coordinate the interdependent roles. As the amount of uncertainty increases, and therefore information processing increases, the organization must adopt integrating mechanisms which increase its information processing capabilities.

***

[*] Reprinted from *Interfaces*, vol. 4, no. 3 (May 1974), pp. 28–36.

Coordination by Rules or Programs

For routine predictable tasks March and Simon have identified the use of rules or programs to coordinate behavior between interdependent subtasks (March and Simon, 1958, chap. 6). To the extent that job-related situations can be predicted in advance, and behaviors specified for these situations, programs allow an interdependent set of activities to be performed without the need for interunit communication. Each role occupant simply executes the behavior which is appropriate for the task-related situation with which he is faced.

Hierarchy

As the organization faces greater uncertainty its participants face situations for which they have no rules. At this point the hierarchy is employed on an exception basis. The recurring job situations are programmed with rules while infrequent situations are referred to that level in the hierarchy where a global perspective exists for all affected subunits. However, the hierarchy also has a limited range. As uncertainty increases, the number of exceptions increases until the hierarchy becomes overloaded.

Coordination by Targets or Goals

As the uncertainty of the organization's task increases, coordination increasingly takes place by specifying outputs, goals or targets (March and Simon, 1958, p. 145). Instead of specifying specific behaviors to be enacted, the organization undertakes processes to set goals to be achieved and the employees select the behaviors which lead to goal accomplishment. Planning reduces the amount of information processing in the hierarchy by increasing the amount of discretion exercised at lower levels. Like the use of rules, planning achieves integrated

action and also eliminates the need for continuous communication among interdependent subunits as long as task performance stays within the planned task specifications, budget limits and within targeted completion dates. If it does not, the hierarchy is again employed on an exception basis.

The ability of an organization to coordinate interdependent tasks depends on its ability to compute meaningful subgoals to guide subunit action. When uncertainty increases because of introducing new products, entering new markets, or employing new technologies, these subgoals are incorrect. The result is more exceptions, more information processing, and an overloaded hierarchy.

DESIGN STRATEGIES

The ability of an organization to successfully utilize coordination by goal setting, hierarchy, and rules depends on the combination of the frequency of exceptions and the capacity of the hierarchy to handle them. As the task uncertainty increases, the organization must again take organization design action. It can proceed in either of two general ways. First, it can act in two ways to reduce the amount of information that is processed. And second, the organization can act in two ways to increase its capacity to handle more information. The two methods for reducing the need for information and the two methods for increasing processing capacity are shown schematically in Figure 1. The effect of all these actions is to reduce the number of exceptional cases referred upward into the organization through hierarchical channels. The assumption is that the critical limiting factor of an organizational form is its ability to handle the nonroutine, consequential events that cannot be anticipated and planned for in advance. The non-programmed events place the greatest communication load on the organization.

FIGURE 1
Organization Design Strategies

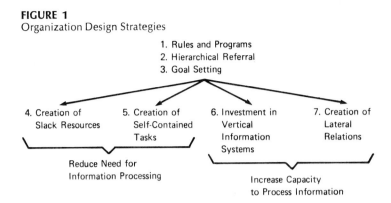

Creation of Slack Resources

As the number of exceptions begin to overload the hierarchy, one response is to increase the planning targets so that fewer exceptions occur. For example, completion dates can be extended until the number of exceptions that occur are within the existing information-processing capacity of the organization. This has been the practice in solving job shop scheduling problems (Pounds, 1963). Job shops quote delivery times that are long enough to keep the scheduling problem within the computational and information processing limits of the organization. Since every job shop has the same problem, standard lead times evolve in the industry. Similarly budget targets could be raised, buffer inventories employed, etc. The greater the uncertainty, the greater the magnitude of the inventory, lead time, or budget needed to reduce an overload.

All of these examples have a similar effect. They represent the use of slack resources to reduce the amount of interdependence between subunits (March and Simon, 1958; Cyert and March, 1963). This keeps the required amount of information within the capacity of the organization to process it. Information processing is reduced because an exception is less likely to occur, and reduced interdependence means

that fewer factors need to be considered simultaneously when an exception does occur.

The strategy of using slack resources has its costs. Relaxing budget targets has the obvious cost of requiring more budget. Increasing the time to completion date has the effect of delaying the customer. Inventories require the investment of capital funds which could be used elsewhere. Reduction of design optimization reduces the performance of the article being designed. Whether slack resources are used to reduce information or not depends on the relative cost of the other alternatives.

The design choices are: (1) among which factors to change (lead time, overtime, machine utilization, etc.) to create the slack, and (2) by what amount should the factor be changed. Many operations research models are useful in choosing factors and amounts. The time-cost trade off problem in project networks is a good example.

Creation of Self-Contained Tasks

The second method of reducing the amount of information processed is to change the subtask groupings from resource (input) based to output based categories and give each group the resources it needs to supply the output. For example, the functional organization could be changed to product groups. Each group would have its own product engineers, process engineers, fabricating and assembly operations, and marketing activities. In other situations, groups can be created around product lines, geographical areas, projects, client groups, markets, etc., each of which would contain the input resources necessary for creation of the output.

The strategy of self-containment shifts the basis of the authority structure from one based on input, resource, skill, or occupational categories to one based on output or geographical categories. The shift reduces the amount of information processing through several mechanisms. First, it reduces the amount of output diversity faced by a single collection of resources. For example, a professional organization with multiple-skill specialties providing service to three different client groups must schedule the use of these specialties across three demands for their services and determine priorities when conflicts occur. But, if the organization changed to three groups, one for each client category, each with its own full complement of specialties, the schedule conflicts across client groups disappear and there is no need to process information to determine priorities.

The second source of information reduction occurs through a reduced division of labor. The functional or resource specialized structure pools the demand for skills across all output categories. In the example above each client generates approximately one third of the demand for each skill. Since the division of labor is limited by the extent of the market, the division of labor must decrease as the demand decreases. In the professional organization, each client group may have generated a need for one third of a computer programmer. The functional organization would have hired one programmer and shared him across the groups. In the self-contained structure there is insufficient demand in each group for a programmer so the professionals must do their own programming. Specialization is reduced but there is no problem of scheduling the programmer's time across the three possible uses for it.

The cost of the self-containment strategy is the loss of resource specialization. In the example, the organization foregoes the benefit of a specialist in computer programming. If there is physical equipment, there is a loss of economies of scale. The professional organization would require three machines in the self-contained form but only a large time-shared machine in the functional form. But those resources which have large economies of scale or for which specialization is necessary may remain centralized. Thus, it is the degree of self-containment that is the variable. The greater the degree of uncertainty, other things equal, the greater the degree of self-containment.

The design choices are the basis for the self-contained structure and the number of resources to be contained in the groups. No groups are completely self-contained or they would not be part of the same organization. But one product divisionalized firm may have eight of 15 functions in the division while another may have 12 of 15 in the divisions. Usually accounting, finance, and legal services are centralized and shared. Those functions which have economies of scale, require specialization or are necessary for control remain centralized and not part of the self-contained group.

The first two strategies reduced the amount of information by lower performance standards and creating small autonomous groups to provide the output. Information is reduced because an exception is less likely to occur and fewer factors need to be considered when an exception does occur. The next two strategies accept the performance standards and division of labor as given and adapt the organization so as to process the new information which is created during task performance.

Investment in Vertical Information Systems

The organization can invest in mechanisms which allow it to process information acquired during task performance without overloading the hierarchical communication channels. The investment occurs according to the following logic. After the organization has created its plan or set of targets for inventories, labor utilization, budgets, and schedules, unanticipated events occur which generate exceptions requiring adjustments to the original plan. At some point when the number of exceptions becomes substantial, it is preferable to generate a new plan rather than make incremental changes with each exception. The issue is then how frequently should plans be revised—yearly, quarterly, or monthly? The greater the frequency of replanning the greater the resources, such as clerks, computer time, input-output devices, etc., required to process information about relevant factors.

The cost of information processing resources can be minimized if the language is formalized. Formalization of a decision-making language simply means that more information is transmitted with the same number of symbols. It is assumed that information processing resources are consumed in proportion to the number of symbols transmitted. The accounting system is an example of a formalized language.

Providing more information, more often, may simply overload the decision maker. Investment may be required to increase the capacity of the decision maker by employing computers, various man-machine combinations, assistants-to, etc. The cost of this strategy is the cost of the information processing resources consumed in transmitting and processing the data.

The design variables of this strategy are the decision frequency, the degree of formalization of language, and the type of decision mechanism which will make the choice. This strategy is usually operationalized by creating redundant information channels which transmit data from the point of origination upward in the hierarchy where the point of decision rests. If data is formalized and quantifiable, this strategy is effective. If the relevant data are qualitative and ambiguous, then it may prove easier to bring the decisions down to where the information exists.

Creation of Lateral Relationships

The last strategy is to employ selectively joint decision processes which cut across lines of authority. This strategy moves the level of decision making down in the organization to where the information exists but does so without reorganizing around self-contained groups. There are several types of lateral decision processes. Some processes are usually referred to as the informal organization. However, these informal processes do not always arise spontaneously out of the needs of the task. This is particularly true in multinational organizations in which participants are separated by physical barriers, language differences, and cultural differences. Under these circumstances lateral processes need to be designed. The lateral processes evolve as follows with increases in uncertainty.

Direct Contact between Managers Who Share a Problem If a problem arises on the shop floor, the foreman can simply call the design engineer, and they can jointly agree upon a solution. From an information processing view, the joint decision prevents an upward referral and unloads the hierarchy.

Liaison Roles When the volume of contacts between any two departments grows, it becomes economical to set up a specialized role to handle this communication. Liaison men are typical examples of specialized roles designed to facilitate communication between two interdependent departments and to bypass the long lines of communication involved in upward referral. Liaison roles arise at lower and middle levels of management.

Task Forces Direct contact and liaison roles, like the integration mechanisms before them, have a limited range of usefulness. They work when two managers or functions are involved. When problems arise involving seven or eight departments, the decision-making capacity of direct contacts is exceeded. Then these problems must be referred upward. For uncertain, interdependent tasks such situations arise frequently. Task forces are a form of horizontal contact which is designed for problems of multiple departments.

The task force is made up of representatives from each of the affected departments. Some are full-time members, others may be part-time. The task force is a temporary group. It exists only as long as the problem remains. When a solution is reached, each participant returns to his normal tasks.

To the extent that they are successful, task forces remove problems from higher levels of the hierarchy. The decisions are made at lower levels in the organization. In order to guarantee integration, a group problem-solving approach is taken. Each affected subunit contributes a member and therefore provides the information necessary to judge the impact on all units.

Teams The next extension is to incorporate the group decision process into the permanent decision processes. That is, as certain decisions consistently arise, the task forces become permanent. These groups are labeled *teams*. There are many design issues concerned in team decision-making such as at what level do they operate, who participates, etc. (Galbraith, 1973, chaps. 6 and 7).

One design decision is particularly critical. This is the choice of leadership. Sometimes a problem exists largely in one department so that the department manager is the leader. Sometimes the leadership passes from one manager to another. As a new product moves to the market place, the leader of the new product team is first the technical manager followed by the production and then the marketing manager. The result is that if the team cannot reach a consensus decision and the leader decides, the goals of the leader are consistent with the goals of the organization for the decision in question. But quite often obvious leaders cannot be found. Another mechanism must be introduced.

Integrating Roles The leadership issue is solved by creating a new role—an integrating role (Lawrence and Lorsch, 1967, chap. 3). These roles carry the labels of product managers, program managers, project managers, unit managers (hospitals), materials managers, etc. After the role is created, the design problem is to create enough power in the role to influence the decision process. These roles have power even when no one reports directly to them. They have some power because they report to the general manager. But if they are selected so as to be unbiased with respect to the groups they integrate and to have technical competence, they have expert power. They collect information and equalize power differences due to preferential access to knowledge and information. The power equalization increases trust and the quality of the joint decision process. But power equalization occurs only if the integrating role is staffed with someone who can exercise expert power in the form of persuasion and informal influences rather than exert the power of rank or authority.

Managerial Linking Roles As tasks become more uncertain, it is more difficult to exercise expert power. The role must get more power of the formal authority type in order to be effective at coordinating the joint decisions which occur at lower levels of the organization. This position power changes the nature of the role which for lack of a better name is labeled a managerial linking role. It is not like the integrating role because it possesses formal position power but is different from line managerial roles in that participants do not report to the linking manager. The power is added by the following successive changes:

1. The integrator receives approval power of budgets formulated in the departments to be integrated.
2. The planning and budgeting process starts with the integrator making his initiation in budgeting legitimate.
3. Linking manager receives the budget for the area of responsibility and buys resources from the specialist groups.

These mechanisms permit the manager to exercise influence even though no one works directly for him. The role is concerned with integration but exercises power through the formal power of the position. If this power is insufficient to integrate the subtasks and creation of self-contained groups is not feasible, there is one last step.

Matrix Organization   The last step is to create the dual authority relationship and the matrix organization (Galbraith, 1971). At some point in the organization some roles have two superiors. The design issue is to select the locus of these roles. The result is a balance of power between the managerial linking roles and the normal line organizational roles. Figure 2 depicts the pure matrix design.

The work of Lawrence and Lorsch is highly consistent with the assertions concerning lateral relations (Lawrence and Lorsch, 1967, Lorsch and Lawrence, 1968).

FIGURE 2
A Pure Matrix Organization

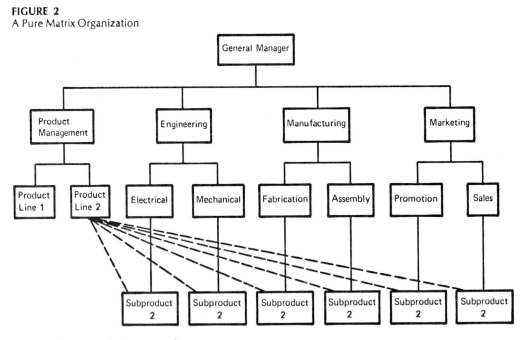

‑ ‑ ‑ ‑ Technical authority over product
‑‑‑‑‑ Formal authority over product (in product organization, these relationships may be reversed)

TABLE 1

	Plastics	Food	Container
Percent new products in last ten years	35%	20%	0%
Integrating devices	Rules	Rules	Rules
	Hierarchy	Hierarchy	Hierarchy
	Planning	Planning	Planning
	Direct contact	Direct contact	Direct contact
	Teams at 3 levels	Task forces	
	Integrating dept.	Integrators	
Percent integrators/managers	22%	17%	0%

Source: Adopted from Lawrence and Lorsch, 1967, pp. 86–138, and Lorsch and Lawrence, 1968.

They compared the types of lateral relations undertaken by the most successful firm in three different industries. Their data are summarized in Table 1. The plastics firm has the greatest rate of new product introduction (uncertainty) and the greatest utilization of lateral processes. The container firm was also very successful but utilized only standard practices because its information-processing task is much less formidable. Thus, the greater the uncertainty the lower the level of decision making and the integration is maintained by lateral relations.

Table 1 points out the cost of using lateral relations. The plastics firm has 22 percent of its managers in integration roles. Thus, the greater the use of lateral relations the greater the managerial intensity. This cost must be balanced against the cost of slack resources, self-contained groups, and information systems.

CHOICE OF STRATEGY

Each of the four strategies has been briefly presented. The organization can follow one or some combination of several if it chooses. It will choose that strategy which has the least cost in its environmental con-

text. (For an example, see Galbraith, 1970). However, what may be lost in all of the explanations is that the four strategies are hypothesized to be an exhaustive set of alternatives. That is, if the organization is faced with greater uncertainty due to technological change, higher performance standards due to increased competition, or diversifies its product line to reduce dependence, the amount of information processing is increased. *The organization must adopt at least one of the four strategies when faced with greater uncertainty.* If it does not consciously choose one of the four, then the first, reduced performance standards, will happen automatically. The task information requirements and the capacity of the organization to process information are always matched. If the organization does not consciously match them, reduced performance through budget overruns, schedule overruns will occur in order to bring about equality. Thus the organization should be planned and designed simultaneously with the planning of the strategy and resource allocations. But if the strategy involves introducing new products, entering new markets, etc., then some provision for increased information must be made. Not to decide is to decide, and it is to decide upon slack resources as the strategy to remove hierarchical overload.

There is probably a fifth strategy which is not articulated here. Instead of changing the organization in response to task uncertainty, the organization can operate on its environment to reduce uncertainty. The organization through strategic decisions, long-term contracts, coalitions, etc., can control its environment. But these maneuvers have costs also. They should be compared with costs of the four design strategies presented above.

SUMMARY

The purpose of this paper has been to explain why task uncertainty is related to organizational form. In so doing the cognitive limits theory of Herbert Simon was the guiding influence. As the consequences of cognitive limits were traced through the framework various organization design strategies were articulated. The framework provides a basis for integrating organizational interventions, such as information systems and group problem solving, which have been treated separately before.

REFERENCES

Cyert, Richard, and March, James, *The Behavioral Theory of the Firm* (Englewood Cliffs, N.J.: Prentice-Hall, 1963).

Galbraith, Jay, "Environmental and Technological Determinents of Organization Design: A Case Study" in Lawrence and Lorsch (ed.) *Studies in Organization Design* (Homewood, Ill.: Richard D. Irwin, Inc., 1970).

Galbraith, Jay, "Designing Matrix Organizations," *Business Horizons*, February 1971, pp. 29–40.

Galbraith, Jay, *Organization Design* (Reading, Mass.: Addison-Wesley Pub. Co., 1973).

Lawrence, Paul, and Lorsch, Jay, *Organization and Environment* (Boston, Mass.: Division of Research, Harvard Business School, 1967).

Lorsch, Jay, and Lawrence, Paul, "Environmental Factors and Organization Integration," Paper read at the Annual Meeting of the American Sociological Association, August 27, 1968, Boston, Mass.

March, James, and Simon, Herbert, *Organizations* (New York, N.Y.: John Wiley & Sons, 1958).

Pounds, William, "The Scheduling Environment" in Muth and Thompson (eds.) *Industrial Scheduling* (Englewood Cliffs, N.J.: Prentice-Hall Inc., 1963).

Simon, Herbert, *Models of Man* (New York: John Wiley & Sons, 1957).

Organizations must balance the need to separate their activities into specialized units and, at the same time, to coordinate these varied units for the efficiency and benefit of the whole. Businesses historically have structured their organizations to respond to these dual needs. The three basic dimensions involved in the choice of a structure are:

1. Functional: a classification based on job activities such as purchasing, manufacturing, sales, finance, and personnel.
2. Product: a classification based on differentiation of goods and/or of services according to distinctions in their manufacture and/or their end use.
3. Area: a classification based on geographical locations whose boundaries are determined by distance, natural, legal, political, and/or cultural considerations.

In domestic organizations, functional structures maximize specialized interests, but coordination across these specializations becomes more difficult. Product structures, by contrast, facilitate coordination among functions for rapid and efficient response, but reduce the ability to develop specialized expertise, particularly in the long term. It seems that when one basis of design is chosen, the benefits of the other are surrendered. How, then, is it possible to design an organization that maximizes both the specialization of one dimension and the coordination of others, simultaneously?

Multinational enterprises, because of their generally large size, often are able to maintain specialized inputs within a product design. Instead of a choice between functional and product structures, their dilemma usually involves a choice between product and area structures. A world-wide product structure maximizes technological coordination between the center and periphery of each product group. It does not, however, facilitate coordination across product groups

READING 4–5

Two Models of Organization: Unity of Command versus Balance of Power*

STANLEY M. DAVIS

within a specific region of the world. This is the benefit of a world-wide area structure.

Given the particular characteristics of an enterprise, what is the best way to organize? When organization is considered synonymous with structure, the dual needs of specialization and coordination are seen as inversely related, as opposite ends of a single variable, as the horns of a dilemma. Most managers speak of this dilemma in terms of the centralization-decentralization variable. Formulated in this manner, greater specialization leads to more difficulty in coordinating the differentiated units. This is why the (de)centralization pendulum is always swinging, and no ideal point can be found at which it can come to rest.

The division of labor into a hierarchical pyramid means that specialization must be defined *either* by function, by product, *or* by area. Firms must select one of these dimensions as primary and then subdivide the other two into subordinate units further

* *Sloan Management Review*, Fall 1974, pp. 29–40. Reprinted by permission.

down the pyramid. The appropriate choice of primary, secondary, and tertiary dimensions is based largely upon the strategic needs of each enterprise. But in all firms it is the result of an implicit assumption that the entire organization cannot specialize by two or three dimensions *simultaneously.* This assumption is based on a monistic pattern of organization with a hierarchy of power and a unity of command, rather than on a dualistic or pluralistic model involving a balance of interest and power.

Two Models of Organization

The structural dilemma poses the ageless question, "If your spouse and a parent were drowning in the river, which one would you rescue first?" The answer of course depends on your environment. In some cultures the blood line comes first. In the United States your spouse comes first; then, if there is time, you save your parent. For our purposes, the question is presented to help determine organizational priorities in business enterprises. However, more and more organizations are unwilling to accept trade-offs. They are creating a structural paradox in order to avoid sacrificing the benefits of either structural alternative. Domestic firms are developing dual structures of functional *and* product dimensions; multinational firms are developing dual structures of product *and* area reporting lines. These dual creations are an attempt to incorporate the best of both structural forms, but they require living with a paradox.

Current wisdom holds that dual structures are appropriate when there are complex and rapidly changing technologies with high interdependencies of either functions, products, or areas. They are said to be *sui generis* and only are appropriate for very particular organizations with unique product/market requirements. This interpretation is misleading, however, because a balance of power in an organization's structure

evolves from the more classical principle of unity of command and not from any fundamentally new organization theory.

Both the "unity of command" and the "balance of power" models develop from a functional hierarchy whose structural form is the pyramid. The product structure maintains the pyramidal framework but sequences the product dimension above the functional one, closer to the apex of the hierarchy. (See Figure 1.) The development of the dual structure, by contrast, represents a shift away from the pyramid, and the hierarchy of power is replaced by the conception of a balance of power. Because most of industry is organized around product-based pyramids, much of the confusion that exists is between this form of organization and the dual or grid design. Some of these differences will now be examined.

First, in the classical evolution from a functional to a product organization, the unity of command is maintained. Managers in functional departments report directly to a general manager for a product line; the general managers report to a single common boss, either a group officer, an executive vice president or the president. In the evolution of a dual structure from a functional organization, the unity of command is not maintained. Product managers and managers of functional departments report to a common boss, but dual sources of authority emanate from them to common subordinates at lower levels.

Second, authority of general managers in the product division structure is vested in their position. It is assumed that as one goes up the hierarchy of command there is a commensurate increase in knowledge. The organization built on a balance of power distinguishes between these two bases of authority. Functional department heads are awarded authority on the basis of their hierarchical position. In contrast, authority is awarded to product, project, or "business" managers on the basis of their knowledge

FIGURE 1
Evolution of Domestic Structures

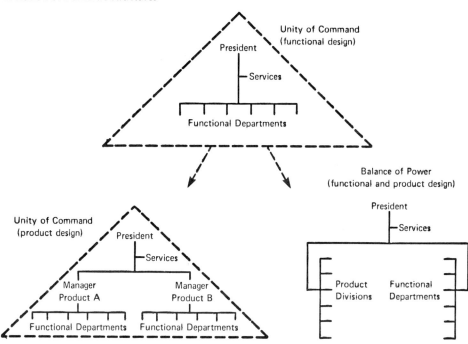

and behavioral skills (their ability to unify the effort among the interdependent functions).

Third, in a functional organization the departments are cost or revenue centers, and profits can be assessed only for the business as a whole. In a product structure each division is a profit center, but the economic performance of the functional departments within can be assessed only on the basis of cost or revenue. In the pluralistic model of organization a number of control systems are possible. In one system, for example, functional department heads watch their costs, and project managers have profit responsibility for their task but do not have formal control over all expenditures. A second method is to use transfer-pricing to fix a portion of the profit responsibility on all managers. Another approach involves "double counting" each dollar of profit. For a manufacturing manager profit

would be defined as "sales revenue less all manufacturing costs and all direct marketing expenses for all products manufactured . . . (as) the total contribution to corporate overhead and net profit."[1] The project manager's contribution would be defined in the same way, and total profits for the functional managers would equal the sum of the project managers' profits.

Fourth, in a product organization the division managers have a permanent body of subordinates, whereas in the pluralistic model product managers may have no supportive staff at all on permanent assignment.

A checks and balances model for management is particularly suited to service and problem solving environments rather than to manufacturing and factory milieux with a constant product flow. Firms that continu-

---

[1] See Vancil [5], p. 85.

ally are faced with temporary projects adopt the task force concept and ultimately formalize it into a permanent project dimension to complement the division of labor by function. Since their environments are in constant and multiple change, it is reasonable that their employees would be able to work comfortably with the ambiguity and flexibility inherent in a balance of power among managers. A major reason why firms with mass production requirements are slower in evolving a dual format, but are now beginning to imitate it, could be because the behavioral flexibility required by the managers in project-work environments is not as *de rigueur* in their own. In other words, the managerial behavior required in mass production environments is unsuitable in a dual structure.

Some firms never feel the need to balance the power between functional and product specialists in their domestic organizations. However, when they expand multinationally they begin to create dual reporting lines. (See Figure 2.) For them, the dual conception of reporting begins in the foreign, not in the domestic, part of the organization, and it may remain there. For example, one may see the general manager of a French subsidiary reporting to a vice president for a product line as well as to a vice

president for Europe. The product vice president may be willing to accept a balance of power in international operations but may be unwilling to accept the parallel ambiguity of sharing the reporting authority of his staff services with corporate staff officers.

Given and Grown Bases of Power

The relative ease or difficulty in developing dual lines of command and a balance of power between functional, product, and area managers depends on which organizing dimension is taken as given and which one must be grown. Domestic companies can develop dual structures by starting with an established functional structure and growing the product coordination. This is easier than starting from a product division structure and trying to grow an independent axis of functional resources. Nevertheless, domestic organizations with a product division structure have progressed in this direction, particularly in the newer technologies and product lines. However, the steps towards dual lines of authority in companies that already have a product division structure tend to be within a division rather than above the division level.

Imagine the reaction of product division managers, who have been nurtured for years on the autonomy of their profit centers, to the suggestion that they relinquish direct line authority over their functional department heads, so that the functions may be centralized. The thought itself is heretical, and any serious consideration is unlikely to come from this level of management. As any student of bureaucracy will attest, it is easier not to grant authority than to recover it once it has been granted. In other words, in an organization with a product division structure it is unlikely that the corporate staff services in manufacturing, engineering, and marketing would become the functional axis of a dual structure. This

FIGURE 2
Organization using Unity of Command Model in Domestic Operations and Balance of Power Model in International Operations

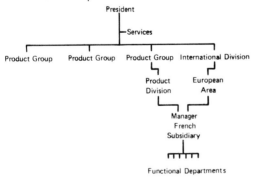

is true especially since the product division managers continue in their product role bereft of direct and complete authority over their functional departments. Still, a multiple reporting system can be developed within a division that maintains the integrity and autonomy of the functional departments, while it grows product managers who supervise the division's various product lines. This is the same as a functionally structured organization evolving into a dual form by growing a product axis.

In a multinational enterprise the resistance to growing a dual reporting structure will be greater among those managers who work along dimensions that historically have been taken as given. It is not inherently easier to take the area or the product dimension as given and to grow the other, because in both cases the functional specializations remain unchanged and are coordinated through the general manager. The

functional department heads will report to the division manager (as in Figure 3) for product A in area X. At the division manager level a choice must be made between reporting to an area manager, to a product manager, or to both.

The reality of dual reporting in multinational firms is not always accepted without problems. A particular company that was organized into world-wide product groups, but that needed to coordinate its Latin American activities across product lines, is an example of how beliefs can be rationalized to fit changed circumstances. A regional manager reported to four product managers in the parent organization who all argued that they had accepted multiple reporting lines but had not separated authority and responsibility. They reasoned that, though they were four individuals, they were all part of the product axis (line). However, they also claimed that it would

FIGURE 3
Evolution of Multinational Structures

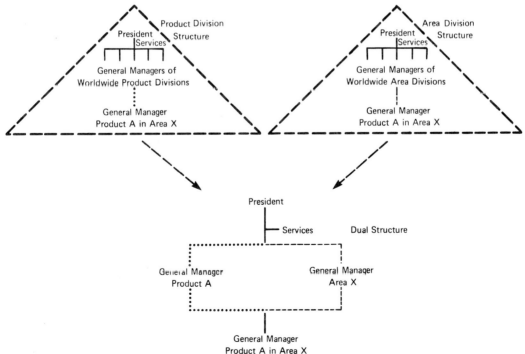

be unworkable for the Brazilian manager to report to the Latin American regional manager and to even one product manager because authority and responsibility would be bifurcated along area and product lines. According to this line of reasoning, reporting to two or more product bosses is acceptable, but reporting to a product boss and a regional boss is not. This is one example of a growing chasm between organizational principles and practical behavior as managers are exposed to the exigencies of a grid structure.

Staff, Line, and the Balance of Power

In both domestic firms with a product division structure and multinational firms structured either by product or by area, the centralized staff services traditionally have existed along a functional dimension, such as engineering, purchasing, manufacturing, marketing, and personnel. According to the principle of unity of command, line personnel are granted authority and responsibility by their superiors which they may in turn delegate to their subordinates. The definition of staff has never been so clear. Generally, staff are resource and service personnel who advise, evaluate, and plan, while line personnel consent, administer, and execute.

Within any one staff function, however, there may be a line of authority. Here some confusion begins. For example, divisional personnel managers usually report to the division general managers. But who can ensure that different policies are not developed by each manager? How can the organization maintain a unified body of personnel policy? Usually this is done in the corporate-level office where staff roles exert authority and the chain of command is not the only integrating mechanism. For these reasons, according to the principles of a grid organization there is no meaning to the staff-line distinction. Writers on organization state that the meaningful distinction is

between "integrating and specialist functions that exercise a mix of both knowledge-based and position-based influence"[2] and that, "a business organized by both resources and programs which are integrated by means of coordination functions is said to have a *matrix organization.*"[3]

The prior existence of centralized staff functions makes it difficult for division managers to accept that the conceptual design of a balance of power can be operational. Instead, they commonly see the desire to shift to dual reporting lines as another replay of traditional staff-line conflict. Managers in divisions are beginning to realize that they do not need direct and/or sole reporting control over plants and sales groups in order to accept profit responsibility for their product. Most people accept that a manager's resonsibility and authority are not equal. That grid structure illustrates explicitly that in most cases more responsibility than authority is delegated. When this occurs, the resource management of functions and the business management of products and/or markets begins to develop as the two dimensions of a grid structure.

From Resolving Conflicts to Managing Them

The principles of pyramidal organization acknowledge and try to resolve conflict among the members, but the source of the conflict is ascribed to human not structural foibles. The grid structure, however, is a greater conflict generator than the pyramid form. Therefore, it puts a heavier burden on behavioral mechanisms for achieving coordination. It also demonstrates that structure itself as a major contributor to organizational conflict, an idea that managers had to acknowledge and ultimately accept as dual structures evolved.

---

[2] See Lawrence and Lorsch [3], p. 170.
[3] See Corey and Star [1], p. 3.

To be effective, all organizations must rely on managers' personal skills to act as mucilage in maintaining a compatible balance of power among the different organizing dimensions. This involves such characteristics as a tolerance of ambiguity, an acceptance of overlapping and dual reporting relationships, and a willingness to arbitrate in face-to-face confrontations. Attempts to routinize conflict resolution has led to the introduction of formal arbitration units in the structure such as Coordinators and Integrating Departments. These are extrinsic to the theoretical principles but are essential to the behavioral reality. Whether formal or informal, the units are behaviorally, not structurally, motivated and, therefore, should be distinguished from the committees that are common to all organizations.

Grid organizations involve different behavior as well as different structure from their pyramidal counterparts. Those that "don't work" usually have grid structures with pyramid-behavior. The refusal to accept trade-offs enables people to tolerate organizational paradoxes at the price of increased conflict and routinized conflict management. This has led to the development of what may be called *antistructures*. Antistructures are designed to be inoperative if the members rely only on traditional coordinating mechanisms. They do not represent the absence of structure in organizations, but rather the fail-safes that are built into the designs to prevent bureaucratization without maintaining or creating chaos. Because the organization's architecture has been laid with competing specialized needs, tensions and conflicts must be negotiated on the basis of behavioral skills. Professional intermediaries, known as counselors, integrators, or coordinators, working in task forces, teams, or departments, have been created in an attempt to institutionalize the grid organization's behavioral requirements. Either they include members of the groups to be coordinated or they are independent

units whose purpose is to accomplish this coordination. Working as individuals or in groups, in temporary or permanent roles, the intermediaries depend on their behavioral skills, more than on their structural placement, for successful resolution of organizational conflicts.

As face-to-face managerial contact becomes increasingly important, a particularly heavy burden is placed on multinational firms because of the distances involved. The new form of organization also requires that people know each other well and, therefore, these companies prefer to develop their management talent internally. It is extremely difficult for someone who thinks in pyramidal terms to be successful in a more pluralistic company environment. This problem is compounded when the individual is from another part of the world. Large investments in manpower planning and in management development are needed to guard against the problems encountered when people work across cultural barriers.

Theory and Practice

Organization theory can start from the beginning to redefine the basis for design. While managers can benefit greatly from the theory, in working toward the new design they must begin with the existing structure of the organization. In a business enterprise this generally involves working with managers who believe in the principles of clarity and unity of command. It then involves developing the organization into one whose managers operate by the principles of paradox and sharing of command. Pressured by the unwillingness to make structural trade-offs and wanting the best of both (if not all) possible designs, managerial behavior changes before managerial belief. A change in practical rationality precedes a change in substantive ideology.

Managerial behavior appropriate in business pyramids is not appropriate to the conditions of life in this nontraditional form. The change is not in structural design alone; it is also a change in technical systems, in organizational culture, and in managerial behavior. Organizations that respond to problems with structural solutions, that do not adapt their systems and managerial behavior to the new design, encounter increased resistance to change and are likely to continue operating in business "as usual." Because the structure and technical information systems are more easily subjected to rational analysis, the human component is likely to be slighted in the design and implementation. This is what happens when one company tries to imitate the structure and methods successfully developed in another organization, without realizing that success is partly due to a good fit between the structure, the systems, and the organization's culture.

The gap between administrative theory and administrative practice continues to exist, although the terms of debate have shifted. The appropriate models for management no longer represent a choice between centralization and decentralization. Many chief executives, for example, would like to increase the unity of effort of the organization's various profit centers without decreasing the autonomy of these units. This is what Alfred Sloan, Jr., set forth in his famous organization statement of General Motors as "decentralized operating responsibility with clearly defined line authority, and coordinated control of policy assured through centralized staff functions."[4] Frederic Donner, past Chairman of the Board and Chief Executive Officer of General Motors, agrees that Sloan's concept "appears, at first blush, to contain an inherent inconsistency."[5] Another chief exec-

utive accepts this paradox under a corporate philosophy called *integrated decentralization.* Many divisional managers, particularly those in foreign or partially-owned subsidiaries, see this as a contradiction in terms or, at best, an impossible dream. In reality, it is a reformulation of the basis for organization.

Starting in the 1920s and 1930s, this reformulation remained within the staff and line principles of the unity of command. The increased diversification and rapid change of the 1960s and 1970s has created a new basis for organization that is completely distinct from the traditional line-staff model yet builds on the principle of "coordinated policy and operational autonomy." The new formulation has evolved from the old one and has the same historical antecedent. The imagery interprets the new principles of organization as either ambiguous and contradictory or adaptable and flexible, depending on whether one is a skeptic or an enthusiast. In either event the theory lagged behind the backed-into reality. Examples, such as the local controller "reporting" up to a functional superior *and* in to a local general manager, have long existed within pyramidal organizations.

The multiplication of this kind of anomaly, along functional, product and area lines simultaneously, has ultimately torn apart the old scaffolding. Organizations that faced rapid change, complexity and diversity of technology and markets, evolved dual or overlapping structures and operating mechanisms. These, in turn, brought about new managerial behavior. The new patterns of behavior often exist with inappropriate principles of organization. Researchers analyze what managers do, yet managers often reject the behavior required by the resultant theories (even if they continue to act in accordance with them). A better correlation between management principles and management experience would help reduce the gap between the

---

4 See Sloan [4].

5 See Donner [2], p. 29.

practitioner's preference for unity of command and the business environment's need for interdependence and shared power.

REFERENCES

1. Corey, E. R., and Star, S. H. *Organization Strategy*. Boston: Division of Research, Graduate School of Business Administration, Harvard University, 1971.

2. Donner, F. G. *The World-Wide Industrial Enterprise*. New York: McGraw-Hill, 1967.

3. Lawrence, P., and Lorsch, J. W. *Organization and Environment*. Boston: Division of Research. Graduate School of Business Administration, Harvard University, 1967.

4. Sloan, A., Jr. *My Years With General Motors*. New York: MacFadden, 1963.

5. Vancil, R. F. "What Kind of Management Control Do You Need?" *Harvard Business Review*, March–April 1973.

The rapid and extensive diversification of major corporations in recent decades has been well documented. Rumelt has found that in a sample of 100 firms selected at random from the 500 largest U.S. industrial companies listed annually by *Fortune* magazine the proportion of firms whose major single business activity accounted for less than 70 percent of total corporate sales had increased from 30.1 percent in 1949 to 64.6 percent in 1969 [20]. Other studies have discovered a similar trend among large British [6], French [18], German [22], and Italian [15] firms.

Organizational change accompanying diversification also has been documented well. Chandler in his landmark study has shown that diversifying firms tend to abandon their original functional organizations (see Figure 1–A) and to adopt instead a product-division form of structure (Fig-

READING 4–6

Diversification Strategies and Organization Policies of Large Diversified Firms*

ROBERT A. PITTS

FIGURE 1

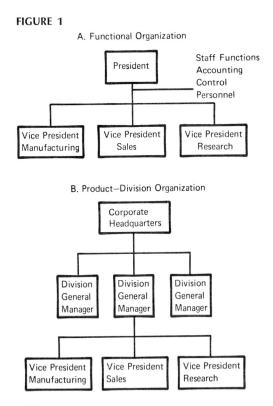

A. Functional Organization

B. Product–Division Organization

ure 1–B) which assigns to each of several relatively autonomous organizational units responsibility for a separate business [5]. The extent to which diversified firms have adopted this organizational form has been documented well. Wrigley [24] has estimated that by 1967 86 percent of the 500 largest industrial U.S. firms had adopted the product-division form of organization, while Fouraker and Stopford [9] found that 89.4 percent of 170 large U.S. firms with substantial investments abroad were organized along division lines. Rumelt, tracing organizational change in the largest 500 U.S. industrial companies over a 20-year time span, found that the percentage of firms having product-division organizations increased from 20.3 percent to 75.9 percent from 1949 to 1969 [20]. Similar studies of British [6], French [18], German [22], and Italian [15] firms indicate that di-

* *Journal of Economics and Business*, vol. 28, no. 3 (Summer 1976), pp. 181–88.

visionalization has accompanied diversification in these countries as well.

Advantages of Diversification and Divisionalization

A variety of advantages of the multi-business divisionalized organization over its predecessor, the single-business functionally-organized firm, has been cited. By enabling an enterprise to operate in a variety of diverse areas, it reduces overall business risk [13]. For this reason, failure in one business area rarely threatens the entire organization. It also provides for more efficient utilization of scarce financial, technical, and managerial resources. For example, it permits easy shifting of funds from divisions in mature, low-growth business to divisions in newer, more dynamic areas [4]. It also provides an opportunity to commercialize more broadly the benefits of technological developments [5, pp. 42–43] and by vastly expanding the number and the variety of promotion opportunities for management personnel, to improve

significantly utilization of this critical organizational resource [16].

Policy Questions and Alternatives

From the standpoint of top corporate management, these new enterprises pose some very difficult questions.

One, **Diversification Strategy** How should a firm attempt to achieve diversification? Should it stress internal generation of new businesses or the acquisition of firms already operating in attractive new fields? If both, then in what combination and with what relative emphasis?

Two, **Location of Activities** Which of a firm's major activities—manufacturing, marketing, research, finance, etc.—should be conducted, respectively, at the corporate and division levels? Should some activities be split between the two? If so, in what proportion?

Three, **Interdivisional Transactions** To what extent and by what means should interchange among divisions—of products, services, and people—be encouraged? For

FIGURE 2
Policy Questions and Alternatives

Policy Questions	Range of Policy Alternatives
1. Diversification strategy	Internal diversification/ diversification by acquisition
2. Location of activities	Primarily at corporate level/ primarily at division level
3. Interdivisional transactions involving products, services, and people	Extensive corporate policies strongly encouraging such transfers/permit each division to determine for itself the extent of its participation in such transfers
4. Performance measurement of division executives:	
a. Impact of organizational performance	Corporate, group, and division performance/division performance only
b. Degree of discretion	Highly discretionary/based on quantitative measures of organizational performance only

example, should a division be permitted to purchase outside the company a product which can be supplied from within? At what price should a product be transferred across division lines? What policies are appropriate with respect to interdivisional transfer of personnel? When a position opens up in a division, for example, should the division in filling it be obliged to consider candidates from other divisions? If so, how should corporate management respond to a refusal by a candidate's superior to release a candidate for transfer to another division?

Four, **Performance Measurement**   How should performance of division managers be assessed? Should it be measured, on the one hand, entirely in terms of the performance of their respective divisions; or should it reflect corporate performance as well? In either case, should it be measured strictly objectively on the basis of accounting data; or should it reflect subjective, judgmental assessments?

Discussion of Policy Alternatives

A fairly persuasive case can be made for either side of each of these questions.

One, **Diversification Strategy**   Diversification by acquisition offers two main advantages over internal diversification. First, it can be accomplished much more rapidly. Second, if payment is made in stock and if the acquiror's stock commands a higher price earnings multiple than that of the acquiree, it results in an immediate earnings per share gain for the acquiror. Internal diversification, on the other hand, has the advantage of being less risky. A firm has time to develop gradually experience in a new field. Internal diversification also provides a firm the opportunity before fully committing itself to test its capabilities against those of competition and to withdraw without large losses if the comparison proves too unfavorable.

Two, **Location of Activities**   In light of the considerable diversity existing, by definition, among the products and the markets of a diversified firm, production and sales activities are likely to be carried out more effectively at the division level. Conversely, financial, accounting, legal, and public relations functions are likely to be performed most efficiently in a centralized fashion at the corporate level.

The proper location of technological research activities presents a real problem. If research is conducted independently by each division, costly duplication may occur. Funds available to individual divisions can be insufficient to underwrite significant research efforts. Centralizing research at the corporate level, on the other hand, while perhaps avoiding these difficulties, raises some others. Corporate research personnel may not understand really the true needs of divisions. This very possibility increases the difficulty of measuring managerial performance since, when research is centralized, a division's performance no longer will depend solely on the achievements of its management team but also on developments occurring in corporate research laboratories.

Three, **Interdivisional Transactions**   Just a single kind of interdivisional transaction —those involving managerial personnel— will be considered here. On the one hand, policies to encourage such transactions would appear beneficial. They would enable a division to draw upon the best management talent available throughout the company when an opening is filled. They also would expand each manager's promotion opportunities well beyond the confines of his immediate division, thereby reducing the likelihood of his leaving the company because of feeling blocked in his career progression.

The main disadvantage of policies in this area is their potentially detrimental impact on division autonomy. To achieve the benefits described above, divisions must be required to submit information on a fairly uniform basis regarding both available managerial candidates and job openings when they occur within their operations [14]. Policies for handling intransigent divisions—divisions unwilling to look elsewhere in the company for a candidate to fill a job opening or those refusing to give up managers to sister divisions—also would have to be developed [21].

Four, **Performance Measurement** These policies detract from a frequently-voiced advantage of the multidivisional over the functional form of organization—namely, the relative ease of measuring managerial performance in the former [10]. When each division management team controls all functions needed to operate its business, it can be held fully accountable for divisional results. When it lacks control over key factors influencing divisional performance, accountability is much more difficult to establish. For example, when technological research is centralized at the corporate level or when divisions are required to give up valued managers to other divisions, divisional performance inevitably becomes a less valid measure of the true accomplishments of division management Under such circumstances, a more subjective, judgmental performance assessment system would appear desirable.

These considerations suggest that the approach a firm takes to measuring performance of division managers probably should depend on the level of autonomy enjoyed by its division. Where autonomy is high, a quantitative measure of division performance would appear to be a quite appropriate measure of managerial performance. When autonomy is low, a more subjective approach would seem to be required.

These four questions provide the focus of the inquiry in this article. The discussion will proceed as follows. First, findings will be presented from three recently completed studies suggesting substantial differences in the way top managements of large diversified firms are answering these questions. Two of the studies have previously been reported elsewhere; the third is reported here for the first time.

The findings indicate that firms pursuing primarily internally generated diversification tend to answer these questions quite differently from those diversifying mainly by acquisition. These differences are explained as the outcome of organizational constraints imposed by diversification strategy. Finally, the implications of these constraints for scholars of business management, practicing executives, and public policy makers are explored.

Research Findings

Berg 1973 The first systematic attempt to determine how these questions are being answered was that of Berg [3]. He examined the size and the composition of the corporate staffs in nine large, growing, highly-diversified firms. Recent diversification activity of four of them which he called diversified majors had been generated primarily internally while that of the remaining five conglomerates had been based importantly on outside acquisitions. His findings which are based on detailed staffing information obtained through personal interviews with corporate-level executives in each of the nine firms studied are reproduced in Table 1. As shown, the diversified majors supported much larger corporate staffs—particularly in research and development—than the conglomerates. While limited to just nine firms deliberately chosen to represent opposite extremes with respect to diversification strategy, Berg's findings suggest that the way a firm responds to question one may constrain severly its response to question two, and vice versa.

TABLE 1
Size and Composition of Corporate Staffs

Companies	Diversified Majors						Conglomerates						
	Company				Four Cos:		Company					Five Cos:	
Functions	A	B	C	X	Total	Avg.	F	G	H	I	J	Total	Avg.
General executives ...	5	5	4	2	16	4	4	1	4	3	14	26	5
Finance	28	61	101	144	334	84	8	22	29	91	106	256	51
(of which control) ..	(10)	(36)	(78)	(107)	(231)	(58)	(6)	(12)	(8)	(38)	(49)	(113)	(23)
Legal-secretarial	4	10	22	42	78	20	1	7	5	6	66	85	17
Personnel adm.	11	6	20	25	62	16	1	2	3	10	20	36	7
Research & dev.	54	130	139	232	555	139	0	0	0	0	0	0	0
Marketing	5	0	34	0	39	10	0	0	0	0	0	0	0
Manufacturing	5	1	0	5	11	3	0	0	0	0	0	0	0
Public relations	1	6	9	16	32	8	5	3	5	6	9	28	6
Purchasing & traffic ...	10	1	33	4	48	12	0	0	0	2	0	2	0
Corporate planning ...	3	3	2	6	14	5	5	4	1	7	9	26	5
Totals	126	223	364	476	1,189	297	24	39	47	125	224	459	92

Note: Numbers shown indicate professional personnel in corporate functions as determined from field research.

Diversified Majors
Bendix
Borg-Warner
Ingersoll-Rand
Company X (unidentified)

Conglomerates
Gulf + Western
Walter Kidde
Lear-Siegler
Litton
Textron

Pitts 1974   Berg's findings stimulated the author to question whether a firm's answer to question one also might constrain its response to question four. Existing evidence on incentive compensation practices in large diversified firms, while extensive, shed no light on this question since data in each case were aggregated in a way which precluded distinguishing among firms pursuing different diversification strategies (see, for example, [23 and 8]). In an effort to generate data which would permit this kind of distinction, the author investigated incentive compensation practices in 11 large diversified firms deliberately selected as representatives of extreme positions along the internal diversification-acquisition diversification spectrum [17]. All 11 which were included in *Fortune's* 1972 directory of the 500 largest U.S. industrial enterprises were operating at the time of the research in at least 12 different three-digit Standard Industrial Classification industries, had operated profitably each year since 1961, and had experienced substantial sales growth since 1961; six of the 11 had achieved recent diversification almost exclusively by internal developments; five, mainly by acquisition. The former were designated internal growth diversifieds (IGDs); the latter, acquisition growth diversifieds (AGDs). These terms were operationalized by computing the dollar sales acquired by each firm between 1961 and 1970 as a percent of its 1970 sales. IGDs were designated as firms meeting the aforementioned four criteria for which the percentage of acquired sales was less than 5 percent; AGDs as those firms for which it exceeded 50 percent.

Information on incentive compensation practices was obtained through personal face-to-face interviews followed up in many cases by telephone and mail communication with the corporate executive in charge of administering the incentive compensation plan in each of the 11 firms studied. Both formal procedures and less formal practices were studied. In firms employing a formula for computing incentive awards, computed

FIGURE 3
Performance Affecting Incentive Awards for
Division General Managers

Performance	Company Type
Division, group, and corporate ...	3 IGDs*
Division and corporate only	3 IGDs, 1 AGD†
Division only	4 AGDs

*IGD = Internal Growth Diversified
†AGD = Aquisition Growth Diversified

FIGURE 4
Top Management Discretionary Influence over
Incentive Awards for Division General Managers

Means of Influence (In Order of Decreasing Influence)	Company Type
Subjective judgments influence allocation of corporate bonus pool to groups, division, and individuals	3 IGDs
One or more variables in bonus formula determined subjectively	2 IGDs
Paid award frequently very different from amount computed by bonus formula ..	1 AGD
Revisions of bonus formula made frequently (more often than once a year)	1 IGD
None of the above	4 AGDs

The following firms participated in this study:

IGDs	AGDs
Borg-Warner	AMF
Corning Glass Works	Gulf + Western Industries
General Electric	ITT
Honeywell	Midland-Ross
3M	Sybron
Westinghouse	

awards were compared with amounts actually paid to participating executives during the year immediately preceding the study.

The results of this investigation are summarized in Figures 3 and 4. The IGDs and AGDs studied did tend to answer question four very differently. While all six IGDs based division general manager incentive awards in part on corporate performance, corporate performance affected divisional general manager awards in only one of the five AGDs examined. In addition, considerably more discretion generally was employed in determining executive performance in IGDs than in AGDs. For example, in all six IGDs, one or another of the four mechanisms for exercising such discretion shown in Figure 4 was being employed; while in all but one of the AGDs, awards were determined by formula based entirely on quantitative measures of divisional performance.

Pitts 1976 These systematic differences in the responses of IGDs and AGDs to questions two and four prompted the author to speculate whether further systematic differences might exist with respect to question three. Investigation of this question was simplified in two respects. First, research was limited to a single aspect of interdivisional transactions—those involving managerial personnel. Second, the extent to which firms had in fact experienced such transactions, rather than the policies encouraging them, were studied.

Ten firms were selected for study. Each had 1973 corporate sales between $500 million and $1 billion dollars, derived less than 60 percent of corporate sales from its largest product-market area, operated in at least five other product-market areas each of which generated more than 5 percent of corporate sales, and reflected this diversity by an organization structure consisting of six or more operating divisions. As in the studies described above, each firm had achieved recent diversification almost wholly by a single route—either by internal expansion or by acquisition. While the IGD-AGD terminology was retained, definitions of these terms were modified slightly. Cumulative dollar sales, at the time of acquisition, of diversifying acquisitions made between 1964 and 1974 was computed as a percentage of each firm's 1964 sales. For IGDs this percentage was set at 5 percent or less; for AGDs at 50 percent or more.

Information on interdivisional managerial transfers was obtained through either a face-to-face or a telephone interview with a corporate executive in each of the 19 firms studied—generally with the corporate vice president of personnel or with his equivalent. For research purposes, a division was defined as the lowest-level organizational unit having responsibility for manufacture and sale of a product line. Two data were obtained on each of a firm's division general managers: first, whether he had ever worked previously in another division of the same company and, second, whether he had done so within the three-year period immediately preceding the research. The percentage of a firm's division general managers falling into either category then was computed. These percentages are shown in Table 2. As it can be seen, interdivisional transfer of management personnel had been far more frequent in all four IGDs than in any of the six AGDs studied.

Explanation of Research Findings

Any generalizations from the findings of these three studies must be qualified in several respects. First, only a small number of firms relative to the population of all diversified firms were examined in each study. Second, investigation was in each case limited to large firms only. Third, because data on dependent variables were not publicly available, accessibility to company management was an important consideration in choosing firms for research. Sample selection was not strictly random. On the other hand, with one or two minor exceptions, firms were selected for study without prior knowledge of their practices with respect to the dependent variables of interest.

In spite of these limitations, these findings do point out some interesting patterns in the way large U.S. firms currently are managing diversity. More specifically, they indicate that successful pursuit of internal diversification may require a quite different set of policies with respect to location of major activities, interdivisional transfer of personnel, and measurement of managerial performance than diversification by acquisition. The purpose here is to speculate on the nature of this requirement.

TABLE 2
Percentage of Division General Managers Who Had Worked in Another Division of the Same Company

Internal growth diversifieds	At Any Time During Their Careers	Within the Past Three Years
A	66%	0%
B	100	62
C	100	44
D	100	56
Average for IGDs	92%	41%
Acquisition growth diversifieds		
M	26%	0%
N	04	03
O	16	16
P	0	0
Q	0	0
R	0	0
Average for AGDs	08%	03%

The following firms participated in this study:

IGDs	AGDs
Corning Glass Works	Alco Standard
Ethyl	Dart Industries
Owens-Corning Fiberglass	Indian Head
Rohm & Haas	Walter Kidde
	Northwest Industries
	SCM

A useful point of departure is consideration of the competence upon which successful diversification by either avenue is based. One perceptive student of corporate strategy has pointed out that, "the strengths of a company which constitute a resource for . . . diversification occur primarily through experience in making and marketing a product line" [1]. Yet, diversifying firms by our definition of this term move into businesses involving entirely new products and customers. Product and market experience gained from their original businesses is likely to be of little direct use in these new ventures. In light of this fact, how can the "distinctive competence" of diversified firms be characterized?

Internal Growth Diversifieds

IGDs first are considered. Their substantial corporate research staffs relative to AGDs suggest that they may possess a primarily technological "distinctive competence." It would appear, for example, that Corning Glass Works' primary competitive advantage when they move into a new business area is its unique technological capabilities in glass manufacture. Similarly, Rohm and Haas' successful diversification appears to have been based importantly on its superior technological competence in several specialty chemical areas. But why centralize this competence at the corporate level rather than dispersing it among divisions? Two factors may account for this. First, an IGD's divisions are likely to be similar technologically since they generally will have been spawned from the same technology. Under such conditions centralization of research avoids costly duplication which would occur if this activity were conducted independently by divisions. Second, centralization permits underwriting of much larger research efforts than could be supported by divisions doing research independently.

Concentrating research at the corporate level involves a cost because it takes away from divisions an activity which vitally can affect their performance. With division autonomy thus substantially reduced, additional reduction in autonomy resulting from policies to encourage interdivisional personnel transfers is perhaps modest and poses few additional costs. With division autonomy relatively low, division management cannot be held entirely accountable for divisional result. This fact helps to explain why IGDs avoid measuring division general manager performance strictly on the basis of quantitative measures of division performance and prefer instead to employ multiple performance measures determined in part subjectively.

Acquisition Growth Diversifieds

AGDs may have considerably more at stake in preserving high division autonomy than IGDs. In fact, an AGD's continued growth may depend to a large extent on its ability to do so. Consider for a moment the difficult situation an AGD faces as it moves into a new business area. Its corporate management, like its counterpart in IGDs, generally will lack experience with respect to the new business' products and markets. AGD top management will suffer an additional handicap. Unlike its IGD counterpart whose unique technological skills can compensate frequently for product and market inexperience AGD corporate management generally will possess no technological competence applicable to a newly acquired business. Consequently, it will be forced to rely much more heavily on the skills and the capabilities residing within its acquired businesses.

This necessity has two important consequences. First, when making an acquisition, an AGD cannot simply acquire the assets, product rights, and distribution channels of a company. It also must secure a company's management talent. Furthermore, in order to ensure the continued success of acquired businesses, it must retain and must motivate acquired managers.

These consequences impose fairly rigid organizational constraints upon AGDs. A manager of an acquired division accustomed typically to many years of operating an independent company is likely to resent infringement upon autonomy—to such an extent, in fact, that he very well may resign rather than subject himself to any appreciable diminution in autonomy. The resignation of key managers in several divisions is likely, in turn, to deal two devastating blows to an AGD. First, performance of the affected divisions is likely to suffer since corporate management—limited to a small number of general managers with lean staffs in finance, accounting, law, and public relations—will generally not itself have sufficient experience in an acquired division's business to manage it successfully. Equally important, any wholesale resignation of top division managers increases an AGD's difficulty in attracting future acquisition candidates, since top management of the latter are likely to scrutinize carefully any acquiror's organization policies and to shun those which do not guarantee divi-

sions of high autonomy following acquisition.

While others have concluded that the unique competence of AGDs is their ability to obtain and to allocate efficiently financial resources, the findings presented here lead to quite a different view [11]. They suggest that equally critical may be their capability to attract, to retain, and to motivate acquired managers. AGDs may be sacrificing deliberately the potential benefits of centralized research and interdivisional transfer of personnel precisely to maintain the extremely high level of division autonomy upon which this capability is based. This view helps to explain the much more objective approach to assessing managerial performance in AGDs as compared with IGDs. Because autonomy of AGD divisions tends to be high, an objective measure of divisional performance becomes a quite valid index of the true accomplishments of their division managers.

Implications

Confident conclusions about the way diversified firms are answering these four questions must await further research of a more statistical nature. Even the prelimi-

FIGURE 5
Summary of Research Findings

		Policy Response	
	Policy Question	IGD	AGD
1.	Diversification strategy	Internal	Acquisition
2.	Location of activities	Large corporate staff	Small corporate staff
3.	Interdivisional transfer of executives	Extensive policies, procedures, and practices to encourage	Few policies, procedures, and practices to encourage
4.	Measurement of divisional general manager performance		
	a. Organizational performance affecting awards	Corporate, group and division	Division only
	b. Top management discretionary influence over awards	Considerable	Little or none

nary studies reported here may be useful to several groups, including students of business management, business practitioners, and public policy makers. For the former, they provide some initial groundwork for building theory relevant to the management of diversity. For example, they represent an initial effort to define such key variables as extent of diversification, diversification strategy, divisionalization, and autonomy. They attempt, further, to trace important relationships among these variables. This effort results in the identification of two very different species of diversified firm—IGDs and AGDs— suggesting a rudimentary classification for diversified firms. These are, after all, the initial steps required in building theory in any area.

Clarification of the organizational constraints imposed by diversification strategy is of potential use to top managers of multi-business firms as well. For example, a better understanding in this area might prevent IGDs and AGDs already possessing organizational characteristics appropriate for their type from making ill-advised shifts in growth strategy. Consider for a moment the plight of an IGD whose stock price is high relative to earnings. Top management of such a firm understandably may be tempted to supplement internal diversification by an occasional bargain acquisition. Yet, the findings presented here suggest that unless the prospective acquisition is operating in an area to which the IGD can apply its technological skills, succumbing to this temptation can result in serious difficulties. Top managers of the acquired firm, for the reasons described above, can be expected to react quite negatively to an IGD's organizational policies. If dissatisfaction results in their resignation, then the performance of the acquired division can be threatened seriously, since corporate management whose competence is building strong businesses around its tech-

nological skill will be unlikely to have much to offer a business unrelated to these skills.

AGDs also might benefit from a better understanding of these constraints—particularly those eager to realize the synergistic potential inherent in the merger of previously independent firms [2]. Realization of this potential requires at least some departure from high division autonomy, since synergy can be achieved only by increasing interdivisional coordination and interdependence. Unfortunately, any departure from high autonomy is likely to make it difficult for an AGD to continue both to attract healthy acquisition candidates and to retain and to motivate managers following acquisition. The unexpected and dramatic profit declines posted by Litton Industries, originally an AGD, in the late 1960s may be directly attributable to such a departure as that company shifted its emphasis from high division autonomy to a synergistic systems organization [19].

Finally, the research can provide useful insights for public policy makers. Spokesmen for this group have long been concerned over the increased opportunities for reciprocity attendant upon diversification [12]. Reciprocity is described as occurring whenever one unit of a company improves its competitive position by utilizing the resources of another. For example, reciprocity is said to occur when a division threatens not to purchase from a supplier unless the supplier purchases from a sister division or when a division uses revenues earned in one division to underwrite predatory pricing activities in another. Interestingly, in trying to stamp out such arrangements, public policy makers have focused their energies mainly against AGDs [7]. Yet, the findings presented here suggest that reciprocity is actually much more likely to occur among IGD divisions because they are typically far more interdependent. The findings suggest that policies to discourage acquisitions can do little to reduce reciprocity; and to be effective in this area, public policy makers will have to tackle the much more difficult task of modifying the internal behavior of IGDs whose diversifying acquisition activities are minimal.

REFERENCES

1. K. R. Andrews, *Business Policy Test and Cases*, eds. Learned, Christensen, Andrews, and Guth, Homewood, Ill., Irwin, 1969, p. 179.

2. H. I. Ansoff, *Corporate Strategy*, New York, McGraw-Hill Book Co., 1965, pp. 75–102.

3. N. A. Berg, "Corporate Role in Diversified Companies," *Business Policy: Teaching and Research*, eds. B. Taylor and K. MacMillan, New York, Halsted Press, 1973.

4. N. Berg, "Strategic Planning in Conglomerate Companies," *Harvard Business Review*, 43: 79–92 (May/June 1965).

5. A. D. Chandler, *Strategy and Structure*, Cambridge, Mass., The M.I.T. Press, 1962.

6. D. F. Channon, *Strategy and Structure of British Enterprise*, unpublished doctoral dissertation, Cambridge, Mass., Harvard Business School, 1971.

7. *Conglomerate Mergers and Acquisitions: Opinion and Analysis*, St. John's Law *Review*, Special edition, Spring 1970.

8. W. L. Davidson, "Executive Compensation in Diversified Companies," *Compensation Review*, New York, American Management Association, Fourth Quarter, 1971, p. 25.

9. L. E. Fouraker and J. M. Stopford, "Organization Structure and the Multinational Strategy," *Administrative Science Quarterly*, 13:47–64 (June 1968).

10. J. C. Kensey, "Dividing the Incentive Pie in Divisionalized Companies," *Financial Executive*, 38:52–67 (September 1970).

11. H. H. Lynch, *Financial Performance of Conglomerates*, Division of Research, Cambridge, Mass., Harvard Business School, 1971.

12. J. W. Markham, *Conglomerate Enterprise and Public Policy*, Division of Research, Cambridge, Mass., Harvard Business School, 1973.

13. Markowitz, *Portfolio Selection: Efficient Diversification of Investment*, New York, John Wiley and Sons, 1959.

14. A. T. Martin, "Skills Inventories," *Personnel Journal*, 46:29 (January 1967).

15. R. J. Pavan, *Strategy and Structure of Italian Enterprise*, unpublished doctoral dissertation, Cambridge, Mass., Harvard Business School, 1972.

16. R. A. Pitts, "Interdivisional Rotation of Middle Managers in Large Diversified Firms," *Academy of Management Proceedings*, New Orleans, La. (August 1975).

17. ———, "Incentive Compensation and Organization Design," *Personnel Journal*, 53: 340–48 (May 1974).

18. G. Pooley, *Strategy and Structure of French Enterprise*, unpublished doctoral dissertation, Cambridge, Mass., Harvard Business School, 1972.

19. W. S. Rukeyser, "Litton Down to Earth," *Fortune* 77:138 (April 1968).

20. R. P. Rumelt, *Strategy, Structure, and Economic Performance of the Fortune "500,"* Cambridge, Mass., Harvard Business School, Division of Research, 1974.

21. R. D. Smith, "Information Systems for More Effective Use of Executive Resources," *Personnel Journal*, 48:454 (June 1969).

22. H. Thanheiser, *Strategy and Structure of German Enterprise*, unpublished doctoral dissertation, Cambridge, Mass., Harvard Business School, 1972.

23. *Top Management Survey*, New York, American Management Association, 1970.

24. L. Wrigley, *Division Autonomy and Diversification*, unpublished doctoral dissertation, Cambridge, Mass., Harvard Business School, 1970.

The phrase "managerial revolution" was coined by James Burnham (5) to describe the increasing dominance of professional managers, first in the large production organizations within society and eventually in society as a whole. The end and aim of the revolution was a managed society, described by Burnham in emerging outline and 25 years later by Galbraith (6) as "the new industrial state." These seminal analysts, however, failed to notice that their revolution, although real enough, was in principle and in fact the *second* sweeping transformation associated with the development of *management* as an activity within society; and, failure of hindsight leading to failure of foresight, they thus mistook the managed industrial society to be a final stage of development rather than a breeding ground for new revolutions as far-reaching and significant as those of the past.

The first managerial revolution, in theory and in fact, was the appearance of management itself as a specialized function within *hierarchical organizations*. This first revolution is still in progress in many parts of the world, and in some it has not even begun. The second revolution, *professionalization*, was stimulated by the separation of ownership and control in the large business organization and by growth in the scale and complexity of managerial tasks. This revolution is essentially complete in North America and in many countries of Europe; however, it is still the critical development in many countries, some of which have made managerial professionalization a deliberate goal of national policy.

The contemporary revolution, however, embodies a different principle, that of *participation*. Its beginnings—in the form of participative management within organizations and in the form of external social participation in the managerial process—appear on all sides and become more prominent every day. Further, participative relationships seem peculiarly characteristic and

The Third Managerial Revolution*

LEE E. PRESTON and
JAMES E. POST

appropriate in postindustrial society, just as hierarchical and technocratic relationships are appropriate for industrializing and mature industrial situations. Finally, and paradoxically, it appears that the participation revolution aims to reestablish some of the natural intra- and inter-organizational relationships that exist in a preindustrial world before the first managerial revolution itself occurs.

THE AMOEBIC ORGANIZATION

In order to examine this paradox, and to lay the groundwork for analysis, let us imagine a primitive or *amoebic organization*, a small group of individuals who perform a few simple tasks cooperatively, without formal internal organization or direction. (Anyone who thinks that nondirected coordination among multiple individuals is impossible is not up on his anthropology) (16). The notion of a single-member organi-

* *Academy of Management Journal*, vol. 17, no. 3 (September 1974), pp. 476–86.

zation is not admissible, but it suggests the "zero value" case for the type of organization that is considered here.

In such an amoebic organization, specialization of function, limitation of responsibility, and control of information—essential characteristics of managerial structures—are unknown. Everything within the organization is related to everything else, and in fairly obvious ways. Similarly, relationships with the external environment are conspicuous throughout the organization. Anything that affects an amoeba in any way affects *all* of it, since in principle it has no separable parts or elements. For convenience, this absence of barriers or separations both within the organization and between it and its environment may be termed "integratedness."

Internal and external integratedness are closely associated; and both, of course, are possible only so long as both the size and the complexity of the organization are severely restricted. The amoebic unit is a primitive organizational form, suitable only for accomplishing primitive tasks. However, the integratedness characteristic of the amoeba may be approximated through new organizational relationships now being brought about by the participation revolution, as will be seen later.

THE FIRST REVOLUTION: HIERARCHIAL STRUCTURES

Amoebic organizations are hard to find in our society, although they abound in the anthropological literature and they are a critical starting point for the analysis of organizational development. The first managerial revolution occurs when *management* appears as a specialized function within the organization, a coordinating and decision-making function different from the specific and separate activities performed. Managerial activity, and hence the hierarchical structures necessary for such activity,

evolves as a result of either (a) increases in the *size* of the organization, even if the increase involves only the repetition of similar activities on a larger scale; or (b) increases in the number of *different* activities being performed, and hence the need for coordination among them. In either case, managerial activity is required to assure that the results of supposedly similar activities are, indeed, similar, and that performance of a variety of specific tasks eventually contributes toward a common goal. As the organization becomes larger and the tasks become more complex, a hierarchy of coordinating points emerges; and these become the successive elements and levels in the traditional management pyramid.

Some authorities—particularly Schein—would restrict the term *organization* to apply only to those task-oriented groupings of individuals in which a formal hierarchy of authority and responsibility had been established (21). Others take a more flexible view, and all recognize the importance of nonhierarchical groups, by whatever name they may be called.

The emergence of management within such groups constitutes a revolutionary development of the first magnitude. It implies the recognition of a separate role of managing or controlling, distinct from the roles required to carry out the operating functions of the group. Recognition of this role also, of course, implies the establishment of a hierarchy in which the manager is distinguished from, and in some sense is superior to, those who carry out the functional tasks. It is significant that the term *management* itself has two important, but quite distinct, meanings. It refers to the *people* who are responsible for making and implementing managerial decisions within microorganizational units (i.e., to the managers considered collectively and not as individuals), and it refers to the managerial *functions* that these people perform. This combination of structural and functional meanings for the term *management* emphasizes the point that managerial functions cannot be seriously thought about without reference to the human beings performing them, and that the position of managers within an organizational structure is ultimately defined not by titles or formal organization charts but by their functional roles.

THE SECOND REVOLUTION: PROFESSIONALIZATION

Conventional analysis of the second managerial revolution begins with Berle and Means' study of the separation of ownership and control in the large corporation (3). Their factual observation was that corporate ownership had become so widely diffused among minority stockholders that effective control of large business units had passed into the hands of nonowning managers. Berle and Means pursued primarily the legal and sociopolitical implications of this development, leaving it to Gordon (8) to investigate its impact on the qualifications and the motivations of the managers themselves.

The separation of ownership and control did not in itself constitute professionalization; however, it did create hospitable conditions. The large numbers of managerial positions created and the constant need for replacement of personnel, plus the increasingly recognized value of specialized skills, led to the development of "salaried experts, trained by education and experience in the field of management . . . [and] responsible for making the decisions which affect not merely the dividends their stockholders receive but also the prices consumers pay, the wages their workers earn, and the level of output and employment in their own firms and in the economy as a whole" (8, p. 318). In short, the *professional* manager emerged as a distinct and important entity, different from both the owner and the functionally specialized employee.

Whether or not the separation of ownership and control has ever been as complete as some analysts have thought (4, 17), the professional character of managerial activity is now universally recognized in our society. Persons aspiring to managerial careers seek the education and experience necessary to become qualified for consideration; and persons confronted with managerial responsibilities by inheritance or routine advancement from lower level positions also turn to training programs and consultants for guidance. Just as nonowning managers have been converted into owners through stock options and bonuses, so owners have converted themselves into professional managers through education and training. The resulting large, competent, and self-motivated cadre of skilled personnel become "The Managers" in Burnham's original analysis (5), "The Technostructure" in Galbraith's *New Industrial State* (6), and the skilled executives of "The Planning System" in his more recent *Economics and the Public Purpose* (7).

There is one fairly significant distinction between the post-revolutionary conditions envisioned by Burnham and by Galbraith. Burnham originally anticipated state ownership of economic resources, so that "the managers will exercise their control . . . not directly, through property rights vested in them as individuals, but indirectly, through their control of the state which in turn will own and control the instruments of production." His central thesis was that "ownership *means* control; if there is no control, then there is no ownership" (5, pp. 72, 92).

Galbraith originally anticipated a more gradual adaptation. Instead of formal elimination of private legal ownership of large scale enterprise, he emphasized that each

. . . individual member of the Technostructure identifies himself with the goals of the mature corporation as, and because, the corporation identifies itself with goals which have, or appear to him to have, social purpose. . . . [Hence,] it will be recognized that the mature corporation, as it develops, becomes part of the larger administrative complex associated with the state. In time the line between the two will disappear. Men will look back in amusement at the pretense that once caused people to refer to General Dynamics and North American Aviation and AT&T as *private* business (6, pp. 166, 393).

In his more recent formulation, Galbraith argues specifically for extensions of the public sector to include both the defense-space establishment and the weaker portions of the "market system" (housing, health, and local transportation, for example) as well. These changes are to be accompanied by the "euthanasia of the stockholders" in large mature corporations; they will be paid off in fixed income securities, and the legal fiction of their ownership thereby eliminated. In this and other ways, the new Galbraithian society will affirm, strengthen, and extend the planning system, simultaneously reorienting it toward "the public purpose" (7, Chaps. 26, 27).

THE MECHANICAL MANAGER

With or without adopting any of these apocalyptic visions, the current management literature—and particularly the textbook literature—focuses almost exclusively on its essential underlying conception, which may be called the "mechanical manager." The evolution of the mechanical manager from the earlier and more primitive concept of "economic man" directly parallels the separation of ownership from control and the increasing sophistication of managerial techniques. Thus, as economic man is the stereotype associated with the household and the owner-managed organization, so the mechanical manager is the stereotype of the professional technocrat in an industrial society.

The tasks and activities of the mechanical manager are now the staples of the management curriculum: defining goals, analyzing alternatives, making decisions, motivating subordinates, and monitoring practice so that policies once decided upon will in fact be carried out. The *compleat* mechanical manager is readily identifiable by the clarity of his vision, the rationality of his decision processes, and the precision of his analytical tools. As Jacoby describes him:

The manager is skilled in allocating scarce resources to the most urgent uses. He knows how to discover new markets and to correlate production with market demand. He is ingenious in financing the enterprise. He designs human organizations. Through his knowledge of people, he selects and welds them into efficient working teams. He plans for the future. He establishes standards of performance. He designs and operates controls of the organization. To do all these things well requires a mastery of the science of management, along with an artistry in its practice that comes with experience (10, p. 70).

The science of management referred to by Jacoby is now almost universally recognized as a study of analytical decision making, primarily in the abstract and without regard to time, space, situation, or organizational context. As Miller and Starr, who have played Geppetto to a whole generation of managerial Pinocchioes, state the case:

Decision making is a root process. It is intertwined with all human activity. These roots are so fundamental to accomplishment that they take on a vital organic meaning without reference to the "real" detail of any particular problem. . . . Few who have not dwelt deliberately and at length on the nature of deciding are aware of how sensibly and straightforwardly decisions lend themselves to theoretical formulation. With a few strong principles we can organize the critical decision elements into basic sets that repeat themselves over and over again in every problem (20, pp. vii–viii).

So powerful a contention can be expected to attract a strong response. Critics of the mechanical manager concept challenge both its descriptive accuracy and its validity as a guide to practical affairs. They ask: Is it true that all, most, or even many managerial decisions can be framed and processed through a single decision theory structure? And, even if so, would the answers thus obtained be really suitable to the problems at hand? More fundamentally, the critics question the very concept of professionalization—with its implications of specialization and remoteness from active participation—as a desirable characteristic of top level decision makers.

Popular criticism of the mechanical manager and his power position within the professional bureaucracy, both corporate and government, has been effectively summarized in Theodore Levitt's *The Third Sector* (18). He points out that the impersonality, narrowness of focus, self-protected behavior, and unresponsiveness of the professional bureaucracies that control the public and the private sectors of our society are being confronted by a "third sector . . . composed of a bewildering variety of organizations and institutions . . . to do things business and government are either not doing, not doing well, or not doing often enough" (18, p. 49). He contrasts the old third sector based on "persuasion and pull" with a new, vigorous, and rapidly growing group of organizations based on "publicity and push." Throughout the third sector, in the past and in the present, the central emphasis has been on *voluntarism*, a willingness on the part of concerned individuals to take upon themselves responsibilities that did not seem to be recognized, or were not well handled, by other elements within society.

Levitt's comments are, as always, stimulating; and his conclusions are almost too optimistic with respect to the power of voluntary organizations to alter basic social relationships. More important, he overlooks the key point that voluntarism implies participation, and that if participative behavior is called into play to deal with aspects of social life neglected by other organizations, it will probably also prove useful—or at least be tried—in the established organizations of the first and second sectors as well. Hence, the true import of Levitt's analysis is not that voluntarism provides an ameliorating force within a professionally managed society, but rather that it constitutes one of the long-term developments associated with the more pervasive *third* managerial revolution itself.

THE THIRD REVOLUTION: PARTICIPATION

As it turns out, both the remoteness of the professional and the pseudo-objectivity of the mechanical manager are now being attacked through a single new revolutionary idea—participation. Participation means the inclusion of persons and groups involved and concerned with the diverse outcomes of managerial activity as participants in the managerial process. Participation is more than simply the receipt of information or the consideration of viewpoints, although recognition by professional managers of the need to take into account the views and attitudes of others may be an opening wedge in the revolutionary process. Participation involves what Bell has described as a shift from the "economizing mode"—characterized by an emphasis on productivity and a rational balancing of ends and means—to a "sociologizing mode," in which there is, first, an effort to establish "social justice by the inclusion of all persons *into* the society," and then an "effort to judge society's needs in a more conscious fashion, and . . . to do so on the basis of some explicit conception of the 'public interest' " (2, p. 283).

In exploring the impact of the participation revolution and the sociologizing (or politicizing) mode on the practice of management within the individual organization, it is important to distinguish between *internal* participation—by persons who might be considered "members" of the managerial unit, such as employees, stockholders, etc.—and *external* participation by "outsiders." Internal participation is the more familiar. A primitive form is based upon the benign but rather naive proposition that subordinates will "feel better" if they have been consulted about some matter involving their activities, even if their consultation has no effect on the eventual results. More sophisticated analyses based upon observational data indicate that the impact of internal participative decision making cannot be clearly ascertained. Mediating factors such as initial motives and attitudes, the visibility of the process, the difficulty of the issues to be settled, amount of information, etc., may exert powerful influence on the outcomes of specific participative decision-making experiences (19). Proposed methods for incorporating internal participation into the managerial process range all the way from informal and occasional consultation of individual workgroups to extensive changes in the ownership and organization structure of enterprises, such as those suggested by the Scanlon Plan, Kelso's "Two-Factor Theory" (15), and the various schemes for worker participation now being adopted in Europe (11, 12, 24, 25, 26). In any event, participative strategies involve structural and behavioral change. As Hunt points out in a recent and highly perceptive handbook of managerial ideas, the central issue to be addressed is "a mounting concern and interest in democratizing authority systems, improving the quality of life within our institutional structures, and meshing organizations more meaningfully with vital human interests" (9, p. 173). He emphasizes that both participative and *counseling* relationships are required, and that facilitating such relationships should be a consideration in the design of organizational structures. Tannenbaum states:

Traditional managerial approaches can be distinguished from participative [ones] by the rules regarding the quality and quantity of exchange within them. In some traditional systems employees exchange compliance for pay; in participative systems they do so for some managerial compliance (plus pay). . . . The possibility of such an expanding exchange relies heavily on the assumption of broad areas of common interest (rather than conflict) between members and leaders of the organization (22, p. 16).

External participation by persons not specifically involved by employment or ownership in the operations of an organization is a newer concept. Its traditional pre-revolutionary forms include governmental rules and formal policies with respect to specific aspects of microunit management, public agency supervision in the regulated sectors of the economy, and occasional public scrutiny of specific firms and their detailed operations in response to economic crises or public outcry. There has also been a tradition in many large enterprises of appointing a few key public figures—presidents of universities or elected officials, for example—to important committees and boards of directors, perhaps as token representatives of society at large. Only recently, however, has the notion that representatives of the *general* public—or of *special* publics, such as community neighborhoods, consumers, customers, etc.—might take significant roles in the formation of microunit plans and decisions. This new concept of representativeness within the management structure is, of course, only one indication of the emerging recognition of organizational social involvement and responsibility and the corresponding participation of society at large in directing and evaluating managerial performance (1; 10, Chap. 8).

The theoretical basis for the participation revolution is provided by the systems approach which, according to Kast and Rosenzweig, offers "an opportunity for some convergence in organization and management theory. [It] provides a basis for integration, by giving us a way to view the total organization in interaction with its environment and for conceptualizing the relationships between internal components or subsystems" (13, p. 9). The essential idea is that a systems analysis, focusing on interrelated components within and among organizations, provides a framework for identifying actual and possible sources of participation and for assessing their relative strengths and involvements with respect to particular issues.

IMPLICATIONS FOR POSTINDUSTRIAL SOCIETY

Internal and external participativeness raise serious issues about the traditional legitimacy and autonomy of managerial organizations, particularly private firms, in our society. At worst, internal participativeness could degenerate into a modern syndicalism, with larger and more rigid collectives of managers, employees, and owners evolving over time. Similarly, external participation could lead to a standoff of conflicting interests that would paralyze micro-unit activity; this danger seems particularly significant with respect to public sector management and the new Galbraithian vision. Even without these dire consequences, as Katz and Kahn point out, "the conflict between rising expectations of involvement and the difficulties of communication and participation in a complicated structure of decision making can have . . . maladaptive effects [such as] . . . apathy or alienation among certain elements, who see themselves hopelessly outside the system; . . .

blind conformity . . . ; [and] . . . ferment without form . . ." (14, p. 470).

On the other hand, attitudes favoring the participation revolution are already well established, and the revolution itself is clearly underway. And, as suggested at the outset, participation may represent a kind of re-creation of the "integratedness," both internal and external, that characterizes the amoebic organization itself. Perhaps the analogy seems strained, but several indicators point in this direction. Internal participation is clearly a reaction against the increasing rigidity and impersonality of hierarchical structures, and against the remoteness and mysticism of professional management. External participation is, at a minimum, a source of information and viewpoint for managers newly aware of multiple complex interactions between their own organizations and the larger society. Indeed, both the reality and the necessity of the participation revolution are seen by some analysts as critical features of the emerging postindustrial society.

Postindustrial society, as envisioned by Bell, is characterized by three key features: (a) a shift of principal economic activity from goods to services, (b) the appearance of "theoretical knowledge" as a principal factor of production and social control, and (c) a resulting "pre-eminence of the professional and technical class" (2, p. 14). A hasty reader might conclude that this is just an updated version of Burnham's "managed society"; however, Bell's further point is that the "technocratic mind-view . . . [with] its emphasis on the logical, practical, problem-solving, instrumental, orderly and disciplined approach to objectives . . ." will not be the governing mode of social decision making and change (2, p. 349). On the contrary, both Bell and Galbraith insist that the "sociologizing mode" and the "political arena" will, and should, become the more prominent and, in effect, final elements in the process of social decision making. The reason, according to Bell, is that "we have become a communal society, in which many more groups now seek to establish their social rights—their claims on society—through the political order." As he sees it, there is "a society-wide uprising against bureaucracy and a desire for participation, a theme summed up in a statement, already a catch-phrase, that 'people ought to be able to affect the decisions that control their lives'" As a result, "the conception of a rational organization of society stands confounded" (2, pp. 364–66).

Paradox upon paradox. First it seems that "knowledge is power," and then—just the reverse—that power is so widely distributed among the substructures of postindustrial society that rationality is "confounded." Can it be that both are true?

The answer, of course, is affirmative. The knowledge that really is power in the postindustrial society is not simply the scientific learning and technical skill of the mechanical manager—necessary and valuable as these are—but the further understanding that these are *not* the final controlling forces in society as a whole. Participation—intraorganizational and extraorganizational (and the two are not as different as they may seem)—is, in fact, the only workable mode of organizational guidance in postindustrial society, and that society will take its evolving shape through the growth and interaction of participative organizations. The third managerial revolution may or may not be the last, but it is certainly the contemporary phenomenon. Hence, the management of participative organizations and processes, and the analysis of the implications of participative behavior throughout society, should be a primary focus of our teaching and study for the remainder of this century.

REFERENCES

1. Adizes, Ichak and J. Fred Weston. "Comparative Models of Social Responsibility," *Academy of Management Journal*, vol. 16, no. 1 (1973), 112–28.

2. Bell, Daniel. *The Coming of Post-Industrial Society* (New York: Basic Books, 1973).

3. Berle, Adolf A., and Gardiner C. Means. *The Modern Corporation* (New York: Macmillan, 1932).

4. Burch, Philip H., Jr. *The Managerial Revolution Reassessed* (Lexington: Health, 1972).

5. Burnham, James. *The Managerial Revolution* (New York: Day, 1941).

6. Galbraith, John Kenneth. *The New Industrial State* (Boston: Houghton Mifflin, 1967).

7. Galbraith, John Kenneth. *Economics and the Public Purpose* (Boston: Houghton Mifflin, 1973).

8. Gordon, Robert Aaron. *Business Leadership in the Large Corporation* (Berkeley: University of California Press, 1961).

9. Hunt, Raymond G. *Interpersonal Strategies for System Management: Applications of Counseling and Participative Principles* (Monterey: Brooks/Cole, 1974).

10. Jacoby, Neil H. *Corporate Power and Social Responsibility* (New York: Macmillan, 1973).

11. Jenkins, David. "Industrial Democracy." *New York Times*, May 13, 1973, Financial Section, p. 1.

12. Jenkins, David. "Industrial Democracy in Sweden," *New York Times*, October 14, 1973.

13. Kast, Fremont E., and James E. Rosenzweig (eds.), *Contingency Views of Organization and Management* (Chicago: Science Research Associates, 1973).

14. Katz, Daniel, and Robert L. Kahn. *The Social Psychology of Organizations* (New York: Wiley, 1966).

15. Kelso, Louis O., and Patricia Hetter. *Two-Factor Theory: The Economics of Reality* (New York: Random House, 1967).

16. Knowles, H. P., and B. O. Saxburg. "Human Relations and the Nature of Man," *Harvard Business Review*, vol. 45, no. 2 (1967), 20–40.

17. Larner, Robert J. *Management Control and the Large Corporation* (New York: Dunellen, 1970).

18. Levitt, Theodore. *The Third Sector* (New York: Amacom, 1973).

19. Lowin, Aaron. "Participative Decision Making," *Organizational Behavior and Human Performance*, vol. 3 (1968), 68–107.

20. Miller, David W., and Martin K. Starr. *Executive Decisions and Operations Research*, 2d ed. (Englewood Cliffs, N. J.: Prentice-Hall, 1969).

21. Schein, Edgar H. *Organizational Psychology* (Englewood Cliffs, N.J.: Prentice-Hall, 1965).

22. Tannenbaum, Arnold S. *Control in Organizations* (New York: McGraw-Hill, 1968).

23. Thompson, James D. "Strategies for Studying Organizations," in Fremont E. Kast and James E. Rosenzweig (eds.), *Contingency Views of Organization and Management* (Chicago: Science Research Associates, 1973), pp. 26–36.

24. Ulman, Neil. "The Worker's Voice," *Wall Street Journal*, February 23, 1973, p. 1.

25. Van de Vall, Mark, and Charles D. King. "Comparing Models of Workers' Participation in Managerial Decision Making," in Desmond Graves (ed.), *Management Research: A Cross-Cultural Perspective* (New York: Elsevier Scientific Publishing, 1973), pp. 95–114.

26. Ways, Max. "More Power to Everybody," *Fortune*, May 1970.

Trying to analyze and present an overall view of evolving organizational forms and structures is like walking into an antique shop and asking, "What's new?". Evolution clearly washes out revolution in structural forms but the old ideas and concepts are being improved upon continually in the hard school of reality. Interesting variations on old structural forms appear at three levels in organizations and each of these levels in turn has undergone steady if not spectacular change.

At the level of the total organization the most promising changes involve an attempt to link strategy to structure in practice rather than in theory, and the design of a two-tiered organization structured to cope with both current operations and future directions.

At the chief executive office level major stress is being placed on the promotion of innovation and the use of a multiple management arrangement usually called the corporate office or the office of the president. The most promising potential for improvement of structural forms at the operational level comes from attempts that link task specialization to integration or coordination in a systematically designed organizational hierarchy.

BASICS UNDERLYING STRUCTURAL CHANGES

A better understanding of the nature of changes in organizational forms at the three levels described above is enhanced if several underlying premises are laid out concisely.

Strategy

First, the presumption is made that strategy does indeed precede structure. Exhibit 1 clearly shows that structure is a tool for implementing strategy. This premise explicitly rejects the organization chart as cast in

Evolving Organizational Forms*

JOHN HUTCHINSON

bronze; rather it is visualized as a flexible instrument designed to facilitate the achievement of a given set of strategies.

Structural Design

The second basic input conceptualizes how a structural design is envisaged by its architect—the turf on which the designer stands. One set of structuralists starts from the point that people are paramount. Organizations they design must fit the existing manpower resources or, at most, require a minimum amount of shifting, hiring, and changing of people. Another underlying principle of organization design holds that information flows should be the major focus. The primacy of information processing and use emphasizes that it is critical to have the right information flowing between the right people and levels so that an optimum amount of information is provided to formulate the decisions shaping the eventual destiny of the company. A third approach considers efficiency as the main point of

* *Columbia Journal of World Business*, Summer 1976, pp. 48–58.

EXHIBIT 1
Strategy Formulaton and Strategy Implementation

Formulation		Implementation
Environmental factors		Objectives
		Structures
Company strengths and weaknesses	Strategy	Processes (planning and control)
Values of key people		People

departure and thus attempts to fit people into the jobs or tasks producing the most efficient result. Major focus in such input-output models is placed in reporting relationships and on planning and control systems to check progress against planned objectives. The final point of take off is to hone in on the task to be done as the vital design element. Here an attempt is made to match up the external environment with the technology and resources (both human and material) that are available in the firm. One of these four basic approaches is usually dominant in the minds of any manager setting up an organizational structure. It is important to recognize this point since the end product is influenced heavily by the bias of the architect—and this tends to limit the degree of flexibility brought to the task at hand.

Evolution

A third factor to consider in giving a perspective on newly evolving forms deals with the concept of how growth in business organizations affects the kinds of structures needed. A typical growth pattern begins with a small, simple one-man operation characterized as an "entrepreneurial" organization. Next in the evolutionary path is the "transitional" stage where product divisions appear. At this point the organization and its people take on a functional aspect, and the chief executive thinks of himself as

an "oilman" or "in chemicals." The zenith of the evolutionary pyramid is reached when the product division evolves into a large and complex multidivisional or multinational company. The chief executive can now be classed as a "trustee" rather than a driving "entrepreneur" or a product-function manager. The obvious point here is that entrepreneurs, functional managers and trustee-type managers have different perspectives and different roles relative to the organization. In the sections that follow the major focus is on phases two and three rather than on the entrepreneurial phase simply because most organizations having major concerns about organizational matters tend to be beyond the early stages of growth. One reference to the entrepreneurial stage does appear however in the discussion of the new ventures concept described below.

ORGANIZATION OF THE TOTAL ENTITY—STRUCTURE IN THE MNC

The MNC is an excellent vehicle in which to examine changing organizational forms because it houses some of the most complex structural formulations in current usage. This section attempts to relate the basic idea that strategy does indeed follow structure by first linking strategic concerns of multinational firms to existing organizational forms and then attempting to evaluate the relative effectiveness of these structures in facilitating the attainment of selected strategies.

In the existing classification of MNCs (which are usually third–stage companies) there are five widely used structure forms. The *international division* appears typically in firms that are first moving into the international area. The division is set up similarly to the domestic product divisions. It may have its own line and staff personnel, and its market is seen as the world rather than a specific geographic area. The second form of structure is the *worldwide product division* where the scope of product sales is extended from the domestic market to a worldwide one. A third alternative is the *area* or *geographic division*. Here separate (but sometimes unequal) divisions are established for, say, Europe, Asia, Africa, and North America. Each geographic entity is theoretically designed to take advantage of the economics of time and place in local market areas. In recent years, the so-called *matrix organization* has come to the forefront. The matrix organization is typically a combination of area or divisional structure with a functional or product division focus at corporate headquarters. In an ideal matrix relationship, a function such as finance works with ("matrixes with") the area division, say Europe, and establishes certain limits, controls, relationships that apply across Europe. This allows the functional expertise at headquarters to be related to and diffused through the various geographic divisions. Serious questions about the balance of power arise in matrix organizations, but when a matrix structure

works properly, specialized skills are readily adopted to meet local conditions. Another relatively new structure that shows signs of continued and rapid development is the *focused market unit*. Focused market units are similar to a combination of product divisions and area divisions but they concentrate on markets rather than products and try to service those markets no matter what geographic or cultural lines are crossed. A well known example of this structure is the strategic business unit concept developed by the General Electric Corporation.

Given the fact that such a wide range of structures exists at the multinational level and keeping in mind the fact that corporate strategies vary in time and in emphasis, the selection of an optimum structure to maximize strategic considerations is a continuing problem for top level management. Exhibit 2 attempts to relate areas of corporate concern to various organizational forms and evaluate the relative suitability of each of these forms to meet corporate criteria. Exhibit 2 is based upon a scheme developed

EXHIBIT 2
Suitability of Basic MNC Organizational Structures to Corporate Concerns

Area of Corporate Concern	Level of Suitability				
	Inter-national Div.	World-wide Product Div.	Area Div.	Matrix	Focused Market Units
Rapid growth	M	H	M	H	H
Diversity of products	L	H	L	H	H
High technology	M	H	L	H	H
Few experienced managers	H	M	L	L	L
Close corporate control	M	H	L	H	H
Close govt. relations	M	L	H	M	M
Resource allocation: Product considerations should dominate	L	H	L	M	M
Geographic considerations should dominate	M	L	H	M	M
Functional considerations should dominate	L	M	L	H	M
Relative cost	M	M	L	H	M

H = high; M = medium; L = low.

by J. W. Widing and simply adapted to show recent changes.[1] The first four columns and all of the rows are taken directly from the Widing article and the focused market unit portion was added to bring the table up to date.

Exhibit 2 indicates that if the main focus of the corporation is rapid growth, as might be the case when a firm attempts to push a new product and gain a competitive advantage before competitors enter the market, then the worldwide product division, the matrix organization, or the focused market unit would be the most suitable kind of organization to adopt. If, on the other hand, the strategic emphasis is on close corporate control because of concern over an issue such as bribery of local government officials, then a worldwide product division, a matrix organization, or a focused market unit would be most suitable. If intimate knowledge of local government operations in the local area is required, Exhibit 2 shows that area divisions are the most utilitarian structural form. The function of this exhibit is to illustrate which of the different structural forms enable strategy to be carried out in the most effective manner. It is only useful after the organization selects its major areas of concern. For example, multinationals under close scrutiny might wish to opt for a matrix organization or a focused market structure to insure close cooperation and coordination with the home office. It issues arise such as those recently faced by the Lockheed Corporation, some of the major oil companies and a multitude of other multinationals, the level of corporate concern about these issues might require some revision in structure to guarantee close corporate control. Exhibit 2 provides a way of assessing in advance those structural forms that are mostly likely to be successful.

---

[1] J. W. Widing, "Reorganizing Your Worldwide Business," *Harvard Business Review*, May–June, 1973.

THE CHIEF EXECUTIVE OFFICE

Moving from the structuring of the total entity to the level of the chief executive office brings out the continuing emergence of the so-called office of the president or its alter ego, the corporate office. The two existing variations on the office of the president format are shown in Exhibit 3.

In the Type I organization the senior vice presidents and the executive office have no direct control over operating or staff units, rather they serve a liaison function between the chief executive office and the operating units. In both Type I and Type II formats the office of the president is a formally established organizational unit where one or more executives can either singly or as a group, act as if they are the president. One man is usually senior to all the others but all individuals in the office can make decisions on matters agreed upon by the members of the office of the president and known to other members of the organization.

The use of the office of the president is advocated for a variety of reasons. Time pressures acting on the chief executive level make the expansion of executive time the major benefit of this form, especially if executives travel a great deal. The office of the president also allows executives to focus on long-range planning, provides balanced representation at the top of the company, and generates a range of skills and experience to cope with external affairs in a complex world environment. Management succession is another matter that comes up on the plus side and social scientists who study this structure say that when the "boxes" are removed there is less inhibition and provincialism in dealings between top executives. Advocates of the approach say that the bottom line result is that better decisions are made faster than in more conventionally designed situations.

EXHIBIT 3
Office of the President

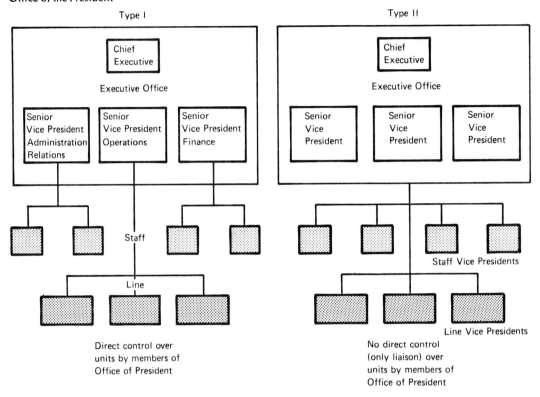

Type I

Direct control over
units by members of
Office of President

Type II

No direct control
(only liaison) over
units by members of
Office of President

For this system to work effectively there must be a well-defined need for a multiple executive rooted in any or all of the items described above. Excellent communications are also critical in the maintenance of a successful office of the president as is personal compatibility among its members. One absolutely essential ingredient here is a strong chief executive who is committed to making it work. If he or she is unwilling to allow people to function in alter ego fashion then the whole concept collapses rapidly.

Examples also exist where the office of the president is not structurally or situationally viable. For example, it might not be particularly suitable when a CEO becomes skilled in his job or a merger calling for complex skills is consummated success-

fully. A lessened need to travel, death, or disablement in the executive office or changing economic conditions can cause it to break down dramatically. In the cost conscious years of the early 1970s several firms decided to drop such a structure to ensure tighter controls and accountability. To quote a top executive in a major insurance company, "A major recession is no place for group management."

There is every indication that tomorrow's environment will be even more demanding than that of the past so it seems probable that complexity alone will promote the use of the office of the president in the future. Present trends show, however, that it will be coupled with the group executive concept to maintain a focus on profitability at the operating level. The office of the president will deal with futuristic matters while a group or divisional executive will hold profit and operations responsibility. This situation is discussed in greater depth at the end of this article.

ORGANIZATION FOR INNOVATION

Organizations can encourage innovation to surface if they provide supportive climates and structures. Actually much of the organization structure should be compatible with the development of innovation but very few firms take the time needed to set up structures appropriate to the development of latent innovative talents. One relatively recent approach to developing innovation is the "new venture" or "new business" group. This particular entity is not designed to develop new products, nor is it related to the ongoing research and development effort; rather it focuses on new ideas or businesses and the encouragement of people in the firm to develop new ideas within the firm rather than taking them outside.

In the past such new venture units have received both good and bad marks. The pluses in terms of business development are quite obvious. If a new venture is successful it can provide financial gains, growth stability, diversification, insurance against competition, penetration into new markets, and new assets. The psychological advantages are that people tend to gain and hold a sense of excitement about new products or new ideas which they help to develop. Management skills grow rapidly in this kind of environment and individuals whose ideas are accepted and utilized tend to stay with an organization rather than seek fulfillment elsewhere.

On the other side of the coin, new ventures departments have been unsuccessful because the concept, the man, the resources, the technology, the market, or any number of other factors have turned sour. The track record under these conditions shows financial losses at worst and overly long periods of gestation at best.

The prime reason for the failure of new ventures is that the corporation is really ill equipped to evaluate new ideas. Few people in large ongoing corporations have the skills required of new venture management, and even the traditional financial organizations serving large companies are ill equipped to advise their clients on how to handle new ventures. There is also a tendency for firms to blow the whistle too soon on new ventures. The kinds of criteria and time dimensions used to evaluate success in large companies have almost no utility in measuring new ventures. Further, the traditional structures for handling new ventures in such firms are inappropriately designed. The new ventures group invariably reports to the wrong place, and it is staffed with the wrong type of skills. All things considered, it is not surprising that many corporations have become disenchanted by the performance of their new venture units.

What then is needed to make new venture units successful? It is quite clear that top management at the CEO level needs to be committed to develop both the business and psychological aspects of the new venture management. Longer time perspectives must be adopted to evaluate these endeavors since most ideas take from three to five years to develop. A structure that allows creative new ventures to take root must be established, and the composition and reporting level of that unit should be designed appropriately. Exhibit 4 shows a typical and recommended reporting level for a new ventures organization.

The structure shown in Exhibit 4 is far less important than how the structure functions and what must be done to maintain it. To obtain operational effectiveness, the new ventures organization should be made

EXHIBIT 4
Structure of the New Venture Group

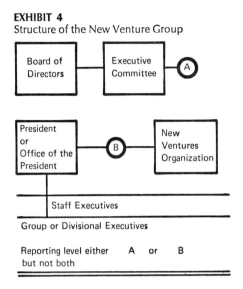

Reporting level either   **A**   or   **B**
but not both

up of a venture company board of advisors (not directors), and the board of advisors should be composed of from three to five members, including one or two insiders and two or three paid outsiders. The executive staff should be no more than three in total including an inside executive, an assistant, and a secretary. The board of advisors, who would serve in staggered two-year terms and not be eligible for reappointment, might consist of a banker, a consultant or professor, and a venture capitalist or market research man. The key here is to ensure that the advisers are well versed in the management of new ventures. The insiders, if they are a team of two, should represent both line and staff functions and serve a maximum term of three years. The most successful managers in new ventures groups have been young men with a reputation to gain and some expertise in marketing and financial matters. Research background seems to have been of little or no help to such managers. The primary focus has been to foster a climate where new and shifting perspectives can flourish. If the new ventures group itself becomes bureaucratic and entrenched there is scant

chance of them turning out anything really novel.

Some added hints useful in considering how to operate new ventures groups effectively are:

- The executive staff must be kept to a minimum.
- Prototypes or patents should be encouraged or even required before even preliminary support is provided.
- Financial support based on progress against a plan is superior to that rooted in vague long-term hope of gain in "rapidly growing" markets.
- The work on a new venture should be done in the product or operating divisions with no special facilities budgeted to the new ventures groups. If a division manager is not willing to buy and/or support a project then it is highly likely that no one else will buy it either.
- The people who develop new ventures should be allowed to manage them. This is one of the secrets of 3M Corporation's success in new venture management.
- Failure in a new venture attempt should not be viewed as a mark of inability. The individual should be allowed to go to his operating home if the new venture fails and be seen as someone who tried and make it rather than as a failure. A chance to reach out for success is a prime motivator in any organization but another is the opportunity to fail.
- Communications should be set up so that the entire organization knows what is going on in any new venture. There is little to be gained by re-inventing the wheel.
- The corporate level should not be involved (after initial approval) until and/or unless large-scale marketing planning and capital commitment is needed. The entry point of the corporation should be between the seed money stage and the growth stage.

In the final analysis the organization must bet on the person and not scuttle projects because results are slow in coming. A climate of tolerant patience is required. The development of a successful new ventures group is an idea that can really fire image and imagination variables. For large corporations the results can even surpass those of R&D activities, and at a much lower cost. With proper thought and care it is possible to organize for innovation, but most organizations have neglected to do the job properly. If, as some pundits say, innovation is on the decline, then organizations should be turning to new ventures departments as a possible way to reverse this negative trend.

ORGANIZATION AT THE OPERATING LEVEL

At the structural level below the total entity and the chief executive office, it is paramount to concentrate on effective operations management. Several types of organizations exist at the operations level, and the key to classifying those organizations rests in the rate of environment change and the technology at stake. Technology here is a very broad-based definition which includes both technical and managerial technologies. Exhibit 5 shows one way of classifying structure in operating companies. The key variable at the top of the chart is environment or rate of change while the left-hand side shows the variable of technology. Environmental rates of change show conditions that are either

stable or unstable while technology exists at some known level or delves into the unknown. Professor William Newman of Columbia University developed this methodology by classifying firms in four categories:

1. Stable.
2. Regulated flexibility.
3. Innovative.
4. Ad hoc organizations.[2]

A stable company might be one that repeats activities in a known stable environment, for example, an oil company opening up another gas station in an area it knows well. Regulated flexibility would be illustrated by a job shop operation while the innovative category would involve a product made on a limited production basis. A temporary or ad hoc organization would be operating in an unstable, unknown environment and might be illustrated by a pilot plant run on an unknown product line.

The key to success in any organization at the operating level is to get the efficiencies or differentiation (specialization) without losing the ability to integrate (coordination) activities. Professors Paul Lawrence and Jay Lorsch at Harvard University concluded that organizations with a task focus and with concern about the way in which differentiation and integration can be achieved have the greatest propensity for overall effectiveness, and their findings comprise the benchmark works in this area.

Exhibit 6 attempts to compile some research findings in the area of organization at the operations level with the Newman scheme of classifying technologies to provide the same kind of guide to action that Exhibit 2 offers in dealing with organization of the multinational firm. The upper part of the exhibit shows that dominant technology by line of business and indi-

EXHIBIT 5
Structure Classification at the Level of the Operating Company

Technology	Environmental Change	
	Stable	Unstable
Known	Stable	Regulated Flexibility
Unknown	Innovative	Ad hoc

[2] William H. Newman, "Strategy and Management Structure," *Journal of Business Policy*, Autumn 1971, vol. 2, no. 1, pp. 56–66.

EXHIBIT 6
Differentiation and Integration Devices

Integrating Devices—Applicability	Dominant Technology (by Line of Business) and Degree of Differentiation			
	Stable (Mass Production)	Regulated flexibility (Job Shop)	Innovative Production (Limited Production)	Temporary or Ad Hoc (New Technology)
	High	Medium	Low	Minimal
Direct control	H	M	L	L
Chain of command	H	M	L	L
Standing plans	H	H	L	L
Budgets with exception reporting	H	M	M	M
General indicators (ROI)	L	M	H	M
Integrators ("Assistant to")	M	H	M	M
Integrating departments	M	H	H	M
Single use plans	L	H	H	H
Ad hoc cross-functional teams (Task Forces)	L	M	H	H
Permanent cross-functional teams	L	M	H	H
Matrix organization	L	M	H	M

cates the degree of differentiation or specialization as going from "high" in stable mass production industries to "low" in temporary ad hoc organizations. The integrating devices listed in the left hand side of the table range from simple direct personal control and the bureaucratic chain of command concept to more sophisticated organizational structures such as matrix organizations. The levels of suitability in the body of the exhibit show which integrating devices are most successful in organizations having different degrees of specialization. For example, direct personal control is highly effective in stable mass-production industries but exhibits a low degree of effectiveness in temporary or ad hoc structures. In contrast, a permanent cross functional team has relatively low utility in a stable mass-production industry but is highly suitable in limited production technologies or temporary ad hoc situations. Again, there are no absolutes in these charts

but they do indicate how certain well-known integrating devices either "fit" (or do not fit) with certain classes of technology. Exhibit 6 emphasizes the point that there is no one utopian way of integrating technologically differing organizations and that coordination devices vary markedly in their effectiveness in diverse technological settings.

Whatever technology exists, certain errors are common in almost every structural design. The first common error is having similar units in different structures. Duplication and diffusion of responsibility invariably cause operating inefficiencies. The second error is setting up a coordinating unit too similar to the unit it coordinates. The net result is that the coordinating unit tends to interfere or even meddle with the operation of the unit it coordinates. A third difficulty is that too many coordinating units are used to coordinate stable production situations. Excessive cost is incurred here with very little return. The final error typically encountered in structuring organizations is that dissimilar units are combined in one structure. This Topsy-like organization makes control and direction very difficult.

Since new studies are continually reporting interesting and utilitarian ways to coordinate activities across differing technological units, the operating level is providing some of the more interesting research being performed in the field of organization structures.

A LOOK AT THE FUTURE

After looking at successively lower sections of the organization, it is fitting that the final section lift its sights to once again consider the total entity. Comments in this section are less data based and more tentative than some of the previous material since dealing with the future involves a certain amount of impressionistic guessing. in the future will have to be more adaptive, more flexible, and more future oriented than their predecessors. It is also If, however, the future is to be somewhat more complex than the past, organizations likely that environmental factors will exert more importance in future-oriented organizations than they have in the past. This means, therefore, that the biggest changes in organization structures will be those that deal directly with managing the future.

In order to correctly assess, evaluate, and even control the future, the vital factors to consider in any organization are intelligence gathering, long range strategic planning, coping and dealing with various external publics, establishing objectives to make sure that strategies are being met, providing for innovative responses to changes in the environment, following up on performance objectives, providing proper structures, and motivating people to meet individual and organizational goals. This sounds like a very big order indeed, but a possible organization structure to expedite the achievement of such results is shown in Exhibit 7.

Exhibit 7 reflects a two-tiered organization with the corporate executive office and its staff being primarily concerned with prediction and adaptation and the group executive and senior vice president level having the primary responsibility for producing goods and services at a profit within the policy guidelines determined in consultation with the executive office. The board of directors would be a much more future-oriented operation than it has been in the past. It would be responsible for making sure the external relationships of the organization are in keeping with the changing social role of the corporation. This means that the board itself requires its own audit staff to look into financial, social, and other critical issues. An ideal staff would be relatively small, perhaps two or three people. It would be comprised of insiders and outsiders who would prepare reports designed to help the board act intelligently on the plans and proposals presented to them by the operating management.

If organizations are going to be more complex in the future, the so-called office of the president is a device which can provide the kinds of balance and skills needed to ensure wise, effective leadership. The previous discussion of the new ventures unit and where it should report would go a long way toward helping to develop innovative ideas without walking away from the fact that the chief innovator in the organization is the chief executive himself.

The staff functions shown in Exhibit 7 indicate a heavier emphasis on "stakeholders" or external publics than is found in most existing organizations. The information and intelligence gathering activity would perform diagnostic activities,

EXHIBIT 7
Proposed Model of a Top Level, Future-Oriented Organization

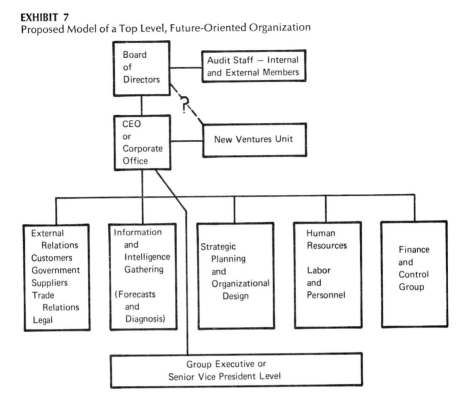

prepare forecasts and feed future oriented data into the strategic planning and organization design units. Since human resources are a critical variable in the success of every organization and since labor and personnel matters require specialized skills, this particular office is elevated above other functional staffs. The finance and control group is set up to advise and guide the office of the president and the directors on how performance has actually been progressing against plans. Scorekeeping must be done well, and capital sources and uses are vital portions of the success mix. External relations cover a variety of areas including dealing with the various "publics," the legal function, and relations with the government, all of which have been increasing in importance in recent years.

The group executive or senior vice presi-

dent level would be structured to resemble existing product or functional organizations. Each would perform as if it is a separate business with separate profit responsibility. In short, the group executives would each head an organization similar to the so-called transitional or product-oriented company described at the start of this report. Research and development activities are not mentioned here specifically since it seems relatively unimportant whether they report at the headquarters level or within the business groups. The size of the company and the importance of technological change in the industry would be the determining variables here.

The organization structure shown in Exhibit 7 is geared to handle the future, the outside, and the anticipation of problems. It is not designed primarily to cope with current or past problems. It provides the organization with seven-league boots, not asbestos shoes to stamp out fires.

Several organizations have already adopted such structures to guide their activities as they move into what they predict to be a much more complex future. It is likely that other organizations, particularly large ones, will construct similar organization structures in the near future. Given the importance of such organizations, any help they can obtain through the use of better organization structures can provide benefits for all segments of our society.

Case 4–1

THE HAMSUN COMPANY

The Hamsun Company has gross sales of approximately $40 million per year, of which 75 percent is derived from publishing. Fifteen hundred persons are employed in the production of publications that range from a variety of specialized business magazines through textbooks, technical books, catalogs, manuals, and even novels. Some are issued weekly, some monthly, and others quarterly or annually. These are produced entirely within Hamsun, from inception of the ideas through their subsequent development and the actual manufacture of the final creative products. Millions of copies are produced each month and distributed in every one of the United States and in 90 other countries throughout the world.

The company describes its business magazines as follows:

> Hamsun publications range from weekies to monthlies, from news magazines to feature publications. All are alike in one basic respect: Each reaches and involves the active interest of key businessmen in a specific market. This is accomplished through precision in every publishing phase: In market definition, by identifying buying influences through censuses and other research . . . in circulation, by scientifically matching distribution to buying influences . . . in editing, by supplementing editorial knowledge and instinct with readership research. The result is a high level of editorial authority and advertising impact.

Exhibit 1 describes the various business publications.

Responsibility for each magazine customarily is shared by a publisher and an editor. The publisher handles the business aspects, including advertising sales and circulation promotion, while the editor supervises the writing and production. In the past they have enjoyed great antonomy in policy and editorial decisions. Performance evaluation has generally been quite informal, but top management is beginning to talk about profit center responsibility.

Hamsun's basic business has been publishing specialized business magazines. To serve as effective advertising vehicles, these magazines must have editorial excellence and must be circulated to key buying personnel. In building the products and distribution, Hamsun publishers and editors have become experts in the markets served by their magazines. Out of this expertise

EXHIBIT 1
Hamsun Company: List of Business Publications

Automatic Systems (monthly) features technical coverage of the design and application of instruments, controls, and systems for measurement, analysis, inspection, testing, computing and data handling, monitoring, and automatic processes. It reaches engineering, management, operations, and procurement personnel working in the process industries as well as the original equipment market.

Automotive News (semimonthly) is the international, technical news magazine of the automotive manufacturing industries. It covers passenger cars, trucks, trailers, and buses; also engines, military vehicles and equipment, recreational vehicles, tractors and farm equipment, construction equipment and industrial trucks, and parts and accessories. The magazine is edited to keep automotive executives informed on the latest automotive designs, developments, and production techniques, both domestic and international.

Brand Name & Trademark Guide (published every four years) shows registered trademarks for all types of jewelry-industry products—from watches, jewelry, gemstones, and silverware to findings, supplies, and equipment.

Car Era (monthly) is designed for the operator of automotive repair and service establishments. It provides technical, merchandising, and management information to help readers compete profitably for motorists' repair and service business.

Car Selling (five issues per year) serves the large buyers and distributors of automotive parts accessories and equipment. These readers determine the stock for the shelves of department store auto centers, discount stores, parts and accessory stores, franchise service outlets, specialty and speed outlets, and diagnostic shops.

Coverage (monthly) is edited for and directed to professional insurance and financial executives: agents, brokers, corporate insurance buyers, and key home office officials. *Coverage* interprets industry, financial, and social trends and their impact on property, liability, life, and health insurance.

Design and Development (monthly) is a technical news service for design engineers and research and development engineers in the original equipment market. It features descriptions of new or improved component parts and materials which can be designed into end products.

Distribution (monthly) is the magazine of physical distribution management, providing traffic and distribution executives with up-to-date information on traffic and transportation, intermodal shipments, containerization, inventory control, order processing, terminal materials handling, and warehouse management.

Electronic Information (monthly) is a new-product publication for engineers, purchasing agents, buyers, and distributor principals who are responsible for the brand selection and procurement of electronic and electromechanical components and equipment. These brand specifiers and buyers are employed by electronic and industrial original equipment manufacturers.

Fleet Journal (monthly) is designed for executives who manage, operate, and maintain the nation's volume truck, bus, and passenger car fleets. Editorial emphasis is on operations, service, maintenance, safety, new products, and industry news interpretations.

Food Equipment Update (quarterly) depicts new products developed for plant support in the food industry. The tabloid format lends itself to high reader inquiry volume.

Food Technology (monthly) is edited for food and beverage manufacturing management in administrative, plant operating, engineering, and other technical functions. An international edition of all issues is read by manufacturers in 100 countries.

Footwear (monthly) serves all segments of the footwear industry. It is the shoeman's source of fashion information, news, and economic data and provides guidance in management, sales, and merchandising to retail footwear establishments.

Gas (monthly) serves the worldwide gas industry. This includes gas gathering, processing, transmission, storage, distribution and the gas department of major oil (production) companies. It encompasses those companies processing and supplying liquified natural gas/substitute natural gas/natural gas and those involved in coal gasification projects. The editorial content is directed to reporting developments and technology useful to personnel responsible for operations and management.

Hardlines Merchandising (monthly) provides management and merchandising and industry and new-product news to retailers, wholesalers, and specialty distributors handling hardware and allied hardline products.

Instrument & Apparatus News (monthly) serves the broad original equipment market, as well as the end user market. It delivers product information covering industrial controls,

Exhibit 1 (continued)

instrumentation, and precision components. Readers of *IAN* are engineering, management, operations, and procurement personnel involved with process/production/manufacturing, product or systems design, and research and development.

Jewelers' Directory is published annually and lists manufacturers and suppliers in more than 1,100 categories of jewelry store products and services.

Jewelers' News (monthly) reports industry news and market information to jewelry retailers, wholesalers, importers, and manufacturers and provides guidance in management, sales, and merchandising to retail jewelry establishments.

Laboratory Equipment Information (monthly) provides product news of biomedical and clinical laboratory instruments, accessories, and computers to medical specialists, scientists, engineers, and technicians involved in patient care, the clinical lab, and selected research branches of the life sciences.

Optics (semimonthly) covers the field of ophthalmic optics—the refracting of the eye and the dispensing and servicing of the prescription. It is also a medium of communication between optical manufacturers, distributors, prescription laboratories, and professional and retail elements.

Owner Driver (bimonthly) serves the independent trucker and the small fleet operator who leases his truck, tractor, or complete rig to major carriers or private fleets or engages in broker operations. Editorial covers equipment, operations, industry news, safety, regulations, and record keeping.

Preview (semiannual) is a four-color advertising and editorial presentation of advance footwear styles designed to provide manufacturers and importers a vehicle for displaying their finest fashions and for buyers to preview them.

Steel Era (weekly) provides news for management executives in the metalworking and metal-producing industries. It reports and interprets business news events in the industry, engineering and production developments, and market and price information. The information for each weekly issue is gathered and prepared by editors and correspondents located in major metalworking and metal-producing centers in the United States and abroad.

Steel Era Metalworking International (monthly) reports on new processes and products for operating management—including production, engineering, and design executives— in metalworking and metal-producing plants in 85 countries outside of the United States. Basic copy is in English, with digests in German, French, and Spanish.

Sterling Index lists and illustrates more than 1,700 sterling flatware patterns made by U.S. silver companies since 1832. An essential reference book for silverware manufacturers, retail jewelers, department stores, antique shops, libraries, etc.

Systems Engineering (monthly) is written and edited for systems engineers involved in the design, production, and testing of electronic equipment and systems. Its editorial content emphasizes both the technical and economic considerations and all of the functions required to build equipment and systems. In addition, the editors analyze the markets which offer the greatest opportunity for systems engineering capabilities. It provides authoritative guidance to engineers responsible for operating in a competitive environment.

Who's Where is published for the annual international automotive service industries show. It is a directory of manufacturing and wholesale personnel attending the show. Officers and directors of the leading industry associations are listed.

over the years, Hamsun has developed a number of auxiliary communications services, all designed to help its thousands of customers define, locate, and sell their markets. Exhibit 2 describes these services.

Middle management complains about the quality of communication in the company. Some deeply distrust the top executives, who tend to be quite secretive about their plans. These executives maintain that they must make some tough decisions on eliminating losing publications. They feel that their deliberations and tentative plans must be kept confidential or morale

EXHIBIT 2
Hamsun Company: List of Services

Advertising Graph Services is an advanced method of measuring the effectiveness of printed communications. Advert-Graph provides not only meaningful measurements of the impact and informative value of advertising and editorial but also related services such as insight studies (exploring in-depth reader awareness); presight studies (testing messages in advance of publication); market-probe studies (eliciting marketing information from selected markets); product testing (actual product and packaging testing by known buyers); sales calls analysis (buyer-oriented sales profiles and tracking studies). These Advert-Graph services are used by outside clients as well as Hamsun publications.

Catalog Division was formed to meet industry's growing needs for more efficient catalog preparation, printing, and distribution. The division has the facilities to provide complete parts and price cataloging in the automotive replacement and other markets. Services include catalog layout, design, and illustration, in addition to printing and distribution of the completed catalogs.

Connely Studios, Inc., provides Hamsun's creative services, made up of creative minds (15 of them) and the discerning eye of a full-time photographer. They offer clients a wide diversification of talent. Geared to handle anything from design, layout, illustration, mechanicals, and photography to the color coordination of huge housing developments along the Atlantic seaboard, the studios are the newest Hamsun acquisition.

Hamsun Book Company publishes a wide range of nonfiction and fiction for the general reader, professionals in many fields, schools, and libraries. The division has over 450 titles currently in print and adds 70–80 new books each year. With over 110 publications in the field, Hamsun Book Company is one of America's largest automotive book publishers. Other areas of interest include arts and crafts, business and technical, journalism, law enforcement, and books for the school-age reader.

Hamsun Data Processing originally was created to support the multitude of in-house activities. It has met that challenge and expanded its scope to outside service bureau activities as well. Hamsun's demand for excellence has resulted in a recognized team of highly accomplished data processing professionals and the most modern IBM computer available. This combination of men and machines strengthens the total capability for supplying the complex information needs of modern business while meeting the data processing requirements of the Hamsun publications and services.

Hamsun Direct Mail Company is staffed and equipped to provide a full range of services for selling by mail. Customers can use a complete package or any of these services: lists, direct mail marketing, and mailing services.

Hamsun Printing Company produces more than 60 million magazines and catalogs per year. More than 300 highly skilled craftsmen utilize the most modern equipment available: computerized photocomposition; electronically controlled cameras; automatic film processors, high-speed web offset presses; sheet-fed presses; saddle-stitch, side-stitch, and perfect binding, as well as mailing. More than 30 publishers as well as manufacturers and merchandising firms enjoy the on-time, high-quality service of this technologically advanced plant.

Hamsun Research Services is one of the nation's largest and most widely respected research organizations. The full-time staff includes over 200 specialists in mathematical statistics, engineering, marketing, communications, psychology, sociology, and economics. HRS provides unique marketing research assistance to leading business, industrial, and governmental organizations. Hundreds of projects are conducted each year on a confidential contract basis. HRS in turn fulfills the research requirements of the Hamsun publications.

Information Services Division represents an extension of Hamsun's long-term policy of continually expanding its marketing services to advertisers. Information Services is an interface between customers and many specialized services available from the company. Among other activities, this division is responsible for Hamsun's new and unique inquiry program—contract fulfillment of reader inquiries for individual manufacturers—and the maintenance of the quality and processing procedures for Hamsun's publications annual 3,500,000 reader inquiries.

Overseas International Press is the company's European sales, editorial, and marketing organization.

Upper State Paper Mill produces a wide variety of high-quality paper products for the printing and packaging industries.

would suffer from wild rumors. Unfortunately, the rumors are already so rampant that one junior manager observes:

> It is not uncommon for juniors to be very suspicious of the principal executives and Hamsun as a corporation, but to have high trust in their individual publisher or editor. By the same token, communications may be well handled within a department, but middle managers are suspicious of all communications from the top. The typical response to any executive communication is not "What did they say?" but rather "I know what they said, but what did they mean?"

Questions

1. How would you organize this company? Draw an organization chart that includes the various publications and communication services. Create and include also any line and staff executive positions and departments you deem desirable. Explain your chart.
2. Compare your chart with the firm's actual organization (to be provided by your instructor). How do they differ? How is yours potentially superior or inferior?

Case 4–2
MILANO ENTERPRISES*

Mr. Milano is concerned about the long-run future of the group of enterprises he personally has built into a flourishing establishment. Located in a Latin American country, Milano Enterprises is recognized as a dynamic factor in the private sector of the nation's economy. In fact, the success of the business complicates its continuation.

Scope of Activities

Mr. Milano, son of Italian immigrants, started in business 45 years ago in a small but growing city. He anticipated a building boom and left the family grocery store to enter the building supply business. Several of Mr. Milano's present companies are a direct outgrowth of this early start. He still owns two regional wholesale companies dealing in building supplies. A separate company imports specialty plumbing items; and another is the national representative of a world-wide electric elevator manufacturer—selling, installing, and servicing elevators for apartment buildings, offices, and warehouses. Currently, the largest company in the building field is a plant of his that manufactures boilers and other heating equipment. Still another plant manufactures electric fixtures.

---

* From William Newman, Charles Summer, and E. Kirby Warren, *The Process of Management: Concepts, Behavior, Practice,* 2d ed., © 1967, pp. 144–52. Reprinted by permission of Prentice-Hall, Inc., Englewood Cliffs, New Jersey.

Mr. Milano's activities in other fields followed a somewhat similar pattern. Foreseeing needs arising out of urbanization and industrialization, he sought to become the import representative for products serving these needs. And, as imports were sharply restricted due to economic and political reasons, he undertook the manufacture of selected items. For example, in the automotive field he has been the Ford representative for many years. One company does the importing of Ford cars, trucks, and parts. In addition, Milano Enterprises owns a controlling interest in several large dealerships. It also represents the British and German Ford affiliates. Both quotas and tariffs place severe restrictions on the number of vehicles that can be imported, and legislation encourages local manufacture. Consequently, a separate company has been established for truck assembly and body manufacture. Also in the automotive area, Milano Enterprises owns a chain of filling stations.

In the office equipment area, Milano Enterprises has separate companies for the importation of duplicating equipment and of typewriters. In addition, there is a substantial and growing unit that manufactures metal furniture for offices.

About ten years ago, a new company was established to manufacture electric refrigerators locally. Compressors are imported, but the cabinets are manufactured in a plant adjacent to the furniture plant. Other Milano units include a large textile plant that weaves and finishes cotton fabrics, a prominent hotel, a soft-drink bottling company, and a small mining-exploration venture.

In total, there are 25 active operating companies ranging in size from 20 to 500 employees. The textile plant and the boiler plant are the largest units in terms of employment. Milano Enterprises owns all or at least a majority of the stock in each of these operating companies. In several instances, the manager of a company owns a minority interest, but he is under contract to Milano Enterprises to sell back his stock at current book value when he retires.

Obviously, a man who can put together such an array of companies in a single lifetime possesses unusual ability. Part of Mr. Milano's success arises from working in growth areas. Within these areas, Mr. Milano has been willing to invest risk capital, but he has been unusually adept at picking particular spots where growth was strong and at adjusting his operations as the economic environment shifted. Also, once an investment has been made, it has been carefully nurtured and controlled. Mr. Milano is modest in manner, eagerly seeks advice wherever he can find it, and works hard in a well-disciplined manner. His personal integrity is widely respected throughout the business community. He is a religious man and highly devoted to hs family.

Present Organization

Each of the 25 companies has its manager, and, with minor exceptions, each has its own offices and other facilities. As might be expected, the central organization reflects its evolutionary background and is not sharply defined. Six people, in addition to Mr. Milano, share in the general directon of Milano Enterprses.

Mr. Lopez has been closely associated with Mr. Milano during most of his business career. Both men are the same age and, like Mr. Milano, Mr. Lopez has had only elementary school education. In general, Mr. Lopez is more concerned with the operation of existing enterprises than with the starting of new ones. He acts as troubleshooter for Mr. Milano, takes care of labor problems when any arise, and represents the Enterprises at various public functions. Managers of the various companies often find that Mr. Lopez is available for consultation when Mr. Milano is concentrating on some new negotiations.

Mr. Peche has been chief accountant for Milano Enterprises for over 20 years. He has an intimate knowledge of the accounting system of each company even though great variation exists in the way records are kept. Mr. Peche keeps a close eye on the profits, liquidity, expense ratios, and other key figures for each of the companies, and calls Mr. Milano's attention to any significant deviations. Mr. Peche works up estimated projections for Mr. Milano's use in negotiations and in arranging financing, and he takes care of tax matters.

Mr. Gaffney has been Mr. Milano's chief associate in the automotive end of the business, although he is 12 years younger. Mr. Gaffney serves as manager of the automobile import company and exercises supervision over European imports, all distributors, and the filling stations. He spends about two thirds of his time with this group of companies but is available for general consultation on other matters. In several new ventures, Mr. Milano has asked Mr. Gaffney to make the preliminary investigation.

Mr. Bolivar is the official representative of Milano Enterprises to the government, obtaining import licenses, which often involve protracted negotiation. Numerous changes in regulations, often without much warning, require Milano Enterprises to maintain an able representative in close contact with administrative and legislative personnel. Also involved is a certain amount of "lobbying" when new legislation is being discussed in the legislature. Mr. Bolivar devotes his full time to this government work and does not get involved in operating problems of the companies.

Mr. Juan Milano is the 32-year-old son of the company's founder. He has been educated abroad. He now works with his father and with Mr. Lopez on special projects, such as several consumer studies (for the hotel, bottling company, gasoline filling stations, and electric refrigerator plant). Because of his education, he often meets with foreign visitors.

Mrs. Rodriques, who has an M.B.A. from a leading American university, serves a dual role. She is a personal assistant and interpreter for Mr. Milano, and as such she has a keen interest in learning the latest developments and management thought of companies abroad. In this capacity, she not only presents the ideas but discusses with Mr. Milano the way they might be related to the Enterprises. Mrs. Rodriques' more formal assignment deals with executive and technical personnel. A few general conferences have been held, but thus far most of the work in the senior personnel field is still in the planning stage. Competent executives are very scarce, and even though

Milano Enterprises has an excellent reputation, executive selection and development has been more opportunistic than programmed.

All of these people are very busy, and there rarely is a time when two or three of them are not working on some pressing current problem. The board of directors of Milano Enterprises is composed of Mr. Milano, his wife, Juan Milano, Mr. Lopez, and Mr. Gaffney. Since most of these people are in frequent informal contact, formal meetings of the board are held only when some official business must be transacted.

Concern for the Future

Even though Milano Enterprises has been successful and is highly regarded in business circles, Mr. Milano is concerned about the future. For one thing, Mr. Milano recognizes that the central organization lacks system and is too dependent upon him personally. He says, "I'm not proud of our organization. All I can say is that thus far it has proved to be adequate."

More pressing is what will happen after Mr. Milano's death. He is in good health, but he is already 65 and wishes to take steps now for the perpetuation of the Enterprises. He would like any reorganization to provide for three objectives:

1. Modern, effective management that will be flexible enough to meet changing conditions as he has had to do over his lifetime.
2. Continuing contribution to the economy of the country, particularly with respect to the initiative and adaptability that free enterprise can provide better than government bureaus.
3. Continuing family ownership of a controlling block of the stock. This does not mean that some of the stock may not be sold publicly, as local capital markets develop, nor does it mean that members of the family will always hold top executive positions unless they are fully qualified to do so.

A banker with whom Mr. Milano has thoroughly discussed this matter urges "decentralization." He advises:

> No one can keep track of all of your companies the way you have because only you have the background that comes from founding and working with these companies and their executives over a long period of years. Consequently, you should follow the practice of the leading U.S. companies by appointing able people as the chief executive of each of your operating units and then decentralizing authority to each of them. You already have this general form, but too many decisions are made in the central office. You should immediately decentralize and find out which of your mangers are competent and which ones have to be replaced. The sooner you start, the better, because it will be some time before all 25 of the companies can stand on their own feet.

The idea of strong managers in each operating company appeals to Mr. Milano, but he is dubious about the long-run effect of such a decentralization. He fears that Milano Enterprises will become primarily a passive holder of investments, and this certainly has not been the key to success in his personal experience. He anticipates that local managements may continue to do well what they are now doing but is worried about their adaptability to changing conditions, the incentive to seek out new opportunities, and some kind of control that spots difficulties early and insures vigorous remedial action.

Since so much is at stake, Mr. Milano decided to call in an international management consultant. On the basis of advice from companies with whom the Milano Enterprises does business and several personal interviews, Mr. Eberhardt Stempel was selected to make a thorough organization study of the Milano Enterprises. Mr. Stempel presented his recommendations orally and then wrote the following summary report.

Recommendations of Management Consultant

International Consultants, Inc.
New York—London—Frankfort—Caracas

Dear Mr. Milano:

You have asked that we briefly summarize the recommendations we discussed in your office a week ago. In the original assignment you requested that we focus our attention on the central management of the Milano Enterprises, and our investigation confirms your diagnosis that major problems of the future lie in this area.

No report on Milano Enterprises can be made without first recognizing past achievements. Milano Enterprises occupies a unique position in the national economy. Highly respected for its growth, financial strength, willingness to back new ventures, and alertness of management—this group of companies has become a recognized leader in the private business sector. The Milano name carries a high and well-deserved prestige throughout the business community.

The crucial question now facing Milano Enterprises is not immediate. Instead, it is how to prepare for the time when you, Mr. Milano, can no longer serve as the guiding force of the combined group. Note, the problem is greater than the continuing direction of present enterprises. In addition, the future management of Milano Enterprises must have wisdom and courage to expand or contract in various lines as economic opportunities change. Any true perpetuation of your leadership must be dynamic, not static.

We believe the best way to perpetuate Milano Enterprises is to build a strong central organization. The present organization is able to cope with the problems it faces only because of long experience in the field and the exceptional talents of the senior executives. To assure maintenance of present success and to provide for growth, a variety of high-grade specialists should be added to the central organization so that expert talent is readily available to help each of the operating companies meet their respective problems. The organization which we believe will best meet future needs is shown in Exhibit 1. This organization is patterned after several of the most successful companies in the world, and it embraces features we have found to be helpful to many of our other clients.

After you have had an opportunity to study this organization carefully, we will be glad to prepare job descriptions and manpower specifications for each of the positions shown on the chart. Before doing so, however, you should be clear in your own mind that this is the direction you wish to follow. We would like to again stress the advantages of this form of organization to Milano Enterprises:

1. A strong central office is provided, including experts in marketing, production, and finance. Every company, large or small, must perform these basic functions well. Consequently, you should have strength to deal with the problems in these areas.

2. Provision is made for current effectiveness. Subsections are provided for industrial engineering, purchasing, marketing methods, accounting, finance, legal advice, and government representation. When these sections are properly staffed, the central office will have talent to help streamline the operations of any existing and newly acquired operating company.

3. In addition, provision is made for growth. The sections on market research, new product development, financial analysis, and public relations will be primarily concerned with finding opportunities for expansion.

4. Senior executives of Milano Enterprises are given titles and recognition commensurate with the important roles they will play in the group itself and in the nation.

We fully recognize that time will be required to find the proper individuals to fill these posts and to get the entire group working together effectively as a team. We believe that you can best serve Milano Enterprises by

EXHIBIT 1

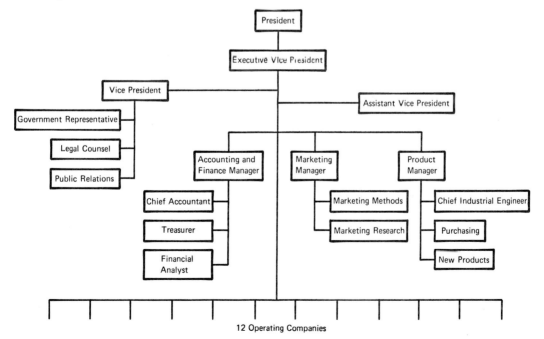

12 Operating Companies

devoting most of your time toward this end. You should anticipate that it may take three or four years before the transition can be completed. It is important that the change be made while you are still able to give it your personal attention and endorsement.

It has been a pleasure to serve you and we shall be happy to be of any further assistance that we can.

Sincerely yours,

Eberhardt Stempel, on behalf of
International Consultants, Inc.

Attachment

Reactions to Mr. Stempel's Recommendations

The central management group had heard Mr. Stempel's oral report, and as soon as they had had an opportunity to review the written summary, Mr. Milano called a meeting for a frank discussion of the recommendations.

Both Mr. Lopez and Mr. Peche expressed grave concern about the heavy overhead expense which the proposed organization would entail. It was far more elaborate than anything they had contemplated, and they felt the central office would be so big that personal contacts with one another would become even more difficult than they already were. Mr. Gaffney said that from the point of view of the automotive unit, he would much prefer to add staff under his immediate direction than be charged for a share of a central office staff which probably would have only superficial understanding of his particular problems. Mrs. Rodriques expressed disappointment that the report was not specifically adapted to the needs of Milano Enterprises. "Except for the special emphasis given government representation, the organization looks as if it was designed for General Electric or Unilever." Juan Milano endorsed this point of view, saying that he did not see how the particular organization would fit the hotel business or the filling station business.

To close the meeting, Mr. Milano made a general statement of his feeling:

> All of us, I'm sure, have been startled by the recommendations. I confess considerable sympathy with most of the points that have been made. And yet I ask myself whether I am rejecting recommendations because they are new and because they cast some reflection on the way I personally have been running the business. We asked Mr. Stempel to come here because we face a grave problem, the most serious problem of my entire life. I personally want to be sure before I reject these recommendations that it is not because they will require a great change in my own behavior, but because I have a better plan for the future of Milano Enterprises. One of the reasons for the success of many of our companies has been a willingness to recognize a need for a change and then to move in that direction aggressively. I would like to think that I am strong enough to apply that same doctrine to my behavior as the head of the Enterprises. Unless we can come up with a better plan, I intend to start to put Mr. Stempel's ideas into effect because time does not permit us to stand still on this issue.

Questions

1. What problems confront Milano Enterprises? Causes?
2. What are Juan Milano Sr.'s objectives? How do they limit his possible solutions?
3. Do you agree or disagree with the banker's recommendations? Why?
4. Do you agree or disagree with the consultant's recommendations? Why?
5. What organizational structure would you recommend to Milano? Why?
6. What other recommendations would you offer Milano?

Case 4–3
GRINDLEY SCHOOL OF BUSINESS

Grindley is a well-known university with a school of business that offers undergraduate and graduate programs. Both are taught by a common faculty which also engages in substantial research, writing, and consulting. It is a large, urban school that endeavors to create knowledge as well as teach it. Some facts:

Grindley University:
   10,000 undergraduate students
    5,000 graduate students
School of Business:
   1,200 undergraduates pursuing a B.S. degree
    300 evening school students
   1,200 graduate students pursuing an M.B.A.
    200 graduate students pursuing a Ph.D.
    150 faculty members

The university and school are organized as in Exhibit 1. The dean of the business school reports to the university president through the provost Reporting to the dean are some staff personnel as well as the directors of the undergraduate, graduate and evening school divisions. The bulk of the personnel reporting directly to the dean, however, are the chairpersons of the ten academic departments, which offer approximately 15 different majors to students.

The faculty members are members of one of the departments, which range in size from 10 to 40 professors and instructors. The chain of command and budget flow are from the president to the provost to the dean (through the associate dean, who helps with the budget) to the department heads. The division directors control relatively few funds, merely enough for administrative expenses of admissions, registration, record keeping, and so on. The department heads exercise the greatest influence on salary increases for individual professors, depending on the budget they can negotiate with the dean. The department heads, the school personnel committee (composed of senior professors), and the dean influence faculty promotions from instructor to assistant professor to associate professor to professor.

EXHIBIT 1
Partial Grindley University Organization Chart: Grindley School of Business

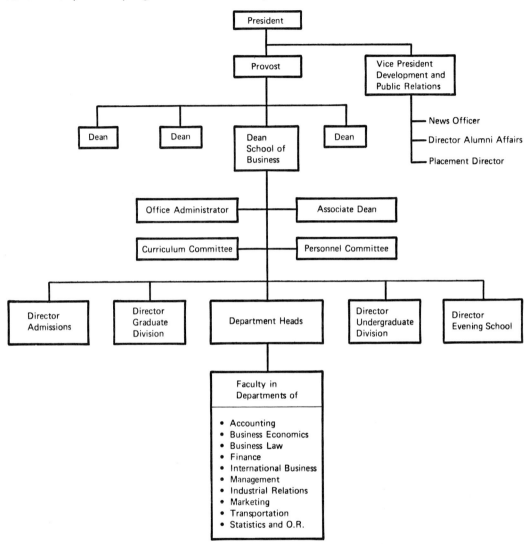

Various complaints are voiced about this system. Some students complain that the caliber of instruction is poor. Since professors' promotions are based heavily on research and writing, they may devote too little attention to teaching and advising. In addition, classes are sometimes taught by part-time instructors who are not clearly qualified or competent. Students also complain about duplication among required courses. In effect, each department has a course that is required of all students in the school. After completing the required courses, a student can major in one of the departments, as well as choosing from any electives. Unfortunately, faculty members in the required courses do not coordinate with one another, so substantial overlap

An extract from the graduate student newspaper gives the students' view as follows:

> Each September a new class of 600 aggressive and highly talented individuals arrives, champing at the bit and ready to take on anything Grindley can throw at them academically. But, for many of the new arrivals, motivation quickly peters out, to be replaced first by dismay, then disillusionment. Many question the wisdom of their decision to attend Grindley; perhaps a rival institution would have lived up to expectations? By their second year in the MBA program, too many students have turned off completely. They sit in the back of the classroom, seldom speak up in class discussion, and generally minimize their involvement with Grindley. Their only apparent concern: get a good job, graduate, and get the hell out of here.
>
> There are several basic causes of this disaffection: The first of these hits the new student hardest; the faculty is disappointing. Grindley has a large faculty of reputed excellence with many outstanding articles and books to their credit. Among these are some who pride themselves on teaching, but the majority emphasize scholarly research and/or outside consulting—to the detriment of their classroom responsibilities, many students feel. As it becomes obvious that most instructors simply are not going to be very demanding of student preparation and participation (the straight, unidirectional lecture is all too common), the typical student reacts in like manner and mentally withdraws from the course.
>
> The second disillusioning factor is the physical environment inside and outside the school. The university is located in a run-down, crime-ridden area of a large, drab city. The classroom building is shared with undergraduate students, and since its builders had not foreseen the rapid expansion of Grindley, it is cramped and overcrowded. In addition, seats are attached to the floor, all faced forward to the lecturer. Communication among the class members is difficult even when the professor desires it. It is much like a high school classroom. A new building complex for Grindley's graduate division has been promised every year, but the university administration is hard-pressed financially, and construction has just never commenced.
>
> Finally, to many students it just doesn't seem that the school is managed very effectively because of the following: registration is an incomprehensible nightmare; all official forms require the signature of a faculty advisor who never seems to be available and apparently couldn't care less about advising anyway; the school seems to be run by secretaries who consider students distinctly inferior beings. When we attempt to diagram the school's administrative structures we find lines of authority cross everywhere. There is no long-range planning function, no working outside advisory board. The top men in the administration seem tired and more concerned with resting on the school's laurels than forging ahead. Grindley appears to have ground to a halt.

Some administrators also have their complaints. To them, too many department heads seem only interested in getting "a warm body" before the required course sections. Consequently, beginning students are upset and gripe to the administrators about the teaching. The administrators in turn feel that these adverse views hinder their efforts to recruit and admit outstanding new students. The administrators (most of whom still teach some classes) feel that they exert little influence over the content, structure, and quality of the educational programs, which seem to consist mainly of unrelated courses. They would like to have a greater voice in what courses are offered and who teaches them. Indeed, the director of the graduate division maintains that he should control the teaching budget, not the department heads. That way, he could tell them whom he wanted to teach in the required courses, that he would pay for professor X but not professor Y, and so on.

The director of the graduate division is also upset because he doesn't have public relations and development (fund-raising) personnel reporting directly to him. These functions are centralized in the university and are available to assist the director, but the university's needs come first, and it shares in any funds raised. The director maintains that this puts him at a disadvantage in competing for students, prestige, and money with other graduate schools of business and management. The president responds that they cannot have the various schools all seeking funds from the same alumni, foundations, and businesses.

Faculty express mixed views about the current situation. Those who have achieved fame through research and publishing (and those who maintain good relations with their department head) tend to be pleased. They teach their desired major, elective graduate courses, and enjoy great autonomy. Those who are in less favorable positions complain about the required undergraduate courses and the teaching hours they are assigned. Some faculty in both groups, however, share the students' and administrators' concerns about the program and instructional quality.

Of all the people at Grindley, the department heads (who are full professors appointed by the dean) are the most satisfied. Although few professors volunteer for the position and they complain about their work loads, they do exercise great influence and enjoy substantial autonomy. Those who chair the most prestigious departments, such as finance, are especially well off because they can negotiate with the dean for substantial departmental budgets which are supplemented by research grants. Some of the less established departments sometimes encounter budget problems resulting in larger classes and smaller stores of office supplies.

Recently, a joint committee composed of students, faculty, administrators, and alumni was formed to recommend structural changes in the school. They are soliciting opinions from the various groups they represent.

Questions

1. What would you recommend to the committee?
2. Draw a new organizational chart for Grindley. How would this improve the present organization?
3. What do you think of the graduate division director's desire to control the teaching budget? How might this be implemented?
4. Where should the development and public relations staff report?
5. Draw colored lines on the present chart and on your proposal depicting the budget flows. How do they differ?

PART
FIVE

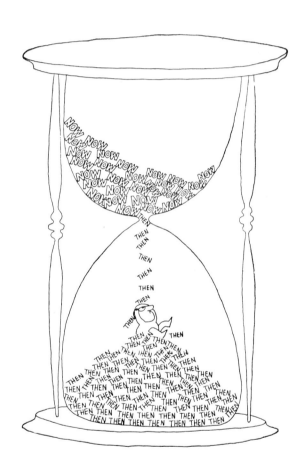

MANAGING
ORGANIZATIONAL
CONFLICT AND
CHANGE

READINGS

5–1

"Eheu! Fugaces: Or, What a Difference a Lot of Days Make," Ogden Nash.

5–2

"Roy Ash Is Having Fun at Addressogrief-Multigrief," Louis Kraar.

5–3

"An Analysis of Intergroup Conflict and Conflict Management," J. David Hunger.

5–4

"Improving Executive Decisions by Formalizing Dissent: The Corporate Devil's Advocate," Theodore T. Herbert and Ralph W. Estes.

5–5

"The Effective Management of Conflict in Project-Oriented Work Environments," Hans J. Thamhain and David L. Wilemon.

5–6

"Seducing the Elites: The Politics of Decision Making and Innovation in Organizational Networks," George Kelley.

5–7

"Power and Innovation: A Two-Center Theory," Eberhard Witte.

5–8

"Theory of Change and the Effective Use of Management Science," Dale E. Zand and Richard E. Sorenson.

5–9

"Management Development *Is* Organization Development," Glenn H. Varney.

CASES

5–1   Race Relations in the U.S. Navy.

5–2   Saint Martin's Challenge.

5–3   Industrial Engineering at Chemtech Corporation.

Eheu! Fugaces: Or, What a Difference a Lot of Days Make*

OGDEN NASH

When I was seventeen or so,
I scoffed at moneygrubbers.
I had a cold contempt for dough,
And I wouldn't wear my rubbers.
No aspirin I took for pains,
For pests no citronella,
And in the Aprilest of rains
I carried no umbrella.

When I was young I was Sidney Carton,
Proudly clad in a Spartan tartan.
Today I'd be, if I were able,
Just healthy, wealthy, and comfortable.

When I was young I would not yield
To comforters and bed socks,
In dreams I covered center field
For the Giants or the Red Sox.
I wished to wander hence and thence,
From diamond mine to goldfield,
Or piloting a Blitzen Benz,
Outdistance Barney Oldfield.

When I subscribed to *The Youth's Companion*
I longed to become a second D'Artagnan.
Today I desire a more modest label:
He's healthy, wealthy, and comfortable.

When I was pushing seventeen,
I hoped to bag a Saracen;
Today should one invade the scene,
I'd simply find it embaracen.

Ah, Postumus, no wild duck I,
But just a waddling puddle duck,
So here's farewell to the open sky
From a middle-aged fuddy-duddle duck.

When I was young I was Roland and Oliver,
Nathan Hale and Simón Bolívar.
Today I would rather sidestep trouble,
And be healthy, wealthy, and comfortubble.

* From *The Private Dining Room* in *Verses From 1929 On* by Ogden Nash. Reprinted by permission of Curtis Brown, Ltd. Copyright 1949, © 1959 by Ogden Nash.

Roy Ash is staking his managerial reputation and a substantial part of his personal fortune—$2.7 million—on an effort to turn around the troubled company that Wall Street analysts privately dubbed "Addressogrief-Multigrief." As both the chief executive and the largest individual stockholder, he has been engaged for the past 17 months in what he calls "a classic case of corporate renewal." The full recovery of Addressograph-Multigraph, he says, will take another four or five years, but the performance so far suggests that he probably won't come to grief.

Ash seems determined to recapture the luster he had in the 1960s as president of glamorous Litton Industries and one of the brightest stars on the U.S. business scene. Litton has faltered since then, and this raised some doubt about the solidity of Ash's achievements. In Washington, he created the idea of an Office of Management and Budget, a considerable accomplishment that was obscured in the general ruin of the Nixon Administration. Now, at 59, Ash seems eager to prove that the managerial success of the glory days at Litton was not a fluke. Speaking of his experience at A-M, he says, "This is kind of Litton revisited."

Rescuing a creaky maker of mechanical office equipment seems a very different kind of challenge from founding and running a high-technology conglomerate, but Ash believes that the right executive guidance can shape up any organization. "At a sufficiently high level of abstraction," he says, "all businesses are the same."

More Agony and Ecstasy

Ash's plans for testing that theory are summed up in the notes that he continually pencils on yellow legal pads. One of the most revealing of these notes says: "Develop a much greater attachment of everybody to the bottom line—more agony and ecstasy." As he sees it, the really important

READING 5–2

Roy Ash Is Having Fun at Addressogrief-Multigrief*

LOUIS KRAAR

change in a company is a process of psychological transformation.

So far, he has flushed out unpromising products, outmoded plants, and surplus personnel—producing a $19.3-million loss for the fiscal year that ended last July 31. To inject more vigor into A-M, Ash has brought in young executives, lowering the average age of the management from 60 to about 40. And by stressing more profitable products, the company has returned to the black for the first half of this fiscal year. But these are only the surface signs of what Ash insists is a much deeper process, "a deliberate attempt to change a corporate culture."

In trying to do that, Ash employs what he calls "immersion management." To reach the core of problems, he probes deeply into operations through relentless questioning,

---

* Reprinted from the February 27, 1978 issue of *Fortune* Magazine by special permission; © 1978 by Time Inc.

Note: Roy Ash is the chief executice officer of Addressograph-Multigraph Co.

which one executive calls "excruciating." Ash batters down bureaucratic practices in the belief that they tend to become an end in themselves. He forbids long memos, which managers submit, he says, "to have the record show the right thing for a defense later." And to make managers fully aware of the impact of their decisions, he demands a penetrating financial analysis of everything the company does or considers doing.

Ash found plenty that seemed to need changing. A-M, in his words, was "slow in pace, conservative in attitude, and living in the past." Its once-dominant line of "clanking machinery" for offset printing and addressing was being overwhelmed by quiet, more efficient electronic products of rivals that include Xerox, I.B.M., and Eastman Kodak. The previous management had floundered about, never coming up with a clear plan for the company's future. Inertia had almost paralyzed its board, which according to one member "kept wishfully thinking that something is going to happen to improve things."

Nothing did happen, however, until one worried director poured out his concern to a personal friend—John Birkelund, president of New Court Securities, the Rothschilds' private investment firm in New York. In the summer of 1976, Birkelund learned that several members of the board wanted a change of direction. Initially acting on his own in hopes of profiting later, he contacted Ash.

If the Worst Happened

After leaving Washington, Ash had retrieved his portfolio from a blind trust, returned to his native California, and fallen into a pattern of "trying to beat the Dow Jones average by a couple of points and blithely doing so." But Ash discovered that just "being a passive investor is not so much fun, it turns out." He had grown restless. Moreover, he dreaded "the really hard

work" of writing a book that he had researched on U.S. presidents as executive managers. "I figured there ought to be something easier than that," he recalls.

Using only publicly available information on A-M (to avoid becoming an insider), Ash made some interesting calculations. Just a glance at the annual report, filled with dark and dreary pictures, convinced him that "this was a company with troubles." But as he looked further, he sensed great potential in a corporation that had amassed assets of more than $400 million, including ample cash (which now totals $50 million). "If the worst happened," he says, "I figured I would double my money." He would be paying $9 a share for a company that could return $18 if liquidated. The "upside gain," as he calls it, would come from redeploying the assets to achieve an even bigger return—if he could run A-M.

But Ash's proposal to invest in the company and run it had to be sold to the cautious directors. In time, they came around. Says Birkelund, who served as a catalyst for the change: "Imagine the credibility of Ash, an outstanding manager who doesn't want a contract and puts his own money at risk."

In late 1976, Ash acquired 300,000 shares (3.6 percent of the total) and a free hand to shake up the company. Birkelund collected a $150,000 fee for lining up Ash and became a director. Anticipating the turnaround, Birkelund's investment house has also purchased about the same number of shares as Ash owns.

Getting Out of the Tower

Ash began his corporate revolution very quietly. The new chairman showed up in Cleveland without a single personal aide to become, he half-jokingly says, "the lion in the den, all alone." He told everyone to continue whatever they were doing and promised, "I'll catch up to you." This helped reassure A-M's management, which was still reeling from past reorganizations and personnel changes that had proved disastrous. "Lots of us," says one vice president, "were damned anxious about how we might fit into his plans."

Instead of immediately starting to revamp the company, Ash spent his first several months visiting its widely scattered operations and politely asking a lot of searching questions. That alone was a dramatic and generally welcomed change. His predecessors had always summoned subordinates to the headquarters building, which had long lived up to its official name, the Tower. But Ash's aim was substantive as well as symbolic. He wanted to get a handle on all the operations and assess the key people who ran them.

Make Them "Requestion Everything"

As he learned about the company, Ash kept jotting down what he saw as the issues that had to be resolved. Those notes, still being revised, became what he calls "my brick pile" for redesigning A-M. They include some 200 items, ranging from problem products to organizational difficulties. Summing up his overall goal in his own form of mental shorthand, he wrote: "Rethink, redesign, rebuild, and re-earn." In the same spirit, he says that he wanted to make the company's executives "requestion everything."

Rather than announcing his ideas, Ash demonstrated them. He left his office door open, placed his own intercom calls to arrange meetings, and always questioned people in person, not in writing. By casually asking office secretaries to suggest ways to "de-bureaucratize" the company, he received some clues about which executives were heavily engaged in paper shuffling. Then he removed some of the company's copying machines "to stop breeding paperwork." Spotting a well-written complaint from an important customer in Minneapolis,

Ash quickly flew off to visit him. As he now explains, "I wanted the word to get around our organization that I'm aware of what's going on."

Soon others began emulating him, even before they grasped his broader objectives. Above all, Ash wanted to "raise the excitement content" of A-M. And he wanted to make its managers personally accountable. "There's nothing like fear of failure," he says, "to motivate all of us."

Ash stirred both excitement and fear by his early discovery that no one in the corporation knew precisely which products were profitable. "I assumed that it was an innocent question," he recalls, "but the data didn't exist." Older hands at A-M had analyzed the profitability of broad product lines that include many different items, but Ash demanded that they break it down further—including the amount of salesman's time devoted to each product. Says one surviving manager: "Roy opened a lot of closets that we hadn't gotten into yet."

Finally, 15 weeks after taking over, Ash gathered five of his key executives in St. Petersburg, Florida, and revealed his ideas for giving the company "a sense of direction." Working from his collection of notes, Ash told them that "I don't have nearly as many answers as you, but I am beginning to know some of the questions." He spent the working weekend reviewing and refining his list of problems, then assigned them to various subordinates with deadlines for action. Accustomed to Ash's style by then, the five had their own pads and pencils ready.

Paths to Thousands of Doors

The catalogue of issues indicated Ash's strategy for turning A-M around. He believes that "it's better to own the market than the product." The main barrier in business today, as he sees it, is not developing new products, but being able to sell them. (This is especially true in office equipment, with average selling expenses of about 40 percent.) Thus A-M's major asset is its 13,000-man sales and service organization, which Ash says "has beaten paths to thousands of doors."

In essence, Ash's plan is to extend the life of the company's mature products as long as possible, while gradually acquiring new electronic office equipment to replace them. A-M steadily continues selling offset duplicators, and expects that its more than 200,000 operating machines will chug along for years—consuming supplies and requiring service. "This company," Ash says, "has a big flywheel that gives us the time and the cash throw-off to do other things." What's more, the corporation's ample hoard of cash, he says, "allows us to deal with this task deliberately, rather than frantically."

But within two weeks of the strategy session in Florida, Ash started shedding what he calls "millstone products"—either unprofitable or unpromising. "One of the things that I learned in Washington," Ash says, "is that a new guy doesn't have a proprietary interest in earlier decisions—or in defending mistakes."

As the c.e.o. began swinging the ax, a sense of alarm swept through the company. But Ash's management style eased the psychic pain. He guided the managers he had inherited into solving their own problems. "Rather than just pronouncing the outcome from on high," he explains, "you lead others through joint analysis to the same conclusion."

Ash concentrated on "structuring the problems"—posing the hard questions, which forced others to provide the answers that determined the fate of dubious products. Canceling the model 9000 lithographic copier, which had been introduced with great fanfare, came as a major blow to sales managers, says Robert Hagy, the senior vice president for marketing. "But when all the facts and figures were in," he adds, "it was the obvious thing to do."

"Why Work on Delta?"

Ash soon found, he says, that "I'm not as cold-blooded as I should be." Last March he brought James Mellor from Litton to be the new president and chief operating officer, and to do the things "that I personally find distasteful." More than a hatchet man, Mellor, 47, is an electrical engineer with 18 years of experience in directing high-technology programs and a desire "to really put my stamp" on A-M. He shares Ash's penchant for letting decisions naturally emerge from the facts.

Armed with his own handwritten copy of Ash's list, Mellor quickly tackled the catalogue of unresolved issues. High on that list were questions about an important new product then under development: "Why work on Delta? What do we expect of it?"

Delta, an offset duplicating system that was supposed to be virtually automatic, had lingered in development for nearly five years and had already cost more than $10 million. Many marketing men at A-M looked on it, remarks one executive, "almost as their salvation." But Ash and Mellor suspected that Delta was another millstone.

Reviewing the Delta R. and D. program last summer, Mellor found that his hardest job was getting information from the managers of A-M's Multigraphics Division. Over a six-weeks span, he spent three 12-hour days questioning them about Delta. "Enough people were emotionally involved and kind of skewed the data, I think unconsciously," he says. "When you've fathered something, it's hard to admit that you've got a mongoloid."

But ultimately Mellor's sharp probing revealed that Delta managers had underestimated almost everything about it—development costs, production costs, the time required to complete it, and the position of competitors. Delta probably couldn't be introduced before 1979, and the analysis indicated that other companies practically had rival products on the shelf. At best, Delta would be a breakeven program within five to seven years.

From Toyshop to Business

By the end of Mellor's final day-long session on Delta, no one was fighting for it. "With all the answers laid out," he says, "a person would have to be very dense to conclude that we should continue." But Mellor softened the blow by immediately declaring that the division's research money would go into making present products more salable, as well as finding new ones.

One of the lessons Mellor brought from Litton, which has taken big write-offs on its office equipment, is the need for R. and D. that "really ties product lines to the marketplace." After scrutinizing A-M's Multigraphics Development Center near Cleveland, he terminated two thirds of the work because it was unrelated to the kinds of future products the corporation wants. The resulting layoffs crumpled morale at the center, Mellor acknowledges. "But those who are bottom-line oriented," he maintains, "recognize that we decided to make a business out of a toyshop."

At Ash's direction, Mellor cleaned up A-M's messy and unprofitable international division. Its managers, who occupied a full floor of the Cleveland headquarters, duplicated the work of domestic divisions. After a month of persistent questions, the answers from the executives involved in the operation reinforced Mellor's solution—abolish the international division. Scores of high-level managers became dispensable. Realizing that this "could cause a lot of trauma to ripple through the company," Mellor fully explained his reasons—in person and in writing—so that "they did not have to hear it from outside or read it in the newspaper." Even some of those who lost their jobs concede that the move was right for the corporation.

The shakeout of the international division led to dramatic cost savings and gave A-M's leaders much better insight into their worldwide operations. Factories in Ohio, Canada, and England that had been turning out similar products and running below capacity now specialize in certain products in order to gain economies of scale. Mellor eliminated a 25-man Brussels office, which he says was "kind of a bureaucratic organization that consolidated information."

Mellor has turned his scalpel to the corporate headquarters staff, and by mid-year will have cut it in half, to 110 people, including secretaries. Part of his purpose is to set an example to operating divisions, which so far have helped reduce total A-M personnel by 1,300 (or 6.5 percent) since Ash arrived. In Ash's view, the personnel cuts not only reduce overhead, but also strip away layers of staff people who stood between him and operations. As Ash explains, "Jim and I like to work directly with guys who are sitting there face to face with the real world."

Eyes for Weak Spots

Despite Ash's emphasis on cool, objective decision making, he is highly sensitive to the need for diplomacy with his board and stockholders. By initiating radical changes slowly and methodically, he won over even the wariest directors. As one says, "Roy had a reputation from Litton of being fast on the draw, but his prudent way of dealing with A-M's problems impressed everyone." For example, when Ash and Mellor decided to drop Vice President Edwin Bruning, whose family owns nearly 3 percent of the corporation, Ash first went to Chicago to break the news gently to the family patriarch, Herbert Bruning.

Ash has not only attracted young executives from outside the company, but also persuaded the holdover managers to adopt his stern disciplines. Hagy, the marketing vice president, a 22-year veteran of A-M, notes that grueling monthly operational reviews force everyone to anticipate problems. "If there's a weak spot," he says, "Ash and Mellor will find it." But they delegate wide authority to the operating divisions, provided that they meet their profitability goals. As a rule, Moller homes in threateningly on any product that fails to provide at least a 20 percent return on investment.

Salesmen Misperceived Themselves

By demanding more of all executives, Ash and Mellor have created an atmosphere of brisk precision. The new senior vice president for finance, James Combes, who held similar posts at NCR and Hertz, observes: "This company is less hung up with committee deliberations and is more action oriented than any I've known. And there's very little political ass protecting."

Much of the turnaround campaign, Ash insists, hinges on "changing the self-perception" of A–M managers. By forcing closer analysis of the company's activities, Ash has laid bare a surprising source of strength that had been neglected. Services and supplies, mainly for the older lines of office equipment, account for 58 percent of the corporation's sales—and an estimated two thirds of its profit. Before Ash pinpointed this basic fact, A–M's research, advertising, and sales commissions were misdirected. As he explains, "Salesmen like to see themselves as offering costly, complex machines, not peddling supplies. We had to adjust their view, not of the company, but of themselves."

Another of the company's mistaken notions about itself, Ash discovered, involves the degree of immediate peril from xerographic copiers, which compete with some of its offset machines. Much of A–M's previous market research was culled from trade journals and guesses, until Ash insisted on a more systematic look at reality. Now the corporation knows that only about 8 per-

cent of its total revenues are exposed to direct competition from such companies as Xerox. As one of the holdover managers says, "That's less than half the threat we thought it was."

Moreover, Mellor notes, A–M "didn't know what were its real winners." As it turns out, a number of the company's newer product lines have carved out significant market niches. "And dominance," Mellor adds, "is what really makes you profitable." Among other things, A–M leads in the growing field of microfiche duplicating, is a major contender in phototypesetters for in-house corporate use, and has sold about 60 percent of the fast-food chains its Documentor point-of-sale systems. Ash is shopping for possible acquisitions of smaller companies with electronic products that A–M can sell.

And a New Name Too

Ash's next dramatic step to reshape company attitudes will be moving its headquarters to Los Angeles in June. Some of his more cynical employees have long assumed that he would find business reasons (complete with statistics) for returning to his sunny home state. But he justifies the move primarily on psychological grounds. "Cleveland is not the environment of new frontier technology in electronics," he says. "We must place ourselves in a setting where—partly through osmosis—we get a different idea of our future." For much the same reason, he wants to change the corporation's name too.

Ash's rapid flow of management buzzwords frequently sound more like academic lectures than the marching orders for an ailing corporation. But he has certainly sparked a lot of substantive change at A–M. Mainly by tightening up its operations and shedding millstones, Ash should boost revenues this fiscal year by 10 percent, to about $650 million, and begin to restore earnings. But just attaining the median return on equity of *Fortune* 500 companies (13.3 percent) will take several more years. And it will require more than positive thinking to thrust the company successfully into electronics.

However things turn out, Ash's efforts appear to have lifted Wall Street's hopes, for A-M shares have already appreciated about 55 percent in a bad market. Ash's own stake in the company has increased in value by $1.5 million. Not bad for a man who says, "This isn't work. It's fun."

THE DYNAMICS OF
INTERGROUP CONFLICT

Research in the area of intergroup conflict has been primarily concerned with conflict arising between two equally powerful groups. An analysis of research done in this area suggests the following conclusions:

1. *Frustration, that is, a blocking of a group's goal attempts, is a significant cause of conflict.* Experiments by Sherif and Sherif (34), Sussman and Weil (41), Blake and Mouton (4), Avigdor (1), Rabbie and Horwitz (29), Wilson and Kayatani (47), Stern, Sternthal, and Craig (37, 38, 39), and Hunger (20, 21) indicate that the frustration of a group's goal attempts by another group results in definite in-group/out-group biasing. Where behavioral measures were used, this frustration also led to verbal, and in some cases, to physical aggression. These findings support Thomas' process model of conflict.

2. *A group's goal attempts can be frustrated in various ways.* Competition in a zero-sum sense (A zero-sum is defined as a game in which the outcomes of the players sum to zero, so that on any given play one player gains precisely the amount that has been lost by his opponent) causes a win-lose syndrome in which both groups realize that their goal attempts are being frustrated or at least threatened. Sherif and Sherif (34), Blake and Mouton (4), and Sussman and Weil (41), used competition between two groups to generate conflict. Two-party competition appears to be a very unstable phenomenon—dissolving often into opponent-centered conflict. The difference between beating an opponent and winning a game is very tenuous in a two-party zero-sum situation.

Rewarding one group and not the other (a zero-sum reward system minus the competition) frustrates the nonrewarded group. This method of developing conflict is well-known to child psychologists and parents

An Analysis of Intergroup Conflict and Conflict Management[*]

J. DAVID HUNGER

everywhere. The experiment by Rabbie and Horwitz (29), in which a toss of a coin dictated which group received portable radios, is an example. Sherif et al. (33), used the same tactic in the instance when only enough ice cream in good containers was available to feed the members of one group. The other group had to settle for ice cream in damaged containers. Avigdor (1), used this technique in the form of circus tickets given to one group and not to the other groups.

Making a non-zero-sum reward to two groups depend upon an agreement which, unknown to them, is very difficult to reach can frustrate the goal achievement of both groups. Stern, Sternthal, and Craig (37, 38, 39) and Hunger (20, 21) utilized this tactic in a bargaining situation in which two

[*] From *Proceedings of the Eastern Academy of Management*, 13th Annual Meeting, 1976, edited by L. K. Bragaw and E. K. Winslow. Reprinted by permission of J. David Hunger and the Eastern Academy of Management.

groups were led to perceive each other as frustrating their goal attempts.

3. *Frustration, although a sufficient condition for conflict, is not a necessary condition.* Manheim (26) showed that behavioral conflict can be induced merely by manipulating a group's perception of its social distance with another group. Although Manheim did not measure for bias effects, it could be suggested that telling a group that another group is very different from it in characteristics important to the task is a method of directly inducing an in-group/out-group bias which, in turn, leads to the behavioral indications of conflict measured by Manheim. Stern, Sternthal, and Craig (37, 38, 39) and Hunger (20, 21) also told high conflict groups that they were different. Their bias results, nevertheless, were confounded with the matrix and aspiration inductions. Manheim's results, however, suggest that it is possible to induce intergroup conflict without a frustration episode by directly manipulating a group's cognitions of the situation.

Other researchers, such as Druckman (15) and Deutsch (9) have found conflict can be manipulated via what Druckman calls the "instructional set." Through variations in the instructional set, Deutsch aroused different attributions of the other's intent, as well as attributions of values to the payoffs. The type of set, contained in the instructions, was shown to affect the players' motivation as well as their game behavior. Druckman (14) created prenegotiation conditions, in a simulation of collective bargaining, that were shown to arouse definitions of the situation as either a win-lose contest or a collaborative problem-solving session. These findings suggest that a group's cognitive definition of the same situation is a determinant of game behavior. This would explain Manheim's findings of behavioral conflict in the absence of frustration. Thus, the structure of the conflict situation must be considered as a major factor in any experiment dealing with intergroup conflict.

4. *Evaluating the in-group higher than an out-group may not, in itself, reflect conflict.* Bass and Dunteman (2) found that groups tend to evaluate themselves higher than other comparable groups even when the groups are merely participating in sensitivity training sessions. Merely being in the presence of *potentially rival* groups may be enough to develop an initial in-group/out-group bias favoring the in-group. Studies by Hunger (20, 21), Harvey (19), Doise (12), Rabbie and Horwitz (29), and Kahn and Ryen (22) appear to support this possibility. This phenomenon may simply reflect a desire for a person to see himself and *his* group in the most favorable light. Thus a person may tend to notice mainly the good points of his group while he continues to see the bad as well as good points of an outgroup. Size of the group may effect this phenomenon (16). A high evaluation of one's own group may also reflect a group's cohesiveness. If so, a positive relationship would be expected between cohesiveness and in-group evaluation. There is some evidence to suggest this relationship (11). Thus, evaluating the in-group higher than an out-group may not, in itself, indicate the presence of conflict.

Studies by Sherif and Sherif (34), Blake and Mouton (4), Hunger (20, 21), and Bass and Dunteman (2) among others, do indicate that the presence of conflict between two groups does act to increase the amount of in-group/out-group bias between them. Sherif and Sherif and Blake and Mouton found that intergroup conflict tends to be accompanied by an increase in the evaluation of one's own group and a decrease in the evaluation (derogation) of the outgroup. Bass and Dunteman and Hunger did not find such an increase in in-group evaluation. These studies reported merely a slight drop in in-group evaluation as the contest got underway. The competitive out-group, however, dropped significantly in evaluation. This evidence suggests that just as conflict cannot be inferred merely by the existence of an in-group/out-group bias, it cannot be inferred merely by an increase in in-group evaluation. It appears that an increasing derogation of the out-group must be present for conflict to be present.

The studies mentioned above appear to fit into Thomas' process model of conflict. Intergroup competition has been used by Sherif and Sherif and by Blake and Mouton, among others, to generate a mutually frustrating situation. A group's goal attempts have also been secretly frustrated by the researchers themselves (1, 20, 21, 37, 38, 39). Such frustrations have normally led to a win-lose conceptualization of the situation. It is at this point that the groups develop opponent-centered attitudes which derogate the out-group (opponent) and often glorify the in-group. If circumstances are right (as they were in the Sherif et al. studies), these attitudes lead to aggressive behavior. This behavior acts to instigate reactions from the other group, thus reinforcing an opponent-centered orientation and generating a "self-fulfilling prophecy" (27) effect.

THE MANAGEMENT OF INTERGROUP CONFLICT

Since it is now recognized that conflict can be functional as well as dysfunctional (8), research emphasis has shifted from resolution to management. Conflict management in the literature still seems to be concerned mainly with reducing conflict to a functional level. The inverse, that is developing conflict where none exists, has just begun to be investigated (31) and could be a future research area of some significance.

Methods of conflict reduction may be categorized on the basis of *how* they work. In any conflict of interest situation based upon an incompatibility of goals, aims, or

values, there appear to be five basic approaches to the resolution of intergroup conflict.

1. *Change the parameters* of the conflict, such as increasingly the supply of a product which is in great demand, so that both groups will be able to achieve their goals. This method aims to resolve the conflict by getting at the underlying source of the problem. Unfortunately, this approach is not always practical in a world of limited resources.

2. *Divide available resources* so that each group is able to partially attain its goal. This is the classic solution of the economist. It includes the techniques of bargaining, mediation, and arbitration which are in great use in today's world.

3. *Isolate the groups* via structural or legal devices so that each group is more independent of the other, and thus less likely to have its goals frustrated by the other. The groups can be isolated structurally in two ways. (a) A buffer can be placed between the conflicting groups. The buffer then has the responsibility of making sure each group attains its goals. If a group does not, the buffer is blamed. Thus hostility is successfully displaced from the out-group to the buffer. (b) The environment of the conflicting groups is modified so that each group is able to achieve its goal independently of the other. Examples of this technique are decentralization and local options.

4. *Reduce ethnocentrism* (in-group/out-group bias) between the groups so that each can perceive each other objectively. The implicit assumption of this approach is that the group will then be able to better resolve the underlying conflict of interest problem. Empirical evidence has shown that in-group/out-group bias can be reduced via superordinate goals and conciliation techniques, such as Blake and Mouton's intergroup "therapy." Research by Stern, Sternthal, and Craig (37) has produced some evidence that an exchange of persons also

acts to resolve intergroup conflict by reducing in-group/out-group bias.

5. *Reduce aggressive behavior* between the groups so that actions of each group will no longer serve to "fan the flame." This approach aims to stop the effect epitomised by the terms *self-fulfilling prophecy* (27) and *Gresham's Law of Conflict* (7). Examples of this approach are cooling-off periods, withdrawal, smoothing attempts, and, of course, surrender. There is little empirical evidence that any of these aggression-reducing methods work to reduce serious intergroup conflict, at least where conflict of interest is concerned. These methods, however, are probably very helpful in reducing aggressive behavior erupting from "nonrealistic" conflict (8) sources such as insanity, drunkenness, or displaced anger (for example, husband yells at wife after boss yells at husband).

Thomas' model suggests that conflict is a process which feeds itself. Thus the model implies that the way to reduce or manage conflict is to break the circle at some point. One could aim at the source of the episode by reducing the cause of the frustration. This would involve any of the first three approaches: changing the parameters, dividing available resources, or isolating the groups (by modifying the environment). One could also aim at the conceptualization aspect of the episode, via the fourth approach, by reducing the in-group/out-group bias between groups. One could also attempt to reduce aggressive behavior by methods mentioned under the fifth approach. To the extent that buffers would serve a displacement of hostility function, isolating the groups may serve to reduce aggressive behavior. (The groups may not act as aggressively toward a buffer as they would toward each other.)

Given (1) that an intergroup conflict situation erupts out of frustration caused by a conflict of interest, (2) that these frustrations cause ethnocentric attitudes (in-group/out-group bias favoring the in-

group), (3) that these attitudes set the cognitive stage for some sort of conflict behavior on both sides, (4) that this behavior generates a feedback effect, and (5) that this feedback tends to reinforce ethnocentric attitudes in both groups, the following key questions arise:

1. *Will reducing the frustrations, by itself, reduce intergroup conflict?* If the conflict has been going on for a long time, it has probably developed aspects of a nonrealistic conflict complete with ethnocentrism and aggression. These could probably keep "fanning the flame" even after the original conflict of interest has been resolved. Generally speaking, however, one probably can assume that reducing a conflict-causing frustration will eventually reduce conceptual and behavioral aspects of conflict.

2. *Will reducing ethnocentrism, by itself, reduce intergroup conflict?* If in-group/out-group biasing results from the frustration of goal attempts, the continued presence of the same frustration should serve to rekindle the conflict. Sherif and Sherif (34) and Blake, Shepard, and Mouton (5) suggest this in their comments concerning the temporary value of the "common enemy" approach. Would not the same criticism pertain to superordinate goals and conciliation attempts if the conflict of interest problem could not be resolved? The Sherifs' many experiments did not resolve this question because they removed the frustration aspects of the situation (competitive episodes and experimenter-induced frustrations) at the same time as they began inserting superordinate goals. A study by Hunger (20, 21) attempted to resolve this question by comparing groups which received an achievable superordinate goal with groups which did not. The frustrating antecedent condition (conflict of interest) was kept constant. Results indicated that the superordinate goal in this situation acted to *retard* the development of felt conflict, rather than to reduce it.

3. *Will reducing aggressive behavior, by itself, reduce intergroup conflict?* A consensus of theory and research findings indicate that reducing aggression will not, by itself, reduce realistic conflict. It is possible, however, that any conflict situation contains a certain amount of nonrealistic conflict generated by the feedback effect. This could be reduced by stopping aggressive behavior.

CONCLUSION

On the basis of this survey of the literature, the process model of conflict appears to be most helpful in explaining the development and management of intergroup conflict. It has been shown that just as conflict can be induced experimentally, it can also be reduced experimentally. The process model suggests various approaches for the management of intergroup conflict. Stern, Sternthal, and Craig (37) are presently engaged in comparing the effectiveness of various conflict reduction techniques. Others such as Robbins (31), are concerned with various techniques to induce conflict. It is suggested that a contingency approach be taken regarding intergroup conflict. A level of conflict which is clearly dysfunctional for one set of groups may be functional for others. A conflict reduction technique may be feasible and effective in one situation, but not in another. Much research is needed before a normative theory of conflict management can be fully developed. The conflict process needs to be more fully defined and quantified to allow the development of better measurement techniques. Research is needed to better pinpoint when conflict is considered dysfunctional. As Robbins suggests, intergroup conflict may be dysfunctional for the people involved but functional for the organization as a whole. For those many situations where conflict is judged dysfunctional, it is important not only to compare the effectiveness of conflict reduction techniques, but also to search for key variables in conflict situations which may determine the appropriateness of these techniques.

REFERENCES

1. Avigdor, R. "The Development of Stereotypes as a Result of Group Interaction." Unpublished Ph.D. dissertation, New York University, 1952. Summarized in *Groups in Harmony and Tension* by Muzafer and Carolyn Sherif (New York: Harper, 1953).

2. Bass, B. M., and Dunteman, G. "Biases In the Evaluation of One's Own Group, Its Allies and Opponents." *Journal of Conflict Resolution*, 7 (1963), pp. 16–20.

3. Berkowitz, I., ed. *Roots of Aggression*. (New York: Atherton Press, 1969).

4. Blake, R. R., and Mouton, J. "Reactions to Intergroup Competition Under Win-Lose Conditions." *Management Science*, 7 (1961), pp. 420–35.

5. Blake, R. R.; Shepard, H. A.; and Mouton, J. S. *Managing Intergroup Conflict In Industry*. (Houston: Tex.: Gulf Publishing Co., 1964).

6. Campbell, D. T. "Stereotypes and the Perception of Group Differences." *American Psychologist*, 22 (1967), pp. 817–29.

7. Coleman, J. S. *Community Conflict*. (New York: The Free Press, 1957).

8. Coser, L. *The Functions of Social Conflict.* (New York: The Free Press, 1956).

9. Deutsch, M. "The Effect of Motivational Orientation Upon Trust and Suspicion." *Human Relations*, 13 (1960), pp. 123–40.

10. Deutsch, M. *The Resolution of Conflict.* (New Haven: Yale University Press, 1973).

11. Dion, K. "Cohesiveness as a Determinant of Ingroup Outgroup Bias." *Journal of Personality and Social Psychology*, 28 (1973), pp. 163–71.

12. Doise, W. "Intergroup Relations and Polarization of Individual and Collective Judgments." *Journal of Personality and Social Psychology*, 12 (1969), pp. 136–43.

13. Dollard, J.; Doob, N.; Miller, N.; Mowrer, O.; and Sears, R. *Frustration and Aggression.* (New Haven: Yale University Press, 1939).

14. Druckman, D. "Prenegotiation Experience and Dyadic Conflict Resolution in a Bargaining Situation." *Journal of Experimental Social Psychology*, 4 (1968), pp. 367–83.

15. Druckman, D. "The Influence of the Situation in Inter-Party Conflict." *Journal of Conflict Resolution*, 15 (1971), pp. 523–54.

16. Gerard, H. B., and Hoyt, M. F. "Distinctiveness of Social Categorization and Attitudes

Toward Ingroup Members." *Journal of Personality and Social Psychology*, 29 (1974), pp. 836–42.

17. Guetzkow, H., ed. *Simulation in Social Science: Readings* (Englewood Cliffs, N.J.: Prentice-Hall, 1962).

18. Harding, J.; Proshansky, H.; Kutner, B.; and Chein, I. "Prejudice and Ethnic Relations," in *The Handbook of Social Psychology*, vol. V. Edited by Gardner Lindzey and Elliot Aronson (Reading, Mass.: Addison-Wesley, 1969).

19. Harvey, O. J. "An Experimental Investigation of Negative and Positive Relations Between Small Groups through Judgmental Indices." *Sociometry*, 19 (1956), pp. 201–09.

20. Hunger, J. D. *An Empirical Test of the Superordinate Goal as a Means of Reducing Intergroup Conflict in a Bargaining Situation*. Unpublished Ph.D. dissertation, The Ohio State University, 1973.

21. Hunger, J. D., and Stern, L. W. "An Assessment of the Functionality of Superordinate Goal in Reducing Conflict." *Academy of Management Journal*, 19 (December 1976), pp. 591–605.

22. Kahn, A., and Ryen, A. H. "Factors Influencing the Bias Towards One's Own Group." *International Journal of Group Tensions*, 2 (1972), pp. 33–50.

23. Kelman, H. C. *International Behavior: A Social Psychological Analysis* (New York: Holt, Rinehart, and Winston, 1965).

24. Landsberger, H. A. "The Horizontal Dimension in Bureaucracy." *Administrative Science Quarterly*, 6 (1961), pp. 299–332.

25. Mack, R. W., and Snyder, R. C. "The Analysis Conflict—Toward an Overview and Synthesis." *Journal of Conflict Resolution*, 1 (1957), pp. 212–48.

26. Manheim, H. L. "Intergroup Interaction as Related to Status and Leadership Differences Between Groups." *Sociometry*, 23 (1960), pp. 415–27.

27. Merton, R. K. *Social Theory and Social Structure* (Glencoe, Ill.: Free Press, 1957).

28. Pondy, L. R. "Organizational Conflict: Concepts and Models." *Administrative Science Quarterly*, 12 (1967), pp. 296–320.

29. Rabbie, J. M., and Horwitz, M. "Arousal of Ingroup-Outgroup Bias by a Chance Win or Loss." *Journal of Personality and Social Psychology*, 13 (1969), pp. 269–77.

30. Rapoport, A. *Fights, Games and Debates* (Ann Arbor, Mich.: University of Michigan Press, 1960).

31. Robbins, S. P. *Managing Organizational Conflict* (Englewood Cliffs, N.J.: Prentice-Hall, 1974).

32. Schmidt, S. M., and Kochan, T. A. "Conflict: Toward Conceptual Clarity." *Administrative Science Quarterly*, 17 (1972), pp. 359–69.

33. Sherif, M.; Harvey, O. J.; White, B. J.; Hood, W. R.; and Sherif, C. W. *Intergroup Conflict and Cooperation: The Robbers' Cave Experiment* (Norman, Okla.: The University Book Exchange, 1961).

34. Sherif, M., and Sherif, C. W. *Social Psychology* (New York: Harper and Row, 1969).

35. Siegel, S., and Fouraker, L. E. *Bargaining and Group Decision Making*. (New York: McGraw-Hill, 1960).

36. Stern, L. W. "Potential Conflict Management Mechanisms in Distribution Channels: An Interorganizational Analysis." *Contractual Marketing Systems*. Ed. by Donald N. Thompson (Boston: Heath-Lexington Books, 1971).

37. Stern, L. W.; Sternthal, B.; and Craig, C. S. "Managing Conflict in Distribution Channels: A Laboratory Study." *Journal of Marketing Research*, 10 (1973), pp. 169–79.

38. Stern, L. W.; Sternthal, B.; and Craig, C. S. "A Parasimulation of Interorganizational Conflict, *International Journal of Group Tensions*, 3 (1973), pp. 68–90.

39. Stern, L. W., Sternthal, B., and Craig, C. S. "Strategies for Managing Interorganizational Conflict: A Laboratory Paradigm." *Journal of Applied Psychology*, 60 (1975), pp. 472–82.

40. Sumner, W. G. *Folkways* (Boston: Ginn, 1906).

41. Sussman, M. B., and Weil, W. B. "An Experimental Study on the Effects of Group Interaction Upon the Behavior of Diabetic Children." *International Journal of Social Psychiatry*, 6 (1960), pp. 120–25.

42. Swingle, P., ed. *The Structure of Conflict* (New York: Academic Press, 1970).

43. Thomas, K. W. "Conflict and Conflict Management." *Handbook of Industrial and Organizational Psychology*. Edited by Marvin D. Dunnette (Chicago: Rand McNally, 1976).

44. Walton, R. E., and McKersie, R. B. *A Behavioral Theory of Labor Negotiations* (New York: McGraw-Hill, 1965).

45. Walton, R. E., and Dutton, J. M. "The Management of Interdepartmental Conflict: A Model and Review." *Administrative Science Quarterly*, 14 (1969), pp. 73–84.

46. Williams, R. M. *The Reduction of Intergroup Tensions* (New York: Social Science Research Council, 1947).

47. Wilson, W., and Kayatani, M. "Intergroup Attitudes and Strategies in Games Between Opponents of the Same or of a Different Race." *Journal of Personality and Social Psychology*, 9 (1968), pp. 24–30.

The corporate executive often is proud of the quality and sophistication of his or her decision making. Increasingly uncertain, complex, and turbulent external environments cause a premium to be placed on the effectiveness with which problems can be identified, alternatives structured and proposed, choices made, and programs implemented.

Sophistication is required to cope with the environment and its impact, which in turn creates the need for specialized planning or other staff groups; full-time professionals with advanced skills are often assigned the task of investigating a problem and recommending solutions to the overloaded line executive (3). Staff analysis is heavily relied upon, for practical reasons of executive time and technical skill limitations; such analysis may possess influence which surpasses that which is warranted, from the effect of the authority of (staff) expertise. Even expert-client confrontation to resolve differences of opinion can result in movement of initial client positions to become identical with those originally made by the experts (12). Analytical breakdowns and insufficiencies (11), improper assumptions (7), or uncertainty absorption (6) are often covered up by the intricacies of the techniques applied to the problem (7). All this can operate to increase the executive's blind acceptance of, and implicit reliance on, the analytical process.

Review and Dissent

Because of potential dangers in approving an inadequate or erroneous analysis, substantial decisions are usually reviewed by the Executive Committee, the Finance Committee, or the board of Directors. Less formally, one's superior may try to pick apart the analysis and recommendations in order to be assured that assumptions and analytical procedures are sound.

READING 5–4

Improving Executive Decisions by Formalizing Dissent: The Corporate Devil's Advocate*

THEODORE T. HERBERT and RALPH W. ESTES

While they are steps in the right direction, the qualifications of the review person or panel members are hardly likely to be specialized enough to allow detailed assessment of the analytical trail followed, to raise issues of alternatives not considered, or to question underlying and implicit value judgments.

The executive decision-making process can be only as effective as the analytical phase allows; yet time and expertise are not normally applied to managing the analytical process. Some assurances of objectivity and control for completeness can enhance the executive's confidence in the proposals submitted and in decisions based on the analyses. The executive is typically a generalist rather than a specialist; he or she relies on

---

* *Academy of Management Review*, October 1977, pp. 662–67.

359

the expertise of another, assuming—or hoping—that the analytical intricacies hidden within the submitted proposal and recommendations are thorough, objective, realistic, and correct.

Formalized Dissent

There are scattered examples of techniques by which control over the decision process is exercised by the executive. Although the techniques differ widely in specifics, they have in common the careful structuring of independent reviews, to balance and test the adequacy of an analytical endeavor. Formal dissenting roles are played by persons investigating the position or proposal of another, bringing to light biases or inadequacies and generating counterproposals.

One of the oldest examples of the formalized dissent role occurs within the Roman Catholic Church; the "Devil's Advocate" (formally termed "promoter of the faith") has been a continuing office since the early 1500s, with the prescribed function of thoroughly investigating proposals for canonization and beatification (10). The Devil's Advocate must bring to light any information which might cast doubt upon the qualifications of the candidate for sainthood. The bestowing of sainthood is not taken lightly. Since it represents extensions of the doctrinal fabric of the church and affects the lives of congregation members, the *negative* side of the proposal for sainthood must be thoroughly and rigorously investigated. *Separation of the functions of promoter and dissenter* ensures that both sides of the question will be thoroughly analyzed and presented, since the roles are not subject to intrapersonal conflict by residing in the same person (9). The very existence of a formal adversary may pressure the promoter to be much more thorough than if only the positive side were presented. (A review of the literature unfortunately reveals no evidence on the effectiveness of the techniques as used in the Catholic church.)

The same dissenting function appears in the Anglo-Saxon legal system. The jury and judge ("executive") examine the merits of the proposal (the prosecution's mustering of all available evidence to show the defendant's guilt) and counterproposal (the defense's presentation of all available evidence to show the defendant's innocence). Carefully structured is the process whereby prosecution and defense attempt to show the fallacies and omissions in the other's presentation to an impartial jury. The system allows complete airing of positive and negative sides of a single question. The verdict ("decision") may then be reached with the benefit of the best possible evidence ("data").

Corporate internal auditors provide a check on investment decisions or other proposals by questioning basic issues of "affordability," helping to ensure that all relevant questions of cost or finance have been addressed by those proposing the investments. Manufacturing firms which operate at the leading edge of technological applications routinely employ outside consulting firms to appraise internally-developed product development efforts.

The British parliamentary system, with its "loyal opposition," balances the unilateral programs of the party in power, questioning almost routinely the government's proposals. The U.S. governmental system builds in a similar dissenting role for those opposed to a proposal ("bill") placed before the legislature, with hearings and debate on the floor of the legislative house.

The efforts of Ralph Nader and consumers' advocate groups also present negative information to the consuming public, balancing what they consider to be one-sided advertising claims. The dissenting role thereby provides more complete information to decision makers who have neither the time nor expertise to gather and analyze data pro *and* con for household consumption decisions.

Academics or learned societies incorporate a formalized dissent procedure to ensure rigorous treatment of the substance of research or theoretical papers. A "discussant" (usually an eager assistant professor), assigned to a paper presented before the society, may gleefully rake over the coals the presenter of an ill-prepared paper.

The Corporate Devil's Advocate

The essence of these techniques can be distilled and formalized for use in corporate decision processes. If volunteering criticism of another's work can be taken as a personal attack, constructive criticism may be withheld. Since the decision process needs valid analytical input to operate as effectively as possible, the assumption cannot be made that discussion and probing questions will control for quality. Contributing one's insights and criticisms does not necessarily follow from the opportunity to contribute; people may choose to withhold their involvement for personal or group-related reasons (1). Institutionalizing the dissent function may help depersonalize the conflict generated by criticism. A critical review by a specialist as technically competent as the staff proposers can help ensure that the analysis is adequate in all major aspects (3).

One benefit which may *not* be readily measurable is the improvement in quality of decision-making input by staff analysts. The analyst's trail to the recommendations, his or her judgments and decisions, are to be traced by another specialist, the Corporate Devil's Advocate; knowledge of such control or follow-up could ensure that controversial, subjective, or value-ridden elements will be minimized. For a process to be effective, it should be measured, evaluated, and rewarded appropriately—and the

critical process is no different (4). Much of what has been said implies that the critical review process can be most appropriately applied to major strategic or other one-time propositions, as opposed to recurring or routine operational matters. But turbulent external environmental conditions, highly technical analytical procedures, subjective or value-laden criteria, or alternatives which embody some risk (as in the reappraisal and reformulation of a firm's strategy in a stable industry) are other conditions in which the process may be of benefit.

The Devil's Advocate starts with the analyst's final copy of the proposal. The Devil's Advocate becomes immersed in the analyst's report only after having conducted an independent audit of the problem situation, to verify that the problem identified or assumed is the real problem. Reconstruction of the analyst's logic and data gives the Devil's Advocate an in-depth trace. Should inconsistencies appear, potential alternatives be omitted from consideration, irrelevant criteria be established, or window dressing be added to impress the executive, the fallacies or inaccuracies must be listed, together with their impacts upon the recommendation. If the proposal is determined to be unsound, a reanalysis of the problem situation should be presented, complete with recommendation and justification.

As soon as the report of the Devil's Advocate is completed, a special confrontation session is held. Proposing analyst and Devil's Advocate each present their own efforts to the decision maker and whatever other executives are appropriate to the session. After formal critique of the proposal, the analyst and Devil's Advocate rationally rebut each others' reports. In the best of all possible worlds, this process may result in a new proposal which eliminates the fallacious parts of both recommendations and is comprised of the soundest elements of each. Failing this synergistic new recommendation, the decision maker must then turn to the task of deciding which—if either—recommendation to accept. The major difference is that shortcomings are now known.

The corporate Devil's Advocate may be an organizational member, an office within the firm, or a group composed of external and independent elements. The approach will vary with the firm, as well as with the nature of the problem and its associated proposal.

The Inside Devil's Advocate

Devil's Advocates who are organizational members may be established in temporary development positions or in permanent career slots. The Devil's Advocate position could be assigned to almost any promising member. Although background, training, and skills would not have to perfectly match the nature of the proposal, a match would probably prove helpful.

Such a position, as a management development device, could be rotated among junior executives with upper-management potential. But the Devil's Advocate should not be exposed to status or rank differentials in the assignment; the analyst whose proposal is critiqued should always be at the same hierarchical level as the Devil's Advocate, to avoid pressure or other repercussions. For practical purposes, the Devil's Advocate might report directly to the president of the firm.

The concept *must* be enthusiastically understood and accepted to be workable. Acceptance by the chief executive and other executives will permit the Devil's Advocate to undertake the role freely, without fear of reprisal or recrimination. Privately, he or she may completely agree with the position of the promoter, but officially he or she *must* oppose and raise doubts about that position. The organization will thus ensure that no project is steamrollered through the decision-making process without full considera-

tion of at least the major disadvantages and alternatives.

A pragmatic disadvantage associated with any specialized unit is the tendency to become differentiated from other organizational units in perspectives on goals, time, and interpersonal orientations (5). Rotating the assignment may help overcome this tendency toward goal displacement.

The External Devil's Advocate

Another general approach to the device is the external, completely independent Corporate Devil's Advocate. This may be a consulting firm contracted to evaluate the proposal and recommendations of an internal analyst group or of another external consulting group. Arm's-length treatment would be relatively assured, even though difficulty might be experienced in recreating the processes through which the conclusions of an internal analyst were derived. Fresh looks at old problems could result in alternatives not previously considered.

Almost any important problem situation could benefit from an independent analysis of the problem definition, nature, and scope. Alternatives presented, or modifications thereof, can offer new insights and controls upon that most most difficult, yet critical, process—executive decision making.

Summary and Conclusions

To ensure valid decision-making inputs, the device of the Corporate Devil's Advocate is proposed. Creating an official "Naysayer," charged with the responsibility of dissenting with recommendations, aids in pointing out logical flaws and other fallacies or inaccuracies in major one-sided proposals.

Since major decisions today are crucial to long-run success in a competitive and volatile market place, the quality of these decisions must be optimized. An important approach is to increase the overall validity of the complete decision-making process, from definition of the problem through to presentation of recommendations deriving from the analysis, and hence to implementation of the decision. An official dissenter can heighten the probability that decisions will be thoroughly researched and proposed solutions soundly based in reality. The Corporate Devil's Advocate also can do much to make sure that marginal or unwise decisions are not made at all.

REFERENCES

1. Carr, David F., Thad B. Green, and Thomas W. Hinckle. "Exploring Nominal Grouping From a Social Facilitation Context," in Dennis F. Ray and Thad B. Green (eds.), *Expanding Dimensions of Management Thought and Action* (Mississippi State, Miss.: Southern Management Association, 1976), pp. 69–81.

2. French, John R. P., Jr., and Bertram Raven. "The Bases of Social Power," in Dorwin Cartwright and Alvin Zander (eds.), *Group Dynamics: Research and Theory*, 3d ed. (New York: Harper and Row, 1968), pp. 259–69.

3. Herbert, Theodore T. "Assumptions and Limitations in Business Policy Educational Technology: Models for Analysis and Innovation," *Journal of Economics and Business*, vol. 28, no. 3 (1976), 209–18

4. Kerr, Steven. "On the Folly of Rewarding A, While Hoping for B," *Academy of Management Journal*, vol. 18, no. 4 (1975), 769–83.

5. Lawrence, Paul R., and Jay W. Lorsch. *Organization and Environment: Managing Differentiation and Integration* (Homewood, Ill.: Irwin, 1969).

6. March, James G., and Herbert A. Simon. *Organizations* (New York: Wiley, 1958).

7. Mason, Richard O. "A Dialectical Approach to Strategic Planning," *Management Science*, vol. 15, no. 8 (1969), B–403–B–414.

8. Methvin, Eugene H. "The Fight to Save the Flint," *Readers Digest*, August 1974, pp. 17–22, 26.

9. Meyer, Herbert H., Emanuel Kay, and John R. P. French, Jr. "Split Roles in Performance Appraisal," *Harvard Business Review* (May–June 1965), 123–29.

10. *New Catholic Encyclopedia*, "Devil's Advocate," vol. 4 (New York: McGraw-Hill, 1967), pp. 829–30.

11. Newman, William H., Charles E. Summer, and E. Kirby Warren. *The Process of Management: Concepts, Behavior, and Practice*, 3d ed. (Englewood Cliffs, N.J.: Prentice-Hall, 1972).

12. Nutt, Paul C. "The Merits of Using Experts or Consumers as Members of Planning Groups: A Field Experiment in Health Planning," *Academy of Management Journal*, vol. 19, no. 3 (1976), 378–94.

13. Thompson, James D. *Organizations in Action: Social Science Bases of Administrative Theory* (New York: McGraw-Hill, 1967).

14. Thornton, Robert L. "Controlling the Technician: The Adversary Approach," *MSU Business Topics* (Summer 1974), 5–10.

To successfully manage complex tasks, project managers must successfully deal with a number of managerial issues. First, they must develop support for their projects from key interfaces within their organizations. Second, they must effectively deal with the inevitable conflict situations which arise in administering their projects. To effectively manage conflict situations, project managers must be sensitive to the potential causes of conflict and to the potential intensity of these situations.

This study investigates four important areas in the management of conflict in project-oriented work environments:

1. Perceived influence methods used by project managers in eliciting support for their projects.
2. The cause and intensity of conflict experienced by project managers in seven areas considered fundamental to project accomplishment.
3. Five distinct modes of conflict resolution are examined and compared with their perceived effectiveness in minimizing conflict situations with project personnel, superiors, and functional support departments.
4. The influence modes of project managers which minimize conflict with key interfaces.

This empirical investigation is based upon a survey of project managers in approximately 150 technology-oriented companies, resulting in a usable sample of 100 project managers. The sample covers a wide variety of project management situations such as airplane production, computer installation, facilities construction, and research and development.

The principal data collection instrument was a survey questionnaire, which was supplemented by interviews with project managers in various organizational settings. The questionnaires and subsequent discus-

The Effective Management of Conflict in Project-Oriented Work Environments*

HANS J. THAMHAIN and DAVID L. WILEMON

sions were designed to measure values on the following three variables:

1. Project manager's perception of influence methods used to elicit support from assigned project personnel and functional support departments.
2. Intensity and causes of conflict experienced by project managers with their superiors, assigned project personnel, supporting functional departments and their immediate team members.
3. Various modes of conflict resolution adopted by project managers.

Influence Methods of Project Managers

The influence methods used by project managers to gain support from project personnel were measured by asking the managers to rank nine methods of influence in terms of how important they felt each was

* *Defense Management Journal*, vol. 11, no. 3 (July 1975), pp. 29–40.

FIGURE 1
Significance of Factors in Support to Project Management

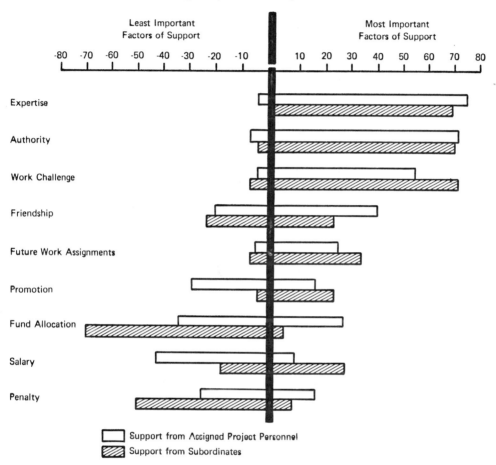

Percentage of replies who ranked powerbase as one of three . . .

Least Important
Factors of Support

Most Important
Factors of Support

-80 -70 -60 -50 -40 -30 -20 -10   10 20 30 40 50 60 70 80

Expertise

Authority

Work Challenge

Friendship

Future Work Assignments

Promotion

Fund Allocation

Salary

Penalty

☐ Support from Assigned Project Personnel
▨ Support from Subordinates

in providing support to their project tasks. More specifically, the framework of this investigation uses French and Raven's[1] typology of interpersonal influences, which had been modified by Gemmill and Thamhain[2]

and used for various power style studies on project managers in situations similar to this one.[3] (The nine influence bases are listed in Figure 1, which also summarizes the rank-order response of this measure.)

[1] J. R. P. French, Jr., and B. Raven, "The Basis of Social Power," in *Studies in Social Power*, D. Cartwright, ed., Ann Arbor, Mich.. Research Center for Group Dynamics, 1959.

[2] A detailed description of the nine measures is provded by G. R. Gemmill and H. J. Thamhain in "Influence Styles of Project Managers: Some Project Performance Correlates," *Academy of Management Journal*, vol. 17, no. 2, June 1974, pp. 216–24.

[3] For further applications of the typology to measure influence methods used by project managers to elicit support, see G. R. Gemmill and H. J. Thamhain, "The Power Styles of Project Managers: Some Efficiency Correlates," *Convention Digest, 20th Annual Joint Engineering Management Conference*, Atlanta Ga., October 30–31, 1972, pp. 89–97; "Project Performance as a Function of the Leadership Styles of Project Managers: Results of a Field Study," *Convention Digest, 4th*

Intensity and Cause of Conflict

The intensity and cause of conflict experienced by project managers was measured using a grid specifically designed for this study. The grid identifies on its y-axis seven different causes over which conflict may arise. The x-axis identifies five interface components where these conflicts occur with:

Subordinates.
Assigned project personnel.
Functional support departments.
Superiors.
Among team members.

Project managers were asked to indicate on a four-point scale the intensity of conflict they experienced for each of the seven causes with each of the five components. The actual measurements and responses are summarized in Figure 2.

Modes of Conflict Resolution

This set of measurements relies on the research of Lawrence and Lorsch,[4] who developed various sets of aphorisms to describe methods of resolving conflict. Fifteen of these aphorisms were selected to match the following five methods identified by Blake and Mouton:[5]

Annual Meeting of the Project Management Institute, Philadelphia, Pa., October 18–21, 1972; and "The Effectiveness of Different Power Styles of Project Managers in Gaining Project Support," *IEEE Transactions on Engineering Management*, vol. 20, no. 2, May 1973, pp. 38–43.

[4] P. R. Lawrence and J. W. Lorsch, *Organization and Environment*, Boston: Division of Research, Harvard Business School, 1967. Examples of aphorisms used in the current research are: Forcing—"The arguments of the strongest always have the most weight"; Smoothing—"Kill your enemies with kindness"; Confrontation—"By digging and digging the truth is being discovered"; Compromise—"Better half a loaf than no bread"; Withdrawal—"When two quarrel, he who keeps silence first is the most praiseworthy."

[5] R. R. Blake and J. S. Mouton, *The Managerial Grid*, Houston: Gulf Publishing, 1964.

FIGURE 2
Mean Conflict Intensity Profile Over Project Life Cycle

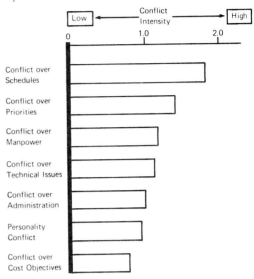

1. *Withdrawal.* Retreating from actual or potential disagreements and conflict situations.

2. *Smoothing.* Deemphasizing differences and emphasizing commalities over conflictual issues.

3. *Compromising.* Considering various issues, bargaining and searching for solutions which attempt to bring some degree of satisfaction to the conflicting parties.

4. *Forcing.* Exterting one's viewpoint at the potential expense of another party. Characterized by competitiveness and a win-lose situation.

5. *Confrontation.* Addressing a disagreement directly. The confrontation approach involves a problem-solving mode whereby affected parties work through their disagreements.[6]

---

[6] For a fuller description of this definition, see R. J. Burke, "Methods of Resolving Interpersonal Conflicts," *Personnel Administration*, July–August 1969, pp. 48–55.

FIGURE 3
The Most and Least Important Modes of Conflict Resolution

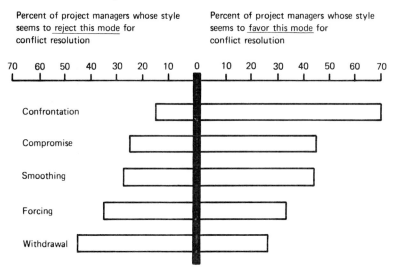

The various models of conflict resolution actually used to manage conflict in project-oriented work environments.

Each aphorism represents folk wisdom about useful methods of handling conflict. They have been used in other research[7] of a similar nature to avoid the potential bias that might be otherwise introduced by the use of social science jargon. In this study the project managers were asked to indicate on a four-point scale their agreement with each of the 15 proverbs as each would apply to resolving conflicts between them and their project personnel, their superiors, and their supporting functional departments. The scores on these proverbs were used as a measure of relative strength for each of the corresponding modes of conflict resolution. Thus, these scores measure the degree or strength at which a project manager adopts a particular mode of conflict resolution in specific personal interface situations. The profile of the five modes is shown in Figure 3.

---

[7] R. J. Burke, "Methods of Managing Superior-Subordinate Conflict," *Canadian Journal of Behavioral Science*, vol. 2, no. 2, 1970, pp. 124–35.

Results of Data

Figure 1 indicates the importance that project managers attach to each of the nine influence bases in gaining project support from their subordinates and assigned personnel. Three of these bases seem to be particularly important for developing support in a project-organized work environment: expertise, formal authority, and work challenge. The three least important influence bases were fund allocation, salary adjustments, and penalty.

Figure 1 also indicates that, in the aggregate, project managers perceive the importance of influence bases in gaining support from their subordinates in approximately the same order as those from assigned project personnel. One noticeable difference between them is work challenge, which seems to be most important in gaining support from subordinates. Taken together, project managers feel that they can enhance the support received from subordinates and assigned project personnel if they emphasize work challenge, expertise, and formal authority. Conversely, they feel least effective in gaining project support when they use fund allocations, salary adjustments, and penalties as primary influence methods.[8] These findings are further supported by the correlation analysis presented later.

While some of the influence bases are ranked lower than expertise, authority, and work challenge (see Figure 1), they also can be important to the project manager in eliciting support for his project. A project manager may use several influence bases to gain support for his project. The specific influence bases used often depend upon the authority he possesses and his knowledge of what motivates various project participants. A project manager, for example, may possess limited authority over his functional interfaces and consequently must rely on other forms of influence, such as friendship ties. Our interviews indicate that many effective project managers "learn" what motivates or induces support from interfaces and adjust their leadership style accordingly. One person, for example, may be primarily motivated by work challenge, while another may be induced by the potentials of future work assignments derived from his satisfactory performance in supporting the project.

---

8 While expertise, authority and work challenge were perceived by 70 percent of all project managers as most important in gaining project support, one cannot relate this finding directly to the most effective leadership style with regard to conflict minimization or project performance. As discussed subsequently, expertise and authority, if used as primary methods of influence, may increase the conflict perceived by project managers. However, as found by Gemmill and Thamhain in previous research, the higher conflict potential created by the project manager's expertise and subsequent greater project involvement may be beneficial to overall project performance and lead to a higher performance rating of the "expert" manager and his team. For details see "Influence Styles of Project Managers: Some Performance Correlates," *Academy of Management Journal*, June 1974, pp. 216–24.

Finally, it is important to note that while a project manager may be limited in his degree of formal authority, he nevertheless often has high degrees of reward power. Rewards a project manager can dispense include offering an interesting work challenge, future work assignments, and promotion. Even though the project manager may not be able to offer some of these rewards directly, he can indirectly influence their outcomes. This capability is usually derived from his position in the organization and its attendant status, and his ability to give performance feedback on his assigned project personnel to the "home manager" of the functional department which directly controls the financial rewards and often substantially influences other rewards, such as promotion and future work assignments.

The intensity of conflict experienced by project managers in various situations has been measured by a four-point scale. Figure 2 indicates the average intensity of conflict perceived by project managers in the sample for various interface situations. As illustrated, conflict over schedules seems to be the major problem, followed by conflict over project priorities and manpower resources. Although these first three areas add up to a cumulative conflict intensity of 4.5, or 50 percent of all conflict measured among the seven categories, considerable conflict seems to exist in other areas, too (see Figure 2). Throughout all seven conflict categories, the perceived intensity of conflict follows a similar rank order. Conflict is most intense in dealings with functional departments, followed by conflict with assigned personnel, conflict between team members, and conflict with superiors, and is weakest in dealings with subordinates.

There are several observations which can be made regarding the intensity and causes of project-oriented conflict. First, a high source of conflict exists with functional departments supporting the project. Much of this conflict can be explained in terms of the authority/priority mix which occurs in project-oriented work environments. Project managers often do not have the authority to direct or to determine the priorities of functional support areas. Thus, conflict often develops over the timing of project activities which, in turn, affect all causes of conflict. Conflict with functional departments also may originate over technical opinions due to the focused expertise of a functional support group and the manner in which a project manager views a particular technical issue. Project managers often stress that they must maintain an overview of the entire project to understand the ramifications of specific technical solutions on the total project as well as how a particular technical approach affects other elements of the project. Since others may not have this overview, conflict may develop over what decisions are "best" for the project.[9]

Conflict with assigned project personnel ranked second to the functional support departments in almost all cases. A comparison of the intensity of conflict between functional support departments and assigned project personnel indicates most project managers have a greater degree of authority and control over assigned personnel. Assigned personnel often bring to a project the parochial viewpoint of their own functional departments. As one project manager stated:

My assigned personnel come from the functional departments and often represent the views of their functional managers. They know when the project is finished that they will probably go back to their originating departments.

At the opposite end of the spectrum it was found that conflict with subordinates ranked lowest in most cases, primarily because project managers tend to have more control over their immediate team members, and team members are often more likely to

project manager than perhaps functional share common project objectives with the departments.

It also is interesting to note the intensity of conflict with superiors over schedules and administrative procedures. Our discussions with project managers revealed that missing schedule targets and milestones can adversely affect their superiors in three principal ways. First, the superior may not recognize the complexities involved in meeting the established project schedule; consequently, disagreements develop. Second, superiors are held directly or indirectly accountable for the overall accomplishment of the project. Third, project scheduling problems can impact on many other areas, such as priorities, manpower resources, administrative procedures, and cost. If any of these areas are affected, it may require the intervention of the project manager's superior and thus result in conflict situations.

Figure 4 summarizes the complex relationships among the various sources of conflict and their causes. The figure only includes the main conflict sources for each category to indicate the importance of a particular source relative to other conflict determinants. More specifically, the sources which are marked in Figure 4 contribute approximately 75 percent of all conflict in each of their categories (rows).

As illustrated in Figure 4, just two sources, functional departments and assigned personnel, contribute to 75 percent of all conflicts over schedules and manpower resources. On the other hand, it takes all five sources to reach the 75 percent level in the personality conflict category. This is indicative of the almost uniform conflict intensity experienced from all five sources over personality conflicts.

The relationship of perceived conflict intensity to the managerial style has been examined within the framework of a correlation analysis. Figure 5 summarizes the association between the intensity of conflict as perceived by project managers and their ac-

---

[9] D. L. Wilemon and J. P. Cicero, "The Project Manager—Anomalies and Ambiguities," *Academy of Management Journal*, Fall 1970, pp. 269–82.

FIGURE 4
Conflict Cause and Sources*

Conflict Cause	Functional Depts.	Assigned Personnel	Between Team Members	Superiors	Subordinates
Schedules	☐	☐			
Project Priorities	☐	☐	☐		
Manpower	☐	☐			
Technical Issues	☐	☐	☐		
Administration	☐	☐		☐	☐
Personality Conflict	☐	☐	☐	☐	☐
Cost Objectives	☐	☐		☐	

Source — Conflict Occurred Mostly With . . .

High —— Relative Conflict Intensity —— Low

High —— Relative Conflict Intensity —— Low (vertical axis)

* The Table includes only the main Conflict Sources for each category (cause). Specifically, the sources which are marked contribute approximately 75 percent of all conflict in their category.

FIGURE 5
Association Between Perceived Intensity of Conflict and Mode of Conflict Resolution* (the figure shows only those associations which are statistically significant at the 95 percent level)

Intensity of Conflict Perceived by Project Manager (PM)	Forcing	Confrontation	Compromise	Smoothing	Withdrawal
Between PM and Personnel	■	✓	✓	✓	■
Between PM and Superior		■	✓		
Between PM and Functional Support Departments	■	■	✓		✓

Actual Conflict Resolution Style

✓ Strongly favorable association with regard to low conflict (- τ).

▨■ Strongly unfavorable association with regard to low conflict (+ τ).

* Kendall Correlation

tual style of conflict resolution as determined from their scores on the aphorisms. Forcing and withdrawal are significantly and positively correlated to increased conflict between project managers and their assigned personnel. This suggests that the more a project manager uses forcing or withdrawal as a mode of conflict resolution, the more conflict he experiences. Conversely, confrontation, compromise, and smoothing are negatively correlated to the same conflict measure. This indicates that managers who rely strongly on compromise, smoothing, and perhaps confrontation in dealing with their personnel experience less conflict than those who neglect these modes.

Figure 5 also indicates the best style for minimizing conflict between project managers and their superiors relies primarily on compromise and avoids confrontation. This suggests that conflict between project managers and their superiors may be reduced if a work environment is established which promotes a free exchange of ideas. It also appears that the project manager should be willing to compromise on certain, perhaps even crucial, issues with his superior at strategic times.

With regard to conflict between project managers and the functional departments that support them, three modes are statistically significant. Most noticeable is the detrimental effect of forcing in dealings with support departments. Also, conflict seems to increase the more the project manager relies on confrontation, while withdrawal tends to minimize conflicts.

The statistically significant findings of the effects of the various conflict resolution styles on conflict intensity are summarized below.

A complimentary measure to the modes of conflict resolution is the management style which project managers employ in dealing with interfaces. Figure 6 summarizes the association between the various influence methods employed by project managers and the intensity of conflict experienced with key interfaces. For example, Figure 6 illustrates the favorable association between conflict intensity and work challenge. Project managers experience less conflict with their assigned personnel and supervisors the more they tend to rely on work challenge as a basis of influence in gaining support for their projects. Further, the ability to use promotion as an influence base appears to have a favorable effect in minimizing conflict between project managers and their assigned project personnel.

Among the influence methods that appear to adversely affect conflict are penalty and authority, which increase the intensity of conflict in dealings with assigned personnel, superiors and supporting functional departments. The use of punishments increases conflict in the project environment for several reasons. First, the use of punishments can cause antagonism toward the project manager. Second, the use of punishments

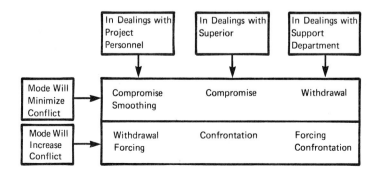

FIGURE 6
Association Between Influence Methods of Project Manager and Their Perceived Conflict Intensity*
(the figure shows only those associations which are statistically significant at the 95 percent level)

Intensity of Conflict Perceived by Project Managers (PM)	Influence Methods as Perceived by Project Managers						
	Expertise	Authority	Work Challenge	Friendship	Promotion	Salary	Penalty
Between PM and Personnel	▪	▪	✓		✓		▪
Between PM and Superior			✓				▪
Between PM and Functional Support Departments		▪					▪

✓ Strongly favorable association with regard to low conflict (- τ).

▪ Strongly unfavorable association with regard to low conflict (+ τ).

* Kendall Correlation

may induce supporting functional groups and assigned personnel to withdraw from fully supporting the project manager. As a consequence, their contribution to the project may be suboptimal. Third, the overuse of punishments against functional support departments and assigned project personnel can escalate and eventually involve the project manager's superior as well as the superiors of those supporting him.

The findings from the correlation analysis are only partially reflected by the descriptive measures on important influence methods perceived by project managers. As deduced from Figure 1, authority was perceived among the most important influence bases by most managers, while penalty methods were seen as the least important. While these two measures are consistent with the association to minimal conflict, authority, which is perceived by 70 percent of all project managers as very important in gaining project support, was found to have negative effects on conflict management.

Even more noticeable is the significantly positive correlation between expertise and conflict intensity in dealings with assigned project personnel, in contrast to the project manager's perception that expertise is one of the most important influence bases in gaining support. This finding can be explained in part by how a project manager uses his expertise. First, it may be demotivating to supporting project personnel if the project manager gets overly involved in the technical details of the project. Many project personnel feel they should have the freedom to make their contribution to the project as long as it does not detrimentally affect the established budget, schedule, and performance objectives of the project. This tends to be a means-to-an-end issue on many projects. Second, since a project manager may be an "expert" in some areas, he can question and more clearly evaluate the contribution of the supporting personnel. This questioning process can create conflict which is not necessarily detrimental. Because of conflict, for example, that develops from the questioning and evaluation process between the project manager and those who support him, new information may be interjected into the decision-making process which can be beneficial to the overall project.

The use of authority also may increase the incidence of conflict with those personnel who support the project. Many project support personnel say they work most effectively when there is a mutual agreement on project objectives and they are subsequently held accountable for the results.[10] This preference is somewhat in contrast to being directed by the project manager. Our observations conclude that the higher the professional status of the supporting project personnel, the more likely it seems that they will strive to achieve the mutually agreed-upon goals for the project without the need for continual direction by the project manager.

These results indicate that expertise and authority assist the project manager in gaining support from project personnel if the personnel respect the manager's expertise and believe he has authority which has been properly delegated.[11] On the other hand, it appears that if project managers overly emphasize their own expertise and stress their authority as a primary influence method, conflict tends to increase.

The study thus proposes that the project manager's effectiveness in managing conflict depends on his ability to create a work environment in which he is perceived by his personnel as emphasizing work challenge

---

[10] D. L. Wilemon, "Project Management Conflict: A View From Apollo," *Third Annual Symposium of the Project Management Institute*, Houston, Tex., October 1971.

[11] This finding is further supported by the research of G. R. Gemmill and H. J. Thamhain, "The Effectiveness of Different Power Styles of Project Managers in Gaining Project Support," *IEEE Transactions on Engineering Management*, vol. 20, no. 2, May 1973, pp. 38–44. The authors concluded that work challenge and expertise as perceived by project personnel are the most important influence bases for establishing a climate of high support, while authority and penalty methods seem to hinder the development of such a climate.

and direct or indirect promotional opportunities as a method of influence. He might further benefit if he uses his expertise judiciously.

Moreover, the data suggests that the more effective the project manager is in providing interesting work to those who support him, the lower the conflict he will experience with his superior. As noted previously, work challenge appears to increase project participation and commitment of interfaces and likely contributes to the project manager's effectiveness. By contrast, the greater the use of penalties in dealing with interfaces, the more conflict the project manager appears to experience and consequently will face in his interactions with his superior.

Management Implications

Project managers often operate in an environment conducive to the generation of intense conflict situations. The nature of project management, the need to elicit support from various organizational units and personnel, the frequently ambiguous authority definition of the project manager, and the temporary nature of projects all contribute to the conflicts which project managers experience in the performance of their roles.

A number of conclusions can be derived from this study which potentially can increase the project manager's effectiveness in the management of conflict and in eliciting support for his project.

Project managers need to use their expertise judiciously. If overused, it can be detrimental and demotivating to project participants since it may discount their contribution; expertise which is wisely used can be important in developing respect and support for project managers.

Conflict with support functional departments is a major concern for many project managers. For the various categories—conflicts over schedules, project priorities, man-

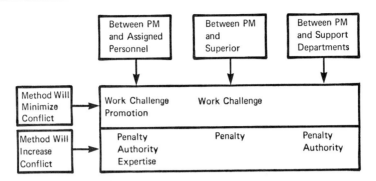

power resources, technical opinions, administrative procedures, personalities, and cost —the study reveiled the highest conflict intensity occurred with the functional support departments. The project manager usually has less control over supporting functional departments than over his assigned personnel or immediate team members, which may contribute to conflict. Moreover, conflict often develops due to the functional department's own priorities, which can impact on any of the conflict categories.

To minimize conflict in these seven areas requires careful planning by the project manager. Effective planning early in the life cycle of a project can assist in forecasting and thus, perhaps, minimizing a number of potential problem areas likely to produce conflict in subsequent phases. Consequently, contingency plans should be developed as early as possible in the life cycle of a project. Top management involvement and commitment in the project also may help reduce some of the conflicts. Good planning is often given insufficient attention by project managers.

Since there are a number of involved parties in a project, it is important that key decisions which affect the project be communicated to all project-related personnel.[12] By openly communicating the objectives and

necessary subtasks involved in a project, there is a higher potential for minimizing detrimental, unproductive conflict. Regularly scheduled status-review meetings can be an important vehicle for communicating important project-related issues.

Project managers need to be aware of their conflict resolution style and its potential effect on key interfaces. As the study suggests, forcing and withdrawal modes appear to increase conflict with functional support departments and assigned personnel, while confrontation, compromise, and smoothing tend to reduce conflict. Again, it is important for project managers to know whether conflict should be minimized or induced. In some instances managers may deliberately induce conflict in their decision-making process to gain new information and provoke constructive dialogue.

A definite relationship appears to exist between the specific influence mode project managers employ and the intensity of conflict experienced with interfaces. Our findings suggest, for example, that the greater the work challenge provided by a manager, the less conflict he experiences with assigned project personnel. One approach is to stimulate interest in the project by matching the needs of supporting personnel with the specific work requirements of the project.

Conflict with functional departments also may be induced by the project manager who overly relies on penalties and authority. Often the overuse of authority and penalties

---

12 D. L. Wilemon, "Managing Conflict on Project Teams," *Management Journal*, Summer 1974, pp. 28–34.

has a negative effect in establishing a climate of mutual support, cooperation, and respect.

In summary, project managers must be aware not only of the management styles they use in eliciting support, but also of the effect of the conflict resolution approaches they employ. For the project manager each set of skills is critical for effective project performance. If a project manager is initially skillful in eliciting support but cannot manage the inevitable conflict situations which develop in the course of his projects, his effectiveness as a manager will erode.

The innovator is like Prometheus and what happened to him is hardly encouraging (5, p. 14).

This article explores a critical dimension of the innovative process: relations with organizational elites. Elite support is necessary for success during the various stages of planning and implementing the innovation program. The elites are those actors within the organization or organizational network who are qualified by "the rules of the game" and their positions of power, to oversee the activities of the organization. As Armstrong notes, elites usually occupy roles involving social control (3, p. 14).

Perspectives on Organizations and Organizational Networks

People will readily admit that governments are organizations. The converse—that organizations are governments—is equally true, but rarely considered (56, p. 16).

The theoretical perspective of organizations taken in this article is a political one (21, 57, 73). Organizations and networks of organizations are viewed as arenas where coalitions representing opposing organizational interests meet in conflict. As Touraine (73) suggests, this model is perhaps more appropriate to public sector organizations, the "private governments" (44), than private sector profit organizations. The process of organizational decision making reflects this conflict of interests and maneuvering for position and power. The basis upon which decisions are likely to be made is not rationality, but rather the reflection of the interests of the dominant coalition.

The goal of the organization or organizational network is not monolithic. Goals are multiple and often contradictory, reflecting the dynamics of the conflict of coalitions and the interests of the organizational actors who make up those coalitions. This process is one of continuous conflict, with goals and programs constantly in the process of negotiation.

The goal of a coalition is a mediated goal. Individual actors coalesce around an issue, each with a different goal or interest. These individual goals are then mediated into a common goal which all within the coalition can agree to support in the decision-making arena. Coalitions are therefore unstable; each actor is getting only part of what he or she wants. If the political risks and costs are greater than the anticipated benefit, the actor will pull out and cut his or her losses. The innovator must constantly guard against withdrawals from a coalition backing the innovation program; withdrawals can lead to stampedes and the collapse of the project.

Seducing the Elites: The Politics of Decision Making and Innovation in Organizational Networks*

GEORGE KELLEY

* *Academy of Management Review*, July 1976, pp. 66–74.

Organizational continuity is provided in two major ways. First, policies or "rules of the game" are developed within the organization or network over time. Because upon losing a round in the organizational arena, the defeated coalition seldom withdraws from the organization or network, conflict is kept manageable by the knowledge that those actors are still within the organization. The losing coalition can bide its time, grow in strength, and fight again. Since coalitions are usually a mediation of individual interests, individual actors in the losing coalition may prove useful to the dominant coalition in an alliance over some other issue.

So "all-out conflict" is checked by the knowledge that "winning" and "losing" are temporary states, that new coalitions will form around new sets of issues, that "friends" and "enemies" change sides and labels as frequently as issues arise, that politics makes for strange bedfellows.

Just as the "rules of the game" keep control over organizational conflict, so the organizational elites could be termed the *referees* to enforce the rules if conflict gets out of hand and to provide organizational continuity, chiefly because they hold the key positions of organizational power. The elites hold similar values and usually work together as a cohesive power bloc.

The elites seldom enter the organizational arena: they are, instead, the spectators. They watch clashes between coalitions of technocrats over policy and programs, usually supporting the winner. The nature of their power is described by Han Fei, an ancient Chinese philosopher (20, p. 336). In his conception of power, Han Fei says that rulers rule not by imposing norms, but by being prerequisite to their imposition. Their power is that of dependency. Elites may not be able to control the decision-making apparatus completely, but they are never excluded from any major decision.

The technocrats of coalitions must be aware of the power of dependency which elites hold over the decision-making arena. The elites do not enter the arena and become bloodied; they instead act as prerequisites to action, controlling support that may be withdrawn at any time. The essential nature of the elite is to be fickle. So the innovator must woo and seduce these fickle elites at critical junctures in the innovative process, to insure the success of the project.

Another aspect of elite power is that of social control (3, 30, 31). Organizational insulation, sanctions, and persuasion techniques are part of the repertoire of control mechanisms; the innovator must be aware of and able to deal with them if they are invoked against him or her. Rival coalitions may attempt to use organizational "cooling-out mechanisms" ('30, 33), devices for allowing those who fail in a power struggle to withdraw with good grace.

Child (13) explores a series of strategies for organizational social control. The innovator must be aware that elites can be co-opted by rival coalitions and social control mechanisms may be turned against both the innovator and the innovative project.

Less developed in Gamson's treatment of social control is isolation. The literature on the elite's control over the decision making arena, that is, control over the agenda of decisions and nondecisions, issues and nonissues is large (4, 5, 29, 52, 79). In keeping with Han Fei's conception of power as dependency, the elite can arrange that controversies never get a hearing, that innovative projects with problems are "cooled-out" by denial of access to the decision making arena.

Within this framework, the innovator must gain leverage over the elites by strategies to elicit their support and to protect the favored position enjoyed by the innovator and the innovative program.

Before developing the strategies, it is helpful to discuss how innovation is viewed in terms of a theoretical framework.

Perspectives on Innovation

Innovations, in order to find support among the organizational elites, must be perceived as essentially conservative. That is, the innovation must be presented in such a way, cloaked in appropriate symbolism, that is appears to fit into the predictability of the elite mind-sets. The need to defend this continuity of mind-set does not argue against change; rather, it argues for change and innovation within the parameters of expectations which the elites have learned to trust.

This mind-set, or system of values, must be understood in order for the innovator to present the program in such a manner as to appear to be working within the elite value system (35). The innovation must not appear to be a challenge to the existing value system, but rather an extension of it. Once the innovator's disruptive implications, real or imaginary, become perceived as a threat to the existing mind-set, the innovation will be resisted and/or eliminated.

Bailey (8) asserts that the study of innovation must be political; innovators must study the competition, to define a situation and have others accept it. When people compete to have an innovation accepted or rejected, they are restricted by the concepts and vocabulary available in their culture. Bailey stresses the importance to the innovator of learning the "repertoires of argument" considered acceptable in various organizational contexts.

One skill that the innovator must develop is the ability to anticipate arguments and to be ready with counterarguments framed in the appropriate jargon, evoking the appropriate symbolism, touching the appropriate bases of the elite target group. Innovators should seek to understand not so much the reasoning of decisions, but the value hierarchy which guides elite decisions with particular emphasis on conflicting value relationships.

In summary, Bailey suggests that in the competition of values, a knowledge of the repertoires of argument and invocation of the relevant and meaningful symbolism (26) is essential to seduce the elite's value hierarchy which affects decision making.

The status of the innovator is also important. The conservative model presented here implies that changes in the elite's environment force a response, either to rectify the environment and restore the status quo, or to modify the organization or organizational network to adapt to the new environment. The adaption process is likely to be an innovative one, but innovation within the mind-set and values of the elite, or at least within their perception of what is "safe" and "familiar," i.e. nonthreatening.

Therefore, the innovator must be nonthreatening. The innovator is the pathfinder. The elites will follow because they trust him or her not to be doing something frivolous or stupid.

The innovation must succeed. Everyone wins: the innovator enjoys increased status and prestige, the elites reap material and symbolic rewards and are likely to be more confident and willing to undertake future innovative ventures.

Failure causes everyone to lose. The innovator loses face, status, prestige. His or her reputation is damaged (7) which limits effectiveness for future innovation ventures. The elites become wary, suspicious, less likely to embark on any new innovation projects.

With all of this at stake, the innovator cannot afford to fail. Strategies of action are needed.

Strategies for Elite Cooperation in Innovation Ventures

. . . Innovation, unlike invention, is necessarily a social process. At least to some degree an innovation has to be a matter of public concern. It therefore becomes subject to debate. In other words an innovation, to a degree varying according to the extent and nature of its ramifying connections, is likely to become the subject of political activities. From this follows that the methods for studying innovation depend upon more general methods for analysing social and political processes (8, p. 323).

The political activities referred to must be anticipated by the innovator, and plans to operate in the political arena must be developed.

The first strategy is to expect the innovative process to involve a high degree of conflict. Change is threatening. Fears of the organizational population must be dealt with by an education strategy that translates the innovation proposal into the appropriate mind-sets, cloaked in the relevant symbolism. But this must not be a one-way process. The elites and rival coalitions must be presented with opportunities to react, to express fears and reservations, to input into the project. In this way, they become ego-involved in the innovation program. The opportunity to express opinions is also a possible "cooling-out mechanism" to deflect criticism. The education program demystifies the innovation, making it translatable and acceptable to the value systems of the organizational populus (57).

Second, opposition to the innovative project must not be stifled or silenced, but defused through the education program; all arguments must be met with facts (9). This strategy also brings the opposing forces out into the open where they can be identified and dealt with openly, avoiding the more risky, and unpleasant, aspects of Byzantine politics.

Finally, the innovation must have a component to deal with conflicts that arise internally, with the supporting coalition, with rival coalitions, and with elites. This component must have people with the time and the patience to engage in legitimate discussion, to answer objections, to allay fears with facts, and to keep the innovation within the "safe" and "familiar" parameters of the organizational value systems.

Marris (49) discusses this process: after the mandate for the innovation has been negotiated with the elites, innovators are impatient to implement it. They think they will save time and energy which might be involved in further conflict by coopting and/or outmaneuvering attempts at organized opposition, by fragmenting criticism and overwhelming it with expert knowledge. The innovator's denial and stifling of legitimate conflict sows the seeds of fear, threat, and distrust that will destroy the innovation at some later stage of the innovative process.

The innovator must deal with legitimate discussion and criticism of the innovation throughout the innovative process. Marris notes that people have to find their own meaning in change before they can live with it. Therefore, innovators must listen as well as explain; the process of modifying and renegotiating the innovation to keep it "safe" and "acceptable" to the organizational populus does not stop at the granting of the mandate, but continues through the innovative process until the innovation is implemented. In the Laumann and Pappi (45) model of community decision-making systems, opportunities for this expression of legitimate discussion are built into various stages.

Absent from the Laumann and Pappi model, but recognized as an important element by Boissevain (10), is the role of the broker. The broker deals in information, in this case, organizational and organizational network information. This is more than a mere boundary spanner role; it is the application of the educational strategy discussed above in a more informal yet more comprehensive way. Just as invisible colleges (18) exist for technocrats and scientific elites, so organizational elites need to obtain highly reliable information on a number of sensitive issues quickly, without formalities and time-wasting red tape. The role of the broker is to supply this type of information quickly and accurately.

The innovator needs to understand the elite decision-making process (some variation of the Laumann and Pappi model perhaps), the politics of the decision-making arena, and how to input into the information system of the broker in order to get positive, reliable information about the innovation project to the elites by yet another channel. The organizational broker can also supply information about elite reactions and attitudes concerning the innovative project that might be unobtainable through other communications channels.

These strategies to seduce and maintain elite support for the innovative project depend on the openness of the innovator's team, as well as educational and communications techniques to help the organizational population accommodate the innovation into their mind-sets.

Conclusion and Caveats

I find the people strangely fantasied;
Possess'd with rumours, full of idle dreams,
Not knowing what they fear, but full of fear . . .
—King John

The conception presented in this article is based upon two major models. First, organizational decision making is the result of conflict between competing coalitions with an organizational elite, holders of positions of power and social control, acting as referees in the decision-making arena. Second, the process of innovation is based on a conservative model, arguing that changes in the organizational or network environment force the elite either to rectify the unbalance and return the situation back to the status quo, or to change the organization or network in order to adapt to the new environment. This adaptive process is usually a process of innovation.

Innovation must be perceived as nonthreatening to the existing mind-sets or

value systems of the organizational population, with emphasis on the organizational elite, to gain and maintain their support for the innovation project. Strategies to gain and maintain elite support are based upon educational and communications techniques which constantly reassure the elite that the innovation is of a nonthreatening nature.

Some warnings and reservations must be lodged against the theoretical framework presented here. Its validity has not been proven by empirical research. As Touraine (73) notes, the arena analogy holds chiefly for public sector organizations. Research studies are also contradictory in terms of how much real power is exercised by elites in the decision-making process.

Burns (11) and Tichy (72) discuss organizational elites in terms of cliques and cabals. Merelman (52) and Wolfinger (79) criticize the "non-decisions" and "non-issues" power of elites. For that conception to be true, they argue, the elites would have to be omnipotent, controlling not only the decision-making process, but the agenda of which issues will be addressed and which decisions decided. Merelman and Wolfinger opt for a pluralist model of decision making as a result of this factor.

Perhaps one of the better attempts to assess elite influences in decision making is the discussion by Chandler, Chandler, and Vogler (12). Their policy analysis develops a typology based on the Lowi and Redford conceptions of elite decision-making dynamics. Chandler, Chandler, and Vogler argue that elites are unconcerned about events at the micro level. At the subsystem level, a larger number of interests are being sought and a larger number of elite concerns are in evidence. At the macro level, the stakes are highest, the rewards greatest, and the preoccupation of the elites most concentrated.

Distributive policies have limited impact, whereas redistributive policies have the greatest impact, and are therefore of the most concern to the elites. The argument here is to concentrate analysis on the macro-redistributive issues and decisions over time, observing who wins and who loses. A coalition that consistently wins seems to deserve the label "elite."

From a research point of view, disagreement over operationalization of "elite," "power," "decision," "non-decision," and other critical variables makes evaluation of the literature difficult. A resurgence in elite studies surveyed by Zartman (80) and Seligman (69) and the increasingly sophisticated research designs and methodologies add fuel to the controversies.

For the innovator, nevertheless, there are case studies that address the question of seducing elite support and stress the importance of their backing for innovation ventures (8, 9, 10). In the midst of conflicting conceptions, strategies to seduce the support of the elite for innovation and further strategies to maintain elite support until the innovation is implemented are available.

REFERENCES

1. Allen, Michael Patrick. "The Structure of Interorganizational Elite Cooptation," *American Sociological Review*, vol. 39 (1974), 393–406.

2. Anthony, L. J. *Accelerating Innovation* (London: Urwin, 1970).

3. Armstrong, John A. *The European Administrative Elite* (Princeton, N.J.: Princeton University Press, 1973).

4. Bachrach, Peter, and Morton S. Baratz. "Two Faces of Power," *American Political Science Review*, vol. 56 (1962), 947–52.

5. Bachrach, Peter, and Morton S. Baratz. "Decisions and Nondecisions: An Analytical Framework," *American Political Science Review*, vol. 57 (1963), 632–42.

6. Bailey, F. G. *Stratagems and Spoils: A Social Anthropology of Politics* (Oxford: Basil Blackwell, 1969).

7. Bailey, F. G. *Gifts and Poison: The Politics of Reputation* (Oxford: Basil Blackwell, 1971).

8. Bailey, F. G. (ed.). *Debate and Compromise: The Politics of Innovation* (Oxford: Basil Blackwell, 1973).

9. Benveniste, Guy. *The Politics of Expertise* (Berkeley: Glendessary, 1972).

10. Boissevain, Jeremy. *Friends of Friends: Networks, Manipulators, and Coalitions* (Oxford: Basil Blackwell, 1974).

11. Burns, Tom. "The Reference of Conduct in Small Groups: Cliques and Cabals in Occupational Milieux," *Human Relations*, vol. 8 (1955), 467–86.

12. Chandler, Marsha, William Chandler, and David Vogler. "Policy Analysis and the Search for Theory," *American Politics Quarterly*, vol. 2 (1974), 107–18.

13. Child, John. "Strategies of Control and Organizational Behavior," *Administrative Science Quarterly*, vol. 18 (1973), 1–17.

14. Cobb, Roger W. "The Belief-Systems Perspective: An Assessment of a Framework," *Journal of Politics*, vol. 35 (1973), 121–53.

15. Coleman, James C. "Loss of Power," *American Sociological Review*, vol. 38 (1973), 1–17.

16. Corr, Edwin G. *The Political Process in Columbia* (Denver, Colo.: University of Denver, 1972).

17. Corwin, Ronald G. "Strategies for Organizational Innovation: An Empirical Comparison," *American Sociological Review*, vol. 37 (1972), 441–54.

18. Crane, Dina. *Invisible Colleges: Diffusion of Knowledge in Scientific Communities* (Chicago: University of Chicago, 1972).

19. Crenson, Matthew. "Organizational Factors in Citizen Participation," *Journal of Politics*, vol. 36 (1974), 356–78.

20. Crew, Ivor (ed.). *Elites in Western Democracy* (New York: Wiley, 1974).

21. Cyert, Richard, and James March. *Behavioral Theory of the Firm* (Englewood Cliffs, N.J.: Prentice-Hall, 1963).

22. Delbecq, André, and Alan Filley. *Program and Project Management in a Matrix Organization: A Case Study* (Madison: University of Wisconsin, 1974).

23. Delbecq, André, Andrew H. Van de Ven, and David H. Gustafson. *Group Techniques for Program Planning* (Glenview, Ill.: Scott, Foresman, 1975).

24. Dolbeare, Kenneth M., and Murray J. Edelman. *American Politics* (Lexington, Mass.: Heath, 1971).

25. Dye, Thomas R., and John W. Pickering. "Governmental and Corporate Elites: Convergence and Differentiation," *Journal of Politics*, vol. 36 (1974), 900–925.

26. Edelman, Murray. *The Symbolic Uses of Politics* (Urbana: University of Illinois, 1964).

27. Edelman, Murray. *Politics as Symbolic Action* (Chicago: Markham, 1971).

28. Field, G. Lowell, and John Higley. *Elites in Developed Societies* (Beverly Hills: Sage, 1972).

29. Frey, Frederik W. "Comment: On Issues and Nonissues in the Study of Power," *American Political Science Review*, vol. 65 (1971), 1081–1101.

30. Gamson, William A. *Power and Discontent* (Homewood, Ill.: Dorsey, 1968).

31. Gamson, William A. *The Strategy of Social Protest* (Homewood, Ill.: Dorsey, 1975).

32. Gitelman, Zvi Y. *The Diffusion of Political Innovation* (Beverly Hills: Sage, 1972).

33. Goffman, Erving. *Frame Analysis* (Cambridge: Harvard, 1974).

34. Gray, Virginia. "Innovation in the States: A Diffusion Study," *American Political Science Review*, vol. 67 (1973), 1174–85.

35. Hage, Jerald, and Robert Dewar. "Elite Values Versus Organizational Structure in Predicting Innovation," *Administrative Science Quarterly*, vol. 18 (1973), 279–90.

36. Halperin, Morton H. *Bureaucratic Politics and Foreign Policy* (Washington, D.C.: The Brookings Institute, 1974).

37. Halperin, Morton H., and Arnold Kantor. *Readings in American Foreign Policy: A Bureaucratic Perspective* (Boston: Little, Brown, 1973).

38. Havelock, Ronald G. *Planning for Innovation Through Dissemination and Utilization of Knowledge* (Ann Arbor, Mich.: Center for Research on Utilization of Scientific Knowledge, 1971).

39. Heydebrand, Wolf. *Hospital Bureaucracy* (New York: Dunellen, 1973).

40. Hilsman, Roger. *The Politics of Policy Making in Defense and Foreign Affairs* (New York: Harper & Row, 1971).

41. Hudson, Liam (ed.). *The Ecology of Human Intelligence* (Middlesex, England: Penguin, 1970).

42. Jacobs, David. "Dependency and Vulnerability: An Exchange Approach to the Control of Organizations," *Administrative Science Quarterly*, vol. 19 (1974), 45–59.

43. Kuhn, Thomas S. "The Essential Tension: Tradition and Innovation in Scientific Research," in Liam Hudson (ed.). *The Ecology of Human Intelligence* (Middlesex, England: Penguin, 1970).

44. Lakoff, Sanford (ed.). *Private Government* (Glenview, Ill.: Scott, Foresman, 1973).

45. Laumann, Edward, and Franz Urban Pappi. "New Directions in the Study of Community Elites," *American Sociological Review*, vol. 38 (1973), 212–30.

46. Laumann, Edward, Lois M. Verbrugge, and Franz U. Pappi. "A Causal Modelling Approach to the Study of a Community Elite Influence Structure," *American Sociological Review*, vol. 39 (1974), 162–74.

47. Levine, Donald N. *Wax and Gold: Tradition and Innovation in Ethiopian Culture* (Chicago: University of Chicago, 1965).

48. Levine, Joel H. "The Sphere of Influence," *American Sociological Review*, vol. 37 (1972), 14–27.

49. Marris, Peter. *Loss and Change* (London: Routledge & Kegan Paul, 1974).

50. Mason, Robert, and Albert N. Halter. "The Application of a System of Simultaneous Equations to an Innovation Diffusion Model," in H. M. Blalock (ed.) *Causal Models in the Social Sciences* (Chicago: Aldine, 1971).

51. Mayhew, Bruce H. "System Size and Ruling Elites," *American Sociological Review*, vol. 38 (1973), 468–75.

52. Merelman, Richard M. "On the Neo-Elitist Critique of Community Power," *American Political Science Review*, vol. 62 (1968), 451–560.

53. Mulkay, M. J. *The Social Process of Innovation* (London: Macmillan, 1972).

54. Nadel, Mark V. "The Hidden Dimension of Public Policy: Private Governments and the Policy-Making Process," *Journal of Politics*, vol. 37 (1975), 2–34.

55. Parry, Geraint. *Political Elites* (London: George Allen & Unwin, 1969).

56. Perrucci, Robert, and Marc Pilisuk. "Leaders and Ruling Elites: The Interorganizational Bases of Community Power," *American Sociological Review*, vol. 35 (1970), 1040–57.

57. Pettigrew, Andrew M. *The Politics of Organizational Decision-Making* (London: Tavistock, 1973).

58. Pfeffer, Jeffrey, and Gerald R. Salancik. "Organizational Decision Making as a Political Process: The Case of the University Budget," *Administrative Science Quarterly*, vol. 19 (1974), 134–51.

59. Prattis, J. I. "Gambling, Fishing and Innovation—A Cross Situational Study of Decision Making," *International Journal of Comparative Sociology*, vol. 14 (1974), 76–88.

60. Press, Charles, and Alan Arian (eds). *Empathy and Ideology: Aspects of Administrative Innovation* (Chicago: Rand McNally, 1966).

61. Pressman, Jeffrey L., and Aaron Wildavsky. *Implementation* (Berkeley: University of California Press, 1973).

62. Presthus, Robert. *Technological Change and Occupational Responses* (Washington, D.C.: U.S. Department of Health, Education, and Welfare, 1970).

63. Presthus, Robert, *Elite Accommodation in Canadian Politics* (London: Cambridge University, 1973).

64. Presthus, Robert. *Elites in the Policy Process* (London: Cambridge University, 1974).

65. Putnam, Robert D. "Studying Elite Political Culture: The Case of Ideology," *American Political Science Review*, vol. 65 (1971), 651–81.

66. Ripley, Randall B., William B. Moreland, and Richard H. Sinnreich. "Policy-Making: A Conceptual Scheme," *American Politics Quarterly*, vol. 1 (1973), 3–42.

67. Salancik, Gerald R., and Jeffrey Pfeffer. "The Bases and Use of Power in Organizational Decision Making: The Case of a University," *Administrative Science Quarterly*, vol. 19 (1974), 453–73.

68. Selevin, Dennis P. "The Innovation Boundary: A Replication with Increased Costs," *Administrative Science Quarterly*, vol. 18 (1973), 71–75.

69. Seligman, Lester G. "Political Elites Reconsidered," *Comparative Politics*, vol. 6 (1974), 299–314.

70. Smith, Michael P. "Elite Theory and Policy Analysis," *Journal of Politics*, vol. 36 (1974), 1006–32.

71. Teulings, W. M., Louis O. Jansen, and William G. Verhoeven. "Growth, Power Structure, and Leadership Functions in the Hospital Organization," *British Journal of Sociology*, vol. 25 (1974), 490–505.

72. Tichy, Noel. "An Analysis of Clique Formation and Structure in Organizations," *Administrative Science Quarterly*, vol. 18 (1973), 194–208.

73. Touraine, Alain. *The Post-Industrial Society* (New York: Random, 1971).

74. Turk, Herman. "Interorganizational Networks in Urban Society," *American Sociological Review*, vol. 35 (1970), 1–19.

75. Urry, John, and John Wakeford (eds.). *Power in Britain* (London: Heinemann, 1973).

76. Von Broembsen, Maximilian H., and Louis N. Gray. "Size and Ruling Elites: Effects of System Growth on Power Structures," *American Sociological Review*, vol. 38 (1973), 476–78.

77. Wamsley, Gary L., and Mayer N. Zald. *The Political Economy of Public Organizations* Lexington, Mass.: Heath, 1973).

78. Wilensky, Harold. *Organizational Intelligence* (New York: Basic, 1967).

79. Wolfinger, Raymond E. "Nondecisions and the Study of Local Politics," *American Political Science Review*, vol. 65 (1971), 1063–80.

80. Zartman, William. "The Study of Elite Circulation," *Comparative Politics*, vol. 6 (1974), 465–88.

The success of innovative decisions depends on the amount of kinetic energy available within the organization to overcome barriers. These barriers can be divided into barriers of will and barriers of capability. Barriers are best overcome through the personal commitment of specific members of the organization who are acting as "promotors."[1] Barriers of will are overcome through "promotors by power"; barriers of capability, through "promotors by know-how." The most favorable situation for overcoming barriers to innovation is a structure in which the roles of promotor by power and of promotor by know-how are both fulfilled, and by two different persons' working "in tandem." This means a two-center theory of innovation in organizations.

The superiority of the tandem structure in obtaining successful innovations is demonstrated through a sample of 233 innovation processes concerning the introduction of computers into German enterprises. The tandem structure was found in just over one third of cases. In comparison with other power structures in the innovation process, the tandem structure was shown to favor more mobilization of organization members, as measured by their number of activities. It did not result in the fastest innovation processes, but it did lead to those with the highest degree of innovation.

The Need for Promotors

In drawing up the desired organizational structure for the promotion of an innovation, we should like to make it clear from the beginning that this kind of organiza-

[1] I use the German spelling of the word rather than the English term *promoter* since the latter denotes in a restrictive way a person promoting another person or thing on a professional basis. See Schumpeter (1912), who uses the word in this sense. The more extensive definition of the term *promotor* was introduced by us in 1966 in our research project on the organization of complex decision-making processes.

READING 5–7

Power and Innovation: A Two-Center Theory*

EBERHARD WITTE

tional concept is not intended to replace the previously existing organization of an enterprise, i.e., it will not eliminate, for example, hierarchies and staff-line structures, exclude the project manager, or make the change agent superfluous. Such dogmatic purism would overlook the fact that every enterprise has to carry out many processes besides innovation. After its introduction, the innovation must be made part of a permanent order and utilized economically in constantly recurring work processes. Suitable structures must even rely on a certain amount of inertia and, consequently, a resistance to innovation (Becker and Whisler, 1967; Shepard, 1967). The organizational concept encouraging innovation is supposed to supplement the lasting order, and must be compatible with the permanent organization.

* Reprinted from *International Studies of Management and Organization*, vol. 7, no. 1 (Spring 1977), pp. 47–70, by permission of the author.

Note: This article is an abstract by the author of his book *Organisation für Innovationsentscheidungen* (Organization for Innovation Decisions). Gottingen: Otto Schwartz & Co., 1973.

The investigation of barriers to innovation has shown that innovation processes do not develop automatically and independently toward a decision favoring the utilization of an invention, but are confronted with barriers of will and capability. To surmount these barriers we need kinetic energy (Lewin, 1961; Knight, 1967), which starts the process and keeps it going until a final decision is reached. We have noted that in cases of barriers caused by rejection or ignorance, opposition to the process is personalized, i.e., it appears in the form of people who either do not want the innovation or are not capable of implementing it. Consequently, the energy necessary to surmount barriers is also furnished by people (suppliers of energy). We have called people who actively and intensively promote an innovation process "promotors." They initiate the process and push it on until the final innovation decision is made, overcoming barriers along the way.

At first sight, the promotor may seem to be an enemy of organization, trying to upset classic principles of organization. For he does not uphold order, stability, and permanence, but strives for change and the elimination of traditional forms of organization. Such an interpretation, which associates the promotor with revolutionary rather than evolutionary activities, would, however, fail to recognize that he works strictly within the hierarchy. When surmounting barriers, he himself employs hierarchic power to advance the process, not adhering to hierarchic restrictions as he does so. In addition to his ordinary, continually repeated tasks, he devotes himself to one special innovation, which—once it has been pushed through—will itself become part of the lasting order. Thus the promotor must detach himself from his hierarchic obligations (Shepard, 1967); only to the extent that he invests energy—either withdrawing it from his regular tasks or furnishing it additionally—in the particular innovation. His principal role is not that of a promotor. The fact is that his tasks leave him enough organizational slack to assume the role of promotor spontaneously. In this respect, however, the hierarchy must be open to innovation. It must leave room for the promotor to enter, establishing and promoting the process.

The full extent of organizational problems connected with promotors becomes apparent if we remember that the innovation process must overcome two different kinds of barriers and that to achieve this aim, it is necessary to employ the energy of power and that of specialized knowledge. We must therefore distinguish between two types of promotors: the promotor by power and the promotor by know-how.

The Promotor by Power

We classify as a promotor by power any person who actively and intensively promotes an innovation process by means of hierarchic power. His defining characteristics are therefore a certain position within the hierarchic structure and, in addition, a certain type of behavior. Typical of his role is that he holds the legitimate power to order sanctions against opponents and provide protection for those who are in favor of innovation (Shepard, 1967). As opponents can be found on all levels, the promotor by power should, in the interest of the innovation, hold a top-management position.[2]

The Promotor by Know-How

We call promotor by know-how any person who actively and intensively encourages an innovation process by means of specific know-how. His position in the hierarchy is immaterial; it should not be assumed even

---

[2] According to the terminology of the behavioral theory of power, the promotor by power has "legitimate" power as well as "coercive" and "referent" power. See Dahl (1957).

that he has a predominantly staff function. It is more likely that the promotor by know-how has a line function in a department whose work routine up to that time has been most closely connected with the innovation (Shepard, 1967). The promotor by know-how may become aware of the potential innovation by recognizing weaknesses within the daily work routine and looking for new methods. But other incentives such as special training or impulses received during visits to fairs or to other firms may also turn a formerly indifferent employee into a promotor by know-how. His interest in the innovation need not be connected with the routine work of his job, but may be based on entirely personal interests. Thus, practically every member of an enterprise can become the promotor by know-how for a certain innovation.

We can see that a promotor by know-how does not start out with complete knowledge, but with interest only. Not until he has acquired a basic, specialized knowledge about the offered object of innovation is he able to display the promoting activity characterizing the behavior pattern of the true promotor. The solitary scientist is no promotor: although he knows the innovation inside out, he does not induce anybody to utilize it in an innovative manner.

The promotor by know-how cannot count on substantial power, and most often on none at all so far as his promoting activities are concerned. In this he differs essentially from the promotor by power. In his case the process-stimulating energy is fed by his know-how, which he increases continually and employs in his arguments with opponents and partisans of innovation.[3] Not only does he study incessantly but he teaches as well. In this way he overcomes the capability barriers to innovation. If we want to

identify him in an empirical manner, we have to assess how often he acts on his own and is noticed by others.

Personal Union of Promotor by Power and Promotor by Know-How

The personal union of promotor by power and promotor by know-how refers to a person who actively and intensively promotes an innovation process by means of both hierarchic potential and object-specific know-how.

The concentration of both promotor roles in one person does not just constitute a mixed case; on the contrary; scientific literature first paid attention to the universal promotor. The innovator in the sense of dynamic entrepreneur, as distinctly described by Schumpeter, can resort to both forms of energy in order to overcome barriers of will and capability. As the enforcer of new combinations he obviously holds enough power to put new ideas into practice. But he is also able to think up these ideas and is sufficiently gifted technically to examine them carefully and transform them expertly into action. The ideal form of the universal promotor first appeared in the innovations of the 19th century; it corresponds to the theoretical concept of the point-in-time, one-man decision.

To identify this personal union empirically, we must consider the hierarchic position of the promotor by power and the object-specific know-how of the promotor by know-how. For the rest, we establish the fact of promotorship according to the frequency of the promotor's action and his impact on others.

Promotor Structures

With our definition of promotors we have established the preconditions for working out the promotor structure we consider the most efficient organization for the pro-

---

[3] In power theory, "expert" power corresponds to the energy of know-how. It is my intention, however, to contrast hierarchic power with object-specific know-how. See Dahl (1957).

motion of innovation. Since it has already become obvious that promotor by power and promotor by know-how contribute to promotion in different ways, and since it is not to be expected that power and know-how are interchangeable without the innovation effect's being limited, it will be necessary for both promotors to do their share. The mere existence of a promotor by power may—because of his hierarchic power—force through an innovation *decision*. But the chosen solution is unlikely to reach a high degree of innovation, i.e., represent a big step into new territory, since the promotor by power neither has the technical insight required for proper evaluation of alternatives nor can hope to be able to put the innovation-decision into practice by himself. The promotor by know-how working in isolation, i.e., without the protection of the promotor by power, is certainly no better off. Although he will be able to plan the innovation project and the method for its implementation, he will be defeated by the barriers of will, or at least be forced to one compromise after the other until the innovation is reduced to insignificance.

In any case, the solitary and unilateral promotor will certainly stand defenseless before one of the barriers to innovation: the barrier of not wanting or of not knowing. This argument does not apply to the personal union of promotor by power and promotor by know-how, for here both promoting elements are—in principle—present, but not in the process-encouraging tension between two organizationally linked supplies of energy. The creative dialogue between the holder of power and the expert is missing; moreover, the energy capacity of the solitary promotor is less.

We therefore assume that a technically first-rate and usable decision can best be achieved when the roles of promotor by power and promotor by know-how are played by two different people. Whereas the promotor by know-how is constantly trying to work out the details and to direct the promotor by power toward the necessary solution, the promotor by power keeps things going, procures budgets for further research and training, and exempts the people participating in the innovation process from routine jobs and shields them against opponents.

Thus the two promotors are not working independently of each other, but in an organizational work-relationship we call "tandem structure." This represents a collaborative structure that is identical with neither the conventional line-connection of two hierarchic authorities nor the staff-line relationship. The promotor by know-how does not regard the promotor by power as a superior in the traditional sense of the word. The promotor by power, on the other hand, does not consider the promotor by know-how an employee with staff functions who merely submits information and acts as a consultant. He does not join the promotor by power on a permanent basis, but cooperates with him—independently of any other long-term jobs—only during this one innovation process. The two promotors can be far removed so far as hierarchic position is concerned; they can, for instance, belong to different divisions or diverge considerably in rank. They do not cooperate out of obligation, but of necessity, as they are both in favor of the innovation and realize that they can push it through only in a joint effort. The combination of promotor by power and promotor by know-how can thus be called a coalition rather than a team.[4]

If we inquire about the special motivation of people acting as promotors by power or know-how, we obtain the most varied explanations, ranging from true love of progress to self-interest. In the case of a successful innovation, the promotor by know-how will certainly be able to count on higher rank

---

4 See Marshak (1955). For the terms *team* and *coalition*, see also Wild (1967).

and a position at the head of a growing department (Sapolsky, 1967). The promotor by power will also be able to expect an increase in his authority. There is no necessity, however, to refer to the motivation structure in order to prove that successful executives are interested in the future development of the enterprise to which they belong. As it is generally assumed that the success of the individual is closely tied to that of the enterprise, promotion chances and financial advantages can be considered a direct consequence.

Thus we have arrived at the desired promotion structure, in which a promotor by power and a promotor by know-how operate in tandem. It is likely that in business practice a greater degree of innovation is achieved by this promotion structure than by any other.

Empirical Proof: The Frequency of Various Promotor Structures

We had available to us a detailed description of 233 innovation processes in German enterprises, obtained in an earlier research project. These were all concerned with the initial introduction of computers in administration. We were able to classify these 233 processes according to their promotor structure. We distinguished five types:

1. The tandem structure. We found 78 cases in which one promotor by power and one promotor by know-how could be identified. We also included in this category nine other cases in which there was more than one promotor by power and/or by know-how, or in which a "personal union" promotor (power and know-how in one man) was supplemented by other promotors.

2. The unilateral power structure. It is typical of this structure that the promotor appears alone, unaccompanied by other promotors. The energy supplied by object-specific knowledge is missing. The structure

also remains one-sided and therefore incomplete in cases in which several promotors by power—i.e., promotors of the same kind—carry on the process.

3. The unilateral know-how structure. Here, too, the innovation is influenced unilaterally, this time by the specific force of the expert's argumentation. The energy furnished by hierarchic power is lacking. Even if several promotors by know-how appear, the structure remains unilateral.

4. The personal union structure. Here the solitary innovator who possesses both hierarchic power and technical knowledge, but who is not connected organizationally with other promotors, characterizes the process. As explained before, we use the term *structure* also for this case, since we analyze the whole process of the innovation decision and not just the isolated activities of this one man. In addition to the "dynamic entrepreneur," a number of other people take part in the process, offering intellectual contributions. But the active and intensive promotion of the process remains in the hands of one person and not—as in our promotor pattern—in the hands of a team working in tandem.

5. The structure without promotors. The processes without promotors constitute the last group. These processes have an organizational, but not a proper promotor, structure, i.e., the structure of the innovation processes is not characterized by the participation of promotors.

These five basic structures occurred in our sample with the frequencies listed in Table 1.

We see that the tandem structure occurs in just one third of the cases. In 50 cases a promotor was not apparent. It may be that in these cases the innovation did not encounter any barriers of will or capability. Another possibility is that the barriers were not recognized or that they were outweighed by the willpower demonstrated by the top authority. We assume the latter explanation

TABLE 1
Promotor Structures of 233 Innovation Processes

Structure	Processes	
	Number	%
Tandem structure	87	37
Unilateral power structure	37	16
Unilateral know-how structure	43	19
Personal union structure	16	7
Structure without promotors	50	21
Total	233	100

to be the correct one, and we expect to find that in these cases the innovation decision is marked by a lesser degree of efficiency. We shall present the pertinent empirical findings later on. The personal union occurs only rarely. That it does occur serves to prove that the old-fashioned entrepreneur still exists today.

All in all, the 233 − 50 = 183 innovations with promotors included 287 promotors: 126 by power, 141 by know-how, and 20 personal unions. The almost even balance between promotors by power and promotors by know-how refutes the assumption that in organizations innovation is achieved solely either by powerful top management or by experts.

Promotor Structure and Number of Problem-Solving Activities

The empirical data allow a count of the number of different problem-solving activities found in the innovation-decision process. The term *activity* is used for every distinct action contributing to the solution of the innovation problem; for details about its measurement, refer to Witte (1973). Our theory that the innovation process is supplied with kinetic energy by the active and intensive participation of promotors leads to the expectation that processes with promotors involve a larger number of activities than those without, and that the tandem promotor structure again encourages greater process activity than do unilateral struc-

tures. The average numbers of problem-solving activities found for the five types of structures are listed in Table 2.

The analysis reveals that the innovation processes without promotors show a very low level of activities, as expected. The tandem structure displays the highest rate of activity, and the unilateral structures are in between. As the activities counted in Table 2 are those of all persons participating in the innovation process, not just of the promotors, it is evident that the promotor is not a solitary innovator, but stimulates activities of others.

Promotor Structure and Duration of Innovation Decision Process

The decision to apply a technological novelty for the first time is a chain of work processes and not a point-in-time decision. Thus, a certain amount of time passes, part of which must be considered working time, as it is taken up with problem-solving activities, the rest being waiting time, i.e., a period without activities. It is therefore difficult to use the duration of a decision process as a scaling factor. Superficial consideration, also adopted by us in the beginning, leads to the conclusion that a short duration can be regarded as "better" innovation behavior. From this point of view, duration is interpreted as a sign of hesitation, lack of daring, or even inefficiency.

In many cases this interpretation hits the core of the problem, but this does not

TABLE 2
Problem-Solving Activities in 233 Innovation Processes

Structure	Average Number of Activities
Tandem structure	57.6
Unilateral power structure	31.5
Unilateral know-how structure	35.1
Personal union structure	26.9
Structure without promotors	13.3

F-test: $P < 0.001$.

necessarily mean that it is always correct. For, first, an innovation process that does justice to the problem and aims at certain goals to be successful requires a minimum period of time to penetrate the complex problem, to gather the necessary information about the novelty and its field of application, to evaluate alternatives, and to finally arrive at a decision. Second, the unavoidable difficulties of the innovation vary from case to case. It is untenable to accept as the ideal figure the hasty innovator who simply brushes aside problems without solving them. Extremely lengthy processes, on the other hand, are not ideal either, for it can be assumed that in this case opponents will delay actions, and barriers of will and capability will be hard to overcome.

Table 3 lists the average number of days the decision process took from its beginning (first problem-related activity) to the final decision. The table shows a tendency toward increased duration in cases involving a promotor by know-how, whereas the participation of a promotor by power shortens the process. The personal union also has an accelerating effect. The tandem structure lies somewhere in between, a fact that can now be explained: the process is subjected to the influence of both the promotor by power and the promotor by know-how. The shortest duration can be registered for processes without promotors. Here the top authority evidently made the innovation decision peremptorily, without going through a proper decision process beforehand. The quality of such a decision will become evident when we assess the degree of innovation.

Upon closer inspection of the findings, one observation seems to stand out: experts slow down the innovation. They go into technical detail, get entangled in contradictions, and seek to achieve technical perfection. When working without the help of a promotor by power, they may not be capable of viewing the specific problem in a larger scope. We realize that promotors by know-how not only are qualified to overcome barriers but can themselves erect barriers by recognizing the difficulties of problems and by informing the other participants of them. They are certainly not naïve innovators. This shows that one should not condemn the delaying effect of promotors by know-how all too quickly. For the difficulties discovered by experts might persist —possibly hidden—and not be coped with in time; thus they might appear much later and entail serious consequences. We can therefore interpret the finding in a different way, viewing the experts as a protection against precipitate and erroneous innovation decisions. We must, however, also take the degree of innovation into account.

Promotor Structure and Degree of Innovation

We should like to compare the different promotor structures according to a measure of the quality of the innovation. An economist would probably look for a measure of the profit or loss caused by the implementation of the innovation to evaluate this. Such a measure was not available to us. Instead, we tried to assess the efficiency of the various promotor structures by measuring the degree of innovation obtained.

In trying to measure the efficiency of the innovation decision by the extent of the innovational step taken, we advanced into unexplored territory in organizational research. Measuring empirical facts presents

TABLE 3
Duration of the 233 Innovation Processes

Structure	Average Duration (days)
Tandem structure	496
Unilateral power structure	379
Unilateral know-how structure	570
Personal union structure	392
Structure without promotors	201

F-test: $P < 0.001$.

major problems. The degree of innovation was not mentioned explicitly in the original records, so it was not possible to set up a direct code, as in the case of process duration or the number of activities. Frequently the innovators themselves did not realize the extent of the innovational step, and, if they did, every one of them applied a different subjective scale. We, on the other hand, had to try to find a scaling system that subjected the 233 investigated innovations to the same assessment.

We therefore chose the lengthy procedures of developing a scale for the degree of innovation by means of interviews. For this purpose we interviewed data-processing experts who had repeatedly participated in computer innovations. They came from both producer and user enterprises and from large, middle-size, and small companies. In addition, advisers in computer application were asked for their opinions.

Each person was interviewed separately, the interview taking one to two full days. We were surprised to find that very soon a homogeneous scale took shape that combined the strictly technological progress of the chosen hardware and software configuration with the novel aspect of the organizational utilization concept of the computer. By taking into account the size of the enterprise and the date of the innovation, an individual degree of innovation could be registered for each of the 233 processes.

If, for instance, in 1965 a large industrial enterprise ordered a central unit with 16 K and equipped it peripherally with a magnetic tape to carry out routine work electronically instead of in the traditional way, this decision constituted a small degree of innovation. If the same decision had been reached by a smaller or by the same company several years earlier, it could be considered a much more daring innovational step, which would, accordingly, warrant a higher assessment, as a certain technological innovation within a particular economic utilization concept constitutes—as a pioneer action—a degree of innovation of the highest level. When in the course of time the same decision is made by other companies, the degree of innovation decreases until one can no longer speak of an innovation.

We thus devised a scale for measuring the degree of innovation. We limited ourselves to a scale with the values "low," "medium," and "high." Our conclusions therefore refer to an ordinal scale and not, as in the previous findings, to a ratio. For this reason we chose the chi-square test to check our hypothesis. This hypothesis states that processes with a promotor structure lead to a decision with a higher degree of innovation than processes without promotor structures. Furthermore, we assume that the tandem pattern results in a higher rating than the unilateral power or know-how structures. The result refers to only 227 innovation decisions, since we were not able to determine a clear-cut degree of innovation in six cases. The data are collected in Table 4.

TABLE 4
Degree of Innovation of 227 Innovation Decisions

Line	Structure	Decisions, Percent Degree of Innovation		
		Low	Medium	High
1.	Tandem structure	27	44	29
2.	Unilateral power structure	33	45	22
3.	Unilateral know-how structure . .	40	40	20
4.	Personal union structure	36	36	28
5.	Structure without promotors	51	31	18
	Total	36	40	24

These data show that processes with promotors reach a significantly higher degree of innovation than those without promotors. We have thus proved that promotors increase not only activity but also the degree of innovation in the final decision.

A comparison of the four different structures with promotors shows the tandem structure with the highest average degree of innovation, followed by the personal union structure, the unilateral power structure, and the unilateral know-how structure, in that order. The differences are not pronounced enough, however, to prove statistically the superiority of the tandem structure over other structures with promotors. Our results are in the expected direction, but the measures available do not allow a stronger confirmation. The tandem structure by itself is statistically significantly superior to the processes without promotors.

A detailed look at the nature of the innovations obtained without the help of promotors confirms their low average degree of innovation. In general, compared with the size of the enterprise, a rather insignificant computer configuration and simple areas of application were chosen. It is interesting that the next lowest average degree of innovation is found for the unilateral know-how structure. This shows that without the protection of a promotor by power, a promotor by know-how is unable to realize ambitious plans.

The tandem structure, with the largest percentage of highly innovative decisions and the smallest percentage of low innovative decisions in Table 4, and with the highest average number of activities in Table 2, appears to be the most effective structure for overcoming innovation barriers. It thus confirms our two-center theory of innovating power.

REFERENCES

Becker, S. W., and Whisler, T. L. (1967) "The Innovative Organization; A Selected View of Current Theory and Research." *Journal of Business*, 40, 462–69.

Cyert, R. M., Simon, H. A., and Trow, D. A. (1966) "Observation of a Business Decision." In A. H. Rubenstein and C. J. Haberstroh (eds), *Some Theories of Organization* (rev. ed.). Homewood, Ill.: Irwin-Dorsey. Pp. 591–605.

Dahl, R. A. (1957) "The Concept of Power." *Behavioral Science*, 2, 201–18.

Irle, M. (1970) "Führungsverhalten in organisierten Gruppen." In A. Mayer and B. Herwig (eds.), *Handbuch der Psychologie*. Band 9. Göttingen: Hogreve. Pp. 521–51.

Judson, A. S. (1966) *A Manager's Guide to Making Changes.* London: Wiley.

Kiefer, K. (1967) *Die Diffusion von Neuerungen.* Tübingen: Mohr.

Kieser, A. (1969) "Innovationen." In E. Grochla (ed.), *Handwörterbuch der Organisation.* Stuttgart: Poeschel. Cols. 741–50.

Knight, K. E. (1967) "A Descriptive Model of the Intra-Firm Innovation Process." *Journal of Business*, 40, 478–86.

LeCompte, K. (1966) "Organizational Structures in Transition." In A. H. Rubenstein and C. J. Haberstroh (eds.), op. cit. Pp. 309–24.

Lewin, K. (1961) "Quasi-Stationary Social Equilibria and the Problem of Permanent Change." In W. G. Bennis, K. Benne, and R. Chin (eds.), *The Planning of Change.* New York: Wiley. Pp. 238–44.

Mann, F. C., and Williams, L. K. (1966) "Observations on the Dynamics of a Change to Electronic Data-Processing Equipment." In A. H. Rubenstein and C. J. Haberstroh (eds.), op. cit. Pp. 336–66.

March, J. G., and Simon, H. A. (1958) *Organizations.* New York: Wiley.

Marschak, J. (1955) "Elements for a Theory of Teams." *Management Science*, 1, 127–37.

Sapolsky, H. M. (1967) "Organizational Structure and Innovation." *Journal of Business*, 40, 497–505.

Schumpeter, J. (1912) *Theorie der wirtschaftlichen Entwicklung.* Leipzig: Duncker and Humblot.

Shepard, H. A. (1967) "Innovation-Resisting and Innovation-Producing Organizations." *Journal of Business*, 40, 470–77.

Walter, H. (1970) "Zusammenhang zwischen Forschung und Entwicklung, Innovation und technischen Fortschritt." In Ifo-Institut für Wirtschaftsforschung (ed.), *Innovation in der Wirtschaft.* München: Duncker and Humbolt. Pp. 30–48.

Wild, J. (1967) *Neuere Organisationsforschung in betriebswirtschaftlicher Sicht.* Berlin: Duncker and Humblot.

Wilson, J. Q. (1966) "Innovation in Organization: Notes Towards a Theory." In J. D. Thompson (ed.), *Approaches to Organizational Design.* Pittsburgh: University of Pittsburgh Press. Pp. 193–218.

Witte, E. (1968a) "Die Organisation komplexer Entscheidungsverläufe." *Zeitschrift für betriebswirtschaftliche Forschung, 20,* 581–99.

Witte, E. (1968b) "Phasen-Theorem und Organisation komplexer Entscheidungsverläufe." *Zeitschrift für betriebswirtschaftliche Forschung, 20,* 625–47.

Witte, E. (1969a) "Mikroskopie einer unternehmerischen Entscheidung. Bericht aus der empirischen Forschung." *IBM Nachrichten, 19,* 490–95.

Witte, E. (1969b) "Entscheidungsprozesse." In E. Grochia (ed.), op. cit. Cols. 497–506.

Witte, E. (1969c) "Entscheidung im aussergewöhnlichen Fall Ein Forschungsbericht." *Harzburger Hefte, 12,* 368–75.

Witte, E. (1971) "Organisatorische Barrieren im Entscheidungsprozess zu Infrastrukturobjekten." In *Grundragen der Infrastrukturplanung für wachsende Wirtschaften.* Schriften des Vereins für Sozialpolitik, vol. 58. Berlin: Duncker and Humblot. Pp. 331–98.

Witte, E. (1972a) "Field Research on Complex Decision-Making Processes—the Phase Theorem." *International Studies of Management & Organization,* II(2), 156–82.

Witte, E. (1972b) *Das Informationsverhalten in Entscheidungsprozessen.* Tübingen: Mohr.

Witte, E. (1973) *Organisation für Innovationsentscheidungen—Das Promotorenmodell.* Göttingen: Schwartz.

Zeleznik, A., and Moment, D. (1964) *The Dynamics of Interpersonal Behavior.* New York: Wiley.

Zander, A.. (1961) "Resistance to Change—Its Analysis and Prevention." In W. G. Bennis, K. Benne, and R. Chin (eds.), op. cit. Pp. 543–48.

Management science seeks to improve the effectiveness of an organization primarily by persuading managers to use the conclusions of rigorous quantitative analysis to allocate resources, design information systems, and make policy decisions. Although precise data on successes and failures are difficult to assess, management scientists have expressed concern about not having very much impact on organizational decisions. Churchman's (1964) survey of the authors of cases in the first six years of *Operations Research* produced no reliable evidence that their recommendations had been accepted. Harvey (1970) and his associates assessed the implementation of their recommendations in all 31 management-science projects conducted by their consulting organization up to 1970 and judged 8 to be failures, 12 partial successes, and 11 successes. Lonnstedt's (1975) survey of 107 operations research studies done before 1971 in 12 Swedish organizations reported that in almost 30 percent of the projects the recommendations had not been implemented. He provided no data on partial implementation.

In recent years management scientists have increased their efforts to understand the implementation process and a body of literature is emerging. Ginzberg (1975) surveyed critically 14 papers on implementation of projects in management science and Lucas (1975) examined six studies in his analysis of why information systems fail. Management scientists are primarily trained in the physical and mathematical sciences and their studies of implementation tend to (1) search empirically for patterns of factors common to different projects (Lonnstedt, 1975; Rubenstein *et al.*, 1967) or (2) focus on a particular conjecture such as a problem-centered or a personality-centered explanation of what affects the success of a management science change effort (Churchman *et al.*, 1957; Huysman, 1970). Both approaches, however, lack an inte-

Theory of Change and the Effective Use of Management Science*

DALE E. ZAND and
RICHARD E. SORENSEN

grating theory that can provide insight into how a large number of variables relate to implementation.

Theory of Change

Behavioral scientists, on the other hand, are primarily trained in the social and psychological sciences and have conducted research for many years on the theory and process of change in individuals, groups, and organizations. Since a management-science project is an attempt to induce organizational change, it seemed desirable to investigate the effective use of management science by using a behavioral theory of change, preferably one which also can organize diverse influences into a small set of variables.

* *Administrative Science Quarterly*, vol. 20, no. 4 (December 1975), pp. 532–45. © Cornell University.

THEORIES OF CHANGE

A management science project translates a problem, such as controlling inventory or choosing among alternative marketing policies, into a mathematical model of relations among key variables and then recommends to the manager a course of action based upon an optimal mathematical solution to the equations in the model. This approach to changing an organization includes the following elements: a problem, a management scientist and manager, and the organization in which they are embedded, consisting of subordinates, several layers of superior managers, and other organizational units interdependent with the manager's unit.

Problem-Centered

The early theories of change held by management scientists centered on defining the problem accurately, using the best analytic techniques, and finding an optimal solution (Churchman et al., 1957; McCloskey and Coppinger, 1956; McCloskey and Trefethin, 1954). It was assumed that managers would readily understand, accept, and implement the solutions of the scientists. Some observers contended, however, that the management scientists were proposing changes with insufficient regard for relevance, timeliness, acceptance, or implementation (Grayson, 1973; Malcolm, 1965; Shycon, 1974).

Personality-Centered

Management scientists then formulated a theory of change which centered on the belief that personality differences between managers and management scientists, primarily their cognitive styles, were obstructing change (Churchman and Schainblatt, 1965; Hammond, 1974; Huysman, 1970). Managers were pragmatic, concrete, and not rigorous conceptualizers, whereas management scientists were analytic, abstract, and rigorous conceptualizers, and these differences would hinder communication and the mutual understanding needed for change. The personality-centered theory of change apparently has a large following as evidenced by the editorial policy of *Interfaces* (1974), a joint quarterly publication of the Institute of Management Sciences and the Operations Research Society of America, the two leading societies in management science, which specifically invites "articles dealing with difficulties in . . . implementation . . . [and] problem solving stemming from the personality differences between managers and management scientists/operations researchers."

Multifactor

Finally, Rubenstein et al. (1967) suggested that a wide set of variables may affect change efforts and enumerated ten variables that could be used in empirical research including level of support by management, technical capability, adequacy of resources, and so on.

Behavioral Theories

Theories of behavioral scientists, however, viewed change as a complex, general social process with many subactivities; for example, conditions conducive to acceptance of change (Linton, 1936), patterns of reaction to change initiatives (Merton, 1957), client opportunities to participate in a change effort (Whyte, 1967), level of trust and the quality of the decision to change (Zand, 1972), initiators of change (Bennis, 1963), organizational methods of inducing change (Zand, 1974), and techniques of diffusing change (Katz and Kahn, 1966).

Theories of both management scientists and behavioral scientists seemed to focus too much on one or another aspect of change without adequately synthesizing the many interacting elements. It seemed desirable to find a theory which would consider not only the relationship between manager and management scientist, but also the influence of other persons and factors. The general theory of change proposed by Lewin (1947) offered the greatest promise, although Kahn (1974) observed that Lewin's theory "is often quoted or paraphrased as a preamble to research, but seldom with any clear indication of how that formulation determined the design of the research that follows its invocation. . . . The schema thus remains not only unelaborated and untested, but really unused. It deserves more serious attention." Thus, the relatively abstract concepts of Lewin's original theory would have to be converted into operational measures.

PROCESS THEORY OF CHANGE

Phases of Change

Lewin's theory conceptualized the present condition or level of activity of a system as a dynamic social equilibrium, that is a state of balance maintained by active driving and resisting social forces. Change then consisted of altering the driving and resisting forces thereby facilitating the movement of the system to a new level of equilibrium.

Lewin (1947) conceptualized change as a process with three phases: (1) unfreezing—behavior that increases the receptivity of the client system to a possible change in the distribution and balance of social forces; (2) moving—altering the magnitude, direction, or number of driving and resisting forces, consequently shifting the equilibrium to a new level; and (3) refreezing—reinforcing the new distribution of forces, thereby maintaining and stabilizing the new social equilibrium.

Lewin also suggested that although common sense might lean toward increasing driving forces to induce change, in many instances this might arouse an equal and opposite increase in resisting forces, the net effect being no change and greater tension than before.

Research

Early research investigated unfreezing and moving by examining a classical approach to change, lecture by scientists, an increase of intellectual driving forces, analogous to focusing on a problem and presenting an expert, optimal solution. Radke and Klisurich (1947) found that lectures by scientists were less effective in changing behavior than individual discussions of reservations about a change with a group (unfreezing) followed by information from scientists (moving). Lewin (1952) examined refreezing and reported that continued implementation of a change was greater among individuals who had made a public commitment to change to a group than among individuals who had not. Coch and French (1948), touching all three phases of the change process, found that work groups participating in the introduction and design of changes in work methods produced more and had less turnover than groups that did not.

Subprocesses

Although Lewin's theory stimulated research, it did not explain what influenced unfreezing, moving, or refreezing. An elaboration of Lewin's concepts, in part suggested by Schein (1964), is outlined because it provided the basic conceptual system used to develop measuring instruments in this research.

Unfreezing This occurs by means of (1) disconfirmation, (2) psychological support, and occasionally, (3) guilt anxiety. Disconfirmation is feedback that one's present behavior is ineffective or not as effective as it might be with reasonable additional effort. The feedback may vary in source, form, and method of transmittal; for example, (a) objective measurements of physical production showing that one's intended level of production was not attained; (b) social comparison showing that one's performance is inferior, in objective of qualitative measurements, to that of another comparable unit; (c) information from important others, such as, superior, peers, or subordinates, indicating that one's intended effects are not being attained; (d) criticism from important others emphasizing that one's behavior is seriously deficient compared to highly-valued, ideal behavior.

Psychological support in unfreezing is an emotional climate that leads one to feel that ineffectiveness is undesirable but can be remedied and that facing up to it is, in the long run, more useful and satisfying than denying it. The difficulty of changing is not diminished, but psychological support provides assurance that change is possible and that one has the physical and mental resources to surmount the difficulties.

Guilt anxiety means increasing people's feelings of shame and embarrassment about their deficient behavior. It is not considered further because its effects are controversial and it was not germane to this research.

Moving   This is concerned with conceptualizing a problem, acquiring information about relevant forces, locating or developing alternative solutions, and choosing a course of action. Moving varies in terms of how a problem is solved and who is involved at a given stage; for example, an order from a higher authority, a recommendation from a management scientist, imitation of another person or social unit, self-directed search, or some of each of these at different times.

Refreezing   This occurs through confirmation, psychological support, and heightened confidence. Confirmation is feedback that performance is effective. It may come from task measurements; from responses of others that verify a new level of effectiveness; from social comparison showing that performance has equalled or exceeded that of another social unit; or from oneself, one's own perceptions and interpretations. Confirmation also may involve rewards such as increased salary, bonuses, promotion, and greater responsibility. Psychological support in refreezing is an emotional climate that leads one to feel satisfaction and pleasure with the new behavior. It is encouragement to practice and use the new behavior, accepting but not being diverted by occasional error, until the behavior is internalized, that is, is more familiar and comfortable than other behavior. Heightened confidence is demonstrated by transferring monitoring and control of the new behavior to the focal unit and encouraging others to adopt the new behavior following the advice and guidance of the focal unit.

Implications for Managers and Management Scientists

Unfreezing seems to be a complex, potentially unstable phase. Management scientists, top managers, and unit managers are attempting to identify the problem, estimate its severity, and assess the need for change. There is uncertainty in forces related to the ability of management to state its problem, the importance attributed to the problem, ideas about the scope of the problem, and awareness of a need for change.

At the same time, the three parties are negotiating a relationship with each other. If their perceptions match and their estimates are similar, and management is open and candid, then there is likely to be a collaborative three-party alliance. However, if the perceptions and estimates of top managers and unit managers differ substantially, then the management scientists may be drawn into a conflict between the parties. The management scientist may see himself as an impartial, objective analyst, but in the dispute, the parties are likely to see him as an ally or an opponent, depending upon whom his views seem to support.

The implication for the problem-centered management scientist is that unless he pays attention to unfreezing, his later efforts to implement a solution may be futile because the organization may not have been ready for change from the outset. When he negotiates his initial relationship, the management scientist will be getting many cues about the balance of forces in unfreezing, to which he should pay close attention.

Strong reservations and resentment by unit managers during unfreezing are likely to cause great difficulties during the moving phase, and if the management scientist proceeds despite these, he meets strong resistance: data are not made available, and managers do not become involved in developing solutions and do not understand the proposed solutions. In short, moving is not favored when management scientists are considered adversaries by managers.

In contrast, moving is favored when, in unfreezing, the need for change is recognized, top and unit managers have congruent perceptions, and managers and management scientists accept each other. It seems to be supported by joint gathering of data, managerial review and evaluation of alternatives, sequential improvement of proposals, and keeping top managers informed of progress. Thus successful moving seems to be a process with open interaction between managers and management scientists, which contributes to incremental improvement of solutions.

Finally, in refreezing, the implication for the management scientist is that his change effort is far from complete when he and the managers agree on a solution. Both must give careful attention to testing the solution and devising standards and measures for evaluating results. It seems especially important that the management scientists give positive feedback to the managers who helped design and implement the solution. Such feedback lets them know whether the risks they took were worthwhile. It also helps sustain the change effort through the initial misunderstandings, mistakes, and decreased performance that frequently occur during the early stages of implementing a change. Refreezing is favored by evidence of success in practice, superior results, positive feedback to managers after using the solution, and application of the solution to other units.

It would be erroneous to conclude from the high correlation between refreezing and level of success that refreezing is the primary cause or a sufficient cause of success. Rather, refreezing and level of success circularly reinforce each other; however, both follow and depend upon the unfreezing and moving that introduce new behavior. If the new behavior is judged more effective than past behavior and refreezing is initiated, then refreezing and level of success will circularly reinforce one another, hence their high correlation. On the other hand, although new behavior may be more effective than past behavior, it tends to attenuate if refreezing is not initiated.

Also, one should not conclude that there are only favorable forces in successful changes and only unfavorable forces in unsuccessful changes. The responses to the questionnaire showed that there were both favorable and unfavorable forces in each phase of change in all projects; however, in successful projects, the number and size of favorable forces in each phase were greater than the number and size of unfavorable forces.

The change framework developed here may be used to understand and improve the ongoing change efforts of management scientists as well as those of managers and staff specialists in an organization. The forces found in each phase of change in this research very likely will be found in other change projects. By examining the balance of favorable and unfavorable forces one could estimate the probability of a successful change and could better propose actions to improve that probability.

REFERENCES

Bennis, Warren G. (1963) "A New role for the Behavioral Sciences: Effecting Organizational Change." *Administrative Science Quarterly*, 8: 125–65.

Berelson, Bernard (1952) *Content Analysis in Communication Research*, Glencoe, Ill.; The Free Press.

Budd, Richard W., Robert K. Thorp, and Lewis Donahew (1967) *Content Analysis of Communications*, New York: Macmillan.

Churchman, C. West (1964) "Managerial Acceptance of Scientific Recommendations." *California Management Review*, 7: 31–38.

Churchman, C. W., and A. H. Schainblatt (1965) "The Researcher and the Manager: A Dialectic of Implementation." *Management Science*, 11: B69–87.

Churchman, C. W., R. L. Ackoff, and E. L. Arnoff (1957) *Introduction to Operations Research*, New York: John Wiley.

Coch, Lester, and John R. P. French, Jr. (1948) "Overcoming Resistance to Change." *Human Relations*, 1: 512–32.

Crowne, Douglas P., and David Marlowe (1964) *The Approval Motive: Studies in Evaluative Dependence*, New York: John Wiley.

Dunnette, Marvin D., John P. Campbell, and Milton D. Hakel (1967) "Factors Contributing to Job Satisfaction and Job Dissatisfaction in Six Occupational Groups." *Organizational Behavior and Human Performance*, 2: 143–74.

Ginzberg, M. J. (1975) *A Critical Survey of Implementation Research*. Working Paper, Massachusetts Institute of Technology, Center for Information Systems Research, Cambridge, Mass.

Goode, William J., and Paul K. Hatt (1952) *Methods of Social Research*, New York: McGraw-Hill.

Grayson, C. Jackson (1973) "Management Science and Business Practice." *Harvard Business Review*, 51: 41–48.

Hammond, John S. (1974) "The Roles of the Manager and Management Scientist in Successful Implementation." *Sloan Management Review*, 15: 1–24.

Harvey, Allan (1970) "Factors Making for Implementation Success and Failure." *Management Science*, 16: B312–20.

Huysmans, Jan H. B. M. (1970) "The Effectiveness of the Cognitive-Style Constraint in Implementing Operations Research Proposals." *Management Science*, 17: 92–104.

Interfaces (1974) 4: Editorial policy.

Kahn, Robert L. (1974) "Organizational Development: Some Problems and Proposals." *Journal of Applied Behavioral Science*, 10: 487.

Katz, Daniel, and Robert L. Kahn (1966) *The Social Psychology of Organizations*: 392–432. New York: John Wiley.

Kerlinger, Fred N. (1964) *Foundations of Behavioral Research*, New York: Holt Rinehart & Winston.

Landy, Frank J., and Robert M. Guion (1970) "Development of Scales for the Measurement of Work Motivation." *Organizational Behavior and Human Performance*, 5: 98–103.

Lewin, Kurt (1947) "Frontiers in Group Dynamics." *Human Relations*, 1: 2–38.

———. (1952) "Group Decision and Social Change. In G. E. Swanson, T. M. Newcomb, and E. L. Hartley (eds.), *Readings in Social Psychology*: 459–73. New York: Holt.

Linton, Ralph (1936) *The Study of Man: An Introduction*: 324–46, New York: Appleton-Century-Crofts.

Lonnstedt, Lars (1975) "Factors Related to the Implementation of Operations Research Solutions." *Interfaces*, 5: 23–30.

Lucas, Henry (1975) *Why Information Systems Fail. New York:* Columbia University Press.

Malcolm, D. G. (1965) "On the Need for Improvement in Implementation of O.R." *Management Science*, 11: B48–58.

McCloskey, J. F., and F. N. Trefethen (eds.) (1956) *Operations Research for Management*. Baltimore: Johns Hopkins.

McCloskey, J. F., and J. M. Coppinger (eds.) (1956) *Operations Research for Management*, Vol. II. Baltimore: Johns Hopkins.

Merton, Robert K. (1957) *Social Theory and Social Structure*: 140–57. New York: Free Press of Glencoe.

Radke, M., and D. Klisurich (1947) "Experiments in Changing Food Habits." *Journal of American Dietetic Association*, 23: 403–9.

Rubenstein, A. H., M. Radnor, N. R. Baker, D. R. Heiman, and J. B. McColly (1967) "Some Organizational Factors Related to the Effectiveness of Management Science Groups in Industry." *Management Science*, 13: B508–18.

Schein, Edgar H. (1964) "The Mechanism of Change." In W. Bennis, E. Schein, F. Steele, and D. Berlew (eds.), *Interpersonal Dynamics:* 362–78, Homewood, Ill.: Dorsey.

Schneider, Joseph, and Edwin A. Locke (1971) "A Critique of Herzberg's Incident Classification System and a Suggested Revision." *Organizational Behavior and Human Performance,* 6: 441–57.

Schultz, William C. (1958) "On Categorizing Qualitative Data in Content Analysis." *Public Opinion Quarterly,* 22: 503–15.

Shycon, Harvey N. (1974) "All around the Model: Perspectives on MS Applications." *Interfaces,* 4: 21–23.

Smith, Patricia Cain, and L. M. Kendall (1963) "Retranslation of Expectations: An Approach to the Construction of Unambiguous Anchors for Rating Scales." *Journal of Applied Psychology,* 47: 149–55.

Sorensen, Richard E., and Dale E. Zand (1974) "Using a Behaviorally Anchored Scale to Measure a Project's Success." In L. Desfosses (ed.), *Decision Sciences: Education and Application:* 7–10, Philadelphia: American Institute of Decision Sciences, Northeast.

Whyte, William F. (1967) "Models for Building and Changing Organizations." *Human Organization,* 26: 22–31.

Zand, Dale E. (1972) "Trust and Managerial Problem Solving." *Administrative Science Quarterly,* 17: 229–39.

———. (1974) "Collateral Organization: A New Change Strategy." *Journal of Applied Behavioral Science,* 10: 63–89.

Management development within organizations is not an abstract process that can be infused into any organization disregarding its tasks, its people, methods, and organizational structure. If the nature and processes of a developmental program are alien to the nature and processes in the organization, it becomes at best an irrelevant program and, at a more serious level, a source of aggravation and frustration to the organizational system, not to mention the people in the organization. *Management Development must be tailored to where the organization is as well as where it wants to be.*

We shall pose four questions, each of which is designed to help explore the assumptions commonly held about organizations. The four questions are: (1) Where in the organization is the relevant knowledge and skills? (2) How does the organization grow? (3) Is the organization a collection of individuals or a collaborative system? (4) What is the most appropriate learning process to develop and utilize the organization's social and human resources?

The answers to these four questions may be drawn from one of two kinds of assumptions concerning the organization. One set of assumptions suggests a more traditional management development program, the other suggests an organization development approach to management development.

Where Is the Relevant Knowledge in the Organization

The first assumption concerns the location of the knowledge and skills in the organization which are relevant to the specific tasks and issues upon which it is working. One assumption is that the relevant operating and managerial knowledge is vested in a few select managerial elite somewhere at the top of the pyramid or at the top of subpyramids in the organizational hier-

READING 5–9

Management Development *Is* Organization Development[*]

GLENN H. VARNEY

archy. Similarly, the knowledge for making changes in the organization and management is vested in these same positions. This set of assumptions suggests that management development prepares people lower down in the organization to eventually enter responsible positions. Development becomes essentially a preparation for entry. The assumption that we can properly prepare people to enter elite positions is parallel to the assumption that we can properly select people for a managerial elite. Thus, where we find traditional management development programs, we frequently find a traditional emphasis upon the use of psychological tests, assessment centers, and other management identification programs. The focus of these programs is not geared to particular organizational issues. Instead they are geared toward selecting an ideal

* This article first appeared in *Journal of General Management*, vol. 4, no. 1 (August 1976), pp. 51–58.

401

man who can manage the organization. If we know what that typical ideal manager looks like in our organization, then we should be able to select future managers on this same basis, and then train them on this basis as well.

The alternative assumption about organization is that the knowledge for its operation, management, and change is widely dispersed among its people and groups. Where this specialized knowledge lies depends upon the specific tasks and issues at hand. The assumption is that it does not necessarily reside entirely at the top of the organization. It also assumes that the location of skill is constantly changing since the tasks and issues are changing, and that the knowledge cannot be ascribed to a specific position or role, but rather to individuals and groups regardless of their formal place in the organization chart. Management development, according to this assumption, is the responsibility of all employees in the organization; initiation and control is located in the people who have knowledge of the development issues. Thus, every employee is a potential manager, depending upon the task or issue to be solved. This contrasts with our usual stereotype of management as a select elite group occupying certain established positions at or near the top of the pyramid.

Based on this assumption, development programs must deal with here-and-now organization issues rather than prepare people to enter a managerial elite of the future. Such an approach provides people with problem-solving skills which can be used now; and emphasizes the collaborative skills needed to work in an organization in which knowledge and skills are widely dispersed rather than centrally located.

How Does the Organization Grow?

A related set of assumptions concerns the basis for organizational growth. One set of assumptions is that the organization grows by following and refining its current methods, procedures, and people. The basis for this assumption is that the organization has arrived at its current condition of success by using these already successful methods. While these may need small refinements, they don't need radical change. Management development, therefore, is most effective if it is focused on reinforcing methods of historical precedent. Similarly, management development needs to refine people's thinking, to help them brush up, and thereby to form pools of ready talent that can fit into the current processes and structures of the organization.

The alternative assumption about organization is that they grow by continually adapting and changing their methods and structures to meet new technologies and behavioral styles. Precedent will always lag behind current needs and demands. Manager development programs, then must provide learning about change—what to change, how to change, and practice in making changes.

Is the Organization a Collection of Individuals or Does it Represent a Collaborative System Which Is More than the Sum Effort and Skills of its Individuals?

One assumption is that the organization is composed of separate individuals, each of whom apply their effort, ideas, and skills regardless of the relationships they have with others in the organization and regardless of their preception of the climate in this organization. This assumption suggests that the prime focus of management development programs should be on the individual, and that conceptual and social skill training of the individual will enhance his effort, his skill, and his ideas. Thus, the individual needs to develop and change, but the system in which he works does not. The individual is developed as though there are no current organization systems of which he is a part. He can temporarily leave that system (physically and psychologically) to receive training and then be returned to the system as a more effective individual.

The alternative assumption is that the organization is composed of closely linked sets of people whose total knowledge and effort is more than the sum of its individuals. These close linkages and relationships require development as well as the individuals in them. The basic issue for a development program then is whether it focuses upon individual development and change without regard to the employee's relationships back on the job, or whether it must incorporate system changes in order for both the system and the individual to develop and change concurrently. An organization development approach as opposed to a purely MD aproach is concerned with the simultaneous development of both the individual and the intricate set of relationships which exist for him back on the job. The premise of O.D. is that change and development cannot occur within the individual without change in the organizational system. Such system changes support and foster the development in the individual. Similarly, the individual feels greater influence in applying his development and learning to the organization and its issues.

What Is the Most Appropriate Learning Process to Develop and Utilize the Organization's Social and Human Resources?

If the previously stated management development assumptions are valid (that we are developing and training employees for eventual entry into a management elite, that the organization grows by refining its methods and people, and that the individual needs development but the organizational system does not), then this suggests

a fourth assumption concerning the learning and development process required for developing managers. The first assumption is that the most effective development can occur through the following sequence: a curriculum is developed by those representing the philosophies and methods of the management elite, that it is based on the historical precedents of the organization, that this curriculum is then "taught" to promising and potential managers. The management development program is responsible for developing and teaching this curriculum; the participants in the program are responsible for absorbing and remembering it as best they can. The relationship between teacher and learner is a traditional one in which the teacher is assumed to know the problems and the answers. The teacher is thus active and knowledgeable, the student is passive and naive. This approach does not preclude, of course, heated group discussions among teacher and student; but the intended curriculum is still the end point of the development sequence. The management development learning model can be pictured as follows:

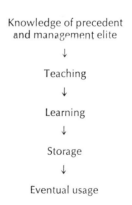

Knowledge of precedent
and management elite

↓

Teaching

↓

Learning

↓

Storage

↓

Eventual usage

Since the participant has had little chance to develop and participate in the curriculum, and has had little opportunity to apply his learnings to his here-and-now organizational issues, evaluation of the management development program and of the participant's learning must necessarily be based on how well the participant has stored his knowledge or how his ideas have been molded to fit in with the company's ideas. Questionnaires, tests, and interviews are frequent follow-ups of management development programs rather than the degree to which the participant has applied his knowledge to immediate organizational issues or changed his organization in some way. Such tests, questionnaires, etc., are entirely appropriate since clear criteria of what the participant should know were established prior to the program and were, therefore, built into the curriculum.

An entirely different learning model follows from the three OD assumptions we have already mentioned (that development must be concerned with actual here-and-now organizational issues and the collaborative skills needed for widely dispersed specialized knowledge, that they must provide learning about change through actual change in the organization, and that the focus of change must be on the organizational system rather than solely on that individual).

First, the OD learning model begins with helping the individual explore and increase his awareness of himself (in the organization). This includes who he is as a person and in relation to other people who are important to him in his work situation. Part of this increased awareness includes the sources of his dissatisfaction and frustration (with self and with his performance) —what he would like to further explore and change in his own behaviors and in his own set of relationships with others who are important to him on the job. Following this awareness, he begins to plan action steps to explore with others these dissatisfactions and frustrations—who to discuss these issues with, natural work situations (meetings, performance evaluation sessions, team-building sessions, etc.) in which to act on these frustrations. The cru-

cial step in the OD learning model is the "action step" actually taken by the participant. And finally, the participant initiates evaluation-research-learning through feedback from others to appraise his actions and their impact on himself and others. This awareness-action-research learning model can be pictured as follows:

Note that the model is circular (rather than the traditional linear model previously described). Learning creates increased awareness for further and perhaps different action which leads to increased learning, etc.

In addition, the OD learning model maximizes a sense of relevance, involvement, and responsibility by the individual. Since the issues for OD come from the individual's own exploration and his own awareness, they are likely to be highly relevant to him. He becomes involved in all phases of the learning model—awareness-action-feedback. For example, he plans and seeks out evaluation—which is a rare occurrence in the traditional learning model. In addition, he takes prime responsibility for the action program—prime responsibility because the cause of his actions are his own (frustrations) and the learnings come from his own experience. He takes the initiative to obtain feedback because he actively wants to learn so that he can become more aware and take more effective action on his own frustrations. Thus the participant is responsible for his own OD/MD program. The management development (OD) coordinator merely facilitates this learning process. Finally the OD learning model results in mutual learning rather than one-way teaching. Those coordinating OD programs are invariably influenced by the increased awareness of individuals about organizational settings. Similarly, employees not directly involved in the OD program are influenced and learn when program participants act upon their increased awareness. And it is in this mutual influence process in the actual work situation that OD tends to change and develop the system as well as the individual.

Assumptions Sometimes Get Confused

It is advisable to explore the methods and values of the organization carefully before dismissing either set of assumptions as invalid. A number of management development programs proceed on the basis of one set of assumptions only to find much later that the basis for this decision was a vague unplanned hope rather than a reality shared by others.

There are a number of research studies concerning training programs which do not take into account the participants' organizational context and relationships and which treat him in isolation from this context. These studies generally indicate that such training programs fail. It has often been found, for example, that participants in a human relations training program tend to gain a more positive attitude toward a participative leadership style. But this favorable attitude tends to decline to its pretraining level when the participant returns to his organization, unless his superior also shares this same attitude. Friedlander (1971) found that a social skills training program for hard-core unemployed had no impact on their performance or retention after job placement; the only thing that did affect the performance and retention was the degree to which the work climate was a supportive one. In both cases, attitude changes resulting from training were temporary and nontransferable from the training situation to the organizational situation. Sometimes, however, the individual does maintain his changed behavior, but the organization cannot tolerate this. Sykes (1962), for example, found that a development program for supervisors which was not congruent with the goals and relationships of its top management caused a number of the supervisors to decide to leave the organization soon after the program was completed.

In the case of OD programs, there must be an agreement between the designers of the management program and those in relevant influential management positions that the development process is part and parcel of the organization process—that the MD/OD program is to be directly applied to immediate organizational issues, that the exploration of these issues will be a crucial part of the program, and that changes in organizational methods, relationships, and personal styles may well follow. The best way to keep the program goals and management goals congruent is to include relevant managers in the OD process.

Once the development programs which match organization goals are in progress, they become meaningful and highly relevant processes for growth—of the individual and the organization. Those in the program know that the organization is with them in their developmental efforts and ready to apply their learnings; and the organization senses a relevance and high regard for the development program.

Nature of an Organization Development Approach to MD

An organization development approach to manager development is a self-instigated developmental process where individuals explore and take steps to change themselves in a direction meaningful to both themselves and the organization.

Typical steps in organization development as it applies to organizational change usually involves the following:

1. Exploration of the problems facing the organization/group/team.

2. Organizational members get together to examine the problems facing their organization.

3. Work together in planning action steps and leverage points for change within their organization.

4. Widening their circle of change and influence in order to bring about viable and realistic change.

5. Instigate the changes.

6. Collect data and feedback to the success of the change.

7. Plan future action steps and changes based on their immediate past experience.

A similar model can be applied to individual change (i.e., MD). The steps when applied to management development are as follows:

1. The individual explores basic problems which he is facing and develops an increased awareness of the things he would like to change.

2. The individual works out (using organizational resources) approaches which he might use to solve the problem or reach goals he wishes to attain.

3. He develops action steps for making change.

4. He enlist the assistance of others within the organization to help him bring about change.

5. He initiates the change.

6. He gets feedback and information from others in the organization on how his new change is working.

7. He then plans the next action step, going through essentially the same processes.

Differences between Traditional MD and an OD Approach to Management Development

More specifically how would traditional MD differ from an OD approach to MD?

The differences as viewed by the author are illustrated below:

MD	OD
1. Packaged programs.	1. Experience based.
2. Responsibility of staff personnel.	2. Responsibility of individual.
3. Inflexible.	3. Flexible.
4. Individual adapts to organization.	4. Individual and organization change together.
5. Safe, predictable.	5. Risky, unpredictable.
6. Individual is passive and inactive.	6. Individual is involved and active in own learning.
7. Highly cognitive (stockpiling information).	7. Cognitive and behavior oriented.

First of all, the developmental processes as usually defined in a management development situation are for the most part self-contained in the training programs. That is, they are usually found in management development programs, courses, and seminars. Contrasted with this, organization development involves open and free experiences associated with daily living and work. With OD the individual may or may not attend courses depending on how they fit his own needs and choices. He is free to make these choices on his own.

Secondly, the responsibility for management development program processes and systems is usually invested in the hands of a management development staff member. On the other hand, under an OD approach the responsibility is vested in the individual, or in some cases a group of people to which the individual is looking for advice and guidance.

Thirdly, under an MD approach, systems and programs remain constant over an extended period of time. That is, once programs are established they stay intact over extended periods of time. OD, on the other hand, is flexible and pliable; there is a high degree of change, and it occurs frequently and quite rapidly. Under MD the individual must adapt to the system. In OD, the individual changes while the system is also changing. In fact, the individual helps to bring about the change in the system.

Fourth, management development processes are relatively safe. They assume that the individual will perform effectively within the context of the programs and procedures which are prescribed. On the other hand, organizational development processes tend to be more risky. The individual may, in fact, experiment with particular learning opportunities and find that they are not suitable for himself. Or, he may develop a particular interest in a field which is not appropriate to the interests of the organization.

Fifth, under an MD approach the individual tends to assume the role of a passive participant, somewhat withdrawn from the organization. He tends to be uncreative and make relatively few contributions to the design of the MD system itself. Contrasted with this, organization development processes require a high degree of involvement of the individual. He is actually very much in it and a part of the process in terms of his own learning as well as learning for the organization.

Sixth, the individual under an MD process is likely to be inactive and inanimate. That is, he sits back and lets it happen to him. In an OD process the individual is vigorously involved in learning. He is moti-vated in terms of doing what is right for himself.

Seventh, management development training is highly cognitive, oriented to storing data and information to be used at some future point in his career. Organization development processes, on the other hand, are action oriented where immediate change and learning takes place. Not only does OD involve cognition, but it is focused on behavior change.

The case for an OD approach to MD seems to outweigh the case for a traditional approach to MD. It appears that management development may not be working in a great many instances, and we may quite likely not be achieving our objectives of fully and successfully designing MD processes to match organizational processes. To fully develop a potential manager, the individual must feel ownership congruity and personal growth between himself and his organization.

REFERENCES

Friedlander, F. and Greenberg, S., "The Effects of Job Attitudes, Training and Organization Climate Upon the Performance of the Hardcore Unemployed," *Journal of Applied Psychology,* vol. 55, pp. 287–95.

Sykes, A., "The Effect of a Supervision Training Course on Supervisors' Perceptions and Expectations of the Role of Management," *Human Relations,* vol. 15, pp. 227–44.

CASES FOR PART FIVE

Case 5–1

RACE RELATIONS IN THE U.S. NAVY

The U.S. Navy was slower to respond to racial problems than the other servives. Perhaps this was because its officers tended to be more elite, its enlisted men were primarily volunteers, and there were relatively few blacks, except for stewards and commissarymen (100 blacks in a ship's complement of 1,300 personnel was not rare).

Nonetheless, with time the racial situation in America came to intrude on the navy's no longer closed society. Black complaints about discriminatory treatment became frequent, and several dangerous incidents occurred on various warships. Typical complaints from black enlisted men concern racist white commissioned officers; lack of remedial training for promotion examinations; more severe punishment meted out to blacks than whites for similar minor infractions; no all-black berthing compartments allowed; restriction of blacks to less attractive jobs in the deck, engineering, and commissary departments, instead of navigation, operations, or electronics; no Afro haircuts, no black films shown in the evenings, and no soul music played on the ship's loudspeakers during holiday routine.

The causes of this situation are of course complex, but a common element has been the insensitivity of almost exclusively white commanding officers to black feelings and aspirations. And outright prejudice is not rare.

The senior naval officer, Admiral Alpha Bravo, determined to take corrective action. As chief of naval personnel before his promotion to chief of naval operations, he had energetically worked to update the navy's image and make it more attractive to young men and women. Revised and more relaxed regulations on haircuts and dress were promulgated, along with many others designed to bridge the gap between civilian and military culture. These orders became famous as "B-grams."

To many officers, however, the B-grams were infamous, for there was widespread disagreement with Bravo's methods and intentions. The traditionalists thought the navy's basic structure was being undermined in a vain search for popularity. This was reinforced when a destroyer commanding officer was removed for what appeared to be just his subordinate's complaints. Nonetheless, Admiral Bravo maintained good relations with Congress and enjoyed a laudatory public press. Applause and resentment were both substantial when the president promoted him to C.N.O., over the heads of 14 admirals senior to him.

The admiral issued directives to commanding officers ordering them to be nondiscriminatory and flexible in relation to minority desires. He realized, however, that orders alone would not be sufficient, because close policing was impossible, some commands were not even aware of their undesired practices, and basic prejudices would remain untouched. Therefore, the admiral appointed a prominent behavioral scientist from a business school to develop a program that would change racial attitudes and behavior in naval commands.

The program developed and implemented was as follows:

1. A team of behavioral scientists was to staff a training center for specialists in human relations.
2. Naval officers were to attend the program full time for several weeks. The program was to utilize a variety of training methods, including lectures on black history and culture, confrontation exercises, and interracial sensitivity training. The intent was to develop substantive knowledge, personnel attitudes, and interpersonal skills.
3. Each program graduate was to be assigned to a naval command as staff advisor to assist the commanding officer in the improvement of the racial climate on his ship or station. One specialist was to be assigned to each station or large vessel and one to a squadron of four to eight smaller ships.

EXHIBIT 1
Military Ranks in U.S. Navy

Navy	Marine Corps
Admiral	General
Vice Admiral	Lieutenant-General
Rear Admiral (Sr.)	Major-General
Rear Admiral (Jr.)	Brigadier-General
Captain	Colonel
Commander	Lieutenant-Colonel
Lieutenant-Commander	Major
Lieutenant	Captain
Lieutenant (junior grade)	1st Lieutenant
Ensign	2nd Lieutenant

An officer with a regular commission is labeled U.S.N. or U.S.M.C. He is usually a graduate of either the naval academy or a college naval scholarship program. His minimum commitment is four years. Some regulars are former enlisted men. An officer with a reserve commission is labeled U.S.N.R. or U.S.M.C.R. He is usually a graduate of a college Reserve Officers Training Corps program or of the three-month Officer Candidate School. His normal commitment is three years. Most officers voluntarily retire (or are involuntarily retired when they are passed over for promotion) at half pay after 20 years' service. Unless they reach the very pinnacle, the rest retire at full pay after 30 years.

The classes consisted of ten participants each. They were selected by the Bureau of Naval Personnel from officers coming up for regular initial appointments or duty transfers. (Ranks of navy and marine corps officers are explained in Exhibit 1.) The following group was typical:

1. Lieutenant (junior grade), U.S.N.R., white, aged 24, 18 months in, two years to serve.
2. Commander, U.S.N., white, age 40, 18 years in.
3. Lieutenant Commander, U.S.N., white, aged 37, 19 years in.
4. Ensign, U.S.N., age 22, black, 0 years in, 4 years to serve.
5. Lieutenant (j.g.), U.S.N.R., black, 2 years in, 1 year to serve.
6. Major, U.S.M.C., white, age 42, 19 years in.
7. Captain, U.S.N., white, age 50, 28 years in.
8. Ensign, U.S.N.R., black, age 23, 2 years service, 1 year to serve.
9. Second Lieutenant, U.S.M.C.R., white, age 22, 0 years in, 3 years to serve.
10. Ensign, U.S.N.R., black, 22 years, 0 years in, 3 years to serve.

Questions

1. What is the change theory underlying this program? What are its assumptions? (E.g., plot the desired changes from faculty all the way to shipboard officers.)
2. What are the problems that you think the program will encounter in actually changing behavior out in the commands? What are the causes of these problems?
3. Analyze the situation of the program graduates.
4. Formulate recommendations to Admiral Bravo to improve the program.
5. What other possible alternatives might exist to change behavior and improve the racial climate in the Navy?

Case 5–2
SAINT MARTIN'S CHALLENGE

Saint Martin's University is a university of 6,000 students in the Northwest. It is well known for athletic success, especially in basketball. The School of Business is one of four undergraduate colleges along with Arts and Letters, Engineering, and Science. Traditionally Arts and Letters had been the largest school (with Business mainly a refuge for the athletes). In recent years, however, Business has grown rapidly, and it shortly will be the largest. Unfortunately, tight economic pressure has restricted faculty growth so that the business school faculty is larger only than engineering, which has a mere 300 students. The dean has pleaded for more teachers to allow the school to reduce teaching load and expand its research, but to no avail. He is even considering resigning to dramatize his discontent over the university administration's treatment of the business school.

The School of Business has been mainly a teaching institution, and its faculty have produced relatively little research. The dean wants to increase research output, partly because he believes it would be the best way to improve the school's reputation and enable it to raise more funds. Following are the comments of two professors on this matter.

Comments by a Teacher-Researcher

About his own work: "Knowledge doubled between 1960 and 1970 and the current doubling will take place in even less time. The university that devotes too much emphasis to current practice trains students about obsolete methods. The focus must be tomorrow's problems as they are being discovered by today's research."

About people in practice: "Time spent with practitioners, with business people and industrialists, means moving back from my proper focus. I do it, but only as the price I must pay to secure the research grants and consulting fees that I need to persevere in my research activities. I don't feel comfortable with practitioners. What I have to say challenges established practice and unsettles personal equities."

About professional societies: "The professional societies to which I belong are oriented to conceptual innovation and change. Such societies provide me with the knowledgeable evaluation of professionals whose opinions I value and with opportunities for publication and reporting."

About students: "I need the feedback that students provide. Much of my intermediate thinking is of the kind that cannot be done in isolation. Students are not committed to current practice. Their response stimulates and motivates me. Furthermore, it is by means of interchange with students that I can evaluate and recruit talent for future help. I hand students half-fashioned material and expect them to work through it to the underlying scientific uniformities. They respond to the excitement inherent in this undertaking. For me there is no difference between research and teaching. If a faculty adheres to research goals, it will merit the support of those who fund academic research and of the superior students who enjoy working at the frontiers of knowledge. However, I can't teach 12 hours a week and advise for another six. I need free time away from students."

About university administrators: "Most university administrators make demands upon my time which I am willing to countenance in return for back-up administrative services, the opportunity to associate with like-minded professionals, and the advantages, if any, of the university's name for publication purposes."

Attitudes about practice-oriented teachers: "The position of teacher-practitioners is difficult to understand. Their opposition to the "publish or perish" dictum is pure rationalization. The universities are full of "mute academicians" who lack the self-discipline to put their thoughts on paper where they will be subject to the scrutiny of other than half-trained minds. Can you convince me that it's more difficult to sound off at the mouth rather than grind out six, seven, or eight drafts of a precisely worded and defensible statement? They say that they sacrifice personal advancement to spend time with their students. My response is whose needs are they serving?"

Comments by a Teacher-Practitioner

About his own work: "Let's not be panicked by the faddists! The role of the university is that stated by Cardinal Newman years ago: Pass on to students the wisdom of the ages. My job is to be in touch with the best in modern business practice, to exemplify it by my behavior, and to communicate it to students."

About people in practice: "The successful business practitioner provides the example for students. My function is to provide a linkage between current practice and the student. I must illustrate my points with current practice drawn from experienced practitioners who opinions will underscore the authenticity of the message I impart."

About professional societies: "The societies to which I belong maintain professional codes and update them by established equities and traditions. Orderly due process is the mode. Informal interchange, most of it oral, and systematic committee work are the instruments. In these societies, I make contacts which are useful to my students and to me personally."

About students: "The personal payback in teaching consists of providing an effective basis for a business career. Substantive knowledge of current practice is accomplished by forceful, organized, and comprehensive classroom presentation. The professional standard is transmitted by personal example and individual conference. A faculty adhering to these arrangements merits the support of business practitioners and will have no difficulty placing graduates."

About university administrators: "Education is a business, and a university lends itself the usual rules of business operation.

Attitudes about research-oriented teachers: "The position of the teacher-researcher is tiresome. They are clamoring for 'writing time' to prepare material for publication that gets them better positions. They have no real interest in either the university or its students. They push the 'research aura' for all its worth to achieve their personal, opportunistic goals. They are never around when students need them, and their classes are usually disorganized and slanted to their own narrow interests."

The Challenge Project

The Challenge Project had been conceived in January as the brain child of the Student Association president, Jim Carroll. On a Sunday afternoon, he had called a meeting of some 40 students, each of whom has previously expressed interest in effecting change at Saint Martin's, and outlined his plans. The group responded enthusiastically. Study groups were immediately formed to audit current practices. The Saint Martin Challenge was born with high hopes.

During the eight weeks of their study, the Challenge groups dug into many issues and their ramifications. Challenge open meetings were heavily attended by students, and the Challenge effort felt it had strong grass roots support. When the booklet "The Saint Martin Challenge" (see the appendix) was published in March it contained the study groups' findings and a list of 54 recommendations for change at Saint Martin's, ranging from abolishing the thesis requirement and the grading system to hiring a director of student affairs and limiting administrative tenure. Student excitement was at a fever pitch, and it was rumored that even some faculty members supported the changes.

In March copies of the document had generated excitement in the students' lounge at Saint Martin's School of Business. The appearance of the little pamphlet entitled "The Saint Martin Challenge" had produced animated discussion and debate among an already restless student body. It had predicted things to come and suggested changes. Now it was November and the mood was strikingly different; disappointment was pervasive. What had happened?

Upon completion of the study, the 40-man Challenge group dissolved but was survived by a five-member Challenge Steering Committee, whose task was to attempt to see the recommendations implemented. Following a conference with the dean, a meeting was scheduled with the faculty.

One Saturday morning in November, Mike Hood, who had chaired one of the original Challenge study groups and had been a founding member of the Challenge Steering Committee, sat alone with his thoughts in the school auditorium. A meeting of the faculty had been held that morning for what he had thought was to vote on acceptance of the proposals, but the professors had now gone, and so, Mike thought, had hopes of seeing the proposals put into effect. The Steering Committee felt that if the faculty would vote acceptance of the proposals, the dean would then be forced to act to implement them.

The faculty vote (Mike thought) was to have taken place this morning. But Mike saw doom in the offing when, as the meeting opened, a notoriously conservative professor rose to address the committee: "Gentlemen, you realize, of course, that we are not prepared to vote on these proposals this morning. To do so would be unthinkably rash." And the debate that took place over the next several hours was fragmented, inconclusive, and showed little support for the proposals. The faculty meeting ended with no action taken—not even an agreement to meet again.

A disappointed Mike now pondered what action to recommend to his fellow students on the Challenge Steering Committee. They had adopted a policy of acting "through the proper channels" in advocating the Challenge recommendations, but all along they had felt strong student pressure for a protest demonstration to make demands instead of recommendations. Mike realized that this pressure would be strengthened by the defeat of his moderate tactics. As Steering Committee Chairman, Mike faced a critical decision: What to do?

Questions

1. How could the dean change the school from its historically predominant teacher-practitioner orientation to the teacher-researcher view? What do you recommend?
2. What was Mike Hood's change theory? Why didn't it work?
3. What should Mike and the steering committee have done differently to promote the desired changes?
4. What are Mike's alternatives now? What do you recommend?

APPENDIX

THE SAINT MARTIN CHALLENGE

Recommendations Summary

1. The dean of the School of Business should be made a full-time administrator who should be paid an administrator's, as opposed to a faculty member's, salary, which is commensurate with the prestige and responsibility of the position.
2. There should be a director of student affairs and a director of public relations in the Business School.
3. The Business School should be reorganized so that the dean has a direct authority line relationship to the director of admissions, the director of alumni affairs, the director of student affairs, and the director of public relations, and a formalized functional relationship with the director of the university placement service.
4. The Business School should have a formal committee chaired by the dean, composed of a faculty representative from each department and at least three students to plan and coordinate the program.
5. The dean should be given budgetary authority to include: payment of salaries to his directors and other administrative assistants, payment of salaries to all clerical personnel, and maintenance of an adequate discretionary fund.
6. There should be an immediate effort initiated to evaluate present costs of programs within the school, including the departments, and to develop a viable and practical budgeting system within the school.
7. The admissions committee should be expanded to include student and more faculty representatives and be given the responsibility of making and evaluating admissions policy.
8. The number of recruiters should be expanded by including the major administrators and, if need be, alumni and students.
9. The present level of recruitment of minority groups should continue and, if possible, increase.

10. Interview procedures should be evaluated to ensure that interviews are available to all applicants and that effective use is made of students as interviewers.

11. A self-evaluating essay question should be added to the admissions application.

12. A full manpower requirements study should be made of the present and future secretarial-clerical needs of the school's administration functions.

13. An assistant director of admissions should be hired immediately.

14. Five full-time secretarial-clerical personnel should be hired immediately, two for the administration office and three for the admissions office.

15. The construction of New Hall should begin as soon as possible, and the need for this should be presented to the board of trustees.

16. The final proposed floor plan of New Hall should be evaluated to ensure that administrative office and student needs will be satisfied.

17. Full use should be made of existing facilities within Wellington Hall to alleviate the present overcrowding of the administrative offices; this should include the conversion of classrooms if necessary.

18. The present $6 portion of the general fee which is returned to the Business School should be increased to provide a wider program of student activities.

19. A high-level group should be formed to evaluate the School of Business, and its recommendations as to where the needs of the school program should rank within the priorities of Saint Martin's University should be submitted to the appropriate decision-making authorities and the board of trustees.

20. The name of the school should be changed, at least in common usage, to Saint Martin's School of Management.

21. There should be specific limits on terms in major administrative offices, and these administrators—particularly the dean—should be selected from among the best of *both* the academic and business communities.

22. Saint Martin's should establish a continuous process to discover what business demands and will demand from students and then relate these to the Business School program appropriately.

23. The lecture method should be deemphasized. Other methods such as cogent class discussion should be used more often. Professors should demand more from the students during such classroom dialogues, producing a challenging environment from which all can learn.

24. More take-home examinations or other examinations requiring thought rather than memorization should be used. There should be time for an adequate review of all examinations, including the final.

25. The size of classes should be as small as possible, and in no case larger than 35.

26. More seminars should be offered.

27. The physical layout of the classroom should be flexible.

28. The Business School should adopt a Distinguished–Pass–No Credit grading system (in replacement of the existing A, B, C, D, fail).

29. Inasmuch as grades may be retained, the full range should apply equally to all courses.

30. Grades should not be released to anyone without the explicit consent of the individual student. Emphasis on grades in recruiting should be lowered.

31. The thesis should be made optional.

32. Meaningful alternatives to the thesis, such as a small seminar, should be widely offered.

33. The core-and-bracket required-course structure should be redesigned by a joint student-faculty group to reflect the current needs of students (approximately 50 percent of a student's courses are required).

34. The core-and-bracket courses should coordinate more fully with other courses.

35. Remedial math training should be offered on a noncredit basis.

36. The school should offer more courses related to consulting.

37. Training in business social responsibility should be offered.

38. There should be a Business Communications general elective course.

39. More courses emphasizing small business and entrepreneurship should be established.

40. The school needs to place more emphasis on management techniques rather than the strictly business approach. We should assess possible additional majors more administratively oriented (e.g., Hospital, Social, Government, and Education Administration).

41. The registration process should aim at providing the courses desired by students in the most efficient manner possible.

42. Students should evaluate the faculty through course questionnaires, and the results should be made public.

43. The *Bulletin* should be revised to better reflect the needs of the Business School, its public relations, and program description.

44. Saint Martin's must assure that the faculty have enough time to teach properly.

45. As much as possible, faculty projects should be related to their classroom work.

46. The present required adviser system should be replaced with an optimal one, in addition to standard sources of information being made available.

47. The present student-to-faculty teaching-hour ratio must be lowered.

48. In-house research studies should be conducted on faculty functioning.

49. Faculty should be reimbursed for the time spent on special administrative committees.

50. Saint Martin's should establish a "Businessmen-in-Residence" Program designed to bring members of top management to the school for an appropriate length of time each semester.

51. Saint Martin's should have a good continuing education program, including a campus Executive Development Program designed to attract both alumni and nonalumni from a wide geographical area.

52. There should be a strong development and research program at the school designed to build good ties with the business community.

53. Contacts between students and alumni should be increased, and alumni should be used in the educational process.

54. Saint Martin's should sponsor more programs designed to increase rapport with all segments of the local community.

Case 5-3

INDUSTRIAL ENGINEERING AT CHEMTECH CORPORATION

The Chemtech Corporation is a large, multiple-products chemical concern. The industrial engineering division is officially "staff" to the plant manager; the director of I.E. reports to an assistant plant manager. However, internally, I.E. is organized into areas and groups paralleling the plant manufacturing divisions and departments. An engineer in industrial engineering normally serves one or two department heads. The engineer's superior, an I.E. group leader, gives official staff support to an engineer's proposals to a production department supervisor while "working for" the superintendent of a manufacturing division.

Industrial engineering performs both measurement and methods studies. Measurement work is an elaboration of the work of the time-study person. The industrial engineer is primarily concerned with deriving figures that can be used to relate production (or other control figures) to labor use. This information may be the basis for individual and group incentive standards or for fixed-pay-labor control plans to provide data to management for evaluation purposes. The techniques have expanded from simple observation with a stop-watch to work-sampling procedures utilizing IBM card

EXHIBIT 1
Parallel Industrial Engineering and Manufacturing Organizations

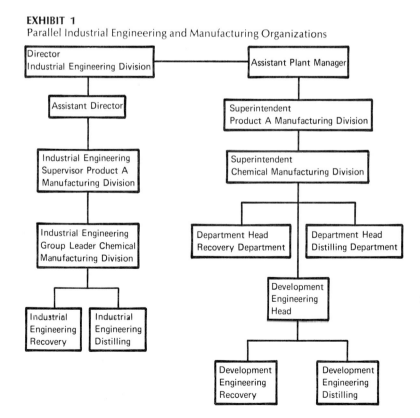

systems and various mathematical correlation techniques with electronic computers. A major part of the measurement work requires the engineer to be on the floor in the production area.

Methods work for the industrial engineering field covers a broad range from modern applications of Gilbreth's therbligs to sophisticated statistical and regression techniques utilizing modern computers. In most cases, methods study on hand motions is done before piece-rate incentive standards are set, but this type of work is of lesser interest. Layout and design have been traditional industrial engineering activities, and a substantial amount of this is done in the company. However, because of the growing field, the interest of the newer engineers is in applications of multiple-regression techniques, linear programming, and inventory control.

Industrial engineering performs both advisory and service work. The solution of recurring work-flow problems may be aided by skilled engineers who can analyze production methods. The use of piece-work systems requires that the production departments call on industrial engineering to develop incentive standards. Another service relationship involves the handling of new and revamped machine layouts and job descriptions when equipment and procedural changes are made.

The plant has a tradition of ensuring strong autonomy for the production organization at the superintendent level. In formal statements of company policy, industrial engineering is clearly subordinated to the superintendent. Industrial engineering is expected to be mainly a service or advisory staff agency, and the superintendent of the chemical manufacturing division is free to decide whether to utilize its services or not.

Service relationships are often neither comfortable nor easy to maintain. And many "advisers" do not wait to be asked. They initiate the contacts with those who are supposed to call on them. Before putting people to work on new activities and techniques, an industrial engineering manager finds it useful to have identified an existing production "problem" that needs solving. Thus, rather than waiting to be called on, industrial engineering spends substantial time in searching for problems on which it can obtain assignments.

In their work in the production department, engineers try to become intimately familiar with what appear to be difficulties. Although they may not be asked to work on these problems specifically, these problems help them to direct their thinking toward the underlying or less-apparent conditions. It is then up the engineers to establish a case for their prospective studies, indicating their estimates of the scope of the problems and potential savings. Approval is required from both I.E. supervision and the chemical plant superintendent.

Although the ideas for assignments have originated with industrial engineers, sometimes they recognize that the nature of the jobs or the personalities of the department heads are such that chances for approval and success will be enhanced if the production people feel it was their idea. This leads to "planting" the idea with a department head. Often, both know whose idea it is, but the fiction ensures cooperation. Actual authorization requires approval by the superintendent, and this little ruse makes it more likely that the department head will be a political ally in future discussions with the superintendent.

The industrial engineering division historically has served as a training area for the whole corporation. In academic achievement and general promise its engineers rank near the top of the firm. Employment in the industrial engineering division gives these people wide access to valuable experience and influential managers. Normal service in the department averages about three years after which the engineers generally move into a production department. The path of promotion is definitely up the line hierarchy. Few desire to stay in technical work, and many are enrolled in the local university's evening M.B.A. program.

Work with Chemical Manufacturing
Division Superintendent

The superintendent of the chemical manufacturing division has a strong personality. He is in his late 40s and started in the division as a development engineer. His education as a chemical engineer and experience as a development engineer have strengthened his interest in the technical aspects of all proposals, and he exercises close supervision over innovative and capital-investment recommendations. Since most innovative ideas that are eventually adopted originate with the division's own development engineers, the superintendent encourages them to talk with him about ideas and demands it when he learns of problem areas.

In addition, the promotion ladder to chemical plant supervisory ranks is through the development engineer position. Accordingly, the superintendent is anxious to give these people as much experience as possible. He encourages (almost indoctrinates) them to work on their own without calling for advisory assistance.

To a significant extent, industrial engineering is management engineering and provides good experience for a future manager. The superintendent is aware of this and wants the development engineers to gain some of this training by performing their own work of this type.

For all these reasons, the chemical plant superintendent is opposed to any extension of industrial engineering activities beyond the relatively routine service work that they have to perform to maintain incentive plans. He discourages what he calls "idle speculation on my time and budget." His intimidation of department heads discourages them from going to him for approval of I.E. projects that they would like to see performed. The superintendent's well-maintained technical expertise subjects department heads to unpleasant grilling when they propose study programs to him.

Work Relationship with Production
Department Supervisors

The supervisor and assistant supervisors all have come up from the ranks in the same department. Their functions consist most simply in getting people on the right jobs at the right time. The recovery department has many types of equipment and a large number of miscellaneous hand operations. All these activities are not performed simultaneously, and it is the responsibility of the supervisors to assign the workers as necessary in order to meet the schedule for each shift. The closeness and accessibility of development engineers and higher supervision relieve them of concern about technological aspects of the equipment.

There is no question that one of the most fertile sources of problem identification is the supervisors. In any dicussion with them, they mention explicit problem conditions. However, the individual supervisor is not inclined to request I.E. assistance on methods problems because of a limited knowledge regarding their functions and lack of reciprocal interactions with industrial engineering. A major part of the supervisors' experience with I.E. has been as unwilling subjects of time studies for incentive pay plans (when they were still hourly paid operators).

With the exception of questions on incentive standards, supervisors seldom initiate interaction with an industrial engineer. On the other hand, virtually every completed assignment by an engineer results in some action by them. In many cases this means new forms and calculations for incentive performance of a crew. Most supervisors see little reason for having group incentive standards and intensely dislike making the necessary calculations. Except for a few initial questions, nothing in their operational job requirements makes it necessary to call in industrial engineering unless new standards are required. They try to avoid the engineer as much as possible.

Because of familiarity and physical proximity, supervisors naturally go to the development engineer or department head when they have problems or ideas. This is also related to the nature of their jobs and their production goals. For the most part, they are concerned with short-term operational matters that demand solutions relatively quickly. When it is necessary to have I.E. do service work (setting a temporary standard), this is an operational matter and they consult an engineer. However, they are not really aware of the I.E.'s availability for advisory problem solving, i.e., methods work, and even if they were, the formal procedure for requesting I.E. services of this nature discourages involvement for a short-term problem.

The Director's Concern

Fundamentally the director of industrial engineering is dissatisfied with the relationship between engineers and production managers. In spite of an accounting procedure under which engineering service is "free' to line managers (they are not directly charged—industrial engineering is absorbed in plant overhead), production departments simply do not consult engineering on important matters as much as is thought desirable by the director and higher management. Since the company has a tradition of great autonomy for line managers, the director doubts that the plant manager would force such consultation on lower managers. Accordingly, the director is wondering how to improve industrial engineering performance so that managers would consider the engineers more helpful.

Questions

1. Analyze why the staff industrial engineers are not consulted by manufacturing management for methods work.
2. What are the possible alternative plans for improving the performance of the industrial engineering staff? What do you recommend?
3. What are the possible alternative plans for improving the relationship between industrial engineering and manufacturing management? What do you recommend? Formulate a systematic change program.

PART SIX

"I'll never make it . . .
I suffer from acrophobia."

MANAGERIAL CAREERS

READINGS

6–1

"Confucius on the Stages of Life."

6–2

"Charles Pilliod Was the Odd Man In at Goodyear," Arthur M. Louis.

6–3

"Why Bosses Turn Bitchy," Rosabeth Moss Kanter.

6–4

"The Management of Stress," Karl E. Weick.

6–5

"An Assessment of Supervisors' Organizational Loyalty," John A. Pearce II.

6–6

"The Black MBA: The Vanguard Generation Moves Up," *MBA*.

6–7

"Tokenism: Opportunity or Trap?" Rosabeth Moss Kanter.

6–8

"Women in Management: An Endangered Species?" John F. Veiga.

6–9

"The Hardest Job of All: Career Planning," Thomas G. Gutteridge.

CASES

6–1   Young Engineers at Dynamic Tech Corporation.

6–2   The Young Supervisor.

6–3   The Case of the Plateaued Performer.

Confucius on the Stages of Life

When I was fifteen, intended to
   live by study
When I was thirty, stand alone
When I was forty, free from
   vacillation
When I was fifty, submit to
   Heaven's will
When I was sixty, know the way
When I was seventy, live in the
   laws of nature.

吾十有五而志於學
三十而立　四十而不惑
五十而知天命　六十而耳順
七十而從心所欲不踰矩

A lot of people were amazed when Charles J. Pilliod, Jr. was appointed president of the Goodyear Tire & Rubber Co. five years ago. Although he had been one of five executive vice presidents with a shot at the job —the final stepping-stone to the position of chairman and chief executive—Pilliod seemed to be burdened with a couple of large handicaps.

Practically his entire career had been spent with Goodyear's foreign operations, including a 19-year stint in Latin America and Great Britain. No one had ever risen to the top at Goodyear without plenty of experience on the domestic side of the business, which last year accounted for about two-thirds of the company's $5.8 billion in revenues. When the presidency opened up in 1972, Pilliod was based in Akron as the head of Goodyear International. But to the rank and file in the domestic operation, he was an obscure figure at best. Few had ever met him, and many—including even some middle-level executives—had trouble placing his name.

Winner by a Clear Margin

His second handicap was that he had never graduated from college. Pilliod's parents had been long on children but short on funds. He had struggled for five semesters in an effort to work his way through two colleges in Ohio but finally gave up in frustration and took a job as a Goodyear trainee. If the professional odds makers were interested in such things, they undoubtedly would have made Pilliod a very dark horse indeed in the run for the Presidency.

To the man empowered to make the choice, however, Pilliod was the winner by a clear margin. Russell DeYoung, who was Goodyear's chief executive at the time, spent several long nights analyzing the records of each candidate. "I took out a pad of paper and wrote down everything I

READING 6–2

Charles Pilliod Was the Odd Man In at Goodyear*

ARTHUR M. LOUIS

could think of with respect to each candidate, and I'd give a plus or minus in each category," he recalls.

DeYoung felt that the crucial considerations were "how they handled their organizations, what their organizations thought of them, how they performed." When DeYoung finished totting up the results, Pilliod, despite his unorthodox background, had thoroughly outclassed the competition. "There wasn't *any* doubt in my mind," says DeYoung. Pilliod became the chief executive in 1974, when DeYoung retired.

Pilliod is not bashful about his success, which he forthrightly attributes to "a desire to excel—a drive to do better than the other guy." He was an ardent athlete in his youth, and the competitive urge carried over into his business career with full force. "I was always looking for something new and different, for ways to improve an oper-

* Reprinted from the May 1977 issue of *Fortune* Magazine by special permission; © 1977 Time Inc.

Note: Charles Pilliod, Jr., is president of the Goodyear Tire and Rubber Co.

ation. I was inquisitive, always trying to find solutions to our problems.

"I worked more than the others; I put in more time. In the process, I also learned a lot. I don't think I was any smarter than anyone else, but if you're working more than the other fellow, you get that much more experience. Each place I went, I did a little better than the guy ahead of me, and in retrospect better than the guy who followed me."

However, Pilliod has yet to prove he can "do better" than DeYoung. Goodyear's financial results have been pretty dismal lately.

Go Climb a Pole

As he made his way to the top, Pilliod sometimes could be difficult to get along with. His colleagues recall that he was a notorious meddler, who would badger people in other departments to do things his way. Within his own jurisdiction, he seemed to be trying to run the whole show himself. Though he might occupy a lofty managerial position, he would get involved in the most picayune details.

As the sales manager in Columbia during the 1950s, for example, Pilliod once ordered one of his top lieutenants to measure the Goodyear display sign atop a 40-foot pole outside a dealership in Bogotá. He had driven past the dealership one evening, and thought the sign did not conform to the company's size standards. He was wrong.

Pilliod was blessed with tremendous physical strength, which he often pushed to the breaking point. "Chuck's around-the-clock involvement with the job has been quite fantastic," remarks a long-time associate. "By the standards of lesser mortals, he certainly has overdone it." Today, at the age of 58, he remains a fitness fanatic, rising at 5:00 in the morning so he can complete a full exercise routine and still get to the office by 7:30. He tugs away at a rowing machine, runs in place, lifts weights, and does the usual calisthenics. He also likes to fish, hunt, ski, and play golf. He can drive the ball more than 300 yards, though his accuracy leaves something to be desired. His handicap is a fairly respectable 12.

The Wrestling Guard

Pilliod likes to brag that he was raised "in the shadow of Goodyear's smoke-stacks." He was born on October 20, 1918, in Cuyahoga Falls, Ohio, just northeast of Akron. His father, a second-generation American of French descent, was a maintenance superintendent at an Ohio Edison plant in Akron and also kept a small farm, where he raised corn, grapes, and chickens. Charles, Jr. was the third of five children.

After attending a Roman Catholic grade school, Pilliod went to public high school, where he made quite a mark as an athlete. He starred in the two roughest interscholastic sports, playing guard for the football team and achieving an unbeaten record with the wrestling team. After graduating in 1937, he wanted to go to college, and then to law school. But his father had lost his job in the depression, and was barely managing to keep the family afloat by running a dry-cleaning business. If he was going to continue his education, Charles, Jr., would have to finance himself.

He made a valiant attempt. He enrolled at Muskingum College, in central Ohio, and took on several part-time jobs while carrying a full load of courses. After two semesters, he dropped out for a year, to help around the house while his mother recuperated from a heart ailment. Then he entered Kent State University, which was located a few miles from home. He attended classes all day, worked at a confectionary for seven hours each night, and then got around to his homework.

In 1941, after three semesters at Kent, he concluded that his schedule was "too much of a grind." He decided to drop out again and get a job with one of the big rubber companies in Akron. He would earn a nice pile of money and then, perhaps, resume his education. Although he was a dropout, he had a glowing letter of recommendation from one of his professors, and Firestone, Goodrich, and Goodyear all seemed interested in him. Pilliod found the offer from Goodyear the most appealing. He joined the company as a production trainee, at 67 cents an hour.

Into the Wild Blue Yonder

Production trainees were supposed to spend three years mastering every task in the Goodyear factories. Most trainees were fired long before the three years were up, but those who completed the course often were promoted to white-collar jobs with the company. Pilliod was assigned to work at the factory from 11 at night until seven in the morning, and sometimes he worked a second shift as well. He also spent several hours a week attending management courses conducted by the Goodyear staff. He did so well that within a year his salary was raised to the trainee maximum—$1.15 an hour. While still technically in the program, he was made a supervisor.

At the time the United States entered World War II, Pilliod was supervising the production of fuel tanks for military aircraft. He was exempt from the draft, but by the summer of 1942 he was feeling conspicuous—and a bit guilty—as a strong, healthy civilian. He enlisted in the Army Air Corps, and trained to become a bomber pilot. When the corps issued a call for pilots interested in flying a mysterious "new airplane," Pilliod volunteered and soon found himself at the controls of a huge B-29.

From bases in China and Indochina he flew about 15 bombing missions against the Japanese. His first mission was part of the first successful run against the Japanese mainland after Jimmy Doolittle's celebrated attack in April 1942. The missions, lasting 15 hours, were nerve-shattering affairs, punctuated by antiaircraft fire. His plane was hit several times, but neither he nor any of his crew was injured.

Years later, as a high-level Goodyear executive, Pilliod visited Japan, and one of his hosts asked him if he knew a certain Japanese city. "Would you like me to draw a diagram of it?" Pilliod replied, "I bombed it." His host, he says, "got a big kick out of it."

After being discharged from the service in October 1945, Pilliod returned to Goodyear. He was put on the staff of Goodyear International—then known as Goodyear Export—as assistant to the general manager. He intended to go back to college the following September. But in the meantime he married his childhood sweetheart, Marie Elizabeth Jacobs (they now have three sons and two daughters). He also became thoroughly engrossed in his work, and he gave up any thought of earning a college degree.

Only about one eighth of the chief executives of Fortune 500 companies did not graduate from college. But from his present eminence, Pilliod can afford to be blasé about his aborted educational career. "I would have liked to have attained the degree," he remarks. "I favor education. It has certain advantages."

Reading Up on Salesmanship

Pilliod had developed a great affection for China during the war, and he persuaded his boss to assign him there. Goodyear then maintained offices in both Shanghai and Canton, and Pilliod was to start out as a salesman. But with the Communists steadily expanding their control over the country, he never did get there. In the spring of

1947, he was transferred instead to Panama, as managing director of the company's subsidiary in that country.

Being the head of Goodyear-Panama was a lot less impressive than it might sound. The subsidiary did not have any production facilities. It consisted only of a sales operation and a decrepit retreading plant. It employed just 20 people altogether and generated about $1 million a year in revenues.

But Pilliod plunged into his job as though the entire future of the corporation depended on his efforts. He demanded that the retreading plant be restored to top condition, and he himself wielded paintbrushes, hammers, and an acetylene torch to help get the chore done. He bought and read half a dozen books on salesmanship, then embarked on a one-man sales campaign, visiting every truck owner in Panama with a fleet of five or more trucks. Pilliod personally provided free pickup and delivery when the fleet owners needed repairs, retreads, or new tires.

Wheels Are Better than Hooves

He would visit the banana plantations in neighboring Costa Rica, drumming up still more business. Most of the plantation owners transported bananas across their property on the backs of mules. They feared that carts, although more efficient, would tear up the irrigated ground. But Pilliod got them to convert to mule-drawn carts— equipped with Goodyear tires, of course— by demonstrating mathematically, and then with field tests, that tires exerted less pressure per square inch than a mule's hoof.

He also succeeded in unloading a huge surplus of foam rubber on the plantation owners. The material had been ordered by his predecessor, who had incorrectly anticipated a postwar boom in the Central American furniture business. Pilliod stuffed the foam into inner tubes, and sold his con-

coction as a shoulder pad for plantation workers who had to tote the heavy banana stems. It was a big hit. Until then, the workers had been using pads made of canvas stuffed with kapok, which tended to abrade the banana skins and were more difficult to clean.

In his four years as managing director of Goodyear-Panama, Pilliod more than doubled the subsidiary's revenues. He increased the company's share of the tire market from 17 percent to more than 35 percent and turned the retreading plant from a chronic money-loser into one of the most profitable in the Goodyear empire.

In 1951, he was sent to Goodyear-Peru, to sell the company's line of industrial products, not only in Peru, but also in Chile and Bolivia. To win new customers, Pilliod decided to peddle his wares to the countless mining companies scattered throughout the Andes. He traveled into areas so remote that few Americans—and certainly no Goodyear salesmen—had gone before him. To establish his good intentions, he would don a protective helmet and lantern himself, and then go crawling through the mine shafts. Invariably, he would come down from the mountains with a briefcase full of orders for Goodyear products such as conveyor belts, rubber hose, and protective rubber coatings.

Ordeal of a Salesman

During one memorable sales trip, he literally almost worked himself to death. In La Paz, Bolivia, he boarded a night train that was to carry him across the Altiplano to the copper mines near Quechisla. His compartment had a broken window, and he woke up in the morning with a bad cold. He spent most of the day touring the dank, cold mines, then took another train to Oruro, where he visited more mines. By the next morning, he had lost his voice, but he plunged boldly on, visiting still more mines near Oruro. By that evening, he was coughing blood.

There weren't any hospitals nearby, so Pilliod went to the local office of W. R. Grace & Co. and explained his plight. The office manager told him to lie down on a bed in a room on the second floor. He called in the local doctor, who diagnosed a severe case of pneumonia. Pilliod remained flat on his back for two days, until some penicillin could be brought in from La Paz. After two more days, he was feeling much better and insisted on continuing his tour.

He traveled to Potosí but almost immediately he had a relapse and had to spend a full day in bed at his hotel. Then he was up again and off to Cochabamba, where he visited a few more mines. Finally he returned to La Paz and then flew home to Lima. "I got some pretty good sales along the way," he remarks. He never bothered to tell his superiors about his illness.

Pilliod was appointed sales manager of Goodyear-Colombia in 1954. As the title implies, he was supposed to manage the sales staff. But he spent much of his time in the field, making sales on his own.

Jack Carter, a colleague from those days, recalls traveling with Pilliod to Sogamoso. "He never had any hesitation to eat in places where flies were crawling over the food, grease and dirt were on the floor, the plates had only been brushed off—not washed. When we went to Sogamoso, it was the time of the bandits. People would travel in convoys. We stayed at a hotel with a single light out front. The room I got had four or five beds. In the morning, you would wake up and find you had roommates. When I opened a window, I found a goat staring me in the face. That kind of facility never bothered Chuck."

Pilliod fancied himself an expert on advertising, and he was always in conflict with the advertising manager, a Colombian named Eduardo Arango. Arango was just as bullheaded as Pilliod, and the two would get into long, loud arguments. On a couple of occasions they nearly came to blows.

Breaking the Cord

One afternoon the sales and advertising departments were making a joint presentation to some Goodyear dealers in Bogotá. The company had just begun producing nylon-cord tires, and in one corner of the room there was a display case, with a large hammer swinging back and forth between a nylon cord and a rayon cord. After a few blows with the hammer, the rayon would break and would have to be replaced, but the nylon seemed impervious to damage.

Arango took the podium. With a mischievious gleam in his eye, he told the assembled dealers: "We all know how strong Mr. Pilliod is. But even Mr. Pilliod couldn't break this nylon cord." Pilliod, taken by surprise, responded instinctively to the challenge. He wrapped the ends of the cord around his hands, strained mightily—and snapped it in two. Most of the advertising staff—but not Arango—laughed.

In 1956, Pilliod was appointed sales manager of Goodyear's subsidiary in Brazil. The Brazilian operation was the largest by far in Latin America and the fourth largest outside the United States—after Canada, Great Britain, and Australia. Though Brazil was recognized as a nation with fabulous economic potential, Goodyear-Brazil was in trouble. Its tire factory, located in São Paulo, had recently experienced a rash of production problems. Sales had fallen off, and the salesmen were demoralized.

Pilliod says that the men who had been running Goodyear-Brazil had failed to respond adequately either to its potential or its problems. "The managing director was not taking the responsibilities of managing the company," he remarks, "and the sales manager was not doing *his* job. I was doing the best sales job in Latin America, so I was sent in to see if I could put some life into the company."

Trophies for the Best and Worst

Pilliod's main challenge was to restore the morale of his salesmen, and he did a masterful job of it. For example, he organized an annual competition between the ten branch offices. The branch that produced the most effective sales presentation received a nice trophy.

The worst branch got a trophy too—a statuette of a straggly-haired, disheveled salesman, holding his nose. The manager of the losing branch was required to display the booby prize in his office. A crude gimmick, to be sure, but it generated incredible enthusiasm among the salesmen. It also generated some heavy betting on the side.

In 1959, Pilliod was promoted to managing director of the Brazilian subsidiary. He took over at a time when Brazil was in the early throes of a grotesque inflation, with prices rising at an average of 30 or 40 percent a year. The economy was thriving despite the inflation, and Pilliod was eager to expand his manufacturing capacity.

But the people back in Akron were reluctant to make any large investments until things became more stable. By borrowing heavily, and using every bit of his cash flow, Pilliod was able to buy an old fabric mill next to the plant in São Paulo and expand his tire-manufacturing facilities. He doubled Goodyear's output in Brazil, and when he left in 1963, the subsidiary was selling everything it could make.

He was assigned next to Goodyear-Great Britain, where he served a brief apprenticeship as director of sales, then became the managing director. The British operation was the jewel in Goodyear International's crown, a substantial company in its own right, with three factories, 7,000 employees, and revenues of nearly $100 million. Even Pilliod will admit that the subsidiary was "in pretty good shape" when he stepped in.

But he still managed to find ways to improve things. He reorganized the sales department, getting rid of what he considered excess personnel—managers and salesmen alike. He greatly expanded the subsidiary's chain of retail stores. And, in what he considers the most important of all his efforts abroad, he built an 833,000-square-foot plant at Craigavon, in Northern Ireland. The facility still is Goodyear's largest industrial-products plant. In the three years Pilliod spent at Goodyear-Great Britain, its sales and revenues grew by an average of 9 percent annually, nearly twice the growth rate before he arrived. The growth rate has slowed down again since his departure, although Pilliod modestly suggests that the economy is to blame.

Two Years on the Road

In 1966, he was called back to Akron to serve as second in command to Richard Thomas, the president of Goodyear International. As director of operations, Pilliod would have day-to-day authority over all of the company's foreign subsidiaries. He didn't want the job, however, and he tried to wriggle out. "Most people in the foreign field are not anxious to get back to the States," he explains. "They like the pay, the perquisites, and the responsibility, the fact that they're running their own show."

Thomas brushed aside Pilliod's protests and ordered him to return. He did so, but he still managed to spend a great deal of his time abroad. Out of the five years he held the job, he spent about two on the road.

Pilliod was promoted to president of Goodyear International in January, 1971, and made a vice president of the parent company as well. Eight months later he was given the more exalted title of executive vice president and was elected to the board of directors.

The president of Goodyear, Victor Holt, was due to retire in July, 1972. The smart money assumed that his successor would be either John Gerstenmaier, the executive vice president in charge of tire manufacturing, or Richard Jay, who was in charge of general products. Pilliod and the two other executive vice presidents—Charles Eaves Jr., in charge of tire sales, and Bruce Robertson, the chief financial officer—were considered marginal candidates.

Line of Succession

One day DeYoung walked into Pilliod's office, and casually inquired about the line of succession at Goodyear International. "Who would take your place if you left this job?" DeYoung asked. Pilliod said his choice would be Ib Thomsen, a native of Denmark, who was serving as director of operations. "And who would replace *him?*" They continued down the hierarchy a few more notches. At last, DeYoung said, "That's fine. You've been elected president of the company, and we've decided to make the announcement this Tuesday." "I was the most surprised guy in the world," says Pilliod.

After Pilliod was made chief executive, his two main rivals also moved up. Gerstenmaier succeeded him as president, and Jay became vice chairman. Robertson is still the chief financial officer, while Eaves retired last year.

As his retirement approached, DeYoung relinquished his authority in stages. He made Pilliod the chief executive on New Year's Day, 1974, but kept the title of chairman until April, when he reached the mandatory retirement age of 65. The procedure seemed a trifle mysterious. Some observers thought DeYoung had been eased out early by Goodyear's directors, because of his par-

ticipation in the company's illegal contribution to the 1972 Nixon campaign. DeYoung had voluntarily confessed to making the $40,000 contribution, but at a dramatic Senate hearing in November, 1973, he gruffly resisted when a senator suggested that he should also repent.

Actually, the manner of DeYoung's withdrawal had a more mundane explanation. By retiring as chief executive just before the start of the year, he got certain tax breaks relating to his deferred income. DeYoung is still a director of Goodyear and is chairman of the executive committee.

Pilliod, by all accounts, had nothing to do with the campaign contribution, but it did haunt the company during the early part of his administration. He found that the publicity had caused "a little bit of a morale problem" among the people at Goodyear. "Some of our people were embarrassed," he says, "but as time went on, it became evident that all these practices were quite prevalent, and ours in relation to others was not unusual. The morale problem soon disappeared."

Pilliod points out that campaign contributions by corporations, although illegal, had been a common practice, and he thinks it was unfair to suddenly make a big fuss about them. "Laws become laws when you decide to enforce them," he says. "Sodomy in the home is illegal, yet you can buy books telling you how to do it. You can find laws on the books against anything, and you can find things that are immoral that the laws don't cover."

R. and D. for Leadership

As one might expect, Pilliod has made some big changes at Goodyear since taking over. He felt that the company had been too slow to produce radial tires for the U.S. market, and he promptly went into radials on an enormous scale. Goodyear now is the largest seller of radials by far in this country, and worldwide it appears to be a close second to Michelin, the French manufacturer.

Pilliod has placed much heavier emphasis on Goodyear's research and development. "I believe that to maintain leadership, that's where we've got to start," he remarks. He also has begun a program to modernize Goodyear's 139 plants and to assure that any new plants will contain the best, most efficient equipment available. "We've had teams traveling all over the world, investigating the latest designs. They've been looking at competitors' facilities, too, when they're able."

Goodyear has had some big problems since Pilliod became chief executive. The company emerged from the economic turmoil of 1974 and 1975 with higher sales but lower earnings. And last year, while revenues were reaching an all-time high (the company is no. 23 on the 500 list), earnings plunged by 24 percent, to $122 million, their lowest level since 1966. Goodyear's domestic production was severely disrupted during the year by a 130-day strike at 15 tire plants. But the greatest drain on earnings occurred in Goodyear International. Its operations were hit hard by soaring inflation and by currency losses.

Going Down the Line

Some of Pilliod's subordinates find it difficult to adjust to his management style. Evidently that style hasn't changed much since the early days in Latin America. He will sit in on the weekly meetings of the production staff and break in repeatedly with his own notions about how to design tire machines. Or he will walk into a sales meeting, grab an artist's rendition of a Goodyear retail store, and pencil in his own modifications. He frequently ignores the chain of command and telephones managers far down the line to discuss their performances and their problems.

His colleagues are surprisingly frank in expressing their reservations about Pilliod. The frankest of all are his two old rivals, John Gerstenmaier and Dick Jay. "He's more dictatorial than previous people I've observed in that office," says Gerstenmaier. "He gives me responsibility, but he steps in with strong suggestions. For example, he will get very much into the detail of our inventory buildup. Within a couple of days, he'll look at this inventory report I received today, he'll spot certain problem areas, and he'll say, 'What the hell's going on?' De-Young wouldn't concern himself with something like unless there was a *major* problem."

As if on cue, Pilliod barged into Gerstenmaier's office while the conversation was taking place, with a copy of the inventory report in his hand. He had marked it up and had attached a long, handwritten note.

Jay says that Pilliod has a tendency to be too rough on people. "He's thoughtless, occasionally. By thoughtless I mean that he will openly criticize someone in a meeting instead of waiting until they're alone. Not everybody is going to be as smart as Chuck, or able to accomplish the things he has. I've seen him tie into someone who was *trying* to do the job right. Later he'll realize he shouldn't have done it. I think I've seen him show regret, though I haven't seen him apologize.

"A company's made up of a great many people, and not all of them are qualified to be chairman of the board. They try to do the best job they can, and if they get scolded because their brilliance doesn't match their leader's, it can lead to low morale. If it wasn't for his egotism, I think we'd all feel more comfortable. But he's got good reason to be egotistical. He's come a long way from less than a standing start. We're all pretty much in awe of him."

"I'd never work for a woman," a woman draftsman told me. "They are too mean and petty."

Research on female workers has for years looked for sex differences on the job. Women, the surveys show, have lower job aspirations than men, less commitment to work, and more concern with friendships than with the work itself. And many people assume that women make poor leaders because their personalities do not allow them to be assertive. Women who do make it to management positions are presumed to fit the mold of the dictatorial, bitchy boss.

To explain why more women don't seek or find career success, many people concentrate on supposed personality differences between the sexes: women's "motive to avoid success" or incapacity to handle power. Or they look at childhood training and educational training: how women learn to limit their ambitions and hide their accomplishments. Because women learn that high achievement means a loss of traditional femininity, they choose to preserve the latter and sacrifice the former.

When I began to study women in work organizations three years ago, I also was looking for sex-related individual differences that would explain women's absence from high-status, powerful jobs. If women were ever going to make it in a man's world, the conventional wisdom said, we would have to get them when they're young and make sure they don't pick up any motives to avoid success or other bad habits. When I looked more closely at how real people in organizations behave, however, the picture changed. I could find nothing about women in my own research and that of others that was not equally true of men in some situations. For example, some women do have low job aspirations, but so do men who are in positions of blocked opportunity. Some women managers are too interfering and coercive, but so are men who

READING 6–3

Why Bosses Turn Bitchy*

ROSABETH MOSS KANTER

have limited power and responsibility in their organizations. Some women in professional careers behave in stereotyped ways and tend to regard others of their sex with disdain, but so do men who are tokens —the only member of their group at work.

So I dropped my search for sex differences, and I concentrated instead on three aspects of a business organization that do the most to explain the conventional wisdom about women: opportunity, power, and tokenism.

Opportunity

Are women less ambitious and committed to work than men? According to one large corporation I investigated, they are. This company has surveyed 111 hourly employees in white-collar jobs about their attitudes toward promotion. Sure enough, the men showed greater motivation to advance in rank than the women, and the men had higher self-esteem, considering themselves

* Reprinted from *Psychology Today* Magazine, May 1976, pp. 56ff. Copyright © 1976 Ziff-Davis Publishing Company.

more competent in the skills that would win them promotions. The women seemed much less interested in advancement, sometimes saying that they cared more about their families.

Yet in this company, like many, there were dramatic differences in the actual opportunities for promotion that men and women had. Men made up only a small proportion of white-collar workers; most were clustered in professional roles with steps toward management positions. Over two thirds of the women were secretaries or clerks in dead-end jobs. They could hope to advance two or three steps up to executive secretary, and there they would stop. Only rarely had a secretary moved up into professional or managerial ranks. No wonder the women found promotion a far-fetched idea.

If the company had looked at women in high-ranking jobs, the apparent sex difference in work attitudes would have vanished utterly. In my interviews, I found that ambition, self-esteem, and career commitment were all flourishing among women in sales jobs, which are well-paid and on the way to top management. Indeed, one successful young woman in the sales force told me she hoped someday to run the company.

Lack of opportunity to succeed, not a personality style that shuns success, is often what separates the unambitious from the climbers—and the women from the men. The great majority of women hold jobs that have short, discouraging career ladders—secretarial, clerical, factory work. When the jobs include opportunities for advancement, women want to advance. But jobs without such opportunities depress a person's ambition and self-esteem, for men as well as women.

The early research that first specified the circumstances under which workers are not highly committed to work or hungry for promotion was all focused on men. Social scientists Eli Chinoy (who studied auto workers), Harry Purcell (meatpackers), and Robert Dubin (factory workers) concluded that the men in these routine jobs behaved just like the typical woman; they defined their jobs as temporary and dreamed of leaving. They claimed to have little interest in climbing to a higher-status job, preferring, they said, "easy work." And they placed a higher value on family life than they placed on their careers. In effect, they adopted values that rationalized the reality of their roles.

Gossip at the Dead End

Opportunity also determines what kinds of relationships a person forms on the job. Workers who have few prospects of moving up and out compensate by making close friends. The very limitations of the job insure that those friends will be around for a while, and one better make sure that at least the social side of an unchallenging job is pleasurable. Being well liked becomes another meaning of success to people in dead-end work, and if you've got the best stories to offer the office, you can add a bit of excitement to mundane work. So it often looks as if women are "talk-oriented," not "task-oriented," in their jobs. Some employers point to the gossipy office coffee klatch as a direct result of women's natural concern with people, rather than with achievement. Instead, I think it is more accurate to say that female socializing reflects the jobs they have.

Highly mobile jobs demand that a person be most concerned with the work. Such jobs make close friendships with co-workers less likely. The corporate world requires its participants to be willing to relocate, to surpass rivals without hesitation, to use other people to advance in status. The aggressive, striving junior executive is as much a creation of his place in the organization hierarchy as is the talkative, unambitious secretary.

A laboratory study by Arthur Cohen clearly showed what happens to young men when their opportunity for advancement is varied. He set up some groups to be highly mobile, with a strong potential for individual promotions, and he set up other groups to believe they had no such potential. The highly mobile groups quickly became more involved with the task they had to do. They dropped irrelevant chatter and reported later that they cared more about the high-power people who were supervising them than about each other. The nonmobile group members, by contrast, concentrated on each other. They virtually ignored the powerful supervisors, because they had nothing to gain from them anyway. They were more openly critical and resentful of people with power.

The Frustrated Fox

People who are placed in dead-end jobs set a self-fulfilling prophecy in motion. Such workers cope with career limitations by giving up hope; like the frustrated fox, they decide they don't want the grapes after all. Instead they create peer groups that give them moral support for not seeking advancement and develop a hostility to outsiders and power figures. Peer groups make a bad job endurable or even fun, but they also put pressure on an individual to stay put. To leave would be a sign of disloyalty. For this reason, the rare man who is offered a promotion out of a dead-end factory slot feels the same ambivalence as the rare secretary who gets a chance at management.

When workers lower their aspirations, their employers logically conclude that they don't have the right attitudes for promotion. The organization decides to invest less of its resources in developing people who seem uninterested, and this decision reinforces the workers' perceptions of

blocked opportunity. The vicious circle is complete.

Power

One of the reasons given to explain why so few women have organizational authority is that people don't like female bosses. In a 1965 *Harvard Business Review* survey of almost 2,000 executives, few respondents of either sex said that they or others would feel comfortable about working for a woman, although the women were more ready to do so than the men. Over half of the men felt that women were "temperamentally unfit" for management, echoing the stereotype of the ineffective lady boss who substitutes pickiness about rules for leadership.

In fact, there is no solid evidence of lasting differences in the leadership styles of men and women. Nor is there evidence that people who work for women have lower morale. Research points in the other direction: those who have worked for a woman boss are much more likely to be favorably disposed toward female leaders.

One clear factor distinguishes good leaders from bad, effective from ineffective, liked from disliked. It is not sex, but power. It is not a matter of personality, but of clout.

Just because people have been given formal authority by virtue of position and title, they do not necessarily have equal access to power in the organization. It is not enough to be the most skillful handler of people in the world. One also needs system-granted power to back up one's demands and decisions and to ensure the confidence and loyalty of subordinates.

System power comes from having influence in the upper echelons of the organization, through membership in informal inner circles and by having high status. As a number of social-psychological studies have shown, people who bring such signs of status and influence into a group tend to be better liked—not resented—and to get their way more often. Organization members, as my interviews revealed, prove to be very knowledgeable about who is in and who is out, and when I asked them to describe desirable bosses, they decidedly preferred those with power to those with style or expertise.

That preference carries real as well as symbolic payoffs. Powerful leaders get more rewards and resources to dispense, and their own mobility promises advancement for the subordinates they bring along. Powerful leaders on the move also pick up a few practices that make them admired. As sociologist Bernard Levenson suggests, promotable supervisors generally adopt a participatory style in which they share information with employees, delegate responsibility, train successors, and are flexible about rules and regulations. They also want to show that they are not indispensable in their current jobs, and they seek to fill the vacancy created by their own advancements with one of their own lieutenants. Since highly mobile people also want to please those above them more than nonmobile people do, they effectively build the relationships that ensure system power.

Punitive, Petty Tyrants

Now consider again the stereotype of the bossy woman boss, who is supposedly rigid, petty, controlling, and likely to poke her nose into the personal affairs of employees. This image is the perfect picture of the powerless. Powerless leaders, men and women alike, often become punitive, petty tyrants. Psychologically, they expect resistance from subordinates. And because they have fewer organizational rewards to trade for compliance, they try to coerce employees into supporting them. Blocked from exercising power in the larger hier-

archy, they substitute the satisfaction of lording it over subordinates. Unable to move ahead, they hold everyone back, and praise conformity to rules rather than talent and innovation.

Burleigh Gardner, a human-relations consultant, reviewed the experiences of women who took over supervisory jobs from men during World War II. He concluded: "Any new supervisor who feels unsure of himself, who feels that his boss is watching him critically, is likely to demand perfect behavior and performance from his people, to be critical of minor mistakes, and to try too hard to please his boss. A woman supervisor, responding to the insecurity and uncertainty of her position as a woman, knowing that she is being watched both critically and doubtfully, feels obliged to try even harder. And for doing this she is said to be 'acting just like a woman,'" In truth, she is acting just as any insecure person would.

We again come full circle. Those who have a favorable place in the power structure are more likely to become effective leaders, to be liked, and thus to gain more power. Sponsorship, for example, is a typical road to the top for many men. The protégé system, whether in academia, politics, or business, is a tough and informal way of keeping outsiders out and making sure the best insiders keep on the fastest track. For this reason, it has been almost impossible for a woman to succeed in business without sponsorship or membership in the company's ruling family. But when women do get real power, whether in politics like Indira Gandhi or in business like advertising-executive Mary Wells, they behave just as well—or badly—as men do.

Tokenism

I studied what happens to women when they do manage to get closer to the top, and I uncovered a range of familiar situations: male managers who could not accept a woman as a colleague without constantly reminding her that she was "different"; women who could not make themselves heard in committee meetings and who felt left out; bright women who hid their accomplishments; a female sales executive who felt that most women should not be hired for jobs like hers; a woman scientist who let another woman in her unit flounder without help; a woman faculty member who brought cookies to department meetings and mothered her colleagues.

All the characters were there, dressed in their sex roles. Yet I saw that even so the play was not about sex. It was about numbers. These women were all tokens, alone or nearly alone in a world of male peers and bosses. When people take on a token status—whether they are female scientists or male nurses or black executives in a white company—they share certain experiences that influence their behavior.

Tokens, by definition, stand out from the crowd. In one company I studied, the first 12 women to go to work among 400 men set the rumor mill in motion. They caused more talk and attracted more attention, usually for their physical attributes, than new male employees. The men tended to evaluate the women against their image of the ideal female rather than the ideal colleague, and the women, under relentless scrutiny, felt they could not afford to make mistakes.

When the token is a black man among whites, a similar reaction occurs. Shelley Taylor and Susan Fiske of Harvard set up an experiment in which they played a tape of group discussions to students. Then they showed pictures of the group and asked the students for their impressions of the discussants. Sometime the photos showed a lone black in an all-white group and sometimes a mixed black-white group. Taylor and Fiske found that the students paid disproportionate attention to the token; they overemphasized his prominence in the group and exaggerated his personality traits. But when the students responded to integrated groups, they were no more likely to recall information about blacks than about whites, and they evaluated the attributes of the blacks as the same as those of the whites.

Hostile, Raunchy Talk

Tokens get attention, but they are isolated on the outskirts of the group. They are reminded constantly of how different they are and what their proper place should be. Other employees sometimes respond to tokens by closing ranks and exaggerating the in-group culture. In several groups of sales trainees I observed, the men's talk got raunchier when token women were present, though they also added elaborate apologies and bows in the women's direction. Tokens have to listen to jokes about people like them, and they face subtle pressures to side with the majority against their kind. Male nurses report the same kind of disguised hostility from the women they work with, who constantly remind them that they do not belong and pose loyalty tests to see if they will side with women against other men. The token is never quite trusted by the rest of the group.

To win the group's trust, tokens often resort to acting out the stereotypical role that members of their sex or race are supposed to play. These roles require them to deny parts of themselves that don't fit the majority group's assumptions, and they make it difficult for the tokens to be ordinary workers doing their jobs. Token women, for instance, may wind up playing mother, sex object, pet, or iron maiden. Token men get caught, too. Lone blacks in groups of white workers, sociologist Everett Hughes found, may play the comedian. Taylor and Fiske's students saw the solo black as taking on special roles in the group, often highly stereotyped. And male nurses, according to Bernard Segal, get inveigled into doing the distasteful chores that the women didn't want to do, which were considered "men's work."

Tokens face additional pressures because they must work doubly hard to prove themselves. "Women must work twice as hard as men to be thought half as good," wrote suffragist Charlotte Whitton; "Luckily, this is not difficult." But it *is* difficult, and takes its psychological toll in emotional stress. Tokens have a shaky identity because of their precarious position; they can't behave in a totally natural way because they are on display all the time.

Many of the supposed personality traits of minority people in white male organizations, then, simply reflect their token status. To avoid the glare of visibility, some tokens try to hide themselves and their achievements. To escape the feeling of being outsiders, some tokens go overboard in adopting the attitudes of the insiders. To win trust and the comfort of being accepted, some play the stereotype that is expected of them.

Yet all of these reactions—which are not necessarily conscious or intentional—are exactly those that prove to the majority that they were right all along. So tokens are kept to a numerical minimum, and another vicious spiral continues.

The Job Makes the Woman

What I am suggesting is that the job makes the man—and the woman. People bring much of themselves and their histories to their work, but I think we have overlooked the tremendous impact of an organization's structure on what happens to them once they are there.

In my approach is right, it suggests that change will not come from changing personalities or attitudes and not from studying sex or race differences. Change will come only from interrupting the self-perpetuating cycles of blocked opportunity, powerlessness, and tokenism.

Take the case of Linda S., a woman who had been a secretary in a large corporation for 16 years. Five years ago, she would have said that she never wanted to be anything but a secretary. She also would have told you that since she had recently had children she was thinking of quitting. She said secretarial work was not a good enough reason to leave the children.

Then came an affirmative-action program, and Linda was offered a promotion. She wavered. It would mean leaving her good female friends for a lonely life among male managers. Her friends thought she was abandoning them. She worried whether she could handle the job. But her boss talked her into it and promised to help, reassuring her that he would be her sponsor.

So Linda was promoted, and now she handles a challenging management job most successfully. Seeing friends is the least of her many reasons to come to work every day, and her ambitions have soared. She wants to go right to the top.

"I have 15 years left to work," she says. "And I want to move up six grades to corporate vice president—at least."

"The driver of a truck carrying high explosives drives more carefully than one loaded with bricks; and the driver of a high-explosives truck who does not believe in a life after death drives more carefully than one who does." That conjecture by author John Fowles illustrates an important point: The potential stress in any activity—whether driving a high-explosives truck or being an executive in a turbulent world—depends partly on the ideas that are in the person's head. That being the case, if you want to reduce stress, you must work on the ideas in your head. Although this prescription may sound simplistic and banal, it isn't.

One thing we know about stress is that it is usually accompanied by feelings of arousal or agitation. A person undergoing stress feels "keyed up." The problem is that when such arousal occurs, thoughts and action become more primitive. As a person becomes more and more agitated, his thoughts become more simplistic, he notices less in his environment, he reverts to his oldest habits, and all complicated responses in his repertoire disappear.

It is my argument that these "terrible simplifications," which occur *after* an increase in arousal, are what make stress appear to be a bad thing. It's not the stress itself that causes havoc but rather the simplifications in analysis and action that follow it. These simplifications in perception and the crudeness of action produce the states of confusion and panic typically associated with stress. Notice that these reactions of confusion and panic occur considerably later in the stress sequence than most people have argued. As a result of this late occurrence, there are several preceding steps that one can take to intervene and dampen the danger. This is the basis for my argument that more head work—and head work of a different kind—might be successful in the management of executive stress.

READING 6–4

The Management of Stress*

KARL E. WEICK

If a major cause of debilitating stress is oversimplification produced by arousal, then to manage stress we have to keep our thoughts and actions sufficiently complicated so that they can register and regulate the complications that originally produced the change in arousal. One of the worst prescriptions for resolving stress is the injunction "Keep it simple." Since the stress already has produced a radical simplification of the responses and ideas a person brings to a situation, more simplification merely compounds this shrinkage in the ability to cope and analyze. If anything, what we need to urge in the case of stress is "Complicate yourself." Intentional complication should both expand the number of responses available to the person and suggest interpretations of the present situation that strip it of its stressful connotations.

Let me give an example. People often report that they feel stress when they are overloaded with more inputs than they can process in a reasonable time. The person looks at his situation with despair and cries, "I can't handle it!" The most obvious solution to this despair is simply to flee. One could do that by physically leaving the situation of overload, by taking refuge in physical illness, or by momentarily going crazy. Suppose, however, the overloaded individual tries to complicate his responses and images by reexamining his assertion "I can't handle it" word by word.

First, he could ask whether the pronoun "I" is appropriate. Is he the only one who can't handle it, or is it, in fact, a problem that most people in this situation couldn't handle? Can the problem be delegated to someone else who *can* handle it? Second, the person under stress can work on the word "can't." Notice that if one substitutes words such as "won't" or "won't be able to" or "am able but don't want to" or "can try to" for "can't," the circumstance that looks hopeless changes dramatically. With each of those transformations—and all of them are plausible in certain circumstances—the person has transformed the situation into quite a different one. It should be emphasized that the sentence "I am able but don't want to handle it" is more complicated than the simple "I can't handle it." It is the power of the "I can't handle it" simplification that has to be undercut by more complicated responses if stress is to be managed.

Third, it is possible to work on the word "handling." Try substituting such less demanding activities as "skimming," "noticing," or "scanning"; the problem will then appear to decrease in magnitude. Finally, precisely what does the word "it" refer to? In all likelihood the person experiencing the stress has some uncertainty about it. Therefore, simply by shifting the definition of the object or problem that can't be handled, some management of the stress may be possible.

The skeptical reader may be saying at this point, "That's simply too glib; the world isn't that simple." The point, however, is that the perception of stressful overload is relative. There is never only one "correct" account of a situation. The world is intrinsically equivocal. In any situation the same set of elements can be interpreted in a vast number of ways, any one of which may be as plausible as another. And any meaning that is ascribed to a situation can be replaced plausibly by other meanings. What I am suggesting is that, in dealing with stress, people should capitalize on these multiple meanings.

Once we realize that stressful situations have considerable latitude for redefinition, we can go further. The original meaning of the word "stress" has a nuance of interest to executives. When people say that a piece of metal is "stressed," they mean that the metal is stationary and that something is done to it. Strain is the result of this stress. Notice that stress occurs when something *external* has been applied. The implication for us is that if an individual sees himself as passive and his fate controlled by others, he is more susceptible to stress in the form of unplanned external events. On the other hand, a man whose self-concept is of a more active nature is less susceptible to stress. Psychiatrist Jordan Scher likes to describe people in terms of actions rather than capabilities. Instead of saying that executives judge, live, experience, think, value, or act, he describes them as judging, living, experiencing, thinking, valuing, and acting. "Only as he is in the act of, only as he is an 'ing' being, is his existence verified and made real," says Scher. If we could persuade people to think of themselves in dynamic rather than static terms, they might be more resistant to stress.

If I think of myself in static terms, I might say that I am a middle manager, my salary equals my age, and, therefore, I am successful. But all of those images are passive—and thus vulnerable. Other people bestow such labels, and that means they also have the power to remove or discredit them. Contrast these vulnerable images with a set that reads, I am thinking, working, improvising, making do, persisting, reflecting. The second set of images is more active than the first. The second implies internal determination, the first external determination. The second is more elusive as a target of stress than the first.

Thus, a form of head work that may help manage executive stress is to think of oneself in dynamic rather than passive terms. This is easier said than done, however, because many people in business are preoccupied with status, titles, job descriptions, and perquisites. This concern with status symbols may heighten vulnerability to stress, because it tends to stabilize the individual, tie his identity to specific objects, and render him a stationary object to which things can happen.

In addition to thinking with dynamic verbs, thinking retrospectively can also be beneficial in stress reduction. Many executives have the misguided belief that people's intentions control their actions. But typically, people know what they have done only after they do it: "How can I know what I think until I see what I say?" Since the meaning of most experiences is clear only *after* the experience has occurred, this belated sense-making can be turned to one's advantage in reducing stress.

When you feel that you are undergoing a stressful situation, the trick is to reexamine retrospectively the actions that you associate with the stressful event. Then force yourself to rewrite history—that is, try to come up with another plausible explanation for the same set of feelings you now have.

Suppose I look back over the last five days when I was trying to get this article into shape. I was grouchy with my family, curt in my conversations with others, withdrawn, sleeping poorly, and so on. However, it is possible for me to reread those events as something over than moderate stress produced by trying to meet a deadline. I could see that same set of events as evidence that I am growing older and more sensitive to small incidents, or as the normal trouble that precedes the moment of truth at a typewriter, or irritation due to teaching commitments rather than writing commitments, or normal irritability due to the heat and humidity of summer. In my case, all of these are plausible interpretations. Notice that the meaning of my agitated last few days, and the likelihood that they are the result of stress, change remarkably depending on which of the interpretations I accept.

Notice also that in my retrospective rewrite of the past few days, I reversed what is usually regarded as the logical order. Most people grow up thinking, "I'll believe it when I see it." But if you accept the idea that the world is inherently equivocal in its meaning, you must turn that assertion around and say to yourself, "I'll see it when I believe it."

When I retrospectively rearranged my last few days, I essentially changed my beliefs first and then noticed events in those days that were consistent with those beliefs. Suppose, for example, that I believe that I am becoming more sensitive to minor incidents; I then see that the supposed big irritants of the past few days were actually quite small. The "reality" of the situation has been changed to fit the explanation of "increased sensitivity of the organism." But what has happened to the stress? If I have simply been oversensitive during the past few days, then I haven't really been under stress. Instead, I have simply registered more vividly more of my surroundings.

So far most of the head work that we have talked about to manage executive stress involves looking backward. However, stress can also be managed in the here and now. The key to this technique lies in a popular theory in social psychology, which argues that an emotion consists of a generalized state of arousal plus a label. The same level of arousal can be interpreted as due to very different emotions. If, for example, I am sitting in an office talking to a subordinate and I feel a general uneasiness and agitation, I might label that diffuse feeling as excitement, fear, or anger. Any of these "emotions" might describe the level of arousal, and the thing that determines which emotion I actually "experience" is the label suggested by the particular context.

Whenever you are tempted to label a set of feelings as "stress," try out a number of different labels. You have to get away from the assumption that a situation is *inherently* stressful or nonstressful. *We* put the labels there, not nature, and since we put them there, we can also remove them.

The stress label can often create a vicious circle. One way we discover "appropriate" labels for our emotions is by looking around at other people to see what they're experiencing. Suppose I have a generalized feeling of arousal, and I puzzle over what that feeling is. As I look around at other people in the situation, I see that they all give off signs of being harried; therefore, I conclude that I am harried and under stress. But those people who look harried may be just as puzzled as I am over what emotion they're experiencing. The minute I conclude that we are under stress, they see my expressive behavior as "proving" that the situation is stressful, and they in turn adopt the "stress" label with more certainty. They act in a stressed fashion, which simply confirms my interpretation of their actions, and this vicious circle continues unchecked.

To break this vicious circle, a person must be aware of the nature of emotional labels and be able to judge emotions in an unsimplified manner.

The importance of being sensitive to complications in expressive behavior is potentially crucial in stress management. We judge emotions by looking at such things as body position, facial expression, expressive behavior, and speech qualities. But if we examine these expressions very carefully, we commonly see that people contradict themselves. They give off a variety of emotions simultaneously. But given our pragmatic interests in everyday life, we tend to see people in simple terms.

The person who is sensitive to the variety of emotions being expressed simultaneously by other individuals is most likely to be able to devise labels other than stress for what is being experienced. And since these labels tend to be self-fulfilling prophecies, the person who can see something other than stress in the faces and bodies of his coworkers should be very successful at reducing the amount of stress experienced in a situation—both by himself and by others.

This management of stress labels, of course, requires some rather refined perceptions. It requires that people notice subtle expressive behavior and potential contradictions in other people. Most important, it can occur only if the observer himself is more rather than less complicated. No one can appreciate and comprehend someone who is more complicated than he is.

One of the interesting properties of stress, and one that is an unusually good candidate for head work, is the feeling in many stressful episodes that the stress will go on forever. It is often not the stress itself that is painful and disabling, but rather the impression that it will never end.

This impression can be countered, first of all, by the experience of living through several stressful episodes and discovering that they do end—that they are finite in magnitude and duration. But for the executive who has not heeded the lesson of experience, there is another way of dealing with this problem. You can think yourself beyond the end of a stressful interlude. By this I mean you visualize your situation in the future perfect tense. You imagine that the situation is already over, and then you look backward to see how that termination was completed. This is an elegant solution because, not only does it show you that the experience will soon be over, it may also suggest a specific way of reaching that point.

Suppose an executive finds himself or herself faced with the question of whether or not to take a promotion that involves relocating his or her family. This classic executive problem is one of the more stressful decisions executives face. No one denies that moving decisions can be painful and disruptive. But it's easy to get trapped into thinking that the momentary pain won't let up and that the stress will go on forever. It is this erroneous projection of a feeling, rather than the pain itself, that reduces the executive's ability to cope.

My suggestion is that the executive transform the question "Will I move?" into the future perfect assertion "I will have moved." By imagining that the event is concluded, the executive can then single out from all possible scenarios a much smaller number that actually could have generated that imagined outcome. Having clarified these intervening activities, the executive then may be in a better position to judge whether he or she should make the move. But for the sake of our present analysis, what is more important is that the executive has put a close on the stressful event. "I will have moved" means that the move is definitely going to be over and done with and presumably that the associated stress will come to an end with it.

Future perfect thinking is especially appropriate for executives because they are often rewarded for their ability to forecast the future. They spend much of their life planning, forecasting, and thinking in the future tense. They wonder about whether the economy will go up or down, whether markets will expand or shrink, whether employment will rise or fall, whether regula-

tions will increase or decrease, and so on. However, the simple future tense is a difficult tense to work with because any possible outcome might occur. Future *perfect* thinking, on the other hand, can make speculation more manageable by focusing on single events. If an event is projected and thought of as already accomplished it can be more easily analyzed.

While the idea of future perfect thinking may be difficult to grasp, you might try this technique devised by one researcher. Suppose that you're trying to write a five-year plan for your department and you get stalled. You experience what some people would call a "writer's block." One way to handle that block is to imagine that it is now six years later. Then write yourself a letter from your boss, congratulating you in great detail on how well your five-year plan worked. Be as specific as possible in the congratulatory letter. Although you are writing a letter of congratulations for a set of activities that have not yet occurred, in doing so you may clarify things you want to accomplish in those five years in a way that thinking in the simple future tense won't.

There's one final activity of the head that can help manage stress: owning up to ambivalent tendencies. Suppose, as an executive, I have an investment in seeing myself as a strong, assertive leader. The opposite of that would be someone who is weak and passive. And that would be a terrible set of traits, right? Wrong! Most psychologists agree that any individual has the capability of exhibiting completely opposite traits. Owning up to these opposing tendencies can be a valuable way of managing stress.

When a person finds himself in a stressful situation, it may not be the events that are producing pain and confusion but rather the efforts the person is making to deny those tendencies that have produced the stressful situation in the first place.

People like to see themselves as able to control their own fate. And one of the main things that precipitates stress is the feeling that "I am losing control." The painfulness of the subsequent stress may result not from the actual fact of losing control but from the individual's unwillingness to admit that he is *capable* of losing control. If he were to accept both his strength and his weakness, if he were to see both sides as true of himself, and if he were to regard himself as a person who is capable of controlling events even while recognizing that there are occasions when he cannot, then he will be in a much better position to manage stress.

As we noted earlier, oversimplification is to be avoided. If the executive compounds the simplification by denying half of the tendencies that he has, then his resources to deal with unanalyzed distress have been reduced drastically.

To summarize, executives have a vested interest in being seen as men of action. Thus, an article that suggests that stress can be managed by thought rather than action might seem subversive, if not silly.

But it is action that is most vulnerable to simplification under the heightened arousal that accompanies stress. And this simplification of action leads to a simplification of thinking. It is this simplification of both action and thought that forces one to miss the nuances in a stressful situation that would allow it to be untangled, defused, and made more manageable.

All of the stress remedies I've proposed are intended to complicate the analyses made of stressful situations in the hope that those situations will be then read accurately. I am not saying that action should be suspended or that action is a bad thing. But I do think that the stereotype of executives as men of action—especially when it is believed by those men—is a simplification that creates additional problems for executives. I am not making the simplistic assertion that "It's all in your mind." But I am saying that your mind is one place where you can do something to help manage a stressful situation.

Attempts to measure the behavioral consequences of an employee's organizational
loyalty have been made in several management studies. Measurements of organizational loyalty that have been used include: a
subordinate's choosing to remain with the
current employer or under the influence
of a particular supervisor;[1] a subordinate's
preference for achieving the goals of the organization rather than those of the individual's profession;[2] and a subordinate's willingness to acknowledge the authority of a
superior.[3]

Despite such diverse operational definitions and variations in methodologies, research has been successful in empirically
validating two benefits of employing loyal
personnel:

1. Supervisors who direct loyal subordinates are more successful in exercising
   control over them. Such supervisors feel
   a greater sense of confidence in their use
   of directives and attempt to influence
   their subordinates more frequently than
   do supervisors whose workers are less
   loyal to the organization.[4]

READING 6–5

An Assessment of Supervisors' Organizational Loyalty*

JOHN A. PEARCE II

2. Supervisors who inspire loyalty in
   themselves and the organization will direct work groups whose productivity
   will be superior to that of less loyal
   work groups.[5]

Under these circumstances, it is understandable that management should attempt
to increase an employee's sense of organizational loyalty in the belief that a loyal
worker will make efforts to further the
firm's objectives. Consequently, the measurement of loyalty properly involves an
evaluation of the worker's attachment to
the organization's objectives, values, survival, and growth.[6] An empirical measure

[1] See, for example, Peter M. Blau and Richard
W. Scott, *Formal Organizations* (San Francisco:
Chandler Publishing, 1962); Rensis Likert, *New
Patterns of Management* (New York: McGraw-
Hill, 1961); or V. V. Murray and Allan F. Coren-
blum, "Loyalty to Immediate Superior at Alter-
nate Hierarchical Levels in a Bureaucracy,"
American Journal of Sociology 72 (July 1966):
77–85.

[2] See Blau and Scott, *Formal Organizations*; or
Alvin W. Gouldner, "Cosmopolitans and Locals:
Toward an Analysis of Latent Social Roles," *Administrative Science Quarterly* 2 (December
1957): 281–306.

[3] Melville Dalton, *Men Who Manage* (New
York: John Wiley and Sons, 1959).

[4] See Blau and Scott, *Formal Organizations*;
John R. P. French, Jr., and Richard Snyder,
"Leadership and Interpersonal Power," in Dorwin
Cartwright, ed., *Studies in Social Power* (Ann
Arbor: Institute for Social Research, University
of Michigan, 1959); or Ronald Lippitt, Norman
Polansky, and Sidney Rosen, "The Dynamics of
Power," *Human Relations* 5 (February 1952):
37–64.

* *MSU Business Topics*, Summer 1977, pp.
50–56. Reprinted by permission of the publisher,
Division of Research, Graduate School of Business
Administration, Michigan State University.

[5] See Blau and Scott, *Formal Organizations*; or
French and Snyder, "Leadership and Interpersonal Power."

[6] Herbert A. Simon, *Administrative Behavior*
(New York: Free Press, 1957).

of organizational loyalty may attempt to gauge the extent to which an employee has assimilated and identified with the values and goals of the organization.[7] Thus, loyalty can be viewed in terms of the degree to which the organization has enlisted the employee's strong personal commitment to "give more than adequately of his time, energy, talents, judgments, ideas, and moral courage in the best interest of the company with which he is affiliated."[8]

Previous studies of organizational loyalty show that many benefits are enjoyed by companies whose employees have a sense of loyalty to their work organizations. Through their attitudes and their behavior, loyal employees enhance the growth and development of their companies. They promote their organizations in the community and support management in periods of reversal and transition, thus helping to provide a united front against the challenges of a competitive environment.

Yet, despite the potential value of loyalty as a partial estimator of an employee's value to the firm, its use has remained limited. The first difficulty is that organizational loyalty cannot be measured directly. The manager is hard pressed to determine which, or how much, of an employee's work-related behavior and attitudes can be attributed to organizational loyalty. Furthermore, since there are few objective measures of this variable, the basis of managerial evaluation of its contribution to employee performance is largely, if not exclusively, subjective. Thus, the manager who is required to submit objective evaluations of employees cannot include a personal estimation of employee loyalty or incorporate it implicitly into objective criteria for other variables.[9]

A second difficulty lies in the fact that it is often hard for managers to determine that behavior which should, at least in part, be interpreted as expressive of organizational loyalty. Few employees behave loyally in all situations. Yet, virtually all employee actions could conceivably be interpreted as having the potential to encompass some degree of loyalty. Therefore, the degree to which a display of loyalty is an intended communication as contrasted to an unplanned by-product of a given employee action is often unclear. Such ambiguity is of particular concern when a worker's behavior could be interpreted as anything from an expression of constructive criticism by a loyal employee to simple malicious disruption by a largely disloyal worker.

A final difficulty is that of determining the intensity of organizational loyalty. Is it important that management concern itself with the degree of worker loyalty or simply that it seek to maintain some minimally sufficient level? In either event, management is faced with the troublesome problem of determining an adequate instrument for the measurement of this intensity.

The Research Objective

To reduce the difficulties limiting development of employee loyalty, progress appeared to be needed in three areas:

1. A definition of loyalty which can be made operational in an organization.
2. Identification of behavior that expresses organizational loyalty.
3. Determinatiton of the attitudinal, demographic, and socioeconomic variables related to organizational loyalty.

These goals provided the impetus for a study of behavior that supervisors consider expressive of loyalty.

------

[7] Harry Levinson, "Whatever Happened to Loyalty?" *Public Management* 48 (June 1966): 160–65.

[8] Nathaniel Stewart, "Organizational Loyalty," *Management Review* 50 (January 1961): 21.

[9] Exceptions would occur when a manager recorded particular behavioral events and their frequency of occurrence, using, for example, the critical incident technique.

Organizational Loyalty Defined

A review of the literature discloses that most researchers view organization-centered loyalties as expressions of employee attitudes, although there has been a lack of unanimity in stating the position explicitly. Definitional weaknesses seem to have arisen when researchers limited themselves to considerations of an emotional or affect-based component of loyalty.[10] An alternative approach has been to define *loyalty* simply as the identification of an employee with the goals of the organization.[11] However, even when using an accepted definition of identification as an emotional tie or concern it appears that researchers have restricted their definitions of organizational loyalty to the affective components of attitudes, although occasionally they have outlined the associated behavioral implications.

An improvement over these approaches is one which views loyalty as a set of object-relevant commitments.[12] The primary advantage of this approach is that a commitment is frequently defined as an attitude.[13] It follows, then, that if loyalty is a set of commitments, and if commitment is an attitude, then loyalty is an attitude or set of attitudes.

Defined as an attitude, organizational loyalty can appropriately be studied from affective, cognitive, and behavioral perspectives, as noted by V. V. Murray and Allan Corenblum.[14]

Thus, a synthesis of published research lends support to the following definition: Organizational loyalty is the attitude of employees predisposing them to respond to individuals, institutions, ideas, or situations with actions they perceive as supportive of the organization.

Behavior Expressive of Loyalty

With this definition, it is possible to describe parameters of behavior expressive of employee loyalty:

1. To minimize the confusion of primarily self-serving actions with more wholly loyal behavior, the studied aspects of behavior generally should not be included in an employee's job description. Specifically, such behavior should (1) be performed without financial compensation, (2) not be directly related to job performance, (3) be performed voluntarily with neither expectation of direct personal benefit nor threat of direct personal penalty, and (4) not be commonly influential in an employee's performance evaluation.

2. The behavior should consist of actions perceived by the employee as supportive of the organization.

3. To avoid the contaminating effects of calculative commitments, the studied behavior should occur away from work or should be at-work behavior peripheral to job performance.

Correlates of Organizational Loyalty

A research project was undertaken to test the hypothesis that organization-centered loyal attitudes actually exist among

---

[10] See, for example, Blau and Scott, *Formal Organizations.*

[11] The studies referred to include the following: Herbert A. Block, *A Concept of Our Changing Loyalties* (London: Columbia University Press, 1934) T. W. Fletcher, "The Nature of Administrative Loyalty," *Public Administration Review* 18 (Winter 1958): 37–42; Levinson, "Whatever Happened to Loyalty?"; and Simon, *Administrative Behavior.*

[12] See Talcott Parsons, *Structure and Process in Modern Societies* (Glencoe, Ill.: Free Press, 1960); or Stewart, "Organizational Loyalty."

[13] See Oscar Grusky, "Career Mobility and Organizational Commitment," *Administrative Science Quarterly* 10 (March 1966): 488–503; or Charles A. Kiesler, "Commitment," in R. P. Abelson et al., eds., *Theories of Cognitive Consistency: A Sourcebook* (Chicago: Rand McNally, 1968).

[14] Murray and Corenblum, "Loyalty to Immediate Supervisor."

supervisors, and to try to determine the attitudinal, demographic, and socioeconomic variables which are correlates of organizational loyalty. This study used the derived definition of organizational loyalty and the parameters of loyal behavior as criteria for selecting aspects of behavior that might be expressions of organizational loyalty.

These criteria were applied to a list of 51 organization-related aspects of behavior used in a research study on employee responsibility.[15] Fourteen of these satisfied all of the selection criteria and were classified as expressive of organizational loyalty. A questionnaire then was developed focusing on the respondents' answers to the following question about each of the kinds of behavior: "To what extent do you agree that the following behavior could fulfill a part of your responsibility to your organization?" The respondents recorded their answers on a five-point scale: (1) strongly agree, (2) agree, (3) even, (4) disagree, (5) strongly disagree. In addition to the 14 loyalty questions, 44 items were included on the form to allow for the study of organizational loyalty correlates.

The questionnaire was distributed to 138 first- and second-level supervisors. They worked in three types of organization: a bank (17 supervisors), a college (11 nonfaculty supervisors), and seven manufacturing firms (110 supervisors). The forms were completed anonymously on a voluntary basis, and all of the supervisors cooperated.

Exhibit 1 displays the major results from a tabulation of the questionnaire responses. For the sake of clarity, supervisors' responses of "strongly agree" and "agree" are consolidated under the heading "agree," and responses of "disagree" and "strongly disagree" are shown under the heading "disagree." The responses of "somewhat agree,

somewhat disagree" are shown in a separate column labeled "even."

The primary insight offered by Exhibit 1 is that the supervisors expressed overwhelming agreement with all 14 of the loyalty-expressive actions as representing behavior that could fulfill a part of their organizational responsibility.[16] The mean percentage of supervisors in agreement with the 14 loyal actions was 81.28 percent, with an average of only 7 percent of the supervisors in disagreement.

It is important to note that these 14 loyal actions are performed without promise of a direct reward and without threat of a direct punishment. Employees expressing their organizational loyalty through any of the off-the-job actions mentioned probably could not expect to be rewarded directly through promotions, wage increases, or improved work appraisals. Nor would they be likely to suffer demotions, wage decreases,

---

[15] John P. Loveland and Jack L. Mendleson, "Employer Responsibility, a Key Goal for Managers," *Human Resource Management* 13 (Spring 1974): 32–36.

---

[16] Actually, 23 of the 51 "responsibility" items satisfied the criteria used to select the behavior expressive of organizational loyalty, and all were included in the study. However, when the data analysis was conducted, it was found that nine of the items were so universally agreed to by the supervisors ($\bar{x} \leq 1.50$; $\sigma \leq 0.65$) that they were not statistically useful in distinguishing levels of organizational loyalty. Thus, these nine nondistinguishing items were eliminated from discussion in the body of this article and from Exhibit 1. These items, showing the respective percentages of "agree," "even," and "disagree," were: Not to engage in theft of organization property, no matter how small (98, 1, 1); To respect all confidences associated with organization position (99, 1, 0); To refrain from any action on the job which could harm the reputation of the organization even though it would not break the organization's rules (95, 4, 1); To make known personal ideas or methods that could benefit the organization regardless of whether I am compensated for these ideas (98, 2, 1); To safeguard information that might be beneficial to competitors (99, 1, 0); To safeguard my own health and the health of my fellow employees (99, 1, 0); To prepare for greater responsibilities (98, 2, 0); To speak favorably of the organization and its management to outsiders (94, 6, 0); To avoid careless actions, either on or off the job, that could compromise or weaken the competitive position of the organization (97, 2, 1). Average percentages were 97.44, 2.11, and 0.44.

EXHIBIT 1
Behavior Expressive of Supervisor Loyalty

Question: To what extent do you agree that the following behavior could fulfill a part of your responsibility to your organization?

Behavior	Agree	Even	Disagree
		(In percentages)	
To refrain from any actions off the job which could harm the reputation of the organization.	93	5	2
To work for only one employer at a time.	85	9	6
To study information related to the job on my own time.	91	6	3
To purchase my organization's products or services rather than those of competitors.	85	11	4
To ensure that my family's conduct reflects favorably on the organization.	71	19	10
To vote for issues and individuals which support the interests of the business community.	72	17	11
To get enough rest and sleep necessary for effective performance on the job.	91	7	2
Not to drink alcoholic beverages immediately before or anytime during the working day.	77	17	6
To return to work promptly after all established work breaks.	96	2	2
To tell management whenever I observe another employee breaking a rule.	54	19	27
To depart work no earlier than the established time.	88	6	6
To be active in groups and clubs which promote the general interests of business.	66	28	6
To hold the goals of the organization above personal nonwork goals which affect the job.	84	11	5
To work at home on my own time if necessary to finish a job.	85	7	8
$\bar{x}_{14} =$	81.28	11.71	7

or more critical work appraisals as a consequence of not behaving in these loyal ways. Thus, these workers' voluntary expressions of organizational loyalty can be viewed as genuine indications of their attitudes.

When combined, the scale values of one to five which the supervisors indicated on the 14 items became their individual loyalty scores, which ranged from 14 points (highest loyalty) to 49 points. These loyalty scores were then compared to the supervisors' responses on questionnaire items regarding demographic and socioeconomic variables, job-pertinent variables, and supervisor attitudes. The results of Spearman rank-order correlation and chi-square analyses show five variables which are significantly related to the supervisors' organizational loyalty

scores ($a \leqq 0.01$): job satisfaction,[17] job motivation,[18] company satisfaction,[19] age, and tenure.

[17] Job satisfaction was measured by the responses to a five-question scale which requested direct indications of the employee's satisfaction with the job and about a willingness to change jobs. For a discussion of the development of the scale, see Arthur N. Turner and Paul L. Lawrence, *Industrial Jobs and the Worker* (Boston: Harvard University, 1965).

[18] Job motivation was measured by the responses to a four-question scale which requested attitudes concerning job boredom, job involvement, willingness to perform extra work, and a perception of relative work effort. For a discussion of the development of the scale, see Martin Patchen, *Some Questionnaire Measures of Employee Motivation and Morale*, Survey Research Monograph No. 41 (Ann Arbor: University of Michigan, 1965).

[19] Based on responses to a four-question scale which requested attitudes concerning the progress

Summary and Conclusions

The research disclosed that supervisors agree to an extensive list of actions—expressive of organizational loyalty—as fulfilling a part of their responsibility to their organization. Without the expectation of direct personal benefits, the supervisors act in support of their organizations in a variety of ways both away from work and in activities peripheral to job performance. Thus, organizational loyalty, as defined in this study, does exist for the 138 supervisors who were questioned and for their nine employers.

With only two exceptions (age and tenure),[20] the strength of organizational loyalty was not significantly related to variations in demographic, socioeconomic, and job-pertinent variables. This suggests that the phenomenon of organizational loyalty is likely to exist at a reasonably consistent level among supervisors, regardless of differences in such variables as sex, race, marital status, supervisory level, salary, education, family size, community population, and second jobs.

Organizational loyalty was found to be significantly correlated with three often-researched attitudes: job satisfaction, company satisfaction, and job motivation. An inference to be drawn from the study of organizational loyalty is that behavior not directly related to job performance but supportive of the organization accrues to those firms that develop job and company satisfaction and job motivation among their supervisors. Indeed, this study has found that supervisors voluntarily govern their behavior in the interest of their organizations in areas that extend considerably beyond the notion of a fair day's work for a fair day's pay.

The idea that loyal behavior is associated with other positive attitudes of supervisors introduces two intriguing possibilities:

1. There may be a causal relationship between supervisors' sense of organizational loyalty and their job-related levels of satisfaction and motivation.
2. A sense of organizational loyalty may vary with supervisors' attitudes toward their jobs and their company.

In either event, it appears likely that organizational development efforts to improve supervisor attitudes and performance will be aided by attention to the effects of the supervisor's sense of organizational loyalty.

---

of the organization, its fairness to employees, its understanding of employee problems, and the willingness of the employee to change organizations. See Turner and Lawrence, "Industrial Jobs and the Worker."

[20] Age and tenure were intercorrelated with a rho of 0.750, at a probability level of 0.0001.

It's been a half dozen years since the first concerted effort to bring more black students into the nation's graduate business schools. From a mere trickle in the 1960s, black MBAs are now flowing into the job market in a steady stream.

Since some graduate business schools contend that their alumni records are not specific as to race, it is difficult to obtain an accurate figure on the number of black MBAs in the job market today. Informed estimates, however, range from 2,000 to 3,000. That means that blacks are beginning to form a critical mass in the nation's large corporations. And many in this vanguard generation, as we call it, are now moving into positions of power and influence. But no one, least of all black MBAs themselves, believes that all barriers have been crossed and all challenges met. As one of the three MBAs profiled below remarked, "We have only reached the threshold."

Nevertheless, minority group MBAs have now been in the marketplace long enough to begin to perceive a pattern of acceptance. The initial reaction to the incursion of blacks into the all-white managements of many corporations was tokenism. The principal requirement of the token black was that he or she be visible to the outside world. In many cases these people have had unique capabilities, but by and large, since they were asked to do nothing more than look black, their capabilities would go undiscovered.

While tokenism continues, a second level of acceptance is what blacks term the *Jackie Robinson syndrome.* Like the Brooklyn Dodger second baseman who broke the color line in the big leagues, blacks are now moving into what has heretofore been forbidden territory in corporate management: line jobs—usually in finance or management—with profit-center responsibilities. The Jackie Robinsons of management are the silent warriors who have opened doors by playing by the rules of the game and

READING 6-6

The Black MBA: The Vanguard Generation Moves Up*

stifling the outrage that is inevitably aroused in such situations.

Finally, the vanguard generation is now producing black MBAs who are not only capable of assuming positions of influence but have the knowledge that they can do so while maintaining their individuality— their own "blackness" as it were. These blacks insist on being accepted for what they do and not because of—or despite —the color of their skin. In the following pages, three MBAs discuss the intricacies of this newly evolving relationship with the corporate world.

"We've Just Reached the Threshold"

When Warren Chatmon graduated from Wharton in 1972 near the top of his class, he had 19 job offers. It was then that he faced perhaps the most important task of his career so far: choosing an employer. "I asked brutally frank questions at all my

* Reprinted with permission from the January 1976 *MBA.* Copyright © 1976 by MBA Communications, Inc.

job interviews," he recalls. "I let them know that if they were looking for window dressing, I wasn't interested."

In fact, at many of the companies where Chatmon interviewed, he sensed an urgency to hire a black. "It was unstated," he says, "but I picked up their thinking. It ran along the lines: "That's great you were on the dean's list, but more importantly you'll help fill our numbers requirement.' "

Today, Chatmon feels the hard questions paid off. As a regional manager for commercial paper underwriting with the investment banking operation of Merrill Lynch, Pierce, Fenner and Smith, he believes that he is in the right company and the right industry. There were two things he liked about Merrill Lynch. First, the company had already met its affirmative action goals, so there was no pressure to hire Chatmon simply to fill a space on a government form. "There was no stroking or party-line patter," says Chatmon of the extensive interviewing he did at the brokerage firm. "They seemed to want talent and ability rather than the correct school tie or a black for the sake of a statistic."

Second, Merrill Lynch was new to the underwriting business, so Chatmon reasoned that the management of this operation would not be tradition-bound. And the job—trading in the commercial paper market to meet corporations' short-term working capital requirements—promised direct contact with client companies sooner than might have been the case in an old-line operation.

Finally, Chatmon feels that his industry is one that rewards performance. "One of the beauties of Wall Street," he says, "is that you can't fake it. If you don't carry your weight, it's discovered early. But if you do produce revenue, they give you your head, so to speak."

A lot of people might look at Chatmon's situation and figure he's got it made. But not Chatmon. To him, while the entry-level barriers for blacks in the white business world are coming down due to equal employment opportunity legislation, the battle for equal treatment in making progress up the ranks has just begun.

"I don't know of any black professional—except maybe some young, naive person who is suffering from delusions of grandeur—who thinks that entry in itself means we've arrived. But we've just reached the threshold," he emphasizes. "I haven't even scratched the surface of the kind of return I'm looking for, and by that I mean getting the greatest possible return for my capabilities. I constantly remind myself that while I've gotten through the door and maybe a little further down the hall than some others, I certainly haven't been seated at the table yet."

Chatmon points out that thus far he's always demonstrated his ability to perform and has never been treated like a token, which he defines as a person encased in black skin who is not required to measure up to a company's normal standards. He maintains that companies don't have to actively recruit qualified blacks because they're available. "It's a disservice to the individual as well as the company when an unqualified black is hired," he says.

Chatmon is descended from a prominent Birmingham family populated by college graduates for three generations. He attended Howard University for two years between the ages of 15 and 17, then dropped out for several years before completing his undergraduate education at Miles College in Birmingham. With a B.S. in industrial relations, he was hired by Sears, Roebuck in Atlanta and eventually became the first black to head up a retail division. He left to work for Exxon as a marketing representative in its southeastern regional headquarters in Charlotte, North Carolina.

At Wharton, Chatmon hedged his bets by taking a double major in corporate finance and marketing. During that summer, he interned at Kidder Peabody, an experience that uncovered his weakness in certain skills and convinced him that he wanted a Wall Street job when he graduated. He hasn't regretted that decision.

Chatmon explains that he's a "very competitive person" who is incapable of taking abuse or hiding his real opinions for the overall good of his black brethren. "I want an opportunity to grow and learn and give it my best shot without being suffocated by self-doubt about whether I'm doing the right thing for the movement every time I speak up or react to an injustice."

He believes that the best contribution he can make to the cause is to excel in his profession rather than by becoming whiter than white. But he admits that he cares what his "brothers" think. "There aren't many of us down here, so there is a kinship. Among ourselves, we have our truest audience. No, I've never been accused of selling out, and if I had been, it would bother me —a lot."

Chatmon is a veteran of the southern civil rights campaign, but says he wasn't much good at the "sit-ins" popular at the time. "I am the type of personality that if someone walked up to me at a lunch counter and spat on me, I'd probably punch him out. That wasn't quite the posture you were supposed to take. So they kept me in the background. I painted signs and shuffled the demonstrators back and forth."

He avoided military service for the same reason. "After I left Howard, Uncle Sam began to make very serious overtures toward my body, and I had to get into school somewhere fast. I would have gone anywhere other than Fort Dix. I just didn't want some big redneck from North Carolina telling me when to get up in the morning and how to tie my shoes."

Chatmon down plays the gains that have come from the civil rights movement. "Suppose you do get to ride in the front of the bus, instead of the back? You should have been able to ride wherever you wanted in the first place."

His father, a prominent businessman in the Birmingham black community, used to say to him, "In all the years we've lived in the South, I've never heard of one white man, acting alone, lynching one black man." Chatmon has attempted to avoid mob psychology ever since and has seen the soundness of his father's observation bourn out in business. He and his wife Jacqueline—a Wharton MBA herself who works for IBM—have no qualms about socializing with their white business associates and friends from graduate school.

He concedes, however, that one of the handicaps for a black in a "people-intense" job such as his is lack of influential contracts that would help bring in new business. "When you're not part of the superstructure [Chatmon's euphemism for white society], you don't have at your fingertips the contacts that may make it a little easier."

Another problem is the ingrained belief, still held by many whites, that the only reason a black has a responsible job is because of external governmental pressure. "When you prove you are capable, you can dispel that idea," he says. "Unfortunately, it is then often replaced by the notion that you are an exceptional black man."

Does Chatmon see any stumbling blocks ahead as he maps his future from his current middle-management perch?

"Are you kidding? Certainly," he says. "The biggest personal career barrier I face as a black is the foregone conclusion that I will not be able to function in the upper echelons of management except as a vice president in charge of industrial relations, community relations, or personnel. And these pre-defined roles preclude my developing in whatever direction my talent and skills take me.

"I've been on The Street now for four years, and I've seen the subtle games that are played," says Chatmon. "I've seen situations where entry was granted but the person is sidetracked into activities where he won't have much client exposure so his ability to move ahead is blocked. This hasn't happened to me yet, but you can be sure I'm on my guard."

Understanding the Subjective Criteria

There is a question that Addison Barry Rand has learned to expect when he talks to black college students. It is usually phrased something like this: "How do you become successful in big business, given the environment, given the fact that you are black?"

Barry Rand, as he prefers to be called, breaks his answer down into two parts. The first is obvious: "You have to meet the company's objective criteria—that is, be technically proficient."

The second is more subtle. "You have to understand the subjective criteria, the social and political climate, that every corporation establishes. You've got to understand which behavioral patterns are taboo in any corporation."

Careful analysis of the social and political climate within Xerox—plus a consistently strong sales record—has brought Barry Rand, who has just turned 31, to the position of manager of the newly created Northern Virgina brank for Xerox. His operation grosses about $13 to $14 million annually and employs about 125 persons.

Many blacks do not have sufficient understanding of the subjective criteria in the corporate world, says Rand. He cites as an example a black friend who was having career problems in the finance section of Xerox's Washington office.

"Finance has a particular environment where you're supposed to look and act in a certain way. But he doesn't. He wears a beard. He wears a large bush. He wears mod clothes, including high heels, and he carries a purse.

"He has his MBA—very intelligent and can do any job that is assigned him. But he doesn't fit the image. He doesn't take a briefcase home filled with papers as some people do. And he doesn't walk down the hall with a brisk, crisp walk—you know, to let people know he's busy.

"It has nothing to do with his performance, but he doesn't fit the image. So he is successful by the *objective* criteria, meaning how you do the job. But he is not successful by the *subjective* criteria. So people assume he is not a hard worker, not a person who puts the corporation first."

Rand says that if his friend gains understanding of the subjective criteria he will win control of the situation. "He can say, 'I don't want to do this because it is not worth me going through.' Or he can say, 'I want this goal; consequently, I am going to have to change my behavior.' He can then make a conscious decision because now he has control."

Another element of the subjective business world is what Rand calls "the after-five environment." "Take a white sales rep," he says. "His best friend might be a white branch manager. So he's privy to a lot of 'after-five' information. He's told where to go and what to do to be successful." So far, blacks are not a part of that network, says Rand, so it is important that they create information networks of their own.

Even then, Rand feels that blacks who have had an early exposure to whites will deal more successfully with the subjective criteria and will, therefore, have a better chance in the corporate world.

In his case the exposure started with the fifth grade and went on to include competition with whites for such positions as captain of the football team and president of his high school class. So when he joined Xerox in 1968, Rand moved into an already familiar environment. "I knew many whites were prejudiced—these people I could deal with. There were also many whites who were willing to help. And there were some who just didn't give a damn."

Rand has encountered but one case of prejudice at Xerox, but that one was serious enough to make him consider quitting. The man, Rand says, was a branch manager who "was prejudiced against anybody who wasn't a WASP." It was, Rand says, a constant cat-and-dog situation, with the branch manager at one point telling him that while he could not fire him, because of his good sales record, he would "damn well" try to slow his career down.

Rand told his wife that he was near quitting, but he hung on in hopes of winning a Sloan fellowship to Stanford's Graduate School of Business. This he did, staying on at Stanford an additional year to get his MBA.

While channels existed within Xerox at the time through which Rand could have sought relief from a prejudiced boss, he says now, "I wasn't smart enough to use them." Winning the fellowship "was like God coming down" to solve the problem.

Rand is not a person who leaves much for a *deus ex machina* to resolve. More typical was the careful sorting out of his prospects and options after dropping out of Rutgers in 1965 following two and a half years of work on a major in political science: "I realized that the only thing that I could do with political science that was really worthwhile was to go to law school. On the other hand, I didn't have an affinity for the sciences, so I couldn't be a doctor and make the kind of money doctors make. I was good in math but that really didn't excite me, so I eliminated being an architect or a mathematician.

"I didn't have any artistic skills. I wasn't a painter; I wasn't a musician. So I sat back and asked, 'What can I offer? What is Barry Rand going to do?'

"At that time I was in retailing. I had been selling for only four months, and I was already the leading salesman. That's when I discovered my talent was in convincing people to do what I wanted them to do. I wanted to stay in marketing, and I

wanted to go with a company that required a degree. It took me six years to get mine [at American University in 1968], and I didn't want to waste the effort. I decided I was going to go with either IBM or Xerox. I made that decision two years before I even started working with Xerox."

When Rand started with Xerox, he had a game plan all lined up: train for five or six months; sell for two years; and be a sales manager for two years. "By the time I'm 30," he told his first branch manager—and on his first day with Xerox—"I want to have my MBA and I want to be a branch manager. He looked at me like I was crazy," says Rand, "but that is exactly what I have done."

For now he counts as his greatest contribution to Xerox his role in "helping blacks get hired, get promoted, and helping to change the environment that blacks have to work in." Rand and other blacks in middle management positions at Xerox have created an informal group to promote black interests. They help blacks at lower levels become more technically proficient.

"Probably, though, our major contribution lies in how to make a black successful according to the subjective criteria: Who should you know? What contacts? What's happening? All the things that help a person make it in the subjective world, all the little innuendoes that you need to make smart decisions. We help each other that way."

Fast Tracking on Merit

"I have been very fortunate," says Richard A. Guilmenot III. And indeed he has been. He has not yet earned a corner office with deep pile carpeting, and the view from his office on the eigth floor of the New York City headquarters of Batten, Barton, Durstine and Osborne, the almost-legendary advertising agency, is definitely less than inspiring. But at the age of 27, this young black man has been able to accomplish what few others, black or white, have been able to accomplish so quickly: he is a senior account executive with a salary in the mid-$20,000 range.

Guilmenot is responsible for the six products in the Gillette Right Guard line of deodorants and antiperspirants. These products bill close to $10 million a year. Since a percentage of the gross billings go to the agency, this puts Guilmenot in charge of an "autonomous profit center," as he calls it, in excess of $1 million.

Part of the good fortune that has helped his career along, he explains, "is the fact that I started out on a very good piece of business. Colgate was a very good piece of business, and Ted Bates was a very good place to start."

"An MBA degree does not prepare you for this business," he says. "It prepares you to learn. When you're starting out in this business you have to be a super 'go-fer.' You can't be afraid to roll up your sleeves and get your hands dirty."

An MBA fresh out of the classroom, Guilmenot says, is a "guy who has little more than energy to contribute to an account group. Sometimes this may mean running a projector or making sure the film is right during a client presentation. Attention to these details can be critical."

Although Guilmenot willingly assumed the "go-fer" job, he knows of other black and white MBAs in advertising who, perhaps out of fear of being stereotyped into the role, refused to play "go-fer." These MBAs he says, have not climbed the ladder as fast as he has.

Guilmenot left Bates for BBDO, lured by the promise of greater responsibility, a hefty salary increase, and the chance to move from a "humdrum account like Palmolive shave cream," with billings around $2 million, to Gillette, a brand leader with annual billings of $10 million. He points out, however, that his relations both with ex-colleagues at Bates and with the agency itself are very cordial. In fact, he says, he's now working on placing two young blacks with Bates. "One of the things I'm proudest of," he says, "is that I'm able to function as an agent in getting more qualified blacks into the business."

This placement role he's playing will, Guilmenot hopes, overcome what he sees as one of the more serious problems facing young blacks: lack of exposure to people who have been successful in business and lack of exposure to career information and opportunities. He adds that there is now developing a core of successful blacks who are meeting with younger blacks, both for socialization and recruitment, making it easier for them to get information and introductions to those who have jobs to offer.

Another problem some blacks face, Guilmenot says, is "separating the bigot from the bastard"—knowing whether you're being harassed because you're black or merely because you're the person with the least status. Guilmenot says he has thus far avoided serious problems with both. "It's not a question of being two-faced," he explains, "it's just a question of getting along with people and doing your job."

For the future, Guilmenot says, he sees himself moving up to the next rung—account supervisor, the position to which he now reports—within the next 12 months, which would be just two years after joining BBDO. "It would be quite an accomplishment for me to become an account supervisor," he admits, both because most of his peers would be older—in their early- to mid-thirties—and also because he would be one of only four or five black account supervisors in the nation.

He says that he has rejected offers to get involved with the marketing of products to the black consumer market. "For me a job is more than a paycheck," he explains. "A learning experience has to be a part of it. I want to learn how to market a consumer product to all people, not just Ultra-Sheen to black people."

Upper-level women at Indsco, especially those in sales, often were more visible than their male peers. As a result, everyone knew about the women. Even women in other divisions who reported they felt ignored and overlooked were known and spotted when they did something unusual.

All the women were the subject of conversation, questioning, gossip, and careful scrutiny. Their positions were known and observed throughout the divisions, while those of most men typically were not. Their names came up at meetings, where they would easily be used as examples. Travelers to other plant locations brought back the latest news about the women, along with other gossip. The women developed well-known names; their characteristics often were broadcast through the system in anticipation of their arrival in another office to do some work.

One woman swore in an elevator, in an Atlanta hotel, while going to have drinks with colleagues, and a few days later it was known all over Chicago that she was a "radical." And some women were even told by their managers that they were watched more closely than the men. Sometimes the manager intended to be helpful, to let the woman know that he would be right there behind her. But these good intentions underscored her isolation and her function as a symbol for women. Tokens, then, performed their jobs under public and symbolic conditions quite different from those of the dominant group.

The point is not that all of these things happen to token women, or that they happen only to people who are tokens. Some young men at Indsco complained that as new hires they felt performance pressures, uncertainties about their acceptance, and either over-protected or abandoned. But these issues were part of a transitional status out of which new hires soon passed, and in any event men did not so routinely or dramatically encounter them.

READING 6–7

Tokenism: Opportunity or Trap?*

ROSABETH MOSS KANTER

Similarly, age and experience helped women to make a satisfactory accommodation, and over time, many women settled into comfortable and less token-like patterns. Some said that there was no problem they could not handle with time and that the manifestations of discrimination in their jobs were trivial.

But still, the issues stemming from rarity and scarcity arose for women in every new situation, with new peers, and at career transitions. Even successful women who reported little or no discrimination said that they had to "work twice as hard" and expend more energy than the average man to succeed.

It is also clear that not all women in the token situation behave alike or engender the same responses in others. There was variety in the individual choices, and there were alternative strategies for managing in the situation. But a system characteristic—

* MBA, January 1978, p. 15ff. This article is adapted from "Men and Women of the Corporation," published by Basic Books, Copyright © 1977 by Rosabeth Moss Kanter.

the numerical proportion of women and men—set limits on behavioral possibilies and defined the context of peer interactions.

Most "tokens" at Indsco already knew the dangers of being few in number. Despite the commitment of management, which tried to live up to its own designation as "a people-conscious organization," the tokens were wary. Many women and minorities, who would otherwise be interested in the growth and challenge that many affirmative action programs offer, said they would not touch such positions: "This label makes it a dead end." Or, in other words: "It's a way of putting us out to pasture." Of course, there was no way to test the reality of such fears, given the short time that the jobs have been in existence, but it could be observed that women or minorities who worked on women's personnel or training issues were finding it hard to move out into other areas.

The question, for tokens, then became, Is the job an opportunity, a trap, or none of the above? Once the question was asked, risks and benefits were weighed before deciding on a strategy to pursue. Sometimes, however, the course was quite rough. What follows are some of the pressures and interactions observed at Indsco.

Because the upper-level women became public creatures, their mistakes or their intimate relationships were known just as readily as other information. Many felt their freedom of action was restricted; they would have preferred to be less noticeable, as these typical comments indicated: "If it seems good to be noticed, wait until you make your first major mistake." Or "It's a burden for the manager who gets asked about a woman and has to answer behind-the-back stuff about her. It doesn't reach the woman unless he tells her. The manager gets it and has to deal with it." And finally, "I don't have as much freedom of behavior as men do; I can't be as independent."

On some occasions, tokens were deliberately thrust into the limelight and displayed as showpieces, paraded before the corporation's public but in ways that sometimes violated the women's sense of personal dignity. One of Indsco's most senior women, a staff manager finally given two assistants (and thus managerial responsibilities) after 26 years with the company, was among the five women celebrated at a civic luncheon for outstanding women in business. On the day of the luncheon, a corsage arrived and, later, a vice president to escort her. So she went, and found she was there to represent the corporation's "prize woman," symbolizing the strides made by women in business. The program for the affair listed the women executives from participating companies, except in the case of Indsco, where the male vice-president escort was listed instead. Pictures were taken for the employee newsletter and a few days later, she received an inscribed paperweight as a memento. She told the story a few weeks after the event with visible embarrassment about being "taken on a date. It was more like a senior prom than a business event."

Yet the senior woman had to go, had to have her picture taken, and had to be gracious and grateful. The reaction of tokens to their notice was also noticed. Many of the tokens seemed to have developed a capacity often observed among marginal or subordinate peoples: to project a public persona that hid inner feelings. Although some junior management men at Indsco, including several fast trackers, were quite open about their lack of commitment to the company and dissatisfaction with aspects of its style, the women felt they could not afford to voice any negative sentiments. They played by a different set of rules, one that maintained the split between public person and private self. One woman commented, "I know the company's a rumor factory. You must be careful how you conduct yourself and what you say to whom. I saw how one woman in the office was discussed endlessly, and I decided it would be better to keep my personal life and personal affairs separate." She refused to bring dates to office parties when she was single, and she did not tell anyone at work that she got married until several months later—this was an office where the involvement of wives was routine. Because the glare of publicity meant that no private information could be kept circumscribed or routine, tokens were forced into the positions of keeping secrets and carefully contriving public performance. They could not afford to stumble.

In men's informal conversations women were often measured by two yardsticks: how, as women, they carried out the sales or management role; and how, as managers, they lived up to the images of womanhood. In short, every act tended to be evaluated beyond its meaning for the organization and taken as a sign of "how women perform." This meant that there was a tendency for problems to be blamed on the sex of a woman rather than on the situation, a phenomenon noted in other reports of few women among many men in high-ranking corporate jobs.

In one case of victim blaming, a woman in sales went to her manager to discuss a customer who was behaving seductively. The manager jumped to the assumption that the woman had led him on. The result was an angry confrontation between the woman and the manager in which she thought he was incapable of seeing her apart from his stereotypes, and he said later he felt misunderstood.

Women were treated as symbols or representatives on those occasions when, regardless of their expertise or interest, they would be asked to provide a meeting with the "woman's point of view" or to explain to a manager why he was having certain problems with woman.

Another way of reducing women to symbols involves stereotyping women's informal roles. In so doing, dominant members of a group can incorporate tokens and still preserve their own identity. In the case of token women in colleague groups at Indsco, four informal role traps were observed. These roles represented familiar categories the men could respond to and understand. Each was formed around one behavioral tendency of the token, building this into an image of the token's place in the group and forcing her to continue to live up to the image; each defined for the dominants a single response to the token's sexuality. Two of the roles make use of men's need to handle women's sexuality by envisioning them either as "madonnas" or "whores" —as either asexual mothers or overly sexual, debased seductresses, perhaps as a function of Victorian family patterns, which encouraged separation of idealistic adoration toward the mother and animalistic eroticism. The others, termed the *pet* and the *iron maiden,* also have family counterparts in the kid sister and the virgin aunt.

The women of Indsco were also aware of another performance pressure: not to make the dominants look bad. Tokenism sets up a dynamic that can make tokens afraid of being too outstanding in performance in group events and tasks. The fears had some grounding in reality. In a corporate bureaucracy like Indsco, where "peer acceptance" held part of the key to success in securing promotions and prized jobs, it was known how people were received by colleagues as well as by higher management. Indeed, men down the ranks resented the tendency for some top executives to make snap judgments about people, after five minutes' worth of conversation, and then try to influence their career reviews and create instant stars. The emphasis on peer acceptance in performance evaluations, a concept known to junior managers, was one way people lower down the managerial hierarchy retained some control over the climbing process, ensured themselves a voice, and maintained a system they felt was equitable. Getting along well with peers was thus not just something that could make daily life in the company more pleasant: it was also fed into the formal review system. One man unwittingly revealed a central principle for the success of tokens in competition with dominants: always stay one step behind, never exceed or excel. "It's okay for women to have these jobs," he said, "as long as they don't go zooming by me."

Can tokens survive the organizational scrutiny? The choices for those in the token position were either to overachieve and carefully construct a public performance that minimized organizational and peer concerns, to try to turn the notoriety of publicity to advantage, or to find ways to become socially invisible. The first course meant that the tokens involved are already outstanding and exceptional, able to perform well under close observation where others are ready to notice first and to attribute any problems to the characteristics that set tokens apart—but also to be able to develop skills in impressions management that permit them to retain control over the extra consequences loaded into their acts. The dexterity required to always do well without generating peer resentment requires both a job-related competence and political sensitivity that could take years to acquire. For this reason, young women just out of college had the greatest difficulty in entering male domains like the Indsco sales force and were responsible for much of the high turnover rate. Women were successful when they were slightly older than their male peers, had strong technical backgrounds, and had previous experiences as token women among male peers.

The second strategy, accepting notoriety and trading on it, seemed least likely to succeed in a corporate environment be-cause of the power of peers. A few women at Indsco flaunted themselves in the public arena and made a point of demonstrating their "difference," by refusing to go to certain programs, parading their high-level connections, or bypassing the routine authority structure. Such boldness was usually accompanied by top management sponsorship. But this strategy was made risky by shifting power alliances at the top. These women, who sought publicity and were getting it in part for their rarity, developed a stake in not sharing the spotlight, often known as the "Queen Bee" syndrome. This second strategy kept the numbers of women down both because the token herself was in danger of not succeeding by choosing such a risky path and because she might keep other women out.

The third choice was accepted more often by the older generation of corporate women, who predated the women's movement and had years ago accommodated to token status. It involved attempts to limit visibility, by becoming socially invisible. This strategy characterized women who tried to minimize their sexual attributes to blend into the predominant male culture, perhaps by adopting "mannish dress," as in reports by other investigators. Or it can include avoidance of public events and occasions for performance—staying away from meetings, working at home rather than in the office, keeping silent at meetings. They avoided conflict, risks, or controversial situations. They were relieved or happy to step into assistant or technical staff jobs such as personnel administration or advertising, where they could quietly play background roles that kept men in the visible forefront —or they at least did not object when the corporation put them into low-visibility jobs, since for many years the company had a stake in keeping its "unusual" people hidden.

Women making this choice did blend into the background and control their performance pressures, but at the cost of limited recognition for their competence. This choice, too, involved a psychic splitting, for the rewards for such people often came with secret knowledge—knowing what they had contributed to an effort that made someone else look good. In general, this strategy, like the last, also reinforced the existence of tokenism and kept the numbers of women down, because it led the organization to conclude that women were not very effective—low risk-takers who cannot stand on their own.

The performance pressure on people in token positions generates a set of attitudes and behaviors that appear sex linked, in the case of women, but can be understood better as situational responses, true of any person in a token role. Perhaps what has been called in the popular literature "fear of success in women," for example, is really the token woman's *fear of visibility.*

The original research that identified the fear of success concept created a hypothetical situation in which a woman was at the top of her class in medical school—a token woman in a male peer group. Such a situation exacts extra psychic costs and creates pressures for some women to make themselves and their achievements invisible—to deny success. Replication of this research using examples of settings in which women were not so proportionately scarce produced very different results.

In sum, organizational, social, and personal ambivalence surrounds people in token situations. It is likely that the burdens carried by tokens in the management of social relations take their toll in psychological stress, even if the tokens succeed in work performance. Research on people in token-like situations has identified a number of psycho-social difficulties, including unsatisfactory social relationships, unstable self-images, frustration from dealing with contradictory demands (from others as well as the self), and insecurity. More serious physical and mental stress has been associated with status incongruities and role pressures at work.

Even the best coping strategy is likely to have some internal repercussions, ranging from inhibition of self-expression to feelings of inadequacy and, perhaps, self-hatred. Self-repression and refraining from certain kinds of expressiveness are part of the culture in large organizations. But tokens especially are in a position where true disclosure to peers is not possible, and tokens may not even easily join work peers in their characteristic modes of tension release—after-work drinks, for example. Finally, to the extent that tokens accept their exceptional status, dissociate themselves from others of their category, and turn against them, tokens may be denying parts of themselves and engaging in self-hatred. This can produce inner tension.

There is a small positive psychological side to tokenism: the self-esteem that comes from mastering a difficult situation and from getting into places that traditionally exclude others of one's kind. If the tokens can segregate conflicting expectations and have strong outside support groups with which to relax, then perhaps a potentially stress-producing situation can be turned into an opportunity for ego enhancement. Indeed, one study showed that the upwardly mobile did not report the physical symptoms otherwise associated with inconsistent statuses. But, on balance, token situations seem more stressful than beneficial.

Perils and Pitfalls of the Token Game

Tokenism is a game of numbers and can be played by everyone. Once the numbers are more balanced, many of the dilemmas disappear. Who among us has not been the skunk at the garden party? The dilemmas result not so much from the individual characteristics of the token as they do from the system of tokenism itself. When tokenism exists it sets real limits on the possibilities for action and for the kinds of interactions that go on in and out of the office.

The token position contains a number of dilemmas and contradictions:

1. Tokens are simultaneously representatives and exceptions. They serve as symbols of their category, especially when they fumble, yet they are also seen as unusual examples of their kind, especially when they succeed.

2. Tokens are made aware of their differences from the numerical dominants, but they must often pretend that the differences do not exist, or have no implications.

3. Tokens are among the most visible and dramatized of performers, noticeably on stage, yet they are often kept away from the organization backstage where the dramas are cast.

4. Tokens are the quintessential "individuals" in the organization, since they stand apart from the mass of peer group members; yet they lose their individuality behind stereotyped roles and carefully constructed public personae that can distort their sense of self.

5. Those situations in which organizational peers are supposedly "relaxing" (after-work drinks, celebratory dinners, sports events) are often the most stressful for tokens, for on such occasions the protection of defined positions and structured interactions disappears. So tokens, paradoxically, may be most relaxed and feel the most "natural" during the official parts of the business day when other people are the most constrained by formal roles.

6. Tokens suffer from their loneness, yet the dynamics of interaction around them create a pressure for them to seek advantage by dissociating themselves from others of their category and, hence, to remain alone.

7. As long as numbers are low, disruptions of interaction around tokens (and their personal problems) are seen by the organization as a huge deflection from its central purposes, a drain of energy, leading to the conclusion that it is not worth having people like the tokens around. Yet the disruptions are primarily a function of the numbers being low and could be remedied by proportional increases.

How the Office Token Is Trapped

Four methods of dealing with tokens without changing their token status have been noted.

1. A token woman sometimes becomes a "mother" to the men in the group. One by one, they bring her their private troubles, and she is expected to comfort them. The assumption that women are sympathetic, good listeners, and easy to talk to about one's problems is common, even though, ironically, men say it was hard to level with women over task-related issues. Many token women act out other parts of the traditional nurturant-maternal role: doing laundry or sewing on buttons for men. This role is comparatively safe. It can, however, have three negative consequences for a woman's task performance: (A) The "mother" is rewarded primarily for service and not for independent action. (B) The dominant power aspects of the maternal image may be feared. Thus the mother is expected to keep her place as a noncritical, accepting "good mother" or lose her rewards. Since the ability to differentiate and be critical is often an indicator of competence in work groups, the mother is prohibited from exhibiting this skill. (C) The mother becomes an emotional specialist. Although the mother may never cry to engage in emotional outbursts she remains identified with emotional matters. In a token position, it is unlikely that nurturance, succor, and expressivity will be

valued or that a mother can demonstrate and be rewarded for critical, independent, task-oriented behaviors.

2. The role of "seductress" or sexual object is fraught with more tension than the maternal role, for it introduces an element of sexual competition and jealousy. The mother may have many sons; it is more difficult for the sexually attractive to have many swains. Men can adopt the role of protector toward an attractive woman, regardless of her collusion, and by implication make her a sex object, a casting that blots out all her other characteristics, reminding her and the rest of the group of her sexual status. In the guise of "helping" her, self-designated protectors may actually create further barriers to the solitary woman's full acceptance by placing themselves between the woman and the rest of the group.

3. The "pet" is adopted by the male group as a cute, amusing little thing and symbolically taken along on group events as a mascot—a cheerleader for shows of prowess. Humor is often a characteristic of the pet. She has to admire male displays, but not enter into them. Shows of competence on her part are treated as special and complimented just because they are unexpected, a kind of look-what-she-does-and-she's-only-a-woman attitude. Such attitudes, on the part of men, encourage self-effacing, girlish responses on the part of solitary women (who after all may be genuinely relieved to be included and petted) and prevent them from realizing or demonstrating their own power and competence.

4. The "iron maiden" is a contemporary variation of the stereotypical roles into which strong women are placed. Women who failed to fall into any of the first three roles, and in fact, resisted overtures that would trap them in a role (such as flirtation), might consequently be responded to as "tough" or dangerous. If a token insisted on full rights in the group, if she displayed competence in a forthright manner, or if she cut off sexual innuendos, she could be asked, "You're not one of those women's libbers, are you?" Regardless of the answer, she was henceforth regarded with suspicion, with undue and exaggerated shows of politeness (by inserting references to women into conversations, by elaborate rituals of not opening doors), and with distance, for she was demanding treatment as an equal in a setting in which no person of her kind had previously been an equal. Women inducted into the "iron maiden" role were stereotyped as tougher than they are (hence the name) and trapped in a more militant stance than they might otherwise take. Whereas seductresses and pets, especially, incurred protective responses, iron maidens faced abandonment. They were left to flounder on their own and often could not find peers sympathetic to them when they had problems.

Token women can have their tokenism institutionalized by accepting role encapsulation and the limitations on demonstrating competence that it implies. Token women must steer a course between protectiveness and abandonment. Either they allow other people to take over and fight their battles, staying out of the main action in stereotypical ways, or they stand much too alone. They may be unable by virtue of scarcity even to establish effective support systems of their own.

Doors to the upper levels of the corporate hierarchy recently have begun to open for women, and most of the time, women themselves have opened these doors. But if the typical career strategies of women in management are indicative of how they pursue career advancement, only a few more doors will be opened in the years to come.

Recent studies have suggested that the number of women in upper-level management positions is beginning to increase. Currently about 2 percent of all women in business are in management positions.[1] The increase can be attributed in part to affirmative action legislation and to more positive social attitudes toward women pursuing traditionally male careers. However, even with all the pressures for change, the relative impact on the corporate hierarchy will be minimal in the years to come. To increase the impact, women will have to take a closer look at their career strategies and values, and they will have to decide whether or not they are willing to play the corporate success game.

The conclusions of this article, based on a cross-sectional study of more than 500 women who hold positions up to the level of vice president, could have far-reaching implications for women in, or aspiring to, management. The women studied (coming from 60 firms, including several on the *Fortune* 500 list, and representing 25 industries) attended career development workshops held during the past four years. In the majority of cases, they were nominated by their firms to attend because of their management potential. The participants averaged 35 years of age; half of them were married; almost all had attended college; and they were earning an average in-

READING 6–8

Women in Management: An Endangered Species?*

JOHN F. VEIGA

come in excess of $16,000. The information received from them was compared to data obtained from men (with similar backgrounds, same average age, and same level of responsibility) who had attended other career development workshops.

In a study of individual career strategies and values, participants were asked to write down their career advice to young persons. Their responses remained anonymous. Here are some examples:

Person A: Don't be a sex symbol or apple polish the boss—do it by merit, being the best worker with the most cooperative attitude.

Person B: Don't be afraid to play politics.

Person C: Continuously develop new skills so as to prepare yourself for advancement.

---

[1] Garda Bowman, N. Beatrice Worthy, and Stephen Greyer, "Are Women Executives People?" *Harvard Business Review* 43 (July–August 1965): 14.

* *MSU Business Topics*, vol. 25, no. 3 (Summer 1977), pp. 31–35. Reprinted by permission of the publisher, Division of Research, Graduate School of Business Administration, Michigan State University.

Person D: Be the well-wrapped package with brains as opposed to the brown paper bag with brains—be noticed.

Person E: Work hard, aim high, learn something new each day, let the sky be your limit.

Few people have difficulty in attributing the advice given by Persons A and D as coming from women. The sex of the remaining persons is not so obvious: B and C were men, and E was a woman. Generally, only about 10 percent of the advice could be readily identified. However, it was possible, upon closer examination, to distinguish some major differences in career perspectives between men and women.

The purposes of the exercise was to get individuals to recognize the limitations of giving or receiving career advice. When the responses were read aloud, it was easy for the participants to see how varied and naive such advice would be. For example, one woman wrote: "Work for a male boss first." A newly promoted man wrote: "If you want to become an executive, look like one." When some of the participants volunteered to elaborate further on their advice, it was evident that these were not frivolous responses but seemed to represent an integral part of the individual's career strategy and values.

By categorizing the advice, two distinct perspectives emerged. For the majority of the 500 men, the common theme expressed was a plan-ahead strategy. Often they stressed a need for planning not only career goals but also the methods of attainment. It was clear that many of the men felt the need to give opportunity a hand. In contrast, women commonly emphasized the value of proving one's ability by doing a good job. The majority expressed advice reminiscent of Horatio Alger, which can best be summarized as a "work hard and some day you will be rewarded for your effort" strategy.

In a related finding, a researcher of factors contributing to women's success in business found that women are culturally conditioned to feel uncomfortable when making demands in their own interest. Such hesitancy, she theorizes, was probably learned at an early age. For example, at a dance, young girls stand "all dolled up against a wall, waiting to be chosen."[2] Such waiting-to-be-picked behavior appears to have carried over into women's career strategies.

It seems that women are taking a myopic view of their careers, almost a short-run perspective of taking care of today and letting the future take care of itself. One woman epitomized this attitude when she said she had no need for specific career plans. "My company knows what is best for me," she said. On the other hand, the men generally were more career wise and questioned the management myth, prevalent until the late 1940s, that good managers, like cream, rise to the top.

Men become more career wise because of their access to what has been described as the "old-boy" network. One executive put this phenomenon simply: "If you are going to play the game, you have to know the rules." Unfortunately, women do not have this access, and there are too few women in management to act as role models and to advise aspiring young women. Myra Strober and Francine Gordon, in *Bringing Women into Management*, point out that because most of today's women have been socialized to believe that management, like fatherhood, is for men, women who aspire to managerial careers need frequent reinforcement of their aspirations."[3] Unfortunately, such reinforcement might be long in coming if women in

---

[2] Margaret Hennig quoted in "Women in Banking: Transition to Management," *Carnegie Quarterly* 24 (Spring 1976): 7.

[3] Francine Gordon and Myra Strober, *Bringing Women into Management* (New York: McGraw-Hill, 1973), p. 79.

management are unable to break what appears to be a self-perpetuating cycle of passive acceptance in career strategy.

Most Women are Unwilling to Play the Game

One remedy for breaking the passive acceptance cycle might be to teach women how to play the game. To some degree assertiveness training has taken this direction. Certainly a nonassertive woman who follows a waiting-to-be-picked strategy will lessen her chance of reaching top management. However, making a woman more assertive and career wise when she is unwilling to play the game is not enough. Basic career motives need to be understood.

Unlike women, most men are expected to play the game. American businessmen often have been characterized as archetypical strivers. In reality, only about one in ten managers can be characterized as possessing the upward or unlimited success orientation.[4] Curt Tausky and Robert Dubin found that many men either are unwilling to play the game necessary to reach the top or do not aspire to top positions. Using the Career Orientations Anchorage Scale (COAS), Tausky and Dubin identified three managerial career orientations: upward, ambivalent, and downward. Male managers with these career orientations were found to possess the following characteristics:

Upward: Value high upward movement; career satisfaction is a function of proximity to the peak.

Ambivalent: Have an uncrystallized career perspective; dissatisfied without advancement but unwilling to actively pursue success.

Downward: Have a limited success perspective; after achieving adequate career rewards, express little interest in further advancement. Career satisfaction is a function of how far they have come in their careers.

Results of several studies which have validated the COAS all have indicated similar career orientation distributions for men in middle management. Male workshop participants included in this study showed virtually no significant differences from the typical pattern. However, when representative women were administered the COAS, some dramatic differences were found. Results are shown in Table 1.

These findings suggest that even fewer women than men (6 percent versus 10 percent) are strivers. Because the sample was an atypical group of women picked for their management potential, a higher incidence of upward orientation could have been expected. A reduction of more than half in the downward category (20 percent versus 47 percent) resulted in almost a doubling of the number of women (74 percent versus 43 percent) in the ambivalent category. The fact that most of the women were in this category suggests they have uncrystallized career perspectives, which is consistent with their shortsighted career strategies. It also suggests that most women value advancement but are unwilling to play the game necessary to achieve success. However, these results may be overinflated. Women have been subjected to pressures from the women's movement as well as

---

[4] Curt Tausky and Robert Dubin, "Career Anchorage: Managerial Mobility Motivation," *American Sociological Review* 30 (October 1965): 725–35.

TABLE 1
Managerial Career Orientation by Sex

Orientation	Women* (%)	Men† (%)
Upward	6	10
Ambivalent	74	43
Downward	20	47

Note: $X^2 = 47.97$, df $= 2$, p $< .001$.
* N $= 194$.
† Tausky and Dubin, p. 729 (N $= 308$).

their organizations' affirmative action efforts. Perhaps some career ambivalence is merely a side effect of these awareness-raising efforts?

As might be expected, most studies show a connection between age and career orientation. By 45 years of age, 73 percent of all males have a downward perspective, in part because these managers have recognized their career limitations and accepted the inescapable fact that only a few will reach the top. In contrast, there is no difference in the career orientation between women over 45 and under 45 years of age. This finding lends credence to the hypothesis that women are being affected by awareness-raising pressures. While only 18 percent of the males over age 45 are experiencing ambivalence, almost four times as many women (70 percent) at this stage in life continue to experience ambivalence.

In a 1976 study,[5] twice as many younger women were found to be highly disillusioned with their present management positions (69 percent) as compared to older women (31 percent). Therefore, despite what might be expected, older women are more likely experiencing career ambivalence because of organizational and societal pressures and not because of unhappiness with present positions. However, since a younger person, male or female, often experiences career ambivalence, it is impossible to determine to what extent the higher level of ambivalence found in women over 45 is a result of awareness-raising pressures and how much might be attributed to the acculturation process found in our society today. Yet, it is possible to conclude that women over 45 are experiencing greater career anxiety than they probably should.

---

[5] John F. Veiga and John N. Yanouzas, "What Women in Management Want: The Ideal vs. the Real," *Academy of Management Journal* 19 (March 1976): 137–43.

TABLE 2
Managerial Career Adaptation Problems Encountered, By Sex

Problem	Women (N = 400) (%)	Men (N = 300) (%)
Choice of anxiety	48.5	23.3
Lack of skill	4.0	33.0
Lack of assurance	20.2	12.3
Lack of information	27.3	31.3

Note: The sample size is a result of the number of managers who indicated some problems in achieving their career goals. Out of 506 women, 400 (79 percent) reported problems. Out of 500 men, 300 (60 percent) reported problems.

Choice Anxiety is a Major Problem

Consistent with the higher incidence of career ambivalence, women also have greater difficulty in making career choices. About 79 percent of the women attempting to develop a career plan express difficulty, as compared to 60 percent of the men. In addition, women express different career adaptation problems than men. Milton E. Hahn identifies four adaptation problems normally encountered when making career decisions: choice anxiety, lack of skill, lack of assurance, and lack of information.[6] Workshop participants were asked to identify problems that they anticipated in accomplishing their career plans. The results, shown in Table 2, were categorized by problem type.

Given the high incidence of ambivalence found in women, it was not too surprising to find almost half with the problem of choice anxiety. Comments such as these were typical: "I have such overriding personal obstacles at the moment that I can't really be as interested as I should be in a career plan." "I'm not sure which way I want to go," and "I just don't know what I really want." Even though their problems varied, many of these women seemed to be

---

[6] Milton E. Hahn, *Planning Ahead After Forty* (Los Angeles: Western Psychological Services, 1973), pp. 2–3.

expressing anxiety over trying to make decisions they were unaccustomed to making. One woman said: "I'm just not accustomed to planning my life the way I want it. I've always accepted things the way they were." Often their expression of choice anxiety sounded like a lack of assurance as well. Hence, even though 20 percent of the problems were classified as a lack of assurance, realistically it was a much greater problem than the table suggests. Surprisingly, lack of skill was rarely mentioned by women even though a great deal of emphasis has been placed on business training for women, primarily because of their lack of business school degrees.

In contrast, the men expressed lack of information and/or skill as their major problems. Statements such as these were common: "I really don't have the educational background to do what I'd really like to do," "I'm not sure what future opportunities are available to me in my present company." The men tended to obscure any choice anxiety or lack of assurance by rationalizing that lack of skill or information was the major obstacle. Those over age 40 tended to fall into the skill trap. They regarded their careers as continuous investments in skill development and often were unwilling to consider any career options requiring them to start over. On the other hand, women seemed to have the greatest difficulty in deciding where they should invest themselves and whether or not investment was really worth it.

Are Women in Management an Endangered Species?

Throughout this article, an attempt was made to avoid any value judgments about which career strategy is best. However, women must become more career wise if they are to survive in the corporate environs. That does not mean that all women should strive for the top. Each one needs to decide where she wants to go, and if the price is worth it.

We all have a choice. We can approach the future as pawns and accept whatever life offers us, or we can recognize our ability to influence our future and take some responsibility for what happens. The outcomes, which vary greatly, often benefit both organization and individual. One woman said: "I've finally discovered that I have wasted a lot of time and energy trying to get a promotion which I thought I wanted. Now that I've decided that goal is not important, to hell with working overtime! I'm going to start taking tennis lessons this weekend." A talented Ph.D. found that by taking an active interest in the direction of her career and by actively pursuing outside opportunities, she won a significant promotion with a major insurance company.

In summary, most of the evidence suggests that it will not be easy for women to assume their rightful place in the corporate hierarchy. While it is clear that, to effect a change, women will have to modify their career strategies, it is unfair to place all the burden for change on them. A great deal still needs to be done to alter the sex-role stereotyping found in business today. Equal pay for equal work has been accepted, but the notion that women and men are interchangeable in management has not.

While there is too much evidence of forward motion to conclude that women in management are an endangered species, it should be recognized that the same pressures that produce change also can be counterproductive. For every woman who achieves a top management position, several others, especially those over age 45, will suffer increased career anxieties and uncertainties. However, along the way women may help modify the corporate environment so that playing the game may become obsolete; or perhaps a new game will emerge.

During the past decade there have been a host of books and articles offering managers how-to advice on securing employment—how to write a dynamic resume, how to conduct a successful job search, how to handle job interviews, and how to switch employers. But the broader problem of planning a career has been largely ignored.

For the past few years I have been conducting research on managerial career patterns and have served as an informal career counselor for a number of MBA students and alumni. In this role I have observed much frustration and disillusionment among MBAs over the progress of their careers. There are three scenarios that recur frequently.

A month or two before graduation, George B., an MBA student, decides it is time to begin his job search. After a few frantic weeks of fruitless hunting he drops by to chat with his advisor.

Asked what kind of job he is looking for, he replies, "Well, I'm really not sure. I kind of enjoyed my marketing courses so maybe that would be a good field for me. Besides, I had sort of hoped that you could give me some ideas about the functional areas, industries, or companies that are likely to offer the best job opportunities."

Unfortunately, George B.'s lack of direction is not atypical. My discussions with colleagues at universities throughout the United States reveal a wide-spread ignorance among MBAs of, first, what kind of job they would like to have and, second, what they have to offer to a potential employer other than the degree common to the approximately 17,000 MBA students who matriculate each year.

In short, many MBA students are ill prepared to make a first-job choice. Others, like George B., find much to their surprise that they have no job offers upon graduation, at which time panic, confusion, and chaos frequently sets in.

The Hardest Job of All: Career Planning*

THOMAS G. GUTTERIDGE

Joseph D. provides a different example of a career crisis. He obtained an MBA degree with a concentration in marketing from a prestigious eastern university in 1965. He accepted a position as a market research analyst at a salary of $11,000 in the headquarters office of a large petroleum company. His career got off to a good start. By 1971 his salary had increased to $21,000, and he was in charge of a five-man analysis team.

Joseph D., however, is discontented with his career progress. While his salary has increased substantially, his level of decision-making responsibility is only slightly greater than it was during the first year or two of his career. He has remained in a staff job in the home office for six years and would like a different type of assignment. He had requested a transfer to the treasurer's office or to a line marketing job.

He was told, however, that he is too valuable in his current assignment to be transferred to another staff position that he was overpaid for a lower-level line position, and too inexperienced to be promoted into a middle- or upper-level line position. Feeling that he is at a dead end in his current job, Joe quits to take a job as a salesman with a company selling computer services.

My research, confirmed by a Harvard Business School study, suggests that Joe's career difficulties are typical of those of many MBAs. Their first job is on staff because of their own and their employer's preference. However, many MBAs discover that, as their careers progress, high salaries inhibit a switch into line jobs. Others find it difficult to cross over from one function to another, for instance, from production to finance. What started as a temporary assignment becomes, not by choice, a permanent career.

Robert J. provides a still different example of a career dilemma. Upon obtaining his MBA in 1964, he went to work for a large consulting firm in New York City. Within a year he was put in charge of major consulting projects throughout the United States. Away from home much of the time, Bob consoled his wife by explaining. "This pace will only last for a couple of years at most and by that time I'll have obtained enough experience to attract a good offer from a client firm. Then I can settle down to a more sedate business executive's life."

Sure enough, Bob received several job offers from client firms and in October 1967 went to Atlanta as divisional personnel manager for a large conglomerate. Faced with a pile of neglected problems, Bob worked long hours and weekends. He brought the personnel situation under control and less than a year later was transferred to another division in Charleston, West Virginia, as plant manager. By the

end of 1972 Bob had received two more promotions, two more transfers, and was earning almost $40,000. He is viewed as a real comer by top management. He appears to be the epitome of an MBA success story.

Unfortunately, Bob has had to pay a price. Unable to cope with her husband's transfers and frequent absences as well as too much socializing of an official nature, Bob's wife divorced him. Ironically, Bob has also begun to question whether this is the kind of life he really wants. Much of the personal enjoyment he once derived from his work has vanished, and he has a nagging feeling that his life is being wasted.

Bob's case is not unique. Promotions, power, and high pay are the supposed ultimate measures of success. Some MBAs have a real need for success, and it satisfies them. Others seek it because they think it will make them happy, and eventually they discover that their careers are not what they wanted after all.

Not all MBAs have careers of unfulfilled expectations and bitter disappointments. Conceivably, the difficulties in the samples discussed could have been largely avoided if the MBAs had heeded Gutteridge's Axiom No. 1:

Each individual must assume the primary responsibility for his own career development, and the best way to do so is to prepare a personal career plan.

In the broadest sense, career planning is the formulation of a life strategy that takes into account a sequence of work activities and job assignments, the organizational settings in which these activities will be performed, the type of career development experiences that will be undertaken, and other similar decisions. Career planning is a series of choices regarding the match-up between an MBA's personal interest, goals, and abilities with the opportunities present in the world of work. (While the guidelines presented here apply equally to men and women, women have special career-planning problems that go beyond the scope of this article.)

It is useful to divide career planning into five phases: (1) determining personal goals and objectives; (2) evaluating personal strengths and weaknesses; (3) analyzing career opportunities; (4) final development and implementation of the career plan; and (5) periodic review and updating of the career plan.

Determining Personal Goals and Objectives

The difficult task of setting down what you really want out of life can be made easier by asking yourself some hard questions and giving yourself honest answers. On the basis of experience (educational, work, personal), what kinds of tasks or activities did you enjoy most? Which did you least enjoy?

If you could have any job you wanted, what job would you choose? Why? What needs would that job fulfill now? A year from now? Ten years from now? At the end of your career?

How important are such factors as income, geographic location, amount of travel, job security, opportunity for independence and autonomy, and company size.

How important are the above factors to your spouse?

What kind of career do you really want and how far up the corporate pyramid do you really want to ascend?

What price are you willing to pay to get ahead? Are you willing to play politics? Are you willing to relocate whenever and wherever your firm directs?

Rank the goals or objectives you would like to achieve during your career and tell yourself why these goals are important to you.

When you have retired, what must you have accomplished to make you feel that your life has been satisfying? How far have you gone toward achieving these things, what remains to be done, and how can you begin to accomplish these unfinished objectives?

When you have honestly answered these questions, you will have a clearer understanding of your goals, values, and priorities. Goal analysis is frustrating and difficult; it requires that you spend hours asking yourself tough questions.

Evaluating Personal Strengths and Weaknesses

The next major step in career planning is to analyze your strengths and weaknesses to determine which are fixed and which can be changed. You can compensate for those weaknesses which are immutable and concentrate on improving those which are more easily remedied.

Develop a list of the ways in which your basic skills can be used. Try not to limit this list to preconceptions about your career. You will be surprised at how many different types of careers can be built from a given set of skills and interests.

Before proceeding to the next major stage in the career plan, you should consider the desires and personal values of others (your spouse, your parents, your in-laws) who are likely to have an influence on your career decisions. To what degree will others determine your geographic location, the type of career you pursue, or the amount of money you must earn?

The extent to which the wishes of others will influence your career plan must be your own decision. But their desires should be considered, and they should be made aware of your career plan.

Analyzing Career Opportunities

You can now begin to focus on specific avenues toward your objective. This means not only specific job offers or promotion and transfer possibilities, but also development activities such as company training programs or returning to school on a full-time basis. (This assumes that you have already generated some career opportunities.)

Career opportunities should be evaluated by considering a variety of issues: the economy as a whole; the labor market for a person with your educational background (the labor market for an MBA, for example, is different from that for an undergraduate business major); the industry; the company; the major unit (division or department); and the specific job or career development opportunity in question. Many MBAs start their evaluation at the level of the job itself. Jobs, however, can change. Company climate and industry health are much more permanent.

The major criterion for evaluating a career opportunity should be the extent to which it will help you achieve both near-term and long-range career goals. Many people do not plan further ahead than their next job (if that far), so they may accept a job which, while superficially attractive (glamorous industry, high pay, desirable location), may be detrimental to their long-run career plans. On the other hand, long-range goals are achieved through a series of intermediate jobs, and if they are too unpleasant, the long-term objectives probably never will be reached.

One additional point. Individuals who are employed should not neglect the career opportunities within their companies. Oddly enough, managers often know more about job prospects outside their company than they do about those inside the firm.

Final Development and Implementation of the Career Plan

At this point in your career plan, you should have a good perspective on your career objectives, your assets and liabilities, the extent to which your career plans are likely to be influenced by the desires of others, and the career opportunities that are available to you. Now, you must put this information together and formulate your career plan. Commit this career plan to writing. This will often spotlight previously unnoticed conflicts and help the planner integrate disparate factors. The career plan should include a listing of your long-term goals and objectives. As a new graduate, these objectives may be vague, but you should have at least a preliminary idea of the final objective of your career.

A plan for accomplishing these goals should include intermediate goals; stepping-stone experiences (jobs, training, functional assignments); a plan for avoiding obsolescence through training; and a decision on your next career move, whether it is your first job, a job change, or further training. Establish schedules and make sure each step is both achievable and worthwhile.

Periodic Review and Updating of the Career Plan

Career planning is an ongoing process, not a single event that is done once and for all. It must be continuously updated to account for changes in oneself, in one's goals, or in the environment. The entire career planning process should be repeated at least once a year.

As you begin to analyze your opportunities and the steps needed to achieve your goals, the goals themselves may change. So may your strengths and weaknesses. The goal of career planning is not to remove uncertainty, but to help you cope with it.

Case 6–1

YOUNG ENGINEERS AT DYNAMIC TECH CORPORATION*

James Mackenzie had been slightly late arriving at his office this morning. He and his wife had celebrated their 20th wedding anniversary at the Elks Club last night, so he had overslept a little. After parking his car in the executive parking lot, he hurried up to his office. It was an office he really liked—plush red carpet, modern paintings (which were colorful and impressive, although he would have preferred more realistic landscapes), and oiled walnut furnishings all testified to his position as manager of the Electronics Research and Development Department for Dynamic Tech Corporation of Chicago. Exhibit 1 gives information on the company.

As Jim stepped off the elevator, he could see a group of engineers outside his office. Frank Nelson stood out with his bushy red mustache, orange shirt, and wide yellow tie. Jim couldn't help wondering where some of his young engineers bought their clothes—and how they could wear them after they bought them. As he got closer, Jim could see that Joe Riley, Nelson Samuels, and Rich Myers were there also; four of the five engineers in his Advanced New Products Group.

Jim figured that they had some technical matter to resolve. The thought gave him ambivalent feelings: pleasure that he could make a decision which he enjoyed doing, but a little anger that work should be held up waiting for him. After all, these engineers were working on a rush project—the final development and testing of the new tactical XXX system for the U.S. Army. Some early models had been field tested in Vietnam with a general conclusion that if the still serious bugs could be ironed out, the XXX system could be of great aid in tactical, nighttime infantry operations. The pressure was on from the military to get the system completed so a production contract could be awarded. In fact, Jim and the company brass had a meeting scheduled with Department of Defense officials that afternoon.

"Good morning, gentlemen," Jim greeted his engineers as he reached the door. The awkward silence in response to his greeting gave Jim an inkling that this was not an ordinary technical problem. After he had hung up his raincoat, had his secretary fetch a cup of coffee, and sat down at his spacious desk, Jim invited the engineers in.

---

* The events in this case occurred in 1970.

EXHIBIT 1
Dynamic Tech Corporation: Partial Organization Chart and Other Information

```
                          ┌──────────────────┐
                          │   President      │
                          │  Robert Oliver   │
                          └──────────────────┘
            ┌──────────────────────┼──────────────────────┐
 ┌──────────────────┐   ┌──────────────────┐   ┌──────────────────┐
 │ Vice President   │   │ Vice President   │   │ Vice President   │
 │Government Relations│  │  Engineering     │   │  Manufacturing   │
 │Jamison McCullough│   │  Foster Jenkins  │   │  Sam Steinberg   │
 └──────────────────┘   └──────────────────┘   └──────────────────┘
              ┌──────────────────┐   ┌──────────────────┐
              │ Vice President   │   │ Vice President   │
              │ Staff Activities │   │     Sales        │
              │  John Sturholm   │   │ William Former   │
              └──────────────────┘   └──────────────────┘
      ┌─────────────────┬─────────────────────┬─────────────────────┐
 ┌──────────────┐   ┌──────────────────┐   ┌──────────────────┐
 │  Manager     │   │  Manager         │   │  Manager         │
 │ Electronics R&D│ │Engineering Design│   │Engineering Services│
 │James Mackenzie│  │ Julian Jaackson  │   │ Richard Higgins  │
 └──────────────┘   └──────────────────┘   └──────────────────┘
         ┌──────────────────┐
         │  Group Leader    │
         │   Testing        │
         │  David Hyland    │
         └──────────────────┘
 ┌──────────────────┐   ┌──────────────────┐
 │  Group Leader    │   │  Group Leader    │
 │Advanced New Products│ │ Basic Research  │
 │ Howard Johannson │   │ Leonard Burke    │
 └──────────────────┘   └──────────────────┘
```

Net sales: $85,000,000.
Government contract percentage of sales: 82%.
XXX system development contract: $1,200,000.
Expected production contract for XXX system: $7,000,000.

Number of engineers employed by company: 83
Number of engineers in Electronics R & D Department: 22.
Corporate headquarters: Chicago (Loop area).
Plant and all engineering: Chicago (south side).

Engineers in Advanced New Products:

Howard Johannson .. age 42   B.S.E., University of Illinois.
Joseph Riley .... age 30   B.S.E., Purdue.
Nelson Samuels .... age 26   B.S.E., Stevens Institute.
Francis Nelson ..... age 25   B.S.E., M.S.E., M.I.T.
Rich Myers .... age 23   B.S.E., M.S.E., Michigan State.

They came in—brightly garbed Frank, almost equally modish Nelson, closecropped and dark-suited Joe, and Rich. Since there was only one chair in the room they all stood rather uneasily in front of their superior's desk (Jim had read in *The Wall Street Journal* that a manager should only have one extra chair in his office; this would supposedly ensure that meetings are short and to the point). "Well?" Jim asked. The engineers looked at each other somewhat anxiously. Silently, Rich Myers withdrew a sheet of paper from his pocket and handed it to Mackenzie. Jim read the note:

> To: Mr. James Mackenzie, Manager, Electronics R&D Department
> From: Engineers in Advanced New Products Group
>
> After much consideration of the military, political, and moral issues involved, the undersigned have agreed that henceforth they will no longer perform any work in continuation of or in conjunction with the XXX system.
>
> (signed) Francis Nelson
Nelson Samuels
Joseph Riley
Richard Myers

With mounting anger and confusion mixed with a slight feeling of panic in the pit of his stomach, James Mackenzie read the note and then looked up at the engineers standing before him.

Questions

1. Analyze the causes of the conflict between the engineers and the company.
2. What do you think are the engineers' objectives?
3. Describe and analyze the pros and cons of Mackenzie's conflict management alternatives.
4. Recommend a course of action for Mackenzie—and for Jenkins and Oliver (see the organization chart) if you think they should become involved.

Case 6–2

THE YOUNG SUPERVISOR*

About three years ago, just two months after reporting to work as the employment manager of a large aluminum manufacturer, John Day received a long-distance telephone call from a Mr. Dave Craft, personnel director of a large manufacturing plant located in a southeastern city which employed approximately 1,600 people. The following conversation took place.

Craft: How are you Johnnie? Al Kline at our K and W plant tells me they sure miss you since you left as their training director. Hope the weather at your new location is more suitable for your wife's health problems.

Day: We're all fine and enjoying the new job and location, thanks. What's on your mind, Dave?

Craft: Just recently at company headquarters, the central staff decided to reorganize the personnel activities of all 12 branch plant operations. I'm not exactly sure why the company wants to reorganize us, but I've

---

* This case was prepared by Professor Charles R. Klasson, University of Iowa. Copyright 1962 by the College of Business Administraton Foundation, University of Texas.

heard it seems they want to get greater control over our operations since the unions got a stronger foothold in the company.

Day: How does this concern me?

Craft: Well, I'm pretty sure four new units will be established—Security, Employment, Employee Relations, and Employee Services—all divisions under my department. I'll need one more supervisor, and I want you for the job.

Day: Wait a minute, Dave. I can't leave this job. I have only been with the company for two months, and, besides, I was hired to set up a new employment department. It would not be very ethical to let my boss down this way after all he has done for me.

Craft: You won't have to let him down, Johnnie, for the reorganization is not scheduled to go into effect for approximately another ten months. That is why I'm trying to line you up now.

Day: I just don't know, Dave. I don't like the idea of leaving so soon after getting on this job.

Craft: Let's be realistic about it, Johnnie. You know very well this would be a major step up for you in our company with good pay and participation in our executive bonus plan. Opportunities for advancement are excellent, and the location of our plant is ideal. I know this will be a difficult decision for you, but give it some serious thought. I will keep in touch with you on any new developments about the reorganization since it is indefinite at this time.

Day: All right, Dave—I'll give it some thought. Thanks for calling. Good-by.

Accepting the New Job

During the following four months, John Day received a number of letters and phone calls from Mr. Craft encouraging him to make the change of jobs. Twenty-eight months ago, John Day accepted a job offer from Mr. Craft as training director of management development, the same position he had held at the company's K and W plant. Organizationally, the training director reported directly to the personnel director. (See Exhibit 1 for organization of the Personnel Department prior to reorganization.) Dave Craft explained to John Day that the reorganization plans were progressing as planned but were as yet not finalized at headquarters; consequently, he could not at that time hire John Day into the company as a supervisor since the plan had not been placed into effect.

Twenty-six months ago, John Day reported to work. That afternoon Day was introduced to all the departmental personnel except the caterer and the plant physician. The company did not maintain a cafeteria staff but instead furnished facilities and utilities to the caterer who contracted with the company for providing food services. Frequently, he was not in the plant. The plant physician was on a retainer and worked only on a part-time basis. Frequently, during the course of the introductions, Craft was called into

EXHIBIT 1
Personnel Department before Reorganization

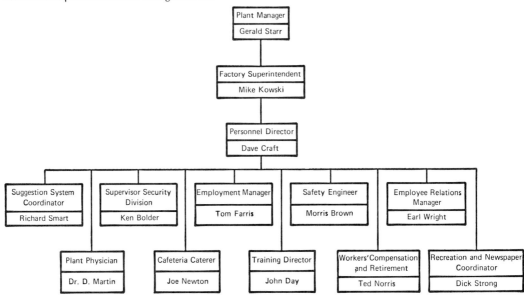

the plant manager's office through an interoffice door which joined the two rooms. During these interruptions little idle conversation took place between the departmental personnel present and Day.

After the formal introductions were over and everyone had left the office, John commented on the number of old-timers that were in the department. The following comments were made by Craft about the personal histories of the people then in his department.

Craft: We've got a fine work group and an awful lot of experience in our department, Johnnie. Respect these men and you'll learn a lot. You probably noticed already that the working relationships between me and my men are very informal and personal. We call each other by our first names. I've gone through plenty in this company with most of the crew. Let me tell you a little about each of them.

Four of my key people are the old-timers you spoke about—Smart, Brown, Farris, and Strong. Everyone of them started as unskilled hourly workers in the production organization over 20 years ago. I don't believe there is any job in the line that one of these men has not filled at one time or another. Soon after I got transferred into this personnel job following my tour in the plant eight years ago, I managed to gradually bring in these experienced men into the department as openings occurred. None of them, like myself, have had any formal training beyond high school, and I don't believe Farris even had that. You are one of the few people in the plant with a college degree.

Joe Newton, the caterer, and I have been working together for five years on running the cafeteria. We get along fine. The "Doc" and I go round and round over these workmen's compensation claims and new hire risks. He's too cautious and believes the men are all trying to get away with something. We have some good "ones" every once in a while.

Ken Bolder, supervisor of Security, has ten years' service with the company and came up through the ranks as an hourly worker, also. He's a good man and should have a good future here. He went to some college for two years. Our employee relations manager, Wright, is a young lawyer. He has a degree from Yale. He has only been with us for two years and doesn't seem to be helping improve union-management relations. It's a fact the union stewards don't like him. Every time a grievance comes to us in the third step, he tries to use some legal technicality in the contract to resolve it. The boys in the shop don't go for this. He may be too young for the job since he is only 33 years old.

Ted Norris, the workmen's compensation and retirement man, came into this department in his present position six years ago after receiving a degree in personnel administration from some business college. It has taken some time, but I believe he has finally learned it takes a little more than book learnin' to get the job done. You know, Johnnie, I guess you're going to be the youngest man in the department at 31. I didn't think about that. Anyway, you should have a pretty good picture of the people you are going to be working with. Try and get along with them all.

Just a couple more things, Johnnie, before I catch my ride home with the plant manager. If you have any problems with the line personnel in doing your job as training director, come and see me about them. I like all of my people to know I have an "open-door" policy at all times. I'm here to help you do your job. Don't forget it! The plant manager, his assistant, and I all came up in the production organization together. We got this plant off the ground, and we want to keep it off. See you tomorrow.

Day: Thanks for taking the time for the introductions and telling me about the people in the department. Good night.

While not working in his private office, Day spent most of his time with supervisors out in the plant coordinating and developing training programs. Consequently, he had little occasion to work or associate with the other members of the personnel department during his first eight months as training director. Throughout this period he, on occasion, casually inquired of his boss as to the progress of the reorganization and was told progress had been made but to be patient.

Announcing the Reorganization

Eighteen months ago, a memorandum from the personnel director requested that departmental members report to the plant conference room for purposes of explaining the company-wide reorganization policy of the personnel departments and for assignment of personnel to the new positions. By about this time, some of the departmental personnel were beginning to wonder whether the reorganization would actually go through since little had been said or done about it for well over a year. At the meeting, Mr. Craft introduced the plant manager, Mr. Starr, who made some generally vague statements about the reasons for the company reorganization after which he turned the meeting over to Craft, who made the following statement.

Craft: I will attempt to explain the new organization as briefly as possible by projecting it on the screen. Please hold all your questions until I am through, at which time I will turn the lights on.

First, the central staff has found it advisable, in the best interest of the over-all company operations, to establish three operating divisions —Security, Employment and Employee Relations, and Employee Services—each headed by a supervisor reporting directly to the departmental personnel director. (See Exhibit 2. The first slide only showed position titles.) Organizationally, the entire department reports and is accountable for its actions and performance to the plant manager. Functionally, the department is also accountable to the company vice president of personnel headquarters through the department head. All company-wide matters referred directly to division heads from central staff counterparts shall be reported to the department head or his representative during his absence. I don't anticipate a large increase in working relationships between the department and central staff. Matters of company-wide concern will be issued to my office in the form of policy directives and procedures which will be dissiminated as required.

The following promotions and transfers will become effective March 1, 1959. In view of the increased responsibilities that will have to be assumed by each new supervisor, length of service diversity of experience were the major factors considered in the promotions, and lateral transfers are not reflected on the screen. Promotions to division supervisors are: supervisor, Security Division, Tom Farris; supervisor, Employment and Employee Relations, Ken Bolder; and supervisor, Employee Services, Ted Norris. In the Security Division no changes are to be made in the staff of 15 inspectors. Earl Wright and Elmer Tread (promoted from quality control) will report to the supervisor, Employment and Employee Relations, respectively, for the employee relations and employment functions. The major change, as you can see, involves the Employee Services Division. Reporting to Ted Norris in this division will be John Day, training director; Dr. D. Martin, physician; Joe Newton caterer; Morris Brown, safety engineer; Richard Smart, suggestion system coordinator; Mel Black (promoted from clerk position within department), workmen's compensation and retirement representative; and Dick Strong, recreation and newspaper coordinator.

Position guides for each new supervisory position will be made available to you by the central staff upon notification of promotions. Each new supervisor will be responsible for organizing and instructing his personnel about any new operational procedures or working relationships deemed necessary. Lights. Now, are there any questions?

EXHIBIT 2
Personnel Department after Reorganization

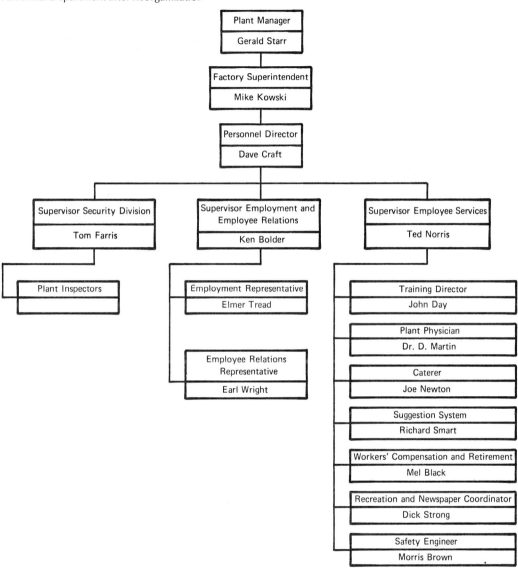

A dead silence and atmosphere of surprise and amazement pervaded the conference room after Craft stopped talking. "If there are no questions, let's call it a day," stated Craft at 4:50 P.M. As the physician walked out the door, he said in a loud voice, "Anybody want to quit?"

Reactions of Personnel to Reorganization

While talking to the casewriter about his reactions and observations to the new reorganization plan and promotions announced by the personnel director, John Day sketched out the following events:

Day: The whole thing came as somewhat of a shock to me. In fact, I was virtually stunned for a moment when I heard I did not get promoted. I had been waiting for almost a year for the promotion. I was not only disappointed but damn mad, since nothing was said or hinted about my not getting one of the supervisory slots even though only three, rather than four, positions were authorized. Rather than exploding at Craft before he had an opportunity to explain to me what had happened, I decided to wait for him to call me in and discuss the whole thing. He never did call me, in fact, he acted as though nothing had happened. After realizing he was not going to talk with me about the whole affair, I decided it would be useless to try and argue or even to discuss the issue with Craft. I felt I'd been had. Apparently, nobody else in the organization was aware that I was hired to fill one of the new supervisory slots.

I was really in a bind because I couldn't afford to make another move so quickly for fear of being labeled a job-hopper. Furthermore, the line-up of people didn't appear to leave much chance of my getting a promotion in the organization.

I wasn't the only one shocked. For two weeks immediately following the meeting, everyone in the department was pretty closed mouth about the new organization plan and promotions except Tom Farris, the new Security Division supervisor. I heard him complaining that his close friend, Dave Craft, dealt him out when he was not promoted to head up his old employment function. Later on he had a showdown with Craft. I understand Craft persuaded him everything would work out fine. They really had an argument over this one.

While not mentioning any names, some of the people under Ted Norris were definitely not happy about having to report to someone other than Craft. In fact, I got pretty close to Ted after the reorganization and enjoyed working with him. As a result of our confidence in each other, he began telling me he was not too happy under the new organizational arrangement. He inferred there was a lot of politics going on that he didn't like. Also, he complained that a number of people in his division by-passed him on some pretty important matters and decisions going to Craft. About six months after the reorganization, Ted let it slip he was in the market for a new job. I can't say that I was surprised.

A couple of other interesting things happened. Almost immediately after the new divisions were set up, every morning about a half hour before working hours started, Craft, Bolder, Farris, and Norris would meet in Craft's office. You could see them all through the glass partitions. A number of us in the department had noticed this practice but did not have any idea as to what went on in these sessions. No formal departmental meetings of all the division heads were held, so these morning meetings may have served that purpose. The other matter concerns a conversation which I had with Craft six weeks after the new promotions were announced. One morning he called me aside and said, "I'm getting you a raise but don't say anything to Norris about it." And that was all there was to it. Next month my check increased.

The work seemed to get done around the office—how efficiently, I didn't know. I had no real problems working with anybody in the department since I spent most of my time in the plant.

Promotion of John Day

Seven months ago, the news got out that Ted Norris was quitting as supervisor of Employee Services after only ten months on the job. Rumors from people in the know had it that he was "fed up with the whole situation." Officially, the announcement was made that Ted Norris had a wonderful opportunity to go to work for a large manufacturing concern as personnel director. Immediately people in the department began speculating as to which one of the "old-timers" would get the job vacated by Norris.

Six months ago, Dave Craft issued a memorandum to all department personnel, announcing that John Day would replace Ted Norris and officially assume his new duties and responsibilities on February 1, 1960. The news of the promotion came as a surprise to everyone in the division, including Day, who had not heard or knew anything about it before receipt of the memorandum. It was plain to see that a number of people in the department were openly disgruntled as one person had stated, "How does the new man rate the job?" Two days later Craft called Day into his office to discuss briefly the promotion.

Craft: Congratulations, Johnnie. Well! I told you to be patient and that I'd get you the promotion I promised you. It wasn't how or when I planned it, but we made it. Now I expect you to start producing. Ted has been instructed to break you in on the job for the next two weeks. You shouldn't have any trouble. After you get acquainted with what's involved, I will want to talk with you regarding some of the weaknesses I noted in Ted's performance which I don't care to see in you. We will want you to continue on as training director until we can find someone to replace you. You won't have to worry about the other jobs in the division—they'll be handled well. Now, any questions?

Day: Yes. I certainly appreciate this opportunity. After not getting one of the new openings last year, I was pretty disappointed. Looks like everything is going to work out okay. Frankly, I didn't expect it.

Craft: Always remember, you've gotta learn to maneuver, John—timing is real important.

Day: Do you have some kind of a job description I can see, Dave, in order to know exactly what my new job entails?

Craft: No, Day. We got some position guides from central staff last year which didn't apply too well to our operation. So we decided not to rely on them. Ted will check you out on what's involved.

For the next two and half weeks Ted Norris acquainted and explained his job to John Day. Day quickly observed that a large part of Ted's time was spent working on workmen's compensation cases and preparing a large number of monthly reports required by state and federal agencies. Near the end of the training period and while out to lunch together, Ted told John about a real serious problem he had and couldn't resolve.

Ted: I've had a rough time with some of the people in my division, John. First, I'm sure they have resented me ever since I took over the job.

John: What do you mean? Everyone in the division has treated me fine.

Ted: Yes, so far, but let's wait and see what happens when you step into my shoes. I'm warning you—expect some trouble. Let me explain by way of a recent example. We've got the staff responsibility for a number of jobs that actually involve a number of different people and organizational units. Take safety, for example. While safety is a basic responsibility of all managers, we prepare all directives and safety procedure for all plant supervisors to follow. On new jobs, Morris Brown, the safety engineer, is called in by the process engineer for purposes of determining what working hazards may be present and to establish appropriate safety procedures, to prescribe safety equipment and clothes if required, and to check on actual compliances to such directives. Last week my phone nearly jumped off the desk, and when I answered it, Larry, foreman of paint spray, cussed me out good for going to the plant manager about the ventilation problems in the spray booths. After I quieted him down, I tried to explain that I didn't go to the plant manager, and, what's more, I knew nothing about the whole incident. I called in Brown, the safety engineer, and come to find out he went to Craft a week ago complaining that the paint shop ignored two notices to repair an erratic exhaust system. Apparently, Craft felt it was serious enough and recommended to the plant manager to shut the defective spray booth down. I found out about the decision after it was made. Oh, yes, Bolder also called after the union filed a grievance on "unsafe working conditions." I was asked why I let that happen. However, Craft, when I asked, didn't seem to think the problem was serious enough to bring it to my attention. It's problems like this you have to watch out for. Brown isn't the only violator. I can't seem to get these people to understand the importance of checking in with me on such matters. You and Dick Strong are the only two who haven't given me trouble on this score. Oh, well, thought this information might interest as well as help you in the future.

Taking Over the Division

The first work day in his new assignment, John Day called a divisional meeting of all personnel in the Employee Services Division for purposes of explaining how the division would operate. Dr. Martin, Joe Newton (the caterer), and Morris Brown, while in the plant, did not attend this meeting. John Day explained that he would be working primarily in the area of training since no replacement was immediately available. This meant that everyone would continue to work pretty much as in the past. It was requested by Day, however, that if problems arose which could not be solved by the responsible individual in the division, that they confer with Day before going to anyone outside the division. Little else was said during this somewhat formal and brief meeting.

While his first two months as employee services supervisor were pretty routine, John Day was kept busy on a special project assignment. The plant manager requested Dave Craft to prepare an "executive inventory evaluation" of all managerial personnel from division heads up to and including superintendents for purposes of appraising available manpower for June promotions and as a basis for all future executive performance appraisals. Craft delegated this assignment to Day five months ago. Since this technique had not been used in the past, Craft told Day to do a complete and quality job and not to worry about the division. The report was to be presented orally before the executive committee around June 1.

It took a while for Day to get used to working for Craft again after working with Ted. Ted constantly checked on the progress of all Day's work in the training area, sought advice in special training problems, and kept John informed of matters of general departmental importance through periodic division meetings. Dave Craft seemed to want his division heads to be pretty much on their own. Official departmental meetings were rarely held. Practically all information from Craft was dissiminated by memorandum.

John Day noticed that the "before-work" get-together among Craft, Farris, and Bolder continued after Norris left the company. A month passed by, and he was not invited to attend. One morning Day casually walked in on one of these meetings. Everyone there looked up indifferently and somewhat surprised. After what seemed to be five minutes to Day, finally Craft said, "Hi, have a seat." Thereafter, all four persons met regularly each morning before work in what was described to be a general "bull session." While business was generally the subject matter, the issues discussed normally concerned over-all plant problems and politics. Day got along very well with Farris and Bolder in the plant although little socializing occurred after hours even while all three supervisors belonged to the same social club. Day felt this group accepted him, for a number of confidential matters were discussed freely in his presence.

One morning three months ago Day received a call from the employment manager, Ken Bolder. The following conversation resulted:

Bolder: Good morning, Johnnie. I'm glad to see you finally found someone to fill your open requisition for training director. Sounds like you're getting a good man.

Johnnie: Oh! I was not aware that I had filled the slot. Who signed the requisition and who is the individual?

Bolder: You don't know?

Johnnie: No!

Bolder: Both Craft and Starr signed and approved an applicant by the name of Morton. I understand this guy is a retired army colonel. His brother is a good friend of Starr, the plant manager. You better see Craft and find out the full story. He's supposed to report for work next month.

Johnnie: You bet I will!

Bolder: One other thing. We've decided to let Earl Wright go. He just generates too much heat and friction between the union and the company. Lately, we've had an international representative down checking into a number of matters with the local union president. This spells more trouble. Even though Dave is out of town, I decided it was time for him to go.

Johnnie: You're making a big mistake, Ken. This guy has finally brought this union crew around to the point where they can't push us around. That's why they're complaining. Do you realize how few grievances have gotten to arbitration since Earl has been with the company? The guy spends half his nights here working on cases.

Bolder: Regardless! If the men are not satisfied, we're in trouble, and they're not satisfied. Have you looked at the absenteeism on "number two line"? You can't run a production operation when people don't show. 'Bye.

After three months on the job, Day was called into Craft's office for his first supervisory "performance review." Craft simply said to Day, "You're doing a good job, and I'm pleased with your performance. I have filled out your 'performance review' and would like you to sign, so we can make it official." No actual review of Day's performance in terms of the factors used took place between the two men. The "performance review" technique was adopted the preceding year by the plant based on its recommended use by the central staff, company headquarters. Day introduced the review procedures to all supervisory personnel who were required to use it semiannually or all unrepresented employees up through and including division supervisors. While still new, the program had not been received well nor properly implemented by most plant supervisors.

Shortly after completing the plant-wide performance review last month, the Executive Promotion Committee convened to receive and consider Mr. Craft's study on the "executive inventory evaluation" which he had been requested earlier to prepare. (This committee was headed by the plant manager who was assisted by the factory superintendent and Craft.) At the request of Craft and the approval of the committee, Day was asked to make an oral presentation of his study and to answer any inquiries the committee members might have. Having made his report, Day sat down and observed the discussion that followed. The "executive inventory evaluation" was all but ignored by the committee. Craft dominated and directed most of the discussion and seemed to have a very strong voice in making final evaluations and promotion recommendations, to the surprise of Day. Of all the available candidates for promotion or transfer to existing departmental or higher openings, few candidates were discussed at any great length before a decision was reached. With the exception of a few minor questions, Day contributed little to the meeting. When it finally ended, Day was puzzled. Since the inventory was distributed two weeks before the meeting, he didn't know how much confidence or value the committee placed in it as a useful tool in arriving at their decisions. No comments to this effect were ever made to Day by any member of the committee even though they continued the use of the inventory thereafter.

Clarifying His Position

After concluding to himself that his attitude towards his job and his boss was beginning to deteriorate, Day decided it was time to have a talk with his boss regarding a few serious problems that had gotten under his skin and with which he wanted some help. The following remarks represent the substance of a conversation Day had with Craft.

Day: I felt it time got an understanding and a ruling on who reports to whom in this department. I'm . . .

Craft: What do you mean?

Day: Just this. For over eight months now, it seems that Joe Newton, the caterer; Dr. Martin; Mel Black; and Morris Brown, the safety engineer, don't know or don't care that I'm supposed to be their immediate supervisor. Take Newton. For over a month complaints were coming in that the cafeteria was not being cleaned up properly after the second shift. I decided to check into it, and after inspecting the cafeteria for eight consecutive working days, I found the complaint was justified. When I brought the complaint to Joe's attention and told him to correct it, he simply said, "Go to hell" and stomped off. That is about all I can take from him. This isn't the first time he has literally ignored a request of mine. I believe he thinks those free hams and turkeys he provides to certain people the year round gives him a free passport around here.

Craft: Don't mind Joe. He is a little hot-head, but for five years I've sorta given him a free rein in handling this catering contract he makes with me each year. But you're right. He should not be doing a poor job down in the cafeteria. You have a right to keep after him. I'll have a talk with him and straighten this out. What else?

Day: Dr. Martin seems to spend more time in your office discussing injury cases, workmen comp cases, and medical employment problems than he does with me. Sometimes he lets me in on decisions you have made, but most of the time he doesn't. I find out by seeing a hiring requisition or an approved claim. Why?

Craft: Martin is doing a good job for you

Day: Yes. Such a good job, Elmer Tread in Employment keeps riding me because he can't fill his open employment requisitions with Martin giving so many 4-D health classifications on the employment physicals. I like to run the division without so much outside help and pressure.

If we're given a job to do, why can't we do it our way and make the decisions—major and minor. Of late, more decisions have been made outside the division than in it.

Craft: There are some matters which require more heads than one, Day, and this is why I'm here—to assist you in such instances.

Day: That's just it. I feel like I'm getting 95 percent assistance instead of five. Take, for example, the Collins' compensation case just last week. We had a good case against this employee, for his workmen's compensation claim was obviously fraudulent. Dr. Martin found nothing physically wrong with his back; the detective we hired took films of this man lifting bails of hay on weekends at his farm. And, furthermore, our lawyer said the man had a weak case legally. But yet you overruled a group of specialists whose opinions I respected and awarded the claims to Collins.

Craft: This was a special case, and you were not made aware of all the facts in the situation. We had no alternative but to agree to the claim. From what you have said so far, I'm sure the problem is not as serious as you believe. Since I have a department heads meeting soon, plan on lunch with me for today, and we can straighten things out.

Questions

1. Does John Day have any problems? What?
2. How has Craft contributed to these problems?
3. How has Day contributed to his situation?
4. What might Day have done differently (if he could go back in time)?
5. What possible courses of action might Day pursue now?
6. What would you recommend for Day? Why?

Case 6–3

CASE OF THE PLATEAUED PERFORMER*

"Grow old along with me, the best is yet to be." When Robert Browning expressed this sentiment, he was not writing as a spokesman for business to promising young executive. Yet in the 19th century, while such poetry may have been out of place in business, the thought was very fitting.

In fact, until quite recently, corporations have been able to reward capable employees with increased responsibilities and opportunities. Based on our recently completed research into nine companies, however, the more prev-

---

* E. Kirby Warren, Thomas P. Ference, and James A. F. Stoner, *Harvard Business Review*, vol. 33, no. 1 (January–February 1975), p. 30ff. Copyright © 1975 by the President and Fellows of Harvard College; all rights reserved.

alent corporate sentiment might be, "Stay young along with me, or gone you well may be."

We found a large number of managers who, in the judgment of their organization, have "plateaued." That is, there is little or no likelihood that they will be promoted or receive substantial increases in duties and responsibilities. These long-service employees are being regarded with growing concern because plateauing is taking place more markedly, and frequently earlier, than in years past. Further, executives feel that plateauing is frequently accompanied by noticeable declines in both motivation and quality of performance.

While plateauing, like aging, is inevitable, in years past it was a more gradual process. For the most part, those who sought advancement in their managerial careers had ample opportunity to get it, within broad limits of ability, while those who did not desire advancement (including competent individuals content with more modest levels of achievement and success) could be bypassed by colleagues still on the way up.

Today the situation has changed. Declining rates of corporate growth and an ever-increasing number of candidates have heightened the competition for managerial positions. The top of the pyramid is expanding much more slowly than the middle, and the managers who advanced rapidly during the growth boom of the 1960s are now at or just below the top. Their rate of career progress has necessarily slowed, and yet they are still many years from normal retirement and with many productive years to go. As these managers continue in their positions, the queue of younger, aggressive aspirants just below them is likely to grow longer, with spillover effects on opportunities and mobility rates throughout the organization.

This is precisely the dilemma confronting Benjamin Petersen, president and chairman of the board of Petersen Electronics.

Petersen founded the company in 1944, and it grew rapidly during the 1950s and 1960s, reaching sales of $200 million in 1968. Growth since then, though, has been uneven and at an average of less than 5% per year. However, 1974 was a good year, with sales and profits showing leaps of 12% and 18% respectively.

Despite the good year, Benjamin Petersen now 61 years old, is concerned about the company as he nears retirement. His major problem involves George Briggs, 53, vice president of marketing, and Thomas Evans, national sales manager, who is 34 years old and one of Brigg's four subordinates. Nor have the implications of the situation between Briggs and Evans been lost on Victor Perkins, 39, vice president of personnel.

Petersen's View of the Predicament

"When we started, a handful of people worked very hard and very closely to build something bigger than any of us. One of these people was George Briggs. George has been with me from the start, as have almost all of my vice presidents and many of my key department heads.

"For the first five years, I did almost all the inventing and engineering work. Tom Carroll ran the plant and George Briggs knocked on doors and sold dreams as well as products for the company.

"As the company grew, we added people, and Briggs slowly worked his way up the sales organization. Eight years ago, when our vice president of marketing retired, I put George in the job. He has market research, product management, sales service, and the field sales force (reporting through a national sales manager) under him, and he has really done a first-rate job all around.

"About ten years ago we began bringing in more bright young engineers and MBAs and moved them along as fast as we could. Turnover has been high, and we have had some friction between our young Turks and the old guard.

"When business slowed in the early 70s, we also had a lot of competition among the newcomers. Those who stayed have continued to move up, and a few are now in or ready for top jobs. One of the best of this group is Tom Evans. He started with us nine years ago in the sales service area. Later, he spent three years in product management.

"George Briggs got him to move from head of the sales service department to assistant product manager. After one year, George Briggs named him manager of the product management group, and two years later, when the national sales manager retired, George named Evans to this post.

"That move both surprised and pleased me. I felt that Evans would make a good sales manager despite the fact that he had had little direct sales experience. I was afraid, however, that George would not want someone in that job who hadn't had years of field experience.

"I was even more surprised, though, when six months later (a month ago) George told me he was afraid Evans wasn't working out, and asked if I might be able to find a spot for him in the corporate personnel department. While I'm sure our recent upturn in sales is not solely Evans's doing, he certainly seems to be one of the keys. Despite his inexperience, he seems to have the field sales organization behind him. He spends much of his time traveling with them, and from what I hear he has built a great team spirit.

"Despite this, George Briggs claims that he is in over his head and that it is just a matter of time before his inexperience gets him in trouble. I can't understand why George is so adamant. It's clearly not a personality clash, since they have always gotten along well in the past. In many ways, Briggs has been Evans's greatest booster until recently.

"Since George is going to need a replacement someday, I was hoping it would be Evans. If George doesn't retire before we have to move Evans again or lose him, I'd consider moving Evans to another area.

"When we were growing faster, I didn't worry about a new challenge opening up for our aggressive young managers—there were always new divisions, new lines—something to keep them stimulated and satisfied with their progress. Now I have less flexibility—my top people are several years from retirement. And yet I have some younger ones—like Evans, whom I would hate to lose—always pushing and expecting promotion.

"Evans is a good example of this; I could move him, but there are not that many *real* opportunities. He could go to personnel or engineering or even finance. Evans has the makings of a really fine general manager. But I'd hate to move him now. He really isn't ready for another shift—although he will be in a few years—and despite what George claims, I think he is stimulating team work and commitment in the sales organization as a result of his style.

"Finally, while I don't want to appear unduly critical of Briggs, I'm not sure he could get the job done in these competitive times without a bright young person like Evans to help him."

Briggs's Account of the Situation

"Before I say anything else, let me assure you there is nothing personal in my criticism of Evans.

"I like him. I have always liked him. I've done more for him than anyone else in the company. I've tried to coach him and bring him along just like a son.

"But the simple truth is that he's in way over his head and showing a side of his personality I've never seen before. I brought him along through sales service and product management, and he was always eager to learn. While I couldn't give him a lot of help in those areas (frankly, there are aspects of them I don't yet fully understand), I still tried, and he paid attention and learned from others as well.

"The job of national sales manager, however, is a different story. In the other jobs Evans had—staff jobs—there was always time to consult, to consider, to get more data. In sales, however, all this participative stuff he uses takes too long. The national sales manager has to be able to make quick, intuitive decisions. What's more, like the captain of a ship, he has to inspire confidence in those below him. If the going gets rough, the only thing that keeps the sailors and junior officers from panicking is confidence in the skipper. I've been there and I know.

"Right now, with orders coming in strong, he can get away with all of his meetings and indecisiveness. The people in the field really like him and are trying to keep him out of trouble. In addition, I have been putting in 60 to 70 hours a week trying to do my job and also make sure he doesn't make any serious mistakes.

"I know he is feeling the pressure, too. Despite the fact that he has been his usual cheery self with others, when I call him in to question a decision he has made or is about to make, he gets very defensive. He was never that way with me before.

"I may have lost a little feel for what's going on in the field over the years, but I suspect I still know more about the customers and our sales people than Tom Evans will ever know. I've tried for the past seven months to get him to relax and let the old man help him, but it's no use. I'm convinced he's just not cut out for the job, and before we ruin him I want to transfer him somewhere else. He would probably make a fine personnel director someday.

He's a very popular guy who seems genuinely interested in people and in helping them.

"I have talked with Ben Petersen about the move, and he has been stalling me. I understanding his position. We have a lot of young comers like Evans in the company, and Ben has to worry about all of them. He told me that if anyone can bring Evans along I can, and he asked me to give it another try. I have, and things are getting worse.

"I hate to admit I made a mistake with Evans, but I plan on seeing Ben about this again tomorrow. We just can't keep putting it off. I'm sure he'll see it my way, and as soon as he approves the transfer, I'll have a heart-to-heart talk with Tom."

Evans's Side of the Story

"This has been a very hectic but rewarding period for me. I've never worked as hard in my life as I have during the last six months, but it's paying off. I'm learning more about sales each day, and more important, I'm building a first-rate sales team. My people are really enjoying the chance to share ideas and support each other.

"At first, particularly with our markets improving, it was hard to convince them to take time to meet with me and their subordinates. Gradually they have come to accept these sessions as an investment in team building. According to them, we've come up with more good ideas and ways to help each other than ever before.

"Fortunately, I also have experience in product management and sales service. Someday I hope to bring representatives from this department and market research into the meetings with regional and branch people, but that will take time. This kind of direct coordination and interaction doesn't fit with the thinking of some of the old-timers. I ran into objections when I tried this while I was working in the other departments.

"But I'm certain that in a year or so I'll be able to show, by results, that we should have more direct contact across department levels.

"My boss, George Briggs, will be one of the ones I will have to convince. He comes from the old school and is slow to give up what he knows used to work well.

"George likes me, though, and has given me a tremendous amount of help in the past. I was amazed when he told me he was giving me this job. Frankly, I didn't think I was ready yet, but he assured me I could handle it. I've gotten a big promotion every few years and I really like that—being challenged to learn new skills and getting more responsibility. I guess I have a real future here, although George won't be retiring for some years and I've gone as high as I can go until then.

"George is a very demanding person, but extremely fair, and he is always trying to help. I only hope I can justify the confidence he has shown in me. He stuck his neck out by giving me this chance, and I'm going to do all I can to succeed.

"Recently we have had a few run-ins. George Briggs works harder than anyone else around here, and perhaps the pressure of the last few years is getting to him. I wish he'd take a vacation this year and get away for a month or more and just relax. He hasn't taken more than a week off in the nine years I've been here, and for the last two years he hasn't taken any vacation.

"I can see the strain is taking its toll. Recently he has been on my back for all kinds of little things. He always was a worrier, but lately he has been testing me on numerous small issues. He keeps throwing out suggestions or second-guessing me on things that I've spent weeks working on with the field people.

"I try to assure him I'll be all right, and to please help me where I need it with the finance and production people who've had a tough time keeping up with our sales organization. It has been rough lately, but I'm sure it will work out. Sooner or later George will accept the fact that while I will never be able to run things the way he did, I can still get the job done for him."

Perkins's Opinions

"I feel that George Briggs is threatened by Evans's seeming success with the field sales people. I don't thing he realizes it, but he is probably jealous of the speed with which Tom has taken charge. In all likelihood, he didn't expect Tom to be able to handle the field people as well as he has, as fast as he has.

"When George put Tom in the job, I have a feeling that he was looking forward to having him need much more help and advice from the old skipper. Tom does need help and advice, but he is getting most of what George would offer from his own subordinates and his peers. As a result, he has created a real team spirit below and around him, but he has upset George in the process.

"George not only has trouble seeing Tom depend so much on his subordinates, but I feel that he resents Tom's unwillingness to let him show him how he used to run the sales force.

"I may be wrong about this, of course. I am sure that George honestly believes that Tom's style will get him in trouble sooner or later. George is no doddering old fool who has to relive his past success in lower-level jobs. In the past, I'm told, he has shown real insight and interest in the big-picture aspects of the company.

"The trouble is he knows he was an outstanding sales manager, but I am not sure he has the same confidence in his ability as vice president. I have seen this time and again, particularly in recent years. When a person begins to doubt his future, he sometimes drops back and begins to protect his past. With more competition from younger subordinates and the new methods that they often bring in, many of our experienced people find that doing their job the way they used to just isn't good enough anymore.

"Some reach out and seek new responsibilities to prove their worth. Others, however, return to the things they used to excel in and try to show that theirs is still the best way to do things. They don't even seem to realize that this puts them in direct competition with their subordinates.

"What do we do about this? I wish I knew! At lower levels, where you have more room to shift people around, you have more options. When the company is growing rapidly, the problem often takes care of itself.

"In this case, I am not sure what I will recommend if Ben Petersen asks my advice. Moving Tom to personnel at this time not only won't help me (I really don't have a spot for him), but it won't help Briggs or Evans either. Moving Evans now would be wasteful of the time and effort we've invested in his development. It may also reverse some important trends Tom has begun in team building within the sales force.

"If Briggs were seven or eight years older, we could wait it out. If the company were growing faster, we might be able to shift people. As things stand, however, I see only one approach as a possibility. And I'm not entirely sure it will work.

"I would recommend that we get busy refocusing Brigg's attention on the vice president's job and get him to see that there is where he has to put his time and efforts. Perhaps the best thing would be to send him to one of the longer programs for senior executives. Don't forget he is a very bright and experienced person who still has a great deal to offer the company if we can figure out how to help him."

What Would You Suggest?

Petersen has agreed to talk with Briggs about Evans tomorrow afternoon. As he thinks about the situation, he wonders what he can do that would be best for the company and everyone concerned. Should he go along with Briggs's recommendation that Evans be transferred to personnel? Or would it be preferable to do as Perkins has suggested and send Briggs to an executive program? As you consider the various perspectives, why do you think the impasse came to be and what do you think could be done to resolve it?

Questions

1. What are Briggs's problems? What are the causes?
2. Why has Briggs's view of Evans changed? Do you agree or disagree with Briggs? Why?
3. What is Evans's potential problem?
4. How has Petersen contributed to the situation?
5. What recommendations would you give Evans? Briggs? Petersen?

AUTHOR INDEX

Auden, W. H., 15

Berlew, David E., 152

Burck, Charles G., 264

Burnham, David H., 35

Confucius, 425

Davis, Stanley M., 287

Estes, Ralph W., 359

Faltermayer, Edmund, 176

Frost, Robert, 175

Galbraith, Jay R., 278

Gutteridge, Thomas G., 470

Hall, Jay, 112

Henry, Harold W., 221

Herbert, Theodore T., 359

Horner, Matina S., 45

Hunger, David J., 353

Hutchinson, John, 316

Johnson, John H., 101

Kanter, Rosabeth Moss, 434, 458

Kelley, George, 376

Kerr, Steven, 211

Kotter, John P., 123

Kraar, Louis, 346

Lawler, Edward E., 26

Locke, Edwin A., 133

Lorange, Peter, 186

Louis, Arthur M., 16, 426

MBA, 452

McCaskey, Michael B., 271

McClelland, David C., 35, 65

Milne, A. A., 263

Nash, Ogden, 345

Pearce, John A., II, 446

Pfeffer, Jeffrey, 142

Pitts, Robert A., 296

Post, James E., 307

Preston, Lee E., 307

Psychology Today, 26

Quinn, James Brian, 194

Redman, Louis N., 207

Renwick, Patricia A., 26

Roalman, Arthur R., 182

Schwartz, Eleanor Brantley, 52

Shakespeare, William, 99

Sorenson, Richard E., 394

Thamhain, Hans J., 364

Vancil, Richard F., 186

Varney, Glenn H., 401

Veiga, John F., 465

Weick, Karl E., 440

White, Bernard J., 74

White, Eberhard, 384

Wiard, Harry, 116

Wilemon, David L., 364

Zand, David E., 394

This book has been set linotype in 10 and 9 point Palatino, leaded 2 points. Part numbers are 30 point Optima and part titles are 18 point Optima. Reading numbers are 12 point Optima and reading titles are 18 point Optima. The size of the text area is 33½ picas by 49 picas.